WHAT

—TO—

WATCH
WHEN

1,000 TV Shows for Every Mood and Moment

WHAT
—TO—
WATCH
WHEN

1,000 TV Shows for Every Mood and Moment

Written by
Christian Blauvelt, Laura Buller, Andrew Frisicano,
Stacey Grant, Mark Morris, Eddie Robson, Maggie Serota,
Drew Toal, Matthew Turner, Laurie Ulster

CONTENTS

A NOTE ON AGE RATINGS

The certification given for each TV program indicates the highest US rating given to an episode across the whole of each TV series. Sometimes the rating is the exception, but it's always good to know whether there's a risk of much more mature content than you would otherwise be expecting. Where no US rating is available, we've provided the UK rating, with "(UK)" following it. In a few cases, there are TV shows with no age rating in either the US or the UK. In situations like this, you will see "NR"—no rating.

US ratings used in this book
TV-G: General audience. Most parents would find this program suitable for all ages.
TV-PG: Parental guidance suggested. This program contains material that parents may find unsuitable for younger children.
TV-Y: All children.
TV-Y7: Directed to older children. This program is designed for children aged 7 and above.
TV-Y7-FV: Directed to older children—fantasy violence. Programs where fantasy violence might be more intense or combative than the TV-Y7 category.
TV-14: Parents strongly cautioned. This program contains some material that many parents would find unsuitable for children under 14.
TV-MA: Mature audience only. This program is specifically designed to be viewed by adults and may be unsuitable for children under 17.

UK ratings used in this book
U: Universal. Suitable for all.
PG: Parental guidance. General viewing, but some scenes might be unsuitable for young children.
12: Video release suitable for 12 years and over.
15: Suitable only for 15 years and over.
18: Suitable only for adults.

Canadian ratings (for reference)
E: Exempt.
C: Children. Programming intended for younger children under the age of 8 years.
C8: Children over 8 years. Programming that is generally considered acceptable for children 8 years and over to view on their own.
G: General. Considered acceptable for all age groups.
PG: Parental guidance. This programming, while intended for a general audience, may not be suitable for younger children under the age of 8.
14+: Over 14 years.
18+: Over 18 years.

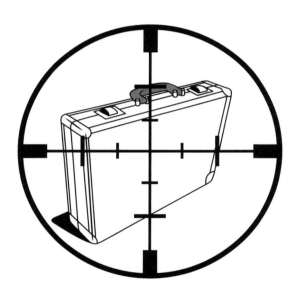

YOU WANT TO GET YOUR PULSE RACING

Written by Drew Toal

Whether it's a modern crime drama or an impossibly bloody fight for the Iron Throne, these shows push your heart into your throat and leave you white-knuckling the television remote. They thrill with tense standoffs, daring heists, killer robots, flawed heroes (superpowered or otherwise), and sometimes just good, old-fashioned detective work. If it's adrenaline you crave, these are the shows for you.

GAME OF THRONES

FANTASY • 2011 • RATED: TV-MA • 57 MINS • SEASONS: 8
PETER DINKLAGE, LENA HEADEY, EMILIA CLARKE

HBO's award-winning adaptation of George R. R. Martin's epic fantasy opus is known for its swords, sex, dragons, and ice zombies. In an era of streaming on demand, *Game of Thrones* quickly became appointment television across the globe.

"Winter is coming." Before the game of thrones ends, these fateful words will be uttered dozens of times, by a huge cast of characters. For Eddard "Ned" Stark (Sean Bean) and his family—the primary protagonists of the series—the motto serves not just as an ominous weather forecast but also as a warning and a promise.

> **"***If you think this has a happy ending, you haven't been paying attention.***"**
>
> Ramsay Bolton (S3 E6)

The Starks are a noble family hailing from Winterfell, a kingdom situated in the north of Westeros. One day, King Robert Baratheon comes to town and recruits his old friend Ned to help him run the fractured government from the capital, King's Landing. Against his better judgment, Ned agrees, a fateful decision that will have far-reaching consequences for the entire world. Ned's family, including his wife, Catelyn; sons, Robb, Bran, and Rickon; daughters, Sansa and Arya; and wards, Jon Snow and Theon Greyjoy, are soon swept from their relatively idyllic existence into a maelstrom of medieval realpolitik. King's Landing is a snake pit, with dueling factions that make our own political divides look extremely quaint in comparison. In *Game of Thrones*, conspiracies, intrigues, and murder are the true currency of the realm—you win or you die.

While a creeping existential threat emerges in the wilderness "beyond the Wall" in the form of an undead army-slash-heavy-handed climate change allegory, warlords across the land ignore the real danger and instead use every tool at their disposal to settle scores and

DEATHS PER SEASON IN *GAME OF THRONES*

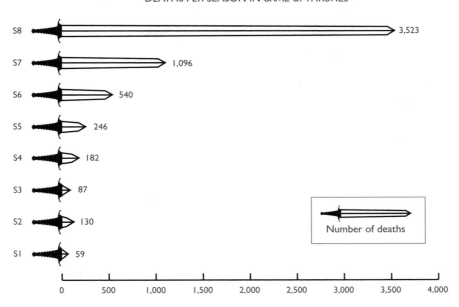

Season	Deaths
S8	3,523
S7	1,096
S6	540
S5	246
S4	182
S3	87
S2	130
S1	59

Number of deaths

squabble over the crown. More often than not, these sadistic machinations leave a trail of bodies that occasionally leads one to wonder whether there will be any subjects left to rule by the time the show ends.

This is no run-of-the-mill swords-and-sorcery TV project. Showrunners David Benioff and D. B. Weiss took George R. R. Martin's beloved books and gave them the true big-screen treatment. Along the way, they even create the longest battle sequence in both TV and film history! Throughout eight seasons, you meet iconic characters and watch them grow—the lucky ones who survive, anyhow—and see allegiances shift. You meet dragons and their "mother," the exiled Daenerys Stormborn of House Targaryen, played by Emilia Clarke. You also meet a rogues' gallery of vicious villains, including the scheming Littlefinger (Aidan Gillen), the brutally sadistic Ramsay Bolton (Iwan Rheon), and, of course,

power-hungry Cersei Lannister (Lena Headey). Characters who are at one time mortal enemies become allies of necessity and then something close to friends. This is not the kind of story in which the good guys always win.

Indeed, in *Game of Thrones*, it's not always clear who the good guys even are. If the show does have a conscience, it comes in the person of Peter Dinklage's Tyrion Lannister, a hard-drinking, melancholic dwarf who also happens to hail from one of the most powerful families in the Seven Kingdoms. Tyrion has a powerful intellect and a biting wit—and also something of a wine dependency. He is a captive witness, as we all are, to a singular adventure and one of the grandest productions in TV history. Even in an era of "prestige TV," *Game of Thrones* pushed the limits of the medium and cemented its place in pop-culture history.

CREATORS: David Benioff, D. B. Weiss PRODUCTION CO: HBO, Television 360, Grok! Studio, Generator Entertainment, Bighead Littlehead

BREAKING BAD

CRIME DRAMA • 2008 • RATED: TV-MA • 49 MINS • SEASONS: 5
BRYAN CRANSTON, AARON PAUL, BOB ODENKIRK

To pay mounting medical bills, high-school chemistry teacher Walter White starts "cooking" and selling crystal meth in secret. Walter soon learns he has a talent for the drug game.

When we first meet Walter (Bryan Cranston), he's not much to look at. Considered a brilliant mind in his younger days, he's now a sad 50-year-old high-school chemistry teacher in New Mexico. After learning he has terminal lung cancer, Walter puts his skills to more unsavory—albeit more lucrative—use. He hooks up with crystal meth enthusiast Jesse Pinkman (Aaron Paul), and the pair form an unlikely, uneasy alliance and a new business.

Walter's initial goal is to financially set up his son, unborn daughter, and wife, Skyler, for when he's gone. He understands the chemistry involved in the drug's production intimately, perhaps better than anyone, but in all other respects, he is in over his head. Jesse and Walter nevertheless dive into their new career

as drug kingpins, learning what to do—and, more often, what not to do—as they go along. Walter makes money, but his noble intentions to support his family quickly give way to his long-suppressed ambition to do something big with his life.

Throughout *Breaking Bad's* five seasons, we meet some memorable characters as Walter builds his empire, including dour fixer Mike Ehrmantraut, businessman Gus Fring, and seedy lawyer Saul Goodman (Bob Odenkirk), whose character was so popular it spawned the spin-off *Better Call Saul* (see p349).

Walter White is no hero, but much of *Breaking Bad's* appeal lies in the actualization of his particular midlife crisis. He's just this guy, living an unremarkable life in the American Southwest, who latches onto a piece of bad news and uses it to get some agency back in his life. He takes his frustrations over his imminent death and channels them into something that reminds him what it's like to feel alive. We can all relate to that.

CREATOR: Vince Gilligan PRODUCTION CO: High Bridge Productions,
Gran Via Productions, Sony Pictures Television, AMC

THE MANDALORIAN

SCI-FI • 2019 • RATED: TV-PG • 30 MINS • SEASONS: 2
PEDRO PASCAL, GINA CARANO, WERNER HERZOG

Beginning on a backwater planet several years after the events of *Return of the Jedi*, this original *Star Wars* series, which helped launch the Disney+ streaming service, follows a gunfighter who earns his keep as a bounty hunter.

In the post-Empire galaxy, the economy isn't exactly booming, but bounty hunting still pays the bills. When one of its practitioners, a gloomy individual known as the Mandalorian (Pedro Pascal), accepts a high-risk, high-reward contract, it brings him into contact with the cutest target he's ever faced—a child of the same species as renowned Jedi Master Yoda.

Bounty hunters have always played an outsized role in *Star Wars* mythology. Boba Fett had just a few minutes of screen time in the original movie trilogy but became one of the most

memorable characters to come out of a franchise packed with ready-made action figures. Although you never saw his face in the first movies, Fett exuded a palpable coolness. He couldn't wield the Force, but you just knew he was more than a match for any Jedi through sheer cunning, toughness, some kind of obscure martial art (probably), and his undeniably cool Mandalorian armor.

> *"I'm a Mandalorian. Weapons are part of my religion."*
>
> **The Mandalorian** (S1 E2)

So it's perhaps no surprise that this iconic armor was chosen as the symbol of the marquee series that helped launch the Disney+ streaming service in 2019. Fun for kids and longtime fans alike, *The Mandalorian* truly embraces George Lucas's interest in westerns and samurai films. Mando is basically Clint Eastwood's "Man with No Name," but in a galaxy far, far away. This lone wolf has a moral code, but seemingly no family or close friends. He lives for the job—until his encounter with "The Child" warms his cold, mercenary heart.

For a franchise often mired in nostalgia, *The Mandalorian* shows how *Star Wars* can still give fans what they want (jawas, stormtroopers, droids), while also telling an original story with universal appeal. This slickly entertaining space western is among the best *Star Wars* offshoots since 1983.

CREATOR: Jon Favreau
PRODUCTION CO: Fairview Entertainment, Golem Creations, Lucasfilm, Walt Disney Studios

THE FLASH

ACTION • 2014
RATED: TV-PG • 43 MINS

Barry Allen is fast. Like, really fast. Faster than Superman fast. So what does he do with this skill? He assumes the mantle of The Flash and uses his powers to fight crime in Central City.

Following a laboratory accident, crime scene investigator Barry Allen (Grant Gustin) falls into a coma. He wakes up to find he can move at a speed far beyond the threshold of normal humans. Taking on the alias of The Flash, Allen learns that he's not the only one with new powers and vows to fight those using their super-power abilities for evil.

As a show about a guy who runs really fast *The Flash* wouldn't be all that interesting, but it delves into some deep philosophical and narrative waters, mostly involving time travel, alternate universes, and temporal paradoxes. With crossovers from *Arrow* (see p36) and *Supergirl* (see p93), this series has created a fun Super Hero universe all of its own across six seasons of speed.

LINE OF DUTY

CRIME DRAMA • 2012 • RATED: 15 (UK) • 60 MINS • SEASONS: 6
MARTIN COMPSTON, VICKY MCCLURE, ADRIAN DUNBAR

Trust no one! This series is far from a standard police procedural—it turns your expectations on their head. In the *Line of Duty* world of anti-corruption, the line between criminals and those charged with keeping them behind bars is blurred, at times beyond recognition.

After a fatal accident during a police terrorism sting gone wrong, anti-terrorism officer Steve Arnott (Martin Compston) refuses to join the department's efforts to cover it up. Shunned by his fellow officers who see him as a turncoat, Arnott's unpopular moral stance is noted by others, and he is recruited to AC-12, a police anti-corruption unit.

Written and directed by Jed Mercurio, *Line of Duty* centers on AC-12's work as it uncovers corruption in the police force. Arnott is suited to the work and soon teams up with an undercover specialist named Kate Fleming (Vicky McClure) to root out officers who skirt or break the law. As Arnott, Fleming, and their boss, Superintendent Ted Hastings (Adrian Dunbar), run down dirty cops, they discover traces of a ringleader with ties to organized crime near the top of the police hierarchy.

The team have yet to identify this mysterious figure, known only as "H," but as they bring down corrupt police during the course of each season, they inch ever closer to revealing the person's identity. Prepare to binge your way through this thrilling series, fella.

> **"***There's a line. It's called right and wrong, and I know which side my duty lies.***"**
>
> **Ted Hastings** (S3 E6)

THE NIGHT OF

CRIME DRAMA • 2016 • RATED: TV-MA • 57–95 MINS • SEASONS: 1
RIZ AHMED, JOHN TURTURRO, MICHAEL K. WILLIAMS

Want an up-close and personal look at the nightmare that is the US criminal justice system? Then this is the series for you. Naz goes out one night and ends up blacking out. When he comes to, he's implicated in a murder he can't be sure he didn't commit.

Naz (Riz Ahmed) needs a break. One night, he "borrows" his father's cab to go to a party. Bystanders, understandably, mistake him for a cab driver. One of these, Andrea, convinces Naz to party with her. Drugs and alcohol are consumed. Things get hazy. When Naz's evening is over, he's left with something measurably worse than a bad hangover.

We don't know whether Naz is guilty, but he's not doing himself any favors with his erratic behavior as the police close in on him. As he awaits his trial, a slightly eccentric lawyer named John Stone (John Turturro) agrees to take his case. The question is: can Naz survive the brutal prison where he's awaiting trial long enough to clear his name?

Whether or not you believe Naz is guilty, seeing him await his day in court at a notorious New York prison is chilling. Ahmed and Turturro both turn in A+ performances in the best crime drama of 2016.

> **" Even if you can't remember anything, you'd know it, you'd feel it. I'm not a murderer. "**
>
> **Naz Khan** (S1 E3)

DEUTSCHLAND 83

SPY THRILLER • 2015
RATED: TV-MA • 42 MINS

Martin Rauch is 24 and ready to do his duty for his country. Sounds like a typical military drama, right? But in '80s East Germany "doing your duty" means training as a spy and infiltrating the West for the Stasi.

Martin Rauch (Jonas Nay) is a young border guard working for the East German military in 1983. In these days before the fall of the Berlin Wall, he's a true believer in the Soviet cause and is willing to do whatever it takes to protect his homeland. It turns out this will require him being whisked off to West Germany, where he will undergo training as a spy and report back to his handlers.

Deutschland 83 is a vibrant one-season Cold War–era thriller, told from the perspective of a young man repelled by Western values but still willing to question the motives of his own superiors. The show was supplemented by an incredible soundtrack straight out of the 1980s and was followed by two sequels.

CSI: CRIME SCENE INVESTIGATION

CRIME • 2000
RATED: TV-MA • 60 MINS

For 15 seasons, this groundbreaking procedural drama spawned not only some incredible forensic investigations but also multiple spin-offs and copycats.

Have you heard of "the *CSI* effect?" It's a term used by legal and law enforcement officials to refer to jurors who expect more forensic evidence during criminal trials, thereby raising the standard of proof for prosecutors. That this forensic crime series has infiltrated culture to such a degree is a testament to its influence.

Starring the likes of Ted Danson, Laurence Fishburne, and Elisabeth Shue over the course of its run, *CSI* takes something kind of gross and boring—police lab work—and turns it into something fun and interesting. Set in Las Vegas, episodes see the team combing dead bodies for evidence and using it to close cases that otherwise might have remained unsolved.

THE BRIDGE

CRIME • 2011
RATED: TV-MA • 60 MINS

In an attempt to highlight problems affecting Denmark and Sweden, a killer leaves parts of two dead bodies on the bridge that spans the border between the countries.

Since its premiere in 2011, *The Bridge* has been remade in both the UK and the US, but nothing beats the original. When what appears to be a bisected dead body is found at the exact center of the Øresund Bridge, which connects Sweden and Denmark, a collaborative investigation is launched between the two countries.

The show plays off of the subtle cultural differences between Denmark and Sweden as it brings together Sweden's Saga Norén (Sofia Helin) and Denmark's Martin Rohde (Kim Bodnia) to interpret the message the killer is trying to send, and crack the case. Running for four seasons, *The Bridge* is a suitably bleak and atmospheric affair, something its various remakes could never quite recapture.

DARK

SCI-FI • 2017
RATED: TV-MA • 60 MINS

Kids are vanishing from the German town of Winden. Why? No one knows. It may have something to do with the wormhole connecting various points in time to a cave system under the town.

Children are disappearing from Winden, and the explanation isn't as simple as kidnappings or runaways. Underneath the town, a series of caves connect to a wormhole that links the present day with 33-year jumps into the past, to both 1986 and 1953. Four families find their lives inextricably linked as the mystery unfolds over three seasons.

For a show to follow through on the logical implications of time travel, paradoxes and all, is an incredibly challenging feat to pull off. This German series does it right, setting up a solid foundation for its foray into multiple timelines and a riddle shrouded in mystery. Does it occasionally make your brain nearly explode? Yes. Should you take notes as you watch? Probably. Is it worth it? Most definitely.

PRISONERS OF WAR

DRAMA • 2009
RATED: 15 (UK) • 50 MINS

Following two Israeli soldiers who come home after years of imprisonment and try to piece their lives back together, *Prisoners of War* is the direct precursor to *Homeland*.

Seventeen years ago, there were no smartphones, Prince and Bowie were still alive, Amazon Prime didn't exist, and in the US Netflix sent DVDs to your home. It would be jarring, to say the least, to disappear for such a length of time, reemerge, and try to make sense of the world and your place in it.

In *Prisoners of War*, two Israeli soldiers, Nimrod (Yoram Toledano) and Uri (Ishai Golan) are released after being imprisoned for nearly two decades. They are celebrities, but find their families have either moved on or barely know who they are. And something about their stories doesn't quite add up. Spanning two seasons, *Prisoners of War* is less glitzy than its US cousin, *Homeland* (see p25), but it also tells a deeper, more believable story.

DUBLIN MURDERS

CRIME • 2019
RATED: TV-MA • 60 MINS

Childhood trauma never really goes away, as two cops discover when they're pulled into a murder investigation and find ghosts from their own pasts dogging their present footsteps.

Adapting a cult book is not for the faint of heart. Adapting two and turning them into a single-season series is downright audacious. Fans should be reassured that this is, for the most part, a faithful adaptation of Tana French's *Dublin Murder Squad* books—specifically *In the Woods* and *The Likeness*—although it's not always as neat a blend as they might like.

Investigators Rob Reilly (Killian Scott) and Cassie Maddox (Sarah Greene) are looking into the grisly murder of a young girl, reminiscent of a killing decades earlier in 1985. This is one of those situations where everyone is a suspect, especially the girl's weirdly creepy family. But our heroic officers also have some skeletons in their own respective closets.

THE BREAK

CRIME • 2016
RATED: 15 (UK) • 52 MINS

Sometimes it feels as though the chief export of small idyllic towns—such as the quaint, Belgian setting of *The Break*—is murder. Luckily, they also trade in tense plots and engaging TV.

In a small town in Belgium, the body of a soccer player is pulled out of the river. Police inspector Yoann Peeters (Yoann Blanc) has just moved back home from Brussels with his daughter and is brought in to help out the local police with the case. He's less than impressed with their level of professionalism when it comes to investigating a murder and quickly determines this was no simple suicide. But then again, when it comes to this case, nothing is simple.

Running two seasons, *The Break* has the usual array of false leads, creepy forests, creepier familial dynamics, and puzzling flashbacks. The real takeaway, though, is Blanc's performance. He looks and speaks like an actual detective, rather than an actor playing a detective on TV.

THE BOYS

ACTION • 2019 • RATED: TV-MA • 60 MINS • SEASONS: I
KARL URBAN, JACK QUAID, ERIN MORIARTY

What happens when superheroes use their superpowers for bad? The Boys are a team of normal-powered people fighting back against superpowered celebs who aren't the heroes they should be. Things could get nasty!

The Boys, an adaptation of the comic book written by Garth Ennis, is less of a harmless Comic-Con thought exercise and more a matter of life and death. In the real world, superhero movies are big business. In the world of The Boys, it's the superheroes themselves who make the money. These demigod influencers are adored by the public, get rich with lucrative endorsement deals, and love taking selfies. Imagine if Harry Styles could fly and shoot deadly lasers out of his eyes, and you get the general idea.

on the radar of Billy Butcher (Karl Urban), a foul-mouthed renegade with quite the story to tell. "See, people love that cozy feeling supes give them," Butcher explains. "But if you knew half the s**t they get up to … F**kin' diabolical."

The Boys creator Garth Ennis has a penchant for spectacular violence that often verges on the cartoonish. The Boys is no exception, but the show also pokes holes in our celebrity-obsessed culture and plays with the idea that absolute power corrupts absolutely. If Superman one day decided to treat people like bugs instead of friends and colleagues, what could we do to stop him? It's a question The Boys aims to find out.

> **" Why have average when you can have extraordinary?"**
>
> Madelyn Stillwell (SI E2)

Every kid wants to be a superhero, and we follow a young woman named Starlight (Erin Moriarty), née Annie January, who plans on joining Earth's most popular "supes" team, The Seven, owned by corporate giant Vought International, whose vice president is the Machiavellian Madelyn Stillwell (Elisabeth Shue). Hughie Campbell (Jack Quaid), on the other hand, is just a normal guy working a normal job. Then one day a terrible accident brings him to the attention of The Seven. It also puts Hughie

CREATOR: Eric Kripke, Evan Goldberg, Seth Rogen
PRODUCTION CO: Amazon Studios, Original Film, Point Grey Pictures, Sony Pictures Television

HAPPY VALLEY

CRIME DRAMA • 2014
RATED: TV-MA • 58 MINS

The West Yorkshire of *Happy Valley* is not exactly the most joyous place on Earth. However, it's well worth a visit in this award-winning crime drama that will leave you emotionally drained.

There are some things you just don't get over, and the suicide of a teenage child is definitely on that list. West Yorkshire police officer Catherine Cawood (Sarah Lancashire) is still struggling with the sudden death of her daughter, Becky, some years before the events of the first season. Becky was driven to suicide after being raped by Tommy Lee Royce (James Norton). Becky's son now lives with Catherine and her sister, Clare, a recovering addict, and is getting into fights at school.

Tommy is released from prison, and this event leads Catherine down a dark and twisting path, but throughout the show's two seasons, she never loses her stoic equanimity. Sarah Lancashire imbues the character with incredible humanity in the face of bleak truths.

RAY DONOVAN

DRAMA • 2013
RATED: TV-MA • 60 MINS

When the rich and famous need a fixer who can smooth out the bumps in their glamorous lives, Ray Donovan is the man. It's a tough, bloody job, but he's good at it—and someone has to do it.

Ray (Liev Schreiber) isn't a creature of Hollywood. He hails from rougher South Boston stock and makes his living as a baseball bat-wielding "fixer," who facilitates many of the onerous tasks needed to keep the lives of LA's monied set running smoothly. *Ray Donovan* doesn't have the traditional atmosphere of a California noir, but it's one of Showtime's most popular dramas of all time for a reason.

Watching Ray try to balance his rather unconventional career with his dysfunctional family—Jon Voight won a Golden Globe for his portrayal of Mickey, Ray's ex-con father—is the true embodiment of the American dream. There was huge disappointment when the show was dropped after seven seasons.

SPOOKS

ACTION • 2002
RATED: TV-14 • 60 MINS

Before *Game of Thrones* became known for inflicting sudden, grisly deaths on beloved characters, there was *Spooks*, a spy thriller focused on the MI-5 branch of the British secret service.

Spooks follows the work of a team of MI-5 officers, headed by the dependable Harry Pearce (Peter Firth), as they defend queen and country against a multitude of global threats (*Spooks* was known in some countries as *MI-5*). The series had a strong list of rotating guest stars, with the ever-present threat of one of them being eliminated in spectacular fashion—in the world of *Spooks*, nobody is safe.

The show became notorious early on in its run. In the second episode, a character played by Lisa Faulkner is gruesomely tortured before being shot in the head, triggering numerous complaints from viewers. Despite the controversy, or perhaps because of it, the show maintained high audience numbers throughout its 10-season run.

HOW TO GET AWAY WITH MURDER

THRILLER • 2014
RATED: TV-14 • 43 MINS

You can learn a lot in an internship, like how to fetch coffee, make copies, and—in some extremely rare cases—how to commit and cover up a murder.

When five first-year law students are selected to intern at a prestigious law firm, little do they know that their personal lives and professional careers are about to be upended in the craziest way possible. Through flashbacks, the series works toward the middle of its story from the beginning and the end. How do they go from accepting their dream legal jobs to disposing of a body and destroying evidence?

In this six-season show, Viola Davis is truly wonderful as the troubled but talented law firm head Annalise Keating. She carries the series, even when the intricate setups in each season—while always fun—sometimes crumble under their ambition when it comes to the payoff.

THE KILLING

CRIME • 2007
RATED: TV-MA • 57 MINS

Nothing beats the original Danish version of this gripping police procedural, which influenced a whole decade of gritty crime dramas.

Detective Chief Inspector Sarah Lund (Sofie Gråbøl) is on her last day at the Copenhagen police department. She's all set to move to Sweden and start her new life there when a 19-year-old girl is raped and murdered and she decides to work one last case. Lund and her incoming replacement, Jan Meyer (Søren Malling), spend the next three weeks investigating a killing that many in Copenhagen do not want them to solve.

Police procedurals historically follow standard formulas. Over three seasons, *The Killing* elevates everything—from the acting to the atmosphere to the red herrings. Its global influence is apparent everywhere. If you've enjoyed a crime drama with a moody tone and high production values in the last decade, you have *The Killing* to thank.

THE KILLING (US)

CRIME • 2011
RATED: TV-14 • 45 MINS

If you're no fan of subtitles but love a dark crime drama, this US remake of the hit Danish series could be the show for you.

There are a few things you should know about *The Killing*. One, it's a remake of a Danish show that nearly everyone on the planet loves. Two, it takes place in Seattle and is filmed in English for the subtitle-averse American public. Three, it rains a lot. And finally, over its four seasons, some of its plot twists mirror a less playful *Twin Peaks* (see p456) in vague but undeniable ways.

Like its Danish counterpart, *The Killing* follows two cops, Sarah Linden (Mireille Enos) and Stephen Holder (Joel Kinnaman), as they investigate crimes. There is some real on-screen chemistry here—Enos and Kinnaman also star together in Amazon's *Hanna* (see p24)—and while it doesn't quite live up to the original, it's still a solid adaptation.

GOMORRAH

CRIME • 2014
RATED: TV-MA • 55 MINS

Naples seems like a wild place. Warring crime factions and deadly internal politics make *Gomorrah* the best mafia show this side of *The Sopranos*.

With all the charm of HBO's *My Brilliant Friend* but with roughly a thousand times more violence, *Gomorrah* follows Ciro (Marco D'Amore), an enforcer for the Naples Savastano crime family, as he negotiates various personal and professional challenges that beset a man in his particular trade. Ciro does his best for his boss, Don Pietro (Fortunato Cerlino), and Don Pietro's son, Gennaro, but he has ambitions of his own.

It's unfairly reductive to call *Gomorrah* a simple crime drama when it's so much more. The interfamily dynamics, the power plays, and even the looks exchanged between characters, all combine to make this a riveting televisual experience. The violence is, if anything, a distraction from the real, more intangible drama in this four-season series.

MAX HEADROOM

SCI-FI • 1987
RATED: 15 (UK) • 60 MINS

The idea of our lives being taken over by television networks seems quaint in the age of the internet. But the underlying anti-corporate message of *Max Headroom* still resonates today.

Now, we worry about disinformation on social media, or tech companies listening to our conversations. Back in the '80s, it was more about subliminal advertising (check out films such as *They Live!*) or TVs melting our brains. And nothing encapsulated that fear better than *Max Headroom*, the short-lived dystopian sci-fi show that ran for two short seasons.

Edison Carter (Matt Frewer) is a reporter for Network 23. After an accident, the network tries to save the brand by downloading his brain into a computer. The result is Max Headroom, a stuttering, wisecracking, digitized version of the man. The show is like nothing else on TV before or since, and Max was, for a time, a virtual celebrity, complete with his own endorsements.

TREADSTONE

ACTION • 2019
RATED: TV-MA • 44 MINS

What's the Bourne franchise without the irresistible charisma of memory-challenged assassin cyborg guy Jason Bourne? We're about to find out!

It can be hard to keep track of all the plot threads of the *Bourne* films, between Jason's past CIA handlers, the multitude of dudes trying to kill him, and the tricks his memory plays on him. But one thing we can be certain about is that Treadstone—the code name for the CIA assassin-training program that spawned Bourne—is at the center of it.

Treadstone's one season gives us a glimpse into the program. In 1973 in East Berlin, a CIA operative, J. Randolph Bentley (Jeremy Irvine), is captured by the KGB and put into a behavioral modification program called "Cicada." Fast forward to the present day, where a Korean general is making statements about the "cicadas" being "activated." Much fighting ensues. If nonstop action is your thing, get on *Treadstone* today.

THE NIGHT MANAGER

SPY DRAMA • 2016 • RATED: TV-14 • 60 MINS • SEASONS: 1
TOM HIDDLESTON, HUGH LAURIE, OLIVIA COLMAN

From the mind of spymaster-turned-novelist John le Carré, _The Night Manager_ follows hotel employee Jonathan Pine, whose particular set of skills proves useful when he is thrust into the murky world of the international arms trade.

After two tours of duty in Iraq, Jonathan Pine (Tom Hiddleston) is settled into civilian life working at the Nefertiti Hotel in Cairo. That all changes when Pine becomes involved with a woman named Sophie Alekan (Aure Atika). She's connected to the powerful Hamid family and passes along sensitive information to Pine concerning a huge international weapons deal between the family and arms dealer Richard Roper (Hugh Laurie).

Using connections from his military days, Pine sends the damning info to British intelligence, but a leak there allows Roper to escape.

We next meet Pine four years later working at a Swiss hotel. When Roper walks back into his life, he has a life-changing decision to make.

> **"** _Nothing quite as pretty as napalm at night._ **"**
>
> Richard Roper (S1 E5)

There's something deliciously understated about _The Night Manager_ that suits Hiddleston's acting style perfectly, while Laurie gives arguably his best-ever performance (both won Golden Globes). Pine is the quintessential le Carré hero, but Laurie's Roper dispenses the better advice. His timely reminder to Pine is one no viewer watching the show should forget: "Anyone can betray anyone, Jonathan."

SONS OF ANARCHY

CRIME DRAMA • 2008
RATED: TV-MA • 45 MINS

Jax Teller is an unconventional CEO dealing with a host of organizational issues—everything from running guns to rival gangs and run-ins with the law.

The above description makes sense as soon as you realize that Jax (Charlie Hunnam) is the head of the Sons of Anarchy Motorcycle Club, Redwood Original (SAMCRO). Loosely based on the real-life Hells Angels Motorcycle Club,

Sons of Anarchy charts the lives of a group of modern-day outlaws carving out a home in California's Central Valley.

Through seven anarchic seasons, SAMCRO fights to stay true to itself while battling enemies both internal and external. Jax struggles with the legacy of his father (who founded the group) and challenges himself with being a better dad to his son, Abel. Having recruited a number of actual Hells Angels members to the cast, _Sons of Anarchy_, at its best, manages to harness an outlaw spirit that brought it a devoted following.

SPIRAL

CRIME • 2005
RATED: 18 (UK) • 52 MINS

Mutilations. Bombings. Corruption. Sex trafficking. Gruesome crimes. It's all there in *Spiral*, where silver linings are rarely found.

Like *The Wire* (see p320), but French, *Spiral* is a dark police show set primarily in the Paris slums, where over the course of seven seasons, corruption and violence run rampant and things generally do not work out in the end.

In Season 1, police captain Laure Berthaud (Caroline Proust) and deputy prosecutor Pierre Clément (Grégory Fitoussi) investigate a crime involving a murdered and mutilated Romanian girl, with the trail implicating the rich and powerful. This is a world in which even the most well-meaning characters are forced into uncomfortable choices between justice and loyalty.

Due to some extremely graphic elements, *Spiral* is not for the fainthearted. But for anyone looking for a journey into the heart of darkness, this is the show for you.

OZ

PRISON DRAMA • 1997
RATED: TV-MA • 60 MINS

Oz is the blueprint. If this 1997 prison drama hadn't been as successful as it was, beloved shows such as *The Sopranos*, *The Wire*, and *Game of Thrones* might never have seen the light of day.

Set in the fictional Oswald State Correctional Facility, *Oz* is HBO's first-ever hour-long drama series and a pioneer of prestige TV. A number of top TV actors, including

Christopher Meloni as an incarcerated serial killer named Chris Keller and Edie Falco as Officer Diane Whittlesey, made their HBO debuts in the show.

Oz unquestionably traffics in shock value and gratuitous violence. The incarcerated population of the unit known as "Emerald City" (minus the skipping along a yellow brick road!) jockeys for influence and power over their fellow inmates and those who patrol the block. But the show was unquestionably ahead of its time, and the influence of its six seasons can still be felt today.

LEGENDS

CRIME DRAMA • 2014
RATED: 15 (UK) • 60 MINS

What happens when an undercover agent gets in too deep and loses track of his real identity? That's the question for the FBI's Martin Odum in *Legends*.

Based on *Legends: A Novel of Dissimulation* by Robert Littell, this tells the story of FBI agent Martin Odum (Sean Bean), whose "legends"—or fake identities—are used to infiltrate criminal enterprises. At the same time, though,

they also serve to mask confusion around his own past. As Odum struggles with his true identity, a deeper mystery reveals itself.

Season 1 of *Legends* is an uneven affair, but stick with it—it finds its voice in Season 2, which focuses more on Odum's past and tells a dual narrative in different time periods, much like Season 1 of *True Detective* (see p28). It's a decidedly more mature approach that plays to Bean's strengths, and a stronger, more cohesive story unfolds. Unfortunately, we'll never see what the series could have become because it was canceled before Season 3.

HELIX

SCI-FI • 2014
RATED: TV-PG (15) • 40 MINS

A team of scientists battle with a super virus that turns people into gross zombies in this sci-fi thriller set in a remote Arctic research facility.

Researchers from the Center for Disease Control, led by Dr. Alan Farragut (Billy Campbell) and Dr. Sarah Jordan (Jordan Hayes), travel to an Arctic research station to investigate an outbreak. What they find there will not be solved by social distancing, and soon all hell breaks loose. The sinister Ilaria Corporation is playing a dangerous game, with its own inscrutable goals. Dr. Julia Walker (Kyra Zagorsky) could be the key to it all.

Finding monsters at isolated Arctic research stations isn't a novel concept—shout out to *The Thing*—but even when the show moves to a remote island in the second and final season, *Helix* has some pretty wild plot developments that push it from science fiction into pure fantasy. But don't worry, that's not necessarily a bad thing.

INFORMER

CRIME • 2018
RATED: TV-14 (15) • 60 MINS

No one likes a snitch, but there's plenty to love about *Informer*, a gripping, disjointed thriller, to make us question everything we think we know.

Police informers are not generally thought of in positive terms. "Snitches get stitches" is the approach of those getting informed on, and police handlers often take a pretty dim view of their sources' moral rectitude.

DS Gabe Waters (Paddy Considine), a counterterrorist agent, recognizes a good informer's value. When a café is bombed, the story jumps back a year to focus on a Pakistani immigrant named Raza Shar (Nabhaan Rizwan) who is working for Waters. By the end, Shar may get worse than stitches.

Running over one tight, eight-episode season, *Informer* has excellent plotting and acting. One thing that sets it apart is how deftly it deals with issues such as immigration, race, criminal justice, and other problems so confounding to both society and television in today's world.

LOCKED UP

PRISON DRAMA • 2015
RATED: TV-MA (18) • 53 MINS

Finished *Orange Is the New Black* and looking for a replacement? This Spanish series (also known as *Vis a vis*) has a similar setup, but with a raunchier, faster-paced quality.

We all do stupid things for love, and Macarena Ferreiro (Maggie Civantos) is no exception. Her boss-slash-lover sets her up to take the fall for his own dodgy accounting practices, and she's sent away to Cruz del Sur prison in Spain. Macarena, like *Orange Is the New Black*'s Piper Chapman (see p357), is not initially suited to prison life, and it's unclear whether she'll last the day, let alone her seven-year sentence. But such circumstances sometimes uncover reserves a person doesn't know they have.

A strong female cast and interesting storytelling choices (direct-to-camera interviews with the inmates, for instance) set this apart from other prison shows, but its four seasons also feature plenty of sex and violence (in case you were wondering).

MARCELLA

CRIME • 2016
RATED: TV-MA (15) • 45 MINS

Blacking out is never fun, even if it's from drinking 10 too many gin and tonics. For Marcella Backland, her memory lapses could leave her with something worse than a hangover.

Marcella (Anna Friel) has been out of the detective game for some 15 years. She left the force to raise a family with her husband, Jason (Nicholas Pinnock). But now Jason is leaving her because he feels as though they've grown apart, while their children are away at boarding school.

So Marcella, her family life in shambles, returns to police work as a serial killer responsible for three unsolved murders reappears. The only problem? She experiences memory blackouts and there's some evidence she gets violent in her fugue state. It's not entirely clear why Marcella is allowed to work at all given her various problems, but this two-season series has a solid gimmick that lends uncertainty to its plot.

WALLANDER

CRIME • 2008
RATED: TV-PG (15) • 90 MINS

If you've not already heard of Kurt Wallander, prepare for a treat. The famously introspective Swedish detective is the godfather of so-called "Scandi Noir."

The British version of the Swedish series *Wallander*, itself based on the books by Henning Mankell, puts Kenneth Branagh in the shoes of the brooding Scandinavian Poirot.

(Branagh would go on to play Poirot in the 2017 film *Murder on the Orient Express*.) Through four seasons, Wallander and his crack team of investigators solve cases in the small Swedish hamlet of Ystad.

The fact that this series is in English but takes place in Sweden is only mildly distracting, while Branagh brings his own flavor to the dour detective. It seems audiences can't get enough of the bleak, washed-out settings of "Scandi Noir," and *Wallander* remains among the first and best of the genre. Come and see where it all started.

SACRED GAMES

THRILLER • 2018
RATED: TV-MA • 50 MINS

This Indian Netflix series is a bit like 24 but set in Mumbai where the Jack Bauer–style main character has 25 days to avert a catastrophe.

Inspector Sartaj Singh (Saif Ali Khan) is having a rough time. He works for an extremely corrupt police force, where his relative honesty has hampered his prospects for any promotion. But when he's contacted by reclusive crime figure Ganesh Gaitonde (Nawazuddin Siddiqui) and told he has 25 days to save the city, his adventure truly begins.

Sacred Games jumps around between different timelines. One follows Gaitonde's life from his earliest days to his becoming nearly a "god," at least in his own mind, while another flashes forward into Singh's journey into the slums of Mumbai. In contrast to many hard-bitten crime dramas, *Sacred Games* can verge on the fantastical over its two seasons, but it's pleasingly weird and artfully shot.

DAMAGES

THRILLER • 2007
RATED: TV-MA • 60 MINS

Lawyers are not generally thought of as warm and cuddly—a stereotype that's reinforced in *Damages*, a high-stakes legal thriller that focuses on a single case per season and messes with your mind by playing with time.

Glenn Close stars as high-powered, ruthless, and controversial attorney Patty Hewes, while Rose Byrne is young, up-and-coming attorney Ellen Parsons in this legal thriller. In Season 1, the attorneys at Hewes & Associates are representing employees of billionaire fraudster Arthur Frobisher (Ted Danson), and things are not always as they seem.

Damages is first and foremost a vehicle for Glenn Close at her most steely and unnerving. The show uses flashbacks to lead the audience off the scent and keeps a single legal narrative going throughout its entire five seasons. This structure makes it stand out among the host of comparable yet more conventional law shows available to watch.

HANNA

ACTION • 2019
RATED: TV-MA • 60 MINS

Based on the 2011 film of the same name, *Hanna* is the story of a 15-year-old girl with incredible abilities who is being hunted by the CIA.

Hanna (Esme Creed-Miles) hasn't had what you'd call a normal childhood. She was born in a CIA facility in Romania, where she and other babies were altered to become genetically enhanced super soldiers. Her father, Erik (Joel Kinnaman), gets Hanna out and raises her in the wilds of Poland, where he trains her to be a peerless hunter and fighter. But the CIA has never stopped looking for its lost asset, and when an agent named Marissa (Mireille Enos) learns of Hanna's survival, the chase is on.

Hanna might be an augmented super teen with an unconventional childhood, but she is also subject to the same wants and anxieties as a normal kid her age. Will she get the chance to lead a normal life at the end of this one-season series? You'll have to watch to find out.

LOST

ADVENTURE MYSTERY • 2004
RATED: TV-14 • 44 MINS

When a plane goes down on a remote beach, neither the survivors nor the viewers are prepared for the strange, borderline supernatural events about to take place.

One of the most popular TV series of all time, J. J. Abrams's island mystery, *Lost,* begins when a commercial flight goes down and the survivors gather on a beach, far from any semblance of civilization. Things quickly go from bad to weird for the group when they learn that the island is not quite as uninhabited as they first thought. Each of the six seasons adds another level of mystery.

Lost is a groundbreaking show in many ways. It's incredibly ambitious (one could argue at times too ambitious), and a major precursor to the current prestige TV era. The ensemble cast are uniformly terrific, and as one mystery is seemingly solved, half a dozen more pop up to take its place. *Lost* is unquestionably the most influential show of the early 2000s.

HOMELAND

**THRILLER • 2011 • RATED: TV-MA • 55 MINS • SEASONS: 8
CLAIRE DANES, MANDY PATINKIN, DAMIAN LEWIS**

Carrie Mathison is a CIA officer who doesn't always play by the rules. Her own zealotry to get the job done often puts her in personal and professional danger, but it's sometimes the only thing that can stop terrorist plots in this post-9/11 thriller.

The first two seasons of *Homeland* are some of the most suspenseful TV that the genre has to offer. Nicholas Brody (Damian Lewis) returns home after years of being held captive by a terrorist leader named Abu Nazir.

Meanwhile, CIA operative Carrie Mathison (Claire Danes) is demoted from her overseas assignment and sent to work at CIA headquarters in Virginia. She suspects that Brody, considered a war hero after his rescue, is allied with Nazir and plotting an attack on the United States. But Carrie is having a hard time getting anyone to listen to her theory, let alone finding proof.

Over eight seasons, Carrie's adventures take her all over the globe, from Afghanistan to Berlin to Brooklyn. She struggles with her own personal demons even as she continually works to thwart deadly plots and make her mentor, Saul Berenson (Mandy Patinkin), proud. It's not always smooth sailing for her, though, while later seasons don't quite maintain the intensity of the early episodes. But any show that counts former US President Barack Obama among its fans, as *Homeland* does, is probably doing something right.

> **"** *It's the lies that undo us. It's the lies we think we need to survive.* **"**
>
> **Carrie Mathison** (S2 E5)

SALAMANDER

**CRIME • 2012
RATED: TV-MA • 40 MINS**

Is *Salamander* a heist show, or is it a political conspiracy thriller? Well, it's a little bit of both and takes some of the best tropes of each to put together two very solid seasons of TV.

This Belgian crime series begins with a bank heist that leads to conspiracies galore. Paul Gerardi (Filip Peeters) is a no-nonsense cop who plays by his own rules and will stop at

nothing to get to the truth (you know the type). When an exclusive bank in Brussels is robbed and many prominent public figures have their valuables stolen, he's put on the case. These dignitaries want the investigation kept under the radar, and it soon becomes clear why. They have secrets, and what originally looked like a simple robbery turns out to be anything but.

In our age of increasing wealth inequality, any conspiracy involving generations of the high and mighty panicking over spilled secrets is a crime story that we can all enjoy.

STARTUP

CRIME • 2016
RATED: 18 (UK) • 44 MINS

The 1995 cult film *Hackers* told us to hack the planet, but the hacker founders of GenCoin take a different route—which first means hacking the venture capital community.

Cyber thrillers come in a number of different flavors. *Mr. Robot* (see p393), for instance, keeps everything super paranoid and unreliable. *Devs* takes a more philosophical bent. *StartUp*,

starring Adam Brody as Nick Talman and Martin Freeman as crooked, self-loathing FBI agent Phil Rask, takes a grittier approach.

Rask blackmails a money launderer named Andrew Talman, who gives the cash to his son, Nick, to move offshore. Nick instead invests in a floundering cryptocurrency startup. But Rask still wants his money. Soon enough, a Haitian gang and the Russian mob get involved, and it's a race to the finish line to see whether Talman and business partner Izzy can raise enough funds for their startup while also managing to avoid getting murdered in the process.

ORPHAN BLACK

SCI-FI • 2013
RATED: TV-MA • 44 MINS

Ever wished you could take over someone else's life and profession and get away with it? If *Orphan Black* is any indication, you should be careful what you wish for.

Where one person sees a tragedy, another smells opportunity. When professional hustler Sarah Manning (Tatiana Maslany) witnesses the suicide of a woman who looks remarkably

like her, she assumes her identity. But what she thought was a standard grift turns into a vast conspiracy, and Sarah learns an impossible truth—that she's a clone, and there's no telling how many versions of herself are out there.

Maslany's performance as the clones has been rightly lauded as one of the most virtuoso television turns in recent memory. Each of her incarnations demonstrates a distinct, utterly memorable personality. In lesser hands, the five-season story might have gone off the rails early on, but thanks to her, it remains one of the better sci-fi dramas of the past decade.

RESIDUE

HORROR • 2015
RATED: 15 (UK) • 43 MINS

For those who want a little more supernatural in their dystopian sci-fi, *Residue* offers ghosts to go along with its suspicious government cover-up.

Starring not one but two *Game of Thrones* (*GoT*; see p8) alumni, *Residue* begins with an explosion at a futuristic UK nightclub and the setting up of a large quarantine zone. Jennifer Preston (Natalia Tena, who played

wildling Osha in *GoT*) is a photojournalist working in the affected area who stumbles onto some disturbing findings. Her boyfriend, Jonas (Iwan Rheon—*GoT* über-villain Ramsay Bolton), is working for the government trying to cover up the mess but is also interested in finding out what is going on.

This one-season series packs a lot of creepiness into its three episodes, and it's cool to see Rheon in a role where you're not rooting for him to die horribly. A great quick watch for those looking for maximum return on minimal time investment.

CLOAK & DAGGER

SCI-FI • 2018
RATED: TV-14 • 44 MINS

Not every Super Hero story has to be on the big screen to be epic. *Cloak & Dagger* shows how lesser-known Marvel properties can still make compelling TV.

There are surprisingly few successful Super Hero duos in the Marvel Cinematic Universe (MCU). Sure, there are sprawling collections of mighty folk like the Avengers or X-Men, but rarely do we see two-person tag teams.

Cloak and Dagger work only as a pair, and not just because of their clever names. Tandy Bowen (Olivia Holt) and Tyrone Johnson (Aubrey Joseph) both grew up in New Orleans, but in vastly different circumstances. After an industrial accident leaves them each with strange powers, they find themselves with a lot more in common and form a deep personal relationship.

Cloak & Dagger is unconventional for a Marvel series and doesn't have any neat analogues. This two-season show is kind of its own thing, and that's refreshing.

GIRI / HAJI

CRIME • 2019
RATED: NR • 60 MINS

Family is everything, but every person's definition of family is a little different. And if that definition includes the word "Yakuza," it's time to run for the hills.

Considering the many different varieties of TV crime shows available, it's a little disheartening to see a relative dearth of streaming options involving the underworld of Japanese gangsters. *Giri/Haji* (Duty/Shame)

seeks to right that wrong as it follows Detective Kenzo Mori (Takehiro Hira) traveling to London in search of his brother, Yuto (Yôsuke Kubozuka). Yuto is on the lam after wronging the Yakuza. True to form, they are none too pleased with him about it, and Yuto is keeping his head down in the UK, where Mori hopes to find him.

Giri/Haji is a taut meditation on family, loyalty, and friendship that never lets up. It has all the dark thrills the Yakuza milieu has to offer but with the twist that the action is mostly set in London. More of this, please.

STATE OF PLAY

THRILLER • 2003
RATED: TV-14 • 52 MINS

An investigative journalist, his cop friend, and two suspicious deaths come together to reveal a conspiracy that reaches right to the top in this taught, London-set political thriller.

When intrepid reporter Cal McCaffrey (John Simm) links the murder of an alleged drug dealer named Kelvin Stagg to the untimely death of a political researcher named Sonia

Baker, it starts a chain reaction that leads to the highest reaches of government. McCaffrey, along with his colleagues Della Smith (Kelly Macdonald) and Cameron Foster (Bill Nighy), are committed to getting to the truth.

Like films such as *All the President's Men* or *Spotlight*, *State of Play* demonstrates the role that journalists still play in holding those in power accountable. The reporters are in over their heads and in harm's way, but they refuse to be silenced—even as a gag order from on high is issued to prevent the story from running and the truth being told.

TRUE DETECTIVE

CRIME DRAMA • 2014 • RATED: TV-MA • 55 MINS • SEASONS: 3
MATTHEW MCCONAUGHEY, COLIN FARRELL, MAHERSHALA ALI

Nihilism, crime, police work, and supernatural happenings are mixed together in deliciously diabolical ways in Nic Pizzolatto's anthology series. If tense Southern Gothic weirdness and philosophical police procedurals are your thing, *True Detective* is the series for you.

Each of the three seasons has its own story and an entirely different cast. In Season 1 of *True Detective*, a 1995 murder in Louisiana sets two homicide cops on a winding path that doesn't end until 17 years later. One of the detectives, Rust Cohle (Matthew McConaughey), struggles with depression and alcoholism. His partner on the case, Marty Hart (Woody Harrelson), is having some of his own troubles at home.

Cohle memorably says, "Time is a flat circle." The show adheres to that idea and bounces between a few different timelines. In 2012 (the present day), Cohle and Hart are being interviewed about their roles in the still-unsolved 1995 case, and Cohle, in particular, is still haunted by the questions that have been left unanswered for nearly two decades. *True Detective*'s first season is still its best.

Season 2 moves from the American South to the sunny shores of California, starring Colin Farrell as a corrupt detective named Ray Velcoro, Rachel McAdams as Detective Sergeant Antigone "Ani" Bezzerides, and Vince Vaughn as a career criminal trying to go straight. Despite the decent performances, strong visuals, and exciting action, this installment lacks the haunting atmosphere that made Season 1 so powerful.

Season 3, starring Mahershala Ali as Detective Wayne Hays and Stephen Dorff as his partner, Roland West, gets back to *True Detective* basics. After two young children disappear in the Ozarks in 1980, Hays and West are brought in to find them. In a future timeline, Hays is being interviewed about the case for a true-crime podcast, even though his memory is failing him and the retired detective becomes increasingly unsure about what's real and what isn't.

Driven by Ali's hypnotic performance, Season 3 also explores issues of racism and class. But ultimately it's the uncertainty of memory, the inability to disentangle the real from the imagined in the face of unspeakable crimes, and the grappling with the past that unites it with the rest of the *True Detective* universe.

CREATOR: Nic Pizzolatto
PRODUCTION CO: Anonymous Content, HBO Entertainment, Passenger

BATTLESTAR GALACTICA

SCI-FI • 2004 • RATED: TV-14 • 44 MINS • SEASONS: 4
EDWARD JAMES OLMOS, KATEE SACKHOFF, JAMES CALLIS

Set in a distant time and an even more distant solar system, *Battlestar Galactica* continually questions what it is that makes us human, as it chronicles a war between colonists and their AI creations.

Battlestar Galactica was an unlikely hit. Loosely based on the 1978 series (see p402), the show found a mainstream audience that eluded the original. A 2003 mini series led to four seasons, each one of which peeled back another layer of history between the humans of the 12 Colonies—a far-flung civilization eons from the original Earth—and their rebellious creations, the Cylons.

As the series begins, the 12 Colonies have enjoyed four decades of relative peace. Following the first Cylon War when the machines rose up against their human masters, the Cylons abruptly vanished, leaving humans to speculate on the fate of their artificial creations. But they weren't really gone—they were just being patient. A coordinated attack decimates the human population, and the few thousand survivors flee on whatever ships remain, including the soon-to-be decommissioned *Galactica*.

There's more bad news for humanity. The upgraded Cylons now look and act exactly like people, to the point where some of these sleeper agents aren't even aware they're Cylons and not humans. Over the next four seasons, the small group of survivors searches everywhere for a new home. As they're being harried across the galaxy, these space refugees are looking for answers and safety, but they're also establishing the rules for their new society.

Battlestar Galactica is a show of its time. There are many not so subtle parallels with the fight against terrorism, which was just getting underway at the time. But many of the questions being asked then—about civil liberties, religious freedom, and free elections—remain unanswered today. From an entertainment standpoint, there's never a dull moment in the series. The Cylons are absolutely ruthless and relentless in their genocidal mission, and every episode is a thrilling fight for survival. But is mere survival enough?

CREATORS: Glen A. Larson, Ronald D. Moore **PRODUCTION CO:** BSkyB, David Eick Productions, NBC Universal Television (2004–2007), R&D TV, Stanford Pictures (II), UMS (2007–2009)

BECK

CRIME DRAMA • 1997
RATED: TV-14 • 90 MINS

The murders are grisly, the divorced detective looks depressed, and the climate is chilly. Welcome to the world of Beck, head of the Stockholm-based Murder Squad.

When we first meet Beck (Peter Haber) and the Murder Squad—which includes his flashier partner, Gunvald Larsson (Mikael Persbrandt)—the team is taking on drug smuggling, serial killers, and a healthy dose of personal tragedy. This sets the tone for the next seven seasons of decapitations, right-wing violence, unhelpful bosses, and child murder. Season 6 sees Kristofer Hivju—best known as *Game of Thrones*'s wildling leader Tormund Giantsbane—join as Beck's partner Steinar Hovland.

Based on the novels by Maj Sjöwall and Per Wahlöö, this long-running crime series deserves plaudits for its incredible stamina alone. Nearly 25 years after it first aired, it still thrills and horrifies just as much today.

SHERLOCK

CRIME • 2010
RATED: TV-14 • 88 MINS

History's greatest detective is plucked out of the 19th century and deposited in modern-day London with some very techie twists.

Breathing new life into an iconic literary character such as Sherlock Holmes can't be easy. It takes superb writing and a truly gifted performer to bring them off the page and back into our hearts. In this update of Sir Arthur Conan Doyle's novels, Holmes (Benedict Cumberbatch) acts as a crime consultant, using his powers of deduction to help police investigations. He's aided by his roommate Dr. John Watson (Martin Freeman), who turns Holmes into a media celebrity by detailing their adventures on his blog. The four-season series also brings in Sherlock's eternal nemesis, the dastardly Moriarty (Andrew Scott).

The show takes some truly creative and imaginative turns, including a Christmas special that sends Holmes and Watson back in time. A compelling series that intrigues and amuses.

JACK TAYLOR

CRIME • 2010
RATED: NR • 90 MINS

In TV series *Game of Thrones*, Iain Glen plays a man of impeccable decency and honor. In *Jack Taylor*, he plays whatever the complete opposite of that is.

Jack Taylor (Iain Glen) isn't what you'd call a gentle spirit. In fact, he was kicked off the police force for assaulting a politician at a traffic stop. He suffers no fools, is as tough as nails, and drinks way too much. But since his dishonorable discharge from the Garda (the Irish police force), he has started a new career as a private investigator, looking into some crimes the police would like to ignore, including some rather gory deaths.

Dressed in his trademark blue overcoat, Taylor is a classic type—cynical and burned out but with a roguish charm—while Galway, a university town on the west coast of Ireland, makes the perfect atmospheric setting for this three-season detective series. It all feels very gloomy—yet vibrant—in the best possible way.

MONEY HEIST

CRIME • 2017
RATED: TV-MA • 70 MINS

One of the best heist shows around, this Spanish thriller follows a crack team of criminals as they attempt a daring billion-euro robbery dressed in Salvador Dalí masks and red overalls.

A mysterious stranger known simply as "The Professor" (Álvaro Morte) puts together a group of thieves and gives them all code names based on cities (Tokyo, Moscow, Berlin, etc.). Their objective? A bold assault on Spain's Royal Mint, which they hope will yield them €2.4 billion with no loss of life. In theory, it's the perfect crime....

But then we all know there's no such thing. You can never predict human behavior perfectly, and hostages, police, and the thieves themselves all act in unexpected ways that threaten to upend The Professor's perfectly laid plan. Full of exciting and unexpected twists, this gripping four-season series—known as *La Casa de Papel* in Spanish—leaves you constantly wondering what's coming next.

SILENT WITNESS

CRIME • 1996
RATED: TV-14 • 120 MINS

Silent Witness **follows a team of forensic pathologists who investigate violent crimes, the likes of which will haunt your dreams for years to come.**

Dr. Sam Ryan (Amanda Burton) is the best forensic pathologist in the business. When we first meet her, she's finding out what happened to a six-year-old girl found floating dead in the river. Dr. Ryan uses her skills to follow a trail of clues invisible to the untrained eye, and following her forensic thought processes is truly fascinating.

There's almost no form of murder or sadistic crime this long-running show hasn't witnessed over its staggering 23 seasons. After leaving the show in Season 8, Dr. Ryan was replaced with an ensemble team, including Dr. Nikki Alexander (Emilia Fox), Jack (David Caves), and Clarissa (Liz Carr), but our appetite for *Silent Witness* has never abated. Here's to 23 more gloriously gruesome seasons.

TRAPPED

MYSTERY • 2015
RATED: TV-14 • 60 MINS

For those who like their noir crime shows extra-desolate and contingent on dangerous weather conditions, Iceland's *Trapped* **is the series for you.**

When a dismembered corpse is pulled out of the water near the eastern Icelandic town of Seyðisfjörður, police chief Andri Ólafsson (Ólafur Darri Ólafsson) is forced to investigate. Complicating matters is the fact that a storm's a-brewin', which will cut the isolated town off from outside help, and the murderer is still, presumably, on the loose.

Taking place against the backdrop of the 2008 financial crisis, this two-season Nordic noir series sees Ólafsson struggling to put aside his small-town ennui and save the day. But is this slightly sad, hirsute local policeman up to the task of solving the crime and bringing the murderer to justice before they kill again?

WATCHMEN

ACTION DRAMA • 2019 • RATED: TV-MA • 60 MINS • SEASONS: 1
REGINA KING, JEREMY IRONS, JEAN SMART

Based on the legendary comic-book series, this adaptation of *Watchmen* is one of the more thought-provoking and gripping single seasons of TV in years, tackling issues of race, love, authority, and family without ever feeling burdened by its own mythology.

The original *Watchmen* comic-book series by Alan Moore and Dave Gibbons has the distinct honor of being the only graphic novel included in *Time* magazine's "All-Time 100 Novels." It's one of the very first books to make the jump from the realm of comics—something traditionally thought of as kids' fare—to a legitimate piece of literature taken seriously by critics. Despite its popular and critical success, the general consensus among fans—as well as series creator Alan Moore—was that *Watchmen* could never be properly translated to the screen. This opinion was only

reinforced by the ponderous 2009 Zack Snyder movie adaptation. Finally, though, more than three decades after its publication, screenwriter Damon Lindelof (*Lost, The Leftovers*) finally cracked the *Watchmen* code with this TV version.

> **"** *People who wear masks are driven by trauma. They're obsessed with justice....* **"**
>
> **Laurie Blake** (S1 E4)

In Lindelof's remix/sequel/prequel, it has been 34 years since the events in the book, and much has transpired since the artificial, Lovecraftian catastrophe manufactured by super-genius Adrian Veidt (aka Ozymandias). For one, Robert Redford is the President of the United States. As commander in chief, the actor, meme, and founder of the Sundance Film Festival has introduced "Redfordations," which offer restitution for victims of racial violence throughout American history.

Not everyone is pleased with President Redford's actions. In Tulsa, Oklahoma, an uneasy peace is about to be shattered. After some bloody encounters with white supremacist group Seventh Kavalry—who all, it should be noted, wear Rorschach masks like the character from the book—local law enforcement decides it would be safer for all involved if police cover their faces to protect their identities. In one particularly

violent instance, later dubbed the "White Night," Seventh Kavalry members launch a coordinated attack against police officers and their families in their homes. Those police who survive—including Angela Abar (Regina King)— are forced to take additional steps to protect their identities and stay safe.

Part of what makes Lindelof's version so refreshing is that instead of trying to animate the graphic novel as a beat-by-beat clone with contemporary actors, it breaks *Watchmen* down into its component parts and uses them to create something entirely new yet faithful to the original. Characters from the original graphic novel, such as Laurie Blake (Jean Smart) are there, but with significant changes. Still, it's hard to categorize, even for Lindelof, who told *Rolling Stone*: "Here's another instance where I want to punch myself in the face: I called this thing a remix, because it doesn't feel like a sequel to me. But it does by

the traditional rules of a sequel, in that this chronologically follows the original. But it's also kind of a prequel, because this story starts in 1921, which predates any of the events of the comic."

It's difficult to say more about the plot without divulging too much, but suffice to say these nine episodes of *Watchmen* have something for everyone, new and old fans alike. And while some were disappointed to hear that there are no current plans to make another season, there is something to be said for leaving when you're at the top of your game.

Watchmen is an entirely original story for our own era, one that also pays homage to the source material. Like the original comic series, it is a dark, dystopian masterpiece.

OTHER SUPER HEROES BASED IN NEW YORK CITY

BRONX

LUKE CAGE
Harlem

NEW JERSEY

PUNISHER
Hell's Kitchen

JESSICA JONES
Hell's Kitchen

DAREDEVIL
Hell's Kitchen

DOCTOR STRANGE
Sanctum Sanctorum

IRON FIST
Chikara Dojo, Chinatown

CENTRAL PARK

AVENGERS
Avengers Mansion

IRON MAN
Stark Tower

THE FANTASTIC FOUR
Baxter Building

MANHATTAN

TEENAGE MUTANT NINJA TURTLES
Manhattan Sewers

QUEENS

SPIDER-MAN
Forest Hills, Queens

BROOKLYN

Also based in NEW YORK
POWER GIRL
CATWOMAN
VIGILANTE
JUSTICE LEAGUE INTERNATIONAL

CREATOR: Damon Lindelof **PRODUCTION CO: DC** Comics, HBO, Paramount Television, Storm Studios, Warner Bros. Television, White Rabbit

CRIMINAL MINDS

CRIME • 2005
RATED: TV-14 • 42 MINS

As one of the most successful and longest-running network crime shows ever, *Criminal Minds* has spawned spin-offs, video games, and copycats.

The first thing you should know about *Criminal Minds* is that, like *CSI* (see p14), it's not necessarily the most realistic portrayal of actual criminal investigations and focuses on criminal profiling. That said, it can still be a lot of fun, and over the course of 15 seasons, its team of crack FBI profilers solves hundreds of cases that have left standard law enforcement officers baffled, sometimes using its skills to anticipate crimes even before they happen.

A rotating cast that includes Mandy Patinkin, Joe Montegna, Thomas Gibson (as the ever-frowning "Hotch"), and Paget Brewster, really keeps the show humming. Episodes such as "The Replicator," about a villain who replicates old crimes the team has solved, might suggest the show's creative juices are starting to run dry, but don't be fooled!

THE STRANGER

MYSTERY • 2020
RATED: TV-MA • 42 MINS

If a strange woman in a cap comes up to you and offers to tell you a secret, do yourself a favor and just run away as fast as you can.

Based on the novel by Harlan Coben, *The Stranger* demonstrates that even the most tranquil towns have dark secrets lingering below the surface. Adam Price (Richard Armitage) has what seems to be a perfect family life. That all goes to hell one day when a young woman in a baseball hat (Hannah John-Kamen) tells him a shattering secret about his wife, Corinne (Dervla Kirwan). Corinne then disappears, and Adam must learn the truth about the stranger and himself.

There are plenty of mysteries to go around in the single season of *The Stranger*, as the titular character is not shy about spreading discord among the townsfolk. Who is she? What does she want? What happened to Corinne? Like any great mystery story, the answers are there, if you know where to look for them.

TRAVELERS

SCI-FI • 2016
RATED: TV-MA • 45 MINS

Citizens of a postapocalyptic future travel back in time to inhabit the bodies of people from our present. Their aim? To use them to try to change their fate.

For our time travelers, the only way to save their present (our future) is to change their past (our present). To accomplish this, they travel back in time and, well, possess people about to die (they know the details from public records) and use them as hosts to accomplish their missions. Although humanity has been nearly wiped out in their own time, thousands of travelers are striving to avert their terrible fate, working in multiple teams.

This three-season series from *Stargate SG-1* creator Brad Wright (see p403) focuses on a single team of travelers, led by Grant MacLaren (Eric McCormack), an erstwhile federal agent. The show doesn't feel especially grounded in science or philosophy but is at its best when the travelers learn to enjoy life for the first time.

BABYLON BERLIN

PERIOD DRAMA • 2017
RATED: TV-MA • 45 MINS

Weimar Germany in 1929 was a global center for arts and culture, but it was built on unstable foundations. *Babylon Berlin* whisks you to the seedy underside of the German capital's gilded age.

This thrilling, sprawling period piece is set in the years just before Hitler comes to power and follows Gereon Rath (Volker Bruch), a police inspector from Cologne who is transferred to Berlin to work on a case involving organized crime. He's helped by Charlotte Ritter (Liv Lisa Fries), a police typist who moonlights as a sex worker.

With a huge budget, incredible production values, talented creators (including Tom Tykwer, director of films such as *Run Lola Run* and *Perfume: The Story of a Murderer*), and a great ensemble cast, *Babylon Berlin*'s two seasons transport you back to a tumultuous period. The society you see there—with a widening gulf between rich and poor and on the cusp of disaster—resonates today.

CONTINUUM

SCI-FI • 2012
RATED: TV-14 • 45 MINS

Featuring a cop from the future stuck in the present, *Continuum* doesn't take itself too seriously, but it is clever and action packed!

Policing the space-time continuum is not a job for the unmotivated. There are thorny legal questions involving predestination and causality, and there are plenty of places (and times) for an enterprising criminal to hide.

When a terrorist group in the year 2077 called Liber8 escapes into the time stream, supercop Kiera Cameron (Rachel Nichols) jumps right in after them. Forget what it must be like for someone from a future where time travel is possible to be trapped in 2012 Vancouver—it doesn't matter, Kiera is far too busy hunting time terrorists.

The overall concept of *Continuum* feels familiar, with the terrorists trying to stop powerful corporations taking over the government. But the story lines and the strength of the lead role keep this four-season series watchable.

GREYZONE

THRILLER • 2018
RATED: 15 (UK) • 45 MINS

Greyzone could be an all-encompassing description of the entire Scandinavian noir genre, but Nordic filmmakers know their business when it comes to crime thrillers.

Victoria Rahbek (Birgitte Hjort Sørensen) is a Danish engineer who works on drones. After Victoria is kidnapped and forced to work against her will by a group of international terrorists, Detective Inspector Eva Forsberg (Tova Magnusson) is in a race against time to prevent the terrorists from killing her and possibly hundreds of other civilians with a drone-based weapon.

You'd think you could see only so many similar landscapes and distressed detectives solving heinous crimes before it got dull. You'd be wrong! *Greyzone* is the latest addition to the increasingly impressive Scandi noir catalog and takes the genre in some new directions. There's only one season so far, but *Greyzone* could be the best yet.

ARROW

ACTION • 2012
RATED: TV-14 • 42 MINS

Stand aside, Batman, there's room for more than one billionaire socialite crime fighter in the DC Universe. *Arrow* follows playboy Oliver Queen as he fights criminals in Starling City.

After being shipwrecked when his father's yacht sinks, scion Oliver Queen (Stephen Amell) spends five years on a mysterious island where he learns tons of cool fighting skills. Eventually, he returns to Starling City, where he assumes the mantle of "The Hood" and fights crime. Through eight seasons and several branding evolutions, Queen becomes known as Arrow (his weapon of choice is a bow and arrow), and the "Arrowverse" is born.

Based on DC Comics's Green Arrow character, the series has spawned a number of spin-offs, from *The Flash* (see p12) to *Supergirl* (see p93) to *Legends of Tomorrow*. The Arrowverse has become its own rich, layered universe, with plenty of simple charms.

THE BLACKLIST

CRIME • 2013
RATED: TV-14 • 43 MINS

If smirks could kill, Raymond "Red" Reddington would be a serial killer. He's an information broker and makes a living knowing more than anyone else—including the US government.

Red (James Spader) is one of the FBI's most wanted criminals. After years spent in service to the government, for the past two decades he's been committing crimes all over the globe with some of the world's worst people. One day, for reasons known only to him, he turns himself in. But what does he want?

In return for immunity and the chance to work with a certain profiler named Elizabeth Keen (Megan Boone), Reddington offers to help the FBI track down not only the most notorious criminals it knows about but also the ones it doesn't know about. Spader delivers a hall-of-mirrors performance, delighting in feeding you answers that you know that they know that he knows are not really answers, but it never ceases to entertain.

THE FALL

CRIME • 2013
RATED: TV-MA • 60 MINS

This British-Irish series is the stuff of nightmares. DCI Stella Gibson is called in to investigate an unsolved murder but soon discovers it's just one in a larger string of cases involving slain women.

The Fall isn't a whodunnit. We find out the murderer's identity almost immediately, and the series instead becomes a cat-and-mouse game between Gibson (Gillian Anderson) and a bereavement counselor named Paul Spector (Jamie Dornan). Set in Belfast, Spector stalks and kills young professional women by night, even as he holds down a job and acts as a loving husband and father by day.

Spector, later referred to as "The Belfast Strangler," leads Gibson on a chase that ends up costing both of them dearly over the course of three seasons. When they finally come face to face, they both already know each other as intimately as we know them.

24

**ACTION • 2001 • RATED: TV-14 • 44 MINS • SEASONS: 8
KIEFER SUTHERLAND, ELISHA CUTHBERT, DENNIS HAYSBERT**

Meet the most indomitable American hero this side of Rambo. Jack Bauer is the federal superagent who races against the clock to stop whatever nefarious agents are threatening the American way of life.

Scripted in "real time," 24 is the quintessential post-9/11 show. In Season 1, Bauer (Kiefer Sutherland) is charged with protecting David Palmer (Dennis Haysbert), a presidential candidate. Things get complicated when Bauer's family is kidnapped and a conspiracy is revealed. The season transpires in the course of a single day—24 hours—where each episode covers roughly one 60-minute period.

Each successive season pits Bauer against increasingly impossible odds, higher global stakes, and more conspiracies within conspiracies. But as the pressure increases, Bauer never gets any more time on the clock. It's always 24 hours. Nuclear weapons, assassinations, dirty bombs, cyberattacks—at one time or another, Jack grimaces and shoots his way through every existential threat to America's sacred freedom.

From a relatively straightforward first season, things ramp up considerably, and the show occasionally veers into some deeply silly plots. Still, 24 never, ever ceases to entertain, and even familiarity with all of Jack's tricks doesn't do much to lessen the thrill when he pulls off another impossible mission.

> **"** *I'm federal agent Jack Bauer, and today is the longest day of my life.* **"**
>
> **Jack Bauer** (S1 E1)

BROADCHURCH

**CRIME DRAMA • 2013
RATED: TV-MA • 48 MINS**

Prepare yourself for an emotional journey and an intriguing investigation as two police detectives seek to solve the murder of a young boy that has rocked a British seaside town.

When an 11-year-old boy is murdered in the fictional coastal town of Broadchurch, it sends the community into turmoil. New arrival DI Alec Hardy (David Tennant), recently put in charge of the local investigative unit, is trying to put his biggest professional failure behind him. DS Ellie Miller (Olivia Colman), who was angling for the job that went to Hardy, is local and knows the townsfolk better than her new boss. But that familiarity presents its own challenges as the investigation continues.

Colman and Tennant are so good that they could make the worst script in the world seem interesting. Fortunately, Chris Chibnall, the writer behind Broadchurch, gave them material worthy of their talents, and all three seasons are deeply layered, engrossing affairs.

TOM CLANCY'S JACK RYAN

ACTION • 2018 • RATED: TV-MA • 60 MINS • SEASONS: 2
JOHN KRASINSKI, WENDELL PIERCE, JOHN HOOGENAKKER

Jack Ryan has military training, but is far more comfortable crunching numbers in an office than taking down bad guys out in the field.

John Krasinski takes the title role of a young CIA analyst in a safe desk job, who's sent into the field after uncovering terrorist activity. From there, he uses his analytical and military skills to combat ruthless international terrorists and cunning power-hungry dictators threatening world safety.

In Season 1, Ryan joins up with James Greer (Wendell Pierce) to track down a powerful international terrorist organization. It's a race against the clock (of course), and he will need to use all of his talents to avert world catastrophe. Season 2 finds Ryan and company in South America, where he gets entangled with a Venezuelan dictator who, it turns out, doesn't care much for the CIA.

The Jack Ryan character, who started life in Tom Clancy's *Ryanverse* novels, has been portrayed by several notable actors in movies. Alec Baldwin played him opposite Sean Connery in *The Hunt for Red October*. Harrison Ford embodied a more mature Ryan in *Patriot Games*. More recently, Ben Affleck took over the Ryan mantle in *The Sum of All Fears*. But Krasinski is the first to take up the name in a TV series, and he does it proud. In every incarnation, Ryan is thought of by his CIA colleagues as a boy scout, and Krasinski's Ryan does have some of the wry charm that served him well as Jim Halpert in *The Office* (see p154). But for the most part, his performance is straight out of the Tom Clancy playbook.

For fans of *24* (see p37) or *Homeland* (see p25), *Jack Ryan* will scratch that same itch. There's lots of intergovernment agency drama, plenty of military action, and occasional snippets of romance. Krasinski might not seem an obvious action hero, but he pulls it off. In fact, there's a good argument for his Jack Ryan being the best yet.

SCREEN APPEARANCES OF MAIN CHARACTERS IN RYANVERSE

	The Hunt for Red October (Feature Film)	Patriot Games (Feature Film)	Clear and Present Danger (Feature Film)	The Sum of All Fears (Feature Film)	Jack Ryan: Shadow Recruit (Feature Film)	Tom Clancy's Jack Ryan (TV Series)
Jack Ryan	✓	✓	✓	✓	✓	✓
Caroline Ryan/Muller	✓	✓	✓	✓	✓	✓
Sally Ryan	✓	✓	✓			
Adm. James Greer	✓	✓	✓			✓
John Clark				✓	✓	
Domingo Chavez			✓			

CREATOR: Carlton Cuse, Graham Roland **PRODUCTION CO:** Genre Arts, Push, Boot., Platinum Dunes, Skydance Television, Paramount Television, Amazon Studios

DAREDEVIL

ACTION • 2015 • RATED: TV-MA • 54 MINS • SEASONS: 3
CHARLIE COX, DEBORAH ANN WOLL, VINCENT D'ONOFRIO

Based on the legendary Marvel Comics hero, *Daredevil* follows Matt Murdock, a lawyer whose blindness has heightened his other senses to an extraordinary degree, helping him fight crime in New York City's Hell's Kitchen neighborhood.

Matt Murdock (Charlie Cox) is a good lawyer. But he's an even better acrobatic vigilante patrolling the streets of Hell's Kitchen by night. A childhood accident left Murdock completely blind, but somehow all his other senses were boosted to an incredible degree. Possessed of an unquenchable thirst for justice that isn't completely satisfied in the courtroom, he suits up and goes looking for bad guys at night. And there's no shortage of petty criminals for Murdock to pulverize.

Murdock may have met his match when he catches the attention of Kingpin (Vincent D'Onofrio), the imposing, bald-pated man who pulls the strings for the criminal element on Manhattan's West Side. Things go from bad to worse in Season 2, as Daredevil meets his long-time rival, The Punisher (Jon Bernthal), a man who is less interested in justice than he is in bloody vengeance. These two vigilantes have markedly different philosophies when it comes to fighting crime, and there's not a chance in Hell's Kitchen they'll be resolved peacefully.

> **"***I'm not seeking penance for what I've done, Father. I'm asking forgiveness ... for what I'm about to do.***"**
>
> Matt Murdock (SI EI)

ALIAS

ACTION • 2001
RATED: TV-14 • 42 MINS

Feisty agent Sydney Bristow was recruited by the CIA—or so she thought. After learning the dark truth about her real employer, Bristow uses her skills to take the organization down from the inside.

In the world of James Bond, spycraft is a pretty straightforward affair. Bond doesn't even bother to pretend he's someone else.

It's just "Bond. James Bond." In the world of *Alias*, things are a bit more complicated. Before she's even finished college, Sydney Bristow (Jennifer Garner) is recruited by the CIA, specifically a secretive unit called SD-6.

The thing is, SD-6 isn't part of the CIA. In fact, it's working to undermine the US government. When Sydney finds out, it launches her into a world of double and triple agents where no one knows who's working for whom. With future star Bradley Cooper and a Renaissance-era conspiracy thrown in for good measure, it all adds up to a wild five seasons.

EDGE OF DARKNESS

CRIME • 1985
RATED: TV-14 • 50 MINS

Nuclear holocaust was very much on the minds of many in 1985, and that anxiety resulted in some incredibly tense and existential TV dramas, none better than *Edge of Darkness*.

Police officer Ronald Craven (Bob Peck) experiences a thing no parent should when his daughter, environmental activist Emma (Joanne Whalley), is shot dead in front of him.

What he originally suspects is a botched attempt on his life quickly reveals itself to be a deeper conspiracy, with implications for nothing less than the fate of the planet.

Edge of Darkness is a product of its time but holds up wonderfully today. (A 2010 movie remake starring Mel Gibson fell flat.) The themes still ring true for those of us worried about environmental degradation and nuclear fallout today. But as a drama alone, this single-season series is a thrilling piece of work that anyone—including those born after the fall of the Berlin Wall—should enjoy.

THE GIFTED

FANTASY • 2017
RATED: TV-14 • 43 MINS

While it doesn't feature the likes of Wolverine or Storm, *The Gifted* still thrillingly embodies the spirit of the X-Men comic-book franchise.

In the classic 1981 comic-book arc "Days of Future Past," the X-Men have been nearly hunted to extinction in a dystopian future. While things are not quite that bleak in *The Gifted*, we're still led to understand that both

the X-Men and the Brotherhood of Mutants have disappeared in its alternative Marvel Universe. Reed Strucker (Stephen Moyer) makes his living as a district attorney who prosecutes mutants and puts them in camps. But everything changes when Strucker discovers that his own kids have latent mutant abilities. To protect them, he takes his family on the run.

Although *The Gifted*'s two seasons lack the star power we expect from the X-Men movies, the series is a solidly entertaining twist on the Super Hero franchise.

WHITECHAPEL

CRIME • 2009
RATED: TV-14 • 45 MINS

A team of detectives in London's Whitechapel district track down copycat killers looking to piggyback on the dubious notoriety of history's most famous murderers.

Copycat serial killers have to be at the absolute bottom of the mass murderer hierarchy. Not only are they contemptible monsters, they're unoriginal to boot.

In 2008, DI Joseph Chandler (Rupert Penry-Jones) must grapple with a series of grisly Jack the Ripper copycat murders when he's posted to Whitechapel to investigate the death of a woman. He works with hard-bitten, street-smart, cynical DS Ray Miles (Philip Davis), who is nearing retirement, and eccentric but knowledgeable (and slightly creepy) Ripper expert, Edward Buchan (Steve Pemberton).

Despite some familiar story lines, this four-season series is intense, atmospheric, and undeniably gripping, providing unexpected twists and turns aplenty.

ARNE DAHL

CRIME • 2011
RATED: TV-14 • 90 MINS

Arne Dahl may sound like the name of a leathery detective with a foul mouth and a gambling addiction, but the truth is he's not even a character in this show.

First things first: the name Arne Dahl refers to the pen name of the writer behind these jaunty crime shows, and not any character contained in them. When three Swedish business guys are murdered, the authorities call in the big guns: the so-called "A-group," which is sort of like the A-Team but Swedish and without Mr. T. What it does have, though, is Paul Hjelm (Shanti Roney), Jorge Chavez (Matias Varela), Viggo Norlander (Claes Ljungmark), and the rest, all bringing different skills to bear in trying to stop the next assassination attempt.

You don't have to be a fan of the books to enjoy the two seasons of *Arne Dahl* mysteries. Anyone who appreciates interesting group dynamics, gruesome murders, and cutthroat Baltic gangs will find something to love here.

HAP AND LEONARD

DRAMA • 2016
RATED: TV-MA • 60 MINS

The success of buddy TV shows can hinge on the chemistry between the two buddies. Do we believe they're actually friends or just playing friends? These two seem like the real deal.

Hap Collins (James Purefoy) and Leonard Pine (Michael K. Williams) are an unlikely pair. Hap is a slightly sad ex-con, and Leonard is a gay Vietnam vet. They're floating around late 1980s-era east Texas when they run into Hap's ex, Trudy Fawst (Christina Hendricks). She has a proposition for the two of them. If they can help her locate a car with the proceeds of a robbery in its trunk, Hap and Leonard will each pocket a cool $100,000. Nothing is that easy, though.

Hap and Leonard exists on its own frequency, in the best way. Every shot looks borderline supernatural, and Willams and Purefoy play off each other beautifully. The three-season show also has interesting things to say on race, sexuality, and friendship.

RUN

THRILLER • 2020
RATED: TV-MA • 30 MINS

When Ruby receives a mysterious text message from an old flame, she embarks on a cross-country adventure 17 years in the making.

Ruby Richardson (Merritt Wever) leads a pretty normal life. Then, one day, she receives a text message out of the blue with just one word: "RUN." Nearly two decades earlier, Ruby and her then boyfriend, Billy Johnson (Domhnall Gleeson), made a pact. If one of them ever texted this word to the other, and got an identical response, they would both drop everything and meet at New York's Grand Central Terminal for a cross-country adventure. Ruby, perhaps stuck in a rut, texts him back and abandons her husband and son for the promise of rekindling an old romance.

This one-season show serves as a cautionary tale about the dangers of excessive nostalgia. Billy and Ruby each have their own reasons for wanting to run, but they soon learn that you can't escape your problems that easily.

MAFIOSA

CRIME • 2006
RATED: TV-MA • 50 MINS

We would all agree that more women should be in positions of power in the worlds of government and business. But what about in TV shows about organized crime? Yep, those too.

When it comes to organized crime, we're not generally talking about a particularly diverse workforce or leadership. Both are predominantly male and, on TV at least, women are relegated to second-class status. In *Mafiosa*, that dynamic shifts spectacularly when a Corsican mafia boss is murdered and leaves leadership of the clan to his niece, a lawyer named Sandra Paoli (Hélène Fillières).

Sandra doesn't have much experience in the mafia business, but her uncle saw something in her. She soon learns she has a talent for her new role, and over this five-season French series, we watch her slowly embrace her new life as a crime boss, confounding those around her who have no idea how to deal with this powerful woman.

PENNYWORTH

CRIME • 2019
RATED: TV-MA • 60 MINS

Everyone loves Bruce Wayne's butler, Alfred. He's old, with impeccable manners, and is always there to pick up Master Bruce when he's down. But where, exactly, did he come from?

Robin is Batman's best-known sidekick, but the truth is that Batman's most-trusted confidant has always been his manservant, the distinguished Alfred Pennyworth. But was Alfred born a bespectacled butler? Surely he had a life before becoming a surrogate father to Bruce Wayne? In this single-season series, we follow a young Alfred (Jack Bannon) and at last learn how he came to work for the Wayne family.

Some people may claim we didn't need to see an origin story about Alfred in swinging '60s London, but there's a stronger argument to be made that we really did. It's well past time for Alfred (Alfie, to his friends) to shine and get out from under Master Bruce's long, pointy-earred shadow.

BEING HUMAN

FANTASY • 2008
RATED: TV-14 • 60 MINS

A trio of roommates who happen to be a vampire, a werewolf, and a ghost, try to make it in the human world.

George Sands (Russell Tovey) and John Mitchell (Aidan Turner) are just like any other people in their mid-20s trying to figure it all out. But rather than worry about buying a home, getting married, or getting a promotion, these two friends have to worry about, um, feasting on the living. Sands is a werewolf, it turns out, and Mitchell is a vampire. Both are trying to go straight, though, and when they move into a new apartment, they make a friend, Annie Sawyer (Lenora Crichlow), a ghost who's haunting their new premises.

Whether vampire, human, or cocker spaniel, most of us just want to be loved and accepted. Running five seasons, *Being Human* is a funny, occasionally touching reminder that we all have some agency in our lives and that no one has to be someone they don't want to be.

NUMB3RS

CRIME • 2005
RATED: TV-14 • 43 MINS

In the movie _Point Break_, FBI agent Johnny Utah's boss tells him they solve crimes by crunching numbers and data, not by surfing. _Numb3rs_ suggests he's right.

TV makes police work seem far more exciting than it is. In real life, catching the bad guys has more to do with sifting through mountains of data than it does thrilling rooftop chases.

This six-season series gives us both. For FBI Special Agent Don Eppes (Rob Morrow), solving crimes is a family affair. He teams up with his brother, Charlie (David Krumholtz), and, occasionally, their father, Alan (Judd Hirsch), to bring in America's most wanted, using both brains and brawn.

Many people wouldn't want to work so closely with a sibling, but these guys make it work. Over six seasons, it is intriguing to see how Charlie and his mathematics—he likes scribbling down complex equations that are clearly complete nonsense—help solve each crime.

JUSTIFIED

ACTION • 2010
RATED: TV-MA • 44 MINS

What would it look like if Wyatt Earp was alive and plying his trade in the present day? Probably something like this contemporary TV western.

Raylan Givens (Timothy Olyphant) is a man out of time. He's basically what would happen if you took Olyphant's character from _Deadwood_ (see p119), stuck him in a time machine, and sent him forward a century.

As a lawman, Givens is more the judge, jury, and executioner type who doesn't have much use for due process. It's a headache for his superiors, so Givens gets busted and sent back to his Kentucky hometown, where this six-season series takes place.

He's joined by Boyd Crowder (Walton Goggins), a criminal who discovers religion in jail. Together, Givens—a man who relies on his quick draw and quicker temper—and Crowder, more cunning and probably more dangerous, make _Justified_ perfect for anyone looking to dig in to a modern-day western.

TINKER TAILOR SOLDIER SPY

SPY DRAMA • 1979
RATED: TV-14 • 50 MINS

One of the greatest Cold War stories ever told, author John le Carré's spy tale has stood the test of time, even as the conflict itself became history.

Like any great spy story, it can be a little hard to follow exactly what's going on at times in _Tinker Tailor Soldier Spy_. We're pretty sure

George Smiley (Alec Guinness) is a good guy, but in the topsy-turvy world of Cold War espionage, who is even sure what that means? After being ousted from his position as deputy head of the British Secret Intelligence Service ("The Circus"), Smiley is pulled into a web of intrigue and feints, with double and perhaps even triple agents! It's wild stuff.

Whether you're a le Carré fan or not, you have to appreciate the care and seriousness with which Guinness treats the material. But you'll have to stay focused to keep up with the labyrinthine twists in this one-season drama.

RUNAWAYS

ACTION • 2017
RATED: TV-14 • 60 MINS

If you think being a teenager is hard, try being one with overbearing super-villain parents. In *Runaways*, a group of six gifted kids use their unique abilities to fight back against their evil progenitors.

At one time or another, every teenager believes that their parents are the greatest villains the world has ever seen. For the Runaways, six teenagers who make a startling discovery about their parents, it's literally true. Part of an evil cabal known as the Pride, their familial guardians are a collection of twisted geniuses and alien malefactors with ill intent. The youngsters use their burgeoning abilities to fight back, and their vicious elders will assuredly do more than ground them.

Brian K. Vaughan, author of *The Runaways'* source material, is one of the most talented comic-book writers working today. With the exception of a few small tweaks, the series is a faithful adaptation of his vision, and a deeply satisfying justification for teen angst.

PRISON BREAK

PRISON DRAMA • 2005
RATED: TV-14 • 44 MINS

Like any good escape tale, *Prison Break* puts together a ragged band of misfits, each with a certain skill, and initiates a Rube Goldberg machine-level of plot devices to liberate our heroes.

After he's framed for killing the brother of the vice president of the United States, things don't look too good for Lincoln Burrows (Dominic Purcell). Luckily for him, his own brother, Michael Scofield (Wentworth Miller), isn't prepared to sit back and do nothing and breaks into Lincoln's prison in order to spring him.

Michael's desperate plan sees him commit armed robbery, knowing it will lead to his own arrest and imprisonment near his brother. It also includes him getting a full-body tattoo of the layout of the prison to help their escape. From there, his plan to win their freedom grows only more elaborate. Later seasons failed to match the thrills of earlier ones, but *Prison Break* is rollickingly good entertainment.

TOP OF THE LAKE

MYSTERY • 2013
RATED: TV-MA • 60 MINS

Most of us are conditioned to associate the rolling hills of New Zealand with hobbits and grizzled wizards. In *Top of the Lake*, the haunting scenery suggests something much more disturbing.

A pregnant 12-year-old girl disappears in a remote New Zealand town, and Detective Robin Griffin (Elisabeth Moss) vows to find her and bring her home safe. The girl also happens to be the daughter of local drug kingpin Matt Mitcham (Peter Mullan). Griffin herself grew up in the town and was raped there when she was 15 and so she has a personal stake in seeing the investigation through. The action moves to Sydney, Australia in Season 2, when, five years after the events of Season 1, Griffin investigates a death at Bondi Beach.

Cocreated by filmmaker Jane Campion (*The Piano*), this is tense and dark, even by the standards of the genre. The hint of violence is never far away, and down under, apparently, no one can hear you scream.

BANSHEE

ACTION • 2013
RATED: TV-MA • 60 MINS

Banshee's **plot is absurd, but undeniably fun. A criminal on the run becomes a small-town sheriff and tries to reconnect with his sweetheart while still being true to his crime-loving nature. What's not to love?**

After serving 15 years in prison for a daring diamond heist and a double-cross gone wrong, a mysterious stranger (Antony Starr) comes to Banshee, Pennsylvania. Through a string of lucky events, he assumes the identity of local sheriff Lucas Hood and tracks down his ex-partner and lover, Carrie Hopewell (Ivana Milicevic). She's in Banshee hiding out from her Ukrainian gangster father and has assumed an alternate identity.

Over four seasons, and many buckets of blood, *Banshee* stays true to itself until the end. The ex-con now known as Lucas Hood certainly isn't a hero, but he's loyal to his friends, loves his daughter, and has a code (of sorts). That'll have to be enough.

SHARP OBJECTS

MYSTERY DRAMA • 2018 • RATED: TV-MA • 53 MINS • SEASONS: 1
AMY ADAMS, PATRICIA CLARKSON, CHRIS MESSINA

They say home is where the heart is, but for *Sharp Object's* Camille Preaker, it's a place of secrets, pain, murder, and one of the creepiest families you're ever likely to meet.

Camille Preaker (Amy Adams) barely made it out of her hometown of Wind Gap, Missouri, in one piece. Now an alcoholic and prone to self-harm, she has, at least, been able to piece together a career. Working as a reporter in St. Louis, Missouri, Preaker warily accepts an assignment from her editor to go back home and investigate the disappearance of two young girls.

Her mother, Adora (Patricia Clarkson), acts as queen of Wind Gap, ruling from the family's large plantation house. The townsfolk, as well as Camille's stepfather, and her younger sister, all tread lightly around Adora, whose Southern gentility masks a barely repressed fury.

Sharp Objects is based on the first novel by Gillian Flynn (*Gone Girl*) and boasts many of her trademark twists and turns. Over the course of eight episodes, you will come to suspect literally everyone of nefarious aims, if not responsibility for the missing girls. The one possible exception is local law enforcement hunk, Chris Messina's Richard Willis. At the end of the day, Camille is a girl who should have stayed gone.

> **"***My demons are not remotely tackled. They're just mildly concussed.***"**
>
> **Camille Preaker** (S1 E2)

45

BODYGUARD

THRILLER • 2018 • RATED: TV-MA • 60 MINS • SEASONS: I
RICHARD MADDEN, KEELEY HAWES, SOPHIE RUNDLE

One of the UK's biggest TV hits of recent years, *Bodyguard* is a tense six-episode series about a conflicted police sergeant assigned to protect a top politician. Creator Jed Mercurio delivers an elaborate puzzle box of conspiracies within conspiracies—and those looking for edge-of-the-sofa thrills will not be disappointed.

David Budd (Richard Madden) is a man who knows how to deal with a tense situation. On a London-bound train, the veteran of the war in Afghanistan uses all of his military training and steely-eyed determination to diffuse a highly dangerous terrorist situation. As a reward for his bravery, he's assigned to bodyguard duty for Julia Montague (Keeley Hawes), an ambitious politician trying to use the general fear of terrorism among voters to catapult her into the office of Prime Minister.

and it has adversely affected his marriage. Far from the charismatic "Young Wolf" he played in *Game of Thrones* (see p8), Madden's David Budd is almost robotic in *Bodyguard*, like he's afraid to allow himself human feelings. But it bears mentioning that if we've learned anything from other bodyguard-themed stories over the years, it's that being in a strained life-and-death situation can lead to some compromising romantic entanglements—something to which Budd is not immune.

Madden's Budd is deadly and highly competent, but also incredibly vulnerable. *Bodyguard* touches on some deeper issues, such as how military veterans in need of help are treated when they come home. That alone makes this show one not to miss, as does its dizzying number of plot twists.

> **"*I'm not the Queen. You're allowed to touch me.*"**
>
> Julia Montague (S1 E2)

Budd doesn't hold with Montague's brand of fear-mongering politics; nevertheless, he's a consummate professional who's willing to do what it takes to get the job done. However, the terrorists Budd thwarted are now looking for revenge. His family isn't safe, and neither is his new charge. Budd suffers from PTSD as a result of his time in the war,

CREATOR: Jed Mercurio
PRODUCTION CO: World Productions

DEXTER

**CRIME DRAMA • 2006 • RATED: TV-MA • 53 MINS • SEASONS: 8
MICHAEL C. HALL, JENNIFER CARPENTER, DAVID ZAYAS**

Historically speaking, most serial killers are rightfully considered to be pretty evil. But what if a serial killer took down other serial killers? It's a delightfully upside-down premise.

One might describe Dexter Morgan as fastidious. As a forensic technician specializing in bloodstain pattern analysis for the Miami police, he's maniacally methodical and observant. He's equally attentive to detail in his other occupation, which involves using his skills—and highly disturbing sociopathic tendencies—to hunt down serial killers.

As a child, Dexter saw his mother brutally murdered right in front of his eyes and is predictably traumatized. Following this hideous crime, he and his sister (Jennifer Carpenter) are adopted by a kindly police officer who recognizes some alarming signs. Rather than let Dexter grow up to be just any old out-of-control psycho, his adoptive father channels his son's troubling quirks in a more productive direction. Dexter understands how serial killers think and operate because, technically speaking, he is one.

Like any show that goes on long enough, *Dexter* has some extremely high highs and some pretty low lows. Season 4, where Dexter befriends and then confronts the Trinity Killer (John Lithgow), is generally considered the show's apex, but Seasons 1, 2, and 7 also deserve plenty of love.

> **"** *I lie to everyone I know. Except my victims, right before I kill them.* **"**
>
> **Dexter** (S2 E11)

LUKE CAGE

**ACTION • 2016
RATED: TV-MA • 55 MINS**

While Spider-Man calls the borough of Queens home and Daredevil patrols Hell's Kitchen, Luke Cage protects Harlem. Cage uses his super body strength to keep his patch safe.

Two years before *Black Panther* took the world by storm, Luke Cage paved the way for black Super Hero leads in the Marvel Cinematic Universe (MCU) when he starred in this two-season series, having first appeared in Netflix's *Jessica Jones* (see p48). Cage (Mike Colter) works odd jobs around town while quietly using his powers for good. By the time Season 2 rolled around, Cage had gone from obscurity to celebrity.

Compared with some of the more recent Marvel films, the stakes may feel lower for Netflix MCU series such as *Daredevil* (see p39) and *Luke Cage*. But the focus on the individual and community is a positive. It humanizes these heroes, especially Cage, in a way that you don't really get in the cinematic releases.

JESSICA JONES

CRIME • 2015
RATED: TV-MA • 56 MINS

Definitely not a comic-book adaptation for kids, _Jessica Jones,_ with its themes of sexual violence and trauma, is arguably the most complex story the Marvel Cinematic Universe has told to date.

Daredevil isn't the only Marvel Super Hero to call Hell's Kitchen home, although Jessica Jones (Krysten Ritter) might bristle at the notion of being called a hero. This three-season series finds Jessica having retired from the noble masked vigilante game (after being forced to use her powers for evil) and starting her own private investigation outfit on the West Side of Manhattan.

Old traumas resurface, though, when a case leads Jessica to discover that the man responsible for her PTSD, Kilgrave (David Tennant in chilling form), is alive and well and causing mayhem. Jessica quickly realizes that the only way she'll be able to move forward is by facing him. Aided by Luke Cage (Mike Colter), she confronts her past.

LUTHER

CRIME THRILLER • 2010 • RATED: TV-MA • 60 MINS • SEASONS: 5
IDRIS ELBA, RUTH WILSON, DERMOT CROWLEY

Do you want a cop who plays by the rules or one who gets results? That's the question John Luther's friends and colleagues must be constantly asking themselves when it comes to the troubled-but-talented police investigator.

From the very first episode of _Luther,_ you get a clear idea of how its titular protagonist (Idris Elba) operates. A gifted detective, he has anger-management issues, and woe betide the criminal who catches him on a bad day. Luther would have lost his job 100 times over if his peers didn't recognize his preternatural talent for cracking the knottiest of cases.

There is no _Luther_ without Elba. Every time he comes on screen, he's seething with barely contained rage. It's impossible to imagine it all working half as well as it does without him prowling through every scene, pitting his next-level sleuthing against some would-be criminal mastermind.

Over five seasons, Luther becomes increasingly entangled with his sometimes nemesis, sometimes friend, Alice Morgan (Ruth Wilson). The psychopathic killer sees in him an intellect to rival her own and decides early on that he is more useful to her alive than dead.

For his part, Luther's damaged personal life doesn't leave much room for friends, so grabbing a coffee with a cold-blooded murderer who sometimes wants to kill him will have to do.

> **"** _I just need a way in, to know what it's like to be him, to not feel anything._ **"**
>
> Luther (SI E3)

LINCOLN RHYME: HUNT FOR THE BONE COLLECTOR

CRIME • 2020
RATED: TV-14 • 43 MINS

A paralyzed detective teams up with a rookie New York police officer to solve cases and track down a notorious serial killer in this single-season thriller.

Based on Jeffrey Deaver's novel *The Bone Collector*—previously filmed in 1999 with Denzel Washington in the lead—this pits the titular Rhyme (Russell Hornsby) and Amelia Sachs (Arielle Kebbel) against the Bone Collector, an infamous serial killer who is still at large in New York City.

So far, so standard, but there's a complicating factor. Rhyme is quadriplegic, paralyzed from the neck down, from an injury he suffered while pursuing the Bone Collector. Together Rhyme and Sachs pool their skills and resolve to put the murderer down for good. While the series could use a pithier title, *Lincoln Rhyme: Hunt for the Bone Collector* hits the right notes over its 10-episode season.

MURDER ONE

CRIME DRAMA • 1995
RATED: TV-14 • 60 MINS

A cult legal classic from *Hill Street Blues* creator Steven Bochco, *Murder One* is less well known than some of his other hits, but its first season (of two) is one of his best. You're in for a treat.

Teddy Hoffman (Daniel Benzali) is a high-powered criminal defense attorney tasked with defending Hollywood bad boy Neil Avedon (Jason Gedrick), who is implicated in the murder of his teenage lover. Other suspects present themselves, including the wealthy Richard Cross (Stanley Tucci), who continually meddles with Hoffman's case.

Season 1 covers just a single case, something that no other series had done before that point. The show laid the groundwork for many of the best legal dramas we've seen over the past three decades. Through its many twists and turns, and dramatic courtroom scenes, the investigation plays out via a story that demands a lot from its audience but rewards those who put in the time.

NARCOS

CRIME • 2015
RATED: TV-MA • 49 MINS

Follow a real-life drug lord's rise to the top of Colombia's most powerful drug cartel. We know how Pablo Escobar's story ends, but this is more about the cocaine-fueled journey.

Pablo Escobar's rags-to-riches story from small-time black-market operator to the world's most powerful and ruthless drug dealer is the stuff of legend, the details of which are by now fairly well known. Despite some minor philanthropic efforts, Escobar is not generally known as a good guy. Still, Netflix does its best to make you cheer for him, and Wagner Moura, who portrays Escobar, plays the role to perfection.

Narcos pairs Escobar's story with that of DEA agent Steve Murphy (Boyd Holbrook), one of the lead investigators in Escobar's manhunt. Their three-season tale spans several decades, starting in 1973, when Escobar links up with Chilean drug dealer "Cockroach" Moreno and an empire is born.

THE SINNER

CRIME • 2017
RATED: TV-MA • 45 MINS

The beach is a place for people to relax, but sometimes your fellow bathers are just inconsiderate. Sometimes, they can even be rude. But is that really a good reason to stab them to death?

One minute, Cora Tannetti (Jessica Biel) is lying on the beach with her husband and young child. The next, she's brutally stabbing some bystander with a paring knife. Life sure comes at you fast! Cora quickly confesses her guilt, but Detective Harry Ambrose (Bill Pullman) thinks there is more to this story than Cora taking offense at some guy catching rays and playing his music too loud.

Each of the three seasons of *The Sinner* is a self-contained story, all featuring Ambrose. Cora's story in Season 1 is about trauma and memory. We know who did the crime, but we don't know why. That "why" drives Ambrose not to accept Cora's admission of guilt at face value. And its gradual unraveling reveals the terrible tragedy that led to the murder.

FINGERSMITH

PERIOD CRIME • 2005
RATED: 15 (UK) • 60 MINS

If you're a con artist or some other kind of thief, it's never a good idea to fall in love with your victims—for one, it's simply bad for business.

Sue Trinder (Sally Hawkins) has had a pretty rough upbringing in the streets of mid-19th-century London. She's a pickpocket (or fingersmith) who's recruited to take part in a potentially lucrative scam by one Richard "Gentleman" Rivers (Rupert Evans). Rivers has made the acquaintance of a young debutante named Maud Lilly (Elaine Cassidy) and has a plan to scam her out of her fortune. This involves Sue acting as Maud's maid. Sue is willing to help him do it—for a cut. But the plot takes an unexpected twist when Sue and Maud fall in love.

This single-season adaptation of Sarah Waters's novel is dark and involving. Will Sue be able to save Maud and outsmart Rivers? Sue thinks she knows all the angles, but does she? Period chicanery at its finest.

CRACKER

CRIME • 1993
RATED: TV-MA • 100 MINS

Before he became the beloved bearded giant known to the world as Hagrid, Robbie Coltrane was the hard-drinking, hard-smoking, hard-gambling criminal psychologist known as Fitz.

In the years before forensics really came into vogue, TV detectives tried to get inside the criminal mind to solve cases. And no one was better at it than Dr. Edward "Fitz" Fitzgerald (Robbie Coltrane), a man of exceptionally poor personal habits but with an exceptionally healthy mind. Fitz is a criminal psychologist, or "cracker," and he's equally great at tracking down criminals and dealing with hangovers.

The three seasons of *Cracker* always leave you wanting more. Younger viewers (18 and older please!) might find it difficult to disassociate the dissolute figure on screen from the jolly bearded giant of their *Harry Potter* youth, but, in every way, Fitz is as memorable a character as anyone you meet at Hogwarts.

LUCK

DRAMA • 2011
RATED: TV-MA • 52 MINS

Anyone who's spent any time at the racetrack knows that it's the best possible spot for people watching, with interesting characters lurking in every direction.

The racetrack is a place where you can witness the whole gamut of human experience in a single afternoon. Hope, love, despair, ecstasy. Oh, and seething, white-hot anger. In *Luck*,

Dustin Hoffman stars as dyspeptic crime boss type Chester "Ace" Bernstein, a cranky ex-con looking for revenge on the unlucky saps who put him behind bars, while setting up a casino at the Santa Anita racetrack.

While *Luck* can be a little too impressed with itself, it's hard to argue with the setting or the talent involved. Hit or miss, series creator David Milch (*Deadwood*, see p119) has a vision, so if you're a Milch fan and haven't seen *Luck* yet, get to it. Note to animal lovers: Season 2 was canceled early allegedly due to the death of three horses during production.

HINTERLAND

CRIME • 2013
RATED: 15 (UK) • 90 MINS

The Scandinavians may be known as champions of noir, but don't overlook the Welsh. Aberystwyth-set *Hinterland* makes their case as noir newbies.

DCI Tom Mathias (Richard Harrington) looks rough. His scowl is a permanent fixture on a grizzled visage, as eternal as the windswept landscape of Aberystwyth, where *Hinterland* is set. He has come here from the big city to deal

with his demons, and his first day on the job is not as straightforward as he hoped it might be. Mathias investigates a disappearance, and he and his partner, DI Mared Rhys (Mali Harries), uncover some dark secrets.

Three-season series *Hinterland* has a lot going for it, including gorgeous scenery and some chewy mysteries. (That it's Welsh only adds to the charm.) Yes, it can become a bit meandering at times, but Harrington's beaten-down-cop-with-nothing-left-to-lose routine is absolutely solid throughout. If this is Welsh noir, the world should have more of it.

LITTLE BOY BLUE

CRIME • 2017
RATED: TV-14 • 60 MINS

Based on the real-life murder of 11-year-old Rhys Jones, *Little Boy Blue* is a dramatic reconstruction of the fraught investigation.

The real-life death of little Rhys Jones in 2007 hit Liverpool hard. On his way home from soccer practice, young Rhys was killed in a gangland hit gone wrong. This four-part, single-season dramatization focuses on a family

and community dealing with grief but also on the ensuing investigation and the battle to bring his killers to justice.

Put under intense pressure to solve a case where everyone already knows the culprit, DS Dave Kelly (Stephen Graham) runs up against one obstruction after another. Knowing who did the crime is not enough, and evidence is scarce. Rather than inserting their own flourishes, which would have cheapened the rawness of the story, the series creators stick to the facts for maximum emotional punch.

THE CHI

DRAMA • 2018
RATED: TV-MA • 60 MINS

From the mind of Emmy Award winner Lena Waithe, *The Chi* transports viewers to the South Side of Chicago.

For her incredible work as a writer on *Master of None* (see p202), Lena Waithe became the first African American woman to win the comedy writing Emmy. Rather than stick to funny fare, she created *The Chi*, a three-season drama with echoes of *The Wire* (see p320)

set in the South Side of Chicago. The story starts when one young man is violently killed, followed by another who witnessed it. These deaths reverberate into the lives of many— including one victim's half-brother, Brandon (Jason Mitchell), and his girlfriend, Jerrika (Tiffany Boone).

The South Side is a sometimes violent place— something the show doesn't shy away from—but there are moments of grace, too. The younger characters, especially Kevin (*Moonlight*'s Alex Hibbert) bring levity and hope to some heavy situations.

SOUTHLAND

CRIME • 2009
RATED: TV-MA • 42 MINS

It turns out the Los Angeles Police Department doesn't have the best reputation. While *Southland* hardly paints a sympathetic portrait, it does let you walk in its cops' shoes for a bit.

When we first meet him, Officer Ben Sherman (Ben McKenzie) is a wet-behind-the-ears rookie learning the ropes from Officer John Cooper (Michael Cudlitz), a complex

character coming to grips with his sexuality. The always-incredible Regina King plays Detective Lydia Adams throughout and is the backbone of the show.

There's something of a documentary feel to this searing five-season series, and it definitely adds to its sense of reality—a quality that often eludes other cop shows of the same type. But ultimately, the appeal of *Southland* rests on strong performances and excellent writing. McKenzie's character, in particular, is a highlight, morphing from untested new recruit into a hardened cynic by the end of the series.

THE DISAPPEARANCE

DRAMA • 2017
RATED: TV-14 • 43 MINS

If you've seen one show about the disappearance of a child, you've seen them all, right? Not necessarily—some are definitely better than others, and this Canadian example is a cut above.

The Disappearance begins when 10-year-old amateur photographer Anthony Sullivan (Michael Riendeau) fails to come home from a birthday treasure hunt. The resulting

investigation leads to some harsh truths about the family and, specifically, the story Anthony's grandfather Henry (Peter Coyote) has told about the true parentage of his son Luke (Aden Young).

Some mystery shows are so intricate that they basically require a PhD to follow. Not so with this one-season addition to the ever-growing stable of missing-child TV dramas. Over six episodes, it strikes a good balance between keeping you guessing and not putting too much pressure on you to keep up.

ER

DRAMA • 1994
RATED: TV-14 • 44 MINS

The show is responsible for launching the careers of George Clooney, and many others. But *ER* is so much more than that—it's one of the longest-running medical dramas in television history for good reason.

Originally created by Michael Crichton, the futurist-author behind the likes of *Jurassic Park* and *Westworld*, *ER* is one of Crichton's more grounded projects, following the day in, day out drama that takes place in County General Hospital in Chicago. Over the years, many, many recognizable faces—including Julianna Margulies, Anthony Edwards, Eriq La Salle, Mekhi Phifer, John Stamos, Noah Wyle, William H. Macy, and more—scrub in and get to work.

The daily grind of an emergency room has more than enough action to fill 15 thrilling seasons, and this crown jewel of medical dramas gives one a genuine appreciation for the real-life heroes who save lives every day.

PRIME SUSPECT

CRIME • 1991
RATED: 18 (UK) • 103 MINS

Until *Prime Suspect's* Jane Tennison came along, gritty TV police work was solely the province of men. She changed all that. Quickly.

Life on the Metropolitan Police force is not easy for a woman, even one as formidable as Detective Chief Inspector Jane Tennison (Helen Mirren). Before she even gets to the business of solving cases, she has to face down rampant sexism and abuse in the workplace. Luckily, she's up to the task. Tennison is a boss who in her quiet way reveals herself as a take-no-prisoners type who will chew these misogynists up and spit them out. All the while solving crimes, too, of course.

In *The Wire* (see p320), perpetually disgruntled Detective McNulty says, "Never trust the bosses." Tennison never does, recognizing that they're only good at getting in her way. The show is tight and tense, and Mirren is, obviously, more than enough reason on her own to check out this seven-season gem.

TRAFFIK

DRAMA • 1989
RATED: 18 (UK) • 53 MINS

The Oscar-winning 2000 film *Traffic* is based on this tense, labyrinthine 1989 miniseries about the international drug business.

The illegal drug trade is a vertically integrated, global economic enterprise that has different parties involved at every step of the process. *Traffik*, a series that inspired the Steven Soderbergh film, focuses on each party in turn, drawing out captivating, parallel story lines around the circuitous heroin business, from a poppy farm to the drug's invasion of a powerful government figure's family.

A British minister named Jack Lithgow (Bill Paterson), poppy farmer Fazal (Jamal Shah), and the English wife of a German smuggler, Helen Rosshalde (Lindsay Duncan), all find themselves connected to this destructive web. *Traffik* is in many ways superior to its Oscar-winning cinematic cousin, if only because it has more screen time to flesh out its vast canvas.

YOU HAVE THREE GENERATIONS ON ONE SOFA

Written by Andrew Frisicano

Picking a show for a range of ages and perspectives can be tough. "What's something that'll keep the kids engaged without putting Grandma to sleep?" you ask. Have no fear! These recommendations—from animation and sci-fi to reality competitions and murder mysteries—deliver the perfect combination of humor, storytelling, and visual pizzazz to hit the mark for more than one age group on the same sofa.

THE SIMPSONS

ANIMATED COMEDY • 1989 • RATED: TV-14 • 22 MINS • SEASONS: 31
DAN CASTELLANETA, NANCY CARTWRIGHT, JULIE KAVNER

Starring America's favorite animated TV family for more than three decades, *The Simpsons* packs popular culture references, witty zingers, satirical jabs, and compelling storytelling into each episode, with a town full of memorable, quirky characters at its disposal.

What does a trip to the fair town of Springfield entail? To start, hop on a skateboard or take the monorail to the hallways of Springfield Elementary School, where class clown Bart (Nancy Cartwright) writes lines on the blackboards in after-school detention. While the show's opening sequence is largely static, you will notice that each episode comes with a new punchline on Bart's board—a hint at the number of inside jokes within each installment. As the opening continues, core members of the family—Homer (Dan Castellaneta), Marge (Julie Kavner), Bart, Lisa (Yeardley Smith), and baby Maggie—congregate on their couch in front of the TV for another rotating gag that highlights the seemingly bottomless well of creativity at work.

The show's best stories—often found in the first 10 seasons—expertly blend character-driven drama, inventive visual jokes, and sharp commentary on the absurdity of modern life: Homer's monotonous job at the power plant (and evil boss Mr. Burns), Bart's puckish antiauthoritarian streak, Marge's long-suffering devotion to her family, and Lisa's often-tested moral center. Springfield has a rich cast of regulars—many with multiple breakout episodes—ranging from pious neighbor Ned Flanders and lovable barfly Barney Gumble to brusque Bozo-like television host Krusty the Clown and Marge's chain-smoking sisters, Patty and Selma.

> *"Kids, you tried your best, and you failed miserably. The lesson is, never try."*
>
> Homer Simpson (S5 E18)

THE DIET OF HOMER SIMPSON

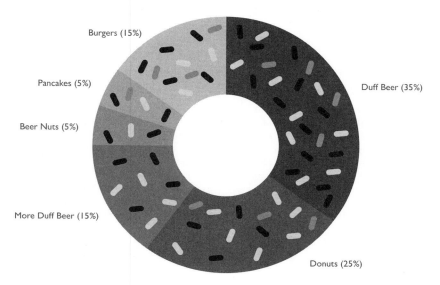

Burgers (15%)

Pancakes (5%)

Beer Nuts (5%)

More Duff Beer (15%)

Duff Beer (35%)

Donuts (25%)

Also remarkable is *The Simpsons'* ability to lure high-wattage guest stars into its world. Movie stars voice semi-regular characters, including Kelsey Grammer as murderous sidekick Sideshow Bob. And lest you forget that the Simpsons live in the real world, other guests appear as themselves, such as Harry Potter writer J. K. Rowling or famously reclusive author Thomas Pynchon.

Some of the show's top work features in its annual "Treehouse of Horror" episodes: vignette-filled anthologies pegged to Halloween that parody classics such as *The Raven*, *The Shining*, and *A Nightmare on Elm Street*. The series' send-up of the latter features a particularly memorable turn by Groundskeeper Willie as Freddie Krueger. The specials are among the show's most creative episodes, with gripping storytelling and plenty of fantastical flights of fancy.

With all the show's dizzying parody and sardonic humor, you might miss that its real heart focuses on the disappointments,

trivialities, and quibbles of everyday life. Along with not-so-typical plot threads, such as Homer's trip into space with an Apollo 11 crew member, or an intergenerational feud with the residents of neighboring town Shelbyville, *The Simpsons* takes on issues such as corporate greed, hypocritical clergy, and even the more mind-dulling aspects of cartoons with its show-within-a-show *Itchy and Scratchy*, a hyper-violent take on *Tom and Jerry*.

From counting down the hours at Moe's Bar to starting another season with its nuclear-energy-themed baseball team, Simpsonsland is the stuff of small-town life. It's as American as a Duff Beer at a Springfield Isotopes ball game or a microwaved convenient-store apple pie, and well worth a visit.

CREATORS: James L. Brooks, Matt Groening, Sam Simon **PRODUCTION CO:** Gracie Films, 20th Century Fox Television, Twentieth Century Fox, Fox Television Animation, The Curiosity Company, Twentieth Century Fox Animation

DOCTOR WHO

SCI-FI FANTASY • 2005 • RATED: TV-Y7-FV • 45 MINS • SEASONS: 12
JODIE WHITTAKER, PETER CAPALDI, MATT SMITH

The Doctor is in! Humanity is in luck, as the titular hero—actually an alien from a planet called Gallifrey—whizzes around time and space in a police-box-shaped ship to keep the universe safe from the forces that would do it harm.

These days, an old-style British police box is more likely to lead you to a devotee of this sci-fi show, a Whovian, than to an officer of the law. The iconic 1960s blue kiosk is the basis for the main character's ship—the interdimensional spacecraft and time machine known as the *TARDIS*—and a definite blast from the past.

But then, watching an episode of *Doctor Who* is a bit like stepping into a time warp. The original series was broadcast from 1963 to 1989 (see p452), and few television shows have enjoyed such a successful second act after a run that long. It is fitting that renewal is a central theme of the show.

Many actors have portrayed the main role of the Doctor. Since the show's relaunch in 2005, each of them has brought their own unique quirks and charms to the character. Due to the nature of being a Time Lord, the Doctor's body regenerates if it is fatally wounded, which means that each new actor assumes the role with a distinct personality. So, as a result, you have Christopher Eccleston's gravitas, David Tennant's freewheeling mania, Matt Smith's sense of adventure, Peter Capaldi's gruffness, and Jodie Whittaker's warmth. Thirteenth Doctor Whittaker is the first woman to take the role and has already made a strong mark with her unguarded portrayal.

Each Doctor is joined by a cast of human friends: in the series' first episodes, Rose Tyler (Billie Piper) provides the template for a trusty companion, while other assistants include Donna Noble (Catherine Tate), Mickey Smith (Noel Clarke), and couple Amy Pond (Karen Gillan) and Rory Williams (Arthur Darvill). You imagine the Doctor would get lonely without all these friends in the TARDIS.

There's also a bevy of baddies that take aim at the Doctor and their companions, including the garbage-can-shaped Daleks, the robotic humanoid Cybermen, the shape-shifting Zygons, and the psychologically menacing Weeping Angels, a true marvel of suspenseful villainery. The logic of the plots might not always get a full explanation, but with the Doctor, it's all about the journey. Trust us: you'll soon be having more fun than you can shake a sonic screwdriver at.

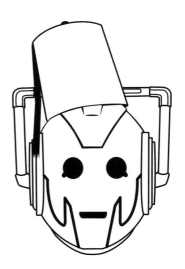

CREATOR: Sydney Newman
PRODUCTION CO: BBC Wales, BBC, CBC

STAR WARS: THE CLONE WARS

ANIMATED SCI-FI • 2008
RATED: TV-PG • 23 MINS

Set a long time ago in a galaxy far, far away, this animated _Star Wars_ spin-off follows familiar Jedi Knights Obi-Wan Kenobi and Anakin Skywalker as they try to bring balance to the Force.

Taking place between _Episode II_ and _Episode III_ of the _Star Wars_ film series, this acclaimed show follows Obi-Wan (James Arnold Taylor), Anakin (Matt Lanter), and new apprentice Ahsoka Tano (Ashley Eckstein) as they traverse the galaxy during the Clone Wars, fighting for the Republic against Count Dooku and the evil Sith.

Computer animation hugely benefits the mission, pulling off impressive sequences, with lightsaber-wielding Jedi Knights and hundreds of clones lurching into battle. The 2008 film of the same name that preceded the series isn't technically part of its seven seasons, but it sets the scene if you're not quite up to speed on your _Star Wars_ space drama.

STAR WARS REBELS

ANIMATED SCI-FI • 2014
RATED: TV-Y7-FV • 22 MINS

A new crew of starship pirates bridges the gap between the _Star Wars_ prequels and the classic set of films, mixing it up with familiar villains, including the iconic Darth Vader.

Callous Imperial functionaries and all sorts of alien species fill new planets on the edge of the galaxy in this series, which adds four seasons of interstellar swashbuckling to the _Star Wars_ story. Protagonist Ezra Bridger (Taylor Gray) is a teenager with a real knack for finding himself on the Empire's bad side in the years before _Star Wars: Episode IV—A New Hope_. As part of the crew of the ship _Ghost_, Bridger spends his time running scams and avoiding the long arm of the Imperial law.

High-speed chases, space dogfights, and plenty of sneaking around are on the menu. While the planets and characters are new, the plucky and talented youngster with a thirst for adventure getting initiated into a greater cause does feel familiar. A fun show for Younglings!

THUNDERBIRDS

SCI-FI • 1965
RATED: TV-G • 50 MINS

Rescuing folks is a family affair for the Tracy clan. Father Jeff and his five sons, all marionettes, operate a fleet of _Thunderbird_ craft that can conquer air, water, and space.

In the year 2065, the Tracy family operates the top-secret International Rescue with the mission of aiding humanity. At their disposal are the titular _Thunderbird_ machines, five distinct ships that range from a submarine to an Earth-orbiting space station. Aided by helper,s including high-society secret agent Lady Penelope and egghead extraordinaire Brains, the crew tackle international intrigue, world-destroying plots, and natural disasters.

A groundbreaking two-season show for its use of "Supermarionation"—sophisticated puppetry combining electronic controls and live-action filmmaking—_Thunderbirds'_ technical triumphs still impress today. While the puppets have some drawbacks, the imagination poured into this show still shines a half century later.

MASTERCHEF

GAME SHOW • 2010
RATED: TV-14 • 42 MINS

Home cooks show off their culinary skills and style in a wide-ranging tournament to decide who will raise the US *MasterChef* trophy.

Unlike the timed cook-off sessions that the show inflicts on its contestants, *MasterChef* itself seems to have no final buzzer. Ten seasons in and the competition is still going strong, with no end in sight. Chefs first face each other in heats, which pare down the field into quarterfinalists and eventually a single winner.

Judges Gordon Ramsay, Aarón Sanchez, and Joe Bastianich have the enviable task of tasting each dish, while offering cooking tips and tricks you might find useful at home. Some challenges ask contestants to fashion dishes using ingredients of their choice; others throw curveballs by introducing mystery products or time restrictions. Thankfully, none of it applies to your culinary efforts at home: just take the lessons on board and proceed at your leisure.

NAILED IT!

GAME SHOW • 2018
RATED: TV-PG • 33 MINS

Amateur bakers whose enthusiasm tends to outpace their skills attempt to craft dazzling baked goods in a series of themed challenges. The judges' favor and a $10,000 (USD) prize is at stake.

It's one thing to burn chocolate chip cookies in the comfort of your own home, it's another to do so in front of a panel of judges and the world. So the contestants taking part in this cooking competition should be commended for their efforts, even if their attempts to bake a cake that resembles Donald Trump end up looking like demonic mannequins.

Hosted by comedian Nicole Byer and celebrated French pastry master Jacques Torres, the four-season show (plus two bonus holiday seasons) is rich in witty banter and gimmicks. The latter include the golden chef's hat awarded midepisode and the panic button that allows for extra help from the judges. Each half-hour episode ends with the least-worst baker being crowned the winner.

CHEF'S TABLE

DOCUMENTARY • 2015
RATED: TV-MA • 50 MINS

In profiling culinary masters who are pushing the boundaries of fine dining at some of the world's best restaurants, *Chef's Table* makes the case for food as a museum-worthy artistic medium.

For these top chefs, eating is a multisensory experience on a par with a night at the opera. Take Argentinian chef Francis Mallmann, whose open-fire cooking pit resembles an ancient ritual, or Grant Achatz, who orchestrates a ballet of sights and sounds with the diner at the center. Other chefs, such as Korean nun Jeong Kwan, envision cooking as a spiritual practice, while farm-to-table proponent Dan Barber uses the meal to highlight the connection between eater and earth.

Chef's Table places these innovators and their food in the context of the global food scene. With six seasons to dig in to, there's a full menu of approaches and exotic locales delivered conveniently to your screen.

CHOPPED

GAME SHOW • 2007
RATED: TV-G • 60 MINS

Invention is the mother of this cooking game show in which contestants compete to make the most of the odd ingredients put in front of them.

Need a good mystery but already run through the whole of *Murder, She Wrote* (see p82)? Anyone looking for some big reveals will be delighted by this cooking competition series, which has racked up an impressive 44 seasons.

Four chefs are asked to craft dishes from boxes of unknown ingredients in three rounds (usually a starter, entrée, and dessert). Each round ends with one chef getting the ax, until a sole survivor remains.

Creativity and the ability to work outside one's comfort zone are key to mastering the show's unusual flavor combinations. In one far-out episode, a dish is made with pungent durian fruit, jiggly lime gelatine, crunchy cheese puffs, and boiled crab legs. If the food doesn't always sound appealing, the pulse-quickening competition more than makes up for it.

ACE OF CAKES

REALITY TV • 2006
RATED: TV-G • 22 MINS

This bustling pastry shop specializes in towering, ambitious designs that are architectural wonders first and food second. See how the cake is baked or, in this case, glued and patched together.

More than mere pastries, the creations at Charm City Cakes are projects to be specced, designed, baked, and iced—all on a tight deadline. Owner Duff Goldman is a tough

taskmaster, keeping his staff of friends on schedule. Unconventional baking methods such as using blow torches and power tools are par for the course, and Goldman's mischievous edge keeps the projects from getting boring.

If you've ever dreamed of having a cake in the shape of a jeep, a race car, or a replica of King Tut's sarcophagus, Goldman and his team are up to the task. Over 10 seasons, their impressive constructions include cakes in the shape of the Hogwarts Express, Wrigley Field baseball park, and the Hubble Space Telescope. It is truly out-of-this-world stuff!

WWE RAW

SPORT • 1993
RATED: TV-14 • 60 MINS

This long-running showcase for sports entertainment's biggest stars delivers drama, trash talk, and bulked-up shirtless bodies slamming against the mat. Cue the entrance music.

For almost 30 years, *Raw* has been the place to get your weekly dose of table-slamming, chair-bashing, spandex-wearing matchups. Along with *SmackDown*, *Raw* provides hours

of scripted drama and rough-and-tumble action for the wrestling-loving masses, narrated to a fever pitch by ringside commentators and cheered on by a rowdy crowd.

Dwayne "The Rock" Johnson is probably the biggest star to grace the ring, but a deep well of talent gets smashed into the show's hallowed turnbuckles over the show's 28 seasons. Look for "Stone Cold" Steve Austin, Undertaker, Bret "The Hitman" Hart, and Shawn Michaels—or dial up any episode from the late '90s "Attitude Era" and trust you'll be in good hands.

GOOD OMENS

FANTASY • 2019 • RATED: TV-MA • 60 MINS • SEASONS: 1
DAVID TENNANT, MICHAEL SHEEN, FRANCES MCDORMAND

Two unlikely friends—an angel and a demon who have been living among us since creation—are the only ones that stand between humanity and Armageddon. The end times are threatening life as we know it and, more importantly, the duo's Earthly vacation.

In the beginning there was heaven and Earth, and along with that, Adam and Eve, the Garden of Eden, and two pesky lieutenants in the battle of good and evil: the louche, demonic Crowley (David Tennant) and the nervous goody-goody called Aziraphale (Michael Sheen). From the start of this story—based on a novel by Terry Pratchett and Neil Gaiman—the pair are harmless, but prone to gaffes. Like when Crowley offers Eve that apple. But then, it's all part of God's plan, isn't it?

Fast-forward to 11 years before the present day and a rather stylized version of our world (Crowley pulls up in a 1930s Bentley) where the duo are enlisted in a plot to kick-start the end of the world. Is the Antichrist's arrival ultimately God's doing? If so, it's clear she has a sense of humor. The devilishly funny scheme stars a satanic order of nuns, every bit as bumbling as Crowley and Aziraphale. If the almighty works through imperfect vessels, she couldn't have picked a more perfectly flawed bunch. Pulling the brakes on the apocalypse—lest they lose their cushy gigs on Earth—is just as tough as it sounds, but nowhere near as unappealing to the pair as eternity.

> **"** *Why did the powers of hell have to drag me into this anyway?* **"**
>
> Crowley (S1 E1)

LARK RISE TO CANDLEFORD

PERIOD DRAMA • 2008
RATED: TV-PG • 60 MINS

If there's a time and place worth looking back to, you could do worse than the late 19th-century English countryside setting of this pastoral tale.

Laura Timmins (Olivia Hallinan) is our guide through this period piece, set when a telegraph delivery was about the most exciting part of your week. Lark Rise and the more bustling Candleford are the twin settings of a drama that unfolds in a cozy corner of Oxfordshire.

After leaving her hometown of Lark Rise, Laura joins Dorcas Lane (Julia Sawalha) in running Candleford's post office. Across four seasons, the community brushes up against mysterious strangers with varying agendas, illness, and long-lost relatives. Much of the joy comes from the period touches, such as neatly constructed dresses and impressively adorned hats. By the end of it, you may be in the market for some fine millinery yourself.

TROLLHUNTERS: TALES OF ARCADIA

ANIMATED FANTASY • 2016
RATED: TV-Y7-FV • 23 MINS

An encounter with a magical amulet on the way to school tosses teenager Jim headlong into a fantastical secret world of trolls and other monsters.

Jim Lake Jr. was minding his own business when fate decided to take the wheel. Jim has become the first human Trollhunter, a position that includes sword-swishing and leading the forces of good against evil. He's not alone though: he's got human classmates Toby and Claire, and troll friends Blinky and AAARRRGGHH!!!

Created by visionary director Guillermo del Toro, *Trollhunters* delivers some impressive artistic direction. Under an unremarkable suburban street lies Heartstone Trollmarket, a gem-filled burg where Jim learns the ropes of his new role. As he engages in battles and subdues villains across three seasons, he puts his newfound skills to the test.

HIS DARK MATERIALS

FANTASY ADVENTURE • 2019 • RATED: TV-14 • 58 MINS • SEASONS: 1
JAMES MCAVOY, DAFNE KEEN, RUTH WILSON

Cleverly mixing escapism, theology, and steampunk-y world-building, this rich fantasy saga is based on Philip Pullman's acclaimed trilogy of books. As she starts tugging at the threads of a massive mystery, young Lyra Belacqua embarks on a quest that takes her to the far reaches of the globe.

As a girl who's grown up in the wood-paneled Jordan College, Lyra Belacqua (Dafne Keen) has been living a sheltered life. When her uncle, Lord Asriel (James McAvoy), returns from an expedition in the snowy north with some startling news, she is thrust out of her comfort zone and into some sinister dealings.

Lyra's world initially seems similar to ours of perhaps a hundred years ago, with some key differences. In this parallel dimension, airships are commonplace, and each child has a "daemon," an externalized part of themselves that takes animal form. In Lyra's case, her loyal Pantalaimon (Pan for short) shifts from ermine to moth to mouse, never going far.

As Lyra digs deeper, she finds all is not hunky-dory. Local children are disappearing at an alarming rate, for one. And grown-ups can be quite untrustworthy. Luckily, she gets some help on the journey, most memorably from a giant armored polar bear.

The plotting can be knotty and the rules of the game aren't always easy to follow. But strong performances—especially from Ruth Wilson as the enigmatic and sinister Mrs. Coulter—will compel you to stow away for the ride. And don't forget there's a giant anthropomorphic bear!

SHARK TANK

REALITY TV • 2009
RATED: TV-PG • 60 MINS

Fledgling entrepreneurs pitch their business ideas to a panel of canny investors in the hope of getting the funding they need to make their companies take flight.

If you've ever hurriedly grabbed a notebook to jot down a "million-dollar idea," then proceeded to lose the note, you may have saved yourself a world of hurt. It's not so easy, as the business owners trying to convince the *Shark Tank* panel to pump capital and resources into their start-ups find out. The bigwigs are quick to remind overeager tinkerers that there's more to a successful business than a stray thought in the shower.

For the past 11 seasons, the Sharks have heard hundreds of ideas, both good and bad. The pitches range from household gadgets and clothing to food and dog treats. The emotional stakes are often high for these would-be tycoons who've poured time, energy, and occasionally their life savings into their ideas.

ICE ROAD TRUCKERS

REALITY TV • 2007
RATED: TV-14 • 46 MINS

Take a trek up north where these cold-weather road warriors deliver supplies to remote communities on the edge of the Arctic Circle, navigating slippery roads in impressive rigs.

The job of a long-haul trucker is difficult enough: tedious routes, long hours, and tight deadlines. Now imagine that the road is not pavement but a melting slick of ice sitting on a frozen lake and the weather outside is cold enough to freeze your toes off. That's what these drivers are up against, delivering goods to the upper limits of the map, navigating snow banks, faulty rigs, and slush at every turn.

Over 11 seasons, the show offers a rare chance to visit some of the world's least-populated areas in Canada and Alaska, but the hectic schedule means there isn't much time for sightseeing. Observing how the drivers manage their sanity in the close quarters of a truck cabin and follow, or bend, the rules of the road, is all part of the thrill.

UNDERCOVER BOSS

REALITY TV • 2010
RATED: TV-14 • 60 MINS

Put on a smile, because that new coworker—the one with the spray tan and flimsy moustache—might be your company head going incognito to get a ground-level look at their operation.

Running a company is hard work, to be sure. But is the CEO, raking in upward of seven figures, working as hard as the lowliest grunt? Over this show's 10 seasons, executives don disguises to work alongside the people turning the wheels. By building trust with their fellow workers, the execs hear unvarnished truths about unsafe conditions, problematic policies, and improvements that could benefit both employees and the bottom line.

Occasionally the boss turns up an unsavory underling who is abusing others and generally making a mess of the operation. When the final reveal comes, punishment is swiftly delivered. But for the good-hearted employees, loyalty and truthfulness pays with praise and a lump sum.

THE MUPPET SHOW

SKETCH COMEDY • 1976 • RATED: TV-G • 30 MINS • SEASONS: 5
JIM HENSON, FRANK OZ, JERRY NELSON

Apologies to all other prime-time players, but the all-singing, all-dancing Muppets host the world's greatest sketch comedy show. Together with a bevy of special guests, these colorful characters deliver a uniquely crafty half hour of television.

If the Muppets seem like naturals at the late-night game, that's because they are. Some of the characters' first appearances were on evening programs such as *The Ed Sullivan Show*, where they played tunes live. After the success of *Sesame Street*, which had the explicit goal of educating kids, Jim Henson and his muppeteers launched this series for adults, and *The Muppet Show* was born.

Loosely following the format of a live televised variety show, the production combines some behind-the-scenes moments and smart use of its guest stars. The ever-responsible and modest Kermit hosts the show, though his efforts are often more like trying to drive a school bus as the wheels fall off. Gonzo the

Great, Miss Piggy, Fozzie Bear, Rowlf the Dog, and really too many others to name serve as the show's meat and potatoes, dazzling audiences with their many masterful turns of phrase and rapturous songs.

The Muppet Show excelled in reeling in the biggest stars: Sylvester Stallone, fresh from the set of *Rocky*, signs autographs and whacks a punching bag. Peter Sellers dons his iconic *Pink Panther* attire, as well as plenty of other notable costumes and accents. Vincent Price gets creepy, and Mark Hamill of *Star Wars* fame pairs with Miss Piggy's Princess Leia. Even jazz maestro Buddy Rich takes part in a drum-off with Animal.

What would a show be without its critics? Well, *The Muppet Show* is lucky enough to have its own in-house commentators, the duo of Statler and Waldorf, heckling the performance from a box in the theater. Like the rest of the gang, the gray-haired curmudgeons are given a spotlight to do their thing, even if that's taking the rest of the proceedings down a peg.

CREATORS: Jim Henson, Jack Burns
PRODUCTION CO: ATV, HIT Entertainment, HA, ITC, The Jim Henson Company

DEADLIEST CATCH

REALITY TV • 2005
RATED: TV-PG • 55 MINS

Commercial fishing boats trawl the ice-cold waters of the treacherous Bering Sea, battling raging currents and exhaustion in search of a lucrative haul of crab.

From one perspective, this series could be called "A Crab's Journey" as it captures one part of your food's path from ocean to plate. For those on board, however, it's far from a pleasure cruise. The grizzled crew, which usually includes one or two new initiates, is faced with whipping winds, cresting waves, listing boats, and big swinging crates of seafood. The name is no joke, as shipmates can fall overboard without warning.

Each fishing season a half-dozen boats (with names like *Northwestern* and *Time Bandit*) jostle to make the most of the tight window, stuffing their hulls with booty. As you might imagine, the language can get kind of salty, but any swearing is smartly masked with a seagull cry or a metal clank.

GOLD RUSH

REALITY TV • 2010
RATED: TV-14 • 45 MINS

Like the 49ers before them, these hopeful prospectors head to the hills, tools in tow, in search of glittery paydirt in the wilderness of Alaska and Canada.

It's been some 150 years since hordes of Americans hopped in their wagons and headed west for the California Gold Rush. These days, would-be miners have to head north instead to find untapped veins of precious metals. These small outfits use backhoes and other heavy equipment to dig for gold, but otherwise the process is remarkably unchanged, tinged with all the hope and anxiety of scratching off a lotto ticket.

These blue-collar crews run 10 seasons of shiny dirt through the sluice to shake loose the valuable nuggets. Their focus is always on the end result—how the numbers add up. Watching with anticipation at the pile of gleaming dust and set of scales, the final weigh-in is a satisfying payoff.

MAN VS. WILD

REALITY TV • 2006
RATED: TV-14 • 45 MINS

Survivalist Bear Grylls jumps out of a helicopter into remote locales and, with scarcely more than a knife and his wits, he is forced to find his way back to civilization.

In the days when almost all travel is reliant on the use of a smartphone, Bear Grylls's wilderness survival skills are something to pay attention to, at least for when your battery eventually dies. The former SAS serviceman airdrops into people-free places—such as a live volcano in Guatemala or the frozen Arctic Circle—and in the process demonstrates how to forage food from local plants and animals, make a shelter out of branches, and navigate the terrain without a map.

The show has been accused of upselling the isolation and danger (where does the camera crew sleep, for instance?), but to watch Grylls bite into fresh scorpion meat or nibble on maggots from a sheep carcass, you can't argue that he hasn't earned his supper.

LEGO MASTERS

GAME SHOW • 2020
RATED: TV-PG • 43 MINS

Brick fans unite! Get some inspiration for your next build with this fun competition that judges contestants' creativity and building skills as they make original LEGO models.

No instructions, no problem. A roadmap won't help you on this game show, which rewards ingenuity and style. Challenges include crafting a complete themed scene from a blank canvas of colored blocks. Think of a massive villain's lair that's closer to a miniature movie set than a children's play toy, or a theme park with functional, moving rides.

Comedian Will Arnett, aka LEGO Batman himself, serves as the cheeky host, while "brickmasters" Amy Corbett and Jamie Berard judge each epic creation with the same attention a food critic would give the finest haute cuisine. After bingeing a few contests (there's only one season so far), you'll be itching to get your hands on something fantastic to build.

AMERICA'S NEXT TOP MODEL

REALITY TV • 2003
RATED: TV-PG • 43 MINS

It's not all beach photo shoots and red carpets for these aspiring models. The road to the catwalk is dangerous with the risk of elimination at every sashay.

Think modeling is all about superficiality? Wrong-o. A lot goes into intricately staged magazine photo shoots and catwalk shows, where a stumble can detract from months of hard work. Tensions can run high in the *Top Model* house, where contestants live while facing challenges that range from strutting and posing (naturally), to rapping and speaking French.

Supermodel Tyra Banks serves as taskmaster, keeping order and doling out advice to the participants. Over 24 seasons there's no shortage of mentor's wisdom—if you go in "smizing" (smiling with your eyes), and flaunt your "flawsomeness," you might come out with a lucrative modeling contract.

TOP GEAR

REALITY TV • 2002
RATED: TV-PG • 60 MINS

Cars, in all their zooming glory, are the thing on *Top Gear*, a series that aims to push the limits of vehicles, whether it's a 10-ton military truck or a race car.

There's more than one way to get from point A to point B, as this auto showcase proves. With 28 seasons of full-throttle driving, *Top Gear* covers a lot of ground, showcasing Porsche, Ferrari, Chevrolet, and every carmaker in between. The hosts, led by the outspoken and at times controversial Jeremy Clarkson, are the sort of garrulous gearheads you might imagine hanging around a garage full of fancy sports cars, and they challenge each other in good-natured races and jaunts.

Other segments focus on subsets of car devotees: fanatics of the three-wheeled Reliant Robin, for example, swap tales about their favored rides. The campervan challenge takes motorhomes to the extreme, with the hosts careening down the road in what's virtually a multi-story abode.

FIXER UPPER

REALITY TV • 2013
RATED: TV-G • 43 MINS

Two married Texans help house hunters find quality properties in need of a little TLC, showing just how much a few touch-ups and a fresh coat of paint can do.

Buying a home can be nerve-racking, with countless pitfalls that can turn your project into a money pit. So, for anxious house hunters, renovators Chip and Joanna Gaines are a godsend. By guiding people through the process, the *Fixer Upper* team can transform any outdated house into a fresh, welcoming abode suited to any needs or budget.

The city of Waco, Texas, is the pair's home base, and the area's ambience and architecture figures strongly into the housing stock and the couple's design choices, which are rich with shiplap walls, wainscoting, and barn doors that give their projects a farmhouse feel. Five seasons' worth of renovations prove that nearly any level of disrepair can be fixed with a sharp eye and some Southern charm.

HOME IMPROVEMENT

COMEDY • 1991
RATED: TV-G • 22 MINS

Tim "The Toolman" Taylor is a pro when it comes to repairing drywall or working a table saw, but the real challenge is managing his household of three boys.

For comedians like Jerry Seinfeld, Roseanne Barr, and Ray Romano, the 1990s provided a great chance to parlay their stand-up material into sitcom gold. In line with those comics, Tim Allen didn't even have to change his first name to play the genial handyman on his own eight-season series. The action bounces between the set of his show-within-a-show to a busy household where his trio of youngsters deal with typical teenage concerns.

Tim's repartee with cohost and straight man Al Borland (Richard Karn) is a highlight—as is his relationship with neighbor Wilson (Earl Hindman), who dispenses advice over the garden fence, his face mostly obscured. Wilson's ready wisdom more than proves the maxim that good fences make good neighbors.

DIY SOS

REALITY TV • 1999
RATED: TV-PG • 30/60 MINS

Handyman Nick Knowles and his squad of home-improvement experts take on jobs big and small for grateful people whose houses need updating, or a complete overhaul.

"Many hands make light work" might as well be the slogan of this beloved, long-running renovation show where crews descend on the homes of normal folks and complete repairs at record speed. The constant for its 29 seasons has been presenter Nick Knowles, in charge of gathering people power and gumption for the ambitious work, and getting to know the stories of those being helped.

The show had its own makeover in 2010, going from leaky taps and crooked blinds, to building entire houses from the ground up. With grander scope, hundreds of volunteers pitch in to help families in need, demonstrating the power of collective action and humanity's best side. The big reveal is always enough for your tear ducts to spring a leak of their own.

ANTIQUES ROADSHOW

REALITY TV • 1997 • RATED: TV-G • 45 MINS • SEASONS: 24
MARK L. WALBERG, SIMEON LIPMAN, LARA SPENCER

Hoarders and keepsake collectors bring their most treasured objects for examination by experts. After discussing their history, and spinning yarns about their probable journeys, the show's appraisers estimate each item's value.

That old vase in your attic? It may be worth thousands. The heirloom painting passed down from your great-great grandma? Worthless. Such are the vagaries of the *Antiques Roadshow*, which is all about putting a story and valuation on old, often one-of-a-kind items.

Based on the very popular UK version (now in its 42nd season), American antique experts in fields such as books, lamps, handmade pottery, decorative arts, and old-school toys and collectibles deliver their spiel about each object brought to them by members of the public in a careful and calming tone. Dropping into conversation some obscure facts and details—such as pointing out a rare misspelling in the dust jacket of a first edition of J. R. R. Tolkien's *The Hobbit*—the appraisers reveal the history of various industries, and the ways people lived and furnished their lives in ages past.

With 24 seasons under its belt, the *Antiques Roadshow* has seen quite a few storage units' worth of items pass through its appraisers' hands. Don't worry if you're not the beneficiary of a large antique china set or owner of a massive grandfather clock, you can still enjoy the tranquillity and richness of the show. In fact, you'd probably be better off not doing your back in and leaving the clock where it is.

AMERICAN RESTORATION

REALITY TV • 2010
RATED: TV-14 • 22 MINS

Skilled metalsmiths give rusted-out dragsters, squeaky bicycles, and other chrome-plated relics a much-needed tune-up, before returning the shiny machines back to their owners.

It's hard to remember a time when most everyday objects weren't designed to be thrown away. *American Restoration* revives that made-to-last past by bringing pieces of history—from old cars to vintage signs—back to life. Set at Rick's Restorations in Las Vegas for its first six seasons, the show sees owner Rick Dale and crew take on various projects, including converting an old gas pump into a change machine. Season 7 leaves Las Vegas to focus on speciality shops around the US.

Watching Rick and co at work, you'll be amazed at how much painting, welding, and fabrication goes into saving the past. The final product is often so dazzling you have to squint to remember what it looked like before. It's a good reminder that the past is still present.

THE JEFFERSONS

COMEDY • 1975
RATED: TV-PG • 22 MINS

This *All in the Family* spin-off featured the Bunkers' neighbors George and Louise Jefferson, who moved from Queens to a "deluxe apartment in the sky" in Manhattan.

With its famous theme song ("Movin' on Up") and high-caliber stars, *The Jeffersons* was a hit right out of the gate. Quick-tempered George (Sherman Hemsley) and his level-headed wife Louise "Weezy" Jefferson (Isabel Sanford) move to a luxurious Manhattan high-rise due to the success of George's dry cleaning business.

With a memorable cast of characters, including wisecracking housekeeper Florence and neighbors Tom and Helen Willis, the show gave its viewers plenty of laughs throughout its 11-season run. In 1981, the show also saw Isabel Sanford become the first black woman to win an Emmy for outstanding lead actress in a comedy series for her role as Louise.

FULL HOUSE

COMEDY • 1987
RATED: TV-G • 22 MINS

A trio of grown guys—the straight man, the funny man, and the cool dude—take on the challenge of raising a trio of girls, while piled into a San Francisco house.

This unconventional family lives up to its name with a cast that's just about big enough to field a football team. There are three men, a baby, two girls, their friends, and that's just at the start. Widower and TV presenter Danny Tanner (Bob Saget), aspiring musician Jesse Katsopolis (John Stamos), and stand-up comic Joey Gladstone (Dave Coulier) are quite a triad of ambition, but their greatest feat is making sure daughters D. J. and Stephanie are in by curfew. The father figures advise the girls on boys and school with real tenderness.

Olsen twins Mary-Kate and Ashley take turns playing the role of little Michelle Tanner, who gets many of the best lines. Eight seasons of light-hearted family fun with one-liners aplenty? "You got it, dude!"

FULLER HOUSE

COMEDY • 2016
RATED: TV-G • 27 MINS

Who says you can never go home again? The grown-up Tanner kids move back into their childhood abode, with their own offspring and extended family in tow, picking up where they left off.

The original *Full House* cast reconvene in their former home (with one notable exception, the Olsens, AWOL). Daddy Danny and Uncles Jesse and Joey pop in occasionally, but it's really all about D. J. (Candace Cameron Bure), now a widow with three sons, and laissez-faire aunt Stephanie (Jodie Sweetin) running the show. Chatterbox best pal Kimmy Gibbler (Andrea Barber), prone to inviting herself for dinner in the original, is a full-time resident with her young daughter.

Of course, things aren't just like the 1990s. Everyone has a smartphone, for one. And the fourth-wall-breaking touches add a nice spin to the largely untouched multi-cam feel of the show. Its five seasons prove that corny dad jokes and soapy heart-to-hearts spring eternal.

BEWITCHED

**COMEDY • 1964 • RATED: TV-G • 25 MINS • SEASONS: 8
ELIZABETH MONTGOMERY, DICK YORK, DICK SARGENT**

Samantha Stephens is a typical 1960s housewife, except she's got an ace up her sleeve—the power to cast spells with a twitch of her nose. With a doting husband and nosy mother, here's what happens when married life gets witchy.

Every marriage comes with some unexpected things—say a weird habit, or a strange quirk. All things considered, adman Darrin Stephens takes it pretty well when he finds out that his new bride, Samantha, is a witch. To make things worse, so is her prodding mother Endora (Agnes Moorehead), who takes full advantage of her ability to appear out of thin air into the couple's lives … literally! Imagine an all-powerful in-law dropping in without warning, before you've even had your morning coffee.

Time and time again, Samantha can't resist using her powers to make the couple's lives easier. From reshuffling their house furniture without lifting a finger, to preparing breakfast in a snap. And who could blame her—witchcraft is the ultimate app. Conspiring against the mixed-species couple are Endora, the deliciously snooty parent who can't help but interfere, and a cast of nosy neighbors. Don't forget Darrin's boss, the high-strung Larry Tate (David White), who's always looking to make a deal, or make Darrin walk on coals for failing to bring in the big accounts.

Speaking of Darrin, you'll notice a shift in Season 5, as the original Darrin (Dick York, a comedic gem) is replaced by the equally capable Dick Sargent. It seems too cruel to pick a favorite, but it's almost hard not to (don't let us sway you).

By Season 2 the couple have a daughter, Tabitha, and with another spellcaster in the house things only get more hectic. Poor Darrin has a knack for finding himself in the wand's path, or as the target of his boss's ire. But the lovable, often blissfully ignorant hubbie is always redeemed. Luckily, Darrin is a good sport who generally shrugs off all the shenanigans with a smile—or due to some magic meddling, doesn't remember just how silly he looked. We can all hope to be so blessed.

> *"So my wife's a witch. Every married man has to make some adjustment."*
>
> **Darrin Stephens** (S1 E1)

ALL CREATURES GREAT AND SMALL

COMEDY DRAMA • 1978
RATED: TV-PG • 50 MINS

Take a trip to the British countryside where vet James Herriot cares for dogs, cats, cows, and pigs, as well as the countless farmers who own them.

Dealing with livestock is easy, but people? Slightly trickier. As refreshing as a drive through crisp, unsullied pastures, *All Creatures*

Great and Small delivers small-town charms set amid the sweeping vistas of the Yorkshire Dales. The 1930s may be a simpler time, but newcomer Dr. Herriot (Christopher Timothy) still has his work cut out in making his way as an animal doctor in a country where you can't throw a rock without hitting a sick dairy cow.

The good doctor soon learns how to avoid a kicking hoof and dodge short-tempered fellow surgeon Siegfried Farnon (Robert Hardy). It may not be a young foal, but this nostalgic seven-season series still has plenty of life in it.

POIROT

CRIME DRAMA • 1989
RATED: TV-14 • 50 MINS

Agatha Christie's legendary detective works his way through the author's extensive casebook—solving 13 seasons of murder mysteries with his signature style, panache, and a twirly moustache.

Who watches the watchmen, or in this case, the ever-vigilant observer, Belgian investigator Hercule Poirot? Well … we do. Seeing the gumshoe at work is like admiring Michael

Jordan effortlessly glide over the competition to the basket. Masterfully portrayed by actor David Suchet, Poirot casually reveals the rot at the heart of genteel society.

Adapting 33 novels and dozens of short stories, mostly set in the 1930s, this is no mere procedural but a towering achievement of crime-solving. Always primly attired in a three-piece suit and homburg hat, the detective hardly breaks a sweat shuttling around labyrinthine manors and rolling estates. And as he often points out in his persistent, quirky manner, paying attention pays off.

LAST OF THE SUMMER WINE

COMEDY • 1973
RATED: TV-PG • 30 MINS

Pity the townsfolk stuck with these retirees, who prove there's no expiration date on boyish tomfoolery or causing low-grade mayhem.

If impish seniors scrounging, cracking jokes, and sipping the odd pint strikes your fancy— or strikes close to home—you'll welcome *Last*

of the Summer Wine, celebrating the laziness and humor of its layabout subjects. Frankly, retirement seems like fun if it's all hanging around with friends and going for walks.

The sitcom's main slackers are the trio of Norman Clegg (Peter Sallis), Foggy Dewhurst (Brian Wilde), and Compo Simmonite (Bill Owen). With a run this protracted, though— 31 seasons, the longest of any live-action sitcom in history—there are plenty of new faces over the years. In fact, you'd be hard pressed to find comic actors of a certain age who haven't appeared in the series.

SPEED RACER

ANIMATION • 1967
RATED: TV-Y7 • 30 MINS

Young drivers everywhere look up to cartoon roadster *Speed Racer*, a wheelman made for the road with quick reflexes and a lightning-fast car at his disposal.

When main character Speed Racer decides to enter a local contest, there are several things going for him. First, as the son of Mom and Pops Racer, there's that born-to-drive

surname. Second, there's free use of his dad's hot rod, the sleek Mach 5, a machine with cool gizmos for besting competitors on the track.

Racing is the family business: Mom, Pop, little brother Spritle, and even mysterious older sibling Racer X are drivers, and Speed (clad in his red racing bandana) is a natural. Dubbed from the Japanese anime *Mahha GoGoGo*, *Speed Racer* brings drama, with assassins and evil racing squads around every hairpin turn. In the original one-season, 52-episode run, Speed goes the distance in search of a good race, traveling from Mexico to Kenya and beyond.

THE DARK CRYSTAL: AGE OF RESISTANCE

FANTASY • 2019
RATED: TV-PG • 60 MINS

The far-off planet Thra, a wondrous land, is in turmoil as the peaceful, mousy Gelfling race live oppressed by their vulturelike overlords, the Skeksis.

If you thought puppet technology had peaked years ago, the visuals of this Jim Henson Company-produced series will knock your

socks off. Frighteningly articulate alien creations stalk this world detailed with breathtaking, nature-documentary-esque CGI vistas and bubbling life. When some good-natured elfin Gelflings get wise to the evil Skeksis, they kick off an epic quest that would make Tolkien blush.

Aliens form just a fraction of the vast universe created for this series. As a prequel to the cult 1982 film *The Dark Crystal*, the 10-episode run continues the sometimes dark tone, where cuteness and grossness meet, danger is real, and the good guys don't always win.

DISENCHANTMENT

ANIMATED COMEDY • 2018
RATED: TV-14 • 28 MINS

Fairy tales get a twisted spin in this humorous visit to a fable-rich land of medieval castles, fire-breathing dragons, and evil stepmothers, starring a beer-swilling, teenage princess.

Don't tell Snow White, but these fantasy creatures belch, swear, and sleep around, ruing the dullness of their storybook lives. Created by Matt Groening, the mind behind

The Simpsons (see p56) and *Futurama* (see p261), the series borrows the visual look and general irreverence of those shows, with slack-jawed, convention-flouting characters.

Princess Bean (Abbi Jacobson), daughter of the king of Dreamland, courts trouble but has no idea what's in store when she meets her demon, Luci (Eric Andre)—a tiny shadow creature with a big mouth—and befriends the outcast accurately named Elfo (Nat Faxon). The characters they encounter, including haughty Prince Merkimer and shape-shifting bear creature Ursula, add to the rich mix.

DEGRASSI: THE NEXT GENERATION

DRAMA • 2001
RATED: TV-PG • 30 MINS

The corridors of Degrassi Community School are rife with all the drama you'd expect from a soap opera injected with raging teenage hormones.

High school is a tough time for everyone. But for those enrolled in Degrassi, it's next level. As well as navigating puberty, tests, and college admissions, these kids and their teachers confront violence, body-image issues, and drugs. Such real-world topics make *Degrassi* relatable, even if the first of its 14 seasons will make you pine for a time before smartphones.

The fourth incarnation of a franchise that began back in 1979, *Degrassi: The Next Generation* makes the most of its diverse and talented rotating cast—including future pop star Drake as basketball-playing Jimmy Brooks— featuring class clowns, theater kids, bookworms, and other archetypes you might remember from your own school days.

SAVED BY THE BELL

COMEDY • 1989
RATED: TV-PG • 22 MINS

Popular Zack, brainiac Screech, and straight-A student Jessie are among the crew who rule the school at Bayside High, much to the chagrin of their principal, Mr. Belding.

Always looking for the easy way out, charming Zack Morris (Mark-Paul Gosselaar) and his pals navigate their way through high school in this teen sitcom. Along the way, Zack's schemes involve everything from convincing the swim team to pose for a calendar, to planting subliminal messages on a mixtape to persuade crush Kelly (Tiffani-Amber Thiessen) to go to the dance. Meanwhile, his nerdy sidekick Screech (Dustin Diamond) comes up with bright ideas that include building a humanoid robot in an attempt to find a new friend.

If four seasons aren't enough, there's a preceding series called *Good Morning, Miss Bliss* and several spin-offs and reboots, notably *Saved by the Bell: The College Years*, in which most of the gang graduate and go to college.

EVERYBODY HATES CHRIS

COMEDY • 2005
RATED: TV-PG • 22 MINS

Comedian Chris Rock brings his childhood to the small screen, narrating stories about getting his bike stolen, landing on the bad side of bullies, and surviving his high-pressure parents.

The way Chris Rock tells it, he saw it all growing up in his Brooklyn neighborhood. The wild characters who inhabit his block serve up some of the best moments, such as the shakedown artists who ask to hold a dollar, and the neighbor selling questionably acquired items from the trunk of his car. Race issues play prominently through the sitcom's four seasons: getting bussed from his majority black area to a school of mostly white kids, Chris is picked first for basketball, despite his lack of skills.

Rock's tiny avatar (Tyler James Williams) is a model of comedic acting, taking lumps from all sides. His tough but loving parents (Terry Crews and Tichina Arnold) similarly knock it out of the park. Everybody may hate Chris, but the perennial underdog is easy to love.

FRIDAY NIGHT LIGHTS

**DRAMA • 2006 • RATED: TV-14 • 44 MINS • SEASONS: 5
KYLE CHANDLER, CONNIE BRITTON, TAYLOR KITSCH**

In Dillon, Texas, football is everything. From its new coach to its star running back, the whole local high-school team is feeling the pressure to take the state title, with the tension finding release on and off the field.

Winning a football game is hard enough. So imagine trying to do it when everyone in your football-crazed town is breathing down your neck. No surprise, then, that Coach Eric Taylor (Kyle Chandler) and his team, the Dillon Panthers, are having a couple of off-field issues. Surely the town's haranguing supporters and busybody parents could use some hobbies of their own?

Based on a true story, which was also spun into a film, *Friday Night Lights* does everything to ratchet up the tension and drama. Dillon is

a town full of people on the brink—of poverty, of personal collapse, of the weight of their own expectations—and the show delivers five seasons of flawed characters looking for gridiron salvation.

A quick look at the team roster presents some obvious issues. There's the enigmatic fullback with a bad drinking problem (Taylor Kitsch), the timid back-up quarterback with abandonment issues (Zach Gilford), and the running back with his eyes set miles ahead on making the pros (Gaius Charles). Almost from the start, the team is in dire straits when its star quarterback (Scott Porter) gets paralyzed during a game. Good thing that rallying the troops is hard-nosed Coach Taylor's speciality. His pregame catchphrase "Clear eyes, full hearts, can't lose" may be the series' most lasting legacy.

HATERS BACK OFF!

**COMEDY • 2016
RATED:TV-14 • 30 MINS**

Pouring boundless energy and optimism into her online videos, delusional internet wannabe Miranda finds the path to YouTube stardom littered with trolls and other catty commenters.

There's something a little off about Miranda, portrayed here—and elsewhere on the web— by comedian Colleen Ballinger. She doesn't realize her lipstick is smeared and that the

singing in her homemade videos is drastically off key. The viral hits don't come easy, but with the help of her creepy but supportive uncle Jim (Steve Little) and bag-of-nerves mom (Angela Kinsey), Miranda is all in.

After her energetic efforts start to become the target of online derision, she locks down her house and invites neighbor Patrick (Erik Stocklin) over to defend her with samurai swords. Of course, a few jealous people can't get in the way of Miranda's dreams or her videos, which become more and more outlandish over the show's two seasons.

ST. ELSEWHERE

DRAMA • 1982
RATED: TV-PG • 60 MINS

Boston's St. Eligius Hospital has seen better days, but its staff haven't given up hope, treating the neediest patients while sorting out their own issues.

Things must be pretty grim if you find yourself at St. Elsewhere, the nickname for this teaching hospital where veteran residents try to prep interns for whatever comes through the door. Like the hospital, the show has a reputation for grittiness, with shooting victims parading in, and unruly patients wandering off. Some of the doctors aren't much better, constantly accused of malpractice, swiping drugs, and otherwise not taking their jobs seriously.

The series' large ensemble cast is its chief lure, and it served to launch some big names, including Denzel Washington. The six seasons also contain plenty of inside jokes: listen for characters from other shows being called over the loudspeaker, and watch for a sequence shot at another fictional Boston landmark, the bar from *Cheers* (see p258).

THE ROYLE FAMILY

COMEDY • 1998
RATED: 12 (UK) • 45 MINS

A British sitcom classic about a Manchester family who never stray far from the TV, holding court as they pile up the cigarette butts and sink deeper into the sofa cushions.

If Jim Royle (Ricky Tomlinson) were any more sunk into his recliner, he might need the jaws of life to get him out. From his perch, Jim regularly spars with wife, Barbara (Sue Johnston); son, Antony (Ralf Little); and daughter, Denise (series cocreator Caroline Aherne), about bills and other hassles.

The name, of course, is an ironic pun on this working-class family's uncouthness. But the genius of the writing and the warmth of the performances over four seasons means everyone—even the Queen herself—will be able to see something of their own family in the Royles. The single-camera production and lack of a cackling audience gives an intimate feel, like you've been invited into their living room. Be prepared to make your own cup of tea, though.

TO THE MANOR BORN

COMEDY • 1979
RATED: TV-PG • 30 MINS

Old money and new money collide when a down-on-her-luck heiress and a supermarket mogul have to share an estate, whose sprawling grounds aren't nearly big enough to keep them apart.

Change is afoot at Grantleigh Manor. After the death of her husband, the aristocratic Audrey fforbes-Hamilton (Penelope Keith) is forced to sell her main palatial home and move to the old lodge on its grounds. The downgraded digs give her a great view of the manor's new resident, the charming nouveau riche Richard DeVere (Peter Bowles). Never one to hold her tongue, Lady Audrey has plenty of opinions on his changes to the place, from the renovated antique fireplace to the hired help.

There are tensions between the two singletons, and their back and forth may remind you of an old married couple. Without giving too much away, you may like to see how matters resolve themselves in the third and final season of this cozy BBC sitcom.

ONLY FOOLS AND HORSES

COMEDY • 1981
RATED: TV-PG • 30 MINS

Fast-talking market trader Del and his half brother Rodney try to get rich quick while doing as little work as possible in this beloved BBC comedy.

Once voted Britain's best sitcom, this classic series follows Derek "Del Boy" Trotter (David Jason) as he hawks wares from his bright yellow three-wheeled van, always with his eyes on something bigger. When he's not sipping cheap vino at the local Nag's Head pub, Peckham boy Del is embarking on new schemes and swindles with the help of younger half brother Rodney (Nicholas Lyndhurst), grandad (Lennard Pearce), and—in later seasons—his uncle Albert (Buster Merryfield).

The show's seven seasons and 16 specials are packed with wonderful characters and comic moments—who can forget Del Boy falling through the bar? Scarily enough, in our scam-filled times some of his plans don't sound so odd: bottling tap water and selling it as "Peckham Spring?" Only a fool would object.

THE VICAR OF DIBLEY

COMEDY • 1994
RATED: TV-PG • 30 MINS

A small country village meets its new vicar, who is, to their surprise, a woman. But her charms and cheery demeanor soon win over the townspeople.

The 1992 Church of England rule change allowing the ordination of women priests provides the basis for this sitcom created by *Notting Hill* writer Richard Curtis. Colorful reverend Geraldine Granger (Dawn French) is just what the bishop ordered for the quiet Oxfordshire enclave of Dibley. Convincing the village's quirky congregation of her worth proves easy compared to some of the other challenges she faces, from giving up chocolates for Lent to remaining humble when her radio hour goes national.

Always game for fun, Granger hosts her share of inventive christenings and weddings during the show's two seasons, including one *Teletubbies*-themed nuptials. The Christmas specials are essential viewing, with even the vicar having trouble celebrating in moderation.

THE WEST WING

DRAMA • 1999
RATED: TV-14 • 44 MINS

Become a fly on the wall in the White House of fictional US president Josiah Bartlet as it contends with global crises, rival lawmakers, and backstabbing staffers in this landmark political drama.

The inner workings of the federal government are hectic and high-stress under Democratic leader Josiah Bartlet (Martin Sheen). Much of the business takes place while characters briskly walk the halls of the White House's hallowed West Wing, with information arriving thick and fast in a barrage of creator Aaron Sorkin's trademark crackling dialogue. Delivering it for all their worth are an idealistic, intelligent, but always relatable team of spin doctors and advisors, including press secretary C. J. Cregg (Allison Janney) and comms director Toby Ziegler (Richard Schiff).

Seven seasons is a long time for any politician, but this series rarely falters. Influential and uplifting, it'll keep you glued right till the end when Bartlet finally gets to pass the baton.

THE ADDAMS FAMILY

COMEDY • 1964 • RATED: TV-G • 30 MINS • SEASONS: 2
CAROLYN JONES, JOHN ASTIN, JACKIE COOGAN

Up is down and black is pitch black in this sitcom about a devilishly twisted gothic family. Every day is Halloween for the Addams clan, a stark contrast to the white picket fences and daffodil gardens of their suburban 'hood.

Even if you aren't familiar with *The Addams Family*'s two-season run in the mid-'60s, you'll likely know the theme tune and its sing-song melody, lurching piano line, and eerie finger snaps. Based on illustrator Charles Addams's print cartoons, this sitcom plowed new TV ground for the macabre along with its similarly Halloweeny competition, *The Munsters* (see p79), which premiered just days later.

Morbid matriarch Morticia Addams (Carolyn Jones) leads the brood along with doting husband Gomez (John Astin). Their extremely tall, organ-playing butler Lurch (Ted Cassidy), witchy frizzy-haired Grandmama (Blossom Rock), and dynamite-happy Uncle Fester (Jackie Coogan) round out the grown-ups,

while kids Wednesday (Lisa Loring) and Pugsley (Ken Weatherwax) prove that the poisoned apple doesn't fall far from the tree. Other uncommon household members include a disembodied hand known as Thing, and the hairy mop that is Cousin Itt. There's never a dull moment to be sure.

As you might imagine, this oddball clan doesn't quite fit into their normal neighborhood. Other quirks include a bear-skin rug that growls at passersby, and Morticia's carnivorous plant Cleopatra, which thankfully doesn't eat people on account of the heartburn. But perhaps their most pointed idiosyncrasy is how, in an era of nagging wives and aloof husbands, Gomez so unselfconsciously swoons for his bride.

For this unique crew, it's all about family. Don't let their house full of torture devices fool you: this is a group who stand by one another—which is all the more impressive considering the daily terrors they have to endure, from elementary school, to puppies, prim neighbors, and even a few sunny days. The horror.

> **"** *When we're together, darling, every night is Halloween.* **"**
>
> Morticia Addams (S1 E7)

CREATORS: David Levy
PRODUCTION CO: Filmways Television

THE MUNSTERS

COMEDY • 1964
RATED: TV-PG • 30 MINS

What happens when there's a family of monsters next door? Like, real monsters? This clan might look like famous movie creepies, but they're as wholesome as apple pie.

You couldn't ask for a better father figure than Herman Munster (Fred Gwynne), a bighearted head of the household who's as innocent as they come, even if he is the spitting image of Frankenstein's monster. Together with his vampiric wife, Lily (Yvonne De Carlo); undead grandpa (Al Lewis); werewolf child, Eddie; and perfectly normal "ugly duckling" niece, Marilyn, the Munsters are a regular collection of backlot odds and ends.

The humor comes from the reactions the family get from the outside world, as well as Grandpa's laboratory tinkering. The show packs quite a few scenarios into its two seasons, from a camping trip to bouts of jealousy, always injecting its wholesome moral lessons with horror-movie strangeness.

AVATAR: THE LAST AIRBENDER

ANIMATED ADVENTURE • 2005
RATED: TV-Y7-FV • 23 MINS

A young hero must learn a mystical martial art that uses psychokinetic powers to control the four elements— then use it to save the world.

Twelve-year-old Aang (Zach Tyler) didn't start the Fire Nation's war, but he's the one who's been preordained to end it. In this world, humanity is split into four tribes dedicated to the elemental forces of fire, water, earth, and air. Only a special individual known as the "Avatar" has the ability to master all four using a mind-powered version of martial arts known as "bending," and bring harmony to the world.

The anime-inspired series draws heavily on East Asian art and culture, bringing ideas about reincarnation and chakras to the fantasy world. It takes Aang three seasons to finish his training—with plenty of stumbling on the way. As he learns, his journey requires patience, so settle in as events build to an epic battle.

THE LEGEND OF KORRA

ANIMATED ADVENTURE • 2012
RATED: TV-Y7-FV • 23 MINS

This follow-up to *The Last Airbender* introduces a new Avatar, the plucky Korra, as she learns to master her skills and navigate a changing world.

Things have evolved quite a bit from the events of *The Last Airbender*, set 70 years earlier. As the newly mantled Avatar, Korra's job is to hone her craft and rise to any challenges. In the bustling Republic City, Korra (Janet Varney), part of the Southern Water Tribe, quickly joins a professional bending league, a new development that packages the martial art for entertainment.

A quick learner, Korra defends the city through four seasons of high-flying action, defeating ne'er-do-wells from all sides while learning to channel her abilities. The battles and settings are visually arresting, taking inspiration from Studio Ghibli movies such as *Princess Mononoke*. As she picks up skills, Korra is well tested in her ability to keep the tenuous peace.

BATMAN: THE ANIMATED SERIES

ANIMATED ADVENTURE • 1992
RATED: TV-PG • 23 MINS

The Dark Knight has never looked better than in this noirish '90s cartoon series, which pits the Gotham City hero against his familiar villains.

Bruce Wayne (Kevin Conroy here) has gone through a battery of versions, from the cartoony 1960s TV series (see p404) to the brooding Christopher Nolan films. This animated version is one of the best. Utilizing a dark color palette and expressionistic angles, its version of Gotham has towering buildings, long shadows, and perfectly timeless retro touches (police airships patrol the sky).

There's the usual cast of characters, including Robin (Loren Lester), Alfred the butler (Efrem Zimbalist Jr.), and police commissioner Gordon (Bob Hastings). The two lengthy seasons allow for plenty of batcave spelunking, bad-guy nabbing, and secret-identity protecting. What else could a young bat fan want?

PINGU

ANIMATION • 1986
RATED: TV-G • 5 MINS

At the South Pole, a family of penguins and their friends excel at short bursts of physical comedy and making gibberish utterances in this stop-motion animated series.

Antarctica is aflutter with activity as Pingu and his family go about their penguin lives, living in igloos, ice fishing, even playing records. Not a bad lot for these birds resigned to the planet's least-populated continent. The mischievous Pingu is also surrounded by several non-penguin friends throughout the series' six seasons, including Robby the seal, and the show's simple clay-animation style is perfect for capturing the figures' amusing skits, such as going to the circus or sledding.

The characters speak in "Penguinese," a constant whir of gibberish sound and syllables (a bit like *Despicable Me*'s Minion-speak), but you'll have no problem deciphering their intent. Especially when one of them lets out a firm negative, or "Noot noot!"

SPONGEBOB SQUAREPANTS

ANIMATED COMEDY • 1999
RATED: TV-Y7 • 23 MINS

The cheerful SpongeBob finds fun and adventure with his underwater friends in Bikini Bottom, a small tiki-fied town on the Pacific ocean floor.

The sea is teeming with life, and nowhere more so than the small enclave that's home to SpongeBob SquarePants (Tom Kenny). The plucky, eternally optimistic cuboid could light up the deepest ocean trench with his megawatt personality and boundless energy. That approach keeps his spirits high while flipping burgers at the Krusty Krab, the restaurant where he works with easily annoyed Squidward (Rodger Bumpass), and gruff boss Mr. Krabs (Clancy Brown).

When he's not working, SpongeBob is usually found hanging out with his starfish pal Patrick and squirrel-in-a-diving-suit Sandy in his pineapple house. SpongeBob is a softy at heart, caring for pet Gary the Snail and serenading others with his ukulele. Soak in the charm with 12 seasons of surreal fun.

TEEN TITANS GO!

ANIMATED ADVENTURE • 2013
RATED: TV-PG • 11 MINS

A sugary-sweet confection with a high-energy filling, this show envisions its Super Hero team as cutely animated kids who bring a keen sense of humor and fun to their exploits.

Teens just have different priorities, as seen in the first episode of *Teen Titans Go!* when the bossy Raven (Tara Strong) wants to watch her favorite cartoon—a show called *Pretty Pegasus*—and sends her teammates on a fools' errand to find a fabled sandwich recipe held in a distant island fortress.

This is Super Hero action as ironic commentary and jokey parody rather than high-stakes heroics. Instead, the crew—who also feature Batman sidekick Robin (Scott Menville), shape-shifting Beast Boy (Greg Cipes), robotic Cyborg (Khary Payton), and laser-blasting Starfire (Hynden Walch)—spend six seasons mostly tracking down snacks, bickering about chores, and generally pranking one another. Typical youngsters.

THE FLINTSTONES

ANIMATED COMEDY • 1960
RATED: TV-G • 27 MINS

"Modern Stone Age family" Fred, Wilma, and baby Pebbles are definitely no grunting cave dwellers—more like your average 1960s suburban residents with some prehistoric touches.

He may live in dinosaur times, but Fred Flintstone (Alan Reed) is still every bit your average working dad. He loves his wife, Wilma (Jean Vander Pyl); his baby daughter, Pebbles; getting sloppy kisses from pet Dino; and going bowling with his buddy, Barney. His work life isn't so different from ours, either, except it involves operating a brontosaurus crane.

Inspired by classic TV sitcoms such as *The Honeymooners*, most episodes of this classic Hanna-Barbera cartoon revolve around a lighthearted husband-and-wife tiff, or a misunderstanding between friends. The threat of Fred getting fired by his quick-to-anger boss Mr. Slate also looms. It's only when alien exile the Great Gazoo shows up in the final sixth season that things get truly weird, so strap in.

WACKY RACES

ANIMATED COMEDY • 1968
RATED: U (UK) • 12 MINS

Teams of cartoon roadsters speed around the globe in odd vehicles trying to foil their fellow racers with outlandish traps and far-out detours.

Formula 1 doesn't have anything on this cross-country tournament, in which 11 cars, driven by cartoon characters from the Hanna-Barbera universe, face off in hope of winning the title "World's Wackiest Racer."

Everything's not quite above board, though, with competitors employing all kinds of conniving moves of questionable legality.

Cars are well-stocked with gizmos, such as Professor Pat Pending's modular Convert-a-Car and Red Max's Crimson Haybailer, a biplane-car hybrid. Combine those with teams such as the Ant Hill Mob, a carful of tiny 1930s gangsters, and arch-villain Dick Dastardly (Paul Winchell), and the drivers are practically falling over each another to put the brakes on the competition. Although it originally ran for only one season, the show was rebooted in 2017.

MISS MARPLE

MYSTERY • 1984
RATED: TV-PG • 53 MINS

Underestimate Miss Marple at your peril. Agatha Christie's senior sleuth is an ace at cracking cases in her home village of St. Mary Mead.

At her age, Miss Marple (Joan Hickson) has seen it all. That's part of why she's so good at rooting out the dark side of the society around her. Drawing on a lifetime of experience, Agatha Christie's slyly cunning crime solver is always able to connect the seemingly random dots by remembering that one fellow in her English village who did something or other.

There are many incarnations of the detective, including ITV's more recent *Agatha Christie's Marple*, but this 1980s BBC dramatization is a uniformly top choice. You could even say Agatha Christie would have approved. Back in 1946, Joan Hickson received a letter from the mystery master herself saying how she hoped Hickson would one day play Miss Marple. These adaptations of all 12 Marple novels over three series are nothing short of delightful.

MURDER, SHE WROTE

MYSTERY • 1984
RATED: TV-PG • 50 MINS

Life imitates art for mystery novelist Jessica Fletcher, who finds malfeasance under every rock in her quaint seaside town, and runs a side hustle as an amateur sleuth.

Where writer Jessica Fletcher (Angela Lansbury) goes, the bodies seem to follow—a pretty disturbing trend when you think about it. The inhabitants of fictional Cabot Cove, a small town in Maine, have a special skill for winding up dead under mysterious circumstances. Hypnotists, congresspeople, musicians, and restaurateurs all find themselves victims over the show's 12 seasons, and Jessica is on hand to figure out who's responsible.

Her writer's eye for detail usually cracks the case, as does her warm demeanor, a veneer that hides the analytical mind at work. She even works on vacation—helping to solve cases while traveling to New Orleans and Hollywood. It's all good fodder for her next page-turner ... and the cycle continues.

MIRANDA

SITCOM • 2009
RATED: TV-PG • 30 MINS

Life is an endless well of humor, amusement, and frivolity for shop owner Miranda. The trouble is, she always seems to be the punchline.

It's too perfect that Miranda lives above a joke shop, though usually the joke's on her. Written and created by comedian Miranda Hart, this three-season sitcom sets her up to take the brunt of the humor, poking fun at her towering height and unladylike mannerisms as she searches for love. She's as likeable and relatable a heroine as you could ask for, with a repertoire of awkward tics played for laughs and a penchant for fourth-wall-breaking asides.

Watching Miranda navigate the dating world, and trying not to scare away prospective paramour Gary (Tom Ellis), is like watching a boxing bout in which the underdog keeps valiantly returning for more punishment. Her mom, Penny (Patricia Hodge), and best pal, Stevie (Sarah Hadland), cheer her on as she goes in for another round.

THE GOLDEN GIRLS

SITCOM • 1985 • RATED: TV-PG • 30 MINS • SEASONS: 7
BEA ARTHUR, BETTY WHITE, RUE MCCLANAHAN

Welcome to 1980s Miami, the land of palm trees, wicker furniture, light pastel tones—and four ladies in their golden years living their lives like there's no tomorrow. Maybe it's time for you to watch them today?

If there's a show with a theme song that perfectly encapsulates its dynamic, it's *The Golden Girls*. As the opening chords of Andrew Gold's "Thank You for Being a Friend" transport you to the sun-dappled bungalow of your dreams, imagine what life could be like in a house of aging ride-or-die pals in sunny Florida. And you couldn't ask for better friends than Dorothy Zbornak (Bea Arthur), Blanche Devereaux (Rue McClanahan), Rose Nylund (Betty White), and Dorothy's 80-year-old mom, Sophia Petrillo (Estelle Getty).

If the premise sounds a bit boring, fear not. These ladies may be closing in on their twilight years, but they haven't lost a step, with quick-witted remarks flying fast and loose around the living room. Each principal leads with a particular brand of humor—there's savvy, wisecracking, old-world Sicilian Sophia; oversexed southern belle Blanche; airheaded comic relief Rose; and level-headed, bone-dry straight woman Dorothy.

When you've lived as long as they have, there's plenty to joke about: unworthy husbands, bad dinner dates, old boyfriends, and the joys of living independently without a man or child calling for you. If life is a banquet, these ladies may worry about the calories but ultimately come back for dessert, with chocolate syrup on top.

Over endless pieces of cheesecake, they find plenty of time for talking about men, relationships, and landing dates with eligible bachelors. I mean, life doesn't end at menopause, you know? There's also the sorting out of those loose ends that come from a life well lived. With all that gentle joking, the theme song reminds you what brings them all together: the bonds between friends. The laughs make those sentimental moments sparkle with a golden hue.

> **"** *People waste their time pondering whether a glass is half empty or half full. Me, I just drink whatever's in the glass.* **"**
>
> Sophia (S5 E14)

CREATORS: Susan Harris
PRODUCTION CO: Touchstone Television, Witt/Thomas/Harris Productions

COSMOS: A SPACETIME ODYSSEY

DOCUMENTARY • 2014 • RATED: TV-PG • 42 MINS • SEASONS: I
NEIL DEGRASSE TYSON

This tour of the universe starts at Earth and moves outward, delivering breathtaking visualizations of far-off worlds and thought-provoking descriptions of impossible sights. For anyone curious about what's up there in the night sky, this is essential viewing.

In the grand scheme of the universe, our world, even our entire galaxy, is just a tiny drop in a vast ocean. It's a humbling thought to ponder as you watch *Cosmos*, which aims to answer the questions of how we got here and where we might be going—in the cosmic sense at least.

Astrophysicist Neil deGrasse Tyson narrates the journey outward past the edge of our solar system, where we observe Voyager I, launched in 1977, hurtling into interstellar space. It's the human-made object farthest from Earth and a reminder of just how far we've come. Like a kindly science teacher, *Cosmos* takes the time to walk you through complex topics such as the wave theory of light, and discoveries from electromagnetism to dark matter.

Our journey here on Earth is part of *Cosmos*, too—after all, our bodies are made from the same stardust as the rest of the planet's life. Meanwhile, the history of astronomy, one of the first sciences, starts shortly after the birth of humankind. Building on cosmologist Carl Sagan's renowned 1980 series, *Cosmos: A Personal Voyage*, this follow-up aims to answer the big questions with a poetic flourish to inspire us all to dream bigger.

NOVA

DOCUMENTARY • 1974
RATED: TV-PG • 60 MINS

Its starlike name belies the vast range of this show, which covers science, history, technology, and the natural world, weighing in on things as global as climate change and as local as sinkholes.

Nova is as dense as a heavy science textbook, but its 47 seasons definitely cover more ground than your average school course. The series asks scientists to explain their work to laypeople. Some of it is complicated stuff, such as the Drake equation, which estimates the probability of ever communicating with extraterrestrial life, and string theory, a complex framework for explaining the universe.

As well as science, *Nova* covers social topics and the natural world, exploring mysteriously abandoned archaeological sites, and the repercussions of human-made climate change. You don't need a track record of staying awake in science class to enjoy this show—just a bit of curiosity and a spare hour.

FAMILY MATTERS

COMEDY • 1989
RATED: TV-G • 30 MINS

If being a nerd is a superpower, then Steve Urkel is a surefire superhero in this comedy about a middle-class African American family.

The teenage neighbor who strolls in whenever they like is a popular sitcom trope, but no one does it better than suspender-snapping, horn-rimmed-glasses-wearing Steve Urkel (Jaleel White). Throughout nine seasons, Steve ingratiates himself with the next-door Winslow clan, who include police officer dad Carl (Reginald VelJohnson) and brainy daughter Laura (Kellie Shanygne Williams).

Steve breaks new ground in the world of nerdery with his particular brand of wiry energy, a teenager with the soul and the cardigan of a senior citizen. His enthusiasm is infectious, as his classmates find out when he leads the group in his pelvis-thrusting Urkel Dance. Steve even goes full nutty professor, inventing a machine to turn into a smooth-talking debonair version of himself.

SAILOR MOON

ANIMATED SCI-FI • 1992
RATED: TV-Y • 30 MINS

A group of schoolkids are given powers to save Earth from destruction in this Japanese anime series that features memorable costumes, magical cats, and powerful crystals.

School was never this intense. Usagi Tsukino (Stephanie Sheh) and her pals are enlisted into the fight against the Dark Kingdom, a truly frightening array of monsters threatening humanity. By uttering the phrase "Moon Prism Power, Make Up," Usagi transforms into a Sailor Guardian, a superpowered hero in a cutesy schoolgirl outfit. As her crew navigates crushes and their school tests, monsters sent by evil Queen Beryl (Cindy Robinson) appear out of the woodwork to challenge the youngsters.

Usagi is klutzy and forgetful, a refreshingly atypical hero who revels in her unabashed love for all things girly throughout this five-season series. As her team assembles, they face danger with style and grace.

STEVEN UNIVERSE

ANIMATED COMEDY • 2013
RATED: TV-PG • 11 MINS

Steven Universe is a normal guy, with some really special roommates— the Crystal Gems—three aliens who teach him to use his own powers to save the world.

The powerful Crystal Gems—Garnet (Estelle), Amethyst (Michaela Dietz), and Pearl (Deedee Magno)—are supercharged warriors from an alien race. Steven (Zach Callison), on the other hand, is half human, half Gem, and faces a learning curve getting his abilities to kick in. As Steven gets up to speed during the show's six seasons, we learn more about the troll-like gemstones in the aliens' chests, their home planet, and how the friends plan to save Earth.

When Steven finally manifests his power as a pink shield, it's a representation of his caring nature and capacity for nurturing. Delivering artfully painted backgrounds loaded with detail and short bite-sized episodes, *Steven Universe* is an easy binge, like cartoon comfort food. Go ahead and dive in!

REGULAR SHOW

ANIMATED COMEDY • 2009
RATED: TV-PG • 23 MINS

Randomness and endless digressions are on order as two 20-somethings—a blue jay and a raccoon who do landscaping at a local park—entertain themselves in this surreal animation.

What's the best way to negotiate a raise? If you're anything like easily distracted friends and coworkers Mordecai (J. G. Quintel) and Rigby (William Salyers), you perform a dance routine for your two bosses, the grumpy human gumball machine Benson and the aloof personified lollipop Pops. The rest of their cohorts are just as odd, and their adventures are only bound by the limits of their weird hobbies. Going to the moon? Hamboning (essentially body-slapping as a form of percussion)? It's all on the menu.

The proceedings are anything but regular in this eight-season series. And its escapades have the unpolished gusto of a college student's senior project. That's not a slight—the show's youthful vigor is enlivening.

A SERIES OF UNFORTUNATE EVENTS

COMEDY DRAMA • 2017
RATED: TV-PG • 50 MINS

The creepy Count Olaf plots against the orphaned Baudelaire children as they work to uncover their family's hidden past with madcap energy.

Things could be better for the three Baudelaire children. As we begin, their parents have just died in a mysterious fire that also turned their house to ashes. The pitch-black opening sets the tone for the fun and mayhem to come in this show based on the book series by Lemony Snicket (pen name of author Daniel Handler).

Violet (Malina Weissman), Klaus (Louis Hynes), and baby Sunny are sent to stay with their scheming distant relative Count Olaf (Neil Patrick Harris). But his creaky abode can only hold the clever kids for so long, and their subsequent travels introduce them to other characters just as unpleasant as Olaf. Their last-minute escapes keep the series churning through three seasons of twisted adventure.

SPEECHLESS

COMEDY • 2016
RATED: TV-PG • 21 MINS

In this heartfelt and hilarious comedy, the DiMeo family buys a rundown house in a new town so their son with cerebral palsy can go to a better school.

The DiMeos are your typical American family, but one you don't see much on TV. Driven mom Maya (Minnie Driver) and calm dad Jimmy (John Ross Bowie) are parents who fight for their three kids tooth and nail, especially eldest, J. J., who has cerebral palsy (played by Micah Fowler who has the condition). Due to his illness, J. J. uses a wheelchair and cannot speak, communicating via a laser pointer to spell words. As a result, the new school pairs him with an aide: groundskeeper Kenneth Clements (Cedric Yarbrough) who becomes a mentor and friend.

It's rare that a show depicts a disabled lead, and rarer still that it can treat the subject of disability with such thoughtfulness and humor. With his sharp wit, J.J. lands some of the best one-liners of the three-season show.

GRAVITY FALLS

ANIMATED COMEDY • 2012
RATED: TV-Y7 • 23 MINS

Strange things happen in the town of Gravity Falls, where twins Dipper and Mabel Pines are sent to stay with great-uncle Stan, and get to know the paranormal creatures around them.

There's something spooky in the woods of Gravity Falls, Oregon, as these youngsters find out while living with their fez-capped great-uncle, or grunkle, who runs tourist-trap museum the Mystery Shack. Uncovering the secrets of the mysterious town keeps the twins busy for two hectic seasons, especially after Dipper (Jason Ritter) finds a cryptic journal detailing the locale's enigmatic history.

You'd expect the glum forests of Gravity Falls to be home to some vampire-esque creatures. But as Mabel (Kristen Schaal) discovers when her boyfriend turns out to be something else entirely, the denizens of these woods are even weirder than that. Mabel and Dipper start work to get to the bottom of it all, while Grunkle Stan (Alex Hirsch) hides a secret.

WE BARE BEARS

ANIMATED COMEDY • 2014
RATED: TV-Y7 • 12 MINS

Something's not quite right about these city-dwelling brothers—they're bears, for one, and despite their attempts to fit in by playing basketball and eating out, urban life is a challenge.

Brothers Grizzly (Eric Edelstein), Panda (Bobby Moynihan), and Ice Bear (Demetri Martin) live in a nice apartment in the San Francisco Bay Area, interacting with the human citizens around them who aren't always accepting of bears in their midst. These ursine individuals aren't scratching themselves in the woods or swatting at salmon—their desires are more commonplace, like wanting their videos to go viral online or launching a food-truck business.

Strolling the city stacked on top of each other, the trio take on the bothersome and irritating aspects of city life with extreme solutions over the show's four seasons. For example, people chatting in a movie theater causes them to become ninja vigilantes, shushing those who make a noise. Bears, they're just like us.

HEARTLAND

DRAMA • 2007
RATED: TV-PG • 45 MINS

Life on this horse ranch in rural Canada offers no shortage of drama as we follow young Amy, who's thrust into the saddle after her mother tragically dies.

In the pastures of Alberta, Canada, Heartland Horse Ranch takes in abandoned and abused animals and nurses them back to health with love and patience. If you think that might be a metaphor for the humans who care for them too, well, you're right. Sisters Amy (Amber Marshall) and Lou Fleming (Michelle Morgan), along with their grandfather Jack (Shaun Johnston) and other ranch hands, work on rehabilitating the steeds while tending to their own wounds.

No mere one-trick pony, this series runs deep, providing 13 seasons of equine caretaking, interpersonal growth, and plenty of lessons learned along the way. The most important lesson, demonstrated time and again, is no matter what the challenge, you've got to get back on the horse.

STAR TREK

SCI-FI • 1966 • RATED: TV-PG • 50 MINS • SEASONS: 3
WILLIAM SHATNER, LEONARD NIMOY, DEFOREST KELLEY

The crew of the _Starship Enterprise_— Captain Kirk, Mister Spock, et al— explore the far reaches of the galaxy in search of intelligent life and alien civilizations. They try to promote peace and justice, but the sentiment isn't always returned.

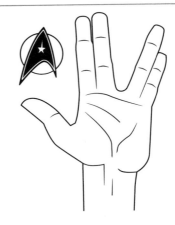

In the 1960s, the Space Race and the challenge to put a man on the moon captivated millions around the globe. _Star Trek_ followed that wave of interstellar interest with a series all about exploring uncharted corners of the Milky Way galaxy. What makes the _Enterprise_ crew's mission so intriguing and relatable here on Earth is that the challenges they find in space— issues such as intolerance, racism, and greed—are similar to those here.

Created by Gene Roddenberry, the show takes its cues from westerns and adventure novels—and would go on to inspire waves of other space dramas, including _Star Wars_ and _Firefly_ (see p91), to say nothing of all the _Star Trek_ sequels, from _Voyager_ (see p134) to the recent _Discovery_ (see p135).

Set only some 200 years from now, the main cast is led by commanding officer James T. Kirk (William Shatner) and consists of science officer Spock (Leonard Nimoy), chief medical officer Leonard McCoy (DeForest Kelley), engineer "Scotty" (James Doohan), communications officer Uhura (Nichelle Nichols), helmsman Sulu (George Takei), and navigator Chekov (Walter Koenig). Of course, with that many personalities traveling the stars, some conflict is inevitable.

THE PRIME STAR TREK TIMELINE

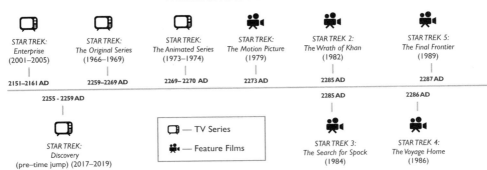

STAR TREK: Enterprise (2001–2005)	STAR TREK: The Original Series (1966–1969)	STAR TREK: The Animated Series (1973–1974)	STAR TREK: The Motion Picture (1979)	STAR TREK 2: The Wrath of Khan (1982)	STAR TREK 5: The Final Frontier (1989)
2151–2161 AD	2259–2269 AD	2269–2270 AD	2273 AD	2285 AD	2287 AD

2255 - 2259 AD		2285 AD	2286 AD
STAR TREK: Discovery (pre–time jump) (2017–2019)		STAR TREK 3: The Search for Spock (1984)	STAR TREK 4: The Voyage Home (1986)

📺 — TV Series

🎥 — Feature Films

The fair-minded Kirk often finds himself advised in two directions by the emotionless-yet-reasonable Spock—who has mixed human and alien-Vulcan heritage—and the more passion-driven McCoy. Likewise, the other cast members reflect a diversity of genders, races, and nationalities, shining a spotlight on the polarization of its era, the 1960s, and a more enlightened future ahead. One notable exchange between Captain Kirk and Lieutenant Uhura features the first kiss between a fictional white male and a fictional black female to premiere on US network television, a big deal at the time.

The crew faces many formidable challenges, from beleaguered Starfleet compatriots—such as a crew member stricken with megalomania and imbued with the power of telekinesis—to a litany of alien species. The lizardlike Gorn make a notable appearance in this series, as do the yeti-inspired salt vampires. Those monster-like creatures are joined by more humanoid races, such as the Klingons and the Romulans, names that will be familiar to most people whether you're a Trekkie or not.

A word of caution: the series' original pilot may throw you. It features a slightly different cast—instead of Captain Kirk, you get to travel the spaceways with Captain Pike (Jeffrey Hunter). After the pilot was rejected, Hunter withdrew from the show, paving the way for Shatner to star in a second more successful pilot.

Likewise, the array of dazzling space gizmos can be a bit overwhelming. As well as the warpdrive (the thing that makes the ship go really fast) and phasers (guns that, don't forget, can be set to stun), there are also transporters that can beam you down to a planet's surface, and tricorders, devices that can be used to do everything from detecting radiation to recording memories (which comes in handy with all the space mischief going on around).

> *"To boldly go where no man has gone before ..."*

Captain Kirk

For all its technology, though, *Star Trek* is really about the core belief that in the future humans will see past differences, and evolve. On the Enterprise, humankind is noble and the crew is open-minded in its exploration of other worlds and cultures. Even when Kirk and crew beat their enemies, they sometimes reach out to their defeated foe to offer help. That's something the world could still learn from *Star Trek* today.

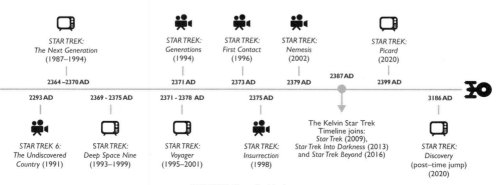

STAR TREK: The Next Generation (1987–1994) — 2364–2370 AD

STAR TREK: Generations (1994) — 2371 AD

STAR TREK: First Contact (1996) — 2373 AD

STAR TREK: Nemesis (2002) — 2379 AD — 2387 AD

STAR TREK: Picard (2020) — 2399 AD

2293 AD — *STAR TREK 6:* The Undiscovered Country (1991)

2369 - 2375 AD — *STAR TREK:* Deep Space Nine (1993–1999)

2371 - 2378 AD — *STAR TREK:* Voyager (1995–2001)

2375 AD — *STAR TREK:* Insurrection (1998)

The Kelvin Star Trek Timeline joins: Star Trek (2009), *Star Trek Into Darkness* (2013) and *Star Trek Beyond* (2016)

3186 AD — *STAR TREK:* Discovery (post–time jump) (2020)

CREATOR: Gene Roddenberry
PRODUCTION CO: Desilu Productions, Norway Corporation, Paramount Television

STAR TREK: THE NEXT GENERATION

SCI-FI • 1987 • RATED: TV-PG • 44 MINS • SEASONS: 7
PATRICK STEWART, JONATHAN FRAKES, BRENT SPINER

The starship and crew—led by sure-handed Captain Jean-Luc Picard—travels the universe discovering new life, conducting interstellar diplomacy, and laying down the law when they have to, in this celebrated follow-up to the groundbreaking sci-fi series.

Every Trekkie has a favorite Starfleet captain, and Captain Picard—portrayed indelibly by Patrick Stewart—is a strong contender against some formidable competition. His enviable leadership skills are a model of clear-headed judgement and principled reasoning.

Along for the ride through space are analytical operations officer Data (Brent Spiner), the bold first officer William Riker (Jonathan Frakes), and visor-wearing engineer Geordi La Forge (LeVar Burton), to name but a few.

The spaceways are still packed with intelligent life, good and bad. Newcomers to the *Star Trek* universe include the bumpy-headed Ferengi, the scaly Cardassians, and the robotic Borg. The Klingons are still there, but now as allies. Picard even helps mediate issues within the Klingon empire. These ridge-skulled aliens remain among *Star Trek*'s most compelling characters, inspired by a warrior's code and with a fully fleshed-out language (which is available for any Klingon enthusiasts to learn who have free time on their hands).

The starship *Enterprise* travels through space for seven seasons, but the show really seems to have all engines blasting around Season 4. Facing plots that threaten to tear their ship apart, Picard and his crew come through by demonstrating humanity's rare and admirable potential for self-sacrifice.

LOST IN SPACE (1965)

SCI-FI • 1965
RATED: TV-G • 51 MINS

The Robinson family are heading into space to colonize a new home when a saboteur in their midst sends their ship off course, stranding them in an unknown alien world.

Imagine it: Earth is desperately overcrowded and humanity is sending one volunteer family to the Alpha Centauri star system to start anew. Did we mention, the year is 1997?

Audiences now know that timeline is a bit off, but these futuristic survivalists—based on the shipwrecked family from *The Swiss Family Robinson* book—have a lot to offer.

Professor John Robinson (Guy Williams), Dr. Maureen Robinson (June Lockhart), their three kids, Major Don West (Mark Goddard), and the deliciously camp Dr. Smith (Jonathan Harris), are a resourceful bunch, good with space hardware and great company for an impending disaster. The group encounters giant monsters, bad space weather, and aliens of all kinds throughout three hectic seasons.

LOST IN SPACE (2018)

SCI-FI • 2018
RATED: TV-PG • 55 MINS

Humanity is once again ditching Earth for greener alien pastures. These travelers are en route to a new paradise when disaster strikes, sending the clan spiraling into the unknown.

The look of this two-season reboot may be totally upgraded from the original's (see p90) retro Space Age feel, but don't think that this new take has completely ignored its predecessor. The precocious Will Robinson (Maxwell Jenkins) is just as brainy as before, and he and the rest of the Robinsons are just as lost. They're not quite as alone, though. This time their spaceship is part of a larger station that's attacked by robotic aliens, depositing the Robinsons on a strange, dangerous planet.

Dr. Smith (Parker Posey)—somewhere between a villain and a misanthropic prankster in the original—is reborn as a mysterious con artist. The actress brings an understated smarm to the character that'll keep you guessing about where the real danger lies.

FIREFLY

SCI-FI • 2002 • RATED: TV-14 • 45 MINS • SEASONS: I
NATHAN FILLION, GINA TORRES, ALAN TUDYK

This ship of space travelers finds that the new frontier of the future is a lot like the Wild West of old as they try to dodge the law and survive on the edge of society.

In the aftermath of an interplanetary civil war, captain of the spaceship *Serenity*, Mal Reynolds (Nathan Fillion), takes on passengers for a fee while making pit stops to scavenge and smuggle. The ragtag group of outcasts on board the spaceship—a sex worker, a pastor, a surgeon, a mercenary, a mechanic, and assorted other crew members—have different motivations for wanting to stay under the radar of the authorities. Without a home to speak of, the travelers create a makeshift world on the ship, falling in love, bickering, and joking like any family would.

Serenity (a Firefly-class spaceship, hence the name of the show) does its best to avoid the rule-enforcing Alliance officers as well as monsterlike Reavers and other scammers, while looting and stealing, mainly from the rich. In addition to a strong American Old West vibe, the show combines costuming and other elements from American and Chinese cultures, the two superpowers that make up the new order. The world is technologically advanced but also seems very lived-in—a future pieced together from scraps.

True to its theme of floating through space, the one-season show offers scant resolution. You'll have to find that in the follow-up film, *Serenity*, which closes the story.

> **"We are just too pretty for God to let us die."**
>
> Mal Reynolds (SI EII)

DOGS

DOCUMENTARY • 2018
RATED: TV-PG • 50 MINS

If you love sharing dog videos on social media, this is the show for you. It examines all kinds of human-canine connections. Meet all manner of pups and the humans who love them.

This six-episode series features dogs of all spots and stripes. Traveling to San Giovanni, a small town on Italy's Lake Como, you meet the loyal labrador that dutifully accompanies his master on a fishing boat each morning and gets a seat at the dinner table each evening. At a birthday party for dogs in Japan, owners speak of their pets like children, holding them close. A young girl in Ohio waits for a service dog that will alert her to dangerous seizures.

One thing is clear, humans depend on their pets as much as their pets rely on them. A rescue organization matches doggos in Texas shelters with owners back in NYC, making a cross-country trek that demonstrates even the greatest effort will be repaid tenfold by a loyal dog. One to watch with the dog.

THE PINK PANTHER SHOW

ANIMATED COMEDY • 1969
RATED: TV-G • 21 MINS

This crazy cat makes mischief, defying all rules or consequences. From the zoo to the department store, the world is the Pink Panther's playground.

The star of these amusing short cartoons is a bit of a cypher. The fuchsia feline is mostly mute, displaying his high-society airs and graces through body language. He keeps himself amused by playing arcade games, practicing his violin, and playing practical jokes on his nemesis, the Little Man. The pair first meet when the Panther tries to convince Little Man, acting as a contractor, to build his dream house, a futuristic all-pink abode.

The *Pink Panther* has had many iterations, but this two-season series shows its comic genius in its purest form. With allusions to timeless silent movie gags and cat-and-mouse chases, it's an addictive pleasure only matched by its catchy, often-covered theme song.

THE MUPPETS.

COMEDY • 2015
RATED: TV-PG • 21 MINS

Kermit, Fozzie, Gonzo, et al star in this mockumentary about a late-night talk show hosted by the mercurial Miss Piggy, with loads of celebrity guests.

Kermit's cheery demeanor and optimism start to show some cracks on this Muppets show for grown-ups. Whether it's the years in Hollywood or the stress of working with his ex—Miss Piggy (Eric Jacobson)—Kermit (Steve Whitmire) is a bit shaggier than usual and prone to snapping at his employees from the stress of pulling together the production.

Seeing the Muppets as real people with real woes can be jarring, and your engagement may vary depending on how successful you think the transformation is. The copious guest stars sweeten the deal, with actors like Elizabeth Banks, Jay Leno, and RuPaul, as well as musical guests including Jack White and Imagine Dragons, dropping in. This show was curtains after only one season, but you can bet the Muppets will have some kind of encore.

SABRINA THE TEENAGE WITCH

COMEDY • 1996
RATED: TV-G • 22 MINS

A teen who discovers she's a witch with magical powers on her 16th birthday tries to live a normal high-school life and keep her spell-casting under wraps.

Sabrina Spellman (Melissa Joan Hart) is your typical everyday teen witch. Set in the Archie comics universe, this is a much gentler version of Sabrina's story than the more recent *Chilling Adventures of Sabrina* (see p398). Sabrina is guided by aunts Hilda (Caroline Rhea) and Zelda (Beth Broderick). And she has a black cat that talks: the hilarious Salem (Nick Bakay), a witch forced to take the form of a cat as punishment.

Rites of passage are given twists, with Sabrina's blunders magnified by her magic powers. As she ships off to college in Season 5, then gets a job in the final seventh season, her aunts depart and we find out whether she was really paying attention through all those lessons.

SUPERGIRL

DRAMA • 2015
RATED: TV-PG • 43 MINS

There's a lot of baggage that comes with following in Superman's footsteps, something that his cousin, Kara Zor-El, aka Kara Danvers, knows all too well.

As Supergirl, Kara (Melissa Benoist) dons the iconic blue-and-red outfit to protect the world from aliens and evildoers while maintaining a secret identity as a mild-mannered reporter. The family history is handy when she can recall, "Wasn't Superman here before?" It's also a bane, when Supergirl finds herself underestimated by friends and foes. It's her quest for equality with Superman as well as in her job that helps make this show feel so vital.

As part of the Department of Extra-Normal Operations (DEO), Supergirl works with a crew of friends including adopted sister Alex Danvers (Chyler Leigh) and tech whiz Winn Schott (Jeremy Jordan). Over five seasons she fends off extraterrestrial baddies and the machinations of LuthorCorp to keep National City safe.

RONJA, THE ROBBER'S DAUGHTER

ANIMATED FANTASY • 2014
RATED: TV-Y7-FV • 25 MINS

A young girl, Ronja, born to the head of a castle-dwelling band of robbers, explores the forest near her home and befriends a boy from a rival gang.

Cloistered castle life is no good for Ronja (Teresa Gallagher), the spirited daughter of bandit Mattis (Rufus Hound). As she starts exploring—and making enquiries about the family business—Ronja learns to hold her own in this medieval fantasy world populated by frightening harpies, dwarves, and other woodland rascals. Her relationship with her family is as much a part of the journey as the battles she fights making her way in the world.

This single season adaptation of the Swedish children's book of the same name is the first television series from Japan's Studio Ghibli, responsible for numerous acclaimed anime films. Ghibli picked a perfect story for this debut effort, just the thing to spirit you away.

QUANTUM LEAP

SCI-FI • 1989 • RATED: TV-PG • 60 MINS • SEASONS: 5
SCOTT BAKULA, DEAN STOCKWELL, DEBORAH PRATT

Physicist Sam Beckett is unstuck in time. Traveling around the 20th century, Sam finds himself thrust into tricky situations—from a bank robbery to a boxing ring—forced to solve problems before he's allowed to continue his travels.

Like so many TV scientists before him, Dr. Sam Beckett (Scott Bakula) was working in his lab one night when something went very wrong. Or did it go right? Now he's flying through time, inhabiting the bodies of strangers while helping them out of a pickle and learning a lesson in the process. Before you know it he's off to another scenario without a minute to catch his breath. Accompanying Dr. Beckett is Admiral Al Calavicci (Dean Stockwell), his cigar-chomping buddy back home who appears as a hologram to advise Sam.

The locations Beckett visits are pulled from the history books, dropping him into hotspots like the American civil rights movement, the war in Vietnam, and even the Kennedy assassination. The outlandishness only elevates from there.

The fact that Sam enters each situation unaware, like someone who's just walked into a film midway, sets up some classic mirror reveals—you see him as Sam, but the mirror shows the character as seen by others. That could be young, old, black, white, man, woman, and beyond. In one episode, Sam transports into the body of a woman who's nearly nine months pregnant. In another, he becomes a chimpanzee.

There's no shortage of brain teasers, including the big question of why this is all happening. The answer has something to do with God, the devil and … well, it doesn't really matter all that much.

What makes *Quantum Leap* so remarkable is its open-hearted approach to some painful history paired with Sam's charm. Even when he's inhabiting the body of a serial killer, or altering the course of history, Sam approaches the situation with compassion and empathy, lest he be stuck there forever. If he's still out there somewhere righting history's wrongs, we're in good hands.

NUMBER OF LEAPS PER YEAR

Leaps before 1950:
1862 = 1x ✳ 1945 = 1x ✳

Leaps after 1990:
1995 = 1x ✳ 1999 = 1x ✳

CREATOR: Donald P. Bellisario
PRODUCTION CO: Belisarius Productions, Universal Television

MACGYVER

**ADVENTURE • 1985 • RATED: TV-PG • 48 MINS • SEASONS: 7
RICHARD DEAN ANDERSON, DANA ELCAR, BRUCE MCGILL**

As a secret agent, MacGyver's special skills are keeping his cool under mega pressure and escaping tricky situations using handy household items. His quick thinking and creativity get him out of almost any jam—you'll never look at duct tape in the same way again.

As far as ex-secret agents with encyclopedic knowledge of chemistry, physics, and all the uses for a Swiss Army Knife go, MacGyver (Richard Dead Anderson) is at the top of his class. He is both a model citizen and a model for nonviolent action heroes everywhere. This is not your average shoot-first, ask-questions-later type brute.

First off, MacGyver hates guns, preferring to use his brain. In one episode he does handle a gun, smashing it and using the pieces to make a wrench. That should give you an idea of where his head is. He then uses the wrench to shut down a runaway nuclear reactor, giving an idea of the stakes. Amazingly, this isn't even the 50th most impressive trick he pulls in the show's luscious seven seasons.

MacGyver is supplied with missions by the secretive Phoenix Foundation. Boss and friend Pete Thornton (Dana Elcar) sends him around the globe to stop assassins, terrorists, and more. MacGyver tends to start episodes elbow-deep in a mission, a little teaser for the post-title main course. You will find yourself going back for seconds.

> **"** *Don't tell me you know how to make a bomb out of a stick of chewing gum.* **"**
>
> **Barbara Spencer to MacGyver** (SI EI)

ROBIN OF SHERWOOD

**ADVENTURE • 1984
RATED: TV-PG • 54 MINS**

Robin Hood and his Merry Men roam Sherwood Forest in this gritty telling of the legend, complete with murder, magic, and plenty of taking from the rich and giving to the poor.

The man with a thirst for justice and a laser-focus arrow, Robin (Michael Praed as Robin of Loxley, then Jason Connery as his successor, Robert of Huntingdon), takes on the fight for the oppressed. His band of outlaws has the usual suspects including Little John (Clive Mantle) and Will Scarlet (Ray Winstone). The crew is what sets this adaptation apart, with a sense of camaraderie among the rough-and-ready fellows.

In just three seasons the rabble-rousers provoke the ire of the ruling classes, all the while winning over the general populace and the fair Lady Marion (Judi Trott). It's to the show's credit that the introduction of sorcery and demons—and the lack of tights—only sharpens the focus on realism.

SHAUN THE SHEEP

COMEDY • 2007
RATED: TV-G • 7 MINS

The sheep have taken over the farmyard. Following the mischievous Shaun, the flock plays around with pigs, dogs, and other creatures while the Farmer's away in this stop-motion series.

Living on a farm, one has to amuse oneself, which is essentially the premise of this series about a sheep who engages in silly antics with the other animals on the farm. What better way to spend a sunny afternoon than to stage an interspecies Olympics with pole vaulting, archery, and gymnastics? When the Farmer comes home, the party's over and the residents go back to pretending to be animals.

The look of Shaun and pals will be familiar to anyone who's seen *Wallace & Gromit,* the clay-animation series in which the sheep previously appeared. That same humor is on full display here as well, with plenty of slapstick stunts and wordless playfulness. The show crams a lot of diversions into its six seasons—it is "shearly" wonderful.

TINY HOUSE NATION

REALITY TV • 2014
RATED: TV-PG • 41 MINS

You can live large in a small house, according to this roving reality show that profiles folks looking to downsize their lives with style.

A bit bigger than a walk-in closet, these architecturally inventive homes are all less than 500 square feet (50 square meters). Experts John Weisbarth and Zack Giffin guide tiny housers through the process from design to construction and moving in. Each of these unique structures brings challenges with it, especially when it comes to getting the approval of opinionated relatives.

Special requests abound over five seasons, like a musician who wants a grand piano in the cozy living quarters or a DJ whose multi-turntable setup is an obstacle turned opportunity. The transformation requires a leap of faith and a powerful imagination, as well as compromise. A tiny house isn't just a place to live, it's a lifestyle change with its own hazards and rewards.

SPY IN THE WILD

DOCUMENTARY • 2017
RATED: TV-PG • 59 MINS

What's the best way to get a good look at a skittish animal in its natural habitat? To do as this show does and create a lifelike animatronic replica with a camera inside, of course.

There's a stranger in their midst. The mechanically minded naturalists of this show have programmed near perfect versions of animals—from elephants and otters to hippos and alligators—and sent them into the wild. The interlopers mimic the movements and sounds of the originals, which helps them gain intimate access. An animatronic wild dog performs a play bow and at the den gets a close-up view of the baby pups at meal time.

Teamwork is important to many animals, and it's incredible that these man-made creations are able to join the team. Not everything goes according to plan, as the "Bad Behavior" episode proves, but the two-season show's range is impressive, following some 30 models into the wide wild world.

WALLACE & GROMIT'S WORLD OF INVENTION

COMEDY • 2010 • RATED: U (UK) • 30 MINS • SEASONS: I
PETER SALLIS, ASHLEY JENSEN, JOHN SPARKES

Slipping some educational content into your TV diet doesn't have to be a chore. Let the industrious Wallace and his canine pal Gromit introduce you to real-world inventions and marvels, in this take on kids programming that should enthrall the whole family.

For master tinkerer Wallace (Peter Sallis) every day is an adventure, starting with a journey through his own custom-built machine of contraptions that do everything from pour his coffee to pull his sweater over his head. He's the perfect person to introduce you to real-life inventors such as the guy who created the pocket calculator and the digital watch (it's Clive Sinclair), or explore the development of the teasmade—a combination alarm clock and tea maker that Wallace is probably upset he didn't invent himself.

Episodes are made up of breakout segments describing real-life history, like the quest for an electric tricycle, or a profile of a thinker whose inventions changed the world or challenged it to dream. Wallace and Gromit serve as your guides, who get up to their own business as well, speaking from the rocket ship they took to the moon and the workshop where they're always tinkering.

Naturally their interest eventually turns skyward, profiling the person behind the largest rocket to launch from the UK and tracing the quest for a workable jetpack. Gustav Mesmer, an inventor with a fondness for building flying machines, brought an artist's touch to the pursuit, creating Icarus-esque wings for himself as well as for his bicycle. None of the creations actually left the ground, but they brought plenty of joy and wonder to those who followed Mesmer's work.

If the fantastical is more your thing, the show is not all science and fact: Wallace and Gromit also take on fictional devices from invisibility cloaks to flying saucers. Just because it hasn't been invented yet doesn't mean it's make-believe, as proven by one "inventor of the week" who, after being told his idea for a prosthetic arm was impossible, created one himself then shared his developments with others around the world.

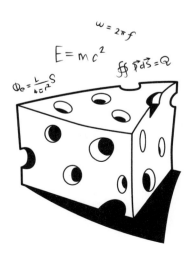

$$\omega = 2\pi f$$

$$E = mc^2$$

$$\oint \vec{p} \, d\vec{s} = Q$$

$$\Phi_e = \frac{L}{4\pi r^2} S$$

INSPECTOR MORSE

CRIME • 1987
RATED: TV-14 • 100 MINS

Mysterious circumstances are de rigueur as Inspector Morse stumbles upon murders most foul in Oxford. Expect sleuthing mixed with a busy schedule of drinking, repressed moping, and listening to opera records.

Unlike most TV detectives, there's something a little sad about Inspector Morse (John Thaw), whose curmudgeonly exterior hides a lifetime of hurt and regret. It's not that serious, though—he's got his beloved crossword puzzles and plenty of classical music albums to keep him company. Inspector Morse is the crime solver most likely to ask your mom out for a date, and, as a member of the Oxford Police's Criminal Investigation Department, he brings a dogged determination to his work.

Over seven series (and five specials) Morse churns through a truckload of cases. His world can be grim, and Morse doesn't always succeed, but his batting average with murders is thankfully better than with the ladies.

RAISING DION

SCI-FI • 2019
RATED: TV-G • 50 MINS

This story of a single mom bringing up her son gets a supernatural spin straight out of a comic book when the child develops special powers.

Superheroes have notoriously challenging parentage. Batman lost his folks early on and Superman's roots were back on Krypton. Dion's dad died in mysterious circumstances. It's good for the youngster (Ja'Siah Young) that he has his mom and protector, Nicole Reese (Alisha Wainwright), close by. Saving the world was never going to be an easy job, as Nicole warns early on. Once Dion starts teleporting and making objects float in the air, it becomes clear just how valuable his skills could be in the wrong hands.

Over the show's single season, Dion's powers soon become mom's woes as the pair unravel the mystery of his talents. And Nicole's ability to navigate this brave new world as a working-class single mom with the usual everyday stresses, is a superpower in itself.

MIDSOMER MURDERS

CRIME • 1997
RATED: TV-14 • 100 MINS

Midsomer may sound beautiful, but it is a dangerous place, and its police force is busy with murder investigations—often several an episode.

The only person busier than the police inspector of this fictional countryside town has to be the undertaker. Bodies pile high, and a walk through the woods is best avoided if possible. Of course, one crime begets another, and it's up to Chief Inspector Tom Barnaby (John Nettles) to unspool the threads of malfeasance. He's in the driver's seat for much of the show's 21 seasons, replaced by his cousin DCI John Barnaby (Neil Dudgeon), from Season 14 on.

With that much mayhem, the area's criminals have to get creative, and murders include victims that are spun to death in a clothes dryer and crushed by a giant wheel of cheese. You almost have to laugh, which is the attitude Barnaby takes, finding dark humor in the unfortunate circumstances.

MERLIN

FANTASY • 2008
RATED: TV-PG • 45 MINS

In this alternative retelling of the legend, Merlin is a wizard-in-training who befriends a not-yet-king Arthur and valiantly serves the court of Camelot.

Typically depicted as a wizened oldster who mentors the young King Arthur, this Merlin (Colin Morgan) is the portrait of the wizard as a young man. At a time when magic is forbidden, Merlin is forced to practice his mystical arts in secret. When Merlin slyly saves Arthur from an assassin, he's assigned to protect the future king, the goofy but good-hearted Arthur Pendragon (Bradley James), so they can both fulfill their destinies.

This isn't quite the legend that you're used to, with changes in characters and relationships that keep you guessing throughout its five-season run. It's a smart move to show the Round Table in this fledgling form, imbuing the centuries-old tale with youthful energy and melodrama that will appeal to all.

BONUS FAMILY

DRAMA • 2017
RATED: 15 (UK) • 44 MINS

This modern Brady Bunch features a Swedish family of two divorcees and their respective broods, plus recent exes, as they learn to get along.

If too many cooks spoil the broth, the four caretakers looking after these three youngsters may spell disaster. Parents and new couple Lisa (Vera Vitali) and Patrik (Erik Johansson) are living together with their respective 10-year-old sons and Lisa's teenage daughter. Their former partners are close by, too, adding humorous commentary to the awkward situations. As everyone gets used to the new normal, including the temperamentally opposed sons, there are growing pains, a few cries of "you're not my real dad," and lots of familial bonding.

Three seasons in, *Bonus Family* has been lauded for its realistic characters who don't always have the answers. Its interlinked web of relationships can be messy, but it's never boring ... for them or for the viewers.

SAMANTHA!

COMEDY • 2018
RATED: 15 (UK) • 27 MINS

Former child star Samantha attempts to revive her flagging career, but her hapless efforts and bossy demeanor only provide comic dividends, not the adulation she craves.

Like leg warmers and big hairstyles, Brazilian TV performer Samantha Alencar (Emanuelle Araújo) peaked in the 1980s. Her children's show made her a household name, but that doesn't count for much these days: she's fallen on hard times. When her ex, Dodói (Douglas Silva), a famous soccer player, returns from prison, Samantha gets a taste of the spotlight and wants it back.

As the misanthropic Samantha tries to claw her way back with the help of her kids and manager, her misadventures send-up celebrity culture and the trappings of post-social-media fame. The show is Netflix's first comedy set in Brazil, and its two seasons (dubbed in English) prove that while Samantha's world might not be ready for her tiara-clad breakout, we are.

YOU WANT TO ESCAPE TO A DIFFERENT TIME

Written by Eddie Robson

Sometimes we want to use TV as a time machine—to put us into a real historical moment, to make a work of classic literature live and breathe, or to send us hurtling into a possible future. And by revisiting old favorites we can take a trip into our own past, with shows that were screamingly contemporary at the time but feel like perfect period pieces today.

MAD MEN

DRAMA • 2007 • RATED: TV-14 • 50 MINS • SEASONS: 7
JON HAMM, ELISABETH MOSS, CHRISTINA HENDRICKS

An engrossing trip through America's 1960s from the viewpoint of a group of ad agency employees, *Mad Men* offers ambiguous characters, seismic social change, simmering office politics, and a lot of really cool outfits.

At the heart of *Mad Men* is the story of two employees at ad agency Sterling Cooper: creative director Don Draper (Jon Hamm), and his new secretary Peggy Olson (Elisabeth Moss). Don is slick, imposing, and good at his job—but there's something oddly blank about him, and we get the sense he constructs his own personal image the same way he conceives new marketing campaigns for clients. Meanwhile, Peggy views her new job

as merely a stepping stone into a creative role in the firm—but in the conservative 1960s, those jobs are filled exclusively by men. This sets her at odds not only with the male employees, but also the female ones, who feel that Peggy thinks she's better than they are.

Yet there are so many other areas of interest in this wonderful series—like Betty, Don's wife, a bored and depressed suburban housewife who doesn't know her psychiatrist is reporting their sessions back to Don. Junior account executive Pete Campbell is an ingratiating creep, but sees the coming changes in women's and civil rights more clearly than most of his colleagues. Office manager Joan Holloway (Christina Hendricks) is initially focused on

getting a husband, but slowly realizes she gets satisfaction through work. There are many more subplots, each offering a compelling reason to watch as the series travels through the decade, eventually landing in 1970.

> ❝*Every decision that [Don] makes is filled with ambiguity.*❞
>
> **Matthew Weiner** (creator/writer/director)

Matthew Weiner's pilot script for *Mad Men* channeled his fascination with the postwar period and frustrations with the limitations of *Becker*, the sitcom he was working on at the time. It scored him a gig writing for *The Sopranos* (see p341), which is a pretty good result in itself—but it was only when the series ended that *Mad Men* took on a life of its own, with AMC making it its first original scripted drama. Taking tonal inspiration from Billy Wilder's film *The Apartment*, Alfred Hitchcock's *North by Northwest*, and Wong-Kar-wai's sumptuous depiction of 1960s Hong Kong in *In the Mood for Love*, Weiner aimed to create a low-key but still visually rich series.

The show's depiction of the 1960s is a huge part of its appeal—it quickly became a byword for a certain type of style, which can be attributed to its keen-eyed production design. The sets are highly controlled—very little of *Mad Men* happens outdoors, instead taking place in carefully constructed interiors. It plays with the viewer's knowledge about what's coming next—a great moment in Season 3 works perfectly because the audience knows the date of the Kennedy assassination, but the characters don't. And then there's the fact that this is a world where nobody bats an eyelid if you drink scotch in your office in the

afternoon. But that's not what makes the series great. From the outset, *Mad Men* is instantly absorbing because its large cast of characters is so vivid and well-developed.

In a TV landscape filled with high-octane thrillers, grisly murders, and gritty police procedurals, *Mad Men* stands out for its subtlety. The stakes are simply whether the characters' lives will turn out like they want to—or in some cases, whether they'll turn out like we want them to. Don frequently leads the audience to believe he has hidden depths, only to revert to his essential shallowness. *Mad Men* trusts you to invest in its stories, and repays you in spades.

DON DRAPER'S CONSUMPTION DURING EPISODE ONE

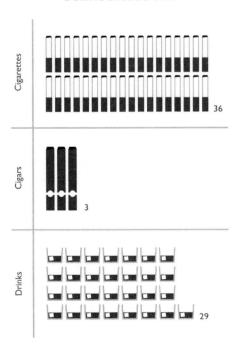

11.22.63

SCI-FI • 2016
RATED: TV-MA • 42–81 MINS

What if you could change history to avert a catastrophe? And should you? These are the questions posed by this one-season series based on a novel by suspense master Stephen King.

When English teacher Jake Epping (James Franco) is shown a time portal in his friend's closet that leads back to 1960, he goes through it with the aim of preventing the assassination of John F. Kennedy in 1963. But he starts to build a life in the past that he becomes reluctant to leave behind—and history resists his attempts to change it.

Franco's performance anchors the premise well, and it gains an extra layer from the conspiracies around JFK's assassination—what if Lee Harvey Oswald (Daniel Webber) hadn't acted alone after all? And how can you avert something if you're not sure how it happened in the first place? The stakes mount as the series goes on, and by the end they couldn't be higher.

TIMELESS

SCI-FI • 2016
RATED: TV-14 • 43 MINS

The theft of an experimental time machine kicks off a breathless chase through American history in a bid to stop the past being changed. It's like _Quantum Leap_ in reverse.

The inventor of the stolen time machine, Connor Mason (Paterson Joseph), assembles perhaps the only elite task force ever to include a history professor—that's Lucy Preston (Abigail Spencer). She's joined by soldier Wyatt Logan (Matt Lanter) and programmer Rufus Carlin (Malcolm Barrett). Their mission is to prevent Garcia Flynn (Goran Višnjić) from crippling the United States by altering its past.

The result of a team-up by the creators of _Supernatural_ (Eric Kripke) and _The Shield_ (Shawn Ryan), _Timeless_ is high-concept action. In an age of increasing serialization, it's refreshing to have a story-of-the-week format and arc plot, with the risk of the past destabilizing the present raising the stakes nicely.

MYSTERY SCIENCE THEATER 3000

SCI-FI COMEDY • 1988
RATED: TV-14 • 90 MINS

The shoestring-budget sci-fi show based around making fun of dopey B-movies went from local TV to a global cult favorite. Sound interesting?

More than 30 years on, it's the show that wouldn't die! Created by Joel Hodgson for Minneapolis-St. Paul station KTMA-TV, _MST3K_ (as it's known by fans) is built around his character Joel Robinson, who is being held aboard a spaceship in an experiment to drive him insane by showing him bad movies. Each movie is screened within the episode, with acerbic commentary from Joel and the robots.

The KTMA-TV episodes are now unavailable, but the show moved to national cable in 1989 and ran for 10 years, and many of these episodes can still be seen, as can both seasons of the 2017 Netflix revival. Mocking bad movies never goes out of date, even if the movies themselves do.

FOR ALL MANKIND

SCI-FI • 2019
RATED: TV-MA • 60 MINS

This series from *Battlestar Galactica* creator Ronald D. Moore builds a fascinating alternative history of the race to put a man on the moon that is both thrilling and terrifying.

In this world, the Russians are the first to land on the moon and NASA comes under pressure to match and surpass them. Apollo 11 is rushed into service, nearly killing its crew.

Nixon wants to establish an American military moonbase. When the USSR lands a woman on the moon, NASA must follow suit. Astronaut Edward Baldwin (Joel Kinnaman), frustrated that Apollo 10 missed the chance of a moon landing, becomes central to the operation.

What makes *For All Mankind*'s one season so effective is the prospect that the space race never ended. We get to see where the NASA program might have gone if it hadn't stopped being a priority in the mid-1970s. The further the series departs from history, the more uneasy it becomes.

THE MAN IN THE HIGH CASTLE

SCI-FI DRAMA • 2015 • RATED: TV-MA • 60 MINS • SEASONS: 4
ALEXA DAVALOS, RUFUS SEWELL, RUPERT EVANS

An intricate take on one of the great "what if?" stories, *The Man in the High Castle* takes you to another time but also shunts you sideways, into a 1960s America under Nazi occupation.

Philip K. Dick's alternative-universe novel *The Man in the High Castle* is set in an America that lost World War II and has been divided between Germany and Japan. In the midst of it all is a banned novel set in an alternative universe where the Allies won the war. It's one of Dick's best and a classic of the genre— but there isn't four seasons of story in it.

In adapting the novel for TV, writer Frank Spotnitz uses Dick's brilliant world-building and most of his characters, but heavily reworks the story into something open-ended.

Design makes a huge contribution, reimagining 1960s America under occupation. Most affectingly, the TV show swaps the banned novel of Dick's original story for documentary footage of the Nazi defeat, which offers Juliana (Alexa Davalos) the realization that the world doesn't have to be like this, and maybe out there is a world that isn't. *The Man in the High Castle* can be a grueling watch at times, but there's hope amid the despair.

> **"** *There's nothing inevitable about good prevailing.* **"**

Frank Spotnitz (creator/writer)

THE AVENGERS

ACTION COMEDY • 1961 • RATED: TV-14 • 60 MINS • SEASONS: 7
PATRICK MACNEE, HONOR BLACKMAN, DIANA RIGG

An extraordinary trip into a strange and comical parallel 1960s, _The Avengers_ steers clear of contemporary issues, yet in many ways reflects the era better than any other show. When it first aired, it also marked a refreshing step forward in TV representations of women.

The Avengers started life as a slightly dour thriller about Dr. David Keel (Ian Hendry), a GP who forms an uneasy crime-fighting partnership with government agent John Steed (Patrick Macnee). Within a few seasons the show had become a baroque action comedy set in its own distinctively skewed version of 1960s England. It's the TV equivalent of watching the Beatles evolve from two-minute beat-pop to elaborate psychedelic ballads.

The Avengers didn't really become what people think of as _The Avengers_ until Steed got the first of his female cohorts: the arrival of Cathy Gale (Honor Blackman), with her judo skills and leather outfits, was a revolution, and their dynamic is still delightful to watch today. Steed is an old-fashioned gentleman, but treats Mrs. Gale (she is widowed) as a complete equal—and usually lets her do the physical fighting, keeping his suit pristine. Cathy was hugely popular with 1960s audiences, a slick action heroine unlike any other character on TV.

Amazingly, the show not only survived Blackman's departure, but went from strength to strength with the introduction of Emma Peel (Diana Rigg). Steed and Mrs. Peel (husband missing, presumed dead) are one of the great couples-who-aren't-a-couple in TV. By this time the pair's brief is absurdly wide-ranging—they might investigate murders, or spies, or just anything unexplained, and their world is full of eccentrics and pop-art stylings. It's a toss-up which Rigg season is the best—the sharp, modish black-and-white one or the wild, psychedelic color one.

Unfortunately things fell apart after Rigg's departure: Linda Thorson as agent Tara King couldn't live up to her predecessors, and though there are still great moments in that final season, the show started to recycle its own clichés. But peak _Avengers_ is pure, glorious escapism—not so much a program, but a way of life.

CREATOR: Sydney Newman
PRODUCTION CO: ABC Weekend Television, Associated British Corporation

THE SINGING DETECTIVE

DRAMA • 1986 • RATED: 15 (UK) • 70 MINS • SEASONS: 1
MICHAEL GAMBON, PATRICK MALAHIDE, JOANNE WHALLEY

An intensely personal, inventive, and multilayered work, *The Singing Detective* is one of the outstanding achievements of British TV drama—a story about escaping the present by going into different versions of the past.

Whenever lists of the all-time great TV writers are compiled, Dennis Potter is always near the top. Having started out writing teleplays in the 1960s, even when he moved on to writing longer pieces, he never wrote a second season of anything. But he did revisit certain themes—sex, illness, memory, the stifling nature of rural life, the potency of popular songs. In *The Singing Detective* he rolled them all into one.

Potter suffered from debilitating psoriasis, which at its worst caused his skin to crack and bleed. He drew on this for the character of Philip E. Marlow (Michael Gambon), a mystery novelist hospitalized by the disease. Irritated by his fellow patients, ashamed of his dependence on the nursing staff, and above all frustrated and bored due to his inability to write, Marlow retreats into his mind.

One thread of this is a 1940s noir thriller incorporating elements from one of his novels, also called *The Singing Detective*. In this, he takes the role of the detective (his name is only one letter away from Raymond Chandler's famous sleuth Philip Marlowe), and works through the plot in his imagination. He also remembers his childhood in the Forest of Dean during World War II, and catching his mother having an affair in the woods.

As the series progresses, the present merges with the real and fictional past in Marlow's mind, and he imagines elaborate musical numbers taking place in the hospital: as Marlow is driven to the brink, reality starts to break down. It's rare for TV drama to be driven by an internal struggle but *The Singing Detective* pulls it off, which is what makes it so compelling and brilliant.

> **"** *You just don't know writers. They'll use anything, anybody. They'll eat their own young.* **"**

Philip E. Marlow (S1 E6)

ANNE WITH AN E

PERIOD DRAMA • 2017
RATED: TV-PG • 44 MINS

This skilful modern take on *Anne of Green Gables* makes great use of the novel's ebullient heroine as she adapts to life on a Canadian farm in the late 19th century.

Don't know why they didn't just call it *Anne of Green Gables*, but yes, it's based on Lucy Maud Montgomery's classic about middle-aged siblings Marilla and Matthew Cuthbert (Geraldine James and R. H. Thomson) who adopt a boy to help on their farm, only for the orphanage to send them a girl instead. Anne (Amybeth McNulty) is a handful, but her enthusiasm wins over her new guardians.

Writer Moira Walley-Beckett's adaptation adds a slightly darker edge to Anne, bringing out the proto-feminist elements of the novel, and strives for a less romanticized view of rural life. Season 1 (which is rooted in the book) was better received than Seasons 2 and 3 (which go in new directions), but the series as a whole has much to offer.

LITTLE HOUSE ON THE PRAIRIE

PERIOD DRAMA • 1974
RATED: TV-PG • 49 MINS

This series about growing up on a small farm in the 19th-century American Midwest lodged the Ingalls family in the minds of a generation.

With nine seasons and more than 200 episodes, *Little House on the Prairie* takes a loose approach to adapting the eight source books (which have since faced some criticism), and a lot of the material is original. The focus is on Laura (Melissa Gilbert) growing up on a farm near Walnut Grove, Minnesota, but the stories concern many of the characters in the immediate community and the hardships involved in agricultural life.

Although the series was created by Blanche Hanalis, Michael Landon (who plays Laura's father Charles) took an active creative role, directing numerous episodes and writing many scripts himself. The show is a classic and quite different from anything you'll see on TV today.

THE WALTONS

PERIOD DRAMA • 1972
RATED: TV-G • 48 MINS

A byword for wholesomeness, *The Waltons* follows a rural Virginia family through the tough times of the Great Depression and World War II.

In 1971 the American TV networks— especially CBS—canceled numerous rural-themed shows to free up space for new series aimed at younger audiences. Perhaps realizing they'd gone too far, CBS introduced *The Waltons* in 1972, created by Earl Hamner Jr. from his own semiautobiographical novel. Richard Thomas stars as eldest son and aspiring writer John-Boy Walton: Hamner himself narrates in character as the older John-Boy.

The series was a big success, winning an Emmy in 1973 and running for nine seasons and six TV movies. While there's undoubtedly a coziness to *The Waltons*, the difficulties of the period add real drama: it follows the Walton children's abrupt loss of innocence as the Depression bites and the war looms.

THE HOUSE OF ELIOTT

PERIOD DRAMA • 1991
RATED: 12 (UK) • 50 MINS

The House of Eliott **combines a key period in fashion, a contrasting sibling relationship, and a struggle against the odds. Like a great outfit, it's perfectly put together.**

In London in the early 1920s, the comfortable lives of sisters Bea and Evie Eliott (Stella Gonet and Louise Lombard) are shattered by the untimely death of their father and the debts he's left them. Penniless, they channel their interest in dressmaking into a fashion house, with the aim of supporting themselves financially.

Creators Jean Marsh and Eileen Atkins had previously had a hit with *Upstairs, Downstairs* (see p124) and it's no surprise *The House of Eliott* was successful too. The surprise is that the BBC canceled it after three seasons, leaving it annoyingly unresolved—but the rise of the Eliott brand, which tracks alongside the emergence of the modern mass-market fashion world—is engagingly dramatized.

MR. SELFRIDGE

PERIOD DRAMA • 2013
RATED: TV-14 • 45 MINS

Everyone knows the name, but this introduces you to the man, dramatizing the struggles of Harry Selfridge (Jeremy Piven) to establish the Selfridge & Co department store.

In 1908, a flamboyant American businessman decides London needs a modern, American-style department store, and identifies a spot at the unpromising end of Oxford Street. When it opens, Selfridge faces a struggle to draw customers—and the years ahead prove bumpy ones for everyone.

Adapted from Lindy Woodhead's biography of Selfridge, *Mr. Selfridge* does an effective job of bringing to life an important part of 20th-century history—the development of modern luxury commerce—in a character-driven way. Over four seasons the series continues up to 1929, wisely focusing the story into windows of a year or so, with much time passing between seasons, and offering numerous engaging threads to follow.

THE COLLECTION

PERIOD DRAMA • 2016
RATED: TV-MA • 60 MINS

While other dramas about the fashion world focus on more glamorous moments, this absorbing series takes place in the years of austerity and rebuilding after World War II.

Created by *Ugly Betty* writer Oliver Goldstick (see p188), *The Collection* concerns brothers Paul and Claude Sabine (Richard Coyle and Tom Riley), who are running their family's fashion house while Paris emerges from Nazi occupation. One brother is charming and has a head for business, the other is misanthropic, creatively brilliant, and secretly gay.

The Collection isn't just about one family, it's about a shattered city trying to regain its identity and come to terms with the events of the war. The sumptuous world of the Sabines is contrasted smartly with the struggles of the less well-off, and both brothers are haunted by secrets that create a backdrop of tension. Frances de la Tour's performance as the Sabines' mother Yvette is a particular joy.

BRIDESHEAD REVISITED

PERIOD DRAMA • 1981 • RATED: 15 (UK) • 52 MINS • SEASONS: 1
JEREMY IRONS, ANTHONY ANDREWS, DIANA QUICK

A stunning adaptation with an extraordinary scope, *Brideshead Revisited* is full of nostalgic melancholy for lost youth and romances that could never quite be. It's faithful to its source material, yet arguably improves on it.

Evelyn Waugh wrote his seventh novel while recovering from a parachute accident during World War II. Encapsulating his nostalgia for the 1920s and '30s, *Brideshead Revisited* was a huge success with a war-weary public when published in 1945. Though the narrative spans a couple of decades, it's not an especially long book, which is what makes this 11-part TV adaptation, screened in 1981, so remarkable.

In telling the story of Charles Ryder (Jeremy Irons) and his connections with the upper-class Flyte family, Waugh depicts the aristocracy's slide into irrelevance, with postwar social upheaval just around the corner. With the benefit of a little extra historical distance, the TV adaptation does this better than the novel, submerging you in the lives of this privileged group, who take their lifestyles for granted. Charles meets Sebastian Flyte (Anthony Andrews) at Oxford University, but only Charles seems to appreciate what they have and how it's slipping away from them. There are a number of love stories along the way (including an unspoken, but blatant, gay relationship between Charles and Sebastian), but the strongest is Charles's adoration of the family's mansion, Brideshead Castle.

Producer and lead writer Derek Granger tried condensing the book into six hours, but felt it lost something, so he expanded the scripts to include everything. The result could have been stodgy and slow, but instead it worked beautifully, capturing an evocation of a certain time, place, and social milieu.

Brideshead Revisited deserves a new audience now because its depth and pacing are more like a contemporary TV drama than anything made at the time. This is more than just an adaptation: it's true "novelistic" storytelling at its very best.

PRODUCTION CO: Granada Television

JEEVES & WOOSTER

COMEDY DRAMA • 1990
RATED: TV-PG • 50 MINS

A pitch-perfect adaptation of the tales of hapless toff Bertie Wooster and his hyper-competent butler Jeeves. These keenly plotted comic escapades offer an alternative to heavier period dramas.

P. G. Wodehouse's *Jeeves* stories are some of the most beloved works of comic fiction ever written—so when sketch duo Stephen Fry and Hugh Laurie were first asked to star as,

respectively, Jeeves and Wooster on TV, they turned it down. They were worried it couldn't possibly do the stories justice, but they also didn't want anyone else to play the characters.

Veteran screenwriter Clive Exton does a fine job of preserving the distinctive rhythms of Wodehouse's prose as well as his benign 1920s/1930s milieu over a four-season run. Bertie's societal misadventures (foolish wagers, aunts assigning him complicated errands) and the looming threat of marriage are tidily resolved and averted by Jeeves, who remains preternaturally calm and untroubled.

MAPP & LUCIA

COMEDY DRAMA • 2014
RATED: TV-PG • 60 MINS

Two upper-middle-class women compete to be queen bee of a small English village in this keenly observed drama of snobbery and one-upmanship, set between the two world wars.

Adapted from a series of comic novels by E. F. Benson, *Mapp & Lucia* takes place in 1930 in the East Sussex village of Tilling. The social center of the village is Elizabeth

Mapp (Miranda Richardson), but her position is threatened by the arrival of the vivacious Emmeline "Lucia" Lucas (Anna Chancellor) —and before long Mapp is plotting to undermine Lucia at every opportunity.

Unfortunately this one-season series didn't grab audiences—a shame, since it offers something different from most modern TV. The stakes aren't life or death, but social position; and the show creates an enclosed world where this is all-important. Immaculately cast, this is very funny indeed.

PENNIES FROM HEAVEN

MUSICAL DRAMA • 1978
RATED: 12 (UK) • 75 MINS

This bleak romantic drama has a simple but effective concept at its core— that people love cheap popular music because it articulates the things they can't express themselves.

Considered by many to be writer Dennis Potter's finest work, *Pennies From Heaven* is set in mid-1930s Britain, where traveling sheet music salesman Arthur Parker (Bob Hoskins) is

frustrated with his inhibited wife Joan (Gemma Craven). When he starts an affair with teacher Eileen Everson (Cheryl Campbell), his life begins an uncontrollable downward spiral.

Arthur is unlikable at times, but the drama works by pitting him against the prudishness of his age, and the scale of the emotions on display more than fills its one season. Potter draws on advertising, children's TV, and, most memorably, light entertainment, with the action frequently pausing for characters to perform gloriously choreographed mimes to period songs. It's heartbreaking stuff.

BOARDWALK EMPIRE

CRIME • 2010 • RATED: TV-MA • 55 MINS • SEASONS: 5
STEVE BUSCEMI, KELLY MACDONALD, MICHAEL SHANNON

Boardwalk Empire challenges The Sopranos for the crown of greatest gangster series ever. Depicting the tensions between the city government, run by criminals, and the federal government, trying to impose order, it explores how the 1920s became a boom time for organized crime in America.

It was inevitable that the age of premium cable TV would eventually set its sights on the Prohibition era, and when it did, it did it right. You couldn't ask for a better star than Steve Buscemi and you couldn't get a more perfect director than Martin Scorsese.

Setting a new standard for TV production values, HBO threw an extraordinary $18 million budget at the pilot (directed by Scorsese, who continued to provide input for the show after it was commissioned). This enabled the crew to build an actual 300 ft (91 m) boardwalk in Brooklyn for filming.

Created by The Sopranos writer Terence Winter (from the book by Nelson Johnson), Boardwalk Empire centers on Atlantic City rather than the more familiar Chicago, and emphasizes the corruption of the era in its focus on Enoch "Nucky" Thompson (Steve Buscemi), who is both a politician and a bootlegger. By his side, young widow Margaret Schroeder (Kelly Macdonald) is troubled by what she witnesses. It's a shame it didn't get a couple more seasons, but Boardwalk Empire is testament to the ability of longform TV to thoroughly explore a time and place.

> **"** *The writing is just impeccable and surprising.* **"**
>
> **Kelly Macdonald** (Margaret Schroeder)

THE UNTOUCHABLES

CRIME • 1959
RATED: 12 (UK) • 50 MINS

This landmark crime series draws on the true stories of the law enforcement squad assembled in Prohibition-era Chicago to put Al Capone behind bars.

Headed by Eliot Ness (played here by Robert Stack), upon whose memoir the series is based, the "Untouchables" were considered incorruptible—Capone had bought off and intimidated so many police officers, it was difficult to make a case against him stick. The show's four-season run ventures far beyond real events, and so most of its story lines are fiction.

Instead, The Untouchables wore its realism in other ways, depicting violence and the tackling of difficult issues. The Capone family were so unhappy with the show that they tried—unsuccessfully—to sue the producers and CBS. Featuring some great guest stars (Lee Marvin, Barbara Stanwyck) and a faster pace than other shows of its era, it's worth making time to watch.

DAMNATION

PERIOD DRAMA • 2017
RATED: TV-MA • 42 MINS

Damnation is set during the Depression, a period under-explored in TV drama, but one full of conflict and juicy themes as the poor become at odds with the rich and powerful.

The strikes of the Great Depression are dramatized via a face-off between two estranged brothers, one a fake preacher with a violent past, the other an ex-con turned detective. *Damnation* is set in Iowa in 1931, and as self-styled preacher Seth Davenport (Killian Scott) rouses farmers to take strike action, detective Creeley Turner (Logan Marshall-Green) is hired as a strikebreaker, using murder to intimidate the protesting farmers.

Damnation only lasted one season, but it uses its well-researched historical setting to make a timely critique of capitalism, without forgetting to include strong character-based drama. It's a slow-burner, with extended flashbacks, but has a clarity of purpose that carries it through.

SHOGUN

PERIOD DRAMA • 1980
RATED: 15 (UK) • 100 MINS

An ambitious piece of event TV, *Shogun* is based on the real-life experiences of English navigator William Adams, who rose to become a high-ranking shogun in early 17th-century Japan.

American TV at the turn of the 1980s was still mostly filled with formula shows, but after the success of *Roots* (see p296) in 1977, the networks became interested in doing historical miniseries. Hence, *Shogun*, a five-part series that topped the NBC prime-time schedule for a week, filmed on location in Japan. It starred Richard Chamberlain as John Blackthorne, the navigator, and scored NBC's highest-ever weekly Nielsen ratings.

In some aspects Shogun has dated, particularly through a modern cultural lens, but it used its huge run time well to communicate Blackthorne's gradual journey to thinking of himself as Japanese. Its scale is impressive and the location work, superbly photographed by Andrew Laszlo, is well worth the trip.

SNOWY RIVER: THE MCGREGOR SAGA

PERIOD DRAMA • 1994
RATED: TV-PG • 45 MINS

Not a lot of TV shows are based on poems, but this "western" spins an epic family saga from one of Australia's most famous works of literature.

Banjo Paterson's 1890 poem, *The Man From Snowy River,* has become part of Australia's national identity and the "Man" of the title, who chases down the escaped colt of a prizewinning racehorse, is a folk hero. This series is set 25 years later, with the "Man," named here as Matt McGregor (Andrew Clarke), having set up a ranch and become a wealthy man, but his cousin Luke (Josh Lucas) believes he's been cheated and wants revenge.

Snowy River is notable for some of the future stars in its cast—Guy Pearce plays Matt's son Rob and Hugh Jackman guests in five episodes of the fourth and final season—but it's also great if you want some slightly gentler drama.

WESTWORLD

SCI-FI • 2016 • RATED: TV-MA • 60 MINS • SEASONS: 3
EVAN RACHEL WOOD, THANDIE NEWTON, ANTHONY HOPKINS

Westworld is the one show you'll discover in this chapter that enables you to escape into the past and future at once. It takes you into a world where humanity has built a fully interactive version of the Old West.

Michael Crichton, writer of *Jurassic Park*, had already had a crack at the concept of "sci-fi theme park goes wrong" when he wrote and directed the 1973 film *Westworld*, about a robot cowboy at an immersive resort going rogue and hunting guests. A tight little thriller, it didn't seem to have ongoing series potential—until writers Jonathan Nolan and Lisa Joy went to town expanding its world for HBO.

From the start, it gives you a point of view closer to the robots—or "hosts," as they're known (have you ever noticed every film and TV show about robots looks for something else to call its robots?). Each day the hosts have their memories erased—but some of this data sits in the recycle bin, like a subconscious.

As they gain access to their past lives, they start to become sentient, and aware of their mistreatment by the guests.

Westworld has stratospheric production values even by current TV standards, as demanded by the expansive and detailed Old West landscape of the park as well as the near-future world of the offices where the hosts are produced and maintained. But it's anchored by the very human struggle of its characters. Dolores (Evan Rachel Wood) seems a minor figure in the daily narrative of the town, but she's also the oldest host still working, with more buried memories than anyone else.

The park is designed as a game, with some tourists happy to play along on the surface, and others going deeper as they try to understand the story lines, and it soon becomes clear that something sinister is going on. Ultimately, this is the story of the hosts—and they're learning humanity from some of the worst of us.

CREATORS: Lisa Joy, Jonathan Nolan
PRODUCTION CO: Bad Robot, Jerry Weintraub Productions, Kilter Films, Warner Bros. Television

BABYLON 5

SCI-FI • 1993
RATED: TV-PG • 43 MINS

A revolutionary series that anticipated how TV—especially American TV— would go in the next 20 years, *Babylon 5* is still one of the most ambitious sci-fi stories ever told.

J. Michael Straczynski conceived *Babylon 5* as a "novel for television." Set in the wake of a war in which Earth was nearly defeated by the Minbari, the eponymous space station is a neutral trading and diplomacy outpost, led by Commander Sinclair (Michael O'Hare) and later Captain Sheridan (Bruce Boxleitner). But tensions remain, not least between alien ambassadors G'Kar and Londo—and a new threat lurks in the shadows.

Babylon 5 demanded a great deal from the audience—the status quo frequently changed over the course of five seasons. But Straczynski was ahead of the game, because the show is perfectly suited to the age of streaming and boxsets, and it's an utter treat for anyone coming to it fresh.

INTO THE BADLANDS

SCI-FI • 2015
RATED: TV-14 • 44 MINS

Imagine America without guns. It's a bold notion but *Into the Badlands* runs with it—straight into a postapocalyptic landscape where crossbows and martial- arts skills are the order of the day.

Created by Alfred Gough and Miles Millar, the team behind *Smallville* (see p423), *Into the Badlands* takes place five centuries after a vast war destroyed civilization. Things have never truly recovered, but everyone now shuns guns. A feudal society has sprung up in middle America, and the series follows the power struggles of the barons who control this territory.

Our focus is on the house of baron Quinn (Marton Csokas), including his wife Lydia (Orla Brady), and head "clipper" (loyal warrior) Sunny (Daniel Wu). The combination of western/samurai stylings, martial-arts action, and postapocalyptic world makes it an engaging prospect, and over its three seasons it offers plenty of twists and turns.

COWBOY BEBOP

SCI-FI • 1998
RATED: TV-MA • 25 MINS

Reckoned by many to be the greatest anime series of all time, *Cowboy Bebop* is a Japanese sci-fi noir western about a mob of bounty hunters trawling the solar system for criminals.

In 2071, 50 years after Earth has become uninhabitable, humanity has spread out across the solar system. Law enforcement is aided by licensed bounty hunters such as those aboard the spaceship Bebop, led by Spike Spiegel (voiced by Steve Blum in the English dub), an exiled former high-ranking member of a crime syndicate. Also working out of the Bebop are a former policeman, an amnesiac con artist, an androgynous teenage hacker, and a superintelligent corgi dog.

The weird, engaging characters and thrilling story line unfurled over one 26-episode season made *Cowboy Bebop* a huge hit in its native Japan, and it's credited with sparking a fresh wave of interest in anime abroad. If you want to give anime a try, this is the place to start.

RIPPER STREET

CRIME • 2012
RATED: TV-MA • 59 MINS

A stylish police procedural set in a vividly realized Victorian London, *Ripper Street* follows a group of Whitechapel bobbies haunted by their failure to catch Jack the Ripper.

Though the show uses the most famous crime of the Victorian era as a hook, it casts its net wider in subject matter—so while the first episode features Ripper-style murders, it's not an entire series about women getting cut up, thankfully. Our leads are the sharp, driven Detective Inspector Edmund Reid (Matthew Macfadyen), dogged Detective Sergeant Bennet Drake (Jerome Flynn), and former US army surgeon-turned-forensic-expert Captain Homer Jackson (Adam Rothenburg).

Over five seasons, the show strikes a nice balance between arc plots and stories-of-the-week—Season 3 contains a great bottle episode where the team works through the night to solve a crime before their suspect is released at dawn.

THE ALIENIST

CRIME • 2018
RATED: TV-MA • 47 MINS

No, it's not about aliens. A future US President assembles an unlikely team to hunt down a serial killer in 1890s New York in this grisly, intense series.

Before becoming President in 1901, Theodore Roosevelt (Brian Geraghty) was commissioner of the NYPD. It's in that role that he appears in this (fictional) yarn about a murderer targeting boy prostitutes. His secretary, Sara Howard (Dakota Fanning), is joined by psychologist (or "alienist") Dr. Laszlo Kreizler (Daniel Brühl) and *New York Times* cartoonist John Schuyler Moore (Luke Evans).

The series is a great example of the possibilities of modern TV: the film rights to Caleb Carr's 1994 novel *The Alienist* were sold before publication, but it proved impossible to squeeze into a single screenplay. Meanwhile, the subject matter was unworkable for American TV at the time. But that all made it perfect fodder for a modern cable series, and finally the book has the adaptation it deserves.

BLACK BUTLER

ANIMATED FANTASY • 2008
RATED: TV-14 • 25 MINS

A startling and surreal Japanese anime take on Victorian Britain, *Black Butler* mixes comedy and horror in its tales of a young aristocrat and his eerily efficient manservant.

Adapted from a manga series (Season 1 tracks close to the comics, while Seasons 2 and 3 diverge into more original territory), *Black Butler* concerns Ciel Phantomhive (Brina Palencia), the 13-year-old head of a wealthy household, served by his butler Sebastian Michaelis (J. Michael Tatum), who is in fact a demon in human form. Sebastian has agreed to help Ciel get revenge for his murdered parents in return for his soul.

The three seasons play fast and loose with history (a mafia group in episode two seems to have stepped out of *Miami Vice*), and it slides freely from light domestic comedy about preparing afternoon tea and cake to brutal fight sequences. But this is exactly what makes it great: there's nothing else like it.

BLEAK HOUSE

PERIOD DRAMA • 2005
RATED: TV-PG • 30 MINS

One of Charles Dickens' finest novels, scripted by one of television's finest adapters of novels, *Bleak House* is a pitch-perfect rendition that makes compulsive viewing.

In Victorian London, a long-running legal battle over an estate causes uncertainty for orphans Ada Clare (Carey Mulligan) and Richard Carstone (Patrick Kennedy), who may be beneficiaries. One of the other claimants, the imperious and cold Lady Dedlock (Gillian Anderson), has a connection to a mysterious dead man, which lawyer Tulkinghorn (Charles Dance) is determined to discover.

Those are just a fraction of the plot threads weaving through *Bleak House*. In an effort to mimic the 20-part serialized publication of the novel, Andrew Davies breaks his eight hours of screentime into 15 episodes (the first is an hour, the rest are half hours), and the result rattles along beautifully. The tone is spot-on and the all-star cast superb.

LITTLE DORRIT

PERIOD DRAMA • 2008
RATED: TV-PG • 30 MINS

Very much a spiritual sequel to the 2005 adaptation of *Bleak House*, *Little Dorrit* applies the same style to another Dickens novel with a huge ensemble cast, to great success.

The "Little Dorrit" of the title is Amy Dorrit (Claire Foy), who has lived her whole life in a debtors' prison with her father, William Dorrit (Tom Courtenay). Arthur Clennam (Matthew Macfadyen) starts to suspect William's impoverished status may not be his own fault after all, and decides to investigate.

Like *Bleak House*, *Little Dorrit* is concerned with the pursuit and loss of money, and it's equally satisfying. Again adapted by Andrew Davies into mostly half-hour episodes, it wasn't written for the streaming age but is perfectly suited to it. The depth of the cast is incredible (Eddie Marsan, Anton Lesser, Annette Crosbie, Freema Agyeman, Robert Hardy, Maxine Peake), meaning even minor characters come vividly to life.

OUR MUTUAL FRIEND

PERIOD DRAMA • 1998
RATED: TV-PG • 50 MINS

An ambitious adaptation of Charles Dickens' longest and most complex novel, *Our Mutual Friend* does a fine job of condensing the sprawling plot into nearly six satisfying hours.

An unreconstructed Scrooge-like figure has left his entire fortune to his estranged son, on the condition he marry Bella Wilfer (Anna Friel), a woman he's never met. The son is set to return from overseas, but never arrives—and his body is dredged up from the Thames....

Our Mutual Friend was the last novel that Dickens completed, and it reflects the increasingly gothic turn of his later works, filled with death and deception. Adapted by Sandy Welch, who specializes in dramatizing 19th-century novels (she went on to do *North and South, Emma, Jane Eyre*, and *The Turn of the Screw*), it's pulled together with skill. A fine cast is rounded out by Steven Mackintosh, Keeley Hawes, and Paul McGann.

ALIAS SMITH AND JONES

WESTERN • 1971
RATED: TV-PG • 60 MINS

***Alias Smith and Jones* was one of the last hits of the golden age of TV westerns, and the first show to be created by one of the titans of American TV.**

Prolific writer/producer Glen A. Larson created more than 20 series during his career, and he conceived *Alias Smith and Jones* using a method that would serve him well on shows such as the 1978 *Battlestar Galactica* (see p402) and *BJ and the Bear*—look for a recent hit film and do something like that. Accordingly *Alias Smith and Jones*—which ran for three seasons—is loosely modeled on *Butch Cassidy and the Sundance Kid* (the title even comes from a line in the film).

Outlaw cousins Hannibal Heyes (Pete Duel and, later, Roger Davis) and Jedediah "Kid" Curry (Ben Murphy) are trying to go straight after securing a conditional amnesty. Their ambiguous status makes them appealing heroes, and like all Larson's shows there's a strong dash of humor.

GUNSMOKE

WESTERN • 1955
RATED: TV-PG • 30/60 MINS

One of the longest-running shows in the history of American TV, *Gunsmoke's* tales of law enforcement in a frontier town were a constant presence throughout the golden age of TV westerns.

Gunsmoke started life as a radio series set in Dodge City, Kansas, and was conceived as a hard-boiled detective drama set in the Old West. It transferred to TV in 1955 as a half-hour, black-and-white show, with James Arness playing sheriff Matt Dillon and Milburn Stone as town doctor Galen "Doc" Adams.

It quickly became the top-rated show on TV, and though its popularity dipped when it expanded to an hour in 1961, it recovered after the move to color in 1966. By its end in 1975, *Gunsmoke* had outlived every other western show. Watching all 635 episodes (over 20 seasons) is a daunting task and some episodes jar with today's cultural sensitivities, but *Gunsmoke* is the epitome of the western genre.

RAWHIDE

WESTERN • 1959
RATED: TV-PG • 50 MINS

At times *Rawhide* achieves a strangely existential quality and an eerie atmosphere—ghost riders and ghost towns both feature—making it one of the best TV westerns ever.

The cattle drive is a staple plot of western movies and *Rawhide* applies it to TV, using the then-common story-of-the-week format of itinerant heroes who get involved in the lives of the people they meet. It's a few years after the end of the Civil War and trail boss Gil Favor (Eric Fleming) is trying to keep his operation running amid the challenging conditions of the frontier.

Clint Eastwood, a defining star of the cowboy genre, got his break on this show as cattle drover Rowdy Yates, facing wolves, anthrax, bandits, and murderers. *Rawhide* was an instant hit, and Eastwood's star quality evident, though he couldn't save the show from cancellation during its eighth season, after Fleming departed.

BONANZA

WESTERN • 1959
RATED: TV-PG • 49 MINS

Bonanza was a series that stood out when first shown, using historical distance to explore issues such as racism and domestic violence that TV networks would have been reluctant to touch in contemporary shows.

A titan of the western genre, *Bonanza* differed from its more action-driven rivals by focusing on the everyday problems of a ranching family on the shore of Lake Tahoe in Nevada. The setting is Ponderosa, the sprawling ranch owned by Ben Cartwright (Lorne Greene), who has three sons, Joe, Adam, and Hoss, by three different wives—which sounds remarkably modern until you learn all the wives have died: that's frontier life for you!

The three sons have different temperaments, which inevitably leads to conflict as they try to run the family's logging and livestock business. This clearly helps the show on its way—running an impressive 14 seasons, *Bonanza* is a true family epic.

DEADWOOD

WESTERN • 2004 • RATED: TV-MA • 55 MINS • SEASONS: 3
TIMOTHY OLYPHANT, IAN MCSHANE, MOLLY PARKER

One of the great "canceled too soon" series, *Deadwood* initially attracted attention for its brutality and creative use of profanity, but quickly proved to be a show of great depth and complexity, anchored by a terrific ensemble cast.

Sometime in the 1970s TV cowboy tales fell out of fashion. Compared to the downbeat, violent, morally ambiguous spaghetti westerns that had taken over from the Hollywood variety, small-screen westerns seemed tame.

With *Deadwood*, writer David Milch (who originally wanted to make a series about ancient Rome, before learning that *Rome*, see p136, was already in development) took advantage of the possibilities at HBO to make a western show that caught up with what cinema had been doing with the genre for 40 years—and surpassed it with its historical detail and sharp character work. It's set in the real town of Deadwood, South Dakota, which was at the center of a gold rush in the 1870s, and many of the characters, including Seth Bullock (Timothy Olyphant) and Al Swearengen (Ian McShane), actually existed.

The tight focus on a small community means you get to know Deadwood inside out as it develops from a camp into a town. The result is a show about how civilization emerges from lawlessness—with a lot of swearing.

> **"** *What's very much alive is the poetry and the characters.* **"**
>
> **Timothy Olyphant** (Seth Bullock)

HELL ON WHEELS

WESTERN • 2011
RATED: TV-14 • 43 MINS

In the wake of the assassination of Abraham Lincoln, an army of workers toils to build the first railroad across the United States, while one man plots to avenge the death of his family.

Cullen Bohannon (Anson Mount) is a Confederate Civil War veteran looking for the Union soldiers who killed his wife and son—but he also needs work, so to support his quest he takes a job as a supervisor on the First Transcontinental Railroad, assisted by freed slave Elam Ferguson (Common). At first it is a means to an end for Cullen, but the railroad business starts to consume him.

We've seen revenge westerns before, but the railroad angle gives *Hell on Wheels* something fresh: the title refers to the camp that moves along with the construction, and it's filled with odd outsider characters. The series' twin driving forces of vengeance and progress are strong, keeping the drama boiling through five seasons.

WAGON TRAIN

WESTERN • 1957
RATED: TV-PG • 60 MINS

Inspired by the film of the same name by John Ford, *Wagon Train* follows a group of pioneers traveling from the Midwest to California, and the people they meet on the way.

Led by wagon master Major Seth Adams (Ward Bond) and later Christopher Hale (John McIntire, who replaced Bond when he died during Season 4), the regular cast anchors the series—but it was always conceived as a semi-anthology. Its substantial budget—40 percent higher than other western shows at the time—enabled producers to snag stars such as Bette Davis, Joseph Cotten, and Peter Lorre to play the guest characters around whom each week's story revolves.

With the budget also paying for location filming, this is very much prestige TV for the 1950s. For that reason, it's perhaps the most watchable of the old western series—just pick an episode from one of its eight seasons that features a favorite actor, and dive in.

GOLD RUSH: THE DISCOVERY OF AMERICA

DOCUMENTARY • 2016
RATED: TV-G • 44 MINS

This documentary series delves into the foundation of modern California in the 19th century, sparked by the discovery of more than $2 billion worth of gold.

Before 1848, fewer than 1,000 non-native people lived in California. By the end of 1849, however, that figure was a staggering 100,000—the population boom was a direct result of gold being found in the Sacramento Valley in early 1848. The Gold Rush was the American dream in its purest form and this five-part series delves into what's become one of the country's founding myths, including the damage it did.

The documentary is peppered with dramatized reenactments, and also examines some less well-known areas—did you know a Silver Rush followed afterward? The terrible treatment of Native Americans is thoroughly covered, as is the fallout when the gold ran out.

GODLESS

WESTERN • 2017
RATED: TV-MA • 41–80 MINS

A New Mexico mining town populated mostly by women is the setting for an Oedipal showdown between two outlaws in this violent, haunting western mini-series from *Logan* writer Scott Frank.

Roy Goode (Jack O'Connell) is on the run from his former partner-in-crime and father figure Frank Griffin (Jeff Daniels), a vicious outlaw whom he's betrayed. Arriving in La Belle,

he's shot by rancher Alice Fletcher (Michelle Dockery), who then nurses him back to health. The majority of La Belle's male population perished in a mining accident and the place is still getting back on its feet—which is bad news, as the ruthless Frank is coming to town.

Godless unfurls slowly and elegantly, giving ample screen time to its ensemble cast. The conflict between Roy and Frank is just part of the story, with the future of the town and its inhabitants also given space to develop. But you know the showdown is coming, and the anticipation is all part of the pleasure.

HATFIELDS & MCCOYS

WESTERN • 2012
RATED: TV-14 • 100 MINS

This docudrama was the History Channel's first-ever scripted series, and employs a big-name cast to tell the story of the most notorious and wide-ranging family feud in US history.

The Hatfield family, led by William Anderson "Devil Anse" Hatfield (Kevin Costner), live on the West Virginia side of the Big Sandy River—the McCoys, led by Randolph "Randall"

McCoy (Bill Paxton), live on the Kentucky side. The two clans both fought for the South in the Civil War, but when the McCoys' lone Unionist, Harmon (Chad Hugghins), is killed by the Hatfields' Jim Vance (Tom Berenger), an escalating feud consumes them for decades.

The sheer weight of historical material keeps this three-part miniseries going, delving into the backgrounds of the two families and establishing the Hatfields' power and influence. Historical fidelity means the story doesn't always fit a satisfying shape, but there's enough real-life insanity to keep you entertained.

THE LONE RANGER

WESTERN • 1949
RATED: TV-G • 23 MINS

The masked hero who roams the land and fights bad guys in this gloriously simple children's western was the first icon of American TV. If you haven't seen it before, now could be the time.

The oddity of the title—the Lone Ranger (Clayton Moore and, later, John Hart) is rarely alone, because he always has sidekick Tonto (Jay Silverheels) with him—is rooted in the

character's origin: a patrol of Texas Rangers is massacred and the sole survivor, John Reid, is rescued by Native American Tonto. After Reid adopts his new identity and mask, he determines to help those in need, rarely waiting around afterward to be thanked.

The genius of the Lone Ranger character was that any kid with a hat and mask could dress up as him. The series' lively storytelling and constant presence on screens (it ran for five seasons, but the first was a massive 78 episodes long) impressed itself firmly on a generation of viewers.

BLACKADDER

COMEDY • 1983 • RATED: TV-PG • 30 MINS • SEASONS: 4
ROWAN ATKINSON, TONY ROBINSON, HUGH LAURIE

The funniest history lesson you'll sit through, *Blackadder* gave birth to one of the great comic antiheroes: a scheming rogue who treats everyone around him badly. But you root for him anyway because he's surrounded by idiots.

Blackadder is several shows in one. Season 1, *The Black Adder*, is set in 1485, and is an alternative history based on the idea that Richard III was killed and succeeded by his nephew Richard IV, who was later written out of history. The show follows his obsequious son Prince Edmund (Rowan Atkinson), who styles himself "The Black Adder," and his sidekicks: the dim Lord Percy and Baldrick (Tony Robinson), his cunning servant. It's good, but the seasons that followed made *Blackadder* an all-time classic.

Blackadder II is set in the reign of Elizabeth I, with Edmund Blackadder as one of her courtiers—and in contrast to his ancestor, he is a sneering, self-centered manipulator. To balance this out, Baldrick's intelligence drops markedly. The budget for this season was smaller, but the writing is sharper, thanks to cocreator Richard Curtis bringing in Ben Elton, fresh from *The Young Ones*. It runs the gamut of comedy from literary and historical inside jokes to slapstick and outright vulgarity.

A lot of *Blackadder's* success is due to Atkinson, who cocreated the show and viewed Blackadder as a man with a modern sensibility who happens to have lived centuries ago, and has no patience with the whims and idiosyncrasies of his age. In *Blackadder the Third*, Edmund is the long-suffering butler to the moronic Prince Regent (Hugh Laurie), and in *Blackadder Goes Forth* he's an army captain trying to escape the futile slaughter of World War I.

Each season has a slightly different tone: *Blackadder the Third* is the most satirical, while *Blackadder Goes Forth* is rightly famed for its gallows humor and moments of poignancy. It's hard to pick a favorite season—it's one of the best pieces of TV comedy ever.

CREATORS: Richard Curtis, Rowan Atkinson
PRODUCTION CO: 7 Network, BBC Worldwide, BBC

THE WITCHER

**FANTASY • 2019 • RATED: TV-MA • 60 MINS • SEASONS: I
HENRY CAVILL, FREYA ALLAN, ANYA CHALOTRA**

Riding into town to fill the gap left by the end of *Game of Thrones*, *The Witcher* is epic fantasy at its most ... well, epic. It wears its classic medieval sword-and-sorcery stylings with total conviction.

Based on a successful series of books by Polish writer Andrzej Sapkowski, the setting is a world known as the Continent and our hero is the taciturn, sword-wielding outsider Geralt of Rivia (Henry Cavill). Geralt is a Witcher, a monster-hunter enhanced by magic: handy in a fight, but his mutant nature makes him unwelcome in taverns. He's destined to meet Ciri (Freya Allan), the tomboyish princess of Cintra—and her quest to find him begins sooner than expected when Cintra comes under attack from its neighbor Nilfgaard.

Your reaction to the above description should indicate whether *The Witcher* is for you. If you think, "*What?,*" then maybe give it a pass; if you think "*TELL ME MORE!,*" then dive right in. What's great about *The Witcher* is its full-blooded commitment to its premise: there will be monsters, magic, and bloody battles, portrayed on a grand scale. Yet its characters— such as sorceress Yennefer (Anya Chalotra) and bard Jaskier (Joey Batey)—are just people trying to get on with their lives, and the depiction of its magical medieval society feels genuinely layered.

"That, to me, is the core of fantasy," explained showrunner Lauren Schmidt Hissrich in a 2019 interview with Collider website, "real people in a crazy environment, dealing with crazy problems ... it reflects on our real world, in big thematic ways, in political ways, and in

cultural ways." The fractious politics of the Continent, with various kingdoms going to war against each other, feels like a timely reminder that our own feudal age isn't all that long ago. And in a time of compromise, Geralt's refusal to settle for the lesser of two evils is a tonic.

> **"They took my choice.
> I want it back."**
>
> **Yennefer** (SI E6)

Right from the opening scenes you get a real sense of a *huge* world, with miles and miles to explore—and the ideal characters to explore it with. Settle in and watch them make their way across the map.

CREATOR: Lauren Schmidt Hissrich
PRODUCTION CO: Netflix, Pioneer Stilking Films, Platige Image, Sean Daniel Company

UPSTAIRS, DOWNSTAIRS

PERIOD DRAMA • 1971
RATED: TV-PG • 50 MINS

A hit on both sides of the Atlantic, this series follows the inhabitants of 165 Eaton Place from the reign of Edward VII to the market crash of 1929.

Upstairs, Downstairs began life as a comedy piece written by actresses Jean Marsh and Eileen Atkins about two housemaids in a Victorian country house. This developed into a drama set in an Edwardian townhouse in Belgravia, focusing on the stories playing out among both the staff and their wealthy employers: hence the title.

The mix between the work of those "downstairs" and the bohemian dalliances and society scandals of those "upstairs" made this one of the most popular dramas of the 1970s throughout its five-season run, and its enduring appeal is clear from the success of the more-than-a-little-similar *Downton Abbey* (see p380). The 2010 revival created by Heidi Thomas, which returns to 165 Eaton Place in 1936, is also worth checking out.

MILDRED PIERCE

DRAMA • 2011
RATED: TV-MA • 65 MINS

Director Todd Haynes specializes in thoughtful 20th-century period pieces, and this five-part miniseries fits in perfectly with his films about women struggling with social constraints.

The 1941 novel by James M. Cain was previously adapted into a noirish thriller that won Joan Crawford an Oscar for her performance in the title role. This version is much more faithful to the book, tracing Mildred (Kate Winslet) through the 1930s as she separates from her husband and tries to support her children alone. The real drama arises from her fractious relationship with her ungrateful daughter Veda (Evan Rachel Wood) and her new beau Monty (Guy Pearce).

Haynes and cowriter Jon Raymond clearly relish the opportunity to put the full sweep of the novel on screen. *Mildred Pierce* has a reputation for being a melodrama, but this version doesn't feel like that at all: it's full of quiet tragedy.

THE CRIMSON PETAL AND THE WHITE

PERIOD DRAMA • 2011
RATED: TV-MA • 59 MINS

Based on Michel Faber's novel about a Victorian prostitute and a feckless perfume heir, this miniseries offers a modern take on the costume drama.

Streetwalker Sugar (Romola Garai) is filled with loathing for the men who abuse her, and is secretly writing a novel about it—but she sees a way out when the wealthy William Rackham (Chris O'Dowd) becomes infatuated with her. Meanwhile, Rackham's wife Agnes (Amanda Hale) is mentally ill, so much so that she refuses to believe in the existence of her own daughter.

The source novel is a huge, intensively researched work, but Lucinda Coxon's script does it justice and the design effectively captures both the seedy and respectable sides of Victorian London. Garai embodies the complex character of Sugar extremely well, and the supporting cast—Gillian Anderson, Richard E. Grant, Shirley Henderson—are magnificent.

THE HOUR

**DRAMA THRILLER • 2011 • RATED: TV-14 • 60 MINS • SEASONS: 2
ROMOLA GARAI, BEN WHISHAW, DOMINIC WEST**

Touted in some quarters as the British *Mad Men*, *The Hour* is in fact something very different—a sinister thriller that smartly weaves fact and fiction.

Set in 1956, the series focuses on the launch of a new BBC current affairs show called, funnily enough, *The Hour*, anchored by Hector Madden (Dominic West). The job of producer has been given to Bel Rowley (Romola Garai), to the horror of some BBC staff members, who consider her too young and too female. With the aid of her best friend, reporter Freddie Lyon (Ben Whishaw), Bel's struggles initially revolve around simply getting the program on air—but with the Suez crisis looming, *The Hour* comes under increasing pressure to conform to the government line.

Either aspect of the show—the workplace drama of the TV studio or the noirish political thriller rumbling in the background—would make a good drama on its own, but by

bringing them together, writer Abi Morgan creates something special. The show is also seriously sexually charged, from the will-they-won't-they relationship between Bel and Freddie, to the amorous adventures of foreign correspondent Lix Storm (Anna Chancellor).

The only downer is that the series got canned after two seasons (be warned, it ends on a cliffhanger), but it's classy, exciting stuff while it lasts.

> **"** *I've always loved drama with a deadline.* **"**
>
> **Abi Morgan** (creator/writer)

THE TRIAL OF CHRISTINE KEELER

**DRAMA • 2019
RATED: 15 (UK) • 58 MINS**

A six-part dramatization of the Profumo affair, the fascinating scandal that took in adultery, politics, Cold War tensions, and the birth of swinging London.

In the early '60s, showgirl and model Christine Keeler (Sophie Cookson) comes to the attention of the press when her boyfriend

Johnny Edgecombe (Nathan Stewart-Jarrett) assaults another man. Her recent affair with high-ranking politician John Profumo (Ben Miles) is exposed, as are her links to osteopath Stephen Ward (James Norton) and Soviet naval attaché Yevgeny Ivanov (Visar Vishka).

Amanda Coe's script avoids sensationalizing the story and focuses on the real person at the center. Keeler has often been depicted as a hapless plaything of powerful men, but here we see her as someone escaping an impoverished childhood and stumbling into something bigger than anyone could have known.

GOOD GIRLS REVOLT

DRAMA • 2015
RATED: TV-MA • 50 MINS

Based on the real-life events of a landmark gender-equality case, *Good Girls Revolt* has the urgency of a story that needs to be told—and tells it in style.

The basis is a book by Lynn Povich, who was one of a group of female employees who sued *Newsweek* magazine in 1970, frustrated at being restricted to lower-paid researcher roles while male writers took credit for their work. The series fictionalizes events—the magazine is cunningly renamed *News of the Week*, and lead Patti Robinson (Genevieve Angelson) is a composite of several women—but it has an important truth at its core.

The drama opens in New York in 1969 and the period is dramatized vibrantly, with the looming lawsuit providing growing tension. Amazon Prime's output tends to be rather male-focused, so it's a real shame it opted to cancel *Good Girls Revolt* after just one season.

PAN AM

DRAMA • 2011
RATED: TV-PG • 43 MINS

An attempt by the ABC network to replicate the success of *Mad Men* for a mainstream audience, *Pan Am* harks back to a pre-9/11 era when air travel was glamorous.

On paper, *Pan Am* has everything going for it. The great cast includes Christina Ricci and a pre-stardom Margot Robbie. It also has gorgeous design, an experienced showrunner in Jack Orman, who'd previously steered *ER* (see p53), and a strong concept, focusing on the friendship and rivalry between a group of Pan Am air stewardesses in the early 1960s. But the show only lasted one 14-episode season before it was canceled.

Arguably *Pan Am* tries to do too much at once: as well as being a glossy workplace soap, it introduces a Cold War thriller element when one of the stewardesses is recruited as an agent by the CIA. But trying to do too much is hardly the worst of sins, and as a stylized trip into the era, it works well.

THE SPY

SPY DRAMA • 2019
RATED: TV-MA • 54 MINS

As tensions rise in the Middle East in the 1960s, Israeli intelligence forces look to an army reject to supply them with information in this riveting thriller based on a true story.

Over one season *The Spy* traces the activities of Eli Cohen (Sacha Baron Cohen), a top Mossad spy, in the years leading up to the Six-Day War between Israel and Syria in 1967. As he goes undercover in Syria, Cohen's efforts to get close to power prove astonishingly successful. Meanwhile, his wife Nadia (Hadar Ratzon-Rotem) is left to bring up their child.

This might be a straight drama, but comedy star Baron Cohen is ideally suited to the role. Having spent years incarnating other characters for his shows, he portrays Eli Cohen's own deceptions with ease. The stakes ratchet up nicely as Cohen climbs the ladder of Syrian society—and a glance at history tells you an explosive conclusion is coming.

OUR FRIENDS IN THE NORTH

DRAMA • 1996 • RATED: TV-MA • 70 MINS • SEASONS: 1
CHRISTOPHER ECCLESTON, GINA MCKEE, DANIEL CRAIG

This epic drama concerned the fluctuating fortunes of four working-class friends from Newcastle over the course of more than 30 years. *Our Friends in the North* was seen as a landmark at the time and its ambition is still impressive today.

The series started life in the early 1980s as a play, where the story ran from Harold Wilson's election as prime minister to that of Margaret Thatcher. Writer Peter Flannery spent over a decade trying to get a TV adaptation off the ground, and the narrative just kept on expanding into a nine-part series. The rich result is testament to the amount of time he took thinking about the characters. We watch as the political idealism of Nicky (Christopher Eccleston) is worn down by bitter experience; the carefree attitude of

Geordie (Daniel Craig) leads him out of his depth; and Mary (Gina McKee) is frustrated by how quickly her options close down when she falls for the charming but feckless Tosker (Mark Strong).

The tight focus on one year at a time is crucial, because each episode tells its own story. The large-scale narrative matched with emotional detail is what TV does so well: you really feel like you've lived a lifetime with these people.

> **"***The personal and the political are connected.***"**
>
> **Peter Flannery** (creator/writer)

THE WONDER YEARS

COMEDY DRAMA • 1988
RATED: TV-PG • 24 MINS

A coming-of-age story that appealed to viewers' nostalgia, *The Wonder Years* has now been around more than long enough to become the object of nostalgia itself.

Created by Neal Marlens and Carol Black, based loosely around their own adolescence in the 1960s and 1970s, *The Wonder Years* may be backward-looking but it's also innovative.

It isn't filmed before a studio audience (a rarity for a sitcom at the time) and its concept means it can't adopt the reset-button tactics employed by other shows: characters have to grow up, the status quo has to change, and over six seasons we see this happen.

The Wonder Years focuses on Kevin Arnold (Fred Savage), a teenager living in middle-class suburbia going through what teenagers go through. The retrospective voiceover from an older Kevin (Daniel Stern) adds a layer to the storytelling, and the result has more depth than your average family sitcom.

LIFE ON MARS

CRIME FANTASY • 2006
RATED: TV-14 • 60 MINS

Its combination of traditional police action, slightly sinister nostalgia, and time-travel weirdness made *Life on Mars* a surprise hit. It catapults you into a hyperreal 1970s world of old TV shows and hazy childhood memories.

Manchester copper Sam Tyler (John Simm) is hit by a car and wakes up in a police station straight out of *The Sweeney*, where DCI Gene Hunt (Philip Glenister) rules the roost. Crass jokes are rife, and regulations are there to be bent. Unable to escape, Sam gets on with solving crimes and catching crooks—and comes to have a grudging respect for Hunt and his methods.

In the title sequence Sam asks, "Am I mad, in a coma, or back in time?" and some viewers, advancing wilder theories, were left fairly disappointed by the final episode (at the end of only Season 2). However, the world of *Life on Mars* is explored further in the 1980s-set sequel, *Ashes To Ashes*.

MINDER

COMEDY • 1979
RATED: 15 (UK) • 50 MINS

This hit series about dubious business dealings is now striking for its depiction of down-at-the-heels London, between the city's fashionable 1960s heyday and its 21st-century gentrification.

The minder of the title is Terry McCann (Dennis Waterman), personal bodyguard to wheeler-dealer Arthur Daley (George Cole), who has an endless supply of get-rich-quick schemes—most of which land him in trouble with the police, incur the displeasure of criminal organizations, or both.

Minder's success comes from the merging of small-time crime stories with a sitcom-style dynamic—Arthur's greed and self-belief clash with Terry's more realistic view, while the pair remain dependent on each other. After Terry's departure at the end of Season 7, the final three seasons feature Arthur's nephew Ray (Gary Webster) with whom he has a distinctly different relationship—but the show still works brilliantly.

WONDER WOMAN

ACTION • 1975
RATED: TV-G • 49 MINS

What the *Batman* TV show is to the 1960s, *Wonder Woman* is to the 1970s—a colorful, and hugely popular take on one of our most famous Super Heroes.

The premise is familiar to generations of Super Hero fans—a member of a civilization of island-dwelling Amazons comes to help humanity at a time of war. Adopting the name Diana Prince (Lynda Carter), she becomes close to American soldier Steve Trevor (Lyle Waggoner). This is the TV show that really lodged the Wonder Woman character in the public imagination.

Season 1 is set in World War II, but Seasons 2 and 3 are effectively a different series. The show was retitled *The New Adventures of Wonder Woman* and set in the present day. This version now seems more of a period piece than Season 1—its colorful style and funky costumes are glorious reminders of the disco era.

CASANOVA

PERIOD DRAMA • 2005
RATED: TV-MA • 60 MINS

The memoirs of Italian romantic adventurer Giacomo Casanova are given an appropriately rollicking treatment by Russell T. Davies. This is a sexy, funny, breathless romp through 18th-century Europe.

Casanova's story has been tackled by two of the best screenwriters British TV has ever had. In 1971 Dennis Potter used it as a loose basis for his first serial. Then in 2005 Davies' one-season, three-part version arrived on the BBC just before his revival of *Doctor Who* (see p58), serving as an effective audition for David Tennant (the estuary accent he used for the Doctor was first aired here).

Tennant plays the young Casanova with cheeky brio. Peter O'Toole plays the older version, recounting his story at the end of his life, and it's this that gives the story weight. Despite the way he glamorizes his frivolous youth and sexual conquests, melancholia creeps in, and the end is deeply affecting.

DARIA

ANIMATED COMEDY • 1997
RATED: TV-14 • 22 MINS

A perfect time capsule of the 1990s, *Daria* was the monotonous voice of a generation. Teenage ennui has rarely been better expressed than in the mundane world of this animated series.

Daria Morgendorffer (Tracy Grandstaff) first appeared as a character in the MTV series *Beavis and Butt-Head* (see p270)—an intelligent, sarcastic teenage girl whose manner rarely shows emotion. In her own show she has a supporting cast who are mostly tragically lacking in self-awareness, from her shallow younger sister Quinn (Wendy Hoopes), neurotic dad, and workaholic mum, to the jocks, creeps, and airheads at school.

Over the course of five seasons the supporting cast develops and becomes more than just the target of Daria's withering commentary. Quinn, in particular, carries a lot of the stories, having more potential for development than Daria. But the show's superb deadpan humor is a constant joy.

MIAMI VICE

CRIME • 1984
RATED: TV-14 • 49 MINS

Nothing is more 1980s than *Miami Vice*. Its focus on aesthetics—the visual style, the killer soundtrack—marked a step toward the more cinematic approach of modern TV.

A lot of American TV from the 1960s and 1970s basically looks the same—especially crime shows, which developed a loosely realist and fairly bland style. *Miami Vice* shook things up, taking influence from music videos (legend has it the original brief was "MTV cops") and making use of visual effects and stereo sound. The main characters, undercover vice detectives "Sonny" Crockett (Don Johnson) and "Rico" Tubbs (Philip Michael Thomas), have up to eight costume changes per episode.

The drive to make *Miami Vice* searingly modern is what makes it such a period piece today—it looks like a spoof of '80s TV. But its mix of real contemporary crime in a neo-noir world over five seasons is still striking.

PICNIC AT HANGING ROCK

PERIOD DRAMA • 2018
RATED: TV-14 • 50 MINS

A school trip in the Australian bush in 1900 goes badly wrong in this creepy and visually stunning series—which makes you glad for modern health and safety regulations.

Based on the 1967 novel by Joan Lindsay (filmed by Peter Weir in 1975), *Picnic at Hanging Rock* concerns three pupils from a girls' boarding school who vanish during the excursion described in the title. Headteacher Hester Appleyard (Natalie Dormer) must deal with the fallout of the disappearances, as hysteria grips the community and parents start to withdraw their daughters from the school.

It seems unlikely that such a short book (and slight, though deeply atmospheric, film) could sustain a six-hour miniseries, but writers Beatrix Christian and Alice Addison expand upon the story intelligently without losing the ambiguity, focusing more on the effect that an unexplained event has than the event itself, as well as the secrets it exposes.

BAND OF BROTHERS

WAR • 2001
RATED: TV-MA • 60 MINS

A landmark in American TV, this war drama, created by Steven Spielberg and Tom Hanks, marked the beginning of big-name talents migrating to the small screen.

Based on the real experiences of the Easy Company from the famous 101st Airborne Division, *Band of Brothers* follows the unit from initial training right up to the end of World War II. Led by Major Richard Winters (Damian Lewis), the company is involved in the Normandy landings, the Battle of the Bulge, and more.

Costing a reported $125 million to make, this 10-part miniseries involved intensive research as well as taking advantage of Spielberg's experience making *Saving Private Ryan*. Hailed as an outstanding piece of filmmaking, it uses the greater screentime of TV to convey the true weight of living through the war. The grueling battle scenes can make it a tough watch, but a rewarding one.

PARADE'S END

PERIOD DRAMA • 2012
RATED: TV-MA • 58 MINS

Adapting Ford Madox Ford's sprawling novel series for the screen is a daunting task—but writer Tom Stoppard manages it with grand aplomb.

Ford Madox Ford unfolds his narratives in a complex, time-hopping, and multistranded way that's really designed for the page. But Stoppard is a formidable writer himself and this rendition—his first foray into TV in 30 years—reshapes the four-book series into a lavish five-hour miniseries. He mostly achieves this by focusing on a World War I love triangle between aristocratic statistician Christopher Tietjens (Benedict Cumberbatch), his unfaithful wife Sylvia (Rebecca Hall), and idealistic suffragette Valentine Wannop (Adelaide Clemens).

The other characters still shine through—Stephen Graham is a revelation as working-class intellectual Vincent MacMaster, in love with the wife of an eccentric vicar (the couple are played by Anne-Marie Duff and Rufus Sewell)—and add light to Ford's bleak story.

DAS BOOT

WAR • 2018
RATED: 18 (UK) • 60 MINS

This is a sequel to, not a remake of, Wolfgang Petersen's film about a German U-boat crew in World War II—a claustrophobic thriller with a new set of characters.

The Oscar-nominated 1981 film of *Das Boot* was more at home on TV—Petersen's original cut was six hours long, and the fullest version is the six-part TV series released a few years later. The 2018 miniseries draws on Lothar-Günther Buchheim's original book and its sequel, expanding its scope to take in French Resistance operations on land.

It zeroes in on desperate struggles within the war, where the moral aspects of the conflict are overridden by straightforward survival. Simone Strasser (*Phantom Thread's* Vicky Krieps), a Nazi translator of French extraction, is sent undercover into the Resistance; on the U-boat, Kapitänleutnant Klaus Hoffman (Rick Okon) struggles to assert his authority. It's tense and grim, but brilliantly done.

THE JEWEL IN THE CROWN

DRAMA • 1984
RATED: TV-14 • 52 MINS

This single-season epic about the final years of the British Raj is a fascinating insight into a national identity, its characters caught between two worlds as the sun finally sets on the Empire.

Based on the *Raj Quartet* of novels by Paul Scott, *The Jewel in the Crown* opens in the fictional city of Mayapore during World War II. Hari Kumar (Art Malik) is an Indian educated in Britain who feels like an outsider in India; his romance with British woman Daphne Manners (Susan Wooldridge) leads to grim consequences when Daphne is raped and Hari is falsely accused.

It's impossible to convey the huge scale of this adaptation here—it continues into the postwar years, taking in dozens of characters—but it's a sweeping, carefully observed piece of work, benefiting from some wonderful location filming in India. The adaptation of Scott's Booker-winning coda to the series, *Staying On,* is also worth looking up.

HOWARDS END

PERIOD DRAMA • 2017
RATED: TV-14 • 60 MINS

This four-episode miniseries captures the rich humor and deep sadness of E. M. Forster's novel—a tale of three families from different backgrounds in early 20th-century Britain.

Forster's work is often characterized by social awkwardness, and *Howards End* concerns the uneasy friendship between the intellectual, bohemian Schlegel family—Margaret (Hayley Atwell), Helen (Philippa Coulthard), and Tibby (Alex Lawther)—and the wealthy Wilcoxes, headed by Henry (Matthew Macfadyen). Matters grow more complicated when Margaret becomes close to the aged Ruth Wilcox (Julia Ormond), and the Schlegels encounter the working-class Bast family.

The script by Kenneth Lonergan (better known for films such as *Gangs of New York*) is sparkling—it's funnier than most comedies, and the cast is extraordinary, especially the Schlegels. This will transport you to 1900s Bloomsbury—a superb piece of work.

TABOO

PERIOD DRAMA • 2017
RATED: TV-MA • 60 MINS

Offering a hallucinatory, violent take on the early 19th century, *Taboo* delves into the British Empire's part in slavery. This is a brutal and thrilling drama.

Created by series star Tom Hardy, his scriptwriter dad Chips Hardy, and *Peaky Blinders* (see p140) creator Steven Knight, *Taboo* brings the stylized approach of *Peaky Blinders* to the world of international trade.

The one-season series is anchored by Hardy's lurid, yet utterly convincing performance as James Delaney, who returns to London following the death of his father, Horace (Edward Fox), after years spent in Africa. Delaney has inherited a small, but valuable stretch of land in America. When he refuses to sell it to the East India Company, the company plans to kill him.

The first half hour throws a lot of backstory at you, but when the plot kicks in *Taboo* is superb, with Delaney walking a fine line between hero and villain.

SHARPE

PERIOD DRAMA • 1993
RATED: TV-MA • 100 MINS

This drama of the Napoleonic Wars, adapted from Bernard Cornwell's popular novels, captivated audiences in the 1990s with its mixture of military heroism and class conflict.

Sergeant Richard Sharpe (Sean Bean) is in service in Portugal when he singlehandedly saves the life of the Duke of Wellington (David Troughton). Promoted to Lieutenant,

Sharpe finds himself at odds with other officers, who have bought their positions rather than earned them—which makes him a perfect hero for a modern audience.

Sheffield-born Bean is so perfect in the lead role that Cornwell tweaked the character's backstory in the novels to give him a Yorkshire accent, despite being from London. *Sharpe's* 16 feature-length episodes track the war from the peninsular conflict of 1809 to the Battle of Waterloo, and beyond, via two episodes set in India. As a whole, the show has a satisfyingly epic scale.

HORNBLOWER

PERIOD DRAMA • 1998
RATED: 15 (UK) • 100 MINS

Following in the footsteps of *Sharpe*, *Hornblower* dramatizes the French Revolutionary and Napoleonic Wars at sea, taking the viewpoint of young Royal Navy officer Horatio Hornblower.

Created by novelist C. S. Forester in the 1930s, Hornblower (Ioan Gruffudd) is loosely based on Lord Nelson and other real naval officers of the period. This series of eight feature-

length episodes draws on the first three novels in the series, starting with Hornblower's voyages as a teenager under the command of the historically real Captain Edward Pellew (Robert Lindsay), who becomes his mentor as the conflict with France deepens.

The end of *Sharpe* left a huge appetite for this sort of drama, and *Hornblower* filled the gap perfectly, marshalling the production values needed to depict battles at sea. Hornblower isn't quite as engaging a character as Sharpe, but Gruffudd carries the action ably, and it won an Emmy for Outstanding Miniseries.

JONATHAN STRANGE & MR. NORRELL

PERIOD FANTASY • 2015 • RATED: TV-14 • 60 MINS • SEASONS: 1
BERTIE CARVEL, EDDIE MARSAN, CHARLOTTE RILEY

Alternately whimsical and sinister, this smart adaptation of the crossover blockbuster novel by Susanna Clarke takes us back to the early 19th century and asks the question: "Why is there no more magic done in England?"

Jonathan Strange & Mr. Norrell was an ambitious commission in which the BBC sadly seemed to lose confidence. The costume drama about magicians seemed ideally suited as a lead-in to Christmas back in 2014, but it was delayed and ultimately aired in May and June 2015, when it got rave reviews, but failed to find an audience. It strongly deserves to find one now.

The premise is that magic used to be commonplace but died out around the Renaissance. Stodgy scholar Gilbert Norrell (Eddie Marsan) has built a personal library of antique magic books, and moves to London with the purpose of reviving England's traditions of practical magic. He takes on Jonathan Strange (Bertie Carvel), a talented younger magician, as a pupil—but their differing approaches set them at odds.

Writer Peter Harness deftly pulls together the threads of Clarke's lengthy novel—the deal made to bring a wealthy man's fiancée back from the dead, the use of magic in the Napoleonic Wars, the unscrupulous hangers-on looking to exploit the return of magic—and never loses sight of the heart of the drama. Before the end, the cost of magic becomes all too clear.

HARLOTS

PERIOD DRAMA • 2017
RATED: TV-MA • 46 MINS

Harlots depicts 18th-century London from the point of view of a slightly different up-and-coming family business: a high-class brothel in Soho, where a mother puts her daughters to work.

Brothels are a staple of "edgy" period drama, but frequently in male-focused stories, and so *Harlots* offers a welcome change. Created by Alison Newman and Moira Buffini, the story concerns a brothel run by whip-smart Margaret Wells (Samantha Morton). In an effort to attract a better clientele, she moves the business to Greek Street in the heart of London—putting her at odds with her old employer Lydia Quigley (Lesley Manville), and the religious puritans trying to clean up the city.

The series strikes a clever balance between delicious melodrama and honest treatment of the very real historical issues raised, as the female characters try to exploit their power over men. There are so many sources of conflict, it's great drama fuel.

STAR TREK: DEEP SPACE NINE

SCI-FI • 1993
RATED: TV-PG • 45 MINS

Widely regarded as the best *Star Trek* series, *Deep Space Nine* took the "Trek" out of the equation by setting its unfolding narrative on a space station.

The planet Bajor has recently thrown off a hostile occupation by the Cardassians, and the Bajorans invite the Federation to take control of the old Cardassian station. Commanded by Benjamin Sisko (Avery Brooks), the renamed Deep Space Nine is soon at the center of tensions when a wormhole is discovered that connects this region of space with another.

In contrast to the cozy relations between the crew in *The Next Generation* (see p90), *Deep Space Nine* is full of conflict, as different parties advance their own agendas. Whereas the modus operandi of previous crews was to cruise the cosmos meddling in situations and then leave, in *Deep Space Nine* they must live with the consequences over seven seasons.

STAR TREK: VOYAGER

SCI-FI • 1995
RATED: TV-PG • 45 MINS

Boldly going in a new direction, *Voyager* gives its new crew a desperate ongoing mission: to travel through uncharted space, and get back home before they all die of old age.

Over the course of *The Next Generation, Deep Space Nine*, as well as the original '60s series, a lot of the *Star Trek* universe had been mapped. To get back that sense of traveling where no one had gone before, the first episode of *Voyager* sees a new crew led by Captain Kathryn Janeway (Kate Mulgrew) zapped by an energy wave 70,000 light-years from Earth—and facing a 75-year return trip.

At first, *Voyager* doesn't feel like much of a departure from *The Next Generation* (see p90). It's only midway through its seven-season run that it develops its own identity. The show offers up some delightfully bizarre episodes, with the addition of Seven of Nine (Jeri Ryan), a human reclaimed from the alien Borg's hive mind, giving it a shot in the arm.

STAR TREK: ENTERPRISE

SCI-FI • 2001
RATED: TV-PG • 45 MINS

Star Trek gets back to basics with a more grounded show from the early days of the Federation, set long before any other *Star Trek* series.

After *Voyager*, the *Trek* franchise needed a shake-up in terms of visuals and storytelling. To this end, *Enterprise* is set in the 22nd century, following the voyages of the first ship to carry that name, under the leadership of Captain Jonathan Archer (Scott Bakula). With this being the first human-built ship capable of traveling at "warp 5" (tens of times faster than the speed of light), new vistas are opening up for the crew.

Enterprise does a good job of striking a balance between the *Trek* aesthetic and the look of real-world space travel, but its first two seasons of largely stand-alone adventures didn't quite catch fire with audiences. The more serialized third and fourth seasons are much more successful, and it's a shame they didn't lead to more.

STAR TREK: DISCOVERY

SCI-FI • 2017 • RATED: TV-MA • 45 MINS • SEASONS: 2
SONEQUA MARTIN-GREEN, DOUG JONES, JASON ISAACS

What happened before Kirk and Spock? Find out in the first *Trek* series designed for the streaming era. *Discovery* expands the old series' story-of-the-week format and adopts a twisting narrative set against a backdrop of interstellar war where not everything is as it seems.

Discovery opens with First Officer Michael Burnham (Sonequa Martin-Green), a human raised by Vulcans, mutinying to prevent a war. She's court-martialed, and conflict breaks out. But while being moved to a new jail, Burnham's vessel gets into trouble and she's rescued by the starship *Discovery*—where Captain Gabriel Lorca (Jason Isaacs) puts her skills to use.

Discovery didn't have a smooth journey to the screen, with showrunners and key writers joining and leaving the project, and at first it

seems unsure about what it wants to be. But this also makes it wonderfully unpredictable. It's refreshing, too, to have a *Trek* show that isn't focused on a starship captain, but on a character with a more uncertain status.

Best of all, you don't have to be vastly invested in *Trek* lore to get it—some of the reveals have more power if you're familiar with the earlier series, but newbies can just dive in and enjoy the best *Star Trek* in decades.

> **"***It's challenging and fulfilling in all the right ways.***"**
>
> **Sonequa Martin-Green** (Michael Burnham)

STAR TREK: PICARD

SCI-FI • 2020
RATED: TV-MA • 45 MINS

While *Discovery* establishes a new set of characters to explore the *Trek* universe, *Picard* taps deep into nostalgia for *The Next Generation*. But it's far from a gentle ride.

Picard picks up the story of Jean-Luc Picard (Patrick Stewart) many years after his last appearance in the film *Star Trek: Nemesis*. In the interim, Picard has resigned from

Starfleet over the treatment of Romulan alien refugees and retired to a vineyard; but he's having unsettling dreams about Data (Brent Spiner), his android officer aboard the *Enterprise*. A young woman named Dahj (Isa Briones) comes to Picard for help and he's shocked to learn she is Data's daughter....

With an epic, cinematic style, *Picard* is faithful to the world of *The Next Generation* (see p90), but adopts the mode of a slow-burning thriller with multiple mysteries over its single season. Weaving a sinister Romulan plot with events aboard an alien cube, it's a feast for *Trek* fans.

MONKEY

FANTASY • 1978
RATED: 12 (UK) • 45 MINS

This retelling of one of the classic works of world literature has a bit of everything—epic fantasy, action, history, and comedy—and gained a worldwide cult following.

Journey to the West, published in China in the 16th century, is probably the most popular book in all of east Asia. It tells of the Buddhist monk Xuanzang's eventful pilgrimage to India to fetch sacred texts, accompanied by Sun Wukong, a monkey born of stone and possessed of magical powers. This latter character was made into the center of a blockbuster adaptation produced for Japanese TV in the late 1970s.

Appropriately for a show about a journey to the west, the two-season series was purchased by the BBC and dubbed into English. It's easy to see why it was a hit. Its mix of high-action sequences and slapstick transcend language barriers, and the novel's episodic style is ideally suited to TV. A classic of its kind.

ROME

HISTORICAL DRAMA • 2005
RATED: TV-MA • 60 MINS

As you might expect from HBO, this lavish drama goes big on the decadence of ancient Rome—but it's also a grand attempt to resurrect the Hollywood tradition of the Roman epic.

Our viewpoint characters in *Rome* are two fictional soldiers in the 1st century BCE, the rogueish Titus Pullo (Ray Stevenson) and the upright Lucius Vorenus (Kevin McKidd).

Their activities bring them into the orbit of lots of names familiar from Shakespeare plays: Julius Caesar (Ciarán Hinds), Mark Antony (James Purefoy), Brutus (Tobias Menzies)….

The series does a good job of depicting Rome across different social strata, and Season 1 builds nicely to the plot to assassinate Caesar (no spoilers on if it succeeds!). Season 2 doesn't quite have the same momentum, and it's no surprise it was the last—but the production values are faultless (it was produced in Italy) and its sheer immersive scale is impressive.

THE LAST KINGDOM

HISTORICAL DRAMA • 2015
RATED: TV-MA • 60 MINS

A thrilling delve into a lesser-explored period of British history, *The Last Kingdom* is ideal if you'd like to watch *Game of Thrones* but can't handle all those dragons.

It's the 9th century. The kingdom of the title is Wessex, and it's the last one because the other six kingdoms of England are being plundered and ruled by invading Vikings. The Northumbrian Uhtred of Bebbanburg (Alexander Dreymon) is forced to pledge his allegiance to King Alfred (David Dawson) to avenge his family and win back his lands.

The show's four seasons are based on a series of books by leading historical novelist Bernard Cornwell. There's real depth to its depiction of the period, giving a sense of how a war was fought at this point in history (it's not pretty and there's a lot of mud!). It's superbly made TV, with action sequences that really hit home, and some of the best cinematography you'll see on the small screen.

ROYAL NIRVANA

PERIOD DRAMA • 2019
RATED: 18 (UK) • 43 MINS

Tired of historical dramas set in times and places you know too well? Try this blockbuster Chinese drama, in which romance and political intrigue clash as a prince falls in love with the same woman twice without realizing.

Adapted by Xue Man Liang Yuan from her own novel, *Royal Nirvana* is set during the Northern Qi dynasty (which ruled in the north of China from AD 550 to 577). It centers on the sensitive Crown Prince Xiao Dingquan (Luo Jin), who believes his soulmate is Lu Wen Xi (Li Yitong), the daughter of a high-ranking civil servant, whom he's never met. His love is based purely on her artwork and beliefs.

But then Xiao Dingquan falls for a new maidservant at the palace ... who is secretly Lu Wen Xi, working undercover in the palace to try to get her father and brother out of jail. That gives you just a small taste of the plot twists in the 60 episodes of this head-spinner of a series.

THE BORGIAS

HISTORICAL DRAMA • 2011
RATED: TV-MA • 52 MINS

The Sopranos of the Renaissance era, The Borgias depicts the demented decadence of one of the most notorious families in history as they ascend to the head of the Catholic Church.

The lurid sex-and-violence-heavy historical drama has become a staple of American cable TV. And if any part of history is crying out for that treatment, it's the Borgias.

Created by Oscar-winning screenwriter and director Neil Jordan, this series centers on Rodrigo Borgia (Jeremy Irons), who uses bribery and corruption to get himself elected Pope Alexander VI.

It all builds nicely, but ends too soon: Jordan wanted at least four seasons so he could cover Alexander's entire reign, but Showtime canceled it after just three. Yet it's still worth watching for its high production values and the characters' thrillingly despicable plotting. If you need to know how it ends, you'll have to pick up a history book.

VERSAILLES

HISTORICAL DRAMA • 2015
RATED: TV-MA • 53 MINS

A century before the French Revolution, another King Louis addresses his own decline in popularity by taking the bold step of building himself a massive new house.

Louis XIV (George Blagden) is now noted for having the longest reign of any French monarch—72 years. But the period dramatized in *Versailles* shows him as a young man, losing the respect and obedience of the French nobility. How does he tackle this? Counterintuitively, by moving out of Paris, and expanding his hunting lodge near the tiny village of Versailles into a palace, enabling his greater plan of centralizing power.

Louis makes for an aloof protagonist, and over three seasons things don't exactly unfold at a breakneck pace—it's about a building project, after all. But it does a great job of shining a light on a period of French history that usually gets ignored in favor of Louis XVI and Marie Antoinette.

WOLF HALL

HISTORICAL DRAMA • 2015 • RATED: TV-14 • 60 MINS • SEASONS: 1
MARK RYLANCE, DAMIAN LEWIS, CLAIRE FOY

Wolf Hall brilliantly dramatizes King Henry VIII's reign from the perspective of the man tasked with getting rid of wife number two.

The first two novels in Hilary Mantel's trilogy about Thomas Cromwell, *Wolf Hall* and *Bring Up the Bodies*, both scooped the Booker Prize (the only time a novel and its sequel have both won), so a BBC adaptation was inevitable. But there was no guarantee it would be this good. Playwright and screenwriter Peter Straughan, writing his first scripts for television, skilfully uses the weight of detail from Mantel's books (which total more than 1,000 pages) to create a textured 16th-century world.

The series details the rise of Cromwell (Mark Rylance) to his position as chief minister to Henry VIII (Damain Lewis), at a time when the king is increasingly dissatisfied with his wife Anne Boleyn (Claire Foy) and wants a way out of the marriage. Mantel's novels are written in the present tense and director Peter Kosminsky responds to this: you really feel like the characters are modern people—because, as far as they're concerned, they are modern people, living through a seismic moment in British politics.

> **"***It is about the politics of despotism.***"**
>
> **Peter Kosminsky** (director)

The language is perfectly executed, neither jarringly modern nor impenetrably archaic. The result is that *Wolf Hall* doesn't feel like a history lesson, but an intense, slow-burning political thriller with high stakes.

CATHERINE THE GREAT

HISTORICAL DRAMA • 2019
RATED: TV-MA • 60 MINS

Chronicling Russia's longest-reigning female ruler, Catherine the Great provides a strong central role for Helen Mirren—her first TV series since Elizabeth I in 2005.

This four-episode miniseries reunites Mirren with screenwriter Nigel Williams, who also wrote *Elizabeth I*, and takes a similar tack by focusing on Catherine's love life—namely her relationship with military commander Grigory Potemkin (Jason Clark). The drama spans most of the latter half of the 18th century, a period widely considered to be Russia's golden age (there's also a 2014 Russian series covering the same subject matter).

It looks stunning, thanks to some excellent location work in Lithuania, and Mirren is as terrific as you'd expect. A few liberties are taken with history, and Williams takes the decision to modernize the language and make liberal use of profanity—but it's a lively take on the period.

THE WHITE QUEEN

HISTORICAL DRAMA • 2013
RATED: TV-MA • 60 MINS

An epic miniseries exploring a slice of 15th-century English history from a fresh perspective. Follow three women as they each try to gain an advantage to put themselves closer to power.

While the Wars of the Roses rage on, Elizabeth Woodville (Rebecca Ferguson), Margaret Beaufort (Amanda Hale), and Anne Neville (Faye Marsay) are all close to the various claimants to the throne. The "White Queen" of the title is Elizabeth, a comparatively low-born woman who won the hand of King Edward IV.

Over the course of 20 years, the characters' machinations play out, often with grim consequences. The 10-part miniseries is adapted by Emma Frost from three novels by Philippa Gregory, so there's a lot of material to draw on and the result is a tumultuous ride. It got a lukewarm reception from critics, but was a hit with audiences, who responded to the high-stakes drama of it all.

THE WHITE PRINCESS

HISTORICAL DRAMA • 2017
RATED: TV-MA • 56 MINS

If you enjoy _The White Queen_, there's more. The 15th-century saga continues as peace finally comes to England—but at the cost of court hostilities between the king and his queen.

The BBC decided not to follow up _The White Queen_, despite a dozen more Philippa Gregory novels covering the Plantagenet and Tudor periods—so the Starz channel stepped in.

The White Princess depicts the marriage of Elizabeth of York (Jodie Comer) and Henry VII (Jacob Collins-Levy), which ends the War of the Roses. Trouble is, the two loathe each other, so this is going to be hard work.

With Emma Frost leading the writing on this eight-part miniseries, it has a similar feel to _The White Queen_ even though the lead characters have all been recast— a pre–_Killing Eve_ (see p368) Jodie Comer is typically brilliant in the title role. It's heightened, for sure, but if _The White Queen_ worked for you, this will, too.

THE SPANISH PRINCESS

HISTORICAL DRAMA • 2019
RATED: TV-MA • 55 MINS

Picking up the thread from _The White Queen_ and _The White Princess_, this tells the story of Catherine of Aragon (Charlotte Hope), the first wife of Henry VIII (Ruairi O'Connor).

Adapted from novels by Philippa Gregory, _The Spanish Princess_ opens with Catherine's arrival in England in 1501. She steps into a terrific piece of teen melodrama—promised to Arthur, Prince of Wales (Angus Imrie) and heir to the throne, she's disappointed to find he's not nearly as romantic as he seemed in his letters. In fact, the true author of the letters was his brother Harry—later to be Henry VIII....

The first season seemed remarkably timely— Catherine's struggles to fit in at court, where she is treated as an outsider, parallel the hostile treatment of Meghan, Duchess of Sussex. The show succeeds in rounding out a historical figure who often gets sidelined, while ramping up the drama to keep things juicy.

PEAKY BLINDERS

CRIME • 2013 • RATED: TV-MA • 60 MINS • SEASONS: 5
CILLIAN MURPHY, HELEN MCCRORY, PAUL ANDERSON

A blood-soaked chronicle of the rise of a Birmingham gangster family after World War I, *Peaky Blinders* is unafraid to be stylized and hyperreal. The show is a glorious contrast to the tone and style of most "straight" TV period dramas.

At the heart of *Peaky Blinders* is a compelling antihero in the form of Tommy Shelby (Cillian Murphy). In some ways, he's an honorable man whose life of crime seems a fair response to how his country has treated him; in others, he's a sadistic brute whom you'd never ever want to meet. Both the writing and Murphy's steely performance form an unsettling portrait of a person whose wartime experiences have left him not caring if he lives or dies—he visibly contemplates suicide several times in the series. He is, you soon realize, an unpredictable man who may not care for consequences.

A modern prestige TV show is expected to travel well around the world, and there's often an urge to make shows relatable to a global audience by not tying them down too firmly to the specifics of a time and place. The risk of this, of course, is that everything ends up feeling the same, as if the stories could take place anywhere. So the success of *Peaky Blinders*, a show rooted in the criminal underworld of Birmingham in the years after World War I, is a welcome reminder that audiences respond when a show is distinctive.

It's also a reminder not to pigeonhole writers. Until the turn of the millennium, Steven Knight was best known for his work for comedian Jasper Carrott (including cowriting all 31 episodes of his sitcom *The Detectives*), and being one of the three creators of game show *Who Wants to Be a Millionaire?* While writing screenplays in the 2000s Knight developed what would become *Peaky Blinders*, drawing on his parents' childhood memories of the big characters who inhabited working-class Birmingham in the interwar period. "In a way I want *Peaky Blinders* to be sort of the view of this world through the eyes of a 10-year-old," Knight said when promoting the first season, "because the men are smarter and stronger and handsomer and the horses are bigger and everything is big and intimidating as a kid."

This notion is key to the aesthetic of *Peaky Blinders* (the title is also the name of the central gang, who have razor blades sewn into the peaks of their caps). While many elements of the show are essential to the era—the aftermath of the war, the British presence in Ireland, narrowing social divisions—it reserves the freedom to paint everything bigger. For example, initially some viewers found the anachronistic music jarring, but the choice of tracks creates a coherent style of dissonant, bluesy rock (Nick Cave, The White Stripes, PJ Harvey) and becomes an attraction in its own right—Anna Calvi's original score for Season 5 is particularly brilliant. The show's cinematography and design are also spectacular; the gang's clothes and haircuts are so immediately identifiable that they've been cosplayed by fans at conventions.

Alongside Murphy's Tommy, that gang also includes some great supporting characters— most notably his aunt Polly (Helen McCrory), who's been running the family while the men were at war, and short-fused brother Arthur (Paul Anderson). Tom Hardy also makes magnificent irregular appearances as Jewish

> *"Any act of violence has a consequence."*
>
> **Steven Knight** (creator/writer)

gang leader Alfie Solomons. However, at the eye of the storm, gang leader Tommy always remains.

As the Shelby empire grows, the stakes get higher and higher—and you don't feel like anyone is safe. For the sheer immersive thrill-ride, few shows can match *Peaky Blinders*.

TOP PEAKY BLINDERS MUSICAL ARTISTS

OF SONG APPEARANCES

CREATOR: Steven Knight
PRODUCTION CO: Caryn Mandabach Productions, Tiger Aspect Productions, BBC

DEATH COMES TO PEMBERLEY

PERIOD DRAMA • 2013
RATED: TV-14 • 58 MINS

This adaptation of P. D. James's sequel to *Pride and Prejudice* refashions Austen's famous romantic heroine into a dogged detective on the trail of a murderer.

Elizabeth Darcy (Anna Maxwell Martin) has been married to Fitzwilliam Darcy (Matthew Rhys) for six years, and to celebrate they invite various friends to a ball at Pemberley. But an argument breaks out in a carriage transporting Lizzie's frivolous sister Lydia, her husband George Wickham, and Captain Denny to the ball, and when their quarrel spills out into the woods, Denny is shot dead. But by whom?

Lizzie's sharpness and proactive nature are recognizable from Austen's novel, so it's not a stretch to see her turn sleuth and try to clear her brother-in-law's name. If you pay attention in this single-season drama, the solution is hiding in plain sight—but there are many juicy revelations along the way.

LOST IN AUSTEN

FANTASY DRAMA • 2008
RATED: TV-14 • 45 MINS

This short one-season series takes a *Life on Mars*–style premise and applies it to *Pride and Prejudice,* when an Austen fan (and hopeless romantic) finds herself trapped in the story.

Amanda Price (Jemima Rooper) is a modern-day Jane Austen fan who, after knocking back a marriage proposal from her boyfriend Michael (Daniel Percival), is surprised to find Lizzie Bennet (Gemma Arterton), the protagonist of *Pride and Prejudice*, in her bathroom. She's even more surprised when Lizzie shows her a secret passage that leads to the novel's world. Trouble is, when she goes down it, she can't find her way back....

Lost in Austen explores the relationship we have with our favorite fiction—would you want to live inside the world of a book, given the chance? What if, by going into it, you ruined it? Amanda's dilemma—does she want to take over Lizzie's role, and can she?—is engagingly played by Rooper.

SENSE AND SENSIBILITY

PERIOD DRAMA • 2008
RATED: TV-14 • 52 MINS

It's a tough act to follow the 1995 film version, but writer Andrew Davies and director John Alexander find their own take, with a dash more sex (practically Davies's trademark) and violence, and less glamour.

Andrew Davies, writer of the blockbuster 1995 version of *Pride and Prejudice*, returns to Jane Austen with this single-season adaptation of one of her most enduringly popular novels. The Dashwood family, including daughters Elinor (Hattie Morahan) and Marianne (Charity Wakefield), are left an unexpectedly small settlement when their father dies.

After seizing the offer of making their home at humble Barton Cottage, the sisters are the object of romantic interest from Edward Ferrars (Dan Stevens), Colonel Brandon (David Morrissey), and John Willoughby (Dominic Cooper). The series has an excellent cast, and Austen's clockwork plotting is always an asset to any adaptation.

CRANFORD

PERIOD DRAMA • 2007
RATED: TV-PG • 54 MINS

This smart combination of several works by Elizabeth Gaskell creates a single-season portrait of life in a secluded mid-19th century town in the north of England.

Gaskell's *Cranford* is one of her best-known novels: here, screenwriter Heidi Thomas combines it with Gaskell's stories *Mr. Harrison's Confessions* and *My Lady Ludlow* to create a multilayered ensemble piece. The ladies of Cranford, including the spinster Jenkyns sisters (Judi Dench and Eileen Atkins), enjoy an orderly and relaxed existence—but the imminent development of a railroad threatens to change the pace of life in the town forever.

The coziness of *Cranford* is nicely balanced by an awareness that nothing can stay the same— Cranford cannot go on entirely untouched by the wave of modernization sweeping Britain. A two-part sequel brings in material from Gaskell's *The Moorland Cottage* and *The Cage at Cranford* to complete the story.

HUNDERBY

PERIOD COMEDY • 2012
RATED: 15 (UK) • 22 MINS

This BAFTA-winning gothic comedy, written by and starring Julia Davis, draws on *Wuthering Heights*, *Jane Eyre*, and *Rebecca*—taking in buried secrets, sexual repression, and bubbly milk.

Hunderby concerns Helene (Alexandra Roach), the sole survivor of a shipwreck, who has washed up in a coastal village. She catches the eye of local pastor Edmund (Alex Macqueen)—but once they're married, Helene finds Edmund much harsher than she expected, and must face hostility from housekeeper Dorothy (Davis), who is strangely obsessed with Edmund's first wife.

The deeply odd tone of *Hunderby* isn't for everyone, but for those who can connect with it, the oddness is the absolute cornerstone of its appeal. Davis uses the historical setting as a means of making her characters even weirder than those in her series *Nighty Night*. Season 1 comes to a satisfyingly absurd end, but the two-part sequel is very welcome.

NORTH & SOUTH

PERIOD DRAMA • 2004
RATED: TV-PG • 58 MINS

A love story played out across the divide of a labor dispute, this outstanding novel of Britain's age of industrialization has always been popular with TV audiences.

Elizabeth Gaskell's 1855 novel *North and South* was based on her own observations of the differences between the London where she had grown up and the Manchester where she lived as an adult. In this version Daniela Denby-Ashe plays the well-to-do, socially conscious Margaret Hale, and Richard Armitage is mill owner John Thornton.

The conflicts in Gaskell's story continue to resonate, which is why it remains popular: Margaret is naive but desperate to improve conditions for workers, while John has a deeper understanding of the situation but not much sympathy for his employees. Each wants the other to come around to their point of view, and this drives the drama briskly along through the four-episode miniseries.

AGENT CARTER

SPY DRAMA • 2015
RATED: TV-PG • 42 MINS

A moody, noirish exploration of the Marvel Cinematic Universe in the aftermath of World War II, *Agent Carter* explores a fresh genre, away from the usual Super Hero business.

British officer Peggy Carter (Hayley Atwell) was instantly popular with viewers of the first 1940s-set *Captain America* movie. But with Cap himself getting frozen for decades at the end of that movie and thawed out in the present day, there didn't seem much room for her to feature in subsequent films—she'd been left behind. TV to the rescue!

Agent Carter ran for just two seasons—one set in New York, one in Los Angeles—but that's actually a benefit. There's no way you can fit *Agents of S.H.I.E.L.D.* into your MCU marathon, but you can easily make room for *Agent Carter*. Its stylish, unique take on the postwar era and the winning presence of Atwell herself are more than enough reason to watch.

THE AMERICANS

SPY DRAMA • 2013
RATED: TV-MA • 49 MINS

The Americans explores the less glamorous side of espionage. No jet-setting around the world here—this is a show about living a lie, under the constant threat of discovery.

One of many excellent shows made by the FX network in the 2010s, *The Americans* follows suburban married couple Elizabeth (Keri Russell) and Philip Jennings (Matthew Rhys), who are actually deep-cover KGB agents. They've been embedded in the US for 15 years, and even their children don't know the truth. This scenario creates a sense of almost unbearable tension: at any moment Elizabeth and Philip's cover could be blown and they'd have to abandon their lives. But when it comes to it, will they?

It's a great premise for exploring questions of identity—personal identity, national identity—and from the beginning, the question of how it will all end hangs over everything. The whole series is a ticking time bomb.

DANGER MAN

SPY DRAMA • 1960
RATED: 12 (UK) • 25/50 MINS

Before James Bond hit cinemas, John Drake was traversing the globe, undertaking covert intelligence operations. The series' slick, moody style made it a hit in both the US and UK.

Originated by Ralph Smart, the concept was developed at one stage by Bond creator Ian Fleming. However, when star Patrick McGoohan (who later turned down the role of 007 in *Dr. No*) was cast, his preferences resulted in key divergences from Bond: no guns and (due to his devout Catholicism) no kissing. *Danger Man* was initially canceled in 1962 after one season, only to be revived in a Bond-inspired vogue for spy drama—running for two more seasons and a two-part special.

Viewed today, *Danger Man* evokes the Cold War era strongly, and captures the globetrotting appeal of Bond well, considering it was all made in the UK. Few TV shows of the 1960s can match it for sheer atmosphere.

THE PRISONER

**SPY DRAMA • 1967 • RATED: TV-PG • 50 MINS • SEASONS: I
PATRICK MCGOOHAN, LEO MCKERN, COLIN GORDON**

No TV show sums up the psychedelic 1960s better than *The Prisoner*. This surreal, visually dazzling spy drama bamboozled viewers on broadcast— but its willingness to ask big existential questions made it an enduring classic.

When *Danger Man* came to an end, its leading man Patrick McGoohan was one of the biggest stars on TV. Whatever he wanted to do next, it would get made. He and one of the *Danger Man* writers, George Markstein, devised a show about a spy who resigns from the service, only to find himself incarcerated in The Village, a resortlike facility, while his employers demand to know the true reason for his resignation. It sounded very much as if it picked up where *Danger Man* left off.

But what McGoohan had in mind was much weirder and more abstract. His central character was never named, being referred to only as "Number Six." Exteriors of The Village were shot in Portmeirion, a stylized Italianate tourist resort in north Wales, and the design of the show was equally strange and whimsical. And while some episodes focused on Number Six's escape attempts, others examined broader concepts of freedom, power, truth, and identity. Many viewers expecting more *Danger Man* were baffled—but its striking visuals, strange imagery, and philosophical approach made it linger in the memory.

Viewed today, its ambition and spirit of experimentation shine through. One week Number Six wakes up in a deserted Village, and half the episode plays out without any

dialogue. In another episode, he's interrogated with a truth serum, and the more serum he's given, the woozier and druggier his flashbacks become. A later episode is a Western, which functions as a commentary on Vietnam (and was considered too contentious to show in America). And the final episode … well, you can make up your own mind about what it means.

The Prisoner now looks like a glorious period piece—but many of the questions it asks are universal and timeless.

> **"*I am not a number.
> I am a free man.*"**
>
> **Number Six** (SI EI)

YOU WANT A COZY NIGHT IN

Written by Laura Buller and Eddie Robson

Some evenings you just want to build a nest on the sofa and curl up in front of the television. Maybe this isn't the night for too much drama—you're in the mood to watch people make their way through life and love, with all the usual chemistry, awkwardness, and humor. Rom-coms, rom-drams, and everything in between, the series in this chapter are the perfect way to unwind. This is TV to shut out the rest of the world.

DAWSON'S CREEK

DRAMA • 1998 • RATED: TV-14 • 60 MINS • SEASONS: 6
JAMES VAN DER BEEK, KATIE HOLMES, MICHELLE WILLIAMS

Four close teenage friends on the brink of adulthood wear their hearts on their sleeves as they negotiate high school and enter college. They are smart and self-aware beyond their years, but plenty of angst lies in store.

Best friends Dawson Leery (James Van Der Beek) and Joey Potter (Katie Holmes) grew up in an idyllic Cape Cod town, loving movies and hanging out together, often with Pacey Witter (Joshua Jackson), who's always up for a laugh, in tow. But the simple stuff is about to get a lot harder. New girl—and maybe bad girl—Jen Lindley (Michelle Williams) moves in from the big city, and high school begins.

Of course, stretching the limits of teen-focused television sometimes made the action a little over-the-top, and the self-absorbed, super-witty, and knowing dialogue was pitched a little high. Plus, none of the cast seemed to have any zits. Yet '90s teenagers couldn't get enough of the immensely appealing, soon-to-be star leads, the music, and the whole adolescent-to-adult experience as portrayed with so much talent and heart.

> " We're growing up, that's all.
> I mean even Spielberg outgrew
> his Peter Pan syndrome."
>
> **Joey** (S1 E1)

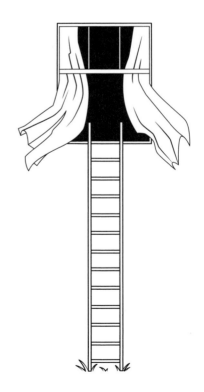

The perils and pains of being a teenager wrap the childhood friends together and sometimes drive them apart as they try to unravel life and figure it all out. Over six seasons, fans watched the characters confront changes, relationship challenges, and a slew of story lines, usually with a good deal of humor and depth. Most of the writing staff were newbies, too, and their anything-goes approach helped this series reach heights well beyond the standards set by typical teen dramas of the time.

CREATOR: Kevin Williamson **PRODUCTION CO:** Outerbanks Entertainment, Columbia TriStar Television, Columbia TriStar Domestic Television, Granville Productions, PGP, Sony Pictures Television

THE OC

DRAMA • 2003
RATED: TV-PG • 44 MINS

A troubled teen winds up in a seemingly untroubled enclave in Orange County, California. But darker secrets lurk beneath the sunny skies of his new home, as he discovers when he begins encountering friends, foes, and lovers.

Problem teen Ryan Atwood (Ben McKenzie) is in for a shock when he moves from the sticks to live in swanky Newport Beach. Helping him settle into his new life is foster brother Seth Cohen (Adam Brody), who guides him through the minefield of school and the unwritten rules of this moneyed community.

The relationships between main characters Ryan, Seth, Marissa Cooper (Mischa Barton), and Summer Roberts (Rachel Bilson) kept viewers tuned in for four seasons. There is plenty of teen angst and a killer soundtrack, but also enough romance and laughter to make the characters relatable. The show also has plenty to say about big issues such as privilege and the meaning of family.

BOYS OVER FLOWERS

ROMANCE • 2009
RATED: TV-14 • 70 MINS

Boys meet girl in this school drama. In this case the boys (all four of them) are the richest and most popular in their private academy, while the girl is a poor but plucky new kid. Who, though, will ultimately win at love?

At the top of the class socially, the boys who call themselves F4 come up against ordinary girl Geum Jan-di (Ku Hye-sun) when she starts attending their upscale school. Unlike her classmates, Jan-di is not obsessed with the group, but leader Gu Jun-pyo (Lee Min-ho) falls for her. At the same time, she is developing a secret crush on another of its members, Yoon Ji-hu (Kim Hyun-joong).

A single-series show based on a Japanese manga comic, this attracted a loyal following for its buzzy pop soundtrack and attractive young male cast. Its stars, especially Min-ho, became as popular as the fictional F4 with obsessed teenage fans, who appreciated the series' binge-worthy, fluffy fun.

SEX EDUCATION

COMEDY • 2019
RATED: TV-MA • 52 MINS

Teenage relationships can be cringe-worthy enough—but what if your mom is a sexpert? Why not try putting all the knowledge she's passed along to you to good use, by opening up a secret sex clinic for your fellow students?

Otis Milburn (Asa Butterfield) is an ordinary school kid. That is, he's a bit shy and awkward around girls, despite the fact he has grown up with almost too much information about sex. Deciding to put his knowledge to use, he sets up a sex-advice clinic for his confused classmates with his bold and bright friend Maeve (Emma Mackey). But as it turns out, Otis might be the one most in need of guidance.

Audiences turned to Otis's advice en masse—this quirky British series' two seasons were a hit in both the UK and US. The show's premise is frank and funny, a perfect mix of hilarious plot lines and poignant touches. As Otis's mom Dr. Jean Milburn, Gillian Anderson breaks boundaries with panache.

JANE THE VIRGIN

COMEDY • 2014 • RATED: TV-14 • 60 MINS • SEASONS: 5
GINA RODRIGUEZ, ANDREA NAVEDO, YAEL GROBGLAS

A baby is not exactly what Miami waitress Jane ordered—but then you never know what's on life's big menu. When a completely unexpected pregnancy flips Jane's world upside down, she enters a spin that never seems to stop. Is her life turning into a Spanish *telenovela*?

Jane Villanueva (Gina Rodriguez) is a bright, bubbly 25-year-old in Miami who loves grilled cheese and God. She's been raised by her mother Xiomara (Andrea Navedo) and her grandmother Alba (Ivonne Coll), who is devoted both to her *telenovelas* (Spanish-language soap operas) and the Catholic church.

Jane works at a posh Miami hotel, while dreaming about becoming a writer and putting romantic distractions (such as boyfriend Michael Cordero Jr, played by Brett Dier) on the back burner. But in a mixup worthy of one of her grandmother's soap operas, Jane is accidentally inseminated on a visit to the doctor, and gives birth to a son. Her boss's son.

From this unusual premise, the five-season series twists and turns its way around Jane's new roller-coaster existence with son Mateo (Elias Jannsen). She wants to do her best for him, but she also yearns to live her life. Some of the plot lines and characters could be lifted straight out of a Mexican soap: there's a love triangle, a kidnapping, a scheming ex, a mystery twin, surprise triplets, a dead husband who suddenly reappears—maybe even a murder. But the show never shies away from Jane's real challenges as a parent, or her relationships, sacrifices, and dreams.

At its heart is the bond between daughter, mother, and grandmother. The love, respect, and wisdom uniting the three generations is handled expertly and realistically, with laughter and tears. Pay this family a visit.

GYPSY

THRILLER • 2017
RATED: TV-MA • 51 MINS

What if you had everything except for what you really wanted? A Manhattan therapist steps outside the boundaries of her perfect life, using her patients' information to fuel her fantasies.

Jean (Naomi Watts) is living the ultimate Manhattan story. She owns a successful therapy practice, and has a happy home with lawyer husband Michael (Billy Crudup).

Yet somehow her glass is half full. She meets Sidney (Sophie Cookson), a barista, and learns that Sidney's ex, Sam (Karl Glusman), is one of her patients. Using Sam's sessions to collect information on her new barista crush, Jean soon finds herself leading a secret double life.

Watts manages the balance between cookie-cutter happiness and the desire for secret thrills with sensitivity in this single-series drama. Trying to figure out why her character takes such extreme risks may yield more questions than answers, but it's an intriguing watch nonetheless.

LOVESICK

COMEDY • 2014
RATED: TV-MA • 24 MINS

Love is all around—but, unfortunately, so are STDs. A young man has the painful task of getting in touch with all of his former partners to pass along some less-than-romantic news.

With a lot of charm but sometimes not much of a clue, Dylan Witter (Johnny Flynn) is not the luckiest in love. Contracting an STD seems very unlucky indeed, but it sends Dylan and his best friends Evie (Antonia Thomas) and Luke (Daniel Ings) on a funny and often touching quest—finding and sharing the news with all the women Dylan has had relationships with.

The show moves between Dylan's past and present with clever flashbacks. All three characters are incredibly watchable, while there's the odd plot twist to keep you guessing, and as many ups and downs as a roller coaster. A three-season series that tells you about true friendship (and maybe, true love) without being mawkish or obvious, it's a surefire cure for whatever ails you.

MODERN LOVE

COMEDY ROMANCE • 2019
RATED: TV-MA • 30 MINS

True love and true stories played out in a city that has heard and seen it all. That's the premise behind this spin-off from a popular newspaper column and podcast exploring love and friendship in modern New York.

Real relationship-based reads come to life in this anthology series. From a blind date gone wrong, to a marriage at a turning point, a friendship that breaks the rules, and a new family trying to impose some, each episode is based on a true confession.

The New York Times' "Modern Love" column has been running every week since October 2004, and this (so far) one-season series captures its diverse picture of modern relationships. The broad variety of tales, trials, troubles, and familiar faces—guest stars include everyone from Anne Hathaway to Tina Fey and Dev Patel—is appealing. While it sometimes risks sliding into sentiment, the quality pulls it through.

THE HOOKUP PLAN

COMEDY • 2018
RATED: TV-MA • 27 MINS

Two years after a breakup, a woman is still struggling to dip her toe in the dating pool. So her best friends decide to fix her up with the perfect man. But is he just a little too perfect ... almost professional?

Elsa (Zita Hanrot) feels like she'll be stuck as a single person forever. So her well-meaning friends Charlotte (Sabrina Ouzani) and Emilie (Joséphine Draï) concoct a plan to help her feel confident again—they secretly hire a male escort to date her. What could possibly go wrong? Almost everything, it seems—though Elsa and escort Jules (Marc Ruchmann) seem to get along just fine.

The premise might be based on deception, but this two-season French comedy is a refreshingly honest watch. Hanrot is a quirky heroine, and her relationships with her friends are true to life, especially when things come to a head. Give it a spin, enjoy the sights of Paris, and find out if money can, in fact, buy you love.

BONES

CRIME DRAMA • 2005
RATED: TV-14 • 40 MINS

A mismatched duo dig into murder cases based on the sketchiest of evidence—often just a pile of bones. But their evident attraction for each other makes this a show worth investigating.

Forensic anthropologist Temperance "Bones" Brennan (Emily Deschanel) and FBI agent Seeley Booth (David Boreanaz) work together to solve crimes that seem unsolvable. The pair are opposites but well matched: Brennan sticks to the facts with a steely resolve, while Booth trusts his gut instinct. Will their respect for each other turn into a deeper attraction?

Over 12 seasons, this comedy drama drew loyal fans for its appealing leads and pleasingly dense plots. Based upon author Kathy Reichs' crime novels, episodes tend to show a killing and someone getting caught. Yet the way they handle procedure, with strong support from the "squints" (the forensic experts who fill in the gaps) gives the show a reliable and steady appeal—no bones about it.

PUSHING DAISIES

FANTASY COMEDY • 2007
RATED: TV-PG • 44 MINS

A pie-maker with the ability to bring people back from the dead puts his skills to good use running a restaurant, helping solve crimes, and finding true love in this one-of-a-kind show.

Pie-shop owner Ned (Lee Pace) has a supernatural skill: he can bring dead people back to life by touching them. There are a couple of catches: when he touches them again, they go back to being dead. If he keeps them alive, someone else has to die. Ned's friend Emerson Cod (Chi McBride) figures out that he and Ned can make some money by reviving crime victims to solve their murders. But things get tricky when one of those victims is Ned's childhood crush, Chuck (Anna Friel).

Despite its quirkiness, wildly vibrant sets and costumes, and fanciful premise, this two-season show is sweet as pie. The love story with a twist is intriguing, and the supporting cast is in turns snappy, sparky, and plain strange. Irresistible entertainment.

CASTLE

CRIME DRAMA • 2009
RATED: TV-14 • 43 MINS

When a famous crime novelist meets a real-life detective, he's so smitten he builds a new character around her. Soon, the pair are writing their own love story.

When a serial killer starts to copy the murders in his books, playboy crime writer Rick Castle (Nathan Fillion) turns to the New York police for help. Intrigued after Detective Kate Beckett (Stana Katic) unravels the mystery, he gets permission to shadow her on the job in order to create a new heroine. At first, no-nonsense Kate finds him annoying, but Rick turns out to be a natural in solving crimes.

The relationship between the two leads offers a nice mix of spiky and sweet. Rick's wisecracking breaks through Kate's tough shell, and she also proves surprising when she lets her guard down. The series stumbles a bit in the final two of its eight seasons, but enjoyable performances, strong storytelling, and a sprinkling of fun helped it grow an audience.

THE OFFICE (UK)

COMEDY • 2001 • RATED: TV-MA • 30 MINS • SEASONS: 2
RICKY GERVAIS, MARTIN FREEMAN, MACKENZIE CROOK

The company slogan may be "life is stationery," but it's all happening at paper firm Wernham Hogg, with an overbearing boss working too hard to be everyone's best friend, a budding romance, and office rivalries aplenty.

The Slough branch of paper company Wernham Hogg is packed with much more than boxes of stationery. At the helm is buffoonish manager David Brent (Ricky Gervais) and his ever-annoying assistant Gareth Keenan (Mackenzie Crook). Meanwhile, comparatively normal Tim Canterbury (Martin Freeman) and Dawn Tinsley (Lucy Davis) make eyes across the office, which is heading for a shutdown.

Gervais and Stephen Merchant's award-winning sitcom follows its characters from the viewpoint of a fly-on-the-wall documentary. Anyone who's ever stuck a passive-aggressive note on a half-empty cup of yogurt in an office fridge will relate to its cringeworthy antics. As uncomfortable at times as a broken office chair, yet as hilarious as a stapler in Jell-o, this mockumentary hit on so many universal truths about office life that it became a franchise in several countries. Gervais in particular is perfect as the non-self-aware, yet still human Brent, while Freeman's bemused Tim is ideal as that guy you always share a laugh with at the photocopier. Along with a strong supporting cast, it all helps create a series you're eager to stay with well past quitting time.

> **"** *Tim's put my stapler inside a jelly again. That's the third time he's done it.* **"**
>
> **Gareth** (SI EI)

MISS FISHER'S MURDER MYSTERIES

MYSTERY DRAMA • 2012
RATED: TV-PG • 60 MINS

A chic private eye solves crimes in 1920s Melbourne. Whether tackling a high-society case or sorting out the low life, this flapper never gets in a flap.

Returning home, Australian heiress Phryne Fisher (Essie Davis) is drawn into a murder case. The local police, headed by Inspector Jack Robinson (Nathan Page), don't take her seriously, but they soon discover that behind the flirtatiousness, fun, and fab wardrobe, Miss Fisher is a smart detective. With her companion Dot Williams (Ashleigh Cummings), she unravels crime after crime like a silk scarf.

Based on the books by Kerry Greenwood, this show not only has a strong female lead of an in-between age, but also a stable of women writers who give it a fresh edge and allow it to pursue some gently feminist themes. Over three series, Fisher's attitude and killer wardrobe have made this a cult favorite.

THE OFFICE (US)

COMEDY • 2005 • RATED: TV-14 • 22 MINS • SEASONS: 9
STEVE CARELL, JENNA FISCHER, JOHN KRASINSKI

It's another nine to five at the Dunder Mifflin Paper Company. The firm is teetering on the brink, and so is the staff. But just like a cookie in your lunch box, something can come along every episode to make you smile.

An ill-matched group of clock-watching, paper-pushing, pen-stealing colleagues work at a struggling paper company in Scranton, Pennsylvania. Their needy boss, Michael Scott (Steve Carell), is a relentless cheerleader, desperate to be loved. But his efforts to win over his staff have the tendency to fall flat. Everyone seems to be going through the motions, one meeting at a time. Yet there is

still plenty on the agenda for this group of coworkers, and following their everyday lives, documentary style, turns out to be a bonus.

The Scranton office is staffed by a group of ultimately loveable characters, even if they don't all come across as such when you first meet them. There's Jim Halpert (John Krasinski), a likeable salesperson who has ambitions beyond playing practical jokes. Dwight Schrute (Rainn Wilson), the target of most of Jim's pranks, is an awkward grump who secretly needs his colleagues so much he would probably turn up at parties if he could. Pam Beesly (Jenna Fisher) is the shy receptionist with hidden depths (and Jim's

---

CLASSIC PRANKS JIM HAS PLAYED ON DWIGHT

Jim hides Dwight's stapler in Jell-o. (S1 E1)

Jim sends faxes to Dwight from "Future Dwight." (S3 E7)

Jim moves Dwight's desk to the men's toilets. (S2 E6)

Jim puts Dwight's stuff in the vending machine. (S2 E11)

Jim wraps Dwight's work area in wrapping paper (or has he?). (S5 E11)

Jim replaces Dwight's pens with crayons. (S2 E21)

partner in crime). Add in others such as world-weary Stanley Hudson (Leslie David Baker), cat-obsessed Angela Martin (Angela Kinsey), flirty Kelly Kapoor (Mindy Kaling), and sad-sack HR executive Toby Flenderson (Paul Lieberstein), and you have the recipe for comedy gold.

The show is based on the British series of the same name (see p153), and many of the US characters are inspired by their UK counterparts. In its first season, *The Office* may have photocopied its parent show a bit too closely, though. American audiences weren't so used to the dark edge and cringeworthy humor. But gradually, the series found its own identity. Its portrayal of boring office life and irritating coworkers remains, but with a touch more optimism in the mix.

Not much goes on at Dunder Mifflin. Only the coffee pot is refreshed. The repetitive hamster wheel of the working day provides a solid theme to explore—and one many people can relate to—but the show keeps going through nine seasons by allowing its characters to grow. In the first few seasons, most of the narrative is set in the office or the warehouse. From a hideous training session and endless, needless meetings, to a performance review that is the stuff of nightmares, and a team-building office Olympic games, there is plenty to empathize with and laugh about. But as things progress, you get to see more of the characters in their out-of-office lives.

You even get to meet one of the fictional crew working on the Dunder Mifflin documentary—if you can believe it.

As much as these changes move the narrative along, a little something of what made the series so good in the first place does end up getting lost on the way here. However, even as *The Office* clocks in for its final episode, its own performance review remains strong. Pull up an uncomfortable desk chair, help yourself to a mug of weak coffee in a "Number One Boss" novelty mug, and enjoy.

> **"** *What're you doing?*
> *I am in the fight of my life*
> *against this computer and*
> *every sale counts!* **"**
>
> **Dwight** (S4 E3)

CREATORS: Greg Daniels, Ricky Gervais, Stephen Merchant **PRODUCTION CO:** Reveille Productions, NBC Universal Television, 3 Arts Entertainment, Deedle-Dee Productions, UMS, Universal Television

I LOVE DICK

COMEDY • 2016
RATED: TV-MA • 25 MINS

Dear Dick: a woman is obsessed with you. Her husband just might be, too. She's also putting down her innermost thoughts about you in letters she never sends. Where will it all end?

Chris Kraus (Kathryn Hahn) is a struggling filmmaker who moves with her writer husband Sylvère Lotringer (Griffin Dunne) to an artsy desert town in Texas. Sylvère has been invited by charismatic cowboy/artist Dick (Kevin Bacon), who soon becomes the object of Chris's obsession. She pours out her feelings to him in a series of unsent letters, prompting her to ask deeper questions about who she is and what she wants.

Based on the memoir-novel of the same name, this one-season series explores some of the big issues about being human—as Chris pushes her own boundaries, everyone is drawn into the chaos. You might think a show this personal would be hard to watch, but strong performances, especially from Hahn, pull you in.

BEING MARY JANE

DRAMA • 2013
RATED: TV-14 • 60 MINS

TV anchor Mary Jane seems to have it all in life—but some things she has a little too much of, including family drama, clashes at work, and most of all, relationship struggles. Can she find a love as strong as she is?

Star anchor of morning show *Great Day USA*, Mary Jane Paul (Gabrielle Union) seems to have a life as polished and perfect as her TV persona. But behind the screen, Mary Jane is not having a great day. Like so many modern women, she's trying to manage the work/life/love balance, often with the advice of her producer and pal Kara Lynch (Lisa Vidal).

In this five-season drama, Union gives her character a breezy bravado that helps get her through anything the series writers throw at her—and that's a lot—as she searches for happiness, stability, and the real unicorn: a dream man. Her true-to-life friendship with Kara, highs and lows included, is especially fun to watch.

SHE'S GOTTA HAVE IT

COMEDY • 2017
RATED: TV-MA • 30 MINS

It's a love quadrangle as a young, independent-minded Brooklyn artist keeps relationships with three different men going at the same time.

Nola Darling (DeWanda Wise) believes in love. And she believes in living on her own terms. Her three romantic partners are the calmed-down grown-up Jamie Overstreet (Lyriq Bent), cool and cultured Greer Childs (Cleo Anthony), and fun-loving Mars Blackmon (Anthony Ramos). Along for the ride are her fearless female friends as she makes art and love in the heart of Brooklyn.

Adapted by Spike Lee from his 1986 film of the same name, this fun and flirtatious two-season series is a portrait of a young, independent black woman. Wise's Nola shares the same vivacious spirit as the movie Nola, but she's also thoroughly modern. Meanwhile, the borough of Brooklyn is a character in its own right, with the show weaving in issues such as gentrification and racism.

THE MINDY PROJECT

COMEDY • 2012
RATED: TV-14 • 30 MINS

A successful New York City doctor grows up hooked on the idea of the perfect romance, but her real-life relationships are far from perfect. Can she find happiness in the big city?

An accomplished obstetrician/gynecologist, Mindy Lahari (Mindy Kaling) is in love with love. While her work life is going well, she can't seem to make her relationships work—forever leading with her heart, only to land on her backside. Among the fellow doctors in contention are posh hunk Jeremy Reed (Ed Weeks) and best pal Danny Castellano (Chris Messina), while a motley crew of other colleagues keep the laughs going.

The six-season comedy is a great vehicle for breakout star Kaling. Her character's mishaps and missteps make it charmingly watchable. Although the premise runs out of steam from time to time, the romantic entanglements are often relatable and realistic, and the mix of wit and rom-com drama is winning.

NEW GIRL

COMEDY • 2011 • RATED: TV-14 • 22 MINS • SEASONS: 7
ZOOEY DESCHANEL, JAKE JOHNSON, MAX GREENFIELD

After yet another breakup, a quirky teacher moves into an LA loft apartment with three single men. Their lives are complicated, silly, sometimes sentimental, and packed with a surprising amount of emotion.

A bit quirky, a bit kooky, but undeniably interesting, Jess Day (Zooey Deschanel) bursts into her new roommates' lives just like she's known to burst into song. They are bartender Nick Miller (Jake Johnson), self-made cool guy Schmidt (Max Greenfeld), and sporty prankster Winston (Lamorne Morris). Together, as they move through different jobs and relationships, and mature (at least a little), their adventures are always engaging. Jess's childhood friend Cece (Hannah Simone) adds an edge to the mix.

Like her friends, Jess lives a more-or-less typical 30-something life, but in true sitcom style, everything is amplified. Over seven seasons, the group's romances—some far-flung and others a bit too close to home—plus their struggles with finding meaningful work, and the milestones they achieve along the way keep you engaged. Deschanel's endearing performance is a particular draw in a show that works to keep things fresh. Even when Jess is no longer the new girl, something different is always just around the corner for each character.

> **"**I'm living with three guys I met on the internet. And yeah, stranger danger is real.**"**
>
> **Jess** (S1 E2)

MOONLIGHTING

COMEDY DRAMA • 1985 • RATED: TV-PG • 60 MINS • SEASONS: 5
BRUCE WILLIS, CYBILL SHEPHERD, ALLYCE BEASLEY

Meet a model who never expected to be a detective, and a private detective who never thought he'd be working for a model. Together, they spy on would-be and maybe-not criminals, cheats, and killers. The main thing to detect? Romance.

After her agent defrauds her, all that model Maddie Hayes (Cybill Shepherd) is left with is her home and the Blue Moon detective agency, she'd owned as a tax write-off. Wisecracking David Addison (Bruce Willis) is the slightly scruffy charmer who runs the agency. Neither one likes the other, but as they work together to solve mysteries, they edge toward that greatest mystery of all: love.

The crime-solving doesn't really matter in this groundbreaking five-season series. Instead, the joy is in the sparkling scripts, the superbly crafted humor, the proper chemistry between the pair, and the playful liberties the writers take with the show. The familiar detective drama premise is completely turned on its head.

Long before breaking the fourth wall between character and viewer was commonplace, Shepherd and Willis smirk and spoof their way through each entertaining episode. The crazy running jokes and copious one-liners are often balanced by a sense of melancholy. Watching the pair fall out with each other while falling in love is a real, grown-up treat. *Moonlighting*'s daring approach had a huge influence on television, and that is no crime.

> *"Hey, we're a team. Partners, now and forever."*
>
> David (S2 E2)

BALLYKISSANGEL

DRAMA • 1996
RATED: TV-14 • 50 MINS

A young British priest gets sent to Ballykissangel, a small town in Ireland. The pub owner warns him that he's in for a chilly welcome, but he eventually warms to the small, gossipy town and its cast of real characters.

Almost before Father Peter Clifford (Stephen Tompkinson) has unpacked his bags in his new parish in rural Ireland, he's run into trouble with his superior, Father MacAnally (Niall Toibin), and bar owner Assumpta Fitzgerald (Dervla Kirwan). It's clear his first task will be to earn the trust of the suspicious townspeople.

Between the pub and the church, everyone knows what everyone else is up to, and surprisingly, it's quite a bit. The writers make the most of the small-town setting that's bursting at the seams with sometimes eccentric, always memorable characters. There are schemers, dreamers, and some pretty suspect holy miracles. Like its beautiful location, this six-season series has an overload of charm.

GAVIN & STACEY

COMEDY • 2007 • RATED: TV-14 • 30 MINS • SEASONS: 3
MATHEW HORNE, JOANNA PAGE, JAMES CORDEN

A couple who speak every day on the phone for work finally meet up in real life. Their backgrounds, families, friends, and worlds collide. Will they hang up or hang on?

Gavin (Mathew Horne) is an Essex man and Stacey (Joanna Page) lives in south Wales. When they decide to get together in person, the two opposites attract. So far, so sweet, but their families and friends can't help but get in the way. Gavin's football-mad best friend Smithy (James Corden) isn't giving up his barstool for Stacey just yet, while Stacey's friend Nessa (Ruth Jones) has a colorful past and is never short of an opinion or two. Romance blossoms into love and marriage, as this ordinary couple make an ordinary life seem ... much less ordinary.

couple's families, portrayed by a brilliant supporting cast that includes Alison Steadman and Rob Brydon, keep things lively.

Injecting a huge dose of comedy into a straightforward romance doesn't always work, but Corden and Jones's well-crafted scripts know where to find the laughs—and a handful of instant-classic catchphrases helps, too. As writers, the pair ensure that even characters who only appear once are full of zing—quite a feat. Although the show runs aground slightly in its final season, a 2019 Christmas special raked in huge ratings (in the UK 17.1 million viewers watched it live or on on-demand in the following week). Funny, sometimes touching, and with fans from Barry Island to Billericay, *Gavin & Stacey* is "lush" entertainment.

> **"** I know it's white, right, but who can honestly say, hand on heart, that they're a virgin these days? **"**

Stacey on wedding dresses (S1 E4)

This comedy with a heart won a legion of fans with its crackling scripts, strong performances, and winning mix of romance and laughs. The likeable loved-up leads are sweet, but often it's the rest of the cast who steal the scenes. Corden and Jones, the show's creators, spark with humor as the perfect sidekicks. And the

CREATORS: James Corden, Ruth Jones
PRODUCTION CO: Baby Cow Productions

GREY'S ANATOMY

DRAMA • 2005 • RATED: TV-14 • 41 MINS • SEASONS: 16
ELLEN POMPEO, SANDRA OH, PATRICK DEMPSEY

Yesterday, they were students. Today, they are interns. Follow a group of trainee medics as they struggle through myriad professional and personal trials. As they learn how to operate at the hospital, they must also figure out how best to operate in real life.

Dr. Meredith Grey (Ellen Pompeo) is scrubbed up and ready to join the other surgical interns starting their medical careers at Seattle Grace Hospital. As they learn and grow through life-and-death situations, the interns depend on each other as friends, sparring partners, and more. While healing patients is the name of the game, they also have to fix their own problems, finding their way as they mature as doctors and people.

The interwoven lives of the group become a huge draw. Alongside Pompeo's Grey, who is the daughter of a prominent surgeon, the original cast includes Derek Shepherd (Patrick Dempsey), Miranda Bailey (Chandra Wilson), Cristina Yang (Sandra Oh), and Richard Webber (James Pickens Jr).

Over its 16 seasons, a few key cast members leave and are replaced, but the show maintains your trust by pressing on with original storytelling and gripping drama. True, there's enough realistic hospital action to earn seasoned viewers an associate medical degree, but there are also laughs, love, and plenty of life lessons. Be sure to book an appointment.

> **"So that's what you do? Kiss McDreamy on your bad days?"**
>
> **Dr. Cristina Yang** (S1 E2)

STATION 19

ACTION DRAMA • 2018
RATED: TV-14 • 43 MINS

Swap doctors for firefighters, and you get this *Grey's Anatomy* spin-off set in a Seattle fire station, following chip-off-the-old-block Lieutenant Andrea "Andy" Herrera and her crew.

Grey's Anatomy began with a lead character in the same line of work as a parent and struggling to emerge from their shadow. The start of *Station 19* takes a leaf out of the same book, with Pruitt Herrera (Miguel Sandoval) stepping down as fire station captain, leaving his daughter Andy (Jaina Lee Ortiz) to forge her own path. From there the show goes for a similar formula, balancing the characters' life-and-death work with their personal lives.

After a decent start, the show makes tweaks for Season 3 that kick it up a notch—including stronger romantic story lines—and it's worth watching in parallel with *Grey's Anatomy* (they air back-to-back on ABC and there are crossovers between the two series). Now they just need a cop show to complete the set.

CABLE GIRLS

PERIOD DRAMA • 2017
RATED: TV-14 • 50 MINS

Four new female employees at Spain's first national phone company in 1928 get a taste of independence in this exuberant drama—before their world is shattered by the Civil War.

Dramas set between the World Wars always have a background tension due to the fact the audience know what's coming, and *Cable Girls* more than most. Lidia (Blanca Suárez), Carlota (Ana Fernández), María (Nadia de Santiago), and Ángeles (Maggie Civantos) are proud to be breaking free of oppressive and limiting social expectations. But we know Madrid will soon be on the front line of the looming conflict.

The series looks wonderful (helped by the '20s fashions) and the romantic story lines, along with the friendships between the characters— a mixed group of personalities drawn together by work—form a huge part of its appeal. Over five seasons, the movement of history pushes them in surprising and heartbreaking directions.

DR. QUINN, MEDICINE WOMAN

WESTERN DRAMA • 1993 • RATED: TV-PG • 60 MINS • SEASONS: 6
JANE SEYMOUR, JOE LANDO, SHAWN TOOVEY

The West has never seen anything wilder: the new doctor in the frontier town of Colorado Springs is a woman. Will she convince the suspicious locals that she's up to the task?

After her father dies, Boston-born Michaela Quinn (Jane Seymour) moves out west to Colorado Springs in 1867. The townspeople are not ready to accept a female physician, so "Mike" must win them over. Local mountain man and friend of the Cheyenne tribespeople Byron Sully (Joe Lando) gives her a welcome helping hand.

As she settles into her new home, Mike gradually earns people's trust—and also earns herself a family, parenting three recently orphaned children. Dr. Quinn is not a typical doctor, and this series is not a typical western.

Alongside the family-friendly drama, the writers touch on political issues, sexism, and the treatment of the poor, African Americans, and Native Americans. Seymour's character fights for the right to do what she wants to do every day, and believes that good medical care should be available to everyone, no matter who they are. Her endearing portrayal of Quinn as compassionate and steadfast earned both Seymour and the show a loyal fanbase.

Of course, the show is fictional and not created to be historically accurate in every way. The forward-thinking, pacifist attitudes of the doctor and her mountain-dwelling pal may not represent the way most frontier people thought at the time. Yet the six-season show stays true to itself and its ideals as family entertainment with a bit of grit.

DRACULA

HORROR • 2013
RATED: TV-14 • 43 MINS

A very different take on Bram Stoker's novel, in which Dracula and Van Helsing join forces to take on a power-hungry chivalric order.

Dracula (Jonathan Rhys Meyers) poses as American entrepreneur Alexander Grayson and enters Victorian London society. His aim is to get revenge on the Order of the Dragon (a real-life organization that had a connection to Dracula inspiration Vlad the Impaler), which hounded him centuries ago. Van Helsing (Thomas Kretschmann) is a former member of the Order, who's also out for vengeance.

This isn't really an adaptation of the novel. Instead, it takes the characters (sometimes just their names—Jonathan Harker, played by Oliver Jackson-Cohen, is a social-climbing journalist) and forges a new story around them. If you're not expecting to see the novel, there's much to enjoy, not the least of which is Rhys Meyers' portrayal. Sadly, it was canned after 10 episodes, cutting it off before the real chaos began.

THE ORIGINALS

FANTASY • 2013
RATED: TV-14 • 42 MINS

This spin-off from *The Vampire Diaries* is based around the original "Original" hybrid, Klaus Mikaelson. The half vampire, half werewolf is the self-styled King of New Orleans' French Quarter.

Introduced in Season 2 of *The Vampire Diaries* (see p417), Klaus (Joseph Morgan) is a member of the "Original" family, the first vampires created a thousand years ago in Norway, and the only one to have werewolf heritage as a result of his mother's infidelity. He and his siblings return to New Orleans— a city Klaus left in 1919—to find his protégé Marcel (Charles Michael Davis) in charge. Meanwhile, werewolf Hayley (Phoebe Tonkin) is pregnant with Klaus's child.

The scale of *The Originals'* family saga is ambitious, and it delves deep into the backstory of *The Vampire Diaries.* For that reason, it makes sense to watch the original series before you tackle *The Originals'* five seasons. But in many ways its complexity makes it the superior show.

TRUE BLOOD

FANTASY HORROR • 2008
RATED: TV-MA • 55 MINS

A world where vampires have come out of hiding forms the backdrop to this dark romance between a telepathic Louisiana waitress and a vampire who fought in the American Civil War.

Developed by Alan Ball (creator of *Six Feet Under*, see p339) from Charlaine Harris's *Southern Vampire Mysteries* novels, the title refers to the synthetic blood that has enabled vampires to be accepted as part of society—at least in theory. In fact, bloodsuckers such as Bill Compton (Stephen Moyer) are still treated with hostility—but not by Sookie Stackhouse (Anna Paquin), who is intrigued to find she is unable to read his mind like she can everyone else's.

True Blood starts in a world like ours—except with vampires—but its mythology spirals as it goes on, bringing in demons, shape-shifters, werewolves, werepanthers.... A great ensemble cast sustains its seven seasons well beyond the Sookie/Bill romance, helped along by a strong thread of humor.

BLOOD TIES

CRIME FANTASY • 2007
RATED: TV-14 • 43 MINS

This series centers on the classic odd couple, but with a twist: she's a private eye, he's the 470-year-old illegitimate vampire son of Henry VIII, who draws comics. Together, they fight crime.

Vicki Nelson (Christina Cox) set up her detective agency after quitting the Toronto Police Service as a result of an eye condition. Investigating the murder of the boyfriend of goth Coreen Fennel (Gina Holden), she runs into comic artist Henry Fitzroy (Kyle Schmid), who is also looking into the case, for fear it'll get pinned on a vampire—such as himself.

Blood Ties is so full of sexual tension—between Vicki and Henry, between Henry and Coreen, between Vicki and her former partner and on-off boyfriend Mike Celluci (Dylan Neal)—it's a wonder there's any room for crime solving. But over two seasons it covers a variety of supernatural mysteries, featuring zombies, ghosts, mummies, and more, making the most of its outré premise.

MOONLIGHT

FANTASY ROMANCE • 2007
RATED: 15 (UK) • 42 MINS

Private investigator and reluctant vampire Mick St. John takes cases in modern-day Los Angeles while trying to keep a low profile. And not fall in love.

When Mick (Alex O'Loughlin) investigates the murder of a college student—which seems to have been committed by vampires—he encounters reporter Beth Turner (Sophia Myles). Mick realizes to his alarm that they've met before: when Beth was a child, he rescued her from the same vampire who sired him—his ex-wife Coraline Duvall (Shannyn Sossamon), a former 18th-century Parisian courtesan.

While Mick's cases provide each episode with their structure, the ongoing hook is very much the relationship between him and Beth. Mick is drawn to her, but also fears they can never have a life together. Not that this means the relationship is endlessly deferred: things develop fast—which is just as well, since the show only lasted one season.

OH MY GHOST

FANTASY COMEDY • 2015
RATED: TV-14 • 60 MINS

The ghost of a young woman who died a virgin is determined to satisfy her lust, so she possesses the body of a timid assistant chef and embarks on a seduction mission.

Shin Soon-ae (Kim Seul-gi) believes the reason she can't move on to the afterlife is that she never had sex, and if she can only possess another woman and lose her virginity, this will resolve her business on Earth. The ideal vehicle for Soon-ae's quest is shy Na Bong-sun (Park Bo-young), who has a crush on her boss, celebrity chef Kang Sun-woo (Jo Jung-suk). As Bong-sun's confidence booms as a result of Soon-ae's intervention, Sun-woo suddenly sees her in a different light.

Oh My Ghost is an odd collision of genres—there's some mystery about Soon-ae's death, too—which it handles gleefully over its one season. As Sun-woo and Soon-ae's relationship progresses, it becomes a thoughtful show about personality and identity, as well as love.

COFFEE PRINCE

COMEDY • 2007
RATED: NR • 55 MINS

A young coffee-shop owner wants to earn his family's approval. A young tomboy just wants to earn money, even if she has to pretend to be a boy. Just what's brewing here?

Choi Han Kyul (Gong Yoo) is the wayward grandson of a coffee heiress. To prove his worth, he opens up a coffee shop. He hires Go Eun Chan (Yoon Eun-hye), a girl often mistaken for a boy who keeps the ruse going to support her family. Despite the pretense, the two grow fond of each other. Will Choi and Go pass the sugar?

Coffee might be black or white, but love isn't always that way. This single-series Korean comedy makes the most of the charisma between the leads to keep viewers hooked despite the somewhat silly premise. As the couple fall for each other, their mixed-up feelings (and a plan to outsmart grandma) add emotional depth to a straight comedy. You will warm to Go as a sweet and relatable heroine.

GENTLEMAN JACK

HISTORICAL DRAMA • 2019
RATED: TV-MA • 60 MINS

A woman returns to her family home in 1830s England, determined to fix up the place and open a coal mine. She also has some secrets under her top hat.

Anne Lister (Suranne Jones) is not an ordinary 19th-century British woman. After inheriting the family estate, bold and brilliant Lister returns to Yorkshire to restore the family fortunes. Other women might marry to fill the coffers, but Lister is not so inclined. She starts a romance with Ann Walker (Sophie Rundle), writing down her feelings in secret code.

Forbidden romance, lavish sets and costumes, family squabbles, and top hats: all the usual things to spot in a period drama are here in this one-season series. But it's the differences that make it so watchable: Jones's character is a woman strong and charismatic enough to prosper in a man's world. Based on Lister's real-life story, the same-sex romance and the story gives this drama rooted in the past a distinctly modern twist.

LIP SERVICE

DRAMA • 2010
RATED: 18 (UK) • 60 MINS

Three gay women in Glasgow experience the ups and downs of love and relationships as they search for their special someone.

Looking for love, whether in all the wrong or all the right places, is always complicated. Frankie (Ruta Gedmintas) has been looking in New York, but now she's back in Glasgow to come to terms with her past. Cat (Laura Fraser) hasn't been looking for a while, but she's decided to reenter the dating game. Meanwhile, Tess (Fiona Button) isn't sure how to look at all.

This two-season series weaves together the sometimes intense, sometimes funny stories of its main characters and their friends in true-to-life situations. A strong cast and excellent writing make for thought-provoking viewing that avoids the usual same-sex stereotypes. Mistakes are made, stuff happens, and sometimes things even work out—and anyone can empathize with things working out.

QUEER AS FOLK

DRAMA • 1999 • RATED: TV-MA • 48 MINS • SEASONS: 2
AIDAN GILLEN, CHARLIE HUNNAM, CRAIG KELLY

Two best friends in Manchester are clubbing and dancing their way into their 30s. When a young man joins the circle, things are bound to change. Is three the magic number?

Stuart Jones (Aidan Gillen) knows he looks good on the dance floor. Handsome, charming, and maybe a little bit full of himself, he is best friends with Vince Tyler (Craig Kelly). Vince has a more low-key, boyish appeal, and a bit of a secret thing for Stuart that never goes anywhere, despite Vince's loyalty to his friend. A brash 15-year-old boy, Nathan Maloney, (Charlie Hunnam) catches Stuart's eye, but won't leave Stuart and Vince alone, thinking he's found love.

One of the first television shows to focus on the everyday lives of gay characters, the show certainly caused a stir (and drew audiences of more than three million). Creator Russell T. Davies did not shy away from any aspect of his character's personal lives. Yet it is the strength of the lead performances, not the racy parts, that drew an audience. Aiden Gillen's Stuart

can be a real piece of work, and Vince has his moments, too, but you still want things to work out for them, despite the occasional broken heart. Hunnam is fun to watch as that annoying teenager who knows everything, but still has a great deal to learn.

It's not all discos and dancefloors. While the show avoids any heavy agenda, it covers quite a lot of issues—from difficult relationships with parents and peers, to homophobia, and knowing when it's time to grow out of the scene and grow up. As in all the most successful dramas, the characters draw you in and keep you wondering. These folks are well worth watching.

> **"**We don't do hammers, or nails, or saws. We do joints and screws, but that's different.**"**
>
> Stuart (S2 E1)

AMAZON RIDERS

ACTION FANTASY • 2016
RATED: TV-PG • 45 MINS

Heroes. Villains. People-eating monsters. Plus, a couple of outsiders who show they have what it takes to do the right thing. What's not to love?

This Japanese show is the perfect introduction to the Kamen Rider genre that tends to feature motorcycle-riding superheroes wearing insect-inspired costumes. In it, an experiment goes wrong. Thousands of artificial life forms called Amazons develop a taste for human flesh. A team of mercenaries gathers to hunt down the Amazons. They encounter Haruka Mizusawa (Tom Fujita), a shy, conflicted loner infected by Amazon cells. Along for the hunt is Jin Takayama (Masashi Taniguchi), a former scientist who wants to crush the flesh-eating monsters as mysterious fighter Amazon Alpha.

This two-season show has less of a focus on special effects than previous Kamen Rider titles and more on developing a deeper backstory. The attempt to develop character over costume makes this a welcome addition.

DARK ANGEL

SCI-FI DRAMA • 2000
RATED: TV-14 • 60 MINS

A genetically engineered supersoldier seeks to evade government capture and search for others like her in post-apocalyptic Seattle.

Max (Jessica Alba) was created in a laboratory as a creepy experiment. Now, 10 years later, she and her "siblings" have escaped, and she spends her days looking for them around the city. After meeting journalist Logan Cale (Michael Weatherly), who is investigating high-level corruption, Max agrees to use her lab-engineered superhero powers to help him. But someone from her past is looking for Max.

Alba puts in a solid performance as the bike messenger by day, supercharged heroine by night in this sometimes overlooked show created by blockbuster film director James Cameron. The series found its feet in its second and final season, after the plot was established and new characters had been added. If you like action with your sci-fi, it's worth experimenting with this.

SENSE8

SCI-FI DRAMA • 2015
RATED: TV-MA • 60 MINS

People—we're all the same, right? What if eight individuals across the globe could suddenly share the same thoughts, skills, visions, and feelings?

Eight complete strangers, all very different, have a strange vision, then find themselves linked mentally and emotionally. They are sensates—connected together even when they are apart. They don't know what is happening or why, or what it means. They get help from another sensate, the mysterious Jonas (Naveen Andrews). Meanwhile, a shadowy figure called Whispers (Terrence Mann) pursues them, hoping to break the connection and use the sensates' powers against them.

Created by the Wachowskis (the brains behind *The Matrix*) and J. Michael Straczynski (creator of *Babylon 5*—see p115), the show features diverse, compelling characters and a creative story. The two seasons use its talented cast to bring complex social issues into the spotlight. Try it—it's not your usual TV sci-fi fare.

STAR-CROSSED

SCI-FI ROMANCE • 2014
RATED: TV-14 • 60 MINS

A human girl and an alien boy fall in love in high school. Some people think all teenage boys are from another planet, but this one is the real deal.

Humans are battling a new alien species, the Atrians, who have crash-landed on Earth. As a little girl, Emery (Aimee Teegarden) protects and befriends alien boy Roman (Matt Lanter). The authorities take him away, and the next time Emery sees him, he has joined her high school as part of an integration program. They renew their bond, but politics and prejudice make things difficult. Will this Romeo-and-Juliet relationship survive?

Stories about disapproved-of teenage romances are nothing new, but one in which the boy is a tattooed alien might offer something different. Teegarden and Lanter create sparks as the sweethearts, while the supporting cast of class clowns, popular kids, and outsiders make things fun. If sweet and soapy sci-fi doesn't sound too alien to you, give this single-season series a try.

LA FEMME NIKITA

ACTION • 1997 • RATED: NR • 60 MINS • SEASONS: 5
PETA WILSON, DON FRANCKS, EUGENE ROBERT GLAZER

A young woman is wrongly convicted of murdering a police officer. She is sentenced to life in prison, but faces a stark choice: join a shadowy group as an assassin, or face death in jail.

Framed for murder and facing a life sentence, Nikita (Peta Wilson) gets a second chance of sorts. If she joins the secret anti-terrorism group called Section One as an assassin, it's a get-out-of-jail card. Nikita is not sure why she has been chosen, but she opts to join the organization, where she falls for her mentor, Michael (Roy Dupuis). However, the group, led by the ruthless Operations (Eugene Robert Glazer) and second in command Madeline (Alberta Watson), want to keep the two apart. The trouble is, when you live in a world of lies, how do you know whom to believe?

Based on the French film *Nikita*, the five-season series was not an exact copy, but equally captivating. The well-crafted characters have to decide when to cross the line between doing their jobs and doing the right thing, and menace is never far away. Wilson's Nikita is an exceptionally strong woman played with intelligence and skill, and Dupuis is ideal as an operative for a secret agency.

Will Nikita find herself again, or disappear into the darkness of the organization? Finding out is a mission well worth undertaking.

> **"** *You could learn to shoot, you can learn to fight, but there's no weapon as powerful as your femininity.* **"**
>
> Madeline (S1 E1)

INSECURE

COMEDY • 2016
RATED: TV-MA • 30 MINS

A young woman in LA juggles work, friends, and relationships while looking for love. Will she trade the insecurity of her 20s for security in her 30s?

Issa Dee (Issa Rae) and her good friend Molly (Yvonne Orji) are making it through life with speed bumps along the way. Whether it's problems at work, relationships gone wrong, the race issues they face as young African-Americans, or just the everyday things that life brings, the pair depend on each other to stay focused. As they head into their 30s, their priorities change, but their bond stays deep.

Cocreator Rae's web series *Awkward Black Girl* was the inspiration for this four-season show. Both Rae and Orji's antics and experiences feel relatable and authentic, and the emotional intensity and on-the-nose humor between the women ring true. This engaging pair strive and sometimes fail, but always share a laugh. Their friendship, if nothing else, is secure.

LIVING WITH YOURSELF

COMEDY DRAMA • 2019
RATED: TV-MA • 26 MINS

A man fed up with life undergoes medical treatment that creates a superior cloned version of himself. There's only room for one of them in this world, but which one?

Miles Elliot (Paul Rudd) feels like he's running on empty. After undergoing a strange treatment at a spa, he wakes up to find himself replaced by a duplicate. The new Miles (also Paul Rudd) is doubly nice, approaching everything, including his wife Kate (Aisling Bea), with enthusiasm. He becomes quite the success, but something's got to give.

It's a fun idea, but there's also food for thought here. Through Miles's predicament, the single season explores what sets us apart. We see situations from the perspective of both Miles and new Miles, which keeps things interesting. Rudd is typically charming in both roles, and Bea is outstanding in what could have been an ordinary part, delivering a performance that deserves its own double-take.

ON MY BLOCK

COMEDY DRAMA • 2018
RATED: TV-14 • 30 MINS

High school is tough, but South Central LA is tougher. Can four teenage friends handle both and make the best of what they've got?

The teenagers live in a rough neighborhood where gang violence is the norm, poverty is all around, and racism is painfully real. Yet this doesn't define them in the same way as their friendship does. Cesar (Diego Tinoco), Ruby (Jason Genao), Jasmine (Jessica Marie Garcia), and Monse (Sierra Capri) live their everyday lives against a difficult background with humor, emotion, and a whole lot of trust for each other.

This three-series show won praise for its diversity and realism. The creators kept the serious stuff on the table, but concentrated on the cast. The issues are there, but it's the fantastic chemistry between the characters that made the show so watchable. They are funny, nerdy, bright, and ultimately uplifting. Spend some time in their neighborhood.

MY SO-CALLED LIFE

COMEDY DRAMA • 1994 • RATED: TV-14 • 48 MINS • SEASONS: 1
CLAIRE DANES, WILSON CRUZ, JARED LETO

Even if you are smart and self-aware, being a teenager can be stupid sometimes. A 15-year-old girl living in a Pittsburgh suburb is trying to figure it all out.

Angela Chase (Claire Danes) wants to be true to herself. She just needs to figure out who that self actually is. Her mother Patty (Bess Armstrong) and father Graham (Tom Irwin) think they know, but as a typical suburban family—albeit with a female main breadwinner—they have their own issues. Angela's old friends think they know her, but her new friends, the uninhibited Rayanne Graff (A.J. Langer) and the misfit Rickie Vasquez (Wilson Cruz), show Angela there is another side to herself. Her crush Jordan Catalano (Jared Leto) is her fantasy.

For a show that lasted just one season, My So-Called Life had a lasting impact. Danes's Angela wasn't like other teen female characters on television. She had a voice, she was candid about her feelings, and she was real. Her narration revealed the scope of the massive changes she was going through. Danes was not afraid to show pain, confusion, terror—all the emotions that were sometimes lacking from more stereotypical portraits of teenage girls at the time. Her character struggled with her white, suburban background and parental expectations, and sometimes these attitudes stuck, no matter how much she wanted to change. Angela was hardly perfect, but Danes was spot-on in the role.

The show broke barriers in several ways. Vasquez played one of the first gender-fluid teen characters on television. Teen sex was a subject for frank discussion, as were traditional gender roles. Other series aimed at teens might have used music and fashion as add-ons, but here both were an integral part of identity. Interestingly, My So-Called Life was also one of the first shows to be the subject of an intensive internet campaign to save it after it was canceled. Why not brighten your own life a little by checking it out?

> **"***I bet people can actually die of embarrassment. I bet it's been medically proven.***"**
>
> **Angela** (S1 E2)

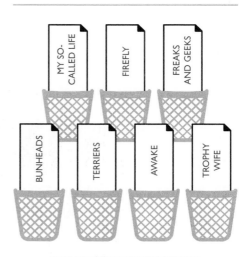

TV SHOWS CONTROVERSIALLY
CANNED AFTER ONE SERIES

CREATOR: Winnie Holzman **PRODUCTION CO:** The Bedford Falls Company, ABC Productions, ABC Video Enterprises, Capital Cities Television Productions

SEX AND THE CITY

COMEDY • 1998 • RATED: TV-MA • 30 MINS • SEASONS: 6
SARAH JESSICA PARKER, KIM CATTRALL, CYNTHIA NIXON

Mainstream TV had never been so frank about the female sexual experience before this iconic 1990s show. So, slip on a pair of Manolo Blahniks (shoes, for the uninitiated), pour a cosmopolitan, and join Carrie and friends in their sexual adventures (and misadventures).

Carrie Bradshaw (Sarah Jessica Parker) writes a column about people's sex lives in New York City, using her own experiences and those of her three best friends as inspiration. While Carrie and her pals search the city for their perfect matches, they already have two in place: their friendship with each other and a shared love of New York City.

This group of friends are no stereotypical besties. Samantha Jones (Kim Cattrall) is a risk-taker and sexual adventurer. In one memorable episode she meets her match in a man who has a sex swing. Although Samantha

vows to have relationships with no strings attached, she discovers there are some ties that bind. Charlotte York (Kristin Davis), who works in an art gallery, is an idealistic achiever, and a true believer in romance, yet is far from timid in her search for Mr. Right. Lawyer Miranda Hobbes (Cynthia Nixon) is the voice of reason and a realist about love. Her on-again, off-again relationship with Steve Brady has its ups and downs, including his testicular cancer diagnosis and her unexpected pregnancy.

> *" Why are there so many great unmarried women, and no great unmarried men?"*
>
> **Carrie Bradshaw** (S1 E1)

SOME OF THE HIGHS AND LOWS OF CARRIE AND BIG'S RELATIONSHIP

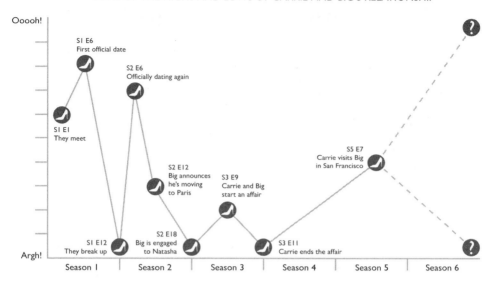

Ooooh!

S1 E6
First official date

S2 E6
Officially dating again

S1 E1
They meet

S5 E7
Carrie visits Big
in San Francisco

S2 E12
Big announces
he's moving
to Paris

S3 E9
Carrie and Big
start an affair

S2 E18
Big is engaged
to Natasha

S1 E12
They break up

S3 E11
Carrie ends the affair

Argh!

Season 1   Season 2   Season 3   Season 4   Season 5   Season 6

Meanwhile, Carrie herself has several love interests—notably Aiden Shaw (John Corbett) and Aleksandr Petrovsky (Mikhail Baryshnikov)—but none can hold a candle to the charismatic Mr. Big (Chris Noth), whom she meets in the very first episode. Each of the four women has their own perspective on love and relationships, so there is plenty for the series to explore.

The show was based on author Candace Bushnell's own newspaper column (which started in *The New York Observer* in 1994) and bestselling book of the same name. Like the source material, the show offers wit and wisdom alongside a look at '90s women's lives and how their place in the greater world can influence their relationships. There is also fashion. The characters became genuine style icons, and each dressed to express: from Samantha's vivid, block colors to Charlotte's classic shift dresses and Miranda's suits. In particular, Carrie's quirky style, mixing high fashion with thrift-store finds (not to mention her nameplate necklace), was an inspiration to many fans.

Sex and the City made stars of all four leads. Their portrayal of loving, loyal female friendship was a joy, as was their honesty about their own desires. Of course, their characters were far from perfect, and none of them ever really had it all, although they gave it a good try.

Looking back now on the series, there are moments that make you wince, and some critics have slammed the women's desperate quest to find a relationship—why do they feel they need a man at all? You could argue they are already complete. They're genuinely happy being single, they're opinionated, they take control of their lives, they're optimistic about the future no matter what, and they depend on the support and acceptance of their female friends.

Four bright, strong female leads. A friendship built on love and respect. And shoes—lots of shoes. *Sex and the City* deserves its accolades.

CREATOR: Darren Star
PRODUCTION CO: Darren Star Productions, HBO, Sex and the City Productions

NORMAL PEOPLE

DRAMA • 2020
RATED: TV-MA • 30 MINS

A small-screen adaptation of Sally Rooney's hit novel about an on-again, off-again young relationship proves just as addictive and heartbreaking as the book.

This 12-episode stand-alone series follows popular athlete Connell (Paul Mescal) and loner Marianne (Daisy Edgar-Jones), who embark on a secret relationship in their last year of school in a small town in Ireland. Like the novel, the 30-minute episodes offer interludes into the pair's lives as they go on to college—and as they try to stay apart but find that they just can't.

Awkward, magnetic, and often steamy, this messy portrayal of young love is phenomenally acted by the two leads (and entire cast), with Mescal and Edgar-Jones conveying perfectly, and often wordlessly, what their characters are thinking. As all-consuming and tantalizing as your first love, this near-perfect adaptation is binge-worthy drama at its best.

SOUNDTRACK

MUSICAL DRAMA • 2019
RATED: TV-MA • 56 MINS

The lives and loves of a group of people living in Los Angeles are interwoven with song and dance in this unusual musical drama series.

Nellie (Callie Hernandez) is a poor little rich girl, with plenty of money but no luck in love. Sam (Paul James) is a rich little poor boy, with abundant singing and songwriting talent but no money. When they connect, their differences nearly keep them apart, but they are soon singing—or rather lip-synching—a love song together.

This show is that rarest of things: a television musical. Even more unusually, no one actually breaks into song. Instead, they lip-synch to a soundtrack of tunes that reveal their feelings. It's a unique approach, a bit too clever at times, but it's easy to get lost in the fantasy. If that sounds like music to your ears, give this 10-episode series a spin.

HART OF DIXIE

COMEDY • 2011
RATED: TV-PG • 60 MINS

A new doctor has big ambitions in the big city. But when things go wrong, she takes a job opportunity in a small southern town. Can this woman from the Big Apple take Bluebell, Alabama?

Dr. Zoe Hart (Rachel Bilson) finds out that her real dad runs a medical practice in the small town of Bluebell—and after he dies, half of it is hers. So, she moves down south, where she encounters hostility from dad's former partner Brick Breeland (Tim Matheson) and his daughter Lemon (Jaime King). Meanwhile, one of her new neighbours is acting more than neighborly.

This show doesn't try to be anything but what it is: quirky and warm entertainment. Over four seasons, there are no complicated backstories, no wrestling with social issues—just a charming story. Yet the story lines are often surprisingly moving, and King in particular is wonderful to watch, as her small town meanie matures—just a little. It's the best possible southern comfort.

NASHVILLE

MUSICAL DRAMA • 2012 • RATED: TV-PG • 43 MINS • SEASONS: 6
HAYDEN PANETTIERE, CLARE BOWEN, CONNIE BRITTON

A country superstar may shine on stage, but there's always someone waiting in the wings to take their place. Follow the rise and fall of the genre's stars in the Music City.

Rayna Jaymes (Connie Britton) is country music royalty, but her crown is aging. Country's new princess is Juliette Barnes (Hayden Panettiere), who even has her eye on Rayna's guitar player and main flame Deacon (Charles Esten). All across Nashville, singers, songwriters, and producers are doing whatever it takes to have a hit record. They don't care whom they push aside on the way up—until they meet them on the way down.

What do you get when you mash up the *Grand Ole Opry* radio show with soap opera? This six-season country music drama, which benefits from a fast-paced story line, wonderful location filming, and a cast of seasoned television actors. Britton is especially

good as the country legend with a heart of gold. What's more, the actors perform the show's original songs themselves.

Nashville's clash between ambition and personal relationships feels all too real, and its portrayal of one character's struggle with addiction is also well judged. Sometimes the soapy stuff overflows, but this show can tug your heartstrings like a good country ballad.

> **"**I don't have friends. I have people who want to be seen with me.**"**
>
> Juliette (SI E4)

THE GET DOWN

MUSICAL DRAMA • 2016
RATED: TV-MA • 52 MINS

A group of teenagers come of age in the South Bronx in 1977. The disco ball is still spinning and hip hop is bubbling underneath. Ready to get down?

Zeke (Justice Smith) is a DJ with a gift for words. He hopes his rhymes will take him to the top with his streetwise graffiti artist partner, Curtis Shaolin Fantastic (Shameik Moore). Mylene (Herizen F. Guardiola),

Zeke's long-time crush, wants to sing her way out of the Bronx. The obstacles all three face are huge—gangs rule the streets, poverty is everywhere, families don't always understand them, and the music business is competitive.

As film director Baz Luhrmann's first TV series, this single-season show looks and sounds amazing. The visuals are authentic and beyond cool. The cast, largely unknown, are genuine and put in the most heartfelt performances, especially Smith's magnetic Zeke. This affectionate portrait of 1970s New York hits all the right notes.

JAM & JERUSALEM

COMEDY • 2006
RATED: TV-14 • 30 MINS

Jennifer Saunders' follow-up to _Absolutely Fabulous_ is a complete contrast—a more sedate series set among the Women's Guild in the small town of Clatterford St. Mary.

Practice nurse Sal (Sue Johnston) loses her job after her husband, the local doctor, dies. At a loss, she joins the Women's Guild at the urging of her friend, indiscreet medical receptionist

Tip (Pauline McLynn). There she finds an odd mix of characters, from Rosie (Dawn French), who suffers from a split personality, to church organist Delilah (Joanna Lumley), wealthy namedropper Caroline (Saunders), and self-appointed chairwoman Eileen (Maggie Steed).

Saunders based the show on her experience of living in a place like Clatterford, and the result is keenly observed: the town is a bubble where minor problems are magnified and gossip spreads like wildfire. Subtler than _Ab Fab_, it's anchored by Johnston's understated but often hilarious turn over its three seasons.

LOIS & CLARK: THE NEW ADVENTURES OF SUPERMAN

FANTASY • 1993
RATED: TV-PG • 46 MINS

One of the smartest Super Hero reinventions, _Lois & Clark_ won over a whole new audience to Superman by bringing its rom-com side to the fore.

In the early '90s, _Superman_ was dead as a film series following the disappointing _Superman IV: The Quest for Peace_. Writer-producer

Deborah Joy LeVine reworked the character for TV, placing the emphasis on Clark Kent (Dean Cain) rather than Superman, and giving Lois Lane (Teri Hatcher) equal prominence. The result, harking back to screwball comedies such as _His Girl Friday_, was a huge hit.

Viewed now, _Lois & Clark_ is a charming halfway house between the camp antics of the 1960s _Batman_ series and today's more character arc-based Super Hero shows. Its willingness to keep moving and not maintain its status quo is laudable, but perhaps also why its popularity dipped sharply in its fourth and final season.

BEAUTY AND THE BAKER

COMEDY ROMANCE • 2013
RATED: NR • 33 MINS

It's a tale as old as time: an international supermodel falls in love with a humble baker and, despite coming from two different worlds, they try to make their relationship work.

The beauty of the title, Noa Hollander (Rotem Sela), is also an heiress, and lives a life of wealth and privilege. The baker, Amos Dahari (Aviv Alush), lives with his parents and

earns minimum wage. They meet in a restaurant in Tel Aviv just as Noa has broken up with her boyfriend, and Amos is about to break up with his girlfriend.

On one level, _Beauty and the Baker_ is a male fantasy of an ordinary guy who gets together with a supermodel, but it has depth as well as gloss, exploring the ethnic divisions between Israelis in a comical way (Noa's family are Ashkenazi Jews, Amos's are Yemenite Jews). Running for two seasons, it was a huge hit in Israel, and spawned an American remake in 2020.

THE GOOD WIFE

DRAMA • 2009
RATED: TV-14 • 43 MINS

When a major corruption and sex scandal results in a state attorney going to prison, his wife revives her legal career to support her family.

Although once an outstanding law student, graduating top of her class, Alicia Florrick's (Julianna Margulies) own career always took a back seat to that of her husband Peter (Chris Noth). But now he's behind bars, the only option is to start climbing the career ladder after 13 years as a stay-at-home mother. Starting from the bottom rung as a junior litigator, Alicia is required to prove herself all over again.

It's easy to see why *The Good Wife* resonated with audiences: the premise starkly lays out the sacrifices women make for men who often aren't worth it, and sets up Alicia with the opportunity to start again. It's a great example of a show that draws you in with the lead character's journey, which sustains seven gripping seasons.

VIRGIN RIVER

ROMANCE DRAMA • 2019
RATED: TV-14 • 45 MINS

A new entry in the "city-dweller makes fresh start in charming small town" subgenre, *Virgin River* offers a greater feel-good factor than most modern TV.

Melinda Monroe (Alexandra Breckenridge) leaves LA to take a job as a nurse in the remote Californian town of Virgin River, hired by mayor Hope McCrea (Annette O'Toole) to assist the grouchy, elderly Doc Mullins (Tim Matheson). But adjusting to life in the town isn't easy, and Mel remains haunted by the unhappy past she's trying to escape.

Based on a series of 21 (!) novels by prolific romance writer Robyn Carr, this one-season show is a departure from Netflix's usual high-concept dramas and compulsive thrillers—it's gunning for an altogether different audience, and does so very successfully. Breckenridge anchors the show with the right mix of steel and vulnerability, and there are enough secrets and conflicts spilling out to spice things up.

MAN SEEKING WOMAN

COMEDY • 2015
RATED: TV-MA • 22 MINS

A surreal take on today's dating scene following 20-something Josh Greenberg as he tries to bounce back from the demise of a long-term relationship.

Josh (Jay Baruchel) is eager to meet women, but his quest is hindered by his reticence, and also by his unimpressive job and apartment. Helping him, in a way, are his assertive and protective sister Liz (Britt Lower), and his best friend Mike (Eric André). But while Liz encourages Josh to find another serious girlfriend, Mike thinks Josh should just look for meaningless sex.

Based on creator Simon Rich's book of short stories, *The Last Girlfriend on Earth*, *Man Seeking Woman* stands out for its weird touches. Over three seasons, plots include Josh's ex turning out to be dating Hitler; Josh going on a date with an actual troll; and Josh and Mike attending a wedding in hell. This odd sensibility is perfect for conveying the disorienting experience of looking for love.

THIRTYSOMETHING

DRAMA • 1987 • RATED: 12 (UK) • 48 MINS • SEASONS: 4
KEN OLIN, MEL HARRIS, MELANIE MAYRON

A group of baby boomers in late-1980s Philadelphia comes to terms with parenthood, career pressures, and no longer being young in this seminal series. If today's 30-somethings want to understand their parents' generation, they should start here.

Michael Steadman (Ken Olin) and Hope Murdoch (Mel Harris) both wanted to be writers, but he's ended up with a steady job in advertising, and she's quit journalism to raise their daughter, Janie. Their social circle includes photographer Melissa Steadman (Melanie Mayron), who is Michael's cousin and has difficulty with relationships; Michael's colleague Elliot Weston (Timothy Busfield), whose marriage to artist Nancy (Patricia Wettig) is troubled; and Hope's long-time friend, politician Ellyn Warren (Polly Draper), who becomes involved with a married man.

Thirtysomething was immediately recognized as something quite different for American TV. More grounded than the glitzy prime-time soaps of the 1980s, its focus is on young, affluent urbanites, who have everyday problems—marital difficulties, thwarted ambitions, terminal illness—and talk about their feelings. At the time, this stirred much debate over whether the show was honest and incisive about contemporary life, or whether its characters were just self-absorbed yuppies who'd never known real hardship.

Yet there's no denying that the series broke new ground in both style and content. The episode "Strangers," broadcast in 1989, revolves around Melissa's gay friend Russell Weller (David Marshall Grant), including

a scene that showed him and his boyfriend in bed together after sex. Homophobic complaints from viewers led to a controversy, causing five firms to pull $1.5 million worth of advertising from the show.

Thirtysomething was canceled after four seasons following a ratings drop (though it was still getting numbers that shows would kill for today). Hugely influential, it stands out just as much today as it did when it first aired—prime-time shows that make drama out of such ordinary matters remain unusual. This is ultimately what makes *Thirtysomething* well worth revisiting—its care and attention to the lives of its characters.

CREATORS: Marshall Herskovitz, Edward Zwick
PRODUCTION CO: The Bedford Falls Company, MGM Television

CASUAL

COMEDY DRAMA • 2015
RATED: TV-MA • 25 MINS

A sister and brother find themselves living under the same roof again after her divorce in this lightly misanthropic take on the contemporary dating scene.

Therapist Valerie (Michaela Watkins) has left her husband after discovering his infidelity, and moved in with her younger brother Alex (Tommy Dewey), perennial bachelor and co-founder of a dating site called Snooger.

Also living with them is Valerie's teenage daughter Laura (Tara Lynne Barr); together all three embark on their own casual relationships.

It's an engaging setup, with the three leads at times at risk of going in deeper than they intended and getting hurt in the process. Watkins shines as the co-dependent Valerie, supported but also trapped by her close friendship with Alex. Sometimes it seems they'll never change—but the fourth and final season puts the characters' journey into fresh perspective.

YOU'RE THE WORST

COMEDY • 2014
RATED: TV-MA • 22 MINS

Two fairly awful people meet at a wedding and start dating, despite neither of them having any interest in a relationship. Can they get over themselves and morph into decent human beings?

Hedonistic PR executive Gretchen (Aya Cash) meets solipsistic writer Jimmy (Chris Geere) as he's being thrown out of a wedding and she's

stealing a gift intended for the bride and groom. The pair embark on a no-strings relationship, but develop deeper feelings for each other despite themselves. Meanwhile the relationships of their friends start to falter.

Despite its cynical premise and tone, *You're the Worst* is very much a romance. Cash and Geere make their off-putting characters an engaging and plausible couple, and you can't help but root for them. The best part is that because they start from such low points, they both have so much room to grow over the course of the show's five seasons.

GIRLFRIENDS' GUIDE TO DIVORCE

COMEDY DRAMA • 2014
RATED: TV-14 • 42 MINS

It's hard to be a self-help writer when your life is falling apart, as this show—obliquely based on a series of self-help books—demonstrates.

Abby McCarthy (Lisa Edelstein) is divorcing her husband Jake Novak (Paul Adelstein), a fairly unsuccessful filmmaker. Her self-help

books focus on marriage and family life, and she fears the professional consequences if it becomes publicly known that her own marriage has failed. She falls back on the support of fellow divorcées Phoebe (Beau Garrett) and Lyla (Janeane Garofalo).

Developed by Marti Noxon (*Buffy the Vampire Slayer, Sharp Objects*), the show adopts the branding of the *Girlfriends' Guide* parenthood books by Vicki Iovine (with three of the five seasons confusingly adopting different titles), but goes for more dramatically juicy territory. A reliably sharp and funny series.

DESCENDANTS OF THE SUN

ROMANCE DRAMA • 2016
RATED: TV-14 • 59 MINS

This sweeping high-stakes romance between an army officer and a doctor mixes genres to great effect, and was a huge hit when it was released.

Special Forces Unit captain Yoo Si-jin (Song Joong-ki) meets assertive surgeon Dr Kang Mo-yeon (Song Hye-kyo) and they start to date. But they quickly realize how different they are—Si-jin's work is violent and secretive, whereas Mo-yeon is committed to protecting life—and the relationship falters. Si-jin is assigned to a peacekeeping mission in Uruk (a fictional country) and when Mo-yeon rejects the romantic overtures of her hospital's director, she's ordered to lead a medical team, also headed for Uruk.

From there, this single-season series swings from asking if its central couple can work, to asking if they can even survive the events they're plunged into. The result is a classy and well-executed piece of melodrama.

WHEN CALLS THE HEART

PERIOD DRAMA • 2014
RATED: TV-G • 42 MINS

Another outsider-in-a-small-town show, this concerns the arrival of a passionate-but-privileged young teacher into a disaster-hit Canadian frontier community in the 1900s.

New in the mining town of Coal Valley, teacher Elizabeth Thatcher (Erin Krakow) is surprised to find daily life harder than in the city, but is determined to adapt to its challenges. She also clashes with dashing Mountie Jack Thornton (Daniel Lissing), who has been assigned by her wealthy father to protect her.

Based on a book by Janette Oke, *When Calls the Heart* was developed by Michael Landon Jr., son of *Little House on the Prairie* (see p108) star Michael Landon, which helps explain its tone. This seven-season drama has a Christian sensibility and found a strong following among viewers who prefer their TV without sex and violence. Despite addressing the difficulties of living in this time and place, it's a gentle watch.

AS TIME GOES BY

COMEDY ROMANCE • 1992
RATED: TV-PG • 30 MINS

After a lost letter pulled them apart, a fluke encounter gives former couple Lionel and Jean a second chance at love. This beloved British sitcom explores the bittersweet experience of rekindling old romance.

In 1953 two lovers, nurse Jean Pargetter (Judi Dench) and army officer Lionel Hardcastle (Geoffrey Palmer), are separated when Lionel is sent off to war in Korea. A letter to Jean never arrives, and eventually the couple go their separate ways. Some 38 years later, Lionel, looking for someone to type up his war memoirs, stumbles upon just the person: Jean.

There is a spark, but is it enough to rekindle love? The pair are both used to their own ways, and there are other potential romantic entanglements to consider. But over time, and nine series, they learn to love again. The appealing mix of sitcom silliness, gentle seriousness, and polished turns from Dench and Palmer made this a BBC sitcom staple.

THIS IS US

DRAMA • 2016 • RATED: TV-14 • 43 MINS • SEASONS: 4
STERLING K. BROWN, CHRISSY METZ, JUSTIN HARTLEY

The disparate lives of a family unfold in this witty and elegantly structured drama that bounces across the US, as well as between the present, past, and future. It's a show about the turning points in our lives and how they shape us.

Kevin Pearson (Justin Hartley) and Kate Pearson (Chrissy Metz) are two of triplets, born in 1980. Their other brother was stillborn, but their parents, Jack (Milo Ventimiglia) and Rebecca (Mandy Moore), chose to adopt Randall (Sterling K. Brown), an abandoned baby born the same day. We join the siblings in the present day, on their 36th birthday. Kevin—now an actor—quits his role in a sitcom, Kate makes a new commitment to lose weight, and Randall tracks down and confronts his biological father.

> **"** *You're not just my great love story, Rebecca. You … you were my big break.* **"**
>
> Jack (S1 E18)

This Is Us has strong comic pedigree: its creator, Dan Fogelman, wrote *Crazy, Stupid, Love* and Disney's *Tangled*. The series began life as a screenplay about sextuplets, but "It wasn't gelling for me as a film," Fogelman said in a 2017 interview for *Deadline*. "I loved the characters, I loved the idea of it, but I just couldn't wrap my head around it as a film.

I struggled to find the point of the ending … So I put it away." When he later revived it as an open-ended TV series, it suddenly worked.

What makes *This Is Us* unusual is its scope: not only in terms of the siblings' geographical separation (Randall lives in New Jersey, Kate and Kevin in Los Angeles) but also how it regularly flashes back to their childhoods and the relationship of their parents in the 1980s—and, later, forward to their futures. It's an ambitious undertaking, but it adds crucial texture to the everyday stories of people approaching middle age.

From such a jumping-off point, the show could easily have descended into syrupyness, but it counters this with a brilliant unpredictability that means you can never get too comfortable. Its popularity in these tumultuous times isn't surprising: *This Is Us* is a series about the things that unite rather than divide us. But it also puts you through the emotional wringer.

TOP-RATED *THIS IS US* EPISODES

 Super Bowl Sunday (S2 E14)

 The Cabin (S4 E14)

 Memphis (S1 E16)

 That'll Be The Day (S2 E13)

 Strangers: Part Two (S4 E18)

 So Long, Marianne (S4 E9)

Pilot Episode (S1 E1)

CREATOR: Dan Fogelman
PRODUCTION CO: Rhode Island Ave. Productions, Zaftig Films, 20th Century Fox Television

BURNING LOVE

COMEDY • 2012
RATED: TV-14 • 22 MINS

This spoof of *The Bachelor* and *The Bachelorette* dating shows benefits from a superb cast and sharp observation, boiling its source material down into bite-size chunks of absurdity.

The title comes from the fact that the man looking for love in Season 1 is firefighter Mark Orlando (Ken Marino, husband of series creator Erica Oyama). The title doesn't make much sense for Seasons 2 and 3, but never mind—just put your feet up and enjoy as *Burning Love* merrily parodies the genre.

Guest stars on *Burning Love* include Kristen Bell, Ken Jeong, Jennifer Aniston, Adam Scott, Michael Cera, Kumail Nanjiani, Paul Rudd, Seth Rogen ... in most cases they're playing contestants who conform to recognizable archetypes, which facilitates some gloriously over-the-top performances. You don't even need to watch dating shows to grasp the humor—it's simply a good vehicle for making characters do amusingly contrived things.

FOREVER

FANTASY COMEDY • 2018
RATED: TV-14 • 30 MINS

A married couple who are stuck in a rut decide to shake things up with a holiday—which leads to them both taking a much bigger step into the unknown than they expected.

Middle-aged, married, childless couple June (Maya Rudolph) and Oscar (Fred Armisen) live a pleasant life in suburban California, taking a vacation at the same lake house each year. Oscar is content, June is restless. One year she suggests that, instead of going to the lake house, they take a ski trip....

It's hard to talk about *Forever* without spoiling the many twists and turns, which is perhaps why it ended after just one season despite getting great reviews. It's fair to say it gets into some very strange and philosophical territory along its unsettling but highly amusing journey. Writers Alan Yang and Matt Hubbard have created a show that shifts, spins, and keeps you guessing, and if you can tune into its frequency, you won't be able to stop watching.

MERCY STREET

HISTORICAL DRAMA • 2016
RATED: TV-14 • 54 MINS

During the American Civil War, two volunteer nurses from opposing sides both find themselves patching up the wounded at a hospital—then one starts to plot against the other.

The Mansion House Hospital in Alexandria, Virginia was a real place: it had been the Mansion House Hotel, owned by the Southern Green family, but the Union requisitioned it and converted it into a hospital. *Mercy Street* takes inspiration from medical records and journals kept by its workers, most notably Mary Phinney (Mary Elizabeth Winstead), whose jealous colleague Emma Green (Hannah James) seeks to bring her down a peg.

It's a superb idea for a drama, and could have supported more than its two seasons. As well as bringing the tensions of the war under one roof, Mansion House was a watershed for women working in medicine. It all combines to create a series that feels highly pertinent in these divisive times.

THE INNOCENTS

FANTASY • 2018
RATED: TV-MA • 50 MINS

Two teenage lovers run away from home, hoping to escape their troubled lives—but problems follow them when it comes to light that one of them has the ability to shape-shift.

After June (Sorcha Groundsell) and Harry (Percelle Ascott) abscond from their native Yorkshire, they're approached by the menacing Steinar (Jóhannes Haukur

Jóhannesson)—and when he touches June, she takes on his form. June doesn't understand what's happening to her, but as she and Harry stumble around London, she's pursued by henchmen working for the possibly-not-trustworthy Bendik Halvorson (Guy Pearce), who runs a commune for "shifters" in Norway.

The use of shape-shifting offers a fresh take on "fantasy as metaphor for teenhood"—all these possible lives are opening up for June, but can she control which one she ends up with? This eight-part one-off serial has a dark tone, but the central romance offers a glimmer of hope.

THE LOVE BOAT

COMEDY • 1977
RATED: TV-G • 45 MINS

A Saturday night staple of US TV for a decade, *The Love Boat* revolves around the crew and passengers on board luxury cruise ship the *SS Pacific Princess*.

A sort of hybrid of scripted comedy and variety show, *The Love Boat's* selling point is that each episode has different guest stars playing the passengers—with each guest-star plot thread written by a different writer.

The eclectic roll-call of actors who guested over the series' nine seasons and five specials includes Gene Kelly, Pam Grier, Janet Jackson, Corey Feldman, Eva Marie Saint, Tim Robbins, and Jamie Lee Curtis—there's even a crossover episode where Charlie's Angels (see p406) solve a crime aboard the vessel.

Its light romantic escapades take a variety of forms (there's a surprising number of ghosts involved), and it's essentially an anthology series with a shared setting and supporting cast. It's easy to dip in and out of—go for one with a guest star you like.

THE PARADISE

PERIOD DRAMA • 2012
RATED: TV-PG • 59 MINS

Relocating Emile Zola's novel *Au Bonheur des Dames* from Paris to north-east England, *The Paradise* tells the story of the country's first department store.

This show arrived on BBC One almost concurrently with the similar *Mr. Selfridge* (see p109) on PBS. It's 1875 and John Moray (Emun Elliott) has grown a small shop into

the grand retail emporium of the title. When Denise Lovett (Joanna Vanderham) takes a job, Moray taps her as a rising star—ruffling the feathers of other employees, as well as the wealthy Katherine Glendenning (Elaine Cassidy), who intends to marry Moray.

It's all quite sumptuous, and the love triangle at the center provides plenty of dramatic fuel, especially with the ambiguity that hangs over Moray and the fate of his first wife. The series struggled to compete with *Mr. Selfridge* and only lasted two seasons, but it's a classy affair.

AUTUMN'S CONCERTO

ROMANCE DRAMA • 2009
RATED: NR • 60 MINS

He's big news, she sells bento boxes. You wouldn't gamble on this couple finding love, but a crazy bet brings them together in this fast-paced romantic drama.

Ren Guang Xi (Vanness Wu) is a college law student and hockey star, with a bright future planned out for him. Liang Mu Cheng (Ady An) hopes to put her tricky past behind her and get an education while working at the school canteen. The pair don't hit it off, but Guang Xi bets his friends he can get a kiss from Mu Cheng within 24 hours, and wins. Against Guang Xi's family's wishes, romance follows.

This highly rated (and wildly popular) single-series drama gave boy-band star Wu a new outlet as an actor, while child actor Xiao Xiao Bin steals every scene he is in as Xiao Le. The show's snappy pace carries the action along, making the romantic elements feel heartfelt and real rather than contrived.

HOW I MET YOUR MOTHER

COMEDY • 2005 • RATED: TV-14 • 22 MINS • SEASONS: 9
JOSH RADNOR, ALYSON HANNIGAN, NEIL PATRICK HARRIS

This sitcom about looking for love in modern-day New York has an intriguing spin: it's a story the main character is telling his kids in the year 2030.

The gimmick of *How I Met Your Mother* is that Ted Mosby (Bob Saget's voice in the 2030 scenes) is unfurling the yarn implied by the title. The identity of the woman he ends up with remains concealed to the audience. The tale he weaves about his younger self (Josh Radnor) and his search for love involves a lot of failed relationships and unsuccessful dates, and so Ted keeps stringing his kids—and us— along, waiting for the revelation that *this* is the woman who turned out to be The One.

Yet all this is somewhat hijacked by the brilliance of the ensemble cast: Alyson Hannigan and Jason Segel as coupled-up friends Lily and Marshall, Cobie Smulders as deadpan news reporter Robin, and Neil Patrick Harris as the materialistic, womanizing Barney.

Much of the funniest material comes from these supporting characters, demonstrated by the popularity of the Robin-focused Season 2 episode "Slap Bet." The way that Barney's play-the-field philosophy pulls against Ted's quest for a steady relationship allows Harris to steal scene after scene.

The success of the show meant the shaggy-dog story went on longer than anticipated, and later episodes in its nine-season run aren't quite as sharp as the early ones. But rest assured, it does eventually deliver on its premise.

ONE TREE HILL

**DRAMA • 2003 • RATED: TV-14 • 42 MINS • SEASONS: 9
CHAD MICHAEL MURRAY, JAMES LAFFERTY, HILARIE BURTON**

This teen show about two rival basketball-playing half brothers ran for so long, it followed its characters well into adulthood—where they continued to carry on the same messy romances and conflicts from high school.

Lucas Scott (Chad Michael Murray) has a grudge against his half-brother Nathan Scott (James Lafferty). Lucas's father Dan (Paul Johansson) abandoned his family to be with Nathan's mother. When Lucas makes the high-school basketball team, Nathan—who's head of the squad—feels threatened. Basketball aside, the two are different—Nathan is cocky but struggles academically, while Lucas is more introverted and literary.

Their rivalry only intensifies as Lucas develops a romantic interest in Nathan's girlfriend, Peyton Sawyer (Hilarie Burton). The romantic entanglements are further complicated by Nathan's attraction to Lucas's best friend

Haley James (Bethany Joy Lenz), and cheerleading squad captain Brooke Davis (Sophia Bush) having designs on Lucas. The debate over who's right for whom is, naturally, a huge part of the show's appeal.

After eking out the high-school drama for four seasons, *One Tree Hill* shifts gear. Although this results in the loss of the original set-up's appeal, it's rewarding to keep following the same characters for so long after most shows would have ended the story.

> *"How many moments in life can you point to and say: 'That's when it all changed.'"*
>
> **Brooke** (S1 E3)

CHEWING GUM

**COMEDY • 2015
RATED: TV-MA • 24 MINS**

An uncomfortable comedy about a religious young woman who wants to have sex but has no clue about how to go about it.

Michaela Coel's one-woman play *Chewing Gum Dreams* drew on her youth as a devout and (for a while) celibate Pentecostalist. This provided her with the TV series' character of Tracey, ill-equipped for the world by her

strict upbringing. Tracey's boyfriend, like her parents, believes in abstaining from sex before marriage, but her veneration of Beyoncé awakens a determination to lose her virginity.

Tracey's awkward sexcapades are an obvious focal point, but much of the humor comes from her unselfconscious narration as she takes us around her humdrum East London estate and expounds her belief she's destined for something greater. Coel's BAFTA-winning performance dominates this two-season series, but Susan Wokoma is also terrific as Tracey's uptight sister Cynthia.

OUTLANDER

PERIOD FANTASY • 2014
RATED: TV-MA • 60 MINS

A nurse from the 1940s falls through time and falls in love with a Highland warrior during the Jacobite rebellion. Can she return home to her husband? Does she want to?

Developed by Ronald D. Moore (of *Battlestar Galactica* fame) from Diana Gabaldon's novels, *Outlander* is a delightfully twisty proposition. When Claire (Caitriona Balfe) finds herself back in 1743 and meets Jamie Fraser (Sam Heughan), they're pursued by the ancestor of her husband, Jonathan "Black Jack" Randall (Tobias Menzies, who also plays hubbie Frank). Claire knows Fraser's proud clan are fighting a losing battle—but can she convince them?

Historical settings have always been popular for romances, and *Outlander* shrewdly mashes up two of them for maximum appeal. Gratifyingly, it never lets the status quo endure for long, putting its characters through the wringer across five seasons—but always remembering to provide good escapism.

THE THORN BIRDS

PERIOD DRAMA • 1983
RATED: 15 (UK) • 98 MINS

One of the highest-rated miniseries in US TV history (second only to *Roots*), *The Thorn Birds* is the saga of a wealthy Australian family from 1915 to 1969.

Based on the novel of the same name by Colleen McCullough (which has sold over 33 million copies worldwide), *The Thorn Birds* was a lavish effort from ABC with a big-name cast including Richard Chamberlain (who'd starred in the 1980 megahit miniseries *Shogun*, see p113), Rachel Ward, Barbara Stanwyck, and Christopher Plummer. Meggie Cleary (Ward) goes to live at her aunt's estate, where she falls in love with handsome, ambitious priest Ralph de Bricassart (Chamberlain).

The production is slightly hampered by the decision to film in California and Hawaii rather than Australia itself (New South Wales doesn't really look like that), but the recreation of the different periods is terrific, and the impossible romance sustains well over seven gripping hours of drama.

GRAND HOTEL

PERIOD DRAMA • 2011
RATED: TV-14 • 45 MINS

This 1900s-set drama has been touted as a Spanish *Downton Abbey*, but that undersells how intense it is. It's a nest of dark secrets, abduction, and murder.

Julio Olmedo (Yon González) visits the high-class Grand Hotel near Cantaloa in northern Spain, where his sister Cristina works as floor manager ... only to learn she's been fired for theft and disappeared. Suspicious, Julio gets himself hired as a waiter at the hotel so he can look into Cristina's disappearance—and is surprised to get help from the owner's daughter, Alicia (Amaia Salamanca), who believes there's something sinister at the heart of the Grand Hotel.

An impossible upstairs/downstairs romance begins between Julio and Alicia—but that's just a fraction of what's in store. Everyone has skeletons in their closet and owner Doña Teresa (Adriana Ozores) uses people's secrets as she tries to keep control of the hotel. It's three seasons of high-octane insanity.

THE TUDORS

HISTORICAL DRAMA • 2007 • RATED: TV-MA • 52 MINS • SEASONS: 4
JONATHAN RHYS MEYERS, MARIA DOYLE KENNEDY

This is the series that kick-started a wave of violent, carnally minded dramas about the ruling classes in various eras of European history. It is still one of the best. Discover the story of Henry VIII, one of England's most extravagant kings, in all its lurid glory.

If you want the rigorous, historically accurate version of Henry's reign, watch the excellent *Wolf Hall* (see p138). If you want a thrillingly heightened period soap opera, *The Tudors* has you covered. Tudor England is a lot cleaner and sexier here than it would have been in real life—this is a hyperreal rendition of the era that uses different historical elements to create an enticing world.

King Henry is played by Jonathan Rhys Meyers, who by Meyers' own admission looks nothing like him. But then this is all about conveying the rock-star charisma that a monarch would have had in the 16th century. Henry makes a great antihero—after all, he bends society to accommodate his own whims and desires. And he gets worse as time goes on—you're worried every time a new wife is introduced.

The Tudors was a ratings smash for Showtime, which gave it full opportunity to tell its expansive story over four seasons—so you can rest assured it doesn't suddenly stop with two wives to go. Of Henry's six brides, Natalie Dormer stands out for her portrayal of a bold Anne Boleyn.

> **"***Showtime commissioned me to write an entertainment, a soap opera, and not history.***"**
>
> **Michael Hirst** (creator/writer)

POLDARK

PERIOD DRAMA • 2015
RATED: TV-14 • 60 MINS

A melodrama about family rivalry, tempestuous romance, and tin mining, *Poldark* shows there's nothing more ruggedly glamorous than riding across the cliffs of 18th-century Cornwall.

Winston Graham's *Poldark* novels were a hit when the BBC first adapted them in the 1970s, and this new version (created by Debbie Horsfield) repeated the trick. Ross Poldark

(Aidan Turner) returns from the American War of Independence to find his father dead, his estate in disarray, and Elizabeth (Heida Reed), his childhood sweetheart, engaged to his cousin. But his fortunes start to improve when he becomes close to his new scullery maid, Demelza (Eleanor Tomlinson).

Over five series, the relations between the characters become ever more tangled, with Ross always quick to take some foolish risk in order to play the hero. It burns brightest in its early seasons, when the Ross/Demelza relationship is still young.

MIDDLEMARCH

PERIOD DRAMA • 1994
RATED: TV-PG • 60 MINS

A superb TV treatment of one of the greatest novels in the English language, *Middlemarch* depicts life in a provincial 1830s town—following several romances along the way.

Victorian door-stopper novels are perfect TV fodder, and there's none better than George Eliot's masterpiece. Intellectually ambitious Dorothea Brooke (Juliet Aubrey) marries the stodgy Reverend Edward Casaubon (Patrick Malahide), setting herself up for disappointment. Dr. Tertius Lydgate (Douglas Hodge) draws ire for his modern medical ideas, and attracts the shallow Rosamund Vincy (Trevyn McDowell). And the arrival of bohemian artist Will Ladislaw (Rufus Sewell) has unexpected consequences....

Andrew Davies' adaptation captures the novel brilliantly, and the casting is immaculate. The misguided characters may have you grousing in irritation at first—but stick with them, as the plot unfurls in a deeply satisfying way.

PRIDE AND PREJUDICE

PERIOD DRAMA • 1995 • RATED: TV-PG • 52 MINS • SEASONS: 1
JENNIFER EHLE, COLIN FIRTH, ALISON STEADMAN

This smoldering adaptation of the classic novel put Jane Austen right at the heart of popular culture, over 180 years after the book was first published. The series started a wave of blockbuster costume dramas and remains a gold standard for the genre.

Elizabeth "Lizzy" Bennet (Jennifer Ehle) is one of five sisters who desperately need to find husbands or they'll have no means of financial support. But Lizzie is determined to marry for love, not money—so the chances of her developing an attachment to the wealthy Fitzwilliam Darcy (Colin Firth), who antagonizes her, seem very remote.

Scriptwriter Andrew Davies has adapted more classic books for TV than anyone else, but thanks to *Pride and Prejudice* he is forever associated with Austen. Davies has spoken of the novel's perfect plotting, which creates a compelling central couple while also making it appear impossible that they can ever get together—the prototype of modern romantic comedy. Even when you know the story, it's compelling to watch it play out.

The casting is uniformly superb, from David Bamber's obsequious Mr. Collins to Julia Sawalha's excitable Lydia. Firth's pitch-perfect performance as Darcy grabs the attention, and it's impossible to read the novel afterward without hearing his voice.

However, it's Ehle who has the trickiest task, doing justice to one of the great heroines of literature, a character about whom many readers have very firm ideas—and she pulls it off brilliantly.

REIGN

HISTORICAL DRAMA • 2013
RATED: TV-14 • 42 MINS

This high-energy series recasts Mary, Queen of Scots as Mary, Teen of Scots, and follows her rise to power as she courts the totally buff heir to the French throne.

The clue that *Reign* isn't your usual historical drama is that it was made for The CW, which is better known for its glossy high-school soaps and superhero shows. Accordingly, it's not the place to look if accuracy is important to you—here creators Laurie McCarthy and Stephanie SenGupta's focus is on taking 16th-century power structures and applying them to teen drama.

Despite its loose relationship to history, France's Wars of Religion make an impact, as does the rivalry between Mary (Adelaide Kane) and Elizabeth I (Rachel Skarsten). But the show never surrenders its essential lightness and campiness throughout its four seasons, remaining a halfway house between reality and a young girl's princess fantasies.

VANITY FAIR

PERIOD DRAMA • 2018
RATED: TV-14 • 46 MINS

Becky Sharp (Olivia Cooke)—a young woman of dubious birth—connives her way into the upper echelons of Regency society in this adaptation of William Makepeace Thackeray's classic novel.

Becky is an ideal antihero for our age: confronted with a society of blatant inequality, she has no qualms about deceiving and manipulating the wealthy into elevating her status. Her naive schoolfriend Amelia Sedley (Claudia Jessie) is her main route of entry—but along the way Becky may ruin Amelia's own chances of happiness with William Dobbin (Johnny Flynn).

Gwyneth Hughes's adaptation deftly trims some of the meandering material from the book's second half, and the script and cast convey Thackeray's wit—Martin Clunes's performance as Sir Pitt Crawley is a particular highlight. The novel has enough incident in it to power two or three seasons of TV, but this squeezes it into seven packed episodes.

VICTORIA

HISTORICAL DRAMA • 2016
RATED: TV-PG • 46 MINS

A biopic of England's most famous queen, depicting Victoria's struggle to assert herself against powerful men who expect her to be compliant.

The Queen Victoria of the popular imagination is an imperious figure, accustomed to power, so it's interesting to see her ascending to the throne as a teenager, lacking in confidence, and intimidated by what she's inherited.

While the courtship of the young Victoria (Jenna Coleman) and Prince Albert (Tom Hughes) is a major feature, the drama—adapted by Daisy Goodwin from her own novel—also speculates on Victoria's almost-romantic relationship with Whig Prime Minister Lord Melbourne (Rufus Sewell).

The fictionalized below-stairs subplots, which add a *Downton Abbey*–quality to proceedings, offer an alternative perspective and convey the complexities of running a royal household. But it's the historical drama at its heart that will keep you coming back over its three seasons.

UGLY BETTY

COMEDY DRAMA • 2006 • RATED: TV-14 • 43 MINS • SEASONS: 4
AMERICA FERRERA, ASHLEY JENSEN, VANESSA WILLIAMS

A fish-out-of-water series about a geeky young woman with zero fashion sense who lands a job at a top style magazine. She views the business as shallow, while her colleagues treat her like a freak. Can they work together?

Based on a successful Colombian *telenovela*, *Ugly Betty* transplants perfectly to New York. Betty Suarez (America Ferrara) is desperate to work in publishing, but *Mode* magazine would not have been her first choice, to say the least. But her lack of glamour is, in fact, exactly why she's been hired to be personal assistant to womanizing editor-in-chief Daniel Meade (Eric Mabius)—the hope is he won't sleep with her like he does most of his PAs.

Of course, Betty is a network TV version of "ugly"—an attractive actress styled with braces, thick glasses, slightly unflattering hair, and a frumpy wardrobe. But within the airbrushed world of *Mode* magazine she stands out enough to get the point across. More relevant than Betty's lack of style is her underprivileged status: whereas her boss,

Daniel, is the son of *Mode's* publisher, and hasn't had to work for his position, Betty is from a poor Latino family and her ambitions are everything to her.

The contrast between the glossy, artificial world of fashion publishing and Betty's humble home life in Queens is nicely managed, and the early episodes play this clash of two worlds heavily for comic effect. What's interesting is how *Ugly Betty* is forced to evolve as the series progresses. Characters such as Amanda Tanen (Becki Newton) and Marc St. James (Michael Urie), who tease and bully Betty at the outset, are in danger of becoming one-note, so they develop depth and some redeeming qualities. Meanwhile, Daniel's respect for Betty grows into genuine fondness.

In its third season *Ugly Betty* starts to lose its way, with the underhanded schemes of creative editor Wilhelmina Slater (Vanessa Williams) pulling too much focus from Betty herself. But at its best, it's a witty, fast-paced, and endearing series that boasts a terrific ensemble cast.

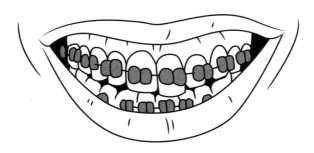

CREATORS: Silvio Horta, Fernando Gaitán **PRODUCTION CO:** Silent H Productions, Ventanarosa Productions, Reveille Productions, Touchstone Television, ABC Studios, Buena Vista Television, Walt Disney Television

BEAUTY AND THE BEAST

FANTASY DRAMA • 1987
RATED: TV-PG • 48 MINS

A literal fairy tale in New York, this reworks the classic story to present us with a more noble Beast, who prefers rescuing women to locking them up until they fall in love with him.

New York lawyer Catherine Chandler (Linda Hamilton) is abducted, beaten, and left for dead—but not by a beast. Instead, Vincent (Ron Perlman) finds her in Central Park and rescues her. He belongs to a community of covert tunnel-dwellers who nurse Catherine back to health—a change that avoids the pair's subsequent romance having an uncomfortable air of Stockholm syndrome.

From there, it becomes a sort of crime drama as Catherine changes careers to become a district attorney, and gets into situations that require Vincent to come to her aid, acting as a guardian angel. The show falters after Hamilton's departure, and the third and final season fails to recapture the original chemistry. Until that point, though, it has much to offer.

BEAUTY AND THE BEAST

CRIME SCI-FI • 2012
RATED: TV-14 • 42 MINS

A loose remake of the 1987 TV series that keeps the romance and crime elements, but also adds a conspiracy-thriller sci-fi thread. It's practically every genre in one.

This time around Catherine Chandler (Kristin Kreuk) is a New York police detective who, nine years prior, was rescued from murderers by a strange creature, but too late to save her mother from being shot. A new case leads her to Vincent Keller (Jay Ryan), a soldier who is listed as killed in action, but who has in fact received an experimental super-soldier treatment that has destabilized his DNA and turned him into something ... beastly.

Using the '80s series as a jumping-off point, the show drifts even further from the classic fairy tale—it perhaps has more in common with *The Incredible Hulk* (see p415). Yet its twists and turns gave it a longer life than the original (four seasons) as our heroes evade the authorities and seek a quiet life together.

SECRET DIARY OF A CALL GIRL

DRAMA • 2007
RATED: TV-MA • 23 MINS

An alternative view of prostitution, as a young, well-educated Londoner leads us through her clandestine life charging wealthy men lots of money for sex.

Adapted from the "Belle de Jour" blog and books by Brooke Magnanti, who worked as an escort while studying for her PhD, *Secret Diary of a Call Girl* stars Billie Piper as Hannah Baxter. Hannah tells her friends and family she's a nighttime legal secretary, but in reality she's a successful high-end prostitute, operating under the name of Belle. She enjoys her work, but can she keep her personal and professional lives separate?

Despite the titillating subject matter, the show—scripted by playwright Lucy Prebble—is a mix of comic escapades and thoughtful drama, with Piper's regular addresses to camera acting as a commentary on, and argument in favor of, her lifestyle.

EASY

COMEDY DRAMA • 2016
RATED: TV-MA • 30 MINS

This anthology of stories about disparate, hipsterish individuals living in Chicago has a loose, low-key style that's the polar opposite of cliffhanger-driven binge-watch TV.

Writer-director Joe Swanberg was central to the "mumblecore" indie film movement of the 2000s, which also saw the rise of actor and filmmaker Greta Gerwig. In *Easy*, he applies his low-budget aesthetic to a series of half-hour stories about modern love set in a shared world. The stand-alone narratives explore gender roles, aging, open relationships, and more, but characters recur and sequel episodes crop up over three seasons.

Easy can seem offputtingly meandering at first—as if it's wilfully refusing to get to the point. But over time it opens up, and its quiet approach yields rewards. The eclectic cast—including Orlando Bloom, Marc Maron, Gugu Mbatha-Raw, and Aubrey Plaza—is a significant bonus.

TALES OF THE CITY

DRAMA • 1993
RATED: TV-MA • 52 MINS

This adaptation of Armistead Maupin's seminal novels about San Francisco's gay community is hugely evocative, and, thanks to a recent revival, has grown into a multigenerational epic.

In the summer of 1976, sheltered and naive Mary Ann Singleton (Laura Linney) arrives in San Francisco and rents an apartment at 28 Barbary Lane from the hippyish Anna Madrigal (Olympia Dukakis). Anna acts as a surrogate mother to her tenants, who include charming young gay man Michael "Mouse" Tolliver (Marcus D'Amico).

The series has a patchwork history: Season 1 was a Channel 4/PBS coproduction, then Seasons 2 and 3 were produced by Showtime with a number of cast changes. The source books were originally serialized in newspapers, so they're perfectly suited to TV, with rolling drama and regular cliffhangers. In 2019 Netflix revived the series for a fourth run, reuniting the characters decades later with great success.

LAST TANGO IN HALIFAX

COMEDY DRAMA • 2012
RATED: TV-14 • 56 MINS

Two former childhood friends, both now widowed and in their 70s, reconnect and fall in love in this touching five-season series praised for its depiction of an elderly couple's romance.

Sally Wainwright was inspired to write *Last Tango in Halifax* by the experiences of her mother, who in her 70s reconnected with a childhood friend and ended up marrying him less than six months later. Wainwright fictionalized this as the romance between Celia Dawson (Anne Reid) and Alan Buttershaw (Derek Jacobi), which supplies an unexpected new chapter in their lives.

This turned out to be the show many viewers were crying out for, and thanks to Wainwright's brilliant character work and witty dialogue, it was a hit: a beguiling story happening to relatable people. Along with the central story line, the experiences of Celia's daughter Caroline (Sarah Lancashire) coming to terms with her sexuality are beautifully observed.

LOVE

COMEDY ROMANCE • 2016
RATED: TV-MA • 35 MINS

The on-off relationship of a chalk-and-cheese couple is explored at length in this frustrating, yet addictive series cocreated by *Knocked Up* and *Trainwreck* director Judd Apatow.

Gus (Paul Rust) has just broken up with his unfaithful girlfriend when he bumps into the self-destructive and discontented Mickey (Gillian Jacobs). Gus, who's a bit too eager to please, is attracted to her, but she isn't attracted to him … until he dates her roommate Bertie (Claudia O'Doherty).

That's far from the end of the travails Gus and Mickey experience in their relationship. Created by Judd Apatow, Paul Rust, and Lesley Arfin, this three-season comedy often jumps through hoops to keep its characters apart—but it succeeds because it's so funny. The sharp writing is brought brilliantly to life by Gillian Jacobs (so good in *Community,* see p212), who makes Mickey the most endearing trainwreck of a human being you could wish to meet.

THE L WORD

DRAMA • 2004 • RATED: TV-MA • 50 MINS • SEASONS: 6
JENNIFER BEALS, MIA KIRSHNER, PAM GRIER

***The L Word* was a landmark—the first US TV drama to focus on a regular cast of gay and bisexual women—and it remains a touchstone today.**

Writer Jenny Schecter (Mia Kirshner) moves in with her boyfriend Tim Haspell (Eric Mabius) in Los Angeles. Her new neighbors are long-term couple Bette Porter (Jennifer Beals) and Tina Kennard (Laurel Holloman), who are seeking a sperm donor so they can have a child. They introduce Jenny to their friends, including café owner Marina Ferrer (Karina Lombard)—with whom Jenny shares an instant attraction.

The characters of *The L Word* exist in a glossy, high-flying milieu but the show needs to keep upping the stakes, so the problems in their comfortable lives become wilder, taking a particularly dark turn in the final season. Despite its groundbreaking nature (it was depicting explicit sex scenes on Showtime when many network shows still wouldn't feature a same-sex kiss), it got some criticism for its depiction of the lesbian community. Cocreator Ilene Chaiken rebuffed this in a 2005 seminar on gay TV: "I won't take on the mantle of social responsibility. That's not compatible with entertainment … I'm not a cultural missionary."

The success of *The L Word* is perhaps down to its mix of representation and sheer escapism. It endured well enough to spawn a 2019 revival, *The L Word: Generation Q,* picking up the story 10 years later.

> **"***I really like telling stories about sex.***"**
>
> **Ilene Chaiken** (cocreator/writer)

YOU NEED A FEEL-GOOD MOMENT

Written by Stacey Grant

Picture this: It's been a long, tiring day. Your brain feels like Swiss cheese and you're desperate for a break, but you're not sure how to go about it. It sounds like you're in need of a feel-good moment. Kick back, relax, and get ready to take a mental vacation for a bit by watching these fun shows.

FRIENDS

COMEDY • 1994 • RATED: TV-14 • 22 MINS • SEASONS: 10
JENNIFER ANISTON, COURTENEY COX, MATTHEW PERRY

Living in New York City is tough, but not if you've got great friends by your side. This cult series follows six adults as they try nabbing their dream jobs, dipping their toes in the dating pool, and having fun together.

Meet your new six best friends: Rachel (Jennifer Aniston), Monica (Courteney Cox), Phoebe (Lisa Kudrow), Chandler (Matthew Perry), Joey (Matt LeBlanc), and Ross (David Schwimmer). This long-running comedy begins with a woman leaving her fiancé at the altar, and ends with that same woman falling in love again. But what happens in between is a wild, hilarious ride.

After Rachel leaves her husband-not-to-be, she's high on her newfound independence, moving into a New York City apartment with her friend, Monica. The lives of Rachel and Monica quickly intersect with Monica's brother, Ross; his friends, Chandler and Joey; and Monica's former roommate, Phoebe.

With six very diverse personalities swirling around each other, expect plenty of love triangles in this sitcom.

> **"***It's a moo point [...] It's like a cow's opinion; it doesn't matter. It's moo.***"**
>
> **Joey** (S7 E8)

The biggest relationship drama, however, involves Rachel and Ross, whose "we were on a break!" scene inspired countless memes and sparked plenty of debates at real-life dinner tables about who was in the right and who was in the wrong. Meanwhile, Chandler and Monica's relationship is smoother sailing, but they aren't without their ups and downs.

The main *Friends* cast broke new ground in the TV world when they all banded together in 2002 to demand equal pay and higher salaries—$1 million an episode, to be exact. This was a record-breaking move and saw women getting the same pay as men. "We were in a position to get it," Matt LeBlanc, who played Joey, told *HuffPost* when asked how those salary negotiations went down. This decision opened the door for future stars to demand seven figures per episode, such as the cast of *The Big Bang Theory* (see p268).

Star wages aside, you'll find yourself falling so quickly for these characters, it'll be hard to decide which friend is your favorite.

CREATORS: David Crane, Marta Kauffman
PRODUCTION CO: Bright/Kauffman/Crane Productions, Warner Bros. Television

LIVING SINGLE

COMEDY • 1993
RATED: TV-PG • 30 MINS

Do you know what inspired *Friends*? Set in Prospect Heights, Brooklyn in the '90s, *Living Single* follows the lives of six successful African-American pals living under the same roof.

Khadijah (Queen Latifah) leads this five-season show as the editor of independent magazine *Flavor*. She's surrounded by her cousin and assistant, Synclaire (Kim Coles), gossip-addicted Regine (Kim Fields), lawyer friend Max (Erika Alexander), and roommates Obie (John Henton), and Kyle (Terrence "T. C." Carson). Together, they experience plenty of love and heartbreak while living together in the building.

The series promoted female empowerment and autonomy, as well as allowing series creator Yvette Lee Bowser to craft a world that didn't directly cater to a white audience. The cast's chemistry simply radiates off the screen, which arguably can be attributed to part of the show's success.

PARKS AND RECREATION

COMEDY • 2009 • RATED: TV-14 • 22 MINS • SEASONS: 7
AMY POEHLER, CHRIS PRATT, NICK OFFERMAN

This political satire follows the exploits of a fictional Indiana town's Parks and Recreation Department as its quirky members work together to enrich their community. The fact their projects never go as planned will keep you laughing from start to finish.

The Parks and Recreation Department is no joke—at least that's how deputy director Leslie Knope (Amy Poehler) sees it. Working to improve the town of Pawnee in Indiana, Leslie is the ultimate go-getter, despite the efforts of department director Ron Swanson (Nick Offerman), who isn't a big fan of the government and tries to lessen his division's impact on the community as much as possible. Thankfully, Leslie's BFF, Ann Perkins (Rashida Jones), is there to help her out on her mission.

The rest of Leslie's coworkers are all over the place—there's Tom Haverford (Aziz Ansari), Leslie's slacker subordinate; April Ludgate (Aubrey Plaza), a cynical intern; Ben Wyatt (Adam Scott), a government official looking to redeem himself; and Chris Traeger (Rob Lowe), an upbeat and health-conscious employee. Rounding out the cast is Andy Dwyer (Chris Pratt), Ann's goofball ex-boyfriend who plays in a band.

Filmed in a mockumentary style like *The Office* (see p153–155), this comedy turns something as straightforward as filling in a pit into a total laugh-riot. Whether the team is displaying inexplicable excitement about miniature pony Li'l Sebastian, getting caught up in the antics of a local cult renting a park, or simply celebrating Galentine's Day, there's never a dull moment in Pawnee.

ONE DAY AT A TIME

COMEDY • 2017 • RATED: TV-PG • 30 MINS • SEASONS: 4
JUSTINA MACHADO, RITA MORENO, TODD GRINNELL

Talk about a full house! Three generations of Cuban Americans live together under the same roof, dealing with real-world issues, while always remembering the importance of family in this sitcom reboot. For every tear that's shed in the household, there's double the amount of laughter.

Newly single mom Penelope (Justina Machado) has a lot on her plate: raising her activist daughter Elena (Isabella Gomez) and athletic son Alex (Marcel Ruiz); battling depression and anxiety after finishing her United States Army service; slowly returning to the dating pool after separating from her husband; and trying her hardest not to let her mother, Lydia (Rita Moreno), get under her skin. Somehow, she manages, but not without help from Schneider (Todd Grinnell), her friend and landlord, whose fancy-free personality is sure to make you fall in love with him.

The series is a remake of the '70s sitcom of the same name, but switches the main characters from a white family to an Hispanic one. The Alvarez family's Cuban heritage plays an important part in the show—and provides a positive Latinx representation that doesn't involve stereotypes. Moreover, the show is female-centric, and explores a coming-out story. One of the characters is nonbinary, and the series respectfully uses their preferred pronouns, educating other characters (and its audience) who don't understand what nonbinary means.

While *One Day at a Time* is entertaining for all ages, it covers several topics most sitcoms would consider taboo for a family show, such as racism, mental health, substance abuse, and immigration. The first step to discussing difficult subject matter is to normalize it, which the series does flawlessly. Unlike other sitcoms, not everything always works out just right for the Alvarezes, and that's OK. They handle whatever curveballs life throws at them together, as a family.

Clearly, this ideal reasonated with audiences. After Netflix canceled the show, there was a fan outcry and Pop TV picked it up for Season 4.

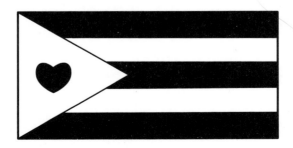

CREATORS: Gloria Calderon Kellett, Mike Royce PRODUCTION CO: Act III Productions,
GloNation Studios, Snowpants Productions, Sony Pictures Television

CUCKOO

COMEDY • 2012
RATED: TV-14 • 30 MINS

Two parents pick up their daughter from the airport after her gap year, only to get the shock of their lives when they discover she's married an out-of-work hippie nicknamed Cuckoo.

This five-season show begins with Rachel (Esther Smith) returning home from a year away to start medical school. With her she brings back an unexpected addition to the family: new husband Cuckoo (Andy Samberg), a shiftless American she's married without the knowledge of her parents, Ken (Greg Davies) and Lorna (Helen Baxendale). Needless to say, dad is less than pleased, immediately trying to get rid of his daughter's new bae by paying him off—a strategy that backfires fast.

Samberg had to leave the show after Season 1, when *Brooklyn Nine-Nine* (see p256) took up his time, but the series cleverly found a way to keep the story going by bringing in Taylor Lautner as Cuckoo's long-lost son. This is a wild ride you won't be able to stop watching.

GREAT NEWS

COMEDY • 2017
RATED: TV-14 • 22 MINS

What if you had to work with your mom? A dream or a nightmare? That's what one daughter has to deal with when her mother gets an internship at her TV news station.

Katie (Briga Heelan) is a producer for the fictional news show called *The Breakdown*. Annoyed that her boss Greg (Adam Campbell) isn't assigning her hard-hitting stories, Katie thinks things can't get any worse ... until the company hires a new intern: Katie's mom, Carol (Andrea Martin). Awkward.

Unsurprisingly, Katie hates that she now works with her mother, quickly trying to get her fired and out of her hair. When that doesn't work, Carol briefly quits, prompting Katie to grow up and learn how to work with her mom. Rounding out the team are coanchors Portia (Nicole Richie) and Chuck (John Michael Higgins), and editor Justin (Horatio Sanz). This two-season show is perfect for mothers to watch with their 20-something daughters.

KATH & KIM

COMEDY • 2002
RATED: 15 (UK) • 26 MINS

As Kath looks to restart her life, her only child Kim's life is falling apart. This beloved Australian sitcom takes you behind-the-scenes of a dysfunctional mother-and-daughter relationship.

Moms are great, except for the fact that they know exactly how to get under your skin. This four-season show introduces us to Kath (Jane Turner), who's excited to start her life with a butcher named Kel (Glenn Robbins). Unfortunately, their relationship hits a snag when Kath's daughter, Kim (Gina Riley), starts staying at Kath's house after having issues with her husband, Brett (Peter Rowsthorn). Of course, once you first move out, you can never really go home again, as Kim learns.

As Kath and Kel prepare for their wedding, Kim and Brett deal with their relationship issues. Yikes. This show is great fun, packed with hilarious lines. Definitely one to watch if you're in a new relationship, or have just gotten out of one.

BOY MEETS WORLD

COMEDY • 1993 • RATED: TV-PG • 23 MINS • SEASONS: 7
BEN SAVAGE, WILLIAM DANIELS, RIDER STRONG

Get ready to start shouting "Fee-hee-heenay," because this coming-of-age show is guaranteed to bring out the goofy kid in you. Follow along as a boy and his pals take on the world ... well, to start with, at least the sixth grade.

Seeing your teacher outside of school is weird enough, but what if you lived next door to him, too? That's what Cory (Ben Savage) has to put up with throughout his school years, never able to pull one over on Mr. Feeny (William Daniels). Of course, it's not for lack of trying, especially with his best friend and total bad boy, Shawn (Rider Strong), as his partner in crime.

> " *Friendship [...] is a real gift.*
> *And it's given with*
> *no expectation and*
> *no gratitude is necessary.* "
>
> Mr. Feeny (SI EI0)

Throughout the course of the series, Cory, Shawn, and Topanga (Danielle Fishel)—Cory's love interest—grow up before our eyes. They begin the series in sixth grade, and end it in college. Toss in Cory's quirky older brother, Eric (Will Friedle), and this fab four will become your new best friends as you watch them experience all the drama of growing up, such as being torn between hanging out with the "cool" kids and your "weirdo" friends, taking your first steps in dating, and the disappointment of not getting into your dream school.

The series, though lighthearted and wholesome overall, isn't afraid to explore more mature topics, such as child abuse, underage drinking, death, and cults. But don't let that stop you from vegging out on the sofa and bingeing on it from start to finish. You'll quickly become engrossed in Cory and Topanga's adorable relationship—a major focal point of the series. Topanga is strong and independent, and Cory is wise enough to respect and adore that about her. Meanwhile, their friend Shawn struggles to find the girl of his dreams, letting both his unconventional family life and stubbornness sometimes get the better of him. Thankfully, Cory and Topanga are always there to help him out, and vice versa. These guys really are the Three Musketeers.

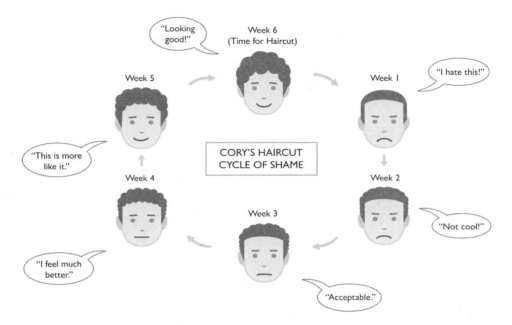

"Looking good!"

Week 6 (Time for Haircut)

Week 5

Week 1

"I hate this!"

"This is more like it."

CORY'S HAIRCUT CYCLE OF SHAME

Week 4

Week 2

Week 3

"Not cool!"

"I feel much better."

"Acceptable."

Boy Meets World wouldn't be the beloved show it is today without the hilarious and dim-witted remarks of Eric. As the series progresses, his personality not-so-subtly shifts from cool older brother to total goofball. In Season 3, episode 17, he admits, "I said to myself, Kyle ... that's what I call myself," which perfectly sums up his oddball personality. Every family has an Eric, someone who can always keep the room laughing and the mood upbeat. Eric's eccentricity is in perfect contrast to Mr. Feeny's no-nonsense demeanor. Though he presents himself as a formidable educator, Feeny always offers an ear to listen and a shoulder to cry on when Cory, Shawn, Topanga, and Eric have a problem they can't solve. His words of wisdom are sure to inspire you as much as they do his students.

As the kids grow up before our eyes onscreen, they expand their friendship squad significantly. Instead of being a fearsome foursome, they later become a beloved group of eight. Meet Angela (Trina McGee), Shawn's girlfriend; Jack (Matthew Lawrence), Shawn's half brother;

and Rachel (Maitland Ward), Eric and Jack's roommate. Together, the group's shenanigan levels double, making it twice as fun to watch how everything plays out.

Though the show is a standard sitcom, it isn't afraid to take some risks and go against its normal setup from time to time, such as the Season 5 episode that acts as a parody of the horror movie *Scream*, slowly "killing off" each of the main characters in a whodunnit style that leaves you guessing until the very end. Another out-of-the-box example is the Season 3 episode in which Cory travels back in time to the 1950s and is mistaken for a Russian spy.

There's always something new and exciting happening in *Boy Meets World*, and you'll find yourself making the Feeny call in no time.

CREATORS: Michael Jacobs, April Kelly
PRODUCTION CO: Michael Jacobs Productions, Touchstone Television

EVERWOOD

DRAMA • 2002
RATED: TV-PG • 60 MINS

Imagine growing up in Manhattan, then being ripped away to live in a tiny Colorado town after your mom dies. That's what two siblings are forced to endure in this family drama.

After brain surgeon Andy (Treat Williams) loses his wife in a car accident, he leaves his hotshot New York City job and moves his two kids, Ephram (Gregory Smith) and Delia (Vivien Cardone), to a small town in Colorado called Everwood that his wife loved. Between losing their mom and moving across the country, Ephram and Delia spend a lot of the series dealing with their grief, as well as having their dad around more, something that didn't happen back in Manhattan because of his hectic work schedule.

This four-season drama is great for fathers and sons to watch together, as Andy and Ephram's relationship begins to grow with each season. *Everwood* proves that good things can come out of tragedy.

LIFE IN PIECES

COMEDY • 2015
RATED: TV-14 • 22 MINS

Looking for the next *Modern Family*? You'll find it in the form of this sitcom about three generations of one family whose stories are told separately, through snapshots of their lives.

Meet the Shorts, whose family tree is the exact opposite of their name. John (James Brolin) and Joan (Dianne Wiest) have three kids, including youngest son Greg (Colin Hanks), and a bunch of grandkids. Everyone has their own story, and each episode is broken up into four parts: three of them involve the adult children and their families, and the fourth one connects all of them together.

Over the course of its four-season run, the series deals with issues around raising kids—from infant to college-age—while also showing the Short patriarch and matriarch's efforts to remain major players in their grown kids' lives. This is a feel-good show that's best watched together as a family.

THE NEW ADVENTURES OF OLD CHRISTINE

COMEDY • 2006
RATED: TV-PG • 22 MINS

Your ex-husband starts seeing someone with the same first name as you. What do you do? If you're old Christine, you seriously ramp up your dating game.

Christine Campbell (Julia Louis-Dreyfus), a single mom who runs her own gym for women, discovers her ex-husband, Richard (Clark Gregg), has a new babe in his life … who is also called Christine (Emily Rutherfurd). Unsure how to proceed, and wanting to keep things with Richard as civil as possible for the sake of their son Ritchie (Trevor Gagnon), Christine decides to find herself a new, better man. Unfortunately, it's not that easy.

While she jumps back into the dating pool, coparents her son, and tries not to kill "New" Christine, she also has to deal with her live-in brother, Matthew (Hamish Linklater), who keeps her on her toes with his quirky personality in this five-season show.

THE MIDDLE

COMEDY • 2009 • RATED: TV-PG • 22 MINS • SEASONS: 9
PATRICIA HEATON, NEIL FLYNN, CHARLIE MCDERMOTT

The Hecks are an Indiana family juggling work, home life, and raising three kids—sometimes not always that well. The Middle is sure to make you grateful for your own wacky relatives, and help you realize some households are even more chaotic than your own.

This sitcom revolves around the point of view of its matriarch, Frankie (Patricia Heaton), someone who eats, sleeps, and breathes for her family. Her no-nonsense husband, Mike (Neil Flynn), is the manager at a limestone quarry.

Their three kids each march to the beat of their own drum: eldest son Axl (Charlie McDermott) is super lazy and narcissistic; daughter Sue (Eden Sher) has a goofy but bubbly personality that makes her the center of ridicule at times; and youngest son Brick (Atticus Shaffer) is a bibliophile whose language disorder involuntarily

causes him to repeat words or phrases. Together, they make up a semitypical, lower-middle-class family.

Frankie feels like she's stuck in a rut in her career, working as a salesperson but with bigger dreams. Thankfully, she has her loved ones to channel her energy into, propelling her into such actions as attending her son's school dressed as a superhero or getting her kids to participate in family dinners—without having the TV on in the living room. Gasp! The Middle lets you laugh at your own family disasters as you laugh along at theirs.

> **"***The truth is, maybe we are just average.***"**
>
> Frankie Heck (S1 E24)

WE'RE HERE

**REALITY TV • 2020
RATED: TV-MA • 59 MINS**

Oh, honey! Get ready for the ultimate drag show experience when three drag queen pros lend their expertise to small-town residents. You'll laugh and cry during every episode.

Join former *RuPaul's Drag Race* contestants Bob the Drag Queen (Caldwell Tidicue), Eureka (David Huggard), and Shangela (D.J. Pierce) as they travel to small, mostly

conservative towns—such as Branson, Missouri—with the goal of putting on a one-night drag show. They're surprisingly successful, with three locals in each city volunteering to be in the show.

While this one-season series itself is fun and memorable, the ultimate goal is to show the townspeople that drag shows can open their hearts and their minds. The queens help people venture out of their comfort zones for one unforgettable night. Many of the drag newbies share how the experience has given them newfound confidence in themselves.

BOB'S BURGERS

ANIMATED COMEDY • 2011 • RATED: TV-14 • 22 MINS • SEASONS: 10
H. JON BENJAMIN, DAN MINTZ, EUGENE MIRMAN

Some dads dream of playing in the NFL. Bob Belcher dreams of running a burger joint. With the help of his family, Bob's Burgers is born. Now he just needs customers to come to him instead of the competition.

Running a restaurant is in the DNA of Bob Belcher (H. Jon Benjamin)—his family has been doing it for generations. Getting to own and operate his hamburger restaurant, aptly called Bob's Burgers, is a dream come true, especially with his wacky family by his side. His wife, Linda (John Roberts), is Bob's polar opposite: where he's pessimism, she's optimism.

Their three kids—socially awkward Tina (Dan Mintz), sound effects-obsessed Gene (Eugene Mirman), and wayward Louise (Kristen Schaal)—all have their own lives going on outside of the family business. Tina spends her days crushing on the son of Bob's rival restaurateur, while

Gene's busy making music, going so far as to create his own fart sounds to use in projects. Meanwhile, Louise plans, schemes, and finds ways to manipulate her family. Put those personalities together with Bob's stubbornness and Linda's laid-back attitude, and you have a houseful of chaotic fun.

> **" You're my family and I love you, but you're terrible."**
>
> **Gene Belcher** (S3 E12)

Bob always has to be on his toes, whether he's convincing a health inspector that his burgers aren't made from human flesh, or learning how to move forward after getting robbed. With a show this savory, you'll definitely come back for seconds.

MASTER OF NONE

COMEDY • 2015
RATED: TV-MA • 30 MINS

Ever wonder what it's like to be a working actor in New York City? Comedian Aziz Ansari loosely bases this show on his own life and experiences.

Meet Dev (Aziz Ansari), an actor living in the Big Apple. In between going on auditions and hanging out with friends Arnold (Eric Wareheim) and Denise (Lena Waithe), Dev is going on dates with Rachel (Noël Wells).

This two-season series is great for foodies because many scenes take place in bars and restaurants all over New York City (and part of Season 2 is spent in Italy where Dev learns how to make pasta). The digital food and dining website *Eater* called it "Netflix's most entertaining food show," so you know there'll be plenty of snackage on screen. Another special part of the series is watching Dev bond with his immigrant parents, played by Ansari's real-life mom and dad. This funny-yet-poignant show is best watched with friends, since the greatest scenes happen when the characters all get together.

BROAD CITY

**COMEDY • 2014
RATED: TV-14 • 22 MINS**

Two 20-something women turn daily life in New York City into one wild, hilarious thrill ride. Nothing's ever boring when you're hanging out with the very funny Abbi and Ilana.

Being a New Yorker can be stressful, but not if you're friends with Abbi (Abbi Jacobson) and Ilana (Ilana Glazer). These BFFs spend five seasons getting into all kinds of shenanigans.

Abbi's an aspiring artist, trying to make it as an illustrator, while Ilana strives to work as little as possible. Ilana's dentist friend with benefits, Lincoln (Hannibal Buress), is always there to help the girls out when they get into trouble.

Broad City is definitely not for younger viewers, as there's plenty of drug use and sex. However, it's great for people in their 20s and 30s to watch, since it tackles issues millennials can relate to, such as dealing with hookups, hustling to make ends meet, and what the "four Rs" really mean: "Reduce, reuse, recycle, Rihanna."

QUEER EYE

**REALITY TV • 2018 • RATED: TV-14 • 45 MINS • SEASONS: 5
JONATHAN VAN NESS, ANTONI POROWSKI, TAN FRANCE**

Five gay professionals use their skills in the fields of fashion, grooming, design, and more to help people upgrade their lives. The reality show is a reboot of the 2000s hit, *Queer Eye for the Straight Guy*.

Stuck in a rut and need to give yourself a makeover? Call the Fab Five, your soon-to-be new favorite superheroes. Each has their own area of expertise: Jonathan Van Ness does grooming, Antoni Porowski knows food and wine, Tan France takes care of fashion, Bobby Berk does design, and Karamo Brown looks after culture and lifestyle. Together, they help people improve aspects of their lives.

Unlike the original Bravo series, this Netflix reboot takes the Fab Five's skills from New York City to the Atlanta metropolitan area. The experts develop relationships with people from all walks of life, whether it's an overworked father of six who isn't taking proper care of himself, a transgender man recovering from top surgery, or a lesbian whose adoptive parents kicked her out because of who she is.

"You're strong, you're a Kelly Clarkson song, you got this."

Jonathan Van Ness (S2 E6)

One of the best aspects of the show is how everyone is valued, no matter what their story. Couple that with the witty and sassy one-liners from the Fab Five, and you have one truly inspiring show. Make sure to have a box of tissues ready, because this show will definitely hit you in the feels.

SHAMELESS

COMEDY DRAMA • 2011 • RATED: TV-MA • 46 MINS • SEASONS: 11
WILLIAM H. MACY, EMMY ROSSUM, JEREMY ALLEN WHITE

What do you do if you are poor, tired, bored, and angry at the world? You steal, trick, and claw your way to the top, of course. At least that's what patriarch Frank and his gaggle of fiesty, law-breaking, and often obnoxious children decide to do.

There's the Brady Bunch, and then there's the Gallaghers. This large, scrappy family of total misfits takes the South Side of Chicago by storm, doing what they have to in order to survive and apologizing for absolutely nothing.

This remake of the hit UK series of the same name follows Frank (William H. Macy) and his cohort of six kids. There's Fiona (Emmy Rossum), who becomes a surrogate mother to the family when their own mother leaves; Lip (Jeremy Allen White), a budding alcoholic with a high IQ; Ian (Cameron Monaghan), a gay teen with the strongest heart; Debbie (Emma Kenney), a spunky kid who takes no prisoners; Carl (Ethan Cutkosky), a roughhouser who sometimes goes too far; and Liam (various actors), the youngest of the rambunctious gang. Together, along with their plucky neighbors, Veronica and Kevin, they do odd (and often illegal) jobs to make ends meet, such as taking exams for other students and selling drugs out of an ice-cream truck in the park.

While this show is centered on a family, it's definitely not appropriate for all ages, and features plenty of graphic sex and nudity. This, though, is part of what makes it so raw and real: many of these intimate scenes aren't included for relationships' sake. Instead, they highlight just another average aspect of life and growing up. Sometimes you're with someone not because you're in love with them, but simply because you're bored or want a warm body.

While *Shameless* is led by Frank, the heart of the show revolves around Fiona and her plight of having to help raise her wayward siblings. Her gumption will inspire all females watching to take charge of their own narrative.

CREATORS: Paul Abbott, John Wells PRODUCTION CO: Bonanza Productions,
John Wells Productions, Warner Bros. Television, Showtime Networks, Sterling Films (V)

SHAMELESS

COMEDY DRAMA • 2004
RATED: TV-MA • 45 MINS

Meet the Gallaghers, a ragged family of misfits doing what it takes to make ends meet in this Manchester-set UK series that inspired the namesake US show.

The British working class is front and center in this 11-season series about alcoholic father Frank (David Threlfall) and his rowdy kids, including eldest child Fiona (Anne-Marie Duff),

who acts as head of the family. She cares for her siblings as best she can, while maintaining a relationship with boyfriend Steve (James McAvoy). Later in the series, you meet the dreaded Maguires, a feared criminal family who quickly get into arguments with the Gallaghers.

As down and dirty as *State of Play* (see p27) creator Paul Abbott's series is, it also finds room for more delicate moments, in particular its treatment of the homosexuality of teen Gallagher, Ian. But outrageous, blackly comic belly laughs are never far away.

TRAILER PARK BOYS

CRIME COMEDY • 2001
RATED: TV-MA • 30 MINS

Welcome to the fictional Sunnyvale Trailer Park, home to three ex-cons who decide to make a living by pulling off petty crimes while avoiding getting busted by the cops.

This 12-season comedy is filmed in a mockumentary style, complete with handheld camerawork. Felons Julian (John Paul Tremblay), Ricky (Robb Wells), and Bubbles

(Mike Smith) team up for various scams and get-rich-quick schemes. Their plans hit snags whenever they run into Jim, the trailer park's alcoholic supervisor, and Jim's colleague and boyfriend, Randy.

The criminal trio treat jail like a revolving door, continually going in and getting out throughout the series. The fact that their illegal schemes usually fail so quickly becomes a running gag on the show that's reminiscent of *Gilligan's Island*'s (see p419) constantly foiled plans. This is a great series to watch when you need a good laugh.

DETECTORISTS

COMEDY • 2014
RATED: 15 (UK) • 30 MINS

Two metal-detecting fanatics share a dream to unearth untold riches in Essex. Their shared goal creates a strong bond between them in this gently funny, understated comedy.

Friends Andy (Mackenzie Crook) and Lance (Toby Jones) are on the hunt for the find of the century buried beneath their feet in the fictional town of Danebury. They attend

a metal-detecting club called the Danebury Metal Detecting Club, or DMDC for short. When they're not looking for treasure, they're dealing with their diverse love lives: Lance hopes to get back with his ex-wife, despite the fact she has a new boyfriend, while Andy dates teacher Becky (Rachael Stirling).

Over the course of the three-season series, the DMDC members encounter plenty of setbacks to their hobby, such as dealing with rival detectorists, uncovering dark secrets, and struggling to make time for their loved ones alongside their beloved pastime.

PROJECT RUNWAY

GAME SHOW • 2004
RATED: TV-PG • 60 MINS

Aspiring fashion designers compete to earn a shot in the cutthroat industry, creating haute couture from materials as diverse as grocery store items and the clothes on their back.

For 18 seasons, this long-running show has been revealing the best and most gifted amateur fashion designers. Join host Heidi Klum and mentor Tim Gunn as they guide creative hopefuls through the rigorous competition. Both fashion editor Nina García and designer Michael Kors have been judges on the series since it began.

In each episode, contestants have to design new fashion pieces to be modeled on a catwalk. Naturally, no two challenges are alike, with many focusing on a designer's creativity, and others testing their resourcefulness.

The ultimate prize is to design a fashion collection for New York Fashion Week. Do you have what it takes?

RUPAUL'S DRAG RACE

GAME SHOW • 2009 • RATED: TV-14 • 45 MINS • SEASONS: 12
RUPAUL, MICHELLE VISAGE, ROSS MATHEWS

Dear drag queens, your makeup's great, your hair's hot, and your outfit came to slay, but you're still missing that crown. Luckily, RuPaul can help. Like he once said, we can't wait to see how this turns out.

If you like drag queens, fab gowns, and having a good time, this is for you. In each season, contestants face a series of challenges to be crowned "America's Next Drag Superstar." RuPaul wears many hats in this series: hosting, mentoring, and serving as head judge. He's assisted by fellow judge Michelle Visage, and at various times Santino Rice, Carson Kressley, and Ross Mathews, as well as star judges such as Ariana Grande and Troye Sivan.

Each episode follows a similar format: contestants must compete in mini and maxi challenges, often creating their own outfits, and showcasing their looks on the runway. The weakest pair then has to fight it out to decide who gets to stay in the competition in a fierce lip-synch battle. Some episodes even throw in a few curveballs, including bringing back previously eliminated queens.

> *"Gentlemen, start your engines, and may the best woman win!"*
>
> **RuPaul** (every episode)

One of the best parts of the show is seeing what sayings RuPaul will come out with next. Quips such as "Impersonating Beyoncé is not your destiny, child" will make even the biggest grump in your house laugh. A hotly-anticipated British version of the show premiered in 2019. You won't want to sashay away.

NATHAN FOR YOU

COMEDY • 2013
RATED: TV-14 • 30 MINS

Need to improve your small business and start to turn a profit? Then call business-school graduate Nathan to help. But be warned, be careful what you wish for!

Armed with his business degree and life experiences, Nathan (Nathan Fielder) sets out to help small companies thrive. Well, kind of. This four-season docu-reality show explores Nathan's totally out-there ideas as he consults on projects ranging from poo-flavored frozen yogurt, to tricking haunted-house guests into thinking they've contracted a disease.

An important aspect of the series is Nathan's social anxiety, something Fielder struggles with himself. He puts his vulnerability on display, telling the Los Angeles Times that he didn't want his TV persona "to feel like a comedy character." So, you know you're getting the real deal when you binge-watch this comedy, which makes the story lines all the more compelling.

RIPPING YARNS

COMEDY • 1976
RATED: TV-PG • 30 MINS

Get ready for some ripping good TV with this collection of thrilling stories all starring Monty Python star Michael Palin in the lead role.

Comedian and writer Michael Palin plays myriad characters in this two-season anthology show, in which each of the nine episodes focuses on completely different characters and plots. His roles span everything from a schoolboy to a bank manager to a prisoner of war, among others, with guest stars such as Ian Ogilvy, Roy Kinnear, John Le Mesurier, Denholm Elliott, and even John Cleese lending support.

Cocreated by Palin and fellow Python Terry Jones, the series parodies pre–World War II schoolboy literature and, through it, different areas of British culture, with pilot episode "Tomkinson's Schooldays" (a take-off of Tom Brown's School Days) helping set the tone. If you're a fan of Monty Python (see p262), this show was made for you.

MOST EXTREME ELIMINATION CHALLENGE

GAME SHOW • 2003
RATED: TV-14 • 30 MINS

This unconventional series mixes comedy with competition by repurposing footage from the hilarious Japanese game show Takeshi's Castle.

The concept of the show, abbreviated to MXC, is simple: two teams compete against each other across various obstacle courses until a winner is crowned. However, MXC is no ordinary game show. The original Japanese audio track is muted so actors Victor Wilson, Christopher Darga, and John Cervenka can provide hysterical voice-overs on each episode, dubbing what the game-show hosts and contestants are saying. The series lasted for five glorious seasons.

Challenges involve contestants having to fly on a rope swing to reach a platform, dodge giant fake boulders while ascending a makeshift mountain, and run across large rolling logs, often resulting in them falling into a mud pit.

PARTY DOWN

COMEDY • 2009
RATED: TV-14 • 30 MINS

So you wanna be a Hollywood star? Looking for fame and fortune? Well, set that dream aside for a bit and get a catering job to make ends meet.

A group of aspiring actors and writers living in LA hope to make their dreams come true, but quickly learn that being a working artist in Hollywood means having to take on a side hustle to pay the bills. So, they turn to catering business Party Down to make a living while waiting for their big break. Henry (Adam Scott), Casey (Lizzy Caplan), Kyle (Ryan Hansen), and Roman (Martin Starr) all work under the leadership of Ron (Ken Marino), an uptight boss whose dream is to manage a soup buffet restaurant.

For two seasons, follow the *Party Down* crew as they work various small-time catering gigs and hope for fame and fortune to strike. Some jobs are more unconventional than others, such as the after-party for an adult entertainment award show.

SUPERSTORE

COMEDY • 2015
RATED: TV-14 • 22 MINS

Looking to make a career change? Maybe try working at a large retail store. The job might stink, but at least you'll have interesting stories to share at parties.

Superstore is to big-box retailers what *The Office* (see p153–155) is to paper companies. Though not filmed in a mockumentary-style format, this sitcom still follows the everyday lives of the employees who work at Cloud 9 store #1217. Single mother Amy (America Ferrera) is the floor manager, who works with new hire Jonah (Ben Feldman), assistant manager Dina (Lauren Ash), associates Mateo (Nico Santos) and Cheyenne (Nichole Bloom), and manager Glenn (Mark McKinney). Together, they strive to make their megastore the best it can be.

Over the course of six seasons, the Cloud 9 team try to work together, despite their differences. If you've ever worked in retail, this is sure to raise some laughs.

THE KING OF QUEENS

COMEDY • 1998
RATED: TV-PG • 22 MINS

You can only choose one of these: a steady job, a beautiful spouse, owning nice things, not living with your father-in-law. If you're Doug Heffernan, you pick the last one every time.

Doug (Kevin James), a delivery driver for the fictional International Parcel Service, has it all, including a loving wife, Carrie (Leah Remini), two great friends Deacon (Victor Williams) and Spence (Patton Oswalt), and a house in Queens. But then his scheming father-in-law, Arthur (Jerry Stiller), moves in after accidentally burning down his own home.

Within the blink of an eye, Doug loses his beloved man-cave basement so that Arthur can have a room. Maybe things wouldn't be so bad if only Arthur wasn't always yelling and complaining, not to mention making outrageous claims, such as having invented the moist towelette. This nine-season sitcom will make you thankful your own in-laws aren't anything like Arthur.

EVERYBODY LOVES RAYMOND

COMEDY • 1996 • RATED: TV-PG • 22 MINS • SEASONS: 9
RAY ROMANO, PATRICIA HEATON, BRAD GARRETT

Join the misadventures of a sarcastic sports columnist as he uses his sense of humor to deal with his overbearing parents, eccentric brother, stressed-out wife, and three kids.

Ray (Ray Romano) and his dysfunctional family are central to this long-running sitcom. When he's not avoiding household and parental duties, leaving everything to wife Debra (Patricia Heaton), he's forced to interact with his manipulative mother Marie (Doris Roberts), stubborn father Frank (Peter Boyle), and New York City cop brother Robert (Brad Garrett).

When the whole family gets together, which is practically daily, there's never a dull moment. Characters play tricks on each other all the time, such as when Marie pretends to teach her daughter-in-law how to make her special meatballs, only to sabotage the recipe and put Ray in the middle of the drama. Or when Robert gets scammed and Ray is forced to come to his rescue to keep the rest of the family from finding out. If you were to look up "whiny" in the dictionary, you'd be sure to find Ray's name right alongside it.

> **"** *So everybody has to do what Raymond wants, right?* **"**
>
> **Robert** (S3 E1)

ARE YOU BEING SERVED?

COMEDY • 1972
RATED: TV-PG • 28 MINS

If you like *Superstore*, double entendres, and humor, then stop what you're watching and start bingeing on this long-running show instead. Working in retail has never been funnier.

This 1970s sitcom about the employees of the clothing departments in a fictional retail store called Grace Brothers, ran for a whopping 10 seasons. Mrs. Slocombe (Mollie Sugden) is a senior sales assistant in charge of the women's department, while Mr. Grainger (Arthur Brough) runs the men's department.

They work with several lower-level sales assistants, each with their own quirks. These include Mr. Humphries (John Inman), who delights in trilling his catchphrase "I'm free!" across the shop floor, and often speaks direct to camera—at a time when breaking the fourth wall was unconventional. The series loves to parody the British class system and thrives on sexual innuendoes. You'll be blushing in no time.

THE CLASS

COMEDY • 2006
RATED: NR • 22 MINS

High-school reunions are so yesterday. It's all about third-grade reunions. In *The Class*, a group of 20-somethings reconnect and share the same gradual realization that growing up sucks.

Ethan (Jason Ritter) thinks he's thought of the best proposal for his girlfriend, whom he met when they were in third grade. He plans to invite their old classmates to help celebrate when he pops the question. Inevitably, that plan backfires. But many of them strike up friendships with each other.

Some rekindle the flame, such as Duncan (Jon Bernthal) and Nicole (Andrea Anders), while Richie (Jesse Tyler Ferguson) and Lina (Heather Goldenhersh) develop new relationships. Toss in the sarcastic Kyle and the even more sarcastic Kat, and the whole school gang is back together in this criminally underrated one-season show. The seven friends may not be at school any more, but they're still learning new stuff every day.

THE CRAZY ONES

COMEDY • 2013
RATED: TV-14 • 30 MINS

Sometimes it's good to be the boss, especially if you're Simon, the head of an ad agency who comes up with the wildest ideas. This was Robin Williams's final TV show before he passed away, and he was funnier than ever in it.

Williams's humor shines brightly as he plays a successful marketer with unconventional ideas, such as convincing Kelly Clarkson to sing a jingle for McDonald's. His more uptight daughter and business partner, Sydney (Sarah Michelle Gellar), does her best to deal with her dad's wacky notions, but it's tough to be a feisty go-getter in such a laid-back working environment.

Luckily she has her coworkers—copywriter Zach, art director Andrew, and assistant Lauren—to help keep her grounded. Together, the marketing team uses their wits and bizarre ideas to seal the deal with their clients on this show that ran for one hilarious season.

EVERYTHING SUCKS!

COMEDY • 2018
RATED: TV-MA • 30 MINS

If *Stranger Things* dominates your vision of the '80s, then *Everything Sucks!* owns the '90s. It's audiovisual club nerds versus drama geeks in this short-lived, nostalgia-filled Netflix series.

The only thing that sucks about this show, set in a town called Boring, is that it only lasted one season. High-school student Luke (Jahi Di'Allo Winston) has the hots for the daughter of Principal Messner (Patch Darragh), Kate (Peyton Kennedy). But she secretly has eyes for Emaline (Sydney Sweeney). When the sets for the school play are accidentally ruined, the drama kids are ready to start smashing skulls—until Luke suggests they team up with him and the rest of the audiovisual club to make a movie. The result is pure hilarious mayhem.

Set in 1996, this series includes as many '90s references as *Stranger Things* (see p446) does '80s ones. It's perfect for millennials who miss their childhood and wish they could go back to simpler times.

DRAMAWORLD

COMEDY • 2016
RATED: NR • 15 MINS

On a scale of one to 10, how much would you be freaking out if you suddenly found yourself in the world of your favorite TV show?

College student Claire (Liv Hewson) would much rather spend her time binge-watching her beloved Korean drama called *Taste of Love* than hanging out with people at parties. She has the hots for actor Joon Park (Sean Dulake) and can't stop fantasizing about him and his enticing show. If only her life were more like the K-drama! Suddenly, thanks to some magic, Claire is sucked into her phone *Jumanji*-style and finds herself IN *Taste of Love*. Now, she's chilling with Joon Park, but fellow outsider Seth Ko (Justin Chon) makes sure she doesn't interfere with the plots. But, of course, nothing goes as planned.

This two-season show features many appearances by famous Korean pop and drama stars, including boy band Super Junior's Choi Si-won.

ENCORE!

REALITY-TV • 2019
RATED: TV-PG • 55 MINS

When it comes to high-school theater, there's usually more drama happening offstage than on. And that drama is still lingering 20 years later in this fun reality show.

Kristen Bell is host and executive producer of this Disney+ reality series about high-school drama classes reuniting to perform encores of the shows they did when they were kids.

Each episode features a different performance, people, location, and year. One installment is about a high-school class from California recreating their 1996 production of *Annie*, while another takes us to Kentucky to watch thespians restage their 1984 musical, *Pippin*.

It's the drama geeks themselves who really make this one-season show special, because many were high-school sweethearts who haven't seen or spoken to each other in decades. One woman is clearly still hung up on her old boyfriend, making for an enticing yet cringy ride.

THE GOOD PLACE

COMEDY • 2016
RATED: TV-14 • 22 MINS

Will you end up in the Good Place or the Bad Place? That is the question. After dying, an amoral girl is mistakenly sent to live in the Good Place.

Get ready for a forking good time with this four-season show. After Eleanor (Kristen Bell) dies, she finds herself in the Good Place, a Heaven-like paradise that only lets in people who've lived virtuous lives. Eleanor realizes she's been sent there by mistake, but she doesn't want Michael (Ted Danson), the person who designed the utopia, to find out.

Eleanor enlists the help of her assigned soulmate, Chidi (William Jackson Harper), to teach her how to be a "good" person. Along the way, Eleanor meets Jason (Manny Jacinto)—who also thinks he's been placed there by mistake—and his soulmate, Tahani (Jameela Jamil). How long can they keep up the charade before it all goes to hell?

COMMUNITY

COMEDY • 2009 • RATED: TV-14 • 22 MINS • SEASONS: 6
JOEL MCHALE, GILLIAN JACOBS, CHEVY CHASE

A smarmy lawyer is disbarred after it is revealed he doesn't actually have a university degree. He enrolls in a community college and forms a pretend study group so he can get closer to his attractive classmate.

Unhappy with putting his life on hold after getting busted for lying about having a degree, Jeff Winger (Joel McHale) plans to get through community college as fast as possible with no distractions. That is, until he meets Britta Perry (Gillian Jacobs), his cute classmate. With one thing on his mind, Jeff tries to form a makeshift study group with Britta so he can get to know her better, but his plan hits a snag when she invites several other students from their class to join the group.

Cue movie-obsessed nerd Abed Nadir (Danny Pudi), overachiever Annie Edison (Alison Brie), former hotshot football star Troy Barnes (Donald Glover), religious do-gooder Shirley Bennett (Yvette Nicole Brown), and Pierce Hawthorne (Chevy Chase), a wealthy tycoon looking for self-discovery. Together, the six of them form an unlikely friendship, continuing to take classes together every semester. When they're not studying, they're begrudgingly helping the dean make Greendale Community College as great as it can be, often with hilarious results. Toss in teacher Ben Chang (Ken Jeong) and you have one seriously eclectic group of people.

Several episodes are parodies of pop culture gems, such as Clint Eastwood's spaghetti western films and *Pulp Fiction*. The live-action show also makes the occasional foray into animation, using everything from traditional 2D forms, to 8-bit video-game stylizations, and stop-motion reminiscent of *Wallace and Gromit* (see p97).

> **"** *I'm a teacher. Wait, that's worse than the truth. I'm a student.* **"**
>
> Jeff (S2 E2)

Season 3 even features a multiple timeline episode that plays out in seven different ways. Titled "Remedial Chaos Theory," the instalment was nominated for an Emmy for Outstanding Writing in a Comedy Series. With so many diverse episodes, it's hard to decide which is best.

CREATOR: Dan Harmon **PRODUCTION CO:** Krasnoff Foster Productions, Harmonius Claptrap, AGBO (as The Russo Brothers), Universal Media Studios (UMS), Sony Pictures Television (in association with)

CRAZY EX-GIRLFRIEND

COMEDY MUSICAL • 2015
RATED: TV-14 • 42 MINS

Would you move across the country to pursue your old boyfriend? That's what one woman does, leaving behind a life in New York City on a whim to reunite with her ex in West Covina, California.

Rebecca (Rachel Bloom) seemingly has it all: an Ivy League education, a hotshot lawyer job in New York City, and a junior partner position, should she accept it. While deciding whether or not to take it she bumps into her old teenage flame, Josh (Vincent Rodriguez III). When Josh says he's leaving NYC for California, she decides to follow suit. On a quest for happiness, Rebecca gets a new job at a law firm and befriends paralegal Paula (Donna Lynne Champlin).

The best part about this four-season show is that it includes original songs in different styles ranging from hip hop to Sondheim, usually sung by Rebecca at key moments. The series also delves into mental illness as it explores Rebecca's psychological issues.

GLEE

MUSICAL COMEDY • 2009 • RATED: TV-14 • 44 MINS • SEASONS: 6
LEA MICHELE, JANE LYNCH, MATTHEW MORRISON

The misfits of a high-school glee club meet its gleaming cheerleaders and musical battle ensues. Songs, drama, and a ton of teen angst follow singing group New Directions' members as they prepare for their biggest challenge ever.

All kids want to do in school is belong, and the students at William McKinley High soon learn that the glee club organized by teacher Will Schuester (Matthew Morrison) is the place to be. Many students join the rejuvenated choir, dubbed New Directions, including enthusiastic show-off Rachel (Lea Michele), footballer Finn, cheerleader Quinn, and bullied Kurt. As Rachel asks in the pilot, "Being a part of something special makes you special, right?"

The glee club's arch-rival is the cheerleading squad, led by Sue Sylvester (Jane Lynch). Sue does everything she can to ruin New Directions, and she's not afraid to fight dirty.

Best known for its cute, catchy covers of popular songs, the show also focuses on more serious issues, such as domestic abuse, eating disorders, and even texting while driving. *Glee* covers topics that nearly all teens can relate to, such as deciding on the best time to lose your virginity or how to gently let down someone who has a crush on you. And if you're not into any particular story line, you can always just bliss out to the fabulous musical numbers.

> *" You can't change your past, but you can let go and start your future."*
>
> **Quinn Fabray** (S3 E11)

THE MARY TYLER MOORE SHOW

COMEDY • 1970
RATED: TV-PG • 30 MINS

This female-centric show about an associate producer changed the game for women's roles on TV and inspired *30 Rock*.

Looking to reinvent herself after her engagement is called off, Mary (Mary Tyler Moore) moves to Minneapolis and gets a job as an associate producer for a TV news station. There, she works with producer Lou (Edward Asner), head writer Murray (Gavin MacLeod), and anchorman Ted (Ted Knight).

As Mary adjusts to her new career path, she also becomes friends with her wisecracking neighbor, Rhoda. The seven-season series was revolutionary, deemed by critics as a show that got rid of the tired, family-friendly sitcom gags. According to *USA Today*, Tina Fey once said the goal of *30 Rock* (see p244) was "to try to be like *The Mary Tyler Moore Show*, where it's not about doing the news."

HAPPY DAYS

COMEDY • 1974 • RATED: TV-G • 30 MINS • SEASONS: 11
RON HOWARD, HENRY WINKLER, TOM BOSLEY

Richie Cunningham has it all: good family, good friends, good fun. This beloved classic, set in the '50s and '60s, follows him and his ragtag group of pals as they come of age in Milwaukee, Wisconsin.

If you're searching for a feel-good show that dreams of yesteryear, look no further. Richie (Ron Howard) grows up in an idealized version of the '50s when times were simpler: no smartphones or social media in sight. Surrounded by his loving family, dad Howard (Tom Bosley), mom Marion (Marion Ross), and sister Joannie (Erin Moran), Richie navigates high school, occasionally getting into trouble. His best friend is rabble-rouser Fonzie (Henry Winkler), a greaser who loves riding his motorbike and being the epitome of cool.

The series involves plenty of story lines about Richie and his buds trying to pick up girls, including his attempts to earn enough money to buy a car to impress the ladies, only to quickly realize it's not the safest of vehicles. Though this is a wholesome family sitcom, *Happy Days* doesn't shy away from certain topics, such as racial prejudice, strippers, and gang wars. But overall the show follows the misadventures of a sweet teen boy who just wants to pick up girls. Before you know it, you'll be pulling a Fonzie and shouting his catchphrase: "Ay-y-y-y!"

> **"***Fonz, you're not jumping over garbage cans on a bike. You're jumping over a shark.***"**
>
> **Richie Cunningham** (S5 E3)

THE ANDY GRIFFITH SHOW

**COMEDY • 1960 • RATED: TV-G • 30 MINS • SEASONS: 8
ANDY GRIFFITH, DON KNOTTS, RON HOWARD**

A widowed sheriff raises his young son in the sleepy town of Mayberry, helped by his aunt and deputy. With minimal crime to deal with, the sheriff spends a lot of time relaxing and fishing with his boy.

While Sheriff Andy (Andy Griffith) keeps things in line in his slow-paced town, his real job is being a father and role model to his son, Opie (Ron Howard). But because it takes a village to raise a child, Andy's deputy, Barney (Don Knotts), and his Aunt Bee (Frances Bavier) both lend a helping hand. Though a good-hearted kid, Opie doesn't stay out of trouble, trespassing on a neighbor's property and falling under the influence of a rogue. But, with Andy's life lessons and guidance, Opie always redeems himself when he messes up.

The comic relief belongs to Barney—Barney thinks he's the best at what he does, but his track record says otherwise. "I had my eye on you right from the start, mister," he loves to say, just as a scammer he naively trusted proves to be, in fact, a scammer. This is a great show to watch when you just want to unwind after a long day.

> **"***Ain't-ain't we a-pickin' our peaches 'fore they're fuzzed up good?***"**
>
> **Sheriff Andy Taylor** (SI E13)

MURPHY BROWN

**COMEDY • 1988
RATED: TV-PG • 30 MINS**

She's middle-aged, she's single, and she's not afraid to get her hands dirty for a great news story. Think you're tough? Odds are, you're no match for journalist Murphy Brown.

Murphy Brown (Candice Bergen) is an investigative journalist and recovering alcoholic who returns to her old stomping ground, a news magazine called *FYI*, after leaving a residential treatment center. In her career so far, she's been seen by colleagues as one of the boys, a hard-hitting media personality who doesn't scare easily. While Murphy is away at rehab, super peppy Corky (Faith Ford) takes over her position and stays on when Murphy returns. Also at the news network is Frank, Murphy's friend and fellow reporter.

This sitcom about a strong woman making a comeback ran for 11 seasons. The final season was a revival, premiering two decades after Season 10, partly in response to Donald Trump's election as president.

COMRADE DETECTIVE

ACTION COMEDY • 2017
RATED: TV-MA • 40 MINS

Move over, *Starsky and Hutch*, there's a new (and bizarre) buddy cop duo in town. They're Romanian, they're anti-capitalists, and they're dubbed by American actors.

Comrade Detective claims to be a 1980s show produced by Romania's then-communist government. It has apparently recently been found and dubbed into English, but things aren't quite what they seem. This one-season show may end up being your new favorite political parody or piece of meta-TV. Buckle up for some retro police fun.

When the partner of Detective Gregor (Florin Piersic, Jr., and dubbed by Channing Tatum) is murdered during a drug bust, Gregor is reassigned a new partner named Iosif (Corneliu Ulici, and dubbed by Joseph Gordon-Levitt). Together, they work to solve the murder of a fellow officer. In the process, they unearth a plot to switch Romania from communism to capitalism.

JUDGE JOHN DEED

CRIME • 2001
RATED: 15 (UK) • 88 MINS

While some shows focus on detectives, and others on lawyers, this crime drama takes a look at another aspect of the legal system: judges. Well, one judge in particular, one who likes to play by his own rules.

Meet your next legal drama obsession. Sir John Deed (Martin Shaw) is a newly appointed High Court judge looking to right the wrongs of the cases that reach his desk. Like many people who've dealt with the judicial system before, John's fed up with many of the law's finer points. Because of that frustration, his methods are considered unconventional, which sometimes lands him in trouble with colleagues, including an Appeals Court judge who happens to be his ex-father-in-law.

While fighting for justice with his cases, John's also on a quest to woo Jo (Jenny Seagrove), part of the Queen's Counsel and an old flame. This six-season series is the missing void in most crime buffs' lives.

THE ROCKFORD FILES

CRIME • 1974
RATED: TV-PG • 60 MINS

Sometimes it takes a con to catch a con, so California criminals beware: LA private eye Jim Rockford is hot on your trail in this classic crime series ... and he's no angel!

Rockford (James Garner) isn't your average private investigator. He has a criminal history—well, sort of. Convicted of a crime he didn't commit, he's pardoned five years later. As a free man, Jim takes on PI jobs, such as tracking down a mistress who's laundering money, and looking into the death of a racecar driver who plummets off a cliff. His retired truck driver dad, Rocky (Noah Beery Jr.), sometimes lends his son a hand in solving cases, as does Dennis Becker (Joe Santos), an LAPD sergeant.

Unlike many other TV private eyes, Jim is easygoing and not a fan of fighting. Spanning over 100 episodes across six seasons, *The Rockford Files* offers a cabinet chock-full of cases for you to get caught up in. You'll be humming its classic theme tune in no time.

CHUCK

ACTION COMEDY • 2007
RATED: TV-14 • 43 MINS

Forget the girl next door. Now, there's the computer genius next door who gets in over his head and needs help from both the CIA and NSA to stay alive. What could he have done?

Twenty-something Chuck (Zachary Levi) is an underachieving computer whiz whose life does a 180-degree turn when he clicks on a mysterious email from his friend in the CIA.

Suddenly, a piece of software containing all of the US's biggest espionage secrets is digitally transferred into Chuck's brain, instantly making him a target for every bad guy in the world. Once the US government learns what has happened, they assign CIA agent Sarah Walker (Yvonne Strahovski) and NSA agent John Casey (Adam Baldwin) to protect him.

For five seasons, Chuck and his entourage work to stop both national and international villains, while trying to blend in and lay low. This zero just went to hero in the blink of an eye and the click of an email.

MONK

CRIME • 2002
RATED: TV-PG • 44 MINS

Criminals may make clean getaways, but the crimes themselves aren't clean, many leaving behind blood, hair, and debris. This makes it hard to be both a detective and a germaphobe.

Detective Adrian Monk (Tony Shalhoub) returns to work after suffering a nervous breakdown over the death of his wife. Now a PI and a consultant for the San Francisco Police

Department's homicide unit, Monk helps solve cases while dealing with his obsessive-compulsive disorder. It's not easy, since Monk has a fear of germs and a long list of other phobias, such as small spaces and heights. Not ideal when you're working on criminal cases.

But Monk's strong attention to detail makes him a valuable asset to the SFPD, especially to Captain Stottlemeyer (Ted Levine) and Lieutenant Disher (Jason Gray-Stanford). Most of the eight-seasons' episodes are standalones, but an overarching story line involves the mysterious death of Monk's wife.

PROFESSOR T.

CRIME • 2015
RATED: TV-MA • 53 MINS

If you thought Sherlock Holmes in *Elementary* was a brilliant, yet insufferable consultant for the police, just wait until you meet Professor Jasper Teerlinck.

Teerlinck (Koen De Bouw) is a professor who teaches criminology at Antwerp University. He's super smart, which sometimes goes to his head as he helps the police with their cases.

Jasper's excellent at what he does, but he's not the easiest to work with, and his methods and personality tend to rub people up the wrong way. Assisted by colleagues Annelies (Ella Leyers) and Daan (Bart Hollanders), he works to solve puzzling cases, such as the attack on a woman on campus that resembles a cold-case crime from a decade before.

Every episode of this three-season crime drama from Belgium will keep you guessing until the big reveal. It's the perfect series for fans looking for another *Inspector Morse* (see p98) or *Sherlock* (see p30).

AGGRETSUKO

ANIMATED COMEDY • 2018
RATED: TV-14 • 15 MINS

Talking animals are the stars in this Japanese cartoon based on the Sanrio character. An overworked red panda spends her days at the office, letting loose at night doing karaoke.

Picture this: you're a 20-something exploited office worker looking to blow off some steam after dealing with your literal pig of a boss. You hit the karaoke bar and rock out to death metal night after night to keep your temper in check. Sounds exhausting, but also kind of fun, right? That's what red panda Retsuko (Erica Mendez) does daily. Her boss is a pig called Director Ton (Josh Petersdorf), who makes Retsuko's work life unbearable. Luckily, her coworkers, Fenneko (Katelyn Gault) and Haida (Ben Diskin), help Retsuko manage her sanity.

This two-season animated show is perfect for anyone struggling in their career. Take it from Retsuko, finding your inner screamo is the best medicine to cure any quarter-life crisis.

F IS FOR FAMILY

ANIMATED COMEDY • 2015
RATED: TV-MA • 30 MINS

"Family" is the F word in this adult cartoon about a five-person household living in the '70s. Watch it to see family life in the time before social media, smart phones, and helicopter parenting.

Frank (Bill Burr) is the patriarch of the Murphy family and husband to Sue (Laura Dern). They have three kids: troublemaker Kevin (Justin Long), bullied Bill (Haley Reinhart), and manipulative Maureen (Debi Derryberry), who are a long way from the *Brady Bunch* (see p253). Frank drinks and drives, asking his son to open a can of beer for him while he's behind the wheel. He's also abusive and neglectful toward his family and constantly comparing himself to neighbors and friends whom he thinks are more successful.

Embracing some dark subject matter, this four-season show stems from the mind of stand-up comedian Bill Burr, who voices the main character. So, expect some seriously witty one-liners.

PINKY AND THE BRAIN

ANIMATED COMEDY • 1995
RATED: TV-Y • 30 MINS

What do you get when you and your partner in crime become famous on the *Animaniacs*? Your own spin-off series about taking over the world, of course!

Well, not quite. Two genetically enhanced lab mice—one a brainiac, the other a doofus—work together to try their hand at controlling everything and everyone. Unsurprisingly, the world-domination plans devised by The Brain (Maurice LaMarche), such as using a growing ray to enlarge both himself and Pinky (Rob Paulsen), always seem to fail, whether due to arrogance, his sidekick's mishaps, or a series of unfortunate events.

Many of the 66 episodes in the series' four seasons are parodies of famous stories, such as *Around the World in 80 Days* and *Robin Hood*, which make the mice's escapades even more entertaining. Strap in for a fun ride, because Pinky and The Brain won't slow down until they … take over the world!

ADVENTURE TIME

ANIMATION • 2010 • RATED: TV-PG • 11 MINS • SEASONS: 10
JOHN DIMAGGIO, JEREMY SHADA, TOM KENNY

Life is just one big adventure for 12-year-old Finn and his shape-shifting talking dog Jake. Join the duo on their crazy adventures as they explore the Land of Ooo, filled with strange and unusual creatures.

Finn (Jeremy Shada) and Jake (John DiMaggio) live in a postapocalyptic world scarred by the impact of a nuclear war, so the characters they meet during their escapades are anything but ordinary in this animated fantasy.

Follow them as they encounter the Ice King (Tom Kenny), who loves to steal princesses, including Princess Bubblegum (Hynden Walch), a feisty candy humanoid who captures Finn's heart. You'll also meet Marceline the Vampire Queen, a sentient computer named BMO, a princess who looks like a cloud, not to mention Jake Jr. and Jake's other four pups. With such a wacky group of pals, you'll never be bored in the Land of Ooo.

Many episodes involve Finn and Jake going on various quests, such as locating an important book that would deem them heroes, traveling to a wicked forest in search of a coveted item, and venturing into the ocean in a submarine to overcome a fear.

Imagination runs wild—literally, in one episode—in this madcap show that's great for kids and kids at heart who are always up for a grand adventure. Who says growing up means having to give up crazy, zany fun? Not *Adventure Time!*

> **"** *Everything ahead of us is totally unknown.* **"**
>
> **Jake Jr.** (S5 E24)

DANGER MOUSE

ANIMATED COMEDY • 1981
RATED: TV-Y7-FV • 25 MINS

Forget Secret Squirrel and Morocco Mole. There's an even better cartoon secret agent duo out there: Danger Mouse and Penfold. They've got their orders and they're off, but will they foil their toady nemesis?

Join spy Danger Mouse (David Jason) and his sidekick Penfold (Terry Scott) as they carry out orders from Colonel K (Edward Kelsey) to

thwart villainous toad Baron Silas Greenback (Kelsey) and his crow henchman Stiletto (Brian Trueman), and save the world. No pressure, right? Luckily, Danger Mouse has a set of special skills, including flexibility and strength. When they're not battling Baron and Stiletto, Danger Mouse and Penfold are fighting the likes of mad scientists, aliens, and a vampire duck named Count Duckula.

The 10-season cartoon is a parody of James Bond and other famous spy stories, including the '60s series *Danger Man* (see p144). The show was later revived in 2015.

CALL THE MIDWIFE

DRAMA • 2012 • RATED: TV-PG • 60 MINS • SEASONS: 9
VANESSA REDGRAVE, LAURA MAIN, JENNY AGUTTER

Based on the memoirs of nurse Jennifer Worth, this series follows the exploits of midwives working in the East End of London in the '50s and '60s. It chronicles how far we've come in terms of medical care, tackling many social issues along the way.

This period drama begins in 1957, during the heyday of the Baby Boom. New midwife Jenny (Jessica Raine) joins a nursing convent run by nuns to help look after the pregnant moms (and often their families) in London's poverty-stricken East End. Jenny's older self (Vanessa Redgrave) narrates the show.

Jenny and her fellow midwives and nuns, including Shelagh Turner (Laura Main) and Sister Julienne (Jenny Agutter), do their best to deliver as many healthy babies as possible, while dealing with various issues, including teen pregnancy, appalling housing conditions, racial prejudice, and prison births.

The midwives have their work cut out for them as the series progresses through the years. With the tensions of the Cold War, the threat of nuclear warfare hovers over the characters, and later the birth control pill changes the game for them.

> **"** *The world is full of love that goes unspoken.* **"**
>
> **Jenny** (S2 E6)

The show refuses to shy away from sensitive issues that can plague women and affect their babies, including incest, domestic violence, miscarriage, prostitution, birth defects, and abortion. It's a female-centric series with powerful roles that will make you stand up and cheer.

GROWN-ISH

COMEDY • 2018
RATED: TV-14 • 22 MINS

The Johnsons' oldest daughter, Zoey, leaves her parents behind for college and loses some of her confidence along the way in this spin-off of *Black-ish* (see p274) starring Yara Shahidi.

Taking its cue from Anthony Anderson's Dre Johnson on *Black-ish*, *Grown-ish* is narrated by Zoey, who's given up her big-fish-in-a-small-pond life as the coolest member of the

Johnson household to become just another college student. While comparisons to 1987's *A Different World* are inevitable, *Grown-ish*, which has three seasons so far, truly stands on its own.

Along with her new college pals, who are exploring gender fluidity along with what it means to suddenly be living in a parent-free world, Zoey stumbles on through, trying new things (like Adderall, the ADHD drug), and seeing if she can find her place. At times she's a bit of a straight man to her wackier friends, who are exploring everything from gender fluidity to figuring out what it means to be "woke."

AMERICAN VANDAL

CRIME COMEDY • 2017 • RATED: TV-MA • 34 MINS • SEASONS: 2
TYLER ALVAREZ, GRIFFIN GLUCK, JIMMY TATRO

Prepare yourself to be shocked. This totally inappropriate yet hysterical sleuthing series holds nothing back in terms of body parts and bodily functions. Crime may not pay, but it might be criminal how much *American Vandal* **makes you laugh.**

This crime satire follows two teens who investigate "serious" cases that have turned high schools upside down—crimes such as salacious graffiti on faculty cars and cafeteria lemonade spiked with a laxativelike substance.

In Season 1, students Peter (Tyler Alvarez) and Sam (Griffin Gluck) team up to unearth the truth about who really drew phallic symbols on 27 faculty cars in the school parking lot. School prankster Dylan Maxwell (Jimmy Tatro) is the number one suspect, but he swears he isn't responsible. Peter and Sam channel their inner Sherlock Holmes and Dr. Watson to delve into the case, even using an evidence board filled with suspects connected by pieces of yarn, just like real detectives do—well, almost!

Season 2 mixes things up a bit as it explores a new case at a different institution, with Peter and Sam travelling to a private Catholic high school to investigate the crimes of the self-proclaimed "Turd Burglar." (Yes, really!) Some vandal has purposely contaminated lemonade, resulting in tons of students simultaneously experiencing diarrhoea. Who is this Turd Burglar, and what is his/her/their endgame? Is it just to wreak havoc, or is there a hidden agenda?

American Vandal is gross, plain and simple, but that doesn't mean you won't laugh from start to finish. The fake seriousness of the situations, which are presented as if the characters were discussing murders instead of pranks, is great when you want to watch a series that doesn't tax your brain too much. You take the show at face value and laugh, or cringe, in the process. Because of the subject matter, the series might not be the most appropriate for tweens and younger teens, but for everyone else, it's terrific fun.

"As a prankster, you gotta respect another prankster."

Dylan Maxwell (S1 E2)

CREATORS: Dan Perrault, Tony Yacenda
PRODUCTION CO: 3 Arts Entertainment, CBS Studios, Funny or Die, Woodhead Entertainment

MISFITS

SCI-FI COMEDY • 2009
RATED: TV-MA • 60 MINS

Being forced to do community service is not great, but gaining superpowers from it sounds worth it. That's what several delinquents discover when their worlds get turned upside down.

Five teenage offenders are sentenced to community service. They all get caught outside during a thunderstorm and mysteriously acquire different supernatural abilities.

Curtis (Nathan Stewart-Jarrett) can rewind time, Simon (Iwan Rheon) can turn invisible, Alisha (Antonia Thomas) can force people to become sexually hysterical, and Kelly (Lauren Socha) can read minds. But fifth member Nathan's powers don't manifest right away.

The quintuplet accidentally kill their probation officer after he is driven insane during the storm and attacks them. How long can they keep the murder a secret, especially now that they have special powers they're learning how to control? This five-season series is perfect for fans of comics and their film adaptations.

PHIL OF THE FUTURE

COMEDY • 2004
RATED: TV-PG • 25 MINS

Note to self: never rent a used time machine—it could malfunction and leave you and your family stranded in a completely different century.

Phil Diffy (Raviv Ullman) is your average teenager: he goes to school, fights with little sister Pim (Amy Bruckner), and has crushes on girls. Oh, and he's from the year 2121, stuck in the present-day after his family's

time machine breaks down. Now they have to carefully blend in with modern society, but it's only a matter of time before someone discovers their secret in this two-season show.

Phil's friend, Keely (Aly Michalka), learns the truth early on. She does what she can to help protect Phil and his family—while also having lots of fun playing with all the exciting, futuristic gadgets they've brought with them. From "Skyack" flying devices to spray food cans, the Diffys may be stuck in the past, but their future looks funny and bright.

THE PROUD FAMILY

ANIMATED COMEDY • 2001
RATED: TV-PG • 30 MINS

You can't pick your family, but if you could, there are far worse options than the Prouds. Grab some Proud Snax and your BFFs, because it's going to be a bumpy ride.

Teenager Penny (Kyla Pratt) is so done with her wacky family. Surrounded by overprotective snack-tycoon dad Oscar (Tommy Davidson), zany mom Trudy

(Paula Jai Parker), and kooky grandma Sugar Mama (Jo Marie Payton), Penny just wants to hang out with her friends and avoid all the responsibilities of growing up. But whenever she runs into trouble, such as having to deal with bullies, she knows her family will be there for her.

The fact that there are plenty of good parent-daughter moments in this animated two-season show makes it especially fun to watch with everyone in the house. You'll be quoting "That's tight," and yelling for Trudy to come fix things before you know it.

DRAKE & JOSH

COMEDY • 2004
RATED: TV-Y7 • 23 MINS

When their parents decide to marry, two teen boys—one a charismatic ladies' man and the other a nerdy goofball—find themselves as the most unlikely of stepbrothers.

Shenanigans ensue when studious Josh Nichols (Josh Peck) is thrown into the same household as popular Drake Parker (Drake Bell). After overcoming their differences, the stepbrothers realize growing up is way more fun with a partner-in-crime. While doing their best to stay out of trouble from their no-nonsense mom and dorky weatherman dad, and avoiding falling for sister Megan's pranks, Drake and Josh take on the struggles of high school. Their wacky friends keep life anything but boring.

This goofy, four-season comedy will have every family member in stitches. The chaotic antics and recurring gags, such as Josh's undying adoration for Oprah Winfrey, and Drake's constant dim-witted remarks, make this a fun watch.

FRESH MEAT

COMEDY • 2011
RATED: TV-MA • 50 MINS

Starting collge is terrifying: new people, new places, and having to clean your own toilet. And being forced to live in a house of oddball strangers doesn't make it any easier.

After each submitting a late application, six students at Manchester Medlock University are forced to live together in an off-campus house instead of halls. Total strangers become housemates in this coming-of-age comedy from the people who created *Peep Show* (see p354). Follow the ups and downs of college life with carefree Vod (Zawe Ashton), quirky Howard (Greg McHugh), anger-prone Josie (Kimberley Nixon), snobby J. P. (Jack Whitehall), sheltered Kingsley (Joe Thomas), and insecure Oregon (Charlotte Ritchie).

Over the course of four seasons, the gang struggle with keeping their grades up, going on dates, partying too hard, and finding the right job. It's the perfect show to watch if you're about to head to or are already at college.

VICTORIOUS

COMEDY • 2010
RATED: TV-G • 24 MINS

You'd never skip class if you went to an epic performing arts high school where aspiring musicians, dancers, and actors give it their all to be the next big stars.

Tori (Victoria Justice) leaves her boring high school behind after getting into Hollywood Arts, a prestigious learning center designed for up-and-coming creators. There she meets several talented kids, including sweet-but-ditzy Cat (Ariana Grande), handsome Beck (Avan Jogia), musical genius Andre (Leon Thomas III), short-tempered Jade (Elizabeth Gillies), and nerdy Robbie (Matt Bennett). Together, along with Tori's sister, Trina (Daniella Monet), they hone their various skills, hoping to make it on to the big screen or into the Top 40.

The show's zany humor never slows down in this four-season sitcom, which includes plenty of fabulous original songs you'll be singing long after you finish binge-watching. The series eventually inspired a short-lived spin-off called *Sam & Cat*.

DICKINSON

PERIOD COMEDY • 2019
RATED: TV-14 • 30 MINS

You've read the poems, now meet the poet. If you think Emily Dickinson was just a sad girl from the 19th century who moped around and wrote weepy verse, you haven't seen *Dickinson*.

Be prepared to meet a whole new Emily Dickinson (Hailee Steinfeld) in this one-season series about the real-life American poet. It's a coming-of-age story about a feisty girl with dreams who wants her voice to be heard. Unfortunately, her father, Edward (Toby Huss), doesn't approve of his daughter's hobby. Her mother, also named Emily (Jane Krakowski), is a housewife, while older brother Austin is engaged to Sue, who happens to be Emily's best friend and crush.

Told in a modern tone, the first season of *Dickinson* follows rebellious Emily's struggle to push back against her parents' desire to find her a suitor. It also explores her revolutionary views of what it means to be an ambitious woman in the 19th century.

LAND GIRLS

PERIOD DRAMA • 2009
RATED: TV-14 • 45 MINS

As Beyoncé once sang, "Who run the world? Girls." Four girls join the Women's Land Army during World War II because they're not going to just sit around and do nothing.

In this three-season period drama, Joyce (Becci Gemmell), Bea (Jo Woodcock), Annie (Christine Bottomley), and Nancy (Summer Strallen) sign up for the Women's Land Army, an organization formed during World War II that allowed women to take over agricultural jobs so the men could go and fight. The girls want to help win the war, although they all enlist for different personal reasons. Life immediately changes for each of them as they adjust to their new surroundings carrying out hard work on the Hoxley Estate.

As the series progresses, new people arrive on the farm, some bringing trouble with them. The girls also find love and heartbreak, so much so that it'll be tough deciding which couple you like most.

PORTLANDIA

COMEDY • 2011
RATED: TV-14 • 22 MINS

Portland, Oregon is a weird town. Really weird. It's the town "where young people go to retire," and all its delightful eccentricities are put on display in this sketch comedy series.

For eight hilarious seasons, Fred Armisen and Carrie Brownstein play a bunch of different characters, including versions of themselves, in this satire. Some of their other characters include a middle-age couple named Peter and Nance, a hipster couple named Spyke and Iris, and two transients named Jeffrey and Quinn.

While Armisen and Brownstein make up the bulk of the cast, stars such as Kyle MacLachlan and Kumail Nanjiani play recurring characters. MacLachlan, for instance, portrays the mayor of Portland, who wants to improve life in the city, but his ideas tend to look better on paper than they work out in practice. Interestingly, his assistant is played by Sam Adams, who was the real-life mayor of Portland for several years.

'ALLO 'ALLO

COMEDY • 1982
RATED: PG (UK) • 45 MINS

What do you get when the Gestapo and escaped Allied POWs hang out under the same roof without the other side knowing? Brilliant comedy.

Exasperated French café owner René (Gorden Kaye) has a lot on his plate in this farce-style comedy. When he's not having affairs with his waitresses, especially Yvette (Vicki Michelle), and trying to hide them from his wife, Edith (Carmen Silvera), he's being dragged into both sides of World War II. The Germans demand he hide stolen objects in his store, while the Resistance uses his café as a safe house for wounded soldiers.

To make a crazy situation even crazier, none of the people from the two sides fighting who use René's business realize who the others are. But René and the viewers know, and it's riotously funny for nine seasons. Keep watching and you'll be repeating its memorable catchphrases, such as "What-a mistake-a to make-a!" in no time.

DAD'S ARMY

COMEDY • 1968
RATED: TV-G • 30 MINS

Join Captain Mainwaring and his squad of senior Home Guard soldiers as they work to protect their coastal community from German invasion in this beloved World War II sitcom.

What do you do when you want to join the military but you're ineligible for service because of your age? You volunteer for the Home Guard. For nine seasons, a group of (mostly) older gentlemen—hence the name *Dad's Army*—help Britain prepare for a German invasion during World War II. Leading the platoon is Captain Mainwaring (Arthur Lowe), followed by laid-back Sergeant Wilson (John Le Mesurier), and dithering Lance Corporal Jones (Clive Dunn).

Wilson subtly and smoothly questions every decision Mainwaring makes, while Jones just panics and flaps. Many of the town's locals join the cause, even though most are pushing the age of 60. How helpful to the war effort can *Dad's Army* be? Have fun finding out!

POSE

DRAMA • 2018
RATED: TV-MA • 60 MINS

Larger-than-life gowns, bitchy banter, and feel-good friendships feature in the African American and Latinx LGBTQ+ scene in the late '80s and early '90s.

In New York City, an underground subculture thrives as queer people of color express themselves through balls—pageantry involving fashion (often drag), dance (especially voguing), and attitude. Members of the ball community belong to Houses—surrogate families headed by a Mother—and these Houses compete in balls for prizes and recognition.

The series focuses on Blanca (MJ Rodriguez), a transgender woman with AIDS who leaves the House of Abundance—run by the great Mother Elektra (Dominique Jackson)—and starts her own House of Evangelista. Billy Porter also stars as Pray Tell, the ball scene's master of ceremonies. This two-season show was praised for having the biggest transgender cast in the history of television.

YOUNG SHELDON

COMEDY • 2017 • RATED: TV-PG • 30 MINS • SEASONS: 3
IAIN ARMITAGE, ZOE PERRY, LANCE BARBER

While his sister learns fractions and his brother chases after girls, child prodigy Sheldon does not feel at all academically challenged and struggles to connect with those around him. Meanwhile, his family struggles to cope with Sheldon's idiosyncrasies and lack of social skills.

A nine-year-old child genius, Sheldon (Iain Armitage) starts high school and tries to understand the world around him. A prequel to *The Big Bang Theory* (see p268), *Young Sheldon* follows the exploits of this budding scientist as he begins high school in a Texas town that values football over academics. Think of it as a portrait of the scientist as a young man.

> **"** *That NASA guy treated me like a child, and I intend to prove him wrong.* **"**
>
> Sheldon (S1 E6)

As Sheldon precociously tries to become the next Nobel Prize winner, his family has different worries for him—they fear that he'll never fit into society. Mary (Zoe Perry), Sheldon's devout Christian mother, prays for her son to adapt to his surroundings, while dad George (Lance Barber) simply rolls his eyes. Sheldon's siblings, twin sister Missy (Raegan Revord) and older brother Georgie (Montana Jordan), just think he's a weirdo and enjoy

giving him a hard time. Rounding out the family is Meemaw (Annie Potts), Sheldon's hilarious grandma, who has a big soft spot for him.

Once he gets out of his head a bit, and really pays attention to other people, Sheldon slowly starts to understand how to bond with them. He may be the next Albert Einstein, but there is definitely a learning curve to social cues.

Jim Parsons, who played the adult Sheldon in *The Big Bang Theory* for all 12 seasons, reprises his role, providing narration as an adult reflecting on his childhood. If Sheldon's mother, Mary, looks familiar it's because she is played by the real-life daughter of Laurie Metcalf, who played Mary in *The Big Bang Theory*. You'll quickly fall in love with young actor Armitage, and his portrayal of the socially inept child Sheldon will make you want to jump into the TV and help him out.

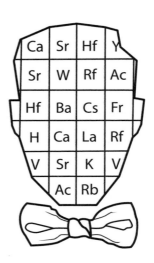

CREATORS: Steven Molaro, Chuck Lorre
PRODUCTION CO: Chuck Lorre Productions, Warner Bros. Television

MOONE BOY

COMEDY • 2015
RATED: TV-14 • 23 MINS

Being the only boy and youngest member of a big family can be tough, but it's easier to handle when you have an imaginary friend who can help guide you through sticky situations.

Martin (David Rawle) is tired of school bullies and his sisters picking on him, so in steps Sean (Chris O'Dowd), his fun imaginary friend. Together, Martin and Sean take on the world ... or at least primary school. Over the course of the series, Martin attempts a number of madcap schemes, such as trying to be an altar boy, against the advice of the more sensible Sean. He also has a crush on his teacher, and generally learns that life comes with serious growing pains.

Though mainly live action, this three-season show, set in a small town in Ireland in the '80s and '90s, incorporates animation into the story lines through Martin's childish drawings. It's a cute coming-of-age sitcom for the kid in all of us.

SCHITT'S CREEK

COMEDY • 2015
RATED: TV-14 • 22 MINS

All good things must end—that's what the wealthy Rose family realize after they lose their fortune and are forced to live in the town they once bought as a joke.

The filthy-rich Roses—patriarch Johnny (Eugene Levy), wife Moira (Catherine O'Hara), and grown-up children David (Daniel Levy) and Alexis (Annie Murphy)—are forced to humble themselves after a "tax issue." The only thing they have left to their name is a tiny town called Schitt's Creek. The Roses are stuck roughing it in the town's motel and struggling to adjust to their new, penniless lives. They try to connect with the locals, but personalities are quick to clash.

This six-season comedy starts off as schadenfreude (joy at the misfortune of other people), but quickly turns to sympathy. Think of it as the quirky offspring of *Arrested Development* (see p274) and *Northern Exposure* (see p237).

UNBREAKABLE KIMMY SCHMIDT

COMEDY • 2015
RATED: TV-14 • 30 MINS

You're rescued from a bunker that's been your home for over a decade, so what do you do next? If you're Kimmy Schmidt, you move to NYC.

After having been abducted and locked in a bunker for 15 years, Kimmy (Ellie Kemper) is rescued and starts over in New York City, leaving the fictional town of Durnsville, Indiana behind. Adjusting to modern life isn't easy. Thankfully, Kimmy runs into Lillian (Carol Kane), who offers her a chance to be roommates with the flamboyant Titus (Tituss Burgess) in an apartment she rents out.

After getting a job as a nanny and settling into the city, Kimmy starts to learn about the life experiences she's missed out on for years. Titus and Kimmy support each other as they negotiate life's ups and downs. This four-season show's quirky humor is great for those who need to escape their own reality for a while.

CRASHING

COMEDY • 2016 • RATED: TV-MA • 30 MINS • SEASONS: 1
PHOEBE WALLER-BRIDGE, JONATHAN BAILEY, JULIE DRAY

This short-lived series nails what it's like to be a young adult trying to get your life together. Packing a mighty punch, *Crashing* is filled with filthy humor, but can also make you swoon and weep in the same episode.

Created by and starring Phoebe Waller-Bridge, who also made the award-winning *Fleabag* (see p340), *Crashing* lets you in on the exploits of a group of 20- and 30-somethings who live together as property guardians in a dilapidated hospital. In order to crash there, they have to protect the building in exchange for low rent.

When Lulu (Waller-Bridge) visits her old friend Anthony (Damien Molony) at the condemned hospital where he lives as a property manager, she gets more than she bargained for, including a new home and six new roommates. As well as Anthony and his fiancée Kate (Louise Ford), she moves in with lascivious Sam (Jonathan Bailey), artistic Melody (Julie Dray), shy Fred

(Amit Shah), and Kate's coworker Colin (Adrian Scarborough)—all vastly different personalities and all hanging out under one condemned roof.

> **"***The main rule about truth songs is just to sing with abandon.***"**
>
> Lulu (S1 E1)

While a comedy about six pals may sound similar to the likes of *Friends* (see p194) or *Living Single* (see p195), this show differs in being serialized, while the humor is definitely in another vein. It's a raw and unapologetically frank series, set in a seriously unconventional location.

YOUNGER

COMEDY • 2015
RATED: TV-14 • 22 MINS

A 40-year-old woman struggling for work is mistaken for a 20-something and sees it as an opportunity to start the career of her dreams in the ageist world of publishing.

When life hands you lemons, you know what to do. Liza (Sutton Foster) is a divorced mom struggling to find a job. After tattoo artist Josh (Nico Tortorella) assumes he and Liza are

both in their late 20s, she crafts a plan to use her youthful appearance to land a role in publishing. When she's hired at Empirical Press as the assistant to the head of marketing (Miriam Shor), she must fight to keep her secret from everyone, including her young coworker, Kelsey (Hilary Duff).

Keeping something like that hidden, especially when your career's on the line, is stressful, but fortunately Liza has her friend and roommate, Maggie (Debi Mazar), to help her out in this seven-season show. Enjoy and don't worry about getting laugh lines!

GILMORE GIRLS

**COMEDY • 2000 • RATED: TV-PG • 44 MINS • SEASONS: 7
LAUREN GRAHAM, ALEXIS BLEDEL, MELISSA MCCARTHY**

A single mother in her 30s does her best to raise her precocious teenage daughter in the fictional town of Stars Hollow, Connecticut. The mother-daughter relationship is central to this comedy melodrama as they deal with love and heartbreak.

Grab your mom and maybe a box of tissues when you start bingeing on this beloved show. Lorelai (Lauren Graham) is a pop culture junkie who balances running a local inn with raising her teen daughter Rory (Alexis Bledel), by herself. It's not easy, but she manages as best she can, thanks to help from friends Sookie (Melissa McCarthy) and Luke (Scott Patterson), as well as her rich parents, who adore their granddaughter.

The family comes together every Friday night to catch up and talk about life. Rory, though always buried in her schoolwork, still makes time for a social life, falling for the likes of new kid Dean (Jared Padalecki), bad boy Jess (Milo Ventimiglia), and charming Logan (Matt Czuchry) over the course of the series. You'll quickly begin debating with family and friends about which boy is best for Rory, so choose your beau wisely.

Gilmore Girls is witty and addictive and it will tear at your heartstring with scenes such as the one when Rory goes through a breakup or when Lorelei tries and fails to develop a better relationship with her somewhat estranged mother.

> **"** *Every relationship is just a big, honkin' leap of faith.* **"**
>
> **Rory** (S6 E12)

THE MARVELOUS MRS. MAISEL

**COMEDY • 2017
RATED: TV-MA • 57 MINS**

Midge proves that women were made for more than just homemaking in the '50s and '60s when she starts a career in stand-up comedy.

This three-season show will transport you back to 1958 as you watch Midge Maisel (Rachel Brosnahan) being left by her husband Joel (Michael Zegen) after his stand-up routine at a comedy club bombs. Heartbroken and drunk, Midge returns to the club and tells the audience her story, much to its delight.

After moving back in with parents Rose (Marin Hinkle) and Abe (Tony Shalhoub), her day job at a department store and her chaotic family life provide great material for Midge's stand-up routines. Manager Susie (Alex Borstein) is there to help Midge learn the ins and outs of her new side hustle, while Midge crosses paths with real-life comedian Lenny Bruce. The first season is a masterclass in comedy writing.

THE GOLDBERGS

COMEDY • 2013 • RATED: TV-14 • 22 MINS • SEASONS: 7
WENDI MCLENDON-COVEY, JEFF GARLIN, SEAN GIAMBRONE

What if your childhood home movies become the next great *America's Funniest Home Videos*? Every embarrassing thing you did growing up, your awkward phases, and bad fashion choices showcased for strangers to enjoy? For show creator Adam F. Goldberg, that's exactly what happens.

The Goldbergs is absolutely the best show to watch if you love all things '80s. From the music to the (questionable) fashion sense, the decade is a time to be remembered— and this sitcom does that in a much more realistic way than *Stranger Things* (see p446). The action is seen through the eyes of Adam (Sean Giambrone), a budding filmmaker who can't go more than 30 seconds without making a pop-culture reference. He never shuts up about movies such as *Star Wars* and *Ghostbusters*, which quickly makes you fall in love with him.

Adam is the quintessential "nerd" who loves doing things such as grabbing his friends and going on a treasure hunt when he finds a map in the attic, just like he's in '80s movie classic *The Goonies*. Adam even finds ways to mesh his love of pop culture with his love life, such as wooing his crush by holding a boombox outside her window à la *Say Anything* (another '80s movie mainstay).

Besides epically parodying famous films and TV shows—seriously, this series pulls out all the stops with amazing music, fantastic wardrobe, and clever writing—*The Goldbergs* never wants for famous guest stars. For a Halloween special, it gets *A Nightmare on Elm Street* actor Robert Englund to don serial killer Freddy Krueger's iconic green-and-red striped sweater and knife glove again. The last time Englund played the character on screen was more than a decade before that episode aired, yet somehow *The Goldbergs* persuades him to return for another performance. It even manages to get musical comedian "Weird Al" Yankovic to play himself in one episode, and it's as hysterical as you'd expect.

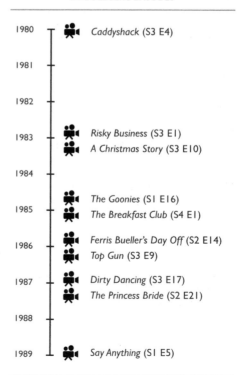

CLASSIC '80S MOVIES RECREATED
IN GOLDBERG EPISODES

1980	Caddyshack (S3 E4)
1981	
1982	
1983	Risky Business (S3 E1)
	A Christmas Story (S3 E10)
1984	
1985	The Goonies (S1 E16)
	The Breakfast Club (S4 E1)
1986	Ferris Bueller's Day Off (S2 E14)
	Top Gun (S3 E9)
1987	Dirty Dancing (S3 E17)
	The Princess Bride (S2 E21)
1988	
1989	Say Anything (S1 E5)

230

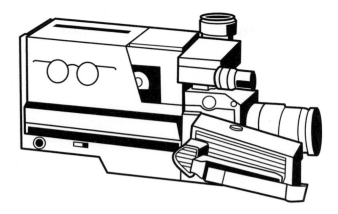

But what really makes *The Goldbergs* stand out isn't the faces you do know, it's the ones you don't. Series creator Adam F. Goldberg brings back many of his childhood pals, ex-girlfriends, and family friends, not to play themselves, but to make fictional cameos. We only learn who they are at the end of each episode, when home video footage that Goldberg shot as a kid is placed next to the reenacted versions. It's unlike any kind of sitcom you've seen before. While the crazy adventures of *Full House* (see p70) aren't based on the showrunner's actual experiences, many of those in *The Goldbergs* are.

> **"***I agree with whatever nonsense your mother just said.***"**
>
> Murray Goldberg (S1 E1)

Of course, Adam wouldn't be the "adorkable" protagonist we love if he didn't have his wacky family to put up with. Beverly (Wendi McLendon-Covey), the family matriarch and Jazzercise enthusiast, loves smothering Adam, as well as older kids Barry (Troy Gentile) and Erica (Hayley Orrantia). His mother doesn't hesitate to insert herself into his life, and does it with so much passion that it's kind of hard to even be mad at her for it. Beverly's the poster child for a mother's unconditional, sometimes neurotic, love.

However, her husband, Murray (Jeff Garlin), is the total opposite: he loves his kids, but he'd rather they be seen and not heard. And when he does hear them, he's probably calling them a moron. Last but not least is "Pops" (George Segal), Adam, Barry, and Erica's maternal grandfather who never seems to have a clue what's going on with the rest of the family's escapades, but he's always down for the ride. In one episode, Adam tricks Pops into taking him to see the movie *Poltergeist* in the cinema by telling him they were going to watch the animated Disney film, *The Great Mouse Detective*. Eventually, Pops wonders where the mouse is, as he's forced to stare at creepy, supernatural things instead.

The Goldbergs may bicker with each other, sometimes saying things they don't mean, but the gang always works it out by the end of the episode. It's a feel-good show that reminds you of the importance of family, no matter how much they annoy you.

FLIGHT OF THE CONCHORDS

MUSICAL COMEDY • 2007
RATED: TV-MA • 28 MINS

Two musicians in a folk-rock band head to New York City from New Zealand to chase success in the cutthroat music industry.

Real-life musicians Jemaine Clement and Bret McKenzie play fictionalized versions of themselves in this two-season show.

While the New Zealand pair's band, Flight of the Conchords, is successful in real life, here they are struggling to find stardom. The show follows Jemaine and Bret as they try getting their group off the ground, without much help from their manager, Murray (Rhys Darby). But fame isn't totally nonexistent: they do have one fan called Mel (Kristen Schaal), who also becomes their stalker.

The duo sing in each episode and the music is woven into the plot, either in the form of one character singing to another or as a character's inner thoughts. Music fans will love this show.

GLOW

COMEDY • 2017
RATED: TV-MA • 35 MINS

Loosely based on an LA women's wrestling show, GLOW takes us back to the 1980s and into the lives of the team's stars as they fight for success and recognition.

A struggling actress named Ruth (Alison Brie in a very different role than Annie Edison in *Community*—see p212) auditions to be part of the Gorgeous Ladies of Wrestling,

aka GLOW. She's kicked out on the first day of tryouts for not creating more of a wrestling identity, so after watching matches and getting more prepared, she returns and nails it—but not without causing drama with her onetime best friend, Debbie (Betty Gilpin).

Over the course of four seasons, we watch GLOW brought to life, alongside fights between members and tensions between Ruth and GLOW director Sam (Marc Maron). Like Ruth says in Season 3, episode 1, "This place can make you a little crazy."

RAMY

COMEDY DRAMA • 2019
RATED: TV-MA • 30 MINS

A first-generation American Muslim struggles with his faith, friends' differing viewpoints, and his relationship with God. It's a lot to handle, and trying to date on top of it all doesn't help.

The son of Egyptian immigrants, Ramy (Ramy Youssef) is a 20-something guy living in New Jersey trying to figure everything out. He lives at home with parents Farouk

(Amr Waked) and Maysa (Hiam Abbass), goes on dates, deals with work drama, and struggles with his American Muslim identity while living in a secular world.

The two-season show is semiautobiographical and called "quietly revolutionary" by *The New York Times* for its central depiction of a Muslim as a regular guy coming of age, not some terrorist or sideplot character. This series will make you think and cheer Ramy on as he tries to find a happy medium between obeying his faith's rules, and letting loose and being a little more carefree.

THE GREAT BRITISH BAKE OFF

REALITY TV • 2010 • RATED: TV-PG • 60 MINS • SEASONS: 10
PAUL HOLLYWOOD, MARY BERRY, MEL GIEDROYC

There are bakers, and then there are *bakers*. This competition show puts cooks to the test to find Britain's best amateur cake makers. Twelve hopefuls spend 10 weeks baking their hearts out, trying to create the best food.

Will the best baker please step forward? That's what everyone wants to know as they watch this delightful competition series. Each season follows a dozen amateur cooks as they compete in various tests, making cakes, bread, cookies, and desserts. Contestants face three challenges in every episode: the Signature, the Technical, and the Showstopper.

The Signature involves hopefuls showing off their baking specialities, aka the creations they've made time and time again, such as a Swiss roll. The Technical puts the bakers' knowledge of their craft to the test with a surprise challenge (occasionally it's something they have never even heard of before). They each have to make the same dish using minimal instructions, such as judge Mary Berry's classic cherry cake. "The recipe is sparse," one contestant regretfully points out in Season 1, episode 1.

Finally, the Showstopper allows bakers to cut loose and really demonstrate their skills. They are told the type of bake, but have to make it really stand out. In one episode, a contestant makes a chocolate cake in the shape of a hat, while another makes a chocolate cake that looks like the Black Forest—even featuring a cute, edible bear on top!

Alongside Mary Berry, baker Paul Hollywood judges the contest, with both providing insights and critiques into why a dish does or does not meet their standards. Rounding out the main cast are co-presenters Mel Giedroyc and Sue Perkins, who explain the rules to the contestants. In later seasons, the likes of Noel Fielding, Sandi Toksvig, and Matt Lucas host the show, and Prue Leith steps in as a judge.

A unique aspect of the series is that the competitors come from all walks of life, varying across age, occupation, and location, and proving anyone can be a talented baker. On your marks ... get set ... bake!

PLEASE LIKE ME

COMEDY ROMANCE • 2013
RATED: TV-MA • 29 MINS

Turns out that being gay isn't a phase, which is apparently news for Josh, who finally opts to come out after his girlfriend dumps him.

When his girlfriend Claire (Caitlin Stasey) breaks up with him because she thinks he's gay—which, surprise, he is—Josh (Josh Thomas) begins a new phase of his life as he comes out. Unfortunately, his newfound sexuality is overshadowed by his mother's deteriorating mental health. Josh moves back in with her and does his best to keep his emotions in check for both her sake as well as his own. His life becomes more complicated when he develops a crush on Geoffrey (Wade Briggs), who works with his pal Tom (Thomas Ward).

Josh is faced with many huge challenges and big life changes throughout the show's four seasons, and does his best to keep his head above water. But, thanks to the supportive people in his life, he manages to tackle his tricky issues with a smile.

RED OAKS

COMEDY • 2014
RATED: TV-MA • 30 MINS

First there was *The Goldbergs*, then there was *Red Oaks*. Coming-of-age story? Check. Set in the '80s? Double check. Wacky antics by fun-loving characters? Check, check, check.

College student David Myers (Craig Roberts) doesn't want summer to come to an end, because then he has to really figure out what he wants to do in life. He starts working at a New Jersey country club and quickly falls for Skye (Alexandra Socha), the daughter of club president Doug Getty (Paul Reiser). Over the summer, David wonders about his future, while his parents, Sam (Richard Kind) and Judy (Jennifer Grey), start to drift apart and attend marriage counseling.

This three-season series was dubbed "one of TV's most underappreciated shows" by online magazine *Vulture*, and for good reason. It explores themes of sexuality and turns character stereotypes, such as the cannabis-smoking best friend, on their head.

ROADIES

COMEDY • 2016
RATED: TV-MA • 60 MINS

Living the rock-star life is the dream. Being on the road, enjoying fame, glory, and fat paychecks—what's not to love? Take a trip with *Roadies* to find out....

Roadies follows the exploits of a road crew for a fictional rock group called the Staton-House Band. Helping make the outfit's multi-city tour successful is tour manager Bill (Luke Wilson), production manager Shelli (Carla Gugino), lighting rigger Kelly Ann (Imogen Poots), financial advisor Reg (Rafe Spall), and sound operator Donna (Keisha Castle-Hughes), among others. The team hits a major setback when they learn some of the crew will lose their jobs, forcing the remaining members to step up their game.

This one-season show take you behind-the-scenes of a band on tour, a set-up that makes perfect sense when you realize that it was created by Cameron Crowe, writer-director of the movie *Almost Famous*, which is also about a touring rock group.

MY MAD FAT DIARY

COMEDY ROMANCE • 2013
RATED: TV-MA • 47 MINS

Surprisingly, it seems attempted suicide and psychiatric hospitals can make for good comedy. Humour comes from unexpected places in this series based on Rae Earl's memoir, *My Fat, Mad Teenage Diary*.

Plus-size Rae (Sharon Rooney), a 16-year-old who has just finished a four-month stint in a psychiatric hospital after attempting suicide,

wants to start over and hide both her mental-health and body-image insecurities. She reconnects with her childhood bestie, Chloe (Jodie Comer), and starts hanging out with her and her friends: Finn, Izzy, Archie, and Chop. But the closer she grows to them, the harder she tries to keep where she's been for nearly half a year a secret. Her cover story? She was in France.

Over the show's three seasons, Rae deals with bad dates, sexual exploration, and learning to love and accept herself (and her mother) for who she is.

SHRILL

COMEDY • 2019
RATED: TV-MA • 30 MINS

Annie is a plus-size woman working to change how society views people's weight. She's tired of being fat-shamed and disregarded just because she isn't model-thin.

This two-season series is based on Lindy West's memoir, *Shrill: Notes from a Loud Woman*. Annie (Aidy Bryant) wants to be a successful journalist, but she's never

given a proper chance because of her size. She can't even go into a coffee shop without someone not-so-subtly encouraging her to lose weight. Her sardonic boss won't help her grow in her journalism career, or let her report on stories that she thinks are relevant and important.

In addition to the work drama in this two-season show, Annie also has to deal with her lazy boyfriend Ryan (Luka Jones), her judgmental mom, and her sick dad. Luckily, her friend and roommate Fran is there to help her through it all.

THE VILLAGE

PERIOD DRAMA • 2013
RATED: TV-14 • 60 MINS

***Downton Abbey*'s aristocrats would be in for quite a shock if they had to live through the 20th century in a working-class family like the Middletons.**

Follow the rough life of Bert Middleton (various actors) across the years in this two-season show. Looking back on his life, Bert takes us through different stages of his adolescence, beginning with his 12-year-old

self in 1914. From there, the series extends into the 1920s, introducing us to Bert's family: loving mother Grace (Maxine Peake), abusive father John (John Simm), and big brother Joe.

The Middletons work on a farm to put food on the table and quickly find themselves caught up in a pregnancy scandal involving a member of the rich Allingham family, who live nearby. This Derbyshire-set drama of everyday folks is perfect for history buffs, as well as anyone who likes traveling back to relive a time before the internet and smartphones took over.

DETROITERS

COMEDY • 2017
RATED: TV-14 • 21 MINS

Just because something's low budget, doesn't mean it's not amazing, right? That's what two BFFs realize as they jump feet first into the chaotic world of advertising.

Sam (Sam Richardson) and Tim (Tim Robinson) are friends, neighbors, and colleagues who work in advertising in Detroit, Michigan. Tim takes over the family business after his dad steps down, prompting him and Sam to create low-budget commercials for businesses, such as Chrysler. Together, along with their assistant, Lea (Lailani Ledesma), they learn advertising is no walk in the park.

This two-season Comedy Central show is quirky and self-aware, making its short run all the more memorable. Jason Sudeikis was both an executive producer and guest star on the show, playing a Chrysler executive named Carter. If you need a new advertising workplace comedy to watch besides *The Crazy Ones* (p210), this is the show for you.

HIGH MAINTENANCE

COMEDY • 2016
RATED: TV-MA • 30 MINS

New Yorkers are a diverse bunch, yet there's one thing some of these different folks have in common: their weed dealer.

Step aside *Breaking Bad* (see p10), you've finally met your match with this HBO show about a guy who delivers weed. Follow along with the appropriately named "The Guy" (Ben Sinclair) as he delivers pot to an eclectic and neurotic group of clients, a different one for every episode. These include an agoraphobic, a workaholic, and a polyamorous couple. The Guy gets to know his customers fairly well, as he has to enter their homes to avoid being spotted selling drugs on the street. As his relationships with them grow, and he gets involved with their often bizarre lifestyles, the plots truly thicken.

Interestingly, the show started out as a web series on Vimeo before moving to HBO. The original series comprises six seasons, while the TV version runs for four.

LODGE 49

COMEDY • 2018
RATED: TV-14 • 51 MINS

Not even Aesop could think up a story this wild. This is a fable about someone who joins a cultlike order offering cheap booze and ideas that are truly out there!

Dud (Wyatt Russell) is having a hard time after first his dad, and then his family business, dies. By chance, or maybe fate, Dud stumbles upon a cult called the Order of the Lynx and meets Ernie (Brent Jennings), a "knight." Although that would probably sound weird to most people, Dud is all for it, and joins the fraternity in the hope of becoming a squire. Meanwhile, Dud's sister, Liz (Sonya Cassidy), is struggling with the massive debt her dad left behind. While one sibling is desperately trying to gain something, the other is frantically trying to lose something.

As Dud spends time in the order and with its members, we follow his search to find more meaning and happiness in his life in this two-season show.

COUGAR TOWN

COMEDY • 2009
RATED: TV-14 • 22 MINS

Being middle-aged is great: you're (maybe) in a strong relationship, you're (hopefully) well into your career, and you've (fingers crossed) got your life together. Well, maybe not for Jules.

Jules (Courteney Cox) is a 40-something, recently divorced real estate agent who's trying to raise her teenage son, Travis (Dan Byrd), while preparing for the next chapter of her life: being a middle-aged, single woman. She's on the prowl for love again but, in short, it's not going as smoothly as she'd like. Laurie (Busy Philipps), Jules's assistant, encourages her to get back out there into the dating pool and have some fun, and she eventually connects with her cute neighbor, Grayson (Josh Hopkins).

As Jules begins to discover herself, there are a lot of new changes to handle all at once in this six-season show. Luckily her best friend, Ellie (Christa Miller), is there to keep her sane, one sarcastic comment at a time.

NORTHERN EXPOSURE

COMEDY • 1990
RATED: PG (UK) • 60 MINS

Congrats! You just finished medical school and are now ready to begin your practice. New York or somewhere tropical sounds fun but, too bad, you're off to Alaska instead!

Graduating from med school and becoming a doctor is all fun and games until you read the fine print. Joel (Rob Morrow) apparently didn't get the memo, because his scholarship requires him to work in Alaska for four years. Bound to the contract, Joel heads north, imagining he'll be working in a large hospital. Nope. He's relocated to a small, remote town that needs a physician.

Things can't get any worse, he thinks, until he meets the townsfolk. Joel encounters wealthy military veteran Maurice (Barry Corbin), and Maggie (Janine Turner), Joel's landlady—someone he quickly develops a love-hate relationship with in this six-season show. Best of luck in your new home, Joel. You'll need it.

THE BOLD TYPE

COMEDY DRAMA • 2017
RATED: TV-14 • 45 MINS

Working for a women's magazine is no walk in the park—especially if you do it wearing high heels. A trio of millennials are put to the test developing their careers in this fun drama.

Three 20-something friends—Jane (Katie Stevens), Kat (Aisha Dee), and Sutton (Meghann Fahy)—work at the fictional global women's magazine, *Scarlet*. A dream job? Maybe. This four-season show follows the trio as they adjust to life in New York City while simultaneously figuring out in which direction they want their careers to go. They each have diverse roles at the company: Jane's a writer, Kat's a social media director, and Sutton's a fashion assistant.

As well as their jobs, the show also chronicles their loves lives, which includes secret relationships and sexual exploration. Based on the career of former *Cosmopolitan* editor in chief Joanna Coles, this is a female-first series that anyone who loves drama will enjoy.

YOU NEED A REALLY GOOD LAUGH

Written by Laurie Ulster

There are times when we must step up and face our troubles head-on … but isn't it more fun to utterly ignore them and have a good laugh? There's a lot to choose from here, depending on your mood: do you need a dry, superior laugh from watching *House*, or a laugh-yourself-silly *Monty Python* moment? Take your pick.

ABSOLUTELY FABULOUS

COMEDY • 1992 • RATED: TV-14 • 45 MINS • SEASONS: 5
JENNIFER SAUNDERS, JOANNA LUMLEY, JULIA SAWALHA

Pour yourself some champagne, sweetie, and smoke 'em if you've got 'em. Now you're ready to join Eddy and Patsy, who live life to excess, are obsessed with fashion, celebrities, and where their next drink is coming from, and yearn for the days when they were Mods in swinging London.

The idea for *Absolutely Fabulous—Ab Fab* for short, because who's got time to say the whole name?—sprang from a sketch by comedians Jennifer Saunders and Dawn French in *French and Saunders* (see p277). The concept? A middle-aged mother acts like a teenager and has to be taken care of by her own teenage daughter, who's like a middle-aged woman.

In *Ab Fab,* PR agent Edina ("Eddy") Monsoon (Jennifer Saunders), and her pal, fashion writer Patsy Stone (Joanna Lumley), are constantly at odds with Eddy's daughter Saffron (Julia Sawalha), who finds the two hard-drinking, chain-smoking women utterly exasperating.

Saunders said in an interview that she took inspiration for the series from '80s female pop group Bananarama, remembering "all the falls" she saw the band make on nights out partying with them—including the time one of them dropped bottom-first out of a taxi into the road. "That's class," she thought. The attitude seems to sum up Patsy and Eddy's world-view perfectly: if you're not drunk and falling out of cars, if you're not shirking responsibility and making bitchy remarks about everyone, you're just not living.

With celebrity cameos galore and plenty of satirical commentary on the fashion world, the show was an international hit, spawning various post-series specials and even a feature film.

CREATORS: Jennifer Saunders, Dawn French (original sketch)
PRODUCTION CO: French & Saunders Productions, BBC, Comedy Central, Oxygen Media

DON'T TRUST THE B----
IN APARTMENT 23

COMEDY • 2012
RATED: TV-14 • 22 MINS

Chloe's a selfish con artist who loves to party and June's an idealist. While they never really change each other, they do become unlikely roommates.

In the first episode, James Van Der Beek (playing a fictionalized version of himself post–*Dawson's Creek*—see p148) reveals the MO of his friend Chloe (Krysten Ritter): she gets new roommates to pay rent up front then becomes so obnoxious to live with that they leave. How does this premise keep going after episode 1? Well, Chloe's new roommate, June (Dreama Walker), proves to be a surprising match for her.

After moving in, June sees the job she came to NYC for fall apart on the first day. Right after, she discovers her fiancé has been cheating on her, and June and Chloe become unlikely friends. It only ran for two seasons, but the show has become a niche cult hit.

I LOVE LUCY

COMEDY • 1951
RATED: TV-G • 30 MINS

It was officially an ensemble comedy, but Lucille Ball as housewife Lucy always steals the show with her elaborate schemes to get into show business, just like her famous bandleader husband Ricky.

Still utterly delightful, *I Love Lucy* has a simple concept: Lucy longs to be famous and often drags best pal Ethel Mertz (Vivian Vance) into her latest plan, ending up in the most ridiculous of situations. Ricky (Desi Arnaz) and Ethel's husband Fred (William Frawley) always get a laugh out of their wives' adventures, but wouldn't change the pair's ways for the world.

Over six seasons, the characters' exploits take place in New York City, Hollywood, and even abroad—one episode finds Lucy in Italy, crushing grapes with her feet and getting into a grape-throwing battle. Among all the wackiness, the show also has its sweet moments, such as when Lucy reveals to Ricky, in the middle of his act, that she is pregnant with their son.

WILL & GRACE

COMEDY • 1998
RATED: TV-14 • 22 MINS

***Will & Grace* was a big deal when it premiered—there were no other shows about the friendship between a straight woman and her gay male roommate.**

It may not seem progressive now, but the show was a groundbreaker. Eric McCormack's Will wasn't a stereotype, nor was he wrestling with his sexuality; he was an out gay man. His friendship with Debra Messing's Grace echoed friendships that were happening everywhere, but rarely represented on screen. He wasn't quite the star of his own story, but it was still a presence that mattered.

The show also features Sean Hayes as Will's flamboyant best friend Jack, and Megan Mullally as Karen, Grace's socialite assistant, whose friendship is just as entertaining. *Will & Grace* has proven its longevity—the initial run lasted for eight seasons, and the show was resurrected for three more seasons in 2017 with the original creators and cast—and Sean Hayes also serving as executive producer.

AMERICAN DAD!

ANIMATED COMEDY • 2005
RATED: TV-14 • 22 MINS

Take a hyper-patriotic CIA agent, add in his family plus a pet goldfish with the brain of a German Olympic skier, and a space alien who spouts inappropriate remarks, and boom! *American Dad!*

This surreal animated comedy started with the idea of a right-wing CIA agent who had a liberal daughter, and from there things just got more bizarre. Patriarch Stan Smith (Seth MacFarlane) does whatever he believes is necessary to keep America safe. He is admired by his loyal wife, Francine (Wendy Schaal), tormented by his left-wing daughter, Hayley, and mildly interesting to his geeky but oddly confident son, Steve. The family shares their home with their fish, Klaus, and a pale-gray space alien named Roger.

At first *American Dad!* struggled to develop an identity distinct from *Family Guy* (see p243), written by the same team. But over 15 seasons it has found its own voice by embracing its weirdness and running with it.

THAT '70S SHOW

COMEDY • 1998 • RATED: TV-14 • 22 MINS • SEASONS: 8
TOPHER GRACE, ASHTON KUTCHER, MILA KUNIS

In the fictional town of Point Place, Wisconsin in the 1970s, a group of teenagers spend most of their free time hanging out in their friend Eric Forman's basement, dodging his hardcore authoritarian dad and well-intentioned mom, and getting high.

That '70s Show relies on its time period for some of its story lines—the kids streak at a school assembly, mom and dad accidentally find themselves at a swinging party, and the first *Star Wars* movie is released—but its biggest laughs come from its characters. There is awkward Eric (Topher Grace), boy toy Kelso, spoiled Jackie, tomboy Donna, sarcastic Hyde, and foreign-exchange student Fez, whose home country is never identified.

But it wasn't just the kids. Eric's dad Red—forever threatening to give people a "kick in the ass"—and mom Kitty, with her high-pitched nervous laugh, star in some of the best episodes, especially the classic "Garage Sale" when both Eric and Donna's parents accidentally eat Hyde's "special" brownies.

If the show has a trademark, it's the "circle" where the gang smokes weed. It's filmed as if the camera's in the center, spinning from one character to the next to suggest they're getting high. While Eric and Kelso left before the show finished its run, both returned for the series finale set on December 31, 1979, bringing the show and the era to an end.

> **"** *You're right, Jackie, the Fonz could beat up Bruce Lee.* **"**
>
> Eric (S1 E4)

DESPERATE HOUSEWIVES

COMEDY DRAMA • 2004
RATED: TV-14 • 42 MINS

Who knew a cul-de-sac could be such a perilous place? The ladies of Wisteria Lane keep up appearances despite breakups and backstabbings, and prove friendship can endure even foul play.

The suicide of a neighbor brings a group of women together: free-spirited Susan (Teri Hatcher), domestic goddess Bree (Marcia Cross), social climber Gaby (Eva Longoria),

career-minded Lynette (Felicity Huffman), and lusty Edie (Nicollette Sheridan). They uncover secrets and solve mysteries—who is that new neighbor hiding in their basement? Is the local pharmacist really a psycho? Can a blender be used as a murder weapon?

This gaggle of suburbanites endure their share of highs and lows over eight seasons, as does the show itself. Plot developments can become outlandish: a plane crash, a body in a freezer, a tornado (resulting in someone impaled on a picket fence). But mostly, this nighttime soap is as sweet as muffins.

FAMILY GUY

ANIMATED COMEDY • 1999
RATED: TV-14 • 22 MINS

Family Guy **is about the Griffins, a pretty normal dysfunctional US family ... except that they include a pretentious, martini-drinking dog and a megalomaniac baby with a British accent.**

At the head of the family is dad Peter (creator Seth MacFarlane, who also voices several other characters), a dullard who's been a safety inspector, a fisherman, a New England

Patriots American football player, and a tobacco lobbyist. Mom (Alex Borstein) is a part-time piano instructor with a taste for sadomasochism, teenage daughter Meg is ridiculed by everyone around her, and son Chris is sweet but dim like his dad. Meanwhile, Brian the dog drinks and smokes, and baby Stewie is an evil genius.

The 18-season series is famous for its cutaways, whether to a throwaway line or an entire scene with no other resonance story-wise. Without them driving its rapid-fire humor, the show wouldn't be the same.

KING OF THE HILL

ANIMATED COMEDY • 1997
RATED: TV-14 • 22 MINS

Hank Hill must be one of the sanest dads on TV—and certainly the sanest animated one. He's an honest, hard-working propane salesman who loves Texas and his family.

Hank (Mike Judge) takes pleasure in things such as propane and golf, and remains perplexed over why others don't share all his values. He's conservative, but never

overbearing, he just wants to mow his lawn, take pride in his work, look after his family, and stand in the yard having beers with his buddies. He's a little confused by his son, Bobby, who prefers comedy to sports and is an oddball kid, but Hank loves him anyway, along with his wife, Peggy, a substitute teacher who's full of ideas that Hank will never quite understand.

King of the Hill is an understated, unassuming show, and always smart and funny. Even when he doesn't comprehend the world around him, Hank remains steadfast and true.

30 ROCK

COMEDY • 2006 • RATED: TV-14 • 22 MINS • SEASONS: 7
TINA FEY, ALEC BALDWIN, TRACY MORGAN

As they say, "There ain't no party like a Liz Lemon party, 'cause a Liz Lemon party is mandatory!" You've seen the memes, now embrace every hilariously ungraceful moment on *30 Rock*, a behind-the-scenes satire about a sketch comedy show filmed at NBC's famous 30 Rockefeller Plaza.

Show creator Tina Fey used her experience as head writer on *Saturday Night Live* as inspiration for her breakout comedy, then added in enough quirks to fill a stadium. As Liz Lemon, she's snack-positive, sex-negative, and alternately super weird and completely relatable. Liz expertly runs a TV show while she lusts after sandwiches, shies away from intimacy, and occasionally dresses up as Princess Leia. The show is packed with wall-to-wall jokes— so many that a blogger clocked one episode as having almost 10 per minute—and a steady stream of pop culture references.

30 Rock is sharply written and full of eccentric characters, but at its heart is the unusual friendship between polar opposites Liz and Jack Donaghy (Alec Baldwin). Jack insists on mentoring Liz, trying to cure her bad habits such as eating cheese at night, gross outfits, and self-deprecation, while Liz brings out Jack's softer side without either of them losing their edge. The pair give the series its strongest one-liners, funniest moments, and most absurd story lines. But side characters shine just as much, from lay-down-his-life-for-NBC Kenneth Parcell (Jack McBrayer)—part of the network's page program for trainees—to actress/singer/narcissist Jenna Maroney (Jane Krakowski), forced to share the show-within-a-show spotlight with unpredictable celebrity Tracy Jordan (Tracy Morgan)—"unpredictable" being a huge understatement.

> **"** *I'm not a creative type like you, with your work sneakers and left-handedness.* **"**
>
> Jack Donaghy (S1 E19)

TASKS KENNETH PARCELL CAN PERFORM

Useful

❌ See his own reflection

❌ Drink hot liquids

Speak French ✅

❌ Choose a political candidate

Speak Mandarin ✅

Win at poker ✅

Can't do ———————— Can do

Speak Latin ✅

✅ Ventriloquism

❌ Save squirrels from hawks

✅ Win a drinking contest

❌ Eat strawberries

Speak backward ✅

❌ Age

Clog ✅

✅ Win a pig-eating contest

Live forever ✅

Useless

A parade of A-list guest stars take on bizarre roles—if you ever want to see Oprah Winfrey as a drug-fueled airplane hallucination, you've come to the right place. Emily Mortimer plays Jack's (brief) fiancée, Phoebe, who has "avian bone syndrome" and says "ow" when anyone touches her. Matt Damon is a pilot named Carol Burnett whom Liz dates (and starts an uprising against), and Jon Hamm is another Liz boyfriend who lives in a bubble of super-handsomeness, but eventually ends up with hooks for hands.

James Franco plays a version of himself with a sexual fixation on body pillows, Carrie Fisher features as Liz's comedy idol who's grown woefully out of touch, and Michael Keaton portrays a maintenance man trying to fix a leak. There's also *Oz* (see p21) star, Dean Winters, as Liz's ungrateful on-off boyfriend who affectionately nicknames her "Dummy." Classic episodes include "Reaganing," which sees Jack enjoy a perfect 24-hour winning streak and guest star Kelsey Grammer trying

to get rich off an ice-cream cake scam; "Kidney Now!," which features a star-studded telethon set up to find a kidney for Jack's father (Alan Alda); "Cleveland," in which Liz discovers that life is kinder and gentler in Cleveland; and "Reunion," in which Liz makes another, more terrible discovery, at her high-school reunion.

30 Rock never got huge ratings, but its fans were passionate, and critics raved. It was constantly up for (and won) awards, and set a record for the most nominations for a comedy show in a single year when it scored 22 Emmy nods in 2009. Every year it was on, *30 Rock* was nominated for multiple Golden Globes and Emmys, winning some and losing others.

The writing staff, led by Fey, created classic lines that always got a laugh and still come in super handy, from "What the what?" to "Never go with a hippie to a second location." The ratings didn't show it, but *30 Rock* is a modern classic: we all want to go to there.

CREATOR: Tina Fey
PRODUCTION CO: Broadway Video, Little Stranger, NBC Studios, NBC Universal Television, UMS

BOTTOM

COMEDY • 1991
RATED: 15 (UK) • 30 MINS

Take two sexist, sex-deprived losers with no jobs and almost no money who don't even seem to like each other very much but live together anyway—and you get *Bottom*.

Created by and starring *The Young Ones* (see p251) alumni, Rik Mayall and Adrian Edmondson, *Bottom* lasted three crazy seasons. The squabbling pair use slapstick violence against each other when they're not concocting ill-fated plans to find women who they believe might wish to have sex with them.

It's a toss-up as to which of the two characters might be dumber: Richie (Mayall), the frustrated virgin who doesn't have any friends; or Eddie (Edmondson), the alcoholic who has to live in Richie's apartment because he can't hold down a job long enough to pay his own bills. Famous for their misogyny, crudeness, and general ignorance about everything, the pair occasionally hit the local pub, but mostly just stay at home tormenting each other.

MORK & MINDY

SCI-FI COMEDY • 1978
RATED: TV-PG • 30 MINS

Mork & Mindy starred up-and-coming comedian Robin Williams as Mork, an alien from the planet Ork who's assigned to observe human behavior and report back to his boss, Orson.

In the first episode, Mork lands in Boulder, Colorado, where he is taken in by Mindy (Pam Dawber). Over four seasons, Mork learns about planet Earth, wears his trademark rainbow suspenders, greets friends and strangers with "Na-Nu, Na-Nu," makes daily reports to Orson, and turns the Orkan expletive "Shazbot" into a household word.

A spin-off of a hugely successful episode of the hit sitcom *Happy Days* (see p214), *Mork & Mindy* was the perfect platform for the unstoppable improvisational talents of Robin Williams. It was his first major acting role, and he built a career on it. It showcased his ability to be utterly absurd and his knack for commenting on our daily lives with the whacked-out view of an outsider who also happens to be an alien.

THE ODD COUPLE

COMEDY • 2015
RATED: TV-PG • 21 MINS

Two divorced men—one a thoughtless, sloppy sports reporter and the other a neurotic, fastidious photographer— share an apartment in New York City … and drive each other crazy in the process. Sound familiar?

It was hardly a new concept: Neil Simon's original play hit Broadway in 1965, followed by a film version, and then various TV series and made-for-TV movies. The 2015 version stars Matthew Perry as Oscar and Thomas Lennon as Felix, and features a few updates. Oscar is now a satellite radio show host instead of a newspaper columnist, and Felix, though still a photographer, does yoga and plays the cello.

Like the original, Oscar and Felix are two halves of the same whole, irritating each other in the same ways they irritated their ex-wives for all three seasons. Unlike in previous versions, Felix gets a girlfriend this time around. But Oscar still hosts poker games, and Felix still cleans them up.

GRACE AND FRANKIE

**COMEDY • 2015 • RATED: TV-MA • 30 MINS • SEASONS: 7
JANE FONDA, LILY TOMLIN, MARTIN SHEEN**

Two women meet in a restaurant, their husbands join them, and their lives change forever. Why? Because their husbands are leaving them ... for each other. *Grace and Frankie*, starring four actors in their 70s, defied all odds to become the longest-running series in Netflix history.

Like *The Golden Girls* (see p83) before it, this comedy looks at what life is like for older women, and reflects the times perfectly. Grace and Frankie's husbands set the story in motion by confessing their 20-year affair and desire to get married, "because we can do that now." But it is Jane Fonda's Grace and Lily Tomlin's

Frankie whose hilarious banter and totally unexpected friendship that got audiences hooked, backed by a strong supporting cast.

Grace, a former cosmetics mogul in tailored suits, and Frankie, a kaftan-wearing vegan hippie artist, move into Grace's beach house together. The unlikely duo—one a driven and buttoned-up martini-lover, the other a free-spirited and wildly impractical pot smoker—start with nothing but disdain for each other, but become BFFs as they navigate a world that dismisses older women—especially unmarried ones. They even start a business together, filling a much-needed gap by creating products for women in their age group: an organic yam-based vaginal lube, an arthritis-friendly vibrator, and a self-lifting toilet seat called the "Rise Up."

Frankie rolls joints and chants while Grace frets about her lost status, but they come together to laugh and cry about the unexpected path they find themselves on. Their grown children patronize them, their ex-husbands worry about them, and eligible men (played by a slew of famous guest stars) date them.

Episodes cover a wide terrain: Frankie is accidentally declared legally dead, they visit their exes and get caught in a lockdown when an orangutan escapes a local zoo, and they even appear on business reality TV show *Shark Tank*. But no matter where their lives take them, audiences stay hooked.

CREATORS: Marta Kauffman, Howard J. Morris
PRODUCTION CO: Skydance Media, Skydance Television

SOUTH PARK

ANIMATED COMEDY • 1997 • RATED: TV-MA • 22 MINS • SEASONS: 23
TREY PARKER, MATT STONE, MONA MARSHALL

South Park is famous for its relentless swearing and its propensity for killing off a character named Kenny. But it's also a subversive, dark, surreal satire that tackles everything from religion, politics, celebrities, and social issues to what it's like just being a kid.

Trey Parker and Matt Stone, who also voice the lead characters, created this show about four elementary school boys in South Park, Colorado, using a unique style of cut-out (albeit now computer-generated) animation.

There's Stan (Parker), the everyman of the group; his best friend Kyle (Stone), the only Jewish kid in the gang; and (Eric) Cartman, the most arrogant, prejudiced, blasphemous one (and a quick fan favorite, despite carrying out some truly alarming antics). Then there's Kenny, who spent the first five seasons of the show getting killed in every episode—resulting in the catchphrases "Oh my God! They killed Kenny!" and "You bastards!" But he would always be back in the next episode, as if nothing had ever happened.

> **"** *Cartman, that's the dumbest thing you've ever said … this week.* **"**
>
> Kyle (S6 E8)

Based on a five-minute stop-motion cartoon made by Parker and Stone in college, *South Park* became a cultural phenomenon on Comedy Central. The show kept getting bigger, resulting in a hit movie in 1999. While controversy frequently rages around the show, viewers keep watching … and laughing their butts off.

NIGHT COURT

COMEDY • 1984
RATED: TV-14 • 24 MINS

During the nighttime sitting of a Manhattan municipal court, the youngest judge in state history—who's also a magician—presides over unpredictable cases with the help of his quirky staff.

Judge Harry T. Stone (Harry Anderson) leads the charge with his innate cheerfulness, his love of singer Mel Tormé, and his unfailing compassion. Also in court every night are prosecutor Dan Fielding (John Larroquette); narcissist "Bull" Shannon (Richard Moll); giant-but-sweet bailiff Roz (Marsha Warfield); and, settling in after Season 3 (of nine), public defender Christine Sullivan (Markie Post), who becomes Harry's love interest. Larroquette was so popular, he won an Emmy four times in a row, before leaving the following year.

Night Court wasn't a show to tackle controversial issues, take big risks, or show the evolution of its characters—instead, it was a dependable, silly comedy meant to give audiences a break from the real world.

RICK AND MORTY

**ANIMATED SCI-FI • 2013 • RATED: TV-MA • 22 MINS • SEASONS: 4
JUSTIN ROILAND, CHRIS PARNELL, SPENCER GRAMMER**

It's sci-fi, it's a comedy, it's an adventure, it's metaphysical ... *Rick and Morty*—a show about an alcoholic, misanthropic scientist taking his nervous grandson on interdimensional adventures whether he likes it or not—is difficult to define.

For a show whose main character operates under the principle that nothing really matters, *Rick and Morty* is surprisingly energetic and whimsical. The stories center on the Smith family: dad Jerry (Chris Parnell), mom Beth (Sarah Chalke), kids Summer (Spencer Grammer) and Morty (Justin Roiland), and Beth's dad, Rick (also Roiland)—but take place in an infinite number of different galaxies and realities. "What about the reality we left behind?" asks innocent, 14-year-old Morty, but Rick doesn't care; there's always another one.

In this cartoon sci-fi world, anything is possible. Rick, when he's finished drinking from the flask he always carries, builds everything from bombs and freeze rays to a butter-carrying robot and a cable box that lets him watch TV across every dimension.

> *"Morty, I'm a drunk, not a hack."*
>
> **Rick** (S3 E4)

Over the seasons, Morty becomes more of a willing participant—invited, rather than dragged, by Rick to the next adventure. There's no specific style to the humor: it can be smart, goofy, or sophisticated. There's plenty of slapstick cartoon violence, mingled with philosophy and social commentary, plus the occasional breaking of the fourth wall, making it one of the most unpredictable shows out there.

MONGRELS

**COMEDY • 2010
RATED: 15 (UK) • 30 MINS**

An adult comedy starring foul-mouthed puppets, *Mongrels* is about five anthropomorphic animals who hang out behind a pub in London (on the Isle of Dogs!), none of whom are actual mongrels.

Two foxes (one of which is described as metrosexual), a cat, a pigeon, and a purebred Afghan hound star in this two-season series that was inspired by the likes of *The Muppet Show* (see p65), *The Simpsons* (see p56), stage musical *Avenue Q*, and *Family Guy* (see p243). To get a sense of its tone, jump right in with the first episode, in which Marion (Dan Tetsell), a Persian alley cat, realizes his owner has been dead for four months and gives the go-ahead to his other kitty friends to eat the corpse.

Episodes also feature cameo appearances (as puppets) by British comedians in small roles. Each episode also has a little song—the one in the pilot is called "Where My Balls At," sung by a cat who's been neutered.

DERRY GIRLS

COMEDY • 2018 • RATED: TV-MA • 25 MINS • SEASONS: 3
SAOIRSE-MONICA JACKSON, NICOLA COUGHLAN

As if being a teenager weren't complicated enough, *Derry Girls* chronicles the adventures of four girls and one boy who go to a Catholic school in early 1990s Derry, Northern Ireland, during the period of violence known as "The Troubles."

One of the funniest premises of the irreverent *Derry Girls*—set during the unfunny time of violent conflict between Catholic Irish nationalists and Protestant United Kingdom loyalists—is that "wee English lad" from London, James (Dylan Llewellyn), has to go to an all-girls Catholic school (where there's no boys' bathroom). If he went to the all-boys school, he'd get beaten up because of his English accent.

James's cousin Michelle (Jamie-Lee O'Donnell), the wild-child troublemaker, introduces him to the rest of her pals: Erin (Saoirse-Monica Jackson), who has a lot of ideas and is sure they're all correct; Erin's cousin Orla (Louisa Harland), who doesn't care what anybody thinks about her and reads Erin's diary; and Clare (Nicola Coughlan), a sweet, easily intimidated girl, and the voice of comparative reason. While the girls get up to the kind of antics you'd expect from teenagers (underage drinking, skipping school), their lives also include bomb scares and military checkpoints. Lisa McGhee, who created the series and writes every episode, grew up in Derry and knows what she's talking about.

The girls (and James) are clearly the stars, with their presumptions, proclamations, and not-so-fantastic choices. But they're not the only ones getting laughs—the adults are just as ridiculous. Erin's grandfather, Granda Joe, gets some of the best lines, especially when he's criticizing Gerry, Erin's good-natured father. Sister Michael, the headmistress of the girls' school, is edgy, sarcastic, and takes no nonsense, except for her own. And there's even a hot priest!

> **❝ *You're a Derry girl now, James.* ❞**
>
> **Michelle** (S2 E6)

If you're not used to the Northern Irish accent, take the time to tune your ear in. The jokes are funny, the timing is spot-on, and the slang is well worth learning. And the music, all from the '90s, is perfection.

CREATOR: Lisa McGee
PRODUCTION CO: Hat Trick Productions

PHINEAS AND FERB

ANIMATED COMEDY • 2007
RATED: TV-G • 23 MINS

All summer long, brothers Phineas and Ferb build elaborate contraptions that disappear by the end of each episode, while their sister Candace tries to bust them before the evidence vanishes.

Don't be fooled into thinking this show's just for kids—*Phineas and Ferb* has universal appeal. In (eventually) intersecting stories, Phineas (Vincent Martella) and Ferb (Thomas Brodie-Sangster) build giant inventions and Candace (Ashley Tisdale) tries to get them in trouble, while family pet/secret agent Perry the Platypus foils evil but inept scientist Heinz Doofenshmirtz from taking over the tristate area. The other kids include Isabel (who's in love with Phineas), Baljeet (an overachiever), and Jeremy (Candace's sweet boyfriend).

Over the four-season show, you will discover Grammy-worthy songs—you'll find yourself humming them hours later—a series of celebrity guest voices, and some of the most creative, inventive stories ever seen on TV.

THE INBETWEENERS

COMEDY • 2008
RATED: TV-MA • 25 MINS

In the pre-Instagram days, four high-school boys who aren't cool enough to be popular and not smart enough to be nerds form a bond.

The show begins when Will (Simon Bird) has to stop going to private school after his parents' divorce and tries to find friends at his new public school. There's Simon (Joe Thomas) the romantic, Jay (James Buckley) the braggart, and Neil (Blake Harrison), who's not that bright. Over three seasons, the four try to impress girls (Simon moons over his crush Carli, while Jay invents sexual exploits), get their hands on alcohol, and navigate around their unpleasant teachers.

Each episode is narrated by Will, but the awkward moments are evenly spread out among the group. The boys' exchanges—when they're not busy embarrassing themselves in public—are both authentic and hilarious, like when they're trying to get a drink at a bar without ID.

THE YOUNG ONES

COMEDY • 1982
RATED: TV-PG • 35 MINS

In the squalid house they share, four college students live together, torment each other, and try to get through the day as ridiculously as they can while they avoid their studies.

This short-lived but popular comedy became a cult hit, thanks to its irreverent, punkish attitude. It attracted some of Britain's best comedians, with guest spots from the likes of Stephen Fry, Hugh Laurie, and Emma Thompson. But it was the core cast viewers loved: Rick (Rik Mayall), who's either studying sociology or domestic science and probably not sure what the difference is; sociopathic medical student Vyvyan (Adrian Edmondson); laid-back Mike (Christopher Ryan); and hippie Neil (Nigel Planer), who supposedly does the cooking and cleaning—but not much of either.

The two-season show also features puppets and long aside segments that had absolutely nothing to do with the plot, making each episode a completely unpredictable ride.

FAMILY TIES

COMEDY • 1982
RATED: TV-PG • 24 MINS

Baby boomers Steven and Elyse Keaton are raising a family with the values they embraced in the 1960s, but their two oldest kids are a Young Republican and a shopaholic.

Michael J. Fox became a star as Alex P. Keaton, the ambitious, Ronald Reagan–loving kid with a fixation on making money. His sister Mallory isn't political, but she's a full-on '80s materialist whose favorite things are boys and shopping. The youngest, Jennifer, is a good-natured tomboy who clearly understands her parents better than either of her siblings.

Steven manages the local public TV station and Elyse is an architect. They don't understand their two oldest kids but they keep on trying. Look out for great cameos from Tom Hanks as the children's alcoholic uncle, and Geena Davis as the family's housekeeper. Most people think the seven-season show became far-fetched when a baby brother arrived toward the end of Season 3, so stick to earlier episodes.

MALCOLM IN THE MIDDLE

COMEDY • 2000
RATED: TV-PG • 22 MINS

Sure, Malcolm is a certified genius, but that doesn't help much in his wildly dysfunctional family, where he has no control over his fiery mother, immature father, or ridiculous brothers.

Malcolm's (Frankie Muniz) brains aren't much help in school, where being in the gifted class does nothing for his social status. At home, his mother Lois (Jane Kaczmarek) flies off the handle at everything, while dad Hal (Bryan Cranston in his pre-*Breaking Bad* years) is well-meaning but generally unhelpful. Oldest brother Francis is in a military school (for the first few seasons), and big brother Reese is a big dumb bully. Little brother Dewey is busy dreaming, and eventually there's also baby Jamie to add to the circus.

While chaos reigns, Lois and Hal's true passion for each other helps keep the family strong throughout the seven seasons. Things are nuts inside the house, but against outside forces they were always—usually—a united front.

MODERN FAMILY

COMEDY • 2009
RATED: TV-PG • 22 MINS

The characters of the three families in this mockumentary are all connected by their patriarch Jay. Get drawn in to their lives as they talk to the camera about relationships, squabbles, and how to raise kids in the modern era.

Featuring a sprawling cast, this genius comedy leaps beyond some of the more outdated and rigid conceptions of the traditional American family found in other mainstream sitcoms. Ed O'Neill stars as Jay, whose daughter Claire (Julie Bowen) has a husband and three kids. Jay's son, Mitchell (Jesse Tyler Ferguson), has a husband and an adopted Vietnamese daughter (and had to come out to his dad three times before it sunk in). Meanwhile, Jay's second wife, Gloria, is Colombian, gorgeous, and decades younger than he is.

A hit for all of its 11 seasons, the show uses a mix of comedy and emotion to demonstrate that family issues are universal, no matter what type of household they're coming from.

3RD ROCK FROM THE SUN

SCI-FI COMEDY • 1996
RATED: TV-14 • 22 MINS

Four aliens pose as a normal, human family in Rutherford, Ohio, while they observe earthling behavior, study the culture, and send back reports to their boss, the Big Giant Head.

In this fish-out-of-water high-concept sitcom, the comedy comes from the aliens' attempts to understand human society. There's Dick (John Lithgow), now the dad of the family and a physics professor; his sister Sally (Kristen Johnston), who became a woman for the Earth visit (there is no gender difference where these aliens come from), resulting in a lot of breast jokes; their dim brother Harry; and Tommy, a teenage boy who has to deal with high school—and go through puberty.

As we get deeper into the show's six seasons, the aliens get more comfortable on Earth and become increasingly interested in the lives they've adopted, as well as the friends they've made. And just wait until you see who plays the Big Giant Head....

MARRIED ... WITH CHILDREN

COMEDY • 1987
RATED: TV-14 • 22 MINS

Tired of all the sitcoms about nice families who always get along? *Married ... with Children* is the polar opposite, starring the crude but hilarious and majorly underachieving Bundy family.

Al Bundy (Ed O'Neill) is a TV-loving shoe salesman. His wife Peggy (Katey Sagal) is never seen without a big bouffant hairdo, high heels, tight pants, and a lot of complaints about Al's lack of sex drive. Kelly (Christina Applegate) is their trashy and dim-bulb daughter, while her brother Bud (David Faustino) is somewhat smarter, but a lot less popular. Along with neighbor Marcy and her husbands, the lineup left no lowbrow stone unturned.

Married ... with Children was the very first show on Fox's prime-time schedule and ran for 11 seasons. In stark contrast to the usual sitcom formula, the characters were crass and selfish, and the cast delivered all their outrageous dialogue with complete conviction.

THE BRADY BUNCH

COMEDY • 1969
RATED: TV-PG • 25 MINS

This sitcom about a widower with three sons and a widow with three daughters who marry and blend their families has been an indelible part of American childhood for generations.

Regular guy and architect Mike Brady (Robert Reed), his wife Carol (Florence Henderson), and their trusty maid Alice are trying to keep the chaos to a minimum in a house with six kids, a dog (at least in Season 1), and all the groovy changes that the 1970s brought to this kitschy, innocuous suburban American family. Everyone struggles to deal with everyone else, but problems are resolved by the end of each episode, and they all learn to get along.

There are classic moments and episodes that are now part of the American lexicon, from "Marcia! Marcia! Marcia!" to "Mom always says not to play ball in the house," followed by the sound of a crash. And no one who grew up with the show will ever forget, "Here's my sister—the new Jan Brady!"

SANTA CLARITA DIET

COMEDY HORROR • 2017
RATED: TV-MA • 30 MINS

A married couple, who are both real estate agents in Santa Clarita, California, have to find a way to cope when one of them suddenly turns into an undead cannibal.

Joel (Timothy Olyphant), Sheila (Drew Barrymore), and their daughter Abby (Liv Hewson) are doing just fine until the day Sheila gets sick, vomits up a storm (and an internal organ), and dies. Or does she? All of a sudden Sheila is awake again, only now she doesn't have a pulse. Or blood. At the same time, her libido is up, her id is running wild, and she's eating raw meat. "How could this happen? We're realtors!" protests Joel when Abby's friend Eric determines that Sheila is undead and will soon be eating human flesh.

Over three seasons, the family's lives get even more complicated as they seek to cure Sheila while keeping her fed along the way. And that means finding people who really *deserve* to be dead, so she can eat them.

IN LIVING COLOR

COMEDY • 1990
RATED: TV-14 • 22 MINS

Not only did *In Living Color* launch some huge careers, this five-season show broke ground by being the first sketch comedy show in America to star a predominantly black cast.

Created by Keenan Ivory Wayans and co-starring some of his talented family members, *In Living Color* broke new ground, providing a stark contrast to the mostly white *Saturday Night Live*. Sketches and characters caught on quickly, making expressions like "two snaps up" and "hated it" from the effeminate reviewers in the recurring "Men on Film" sketch into instant catchphrases.

Along with the Wayanses, the not-yet-famous cast included Tommy Davidson, David Alan Grier, Jamie Foxx, Jim Carrey, as well as Jennifer Lopez doing dance moves choreographed by Rosie Perez. Characters like Homey D. Clown and the inept Fire Marshal Bill and sketches like "The Homeboy Shopping Network" became TV classics.

WHAT WE DO IN THE SHADOWS

COMEDY HORROR • 2019
RATED: TV-MA • 22 MINS

This mockumentary about a group of vampires living together in Staten Island, New York, features a stream of celebrity cameos.

Based on the 2014 film, this horror comedy follows four vampire housemates who have been living together for centuries. There's Nandor the Relentless (Kayvan Novak)—"because I never relent"—who depends on his human assistant to take care of him. Then there's Laszlo (Matt Berry) and Nadja (Natasia Demetriou), a married vampire couple with very high sex drives, and Colin Robinson (Mark Proksch), an energy vampire who drains humans by boring or enraging them.

Celebrities love guest-starring on this two-season series, from Dave Bautista and Tilda Swinton, to Wesley Snipes, Mark Hamill, and *Sixth Sense* star Haley Joel Osment (already famous for seeing dead people).

AFTER LIFE

COMEDY DRAMA • 2019
RATED: TV-MA • 30 MINS

A dark comedy from Ricky Gervais about a semi-suicidal man who gives up on caring about almost anything after his wife dies of cancer. It may sound grim, but it's also very funny.

Tony (Ricky Gervais) is mourning his wife and the joy has gone from his life, so he spends his days insulting coworkers, innocent strangers, and even random primary school kids he passes on his way to work. One particularly explicit insult directed at a young, pint-sized, red-haired bully creates a moment that is shocking, tragic, and amusing all at the same time, in true Gervais form.

But thanks to a widow he meets (*Downton Abbey*'s Penelope Wilton), a new coworker, his dad's nurse, his love for his dog, and the videos his wife made for him before she died, Tony slowly comes alive again, finding his redemption in connection. It's dark stuff, indeed, but this two-season show is also full of razor-sharp comedy.

MAN LIKE MOBEEN

COMEDY • 2017
RATED: TV-MA • 23 MINS

Mobeen is trying to stay out of trouble, but it's not easy living in Small Heath, taking care of his 15-year-old sister, and attempting to be a good Muslim at the same time.

Mobeen (Guz Khan) is trying to escape his past as a drug dealer, but he's always eyed suspiciously by the local police. However, even while he's being pestered by the cops, or having to deal with his friends' terrible choices—such as his pal Eight (Tez Ilyas) buying a laptop from a stranger that turns out to be a dead cat in a bag—he's determined to be a better person.

Over three seasons, this one-of-a-kind Birmingham-set comedy explores everything from Brexit to letting your sister go to the school prom, and viral dog-punching videos. Take the chance to look at the world from the point of view of a Muslim man who's just trying to do the right thing—and knows how to laugh about it.

PEOPLE JUST DO NOTHING

COMEDY • 2014
RATED: 15 (UK) • 30 MINS

If *The Office*'s David Brent were younger and involved in pirate radio, he'd be one of the not-very-successful but overly confident MCs in this original British comedy.

Now with five seasons under its belt, this mockumentary started out as a series of online shorts that got so popular that its stars and creators—Allan Mustafa (arrogant "MC Grindah"), Steve Stamp (dopey "Steves"), Asim Chaudhry (entrepreneurial "Chabuddy G"), and Hugo Chegwin (loyal "DJ Beats")—were hired to turn it into a TV series. The show is about a group of MCs and DJs who run a pirate radio station called Kurupt FM that broadcasts garage and drum-and-bass music.

The documentary concept gives them plenty of opportunities to talk directly to the camera as they ooze confidence, completely oblivious to the reality of their non-rise to fame and lack of influence on anyone more than a few miles away from the transmitter.

BROOKLYN NINE-NINE

COMEDY • 2013 • RATED: TV-14 • 22 MINS • SEASONS: 8
ANDY SAMBERG, MELISSA FUMERO, ANDRE BRAUGHER

This ain't your average police station. At the 99th precinct in Brooklyn, immature (but talented) NYPD Detective Jake Peralta and the rest of his quirky coworkers solve crimes, throw jokes around, and vie for the approval of by-the-book Captain Holt.

The show is centered on Jake (Andy Samberg), a man-boy who's great at closing cases despite—or perhaps because of—his very chill style. While there's comedy to be milked from his conflicts with Holt (Andre Braugher) and the varying abilities of his colleagues, *Brooklyn Nine-Nine* also has an optimistic heart.

Running themes include Jake and Sergeant Amy Santiago's will-they-or-won't-they romance, Charles Boyles's culinary obsessions, and Lt. Terry Jeffords's love of yogurt.

You will also learn to love Jake's penchant for repeating a phrase said by someone (usually Amy) and announcing that it's the title of their sex tape. And Jake's obsession with the movie *Die Hard* crops up in many episodes, even one in which he gets to reenact the plot—sort of—in Season 3.

Less intense than other popular cop shows, *Brooklyn Nine-Nine* can also be quite touching. Story lines include such subjects as the complexities of sexual harassment cases, and coming face-to-face with racial profiling, as well as featuring characters who have had to come out to their parents. The series tackles these and other sensitive issues with sincerity without ever giving up its comedy roots.

BLACK BOOKS

COMEDY • 2000
RATED: TV-PG • 25 MINS

Bernard Black owns a bookshop in London, but has no interest in sales or customers. He's constantly irritated by everybody, tolerating only his assistant Manny, and best friend Fran.

Bernard (Dylan Moran) is perpetually annoyed by customers who dare to show up at his shop and treat it like a library, so he hires Manny (Bill Bailey), his polar opposite, to help out.

Bernard doesn't really want to sell books, as then he'd have to do more work, such as ordering more stock! Instead he spends this sitcom's three seasons drinking, smoking, and yelling at people. Optimistic Manny wants to change things. The first time Bernard leaves him alone in the shop, customers flood in, thrilled to shop without the verbal abuse.

Fran runs the gift shop next door called Nifty Gifts and, as she admits, sells a lot of "wank." She's also the only one who can get through to Bernard, who avoids common sense like the plague.

ELLEN

COMEDY • 1994
RATED: TV-14 • 22 MINS

Ellen was a simple sitcom (modeled slightly after Seinfeld) about a bookshop owner in Los Angeles named Ellen, and her friends and family. Then, in Season 4, things changed.

Ellen spent the first two seasons running her bookstore and dating men, but by the third, she had left the dating to her friends and was focused more on her business. When the network suggested she get a puppy to spice things up, star Ellen DeGeneres and the writers decided it was time for their main character to come out of the closet— a radical move for the times.

In the famous "The Puppy Episode," Ellen finally comes out as gay at a special gathering of her friends after first denying it to herself and others. The episode scored the show its highest ratings ever, but it was canceled after just one more season, and it would be years before the real Ellen became the beloved superstar she is today.

TAXI

COMEDY • 1978
RATED: TV-PG • 24 MINS

Inspired by an article in New York magazine, Taxi is a smart and funny, but also poignant look at a group of cab drivers dreaming of better things in a grungy garage.

Alex Rieger (Judd Hirsch) is the only one in the bunch who calls himself a cab driver. Tony (Tony Danza) is a boxer who loses more fights than he wins; Bobby (Jeff Conaway) is an actor dreaming of his big break; Elaine (Marilu Henner) works at an art gallery and plans to run her own one day. Their dispatcher is the belligerent Louis De Palma (Danny DeVito), who also rules over Latka (Andy Kaufman), the garage's sweet immigrant mechanic, and Reverend Jim (Christopher Lloyd), who never recovered from the drug-addled '60s.

During the show's five-season run, guest stars such as Ruth Gordon, Ted Danson, Tom Selleck, and Tom Hanks all turned up. It also scored 31 Emmy nods, winning 18—three of them for Outstanding Comedy Series.

NEVER HAVE I EVER

COMEDY • 2020
RATED: TV-14 • 28 MINS

A coming-of-age rom-com about 15-year-old Devi Vishwakumar, a nerdy Indian-American girl, narrated by tennis great John McEnroe. Wait, what?

It's sophomore year of high school and Devi (Maitreyi Ramakrishnan) embarks on a plan to be cool, get hot, and snag a boy. Devi has an overbearing mother, two best friends, a debilitating crush, and an academic rival.

Sounds like a standard teen comedy, but this 10-part series (one season so far), co-created by Mindy Kaling and partly inspired by her own adolescence, is a fresh take on the genre.

Having John McEnroe as a narrator shouldn't work, but it does—he's funny and unapologetically weird. Refreshingly, Devi's Indian culture, and her complex relationship with it, is also in the foreground throughout. And Ramakrishnan, discovered through a global casting search, truly shines as witty and self-assured Devi—especially when grappling with her grief over her father's death.

CHEERS

**COMEDY • 1982 • RATED: TV-PG • 22 MINS • SEASONS: 11
TED DANSON, SHELLEY LONG, RHEA PERLMAN**

As the theme song says, "Sometimes you wanna go where everybody knows your name." The Cheers bar is a place you want to hang out, where the jokes fly fast and furious, delivered by a cast of characters you can't help but love.

If you've ever, even for a minute, aspired to write a sitcom pilot, *Cheers* sets the gold standard. Since the series ran 11 seasons, you'd think the first episode wouldn't be so important, but it sets up the location, characters, and the key relationships so perfectly, it's like watching a sitcom symphony.

> *" If ignorance is bliss,
> this is Eden."*
>
> **Diane Chambers** (S3 E16)

When *Cheers* premiered, the focus was on its two stars: Sam Malone (Ted Danson), an ex-professional baseball player, recovering alcoholic, and womanizer who owns the bar, and Diane Chambers (Shelley Long), a snobby intellectual who takes a job as a waitress at the bar after her fiancé abandons her in episode 1. They had incredibly strong chemistry—the writers said they took inspiration from Spencer Tracy and Katharine Hepburn.

The other characters provide a perfect back-up chorus. Behind the bar is the relentlessly agreeable but slow-witted Coach (Nicholas Colasanto). When Colasanto died between Seasons 3 and 4, Woody Harrelson

stepped in as Woody Boyd, equally clueless and just as kind. Carla, the other waitress, is a single mom living a tough life with an easily ignited temper, who almost hero-worships Sam. The bar's regular customers include Norm, an accountant who's always hiding from his wife, and Cliff, a know-it-all whose facts are never quite accurate, not to mention—from Season 3—psychiatrist Dr. Frasier Crane (Kelsey Grammer), who would later get his own spin-off (see *Frasier*, p259). When Diane leaves town to become a writer, Kirstie Alley steps in as Rebecca Howe, who seems like a confident businesswoman, but is revealed to be more and more neurotic as time goes on.

Season 1 got terrible ratings, but soon picked up steam thanks to adoring critics, Emmy Awards, and the support of the head of NBC Entertainment, Brandon Tartikoff. By Season 2 it was a top-rated show, and the 1993 finale was watched by 80 million viewers. Wouldn't it be great if we all had a Cheers around the corner....

CREATORS: James Burrows, Glen Charles, Les Charles
PRODUCTION CO: Charles/Burrows/Charles Productions, Paramount Televsion

FRASIER

COMEDY • 1993
RATED: TV-PG • 22 MINS

Funny, sharp, and witty, this *Cheers* spin-off finds psychiatrist Frasier Crane hosting a radio advice show and taking in his police detective father after he's shot on duty and forced to retire.

Kelsey Grammar plays the title character, who is back home in Seattle from Boston, and David Hyde Pierce is his brother, Niles, also a psychiatrist, and even more snobby

and refined. John Mahoney is their down-to-earth dad, Martin, who moves in with Frasier along with live-in physical therapist and caregiver Daphne (Jane Leeves) and a hideous pea-green recliner chair that seriously offends Frasier's sense of good taste.

Frasier's partner at the radio station, producer Roz (Peri Gilpin), also provides a voice of reason as she gets to know the family well. One of the most successful television spin-offs ever, the show ran for 11 seasons and won the Emmy for Outstanding Comedy Series five years in a row.

WKRP IN CINCINNATI

COMEDY • 1978 • RATED: TV-PG • 25 MINS • SEASONS: 4
HOWARD HESSEMAN, GARY SANDY, LONI ANDERSON

An easy-listening radio station in Cincinnati gets a shock when a new programme director arrives and changes its output to rock 'n' roll overnight. The staff and bumbling manager have very mixed reactions.

DJ Dr. Johnny Fever (Howard Hesseman) is delighted when he is woken from his easy-listening stupor and allowed to play rock 'n' roll on air—and finally gets to say the word that got him fired from his last big job: "Booger!" Program director Andy Travis (Gary Sandy) adds smooth-talking funky DJ Venus Flytrap (Tim Reid) to the staff to liven things up for the night shift.

Andy also promotes Bailey Quarters (Jan Smithers), the painfully shy but underused woman helping schedule ads. Rounding out

the ensemble is Arthur Carlson, technically in charge but inept, and Les Nessman, the newscaster who dreams of having his own helicopter, and walls around his cubicle. Jennifer Marlowe (Loni Anderson) is the glamorous receptionist lusted after by sales manager, Herb Tarlek. Andy soon realizes Jennifer is the glue that keeps the station together, and the one person who can keep Carlson out of everybody's hair.

But at WKRP everybody is lovable in their own way. The show stayed funny more than four seasons, even during story lines that included Russian dissidents, bomb threats, draft dodgers, and the famous, and many say funniest, "Turkeys Away" episode, where Carlson and Nessman (off camera) cook up a Thanksgiving promotion scheme that involves throwing live turkeys out of a helicopter.

RED DWARF

SCI-FI COMEDY • 1988
RATED: TV-14 • 30 MINS

On a space mining ship called *Red Dwarf*, an underachiever from Liverpool wakes up three million years into the future and discovers he's the last human being alive in the universe.

In episode 1, Dave Lister (Craig Charles) is given a choice: go into stasis as punishment or reveal the location of the cat he's stashed on board to have it dissected. He chooses stasis, and then a radiation leak kills the rest of the crew. The ship's computer wakes him up, once it's safe—3 million years later.

Over the sitcom's 13 seasons, Lister has only a few companions. There's the ship's computer, Holly, who is initially male, but later switches to female. Rimmer (Chris Barrie) is a hologram of Lister's boss, made by Holly to keep Lister from going crazy alone, while Cat (Danny John-Jules) is a humanoid cat descended from the pet Lister was protecting. In later seasons, they're joined by Kryten (Robert Llewellyn), a robot Lister finds and repairs.

THE HITCHHIKER'S GUIDE TO THE GALAXY

SCI-FI COMEDY • 1981
RATED: TV-PG • 33 MINS

Long before the 2005 movie of the same name, this comedy series delighted fans of Douglas Adams's novel and general audiences alike.

Arthur Dent (Simon Jones) is rescued by his alien friend Ford Prefect (David Dixon), who hitches a ride on a spaceship when Earth is scheduled for demolition by the Vogons. The TV series lasted for only one season, but it was a memorable ride, featuring characters such as the two-headed, three-armed Zaphod Beeblebrox, and Marvin the Paranoid Android.

To keep the whimsy of the novel, the titular *Guide*—an electronic book Ford hands to Arthur while hiding on the Vogons' ship—delivers its information in narrated, animated segments. It provides information on all the species, planets, and habits Arthur needs to know during his journey, including its key instruction on the front cover: "Don't panic."

THE ORVILLE

SCI-FI COMEDY • 2017
RATED: TV-14 • 44 MINS

Hundreds of years in the future, the crew of the *USS Orville* represent Earth's Interstellar Fleet as they explore space, meet new alien species, and deal with the relationships and complications of their daily lives.

Seth MacFarlane (creator of both *American Dad!* and *Family Guy*—see p242–243) took his love for *Star Trek* (see p88), combined it with comedy, and created a two-season show that manages to stay true to its sci-fi roots, create dramatic tension, and still be both funny and touching. There are philosophical stories—a planet ruled by social media, an all-male species that alters the gender of its children—as well as bigger arcs that place *The Orville* as the only ship that can save the galaxy.

The characters, from the human crew to a robot named Isaac and a gelatinous alien named Yaphit, are compelling and, above all, amusing.

FUTURAMA

SCI-FI COMEDY • 1999 • RATED: TV-PG • 22 MINS • SEASONS: 7
BILLY WEST, KATEY SAGAL, JOHN DIMAGGIO

Philip J. Fry, a pizza-delivery boy disappointed with life, falls into a cryogenic chamber on December 31, 1999, and wakes up on New Year's Eve—1,000 years later! He quickly adapts and gets a new life ... as a delivery boy.

Fry (Billy West) tracks down his very *very* distant nephew, Professor Hubert J. Farnsworth (also voiced by Billy West), a 160-year-old inventor who needs a crew for his interstellar delivery service, Planet Express. Fry is joined by Bender (John DiMaggio), a sarcastic, selfish, alcohol-swilling robot, and one-eyed Captain Turanga Leela (Katey Sagal), who appears to be the only one of her kind.

Planet Express also has an intern, Amy, whose rich parents own the western hemisphere of Mars; Doctor Zoidberg, an incompetent walruslike alien; and Jamaican accountant

Hermes Conrad, an expert at numbers and a former Olympic limbo champion.

The show has frequent admiring nods to *Star Trek* (see p88), including guest appearances by almost all of the original series' cast, and celebrity cameos, from an army of butt-kicking Lucy Lius to famous people voicing versions of themselves as heads preserved in glass jars. Among the very best: John Goodman in top form as a rampaging robot Santa who rips the heads off naughty children and stuffs toys down their necks.

> **"*I'm so embarrassed. I wish everybody else was dead.*"**
>
> Bender (S4 E13)

AVENUE 5

SCI-FI COMEDY • 2020
RATED: TV-MA • 30 MINS

Forty years in the future, a group of rich, spoiled tourists and inept crew members are knocked off course and stranded aboard a luxury commercial spaceship for three years.

"Set your phasers to fun!" says Captain Ryan Clark (Hugh Laurie) to his passengers, moments before *Avenue 5* gets knocked off its trajectory. Instead of heading home, they're

now three years away, and everyone is mad. Things get worse: they discover Clark was only hired to play a captain, and doesn't know anything about how to fly a spaceship.

Turns out there's an entire fake crew of people who look like they know what they're doing, while the real experts labor below deck. But since this is a commercial flight, it seems in everyone's best interest to keep thinking Clark is their fearless leader. Soon the lines between deceptive fiction and reality are so blurred that nobody has any idea what's really going on in the first season.

MONTY PYTHON'S FLYING CIRCUS

SKETCH COMEDY • 1969 • RATED: TV-MA • 30 MINS • SEASONS: 4
JOHN CLEESE, ERIC IDLE, MICHAEL PALIN

Monty Python's Flying Circus is
**a surreal mix of absurdities, social
commentary, whimsical animations,
unabashed silliness, and a lot of men
in dresses. Its catchline, "And now for
something completely different," is a
perfect description of what happens
in every episode.**

For their landmark comedy series,
incomparable and irreverent writer-
performers the "Pythons"—Graham
Chapman, Eric Idle, Terry Jones, Michael Palin,
Terry Gilliam, and John Cleese—created

characters, situations, and sketches that
amused themselves, and each other, and
(eventually) viewers across the globe. It's hard
to believe it only ran for four seasons.

Animations suddenly appear from out of the
blue, stopping sketches in midflow and starting
new ones, or sometimes continuing them.
Characters move from one sketch to the next;
new characters pop up in the middle of
sketches to end them, or just to shout
something and disappear. In the much-loved
"Dead Parrot" sketch, an irate John Cleese
tries to return his parrot because it's dead,

WE INTERRUPT THIS ARTICLE TO ANNOY YOU AND GIVE YOU A DIAGRAM
SHOWING HOW MONTY PYTHON SKETCHES ARE (NOT AT ALL REALLY) LINKED

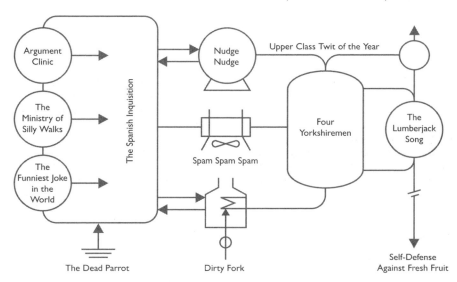

despite the insistence of pet-shop owner Michael Palin that it is "resting," "stunned," and "probably pining for the fjords." Things get increasingly more absurd until Cleese's character decides it's all "getting too silly" and Graham Chapman, dressed as a colonel, orders things to end, turning to camera and commanding everyone to "Get on with it."

There are continuing jokes, such as "nobody expects the Spanish Inquisition!," but also super-quick and unforgettable sketches, such as the 20-second "Fish-Slapping Dance" sketch, in which a man dances and continually slaps another man with a fish. Finally, the slapped man pulls out a larger fish, and uses it to slap the first man into the water. The end features one of Gilliam's animations—the man in the water is eaten by a giant, very ugly fish. Decades later, it still makes you laugh, even when you watch it over and over again.

Monty Python thrived on juxtaposition. The humor goes from the purely physical (silly walks), to conversations full of eloquent language. Sometimes, the Pythons are plain ridiculous; other times they remain steadfastly serious in the most ludicrous situations. Some sketches are only as long as a sentence. Occasionally, the Pythons even apologize on screen for the terribleness of their show. At other times, the opening theme or the credits turn up in the wrong place in an episode, just for fun.

> **"** *Python was in your face, challenging, and very silly.* **"**
>
> Eric Idle

Even if you haven't seen the show, you still probably know about some of its most famous moments. Can anyone look at a can of spam in a grocery store without thinking about a

group of Vikings in a greasy-spoon café singing "Spam, spam, spam, spam, spam, spam" to a frustrated couple who want their breakfast without spam? Or how about "The Lumberjack Song," in which a group of singing Mounties are happy to provide backup vocals to one of their own until he announces, mid-song, that he likes to "cut down trees, wear high heels, suspenders and a bra?" Then there's Eric Idle's insistent badgering of Terry Jones about his sex life with his wife, with a relentless "nudge nudge, wink wink, say no more" elbowing. When he finally asks Jones if he has ever "slept with a lady" and Jones answers yes, Idle responds: "What's it like?" It's one of the few *Python* sketches that ends with a punchline.

The group went on to make movies, documentaries, records, and books together— not to mention their own solo projects—with great success, but the *Monty Python's Flying Circus* TV series remains a legendary, quotable, superbly silly, and cunningly clever classic.

CREATORS: Graham Chapman, Eric Idle, Terry Jones, Michael Palin, Terry Gilliam, John Cleese
PRODUCTION CO: BBC, Python (Monty) Pictures

FUTURE MAN

SCI-FI COMEDY • 2017
RATED: TV-MA • 30 MINS

After Josh, a janitor who still lives with his parents, finally beats a supposedly unbeatable video game, things start to get weird. Two of its characters come to life and ask him to save the world.

The first thing you need to know is that Seth Rogen and Evan Goldberg (*Sausage Party, The Interview*) are among *Future Man*'s executive producers, which should give you some idea of its absurdish tone. Game characters Tiger (Eliza Coupe) and Wolf (Derek Wilson) drag loser janitor Josh (Josh Hutcherson) off to save the past, and therefore the future— and have no idea what Josh means when he tells them they're just ripping off the plot of cult movie *The Last Starfighter*. Whenever they return to the present, they discover repercussions to the changes they've made.

Over two seasons, crude jokes and references to other sci-fi films such as *The Terminator* are wrapped up with the very silly idea that Josh has the skills to be a hero at all.

GREEN WING

COMEDY • 2004
RATED: 15 (UK) • 51 MINS

A hospital show that's almost never about anything medical, *Green Wing* takes a bunch of outrageous characters and slaps them together, adding soap opera-style plot twists and a touch of sketch comedy.

One of *Green Wing*'s trademarks is the way the action suddenly slows down or speeds up, helping characters milk the moment or beat hasty exits, depending on the scene. This makes it a slightly strange hybrid between a sketch show and a sitcom, featuring absurd but occasionally relatable situations, such as the love triangle between Caroline Todd (Tamsin Greig) and two other doctors.

Among the memorable characters—such as Harriet Schulenburg (Olivia Colman), an exhausted mom who works in administration— are stories involving blackmail, various naked people, local politics, and someone beaten to death with a stuffed heron. Season 2 (the last) bowed out with a 90-minute special.

HOUSE M.D.

COMEDY DRAMA • 2004
RATED: TV-PG • 44 MINS

What's so funny about a drama featuring a brilliant but abrasive pain killer-addicted doctor who has a knack for diagnosing difficult cases? The hilarious dialogue.

Dr. Gregory House (Hugh Laurie) is a sharp-tongued diagnostic genius heading up a team of doctors in this mystery drama series. "Everybody lies" is House's reason for his visible contempt for patients, but over eight seasons, he and his team figure out some tricky diagnoses. Along the way, House torments everyone who works with him, from his boss to his beleaguered underlings. His best friend, Dr. Wilson (Robert Sean Leonard), is probably the only person who likes him.

While there's no shortage of compelling, dramatic stories and characters, *House*'s biting wit will make you laugh even in the darkest moments. There's also a running joke about lupus, which manages to be funny without really being funny at all.

M*A*S*H

COMEDY DRAMA • 1972 • RATED: TV-PG • 25 MINS • SEASONS: 11
ALAN ALDA, LORETTA SWIT, GARY BURGHOFF

In the thick of the Korean War, a motley group of doctors, nurses, and support staff run the US Army's Mobile Army Surgical Hospital 4077, staving off their fears, nightmares, and homesickness with laughter wherever they can find it.

Lasting more than three times longer than the Korean war itself, M*A*S*H took the grimmest of concepts—a mobile hospital where combat soldiers are quickly stitched up, then sent somewhere else to recover—and made it funny, without ever losing the horror of war. As they operate on one patient after another, surgeons Hawkeye (Alan Alda) and Trapper John (Wayne Rogers) keep the jokes going, irritating Margaret "Hot Lips" Houlihan (Loretta Swit) and the narrow-minded Frank Burns, and amusing company commander Henry Blake, company clerk Radar O'Reilly, dress-wearing soldier Max Klinger, and chaplain Father Mulcahy. While the network insisted on using a laugh track, producers convinced it to keep it out of the operating room. When the BBC aired the show, it removed the laugh track entirely.

Over the seasons, the tone shifted. As the writers explored darker themes, the jokes got even better, steering away from easy wisecracks about nurses' bodies and heading into smarter territory. Actors moved on and new characters came in: Colonel Potter, a career army man with a collection of homespun expressions ("Horse hockey!" "Pony pucks!"); devoted family man B. J. Hunnicutt; and intellectual snob Charles Emerson Winchester III.

> **"** If I had all the answers, I'd run for God. **"**
>
> Max Klinger (S4 E4)

All the characters grew over time, getting deeper and richer along with the tone of the show. Without losing its comic edge, M*A*S*H took on more complicated stories, and even experimented with its own format, creating innovative episodes that explored new kinds of storytelling and tackled controversial subjects. Alan Alda took on more creative responsibilities behind the scenes and became the first person to win an Emmy for acting, writing, and directing on the same show.

The series ended on February 28, 1983, with a two-hour finale (directed by Alda). It still holds the record as the most-watched TV drama episode in American history.

CREATOR: Larry Gelbart
PRODUCTION CO: 20th Century Fox Television

EPISODES

COMEDY • 2011
RATED: TV-MA • 30 MINS

A successful British husband-and-wife TV writing team move to Los Angeles to make a US version of their show, with Matt LeBlanc as their new lead.

Sean and Beverly Lincoln (Stephen Mangan and Tamsin Greig) are high on their success, so when Hollywood comes calling, they answer. But they soon find out the executive who hired them has never watched their series, and Hollywood is full of insincere sycophants. They're also given Matt LeBlanc as their new lead. The ex-*Friends* (see p194) star plays a fictionalized version of himself who's desperate for a career boost. "Don't let them force you to cast anyone you don't want," he tells them, right after they discover they have no choice about his casting.

With its focus on Brits Sean and Beverly, the five seasons give an outsiders' view of Hollywood in all its weird glory. No spoilers, but the writers knew the show was ending and made the finale … let's just say, very meta.

EXTRAS

COMEDY • 2005
RATED: TV-MA • 30 MINS

Andy Millman and his friend Maggie Jacobs work as extras in TV shows and movies. But while she's happy with how things are, he's on a perpetual quest for more screen time.

Andy (Ricky Gervais) goes from trying desperately to get even *one* on-camera line to becoming the star of his own bad sitcom. Devised, written, and directed by *The Office* (see p153) creators Gervais and Stephen Merchant, the show takes a cynical, inside look at the film and TV industries as Andy attempts to get acting jobs that mean something.

One of the many highlights of the show's two seasons (plus a Christmas special) are the A-list celebrities who happily send themselves up for a laugh. Alongside the likes of Patrick Stewart, Ben Stiller, and Kate Winslet, the best guest award has to go to David Bowie, who meets Andy at a party and immediately creates a song about a "pathetic little fat man" who's a "fat waste of space" in response.

KIM'S CONVENIENCE

COMEDY • 2016
RATED: TV-14 • 22 MINS

Kim's Convenience takes the stereotype of a Korean family owning a downtown corner store and shows the reality— and, of course, the comedy—of life as an immigrant in Canada.

Mr. Kim ("Appa" to his grown kids) and Mrs. Kim ("Umma"), both teachers back in Korea, run Kim's Convenience in Toronto. Appa (Paul Sun-Hyung Lee) has opinions on everything from gender and race to shoe color. Umma (Jean Yoon) is a meddler, always looking for a nice Christian boy for her daughter.

Their kids are true Canadians who don't understand their parents. Janet (Andrea Bang) gets the brunt of their attention, but her brother Jung (Simu Liu), who works at a car rental company, relishes the distance he has from his dad, although they get closer over the show's four seasons. The series explores running a business, culture clashes, and generational differences with heart and good humor.

COUNT ARTHUR STRONG

COMEDY • 2013
RATED: TV-PG • 30 MINS

When Michael Baker is hired to write a biography of the father he didn't really know, he must rely on the memories of his dad's former comedy partner, the delusional Count Arthur Strong.

Steve Delaney, who cocreated this three-season series with Graham Linehan (*Father Ted*, see p269), plays the title character, a washed-up music-hall performer who now spends most of his time in a local café. He regards himself as a showbiz legend, and retains an inflated sense of his own importance and a determination to do what he wants even when everyone around him suggests otherwise.

He's also clumsy, not very astute, and the king of the malaprop—as well as an aging actor who will take any excuse to perform again, whether it's to a group of people hiding from a riot, a crew making a documentary about Michael (Rory Kinnear), or a woman who thinks her house needs an exorcism. This is one comedy you can count on for laughs.

I'M ALAN PARTRIDGE

COMEDY • 1997
RATED: TV-MA • 29 MINS

Former TV presenter Alan Partridge thinks he's still a star, even though he's now living in a cheap hotel and DJs during the graveyard slot at a local radio station.

Steve Coogan is Alan Partridge, a character he created who was already well known to British audiences from previous radio and TV shows. This series picks up after he's lost both his wife (who's now living with a fitness instructor), and the BBC talk show he was hosting. Now longing to get back the stardom he once had, he keeps trying to revive his career (with some success) with the help of his personal assistant Lynn, who remains loyal despite his high demands and contemptuous treatment. She handles professional tasks as well as personal ones, buying him medical supplies for a series of grossly unpleasant ailments.

Full of hilariously cringeworthy humor, the show ran for two seasons, and won BAFTAs for best sitcom and best comedy actor.

TOAST OF LONDON

COMEDY • 2012
RATED: 15 (UK) • 23 MINS

Steven Toast is a middle-aged British actor whose life is not going the way he planned. The play he's starring in is terrible, his pompous agent is useless, and he just got divorced.

And that's just the beginning. Toast has many more humiliations and frustrations to undergo during this series' three seasons, from winning a worst actor award to losing £2,000 to Andrew Lloyd Webber in a poker game, and developing an unhealthy obsession with actor Jon Hamm (*Mad Men*) after a head injury. Oh, and starring in a play so awful that people in the street throw vegetables at him.

It doesn't help that he's full of himself and always thinks he deserves better, without much evidence to support it. Toast is played by Matt Berry, who not only sings the theme tune, but also bursts into songs throughout the show, breaking the fourth wall to perform to the audience directly, with other cast members joining in.

THE BIG BANG THEORY

COMEDY • 2007 • RATED: TV-14 • 22 MINS • SEASONS: 12
JIM PARSONS, JOHNNY GALECKI, KALEY CUOCO

The *Big Bang Theory* started with a premise much simpler than the actual Big Bang theory: two brilliant scientists, also roommates, can work out the most complicated theories in the universe, but have trouble navigating everyday life, especially when it comes to women.

Sheldon Cooper (Jim Parsons) and Leonard Hofstadter (Johnny Galecki) are both physicists at Caltech (the California Institute of Technology), a research university. Penny (Kaley Cuoco) is a waitress who moves in across the hall from their apartment, and instantly Leonard is smitten. This is the central (but not the only) romance on the show, and Penny is the catalyst for the guys and their equally nerdy friends to realize how little they know about real, nonlaboratory life. Those friends include Howard, an aerospace engineer who designed a zero-gravity toilet for the International Space Station, and Raj, a rich astrophysicist.

In the company of neuroscientist Amy, microbiologist Bernadette, physicist Leslie, dermatologist Emily, and comic book–store owner Stuart, the gang struggle with dating, professional jealousy, social awkwardness, and exactly where they should all sit on the sofa. Throughout all of this, they eat a lot of takeout and watch hours of TV together. Super-brainy Sheldon, who began college at age 11, earned a PhD at 16, and has an IQ of 187, still doesn't understand sarcasm, making Leonard the straight man who has to explain Sheldon's behavior to other people.

Despite all the science themes and situations, the pair's monikers are telling: they were named after Sheldon Leonard, the actor, producer, director, and writer known for his work on classic TV comedies. Although there are science jokes and problems, and there was a real science advisor on set, the core of the show is always its eccentric characters.

The Big Bang Theory became the longest-running multi-camera sitcom in history, and guest stars flocked to it, from actual *Star Trek* (see p88) actors—an obsession of the characters, of course—to real-life scientists such as Stephen Hawking and Microsoft cofounder Bill Gates. It ended its run with a special one-hour episode, a post-show special, and a spin-off called *Young Sheldon* (see p226).

CREATORS: Chuck Lorre, Bill Prady
PRODUCTION CO: Chuck Lorre Productions, Warner Bros. Television

FATHER TED

COMEDY • 1995
RATED: TV-MA • 25 MINS

On the fictional Craggy Island off the west coast of Ireland, three Catholic priests live together in the parish house where they've been banished by their bishop for a range of very good reasons.

Why is Father Ted (Dermot Morgan) sent to a remote island? While he was never formally charged, he was investigated for stealing money from a child so he could use it to go to Las Vegas. His explanation that it was "just resting" in his account quickly became a catchphrase with fans of the show.

But Father Ted's not the worst offender in his priestly bunch. Father Jack is there because of his alcoholism and womanizing (!)—he also does a fair amount of swearing—while all we know about simple-minded Father Dougal is that he was involved in the "Blackrock Incident," which involved nuns. Their adventures include rabbit infestations, snitching on a philandering milkman, and navigating the lingerie section of a department store.

MEN BEHAVING BADLY

COMEDY • 1992
RATED: TV-PG • 30 MINS

On paper, at least, the main characters in Men Behaving Badly are far from likeable: they come across as a pair of disgusting, politically incorrect bachelor roommates. Thankfully, though, they're still very funny.

Based on a novel by Simon Nye, the show features Gary (Martin Clunes), who owns an apartment and initially shares it with Dermot (Harry Enfield), who keeps forgetting to pay the rent. After Season 1, Dermot is replaced by Tony (Neil Morrissey) for the next five seasons, who quickly becomes infatuated with upstairs neighbor Deborah (Leslie Ash).

Whether it's Gary and Dermot or Gary and Tony, there's a lot of beer drinking and boob talk. The show wasn't meant to endorse their boorish behavior, but to show how ridiculous and funny they were. Gary even has a girlfriend, Dorothy (Caroline Quentin), who puts up with him despite his dead-end job, and Deborah still sees Tony's good side.

SPACED

COMEDY • 1999
RATED: TV-14 • 25 MINS

This era-defining comedy was the springboard for the careers of many involved. If you're a fan of the movies Hot Fuzz or Shaun of the Dead, what are you waiting for?

Writer Daisy (Jessica Stevenson) and wannabe comic-book artist Tim (Simon Pegg) create a fictional history together to convince landlady Marsha to give them an apartment—and then have to keep up the façade. Inspired by shows such as The X-Files (see p442) and The Simpsons (see p56), Spaced is filled with pop-culture references and homages to movies, comics, and video games.

Over its two seasons, Daisy and Tim keep insisting they're not a couple to everyone around them: their conceptual-artist neighbor Brian, his girlfriend Twist (who claims to work "in fashion" but works in a dry cleaner), and Tim's friend Mike, a military-obsessed weapons expert. And yes, romantic tension brews, despite their insistence to the contrary.

BEAVIS AND BUTT-HEAD

ANIMATED COMEDY • 1993
RATED: TV-14 • 15 MINS

Two inarticulate, dumb, sex-obsessed teenage boys spend their days on their sofa watching TV, making fun of music videos, and cracking each other up.

Mike Judge, who would go on to write *Office Space, Idiocracy, King of the Hill* (see p243), and *Silicon Valley* (see p351), wrote, directed, and voiced both title characters over eight seasons of this jittery cartoon. The show taught a generation of MTV viewers in the 1990s that it was okay—maybe even necessary—to giggle every time anyone said something that sounded a little bit dirty.

Beavis and Butt-Head pick apart music videos, and have insults for anything they think "sucks." Occasionally, they also get up from the couch to do something destructive, such as dropping bowling balls containing explosives from rooftops. And sometimes they even go to school, where they find countless targets for their happy derision and distinctive laughter. Uh-heh-heh-heh-heh-heh.

CATASTROPHE

COMEDY ROMANCE • 2015
RATED: TV-MA • 25 MINS

American Rob meets Sharon, an Irish elementary school teacher, on a business trip to London, and after a quick fling, she finds out she's pregnant.

"I don't know what to do when you get pregnant by a stranger. I don't know the etiquette," Sharon tells Rob during their first conversation about her pregnancy. And so begins the relationship at the center of *Catastrophe*, a smart British romantic comedy series created by, written by, and starring Rob Delaney and Sharon Horgan as the suddenly-rushed-into-things couple.

"A terrible thing has happened. Let's make the best of it," he says, and so they embark on a relationship, with all of its complications, including Rob's eccentric mother (Carrie Fisher), Sharon's judgmental brother Fergal, and various unpleasant friends. Each of its four seasons brings a new shift in their situation and dynamic, unforeseen obstacles, and banter that will make you laugh out loud.

MAD ABOUT YOU

COMEDY • 1992
RATED: TV-PG • 22 MINS

If you like watching New Yorkers obsess about everything from their jobs to their dog, and how to afford a parking space in Manhattan in the 1990s, this is the show for you.

Helen Hunt and Paul Reiser are Jamie and Paul Buchanan, a PR specialist and a documentary filmmaker living in the Big Apple with their dog, Murray, who's often chasing an invisible mouse. While the show has scads of amazing recurring guest stars (Mel Brooks, Cyndi Lauper, Carol Burnett, Lisa Kudrow, Alan Ruck), its magic comes from the chemistry between its two stars, whose characters argue, plan and plot, bicker, resolve, and still have fun.

In 2019, they reprised their roles for a limited-run eighth season that revisits Jamie and Paul Buchanan 20 years later. In the new version, they're empty-nesters now that their daughter (born in Season 5 of the original series) has gone off to college.

MR. BEAN

COMEDY • 1990
RATED: TV-PG • 25 MINS

Rowan Atkinson stars in this comedy about a childlike man with an elastic face and a lot of confusion about how to do what everybody else considers ordinary tasks.

The show and the character became a global phenomenon—helped, no doubt, by the fact that Mr. Bean almost never speaks, giving him universal cultural appeal. Over 15 episodes,

Atkinson uses his amazingly flexible facial features and his gift for physical comedy to have Mr. Bean struggle his way through everything from changing into a bathing suit to trying to eat candy in church.

While Atkinson himself described the character as a child inside a man's body, the show's opening sequence, which depicts Mr. Bean falling to the ground in a beam of light shining from above, suggests something else. Is he an alien? It's never clarified, but it would explain his complete lack of understanding of everything the rest of us takes for granted.

THE IT CROWD

COMEDY • 2006
RATED: TV-14 • 25 MINS

In the basement IT department of a London corporation, the technically inept Jen attempts to supervise the socially inept Roy and Moss, two techies who see straight through her.

When Jen Barber (Katherine Parkinson) bluffs her way into a job at Reynholm Industries, things don't turn out the way she hopes. Sent to the basement, she finds herself in charge of

the company's IT department. Work-shy Roy Trenneman (Chris O'Dowd) does everything he can to avoid helping anyone—"Have you tried turning it off and on again?" is his stock reply to those who dare seek his advice. And Maurice Moss (Richard Ayoade) struggles with the simplest of everyday tasks.

Over four seasons, the trio adjust to each other, uniting on a variety of absurd adventures. Full of wonderful characters, surreal situations, and hilarious lines, this show from *Father Ted* (see p269) creator Graham Linehan is British TV comedy at its best.

THE LETDOWN

COMEDY • 2017
RATED: 15 (UK) • 30 MINS

Audrey is a new mom who spends her days dealing with a combination of utter exhaustion and an ongoing identity crisis as she tries to be a good parent to her daughter Stevie.

Alison Bell cocreated, cowrites, and stars as a new mom whose husband stays far away from his fatherly responsibilities in this Australian sitcom. Her character Audrey finds herself in

hilariously relatable situations, from driving around all night (and being harassed by a drug dealer), to being asked to leave a party because Stevie won't stop crying, and struggling to keep up her sex life when her breast milk starts leaking. She also joins a parents' group, which makes things both better and worse.

The two-season show searches for the funny side in parenting's darkest moments with plenty of wit, poking fun at the mommy wars and gender stereotypes—including a dad who has the gall to define looking after his own child as "babysitting."

POLICE SQUAD!

CRIME COMEDY • 1982
RATED: TV-PG • 24 MINS

A hilariously silly satire of police procedural dramas from the production team behind the *Airplane!* movies, starring Leslie Nielsen as deadpan Detective Frank Drebin.

Nielsen had a long career of playing serious roles before he starred in movie spoof *Airplane!* in 1980. In this single-season, six-episode series, he draws on that TV drama experience to play the straight man in a world of crazy people. Drebin never loses his deadpan responses, no matter what silliness springs up around him.

Every episode had a title, but the one announced by the narrator never matched what was on screen, and in a running gag, celebrity guest stars were often murdered during the opening credits. With its broad parody, sight gags, wonderfully terrible puns, non sequiturs, and rapid-fire jokes, *Police Squad!* was a cult hit, later spawning *The Naked Gun* film series.

RAKE

COMEDY DRAMA • 2010
RATED: NR • 54 MINS

Richard Roxburgh is Cleaver Greene, a self-destructive lawyer in Sydney, Australia, who frequently finds himself defending guilty clients in his brilliant and unorthodox style.

Roxburgh cocreated and stars in this show that takes on Australian politics and media with its outlandish stories. Loosely based on infamous Australian lawyer Charles Waterstreet, antihero Greene is both endearing and infuriating. He is a disappointment to his family and friends—even sleeping with his best pal's wife—but a ray of legal sunshine to his frequently terrible clients.

He defends bigamists, cannibals, and even murderers. While his personal life is a mess, he's always a star in the courtroom. Look out for guest appearances by the likes of Cate Blanchett, Toni Collette, Hugo Weaving, Rachel Griffiths, and Sam Neill (in a shocking role you won't be expecting) during the show's five-season run.

THE THIN BLUE LINE

COMEDY • 1995
RATED: TV-PG • 41 MINS

This sitcom about the goings-on at a fictional English police station stars Rowan Atkinson as an inspector who takes his job far too seriously.

Inspector Raymond Fowler (Atkinson) runs his station with rather more devotion than he should. A stickler for rules and regulations, he does everything by the book. Inspector Grim (David Haig) heads up the Criminal Investigation Department and is just as rigid—and while neither of them is terribly competent, they're still competitive.

Supporting them are Sergeant Patricia Dawkins (Serena Evans), Fowler's girlfriend, who longs for more attention. There's also Kevin Goody (James Dreyfus), a simple sort who just likes to wear a uniform; Maggie Habib (Mina Anwar), whose socially progressive views are shared by almost no one; and Frank Gladstone (Rudolph Walker), who's close to retirement. Created by *Blackadder* (see p122) writer Ben Elton, this underrated sitcom ran for two seasons.

BARNEY MILLER

COMEDY • 1975
RATED: TV-PG • 22 MINS

This low-key 1970s sitcom took place almost entirely in the squad room of a New York City police precinct, peopled by a group of eccentric-but-solid detectives.

This isn't about punchlines or catchphrases; *Barney Miller* is a workplace show that derives most of its humor from the parade of New Yorkers brought in by its quirky-but-competent cops, including the stalwart Captain Miller (Hal Linden), the deadpan Sergeant Fish (Abe Vigoda), earnest Detective "Wojo" (Max Gail), and flashy intellectual Detective Harris (Ron Glass). Their rambling, distracted inspector (James Gregory) also regularly drops by to poke his nose in.

Occasionally, a story would take place on a stakeout or in a detective's home, but most of the action stayed within the precinct. The writers balanced the jokes perfectly with the officers' real-life issues as they talked things out over a lot of terrible coffee.

IT'S ALWAYS SUNNY IN PHILADELPHIA

COMEDY • 2005
RATED: TV-MA • 22 MINS

Five self-involved, unlikable friends and family members run Paddy's Pub in this politically incorrect comedy that's cleverer than it looks at first glance.

It's not *always* sunny in Philadelphia, at least not around this crew. Rob McElhenney and Glenn Howerton created and star in this show about a bunch of jerks who frequent an Irish bar in Philadelphia. In addition to a steady stream of insults and schemes, they also use blackmail to manipulate each other or simply amuse themselves.

Charlie (Charlie Day) does most of the work. Mac (McElhenney) is the tough-guy bouncer. Dennis (Howerton) is a narcissist and sexual predator and his twin sister Dee (Kaitlin Olson) gets picked on by them all. Frank (Danny DeVito) is Dennis and Dee's dad—and possibly Charlie's, too. The show's 14-season run is a record for a live-action US sitcom.

SLEDGE HAMMER!

ACTION COMEDY • 1986
RATED: 12 (UK) • 23 MINS

Dirty Harry meets Get Smart in this satire about a macho cop whose love for his .44 Magnum Smith & Wesson is topped only by his "I Heart Violence" bumper sticker.

David Rasche is Sledge Hammer, an exaggerated stereotype of the edgy cop who pursues justice in his own unique and violent way. He loves his gun so much that he sleeps and showers with it, takes it fishing (because "fishing poles are for geeks"), and calls it his best friend. His boss Captain Trunk is always yelling at him, chugging Pepto-Bismol, and complaining to others about his wayward inspector.

The show was created by Alan Spencer, who wrote the first script for it when he was just 16. The project sat around for eight years after he first sent it to some network execs, who were reportedly "appalled" by what they read. Guess he had the last laugh, though—at least for the two seasons it was on.

ARRESTED DEVELOPMENT

COMEDY • 2003
RATED: TV-MA • 22 MINS

The dysfunctional Bluth family is rich and successful ... until their patriarch, George, is arrested for stealing massive amounts of money, and sent to jail. Time for a lifestyle adjustment!

Son Michael (Jason Bateman) steps up to run the family company, keep everything going, and try to stay sane when the rest of the Bluths were never very sane to begin with.

Every member of the family is ridiculous in their own unique way, from terrible magician George II (Will Arnett), to mom Lucille (Jessica Walter), who's never without a drink. And George Sr. (Jeffrey Tambor) is still manipulating everyone, even from jail.

While it's not a mockumentary, the show's five seasons are narrated by its executive producer, Ron Howard, with a trademark: right after something is stated clearly and unequivocally, Howard's voice is there to explain, offer commentary, contradict, or correct. It makes for some of the show's funniest moments.

BLACK-ISH

COMEDY • 2014 • RATED: TV-14 • 22 MINS • SEASONS: 6
ANTHONY ANDERSON, TRACEE ELLIS ROSS, MARSAI MARTIN

Andre and Rainbow Johnson both have high-end professional jobs, a big house in the suburbs, and four beautiful, smart children. But raising a black family in a predominantly white neighborhood—and culture—makes them worry: have they assimilated too much?

Kenya Barris created this sharp, funny sitcom based on his own experience and anxieties. The Johnson family live in a fancy suburban area. They have high-paying, great jobs (one's an advertising exec, the other an anesthesiologist), but lament that their kids have lost touch with their cultural legacy.

Andre (Anthony Anderson), Rainbow (Tracee Ellis Ross), and Pops (Laurence Fishburne), Dre's dad, try to teach their prep-school kids, but the kids are full of smart comebacks. They insist they don't need any parental wisdom. Episodes raise questions about race that aren't always talked about, showing how people

really think as well as what they try to avoid discussing ... but the show keeps its humor along the way.

> **"** *For Junior, nerd is the new black.* **"**
>
> Andre (S1 E3)

The funniest episodes? The one in which the Johnsons get upset about not being invited to pool parties, suspecting it's because of the stereotype that black people can't swim—but then Andre actually can't. Then there's the one in which Andre bemoans the fact his kids' school recognizes Columbus and St. Patrick's days, but not Juneteenth. So, we get a musical history (from the cast AND in a *Schoolhouse Rock*–style cartoon) to celebrate it.

OFFSPRING

COMEDY DRAMA • 2010
RATED: 15 (UK) • 43 MINS

Doctor Nina Proudman is an obstetrician with a messy family, rich fantasy life, and highly unpredictable reality. Oh, and an ex-husband who likes blowing up her personal belongings.

Offspring is a hit show from Australia, populated by lovable weirdos. As well as Nina (Asher Keddie), there's her sister, Billie (Kat Stewart), a former wild-child-turned-rea-

estate-broker who fights with Nina, but loves her. Jimmy is their sweet little brother who seems aimless, but slowly finds more purpose as the show progresses. Meanwhile, midwife Cherie is one of Nina's colleagues—and has a surprise that will make her part of the family.

But it's Nina who's the main star of this seven-season show. Her ongoing voice-over narration, and her fantasies about the handsome doctors she works with, really take you inside her head. *Offspring* has its fair share of serious drama to invest in, but it always finds the laughs to balance things out.

THE FRESH PRINCE OF BEL-AIR

COMEDY • 1990
RATED: TV-PG • 22 MINS

As explained to perfection in the theme song, teenager Will Smith moves from Philadelphia to Bel Air, Los Angeles, to live with his rich aunt and uncle.

Will Smith stars in this six-season sitcom about a street-savvy teen who gets a major lifestyle upgrade. Culture clashes are played for laughs

as his new family adjusts to having him around. There's snobby uncle Phil (James Avery), the more understanding Aunt Vivian (Janet Hubert, then Daphne Reid), plus cousins Carlton, Hilary, and Ashley. Even the family's butler finds Will's casual attitude a challenge. The family learns from each other, no matter how resistant they are.

Music legend Quincy Jones was a producer on the show, which featured a raft of celebrity cameos, from Reverend Jesse Jackson, Queen Latifah, and Vanessa Williams to Tyra Banks, Chris Rock, and Kareem Abdul Jabbar.

WELCOME TO SWEDEN

COMEDY • 2014
RATED: TV-PG • 22 MINS

Bruce Evans is in love! He quits his job and moves to Sweden with his girlfriend, which would be fine if only he knew the language or had a job.

Bruce (Greg Poehler, who created the show) is a money manager for celebrities, some of whom aren't thrilled that he has quit his job and moved abroad. His boss (played by Greg's real-life sister Amy Poehler, who's also one of

the show's executive producers) says she was going to fire him anyway, but his clients—who include rock star Gene Simmons and *Parks and Rec*'s (see p195) Aubrey Plaza—want him back.

Emma, Bruce's girlfriend, is grateful that he gave everything up for her, but her parents feel the absolute opposite, especially since Bruce doesn't have any prospects. What he does have is a bad habit of embarrassing himself, especially when he's trying to speak Swedish or adjust to his new culture. Celebrity cameos from Paul Simon and Will Ferrell liven things up over the show's two seasons.

CHAPPELLE'S SHOW

COMEDY • 2003
RATED: TV-MA • 22 MINS

Dave Chappelle and Neal Brennan created this hit for Comedy Central, which features Chappelle's stand-up, live musical performances, and sketches that hit on contemporary and often controversial topics.

It's a toss-up as to what people remember most about this show—Chappelle's one-off episode as Rick James with its "I'm Rick James, bitch!" catchphrase, or the scandal caused by Chappelle's exit from the show three episodes into Season 3. While he regretted the Rick James sketch's popularity, he never regretted leaving the series behind.

But while it lasted, *Chappelle's Show* made audiences laugh with sketches such as the spoof of documentary series *Frontline*, and a game show called *I Know Black People*, where nonblack contestants tried to answer simple questions about African-American culture. High-profile guests on the series included John Mayer, Snoop Dogg, and Kanye West.

NOT THE NINE O'CLOCK NEWS

SKETCH COMEDY • 1979
RATED: TV-PG • 25 MINS

Late in the 1970s, Margaret Thatcher was British prime minister, and the time was ripe for a new satirical sketch show: *Not the Nine O'Clock News*.

Rowan Atkinson, Pamela Stephenson, Mel Smith, and Griff Rhys Jones star in this sketch comedy series addressing everything current, from politics to celebrities to NASA space launches. Produced by John Lloyd (*Blackadder*, p122), the show begins with the same ticking clock that featured on the real *Nine O'Clock News*—at the time the BBC's flagship news program. After that, though, all bets are off.

The humor is never less than razor-sharp as none of the sketches are allowed to go on long enough to fizzle out. Quick jump cuts, plus the use of real news footage, observational comedy, and tight edits set this four-season show apart.

THE CATHERINE TATE SHOW

SKETCH COMEDY • 2004
RATED: TV-MA • 30 MINS

If you only know Catherine Tate from *Doctor Who* and the US version of *The Office*, dig into the BBC archives to see her star in her very own sketch show.

In the shows three seasons, Tate plays a huge range of different characters, including a woman who jumps at every noise, an over-excited waitress named Amanda, a wayward nurse called Bernie, and a teenage girl named Lauren Cooper with the catchphrase, "Am I bovvered?" Lauren was so popular that "bovvered" was added to the *Oxford English Dictionary* in 2006.

Tate isn't just a master of creating characters and accents, she is also dedicated to looking the part. It took her three-and-a-half hours to get into makeup as "Nan," her most famous character, a foul-mouthed grandmother with opinions about everything and everyone—and none of them good.

FRENCH AND SAUNDERS

SKETCH COMEDY • 1987
RATED: TV-PG • 30 MINS

In a sketch series that would eventually spawn *Absolutely Fabulous*, writers and performers Dawn French and Jennifer Saunders spoof movies, TV shows, pop idols, pop culture, and even themselves.

Everything was ripe for satire in this six-season show (plus numerous specials), from British daily life to top celebrities. As well as creating their own characters, French and Saunders created increasingly bigger-budget parodies of films from *Whatever Happened to Baby Jane?* to *Pulp Fiction*. Favorite music parodies include their takes on Madonna and ABBA.

French and Saunders won viewers over by turning the tables on shows such as *Monty Python* (see p262), which featured men dressed as women. The duo would get padded up and transform into Jim and Jim, two dirty old men who couldn't stop talking about how they were God's greatest gift to women as they scoffed down snacks on the sofa or sat in the pub.

THE KIDS IN THE HALL

SKETCH COMEDY • 1988 • RATED: TV-PG • 24 MINS • SEASONS: 5
DAVE FOLEY, SCOTT THOMPSON, MARK MCKINNEY

Taking some of its cues from *Monty Python's Flying Circus*, this Canadian sketch show combines live stage performance with filmed sequences with brilliant results.

The five all-male "kids" wrote the show and played almost every role. When female characters were called for, on went the dresses and wigs. Separated by brief musical segments with black-and-white footage of Toronto street scenes, the sketches range from pointed and edgy to downright goofy. It is so loved that Amazon has commissioned eight new episodes.

Popular recurring characters include gossiping secretaries Cathy and Kathie (Bruce McCulloch and Dave Foley), the love-starved Chicken Lady (Mark McKinney), and Buddy Cole (Scott Thompson), a socialite whose pen pal is Queen Elizabeth II.

The prerecorded segments provide some of the show's most viral clips. "30 Helens Agree," for example, unites a group of Helens in a field to opine on everything from tattoos to coleslaw.

> **"***I'm crushing your head, I'm crushing your head. Crush. Crush.***"**

The Head Crushing Guy (multiple episodes)

SEINFELD

COMEDY • 1989 • RATED: TV-14 • 22 MINS • SEASONS: 9
JERRY SEINFELD, JULIA LOUIS-DREYFUS, JASON ALEXANDER

It may be remembered as "a show about nothing," but *Seinfeld* is considered one of the greatest sitcoms of all time. Comedian Jerry Seinfeld plays a fictionalized version of himself who riffs, whines, argues, and laughs about the minutiae of everyday life with his three best friends.

Those pals are George (Jason Alexander), ex-girlfriend Elaine Benes (Julia Louis-Dreyfus), and neighbor Cosmo Kramer (Michael Richards). Throughout the show's nine seasons, they're constantly getting together to talk about life and the off-the-wall situations they find themselves in, whether it's in Jerry's Upper West Side apartment, grabbing lunch at Monk's café, or simply waiting in line. And when they talk, boy, do they talk.

Some of the episodes are so famous that even people who never watched *Seinfeld* are familiar with the stories. "The Contest" involves the four friends competing to see who can go the longest without masturbating (although no one ever uses that word, substituting a series of euphemisms), and added the phrase "master of my domain" to the American lexicon. "The Soup Nazi" was based on a real-life, NYC soup vendor and provided another famous catchphrase with "No soup for you!"

There was also "The Chinese Restaurant," set in real time, which had George, Jerry, and Elaine spending the entire episode waiting for a table. Over 180 episodes, the gang had lively conversations about shirt buttons, quiet talkers, cleavage, laundry, and, of course, dating. Cocreator Larry David used his own experiences as material, as did the other writers, and that's the real truth of what the series is about: where a comedian gets his material. The show always had a scene of Jerry doing his stand-up act to drive the point home.

Always funny, never sentimental, the show was full of memorable phrases, including the now-immortal "Yada, yada, yada"—the perfect way to avoid getting into the details of something you've done that you don't really want to talk about. *Seinfeld* became the centerpiece of NBC's "Must-See TV" on Thursday nights throughout the 1990s and has become an indelible part of American culture.

> **"** *That's the true spirit of Christmas; people being helped by people other than me.* **"**
>
> Jerry Seinfeld (S4 E13)

CREATORS: Larry David, Jerry Seinfeld
PRODUCTION CO: West-Shapiro, Castle Rock Entertainment

THE DICK VAN DYKE SHOW

COMEDY • 1961
RATED: TV-G • 25 MINS

This sophisticated, well-written, and delightful comedy about the head writer of a TV show and his family and friends will surprise you with how well it still holds up, decades later.

The show follows Rob Petrie (Dick Van Dyke), his wife Laura (Mary Tyler Moore), fellow writers Buddy (Morey Amsterdam) and Sally (Rose Marie), and Rob and Laura's neighbors, Jerry and Millie. During the day, Rob, Buddy, and Sally write the fictional *Alan Brady Show* (with Brady played by Carl Reiner, who created *The Dick Van Dyke Show*), and get extra laughs whenever Buddy torments show producer Mel Cooley with his one-liners.

Laura was a revolutionary character at the time—not only was she just as smart and funny as her husband, she also (gasp) wore trousers! The Petrie family, with their son, Ritchie, host the greatest dinner parties ever, where guests perform fantastic musical numbers, and the cocktails flow.

THE LARRY SANDERS SHOW

COMEDY • 1992 • RATED: TV-MA • 30 MINS • SEASONS: 6
GARRY SHANDLING, JEFFREY TAMBOR, RIP TORN

This show-within-a-show satire stars Larry Sanders, host of a late-night TV show who is confident and gregarious in public, but insecure and neurotic behind closed doors, frequently in need of the protection of his producer, Artie.

The only person more neurotic (and yet more arrogant) than Larry (Garry Shandling) is his TV sidekick Hank (Jeffrey Tambor), who dreams of a more personal relationship with Larry but is doomed never to get it.

Artie (Rip Torn), a hard drinker with a legendary career and a love of salty dog cocktails, keeps the show running with a smooth but tight grip. He's helped along by the rest of the staff: Larry's assistant Beverly (Penny Johnson Jerald), writers Phil (Wallace Langham) and Jerry (Jeremy Piven, who doesn't last all six seasons), talent booker Paula (Janeane Garofalo)—later replaced by Mary Lou (Mary Lynn Rajskub)—and Hank's assistant Darlene (Linda Doucett), later replaced by Brian (Scott Thompson).

Despite his fame, success, and power, Larry remains perpetually worried about his popularity and is completely self-obsessed, never missing the chance to watch his own show at the end of the night.

The concept paved the way for a steady stream of A-list celebrities to play fictional versions of themselves on the series, which allowed for hilarious temper tantrums, real musical performances, and unforgettable scenes, such as a bathrobe-wearing David Duchovny hitting on a very nervous Larry.

BETTER THINGS

COMEDY • 2016
RATED: TV-MA • 25 MINS

Sam Fox is a raspy-voiced, smart but exhausted actress in Los Angeles, raising her three daughters on her own, and dealing with her British mom, who's starting to lose it.

Pamela Adlon cocreated, directs, frequently writes, and stars in this semiautobiographical four-season show about life in Hollywood. As a woman in her 50s who shoulders all the household burdens along with keeping her career going, Sam is witty and edgy, but also full of heart. She deals with her independent-minded older daughter, the androgynous and demanding middle one, and the sweet, generous youngest one who often redeems the whole gang.

Sam is flawed and doesn't hide it. She gives the show an honesty that bursts through the Hollywood bubble, making even the most ludicrous situations feel real, thanks to both her humor and her empathy. There really is no other show on TV with this point of view.

BLUNT TALK

COMEDY • 2015
RATED: TV-MA • 30 MINS

Patrick Stewart likes being funny! Thus *Blunt Talk* was born, starring Stewart as Walter Blunt, a British newscaster trying to make it big in the world of American nightly cable news.

Blunt Talk's producer, Seth MacFarlane, knew about Stewart's funny side, so he had Jonathan Ames create this two-season series for him, setting the actor free to indulge his silly side.

Blunt stumbles through life and his surprise success (despite a series of on-air mishaps, including passing out cold during his show). He struggles with automatic sinks and paper toilet covers, discovers he's circumcised and never knew it, and picks up a transgender prostitute.

Blunt is aided by his trusty manservant Harry (Adrian Scarborough), who's fiercely loyal and loves to drink and gamble, but that doesn't help much with Blunt's ex-wives, children, and other problems. It's a far cry from Shakespeare or Captain Picard, which is probably why Stewart has so much fun in the role.

SOAP

COMEDY • 1977
RATED: NR • 22 MINS

"This is the story of two sisters— Jessica Tate and Mary Campbell," began the opening sequence of this over-the-top soap opera parody about the outrageous misadventures of two Connecticut families.

The first ever US show to have a "viewer discretion" warning, *Soap*'s wild plots include murder, exorcism, cults, the Mob, alien abduction, kidnapping, and dozens more controversial subjects. But it does it all with broad humor and characters you care about, no matter how wacky things get over the four seasons. Episodes begin with narrated recaps and end with a list of deadpan questions about what would happen next.

Breakout stars include Billy Crystal as Jodie, the Campbells' gay son. Robert Guillaume plays the Tates' butler, Benson (some might remember his own spin-off). Richard Mulligan plays Mary's second husband, Burt—his facial expressions alone deserve a mention.

CALL MY AGENT!

COMEDY • 2015
RATED: 15 (UK) • 52 MINS

A French workplace comedy about one of the biggest talent agencies in Paris, Call My Agent! shows its hardworking agents juggling schedules along with the egos of their famous, demanding clients.

In the show's first episode, the founder of the Samuel Kerr Agency has his last meeting with his staff before taking his first vacation in eight years. One of the agents hedges on what's happening with a famous client, and an assistant gets berated by her boss, flees in tears, and then quits. The tone is set.

Then they learn their vacationing leader has died—and the power struggle begins. Four agents—Mathias (Thibault de Montalembert), Andréa (Camille Cottin), Gabriel (Grégory Montel), and Arlette (Liliane Rovère)—struggle to keep their clients, negotiate contracts, fight off a rival agency, and make their mark. The three-season series features guest appearances from French movie stars, such as Isabelle Adjani and Juliette Binoche.

NEWSRADIO

COMEDY • 1995
RATED: 12 (UK) • 22 MINS

This vastly underrated sitcom covers the day-to-day workplace lives of the on-air and off-air staff at New York City's #2 rated all-news station, led by the boyish-looking news director Dave.

Dave Foley plays the fresh-faced news director Dave Nelson, trying to corral his offbeat employees. Facing the public are pompous coanchor Bill McNeal (Phil Hartman) and sophisticated co-anchor Catherine (Khandi Alexander). Other regular faces include reporter/producer Lisa (Maura Tierney), reporter Matthew (Andy Dick), electrician Joe (Joe Rogan), and secretary Beth (Vicky Lewis).

Sharp and funny, NewsRadio gets its humor from its characters, so plots are kept simple: a funny episode is when Bill is forced to quit smoking, so Dave gives up coffee in solidarity. It never spiked in the ratings, but the show managed to last five seasons due to its tight writing and cast chemistry.

WORKIN' MOMS

COMEDY • 2017
RATED: TV-MA • 22 MINS

As its title makes clear, this Canadian sitcom focuses on a group of friends facing the day-to-day challenges of being working moms as they juggle parenthood, careers, and love lives.

This serialized comedy explores the dark moments of motherhood as well as the absurd. Star Catherine Reitman created the show after she broke down in front of her coworkers when she was teased about missing Mother's Day on a film set. And the writers' room? All female, along with the camera crew.

Over its four seasons, the moms deal with postpartum depression, take business calls while they pump milk in the toilets, and other maternal challenges. It's a navel-gazing look from a group of mostly privileged women, but it mines the outrageous double standards and pressures that mothers face when returning to work for both comedy and compassion.

ATLANTA

COMEDY DRAMA • 2016
RATED: TV-MA • 25 MINS

Earnest "Earn" Marks, an Ivy League dropout living in Atlanta, is in a dead-end job. Things start to change when he begins managing his cousin Paper Boi, whose rap career is on the rise.

Actor, director, musician, and writer Donald Glover created this semiautobiographical comedy drama that manages to be as satirical as it is realistic. Earn (Glover) and Paper Boi (Brian Tyree Henry) are moving up in the Atlanta music scene, trying to make life better for themselves and their families. There are constant, intense contrasts: one minute Earn is at a party full of rich people, the next he's not sure where he's sleeping that night.

While the show dives deep into cultural, social, and economic issues, it also manages to be funny. In Season 1 (of four), an obnoxious and entitled version of singer Justin Bieber is played by a black man (Austin Crute). This is a show that shatters expectations for the better in every episode.

FAWLTY TOWERS

COMEDY • 1975
RATED:TV-PG • 30 MINS

Only two six-episode seasons were made of this classic British sitcom about an unlikable seaside-town hotel owner who can't stand most of his guests.

The series was created by John Cleese and his wife at the time, Connie Booth, inspired by the real-life owner of a hotel Cleese and his fellow *Monty Python's Flying Circus* (see p262) members once stayed in. The owner hated them—he even threw performer Eric Idle's suitcase out of the building—so Cleese created Basil Fawlty, a snob who fawns over the rich and resents having to be remotely pleasant to anybody else.

The one person Basil (Cleese) is afraid of is his wife Sybil (Prunella Scales), who's a better manager than he is—despite being chronically lazy—and can usually silence him with a sharp "Basil!" The show made use of Cleese's abilities for physical comedy and spitting out hilarious insults at anyone in his vicinity.

NEWHART

COMEDY • 1982
RATED: TV-PG • 24 MINS

Dick and his wife Joanna run a small-town inn that attracts more than its fair share of oddballs—sometimes guests, but usually the locals.

Bob Newhart uses his sane-guy-surrounded-by-weirdos expertise to play Dick, a writer from Manhattan who starts out running the inn in Vermont with his wife, then (by Season 2) becomes a local TV talk-show host. The townspeople are a bunch of eccentrics, from the perpetually confused handyman George, to Leslie, an heiress who works for Dick and Joanna as a maid. There's also local café owner Kirk, a compulsive liar, who eventually sells his restaurant to brothers Larry, Darryl, and … Darryl.

The show went through a lot of changes through its eight seasons, but is most famous for its series finale, which—without ruining things—changed everything that had happened before, with a nod back to the original *The Bob Newhart Show* of the 1970s.

ARCHER

ANIMATED COMEDY • 2009
RATED: TV-MA • 22 MINS

This raunchy animation combines a parody of the secret agent genre with a workplace comedy about the agents and operations at ISIS, an international spy organization.

Sterling Archer (code name "Duchess") is the best agent at the International Secret Intelligence Service. He's also a narcissist and womanizer, and spends the agency's money without a second thought. You know who's worse? His mom Malory, who's the director of ISIS ... so yeah, she's his boss. It's difficult to sum up *Archer*—each of the 11 seasons is completely different: the missions, the settings, and even the agency itself. There's also an entire season that takes place in Sterling's subconscious while he's in a coma.

The show is full of twists and turns, crass humor, and utterly ridiculous but thoroughly memorable characters, helped along by a voice cast that includes H. Jon Benjamin, Jessica Walter, and Aisha Tyler.

GET SMART

SPY COMEDY • 1965
RATED: TV-G • 25 MINS

This goofy spy satire stars Don Adams and Barbara Feldon as secret agents saving the world from an evil organization called KAOS.

Created by Mel Brooks and Buck Henry, *Get Smart* follows Maxwell Smart (Adams) and Agent 99 (Feldon), who work for CONTROL and report to a man they just call "Chief." A splendid send-up of the secret-agent genre, it has an endless series of hilarious and imaginative spy gadgets, from Max's shoe phone to transparent cones of silence.

It also has catchphrases galore, such as Max's convoluted explanations that begin with "Would you believe ... ?" and end with "Sorry about that, Chief." The five-season series won Emmys for writing, directing, and acting, and despite (or because of) its general goofiness, attracted guest stars such as Johnny Carson, James Caan, and Carol Burnett. It even spawned a movie with the original cast called *The Nude Bomb* a decade later.

JONATHAN CREEK

CRIME COMEDY • 1997
RATED: TV-MA • 60 MINS

With a main character who lives in a windmill and does magic tricks, *Jonathan Creek* takes the mystery genre and gives it a spin, focusing not on who did the murder but on how it was done.

Jonathan Creek (Alan Davies) designs illusions and tricks for a magician. His skills come in especially handy when he teams up with investigative journalist Maddy Magellan (Caroline Quentin), who has a knack for sneaking into crime scenes and convincing a reluctant Jonathan to get involved. Together the two figure out how "impossible" crimes are committed. When Quentin left after Season 3 (of five), Jonathan got a different new partner for each subsequent season.

So how is all this a comedy? Sometimes it's down to the absurdity of the crimes themselves—like when a fly lands on a fax and gets mistaken for a comma, which somehow results in a fatality—but it's mostly a result of the sparky dialogue.

HAPPY ENDINGS

COMEDY • 2011
RATED: TV-14 • 22 MINS

This ensemble comedy about six friends in Chicago kicks things off with a ruined wedding, which sees the bride run off with a guy on rollerblades she doesn't even like that much.

And it just gets weirder from there, but these pals stick together anyway. There's Alex (Elisha Cuthbert), the runaway bride who returns with cornrows and some good reasons for leaving when she did; Dave (Zachary Knighton), the dumped groom who likes V-neck shirts way too much; Jane, Alex's high-strung sister with a wild past; and Alex's husband Brad, who's also best friends with the guys. And don't forget Max, the gay guy who's also very much a bro; and Penny, who's always looking for a boyfriend.

The three-season show is famous for the "pile-on," when the characters keep repeating an insult to whoever does something dumb. But it always backfires when they try it with other people around. The show is quirky and funny, and manages to add an edge to sitcom.

KEEPING UP APPEARANCES

COMEDY • 1990
RATED: TV-PG • 30 MINS

Social climber Hyacinth Bucket—she'd like you to pronounce it "bouquet," please—is always trying to prove that she's a legitimate member of the upper class. She isn't.

"Richard, you know I love my family, but that's no reason why I should have to acknowledge them in broad daylight." That line tells you everything you need to know about Hyacinth (Patricia Routledge), who spends much of her time explaining to her husband, Richard, exactly what he or someone else is doing wrong, and what he's supposed to do about it. She may come from a working-class family, but she doesn't want anyone to know it.

Every episode of the five-season series reinforces its premise in new and funnier ways, and every new adventure—a search for a country cottage, a trip to an art exhibition, a phone call from someone looking for Chinese takeout—brings new gems of conversation from the redoubtable Hyacinth.

SCRUBS

COMEDY • 2001
RATED: TV-14 • 22 MINS

Great music, surreal fantasies, and the antics of a bunch of medical interns and professionals at a teaching hospital—scrub up and join the team.

Scrubs stars Zach Braff as brand-new hospital intern John "J. D." Dorian. J. D. also provides a voice-over narrating his reality as well as his fantasies about what he wishes or dreads might happen. As the nine seasons progress, he slowly rises up the ranks of the hospital. His best friend and fellow intern is Turk (Donald Faison), who's more confident but still compassionate. J. D.'s love interest is Elliot (Sarah Chalke), an overachiever given a boy's name by her dad, who is lacking in social skills.

Music was a major part of what made *Scrubs* stand out, and the producers admitted that sometimes its music montages were chosen before scripts were written. The show aired a finale at the end of its eighth season, then got renewed for another year, and moved the action to a medical school.

RITA

COMEDY • 2012
RATED: 15 (UK) • 40 MINS

This Danish TV series follows the ups and downs of Rita Madsen, a single mom and a teacher at a private school, who relates more to her students than the other adults.

Rita (Mille Dinesen) may be a teacher, but she's also a rebel—in the very first scene of the show, she's smoking in a school toilet and correcting the grammar of graffiti that says (accurately) that she's f***ing the principal. She speaks her mind to the student's parents, even if it means unpleasant truths: "Whether you like it or not, you have a very annoying child."

But Rita does love her students, and has three kids of her own: daughter Molly and son Ricco, who are grown up and have moved out, and Jeppe, the youngest, who still lives with her and is coming to terms with being gay. Rita is an imperfect and complex woman with strong opinions who sometimes has to come face-to-face with her own mistakes in this funny and poignant four-season show.

WHITE COLLAR

CRIME COMEDY • 2009
RATED: TV-PG • 40 MINS

Con man Neil Caffrey trades his expertise in white-collar crime for his freedom after he's recaptured by FBI Special Agent Peter Burke following a prison break.

Matt Bomer is Neil, who breaks out of prison, gets caught, and becomes a criminal consultant for the White Collar Crime Division of the FBI. He's a forger and a skilled con man with fancy taste: he likes art, good wine, and expensive suits. Tim DeKay is Peter, a by-the-book, happily married FBI agent who catches Neil and is rewarded by getting to butt heads with him on a regular basis now that they're working together.

The six-season series mixes drama with lighter moments and fuels its ongoing stories with multiple plot twists and turns to keep viewers on edge. The professional relationship between Caffrey and Burke turns into more of a friendship, but even then they don't quite trust each other, which keeps it fun.

YEAR OF THE RABBIT

CRIME COMEDY • 2019
RATED: 15 (UK) • 25 MINS

A dark comedy about an unlikeable drunk detective hunting down criminals in 1880s London. This may be the world's first Victorian police comedy.

Mutton-chopped Detective Inspector Rabbit (Matt Berry) drinks and solves crimes pretty well, except that he's getting older, so his boss, Chief Inspector Wisbech, assigns him a partner: the young, sweet Sergeant Strauss. They become a trio when Mabel, Wisbech's adopted daughter, joins them to become London's first female police officer.

The trio encounter murderers and stalkers, youth gangs, snipers, jewel thieves, spiritualists, and even the Elephant Man (the nickname of the real-life, severely deformed Joseph Merrick). But no matter how successful he is, Rabbit still faces the disdain of Wisbech, who likes to admonish him with the memorable line, "Remember who wipes your arse, Rabbit." Oh yes—nearly everyone in this one-season show is foul-mouthed.

YOU WANT TO LEARN SOMETHING NEW

Written by Christian Blauvelt

There are times when you feel ready for a challenge. If you want to soak up something new and exciting, there are plenty of TV shows out there to satisfy your thirst for knowledge. But none of these shows bear any resemblance to homework. A spoonful of entertainment makes the educational value here all the more tantalizing. You may find your IQ going up, and not just when watching *QI*....

THE CROWN

HISTORICAL DRAMA • 2016 • RATED: TV-MA • 60 MINS • SEASONS: 3
CLAIRE FOY, MATT SMITH, OLIVIA COLMAN

You may think you know all there is to know about the British royal family, but writer-creator Peter Morgan goes deeper, finding the personal in the pageantry throughout this decades-spanning portrait of Queen Elizabeth II.

Next to the word "continuity" in the dictionary should be a picture of Queen Elizabeth II, who, as much as anyone, has symbolized Britain in its emergence from the austerity of the postwar years into the bold modern age. What Shakespeare did for the Plantagenet kings of the 15th century, creator Peter Morgan has done for Elizabeth in *The Crown*, hiring some of the finest actors of our time to portray the monarch and her family across the decades. First wielding the sceptre is Claire Foy, who plays Elizabeth in Seasons 1 and 2, which span from her

marriage to Prince Philip (Matt Smith) in 1947 to the birth of her youngest son, Edward, in 1964. For the next two seasons, Oscar-winner Olivia Colman inherits the throne, while Imelda Staunton will pick up the reins of power for the fifth and final season.

Like Shakespeare, Morgan, who has written or cowritten every single episode—a rare and monumental achievement in television—tells a story of changing times through the lens of the monarchy, seeking to find the humans behind the honorifics. Scandals abound: Elizabeth clashes with her sister, Princess Margaret (Vanessa Kirby in Seasons 1 and 2, Helena Bonham Carter in 3 and the upcoming 4), over her love affairs. She also confronts her estranged uncle, the Duke of Windsor (Alex Jennings in Seasons 1 and 2, Derek Jacobi in Season 3), who abdicated as King Edward VIII in order to marry American divorcée, Wallis Simpson. And then there's the matter of her son, Charles, and his burgeoning romance with Camilla Shand.

Morgan goes far deeper than the tabloid headlines, and the results are sympathetic and even touching. Many episodes explore

> *"I thought … A young queen, a middle-aged queen, and an old queen."*
>
> Peter Morgan (creator)

BRITISH PRIME MINISTERS IN POWER DURING THE REIGN OF QUEEN ELIZABETH II

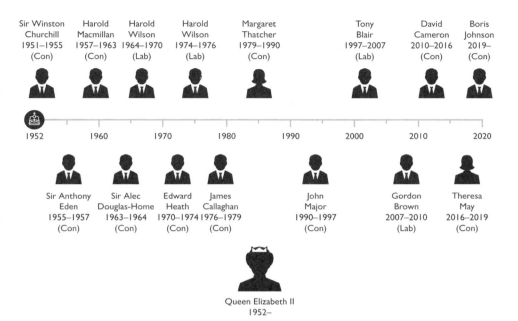

| Sir Winston Churchill 1951–1955 (Con) | Harold Macmillan 1957–1963 (Con) | Harold Wilson 1964–1970 (Lab) | Harold Wilson 1974–1976 (Lab) | Margaret Thatcher 1979–1990 (Con) | Tony Blair 1997–2007 (Lab) | David Cameron 2010–2016 (Con) | Boris Johnson 2019– (Con) |

| Sir Anthony Eden 1955–1957 (Con) | Sir Alec Douglas-Home 1963–1964 (Con) | Edward Heath 1970–1974 (Con) | James Callaghan 1976–1979 (Con) | John Major 1990–1997 (Con) | Gordon Brown 2007–2010 (Lab) | Theresa May 2016–2019 (Con) |

Queen Elizabeth II
1952–

events that are less widely known: Charles's lonely education at Scottish boarding school Gordonstoun (the school has protested over the show's stern depiction); the Queen's regret over her response to the 1966 disaster in Aberfan, Wales, in which 144 people, mostly children, were killed by a mining-related landslide; and the relationship of Philip with his mother, Princess Alice, who lived a life of simplicity and poverty as a nun in Greece.

Quirkier story lines present themselves, too: Princess Margaret finds an unexpected bond with the similarly ribald Lyndon Johnson; Winston Churchill protests against the marriage of Elizabeth to Philip because of the startling presence of high-ranking Nazis in the future Duke of Edinburgh's family tree; and Philip's obsession with the moon landing.

Morgan has built much of his career around the royal family. He wrote the 2006 film *The Queen*, which won Helen Mirren an Oscar for her portrayal of Elizabeth II navigating the aftermath of Princess Diana's death. That then led to a 2013 stage play, also starring Mirren, called *The Audience*, which depicted the Queen's meetings with her first 12 prime ministers. When Netflix wanted to adapt the play, the result, ultimately, was *The Crown*.

Though it has won numerous BAFTAs and Emmys, *The Crown* has raised eyebrows over the staggering sums of money Netflix has reportedly invested in the show—however, rumors that it is "the most expensive TV series ever" have been refuted by Morgan as inaccurate. But if there ever was a show that merited the royal treatment, this is it.

CREATOR: Peter Morgan
PRODUCTION CO: Left Bank Pictures, Sony Pictures Television Production UK

CHERNOBYL

DRAMA • 2019 • RATED: TV-MA • 65 MINS • SEASONS: 1
JARED HARRIS, STELLAN SKARSGÅRD, EMILY WATSON

You know radiation is dangerous. But you'll probably have no idea how dangerous until you see this miniseries about the 1986 nuclear disaster, the heroes who tried to contain it, and the bureaucrats who attempted to cover it up. Things get bleak. Very bleak.

It's no spoiler to say that Jared Harris's Valery Legasov, who led the investigative commission into the notorious Chernobyl nuclear power plant meltdown, ultimately takes his own life: he does so in the first minutes of Craig Mazin's harrowing five-and-a-half-hour HBO epic. The series flashes back from there to the horrific night of April 26, 1986, when Reactor Number Four at the Chernobyl Nuclear Power Plant near the town of Pripyat in present-day Ukraine melted down.

The miniseries becomes an anatomy of a disaster, as power-plant officials insufficiently follow protocols—exposing their workers, firefighters, and other emergency responders, as well as the people of Pripyat and beyond, to lethal levels of radiation. It's all filmed with a veneer of color-drained late-Soviet decay: the production was shot at Chernobyl's "sister" nuclear power plant in Lithuania with the former USSR republic's capital Vilnius standing in for Pripyat. Debate continues about how dangerous the radiation around the actual Chernobyl facility still is, with few permanent residents nearby, but tours to the site are surging in popularity following the release of the HBO show.

Chernobyl can be hard to watch. It's frustrating seeing responsibility-deferring bureaucrats impede the investigation into the meltdown's causes, and heartbreaking when one of the main characters, a firefighter, suffers so dearly from acute radiation sickness. And then the pets start dying.

If you can brace yourself, Mazin's series has much to reveal about not just how the Chernobyl disaster happened, but why it happened. It's been criticized as anti-Soviet propaganda by the Russian Communist Party for implying the disaster hurried the USSR's demise (though Russia's culture minister did praise it). And while it's true the show features inaccuracies, the backlash seems apt for a story about what happens when face-saving takes priority over the truth.

CREATOR: Craig Mazin
PRODUCTION CO: HBO, Sister Pictures, Sky Television, The Mighty Mint, Word Games

THE ASSASSINATION OF GIANNI VERSACE

CRIME DRAMA • 2018
RATED: 15 • 53 MINS

This miniseries about the fashionista's murder explores homophobia in the US media and law enforcement—while also delivering a manhunt thriller.

No one understands where the sordid and the substantial meet better than producer Ryan Murphy. As he did in *The People Vs. O. J.*

Simpson (see p295), Murphy takes a tabloid saga and reveals what it says about society. Édgar Ramírez plays Versace, with Ricky Martin as Antonio D'Amico, his partner, and Penélope Cruz as Donatella, his sister.

The real drama comes from Darren Criss as Versace's murderer Andrew Cunanan, who struggled with his own homosexuality, without the benefit of wealth and fame that shielded his victim. Over nine chilling episodes, Murphy shows how the intolerance of the time resulted in the trivialization of Versace's death, just as it put Cunanan on his path to becoming a killer.

FOSSE/VERDON

DRAMA • 2019 • RATED: TV-MA • 60 MINS • SEASONS: 1
SAM ROCKWELL, MICHELLE WILLIAMS, MARGARET QUALLEY

Bob Fosse and Gwen Verdon reinvented the choreography of the musical in the mid-20th century with their unique blend of physicality and drama. But this dynamic duo of the dance floor brought a little too much drama into their personal lives, too.

Married to each other as well as married to their work, Bob Fosse and Gwen Verdon exploded onto both Broadway and the big screen in the late 1950s. As Fosse, Sam Rockwell captures the obsessive self-absorption of an artist who—with his "jazz hands" and turned-in toes—was essential to the development of modern dance, even if he was someone you'd probably never want to know in person. And Michelle Williams transforms herself to become Verdon—adopting the dancer's unusual voice so perfectly that an Emmy and a Golden Globe followed. *Fosse/Verdon* shows how the couple developed their beloved "Who's Got the Pain?" mambo for

the Broadway musical *Damn Yankees*, as well as Fosse's evolution into an acclaimed film director—including his meticulous work on *Cabaret*.

Part of the joy of this eight-episode miniseries is watching how iconic musical moments came together before seeing them reenacted almost perfectly on screen. What also emerges is a potent examination of Fosse the workaholic. The multitalented artist would live life so full-throttle that he'd die, looking far older than his years, at the age of 60.

> **" *The ones who die young, those are the ones who live forever.* "**
>
> **Gwen Verdon** (E4)

I, CLAUDIUS

HISTORICAL DRAMA • 1976
RATED: 15 (UK) • 52 MINS

This 12-part saga about the early years of the Roman Empire is a who's who of outstanding British acting talent—and a decent primer for anyone interested in the ancient world.

The single-season series covers five emperors of the Julio-Claudian dynasty, which kicked off the Roman Empire. The limping, stuttering Claudius (Derek Jacobi) narrates on the ambitious and ruthless ebb and flow of imperial rule, before finally getting to wear Caesar's laurels himself as emperor number four.

Brian Blessed kicks things off as Augustus, followed by George Baker as Tiberius, who left much of the day-to-day work of ruling to the head of his guard, Sejanus (Patrick Stewart). John Hurt comes next as the wonderfully mad Caligula, and then there's Claudius himself, who tried to restore sanity and reason to Roman rule. Rome may have eventually fallen, but this 1970s series still holds up remarkably well—we come to praise *I, Claudius*, not to bury it.

JESUS OF NAZARETH

DRAMA • 1977
RATED: TV-G • 180 MINUTES

The pedigree of the talent both in front of and behind the camera could not be more prestigious, and the result is a truly superlative retelling of the Gospels.

Unfolding over six hours, this biblical miniseries stars Robert Powell as Jesus, but it's the supporting players who really stand out: Anne Bancroft as Mary Magdalene, Michael York as John the Baptist, Peter Ustinov as Herod the Great, Christopher Plummer as his son Herod Antipas, and James Earl Jones, Fernando Rey and Donald Pleasence as the Three Wise Men.

Beautifully told and acted, *Jesus of Nazareth* might be the best filmed version of the life of Christ we have. In two parts, it's lovingly directed by Franco Zeffirelli and written by the woman responsible for perhaps more Italian cinematic masterpieces of the last century than anyone else: Suso Cecchi d'Amico, who also wrote *Bicycle Thieves* and *The Leopard,* among other classics. A must see.

MEDICI: MASTERS OF FLORENCE

HISTORICAL DRAMA • 2016
RATED: TV-14 • 60 MINS

Dustin Hoffman plays a member of the notorious family who steered Florence through much of the Renaissance in this tunics-and-testosterone drama.

The star of *The Graduate* and *Tootsie* plays Giovanni de'Medici, founder of the Medici bank and arguably the most important early member of the family who wielded extraordinary power over Florence for centuries. He only appears in a few episodes of Season 1, with the focus quickly shifting to his son Cosimo, played by *Game of Thrones* (see p8) alumnus Richard Madden.

Medici is historical fiction as lusty soap opera. In Seasons 2 and 3 (the last), the action shifts ahead several decades to shine a spotlight on Cosimo's grandson, Lorenzo, and his battles with Jacopo de' Pazzi (Sean Bean), among others. If the series' value as history is questionable, its value as drama is not.

BOBBY KENNEDY FOR PRESIDENT

DOCUMENTARY • 2018
RATED: TV-MA • 60 MINS

Bobby Kennedy inspired a generation with his civil rights politics. Never-before-seen footage helps power this look at what might have been.

Unfolding in four parts, Dawn Porter's one-season documentary series looks at the real man behind the figure who defined US

progressive politics in the late 1960s. Archival footage and recorded conversations between Kennedy and his brothers, John and Ted, make for an especially rich and personal telling.

Reflections by those who knew him form the emotional heart of the documentary. Harry Belafonte, Dolores Huerta, John Lewis, and others reveal what Kennedy was like in person and what he meant to their own fights for racial equality and economic justice. Together, they paint a portrait of what the US might have been had Kennedy not been assassinated in 1968.

BOLÍVAR

HISTORICAL DRAMA • 2019
RATED: TV-MA • 52 MINS

Simón Bolívar, the great hero who won independence for much of Spanish-speaking South America, gets the soap-opera treatment in an epic single-season, 60-episode series.

Luis Gerónimo Abreu stars as Simón Bolívar, "El Libertador," in this decades-spanning look at the life of the military leader. While still in his 20s, Bolívar threw off the shackles of Spanish

rule across what is today Venezuela, Colombia, Panama, Ecuador, and Bolivia (named after him), achieving lasting independence for the region by the time he was 37.

This Spanish-language Colombian show combines military history—including a lot of marching around and staring at maps—with flashbacks to Bolívar as a younger man (played by José Ramón Barreto) and the many loves he had along the way. This is a *telenovela*, so every battle comes with some bodice-ripping as well. But if its intent is to humanize a legend, it more than succeeds.

JOHN ADAMS

HISTORICAL DRAMA • 2008
RATED: TV-14 • 75 MINS

Paul Giamatti plays a defining, if slightly overlooked, Founding Father in this story of the American Revolution and the early days of the US.

All the statues of Founding Fathers in the US are of George Washington and Thomas Jefferson, while Benjamin Franklin at least gets his face on the $100 bill. John Adams feels neglected by comparison, but HBO's miniseries

sought to correct that by showing the hard work Giamatti's Adams put into the cause of American independence, which culminated in him becoming the second US president.

All the other famous names are here, too: David Morse plays Washington, Tom Wilkinson is Franklin, Tom Hollander is King George III, Laura Linney is Adams' wife Abigail, and, in a particularly inspired bit of casting, Rufus Sewell is Alexander Hamilton. *John Adams*'s seven episodes are an unsentimental look at the passion, resilience, and sometimes sacrifice required to build a new nation.

A VERY ENGLISH SCANDAL

DRAMA • 2018
RATED: TV-14 • 60 MINS

Intolerance can lead to extreme behavior. That's the case in this sad, strange true-crime drama, in which an MP's desire to cover up his sexuality led to attempted murder.

If you're old enough, you may have heard of the Thorpe Affair. In the late 1970s, Liberal member of parliament Jeremy Thorpe, once the leader of his party, was charged with hiring a hitman to murder Norman Scott, his former lover. Scott threatened to expose their affair, which would have been the end of Thorpe's political life.

The BBC's three-part miniseries boasts an impressive cast—Hugh Grant plays Thorpe, with Ben Whishaw as Scott. Brilliantly written by *Queer as Folk* (see p165) creator Russell T. Davies, *A Very English Scandal* excavates the specifics of the case to demonstrate just how much has changed in British society's attitudes toward the LGBTQI+ community.

HORRIBLE HISTORIES

HISTORICAL COMEDY • 2009
RATED: TV-PG • 30 MINS

Just how crazy was Caligula? Well, consider that he tried to make his favorite horse Incitatus a consul of Rome. The comedy in this kids' history show writes itself.

Picture *Blackadder* (see p122) reimagined for the under-13 set. That's the sensibility of this juvenile sketch comedy based on the popular book series of the same name. Each episode includes an original song and skits on a related subject: for instance, imagine an overview of King Georges I to IV presented as if the four monarchs were members of a boy band.

As the title suggests, *Horrible Histories* lingers on some of the gorier, grislier, gross-out details of the past. Its accuracy has also come under criticism at times—one episode attributed Richard III's nastiness entirely to Shakespeare's literary invention when there is considerable evidence that he was a terrible king. But as a history show for beginners, you could do worse.

LORENA

CRIME DOCUMENTARY • 2019
RATED: TV-MA • 60 MINS

The notorious case of a woman who cut off her husband's penis became a cultural obsession in the US. This documentary series reveals the alleged abuse that drove her to the act.

The #MeToo era has forced a reappraisal of some of the more lurid stories of the past. Among them is the saga of Lorena Bobbit and her ex-husband, John, who made headlines in 1993 after she committed a shocking act of mutilation against him. At the time, she was presented as the wife from hell and, as an immigrant from Ecuador, there was more than a xenophobic tinge to her portrayal in the US press.

This Amazon-produced documentary series gives Lorena a voice: she discusses the alleged abuse—including claims of repeated rape—that John subjected her to that drove her to breaking point. It shows that what was once considered salacious may, in fact, deserve your sympathy instead.

THE PEOPLE VS. O. J. SIMPSON

**DRAMA • 2016 • RATED: TV-MA • 50 MINS • SEASONS: 1
STERLING K. BROWN, SARAH PAULSON, COURTNEY B. VANCE**

It was "the trial of the century" back in the 1990s—not just for the mystery and salaciousness of the case itself, but also for what it said about race, class, sexism, and celebrity in America.

Want to know what that famous line "If it doesn't fit, you must acquit" was all about? Look no further. It came from the court case that breathed new life into supermarket tabloids in the US, and all but single-handedly created the idea of pundit-driven 24-hour cable news. In 1994, O.J. Simpson, the beloved football-phenomenon-turned-movie star-turned-sports-presenter, was charged with murdering his wife and an acquaintance who was in the wrong place at the wrong time.

Ryan Murphy's 10-episode miniseries barely examines Simpson (Cuba Gooding, Jr.) himself. Instead it looks at how the months-long trial became a lens for understanding a divided America where the truth increasingly came to matter less than spin, hype, and fame. Sarah Paulson shines as prosecutor Marcia Clark, and Sterling K. Brown will rip your heart out as her colleague, Christopher Darden.

Like the sensation around the trial itself, the series swerves from the profound to the puerile—this, after all, was the case that first elevated the Kardashians to national prominence (watch out for Selma Blair as Kris Jenner and David Schwimmer as Robert Kardashian). However, it does so in such a way that your obsession is sure to follow.

WORMWOOD

**DOCUMENTARY DRAMA • 2017
RATED: 15 (UK) • 41 MINS**

Might the death of a willing subject of a CIA-sponsored experiment have been something even more sinister? This docudrama uses reenactments and interviews to get closer to the truth.

Errol Morris is one of the most celebrated documentarians in US film history. In *The Thin Blue Line*, he pioneered a new reenactment-driven approach to true crime, before winning

an Oscar for *The Fog of War* in 2004. But he went truly longform with *this* six-part miniseries for Netflix about the mysterious death of a CIA officer in 1953.

Project MKUltra was a shadowy biological warfare program put into action by the CIA as the Cold War heated up. One of its agents, Frank Olson, took an experimental dose of LSD as part of the agency's inquiry into the possibility of "mind control." A week later, he died after falling out of a window. Was it suicide? Murder? Morris heads down a rabbit hole to try to find out.

ROOTS (1977)

HISTORICAL DRAMA • 1977 • RATED: TV-MA • 70 MINS • SEASONS: I • LEVAR BURTON, LESLIE UGGAMS, BEN VEREEN

It was the most-watched miniseries in US television history. It also happened to be the best. Over 40 years later, this multigenerational chronicle of an African American family's journey from slavery to freedom retains its power.

It's the stuff of nightmares: being kidnapped from your family, placed in chains, and taken across the ocean to be enslaved in a foreign land for the rest of your life. A life that is no longer your own.

That's what happens to Kunta Kinte (LeVar Burton) in the first episode of this landmark miniseries adapted from author Alex Haley's novel. Haley wrote the book after looking into his family tree, tracing himself back to Kunta, who was born in the 1750s as one of the Mandinka people in what is now present-day Gambia. One of the most harrowing, upsetting moments in all of television history is when Kunta, now enslaved in America, is repeatedly whipped until he identifies not by the name of his birth, but by the one given to him by his

master: Toby. The story continues with Kunta's descendants Kizzy (Leslie Uggams), "Chicken" George Moore (Ben Vereen), and Tom Harvey (Georg Stanford Brown), as they continue their fight for freedom and, following the end of slavery after the American Civil War, discover that their struggles are far from over.

Roots features an amazing cast, music by legendary producer Quincy Jones, and has the very definition of epic sweep. A sequel series, *Roots: The Next Generation*, aired two years later and brought the story of Kunta's descendants up to the late 1970s, with James Earl Jones playing Haley himself.

Sequels aside, the original run of *Roots* remains one of the most potent dramatizations of American slavery ever put on screen. Its last episode, which aired on January 30, 1977, drew 100 million US viewers, which was well over a third of the nation's population at the time. It remains the second highest-rated broadcast of a scripted program in US TV history.

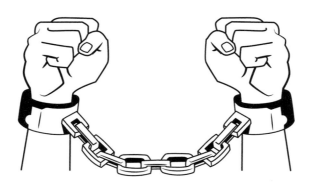

CREATORS: David L. Wolper, Alex Haley
PRODUCTION CO: David L. Wolper Productions, Warner Bros. Television

ROOTS (2016)

HISTORICAL DRAMA • 2016
RATED: TV-MA • 90 MINS

Although Alex Haley's original mini-series was one of the most-watched programs ever in the US, it was far from accurate. This remake reflects up-to-date research and sensibilities.

How do you repeat something as monumental as the original *Roots*? You reinvent it. This reimagined miniseries adds nuance to some of the plot points explored by author Alex Haley in the original. His ancestor Kunta Kinte's village in present-day Gambia, for example, becomes a sprawling city. But beloved characters also return: Forest Whitaker plays Fiddler and Anika Noni Rose is the heartbreaking Kizzy.

Beyond Haley's at-times questionable scholarship, other elements from the 1977 version also haven't aged well—a subplot about a guilt-ridden slaveship captain is cut, while this time O. J. Simpson does not show up as one of Kunta's tribesmen. This is a welcome and satisfying makeover of a classic story for the 21st century.

THE UP SERIES

DOCUMENTARY • 1964 • RATED: TV-14 • 60 MINS • SEASONS: 9
JACQUELINE BASSETT, TONY WALKER, BRUCE BALDEN

It's an experiment unparalleled in TV history: in 1964, ITV profiled a number of British seven-year-olds from different backgrounds. Every seven years since, a new installment has been filmed to reveal what's happened to them. These "kids" are now in their 60s.

Does the economic background you're born into affect the entire direction of your life? That's the underlying premise of *The Up Series*, which in 1964 began following a group of British schoolchildren from diverse circumstances. In that first episode, "Seven Up!," the children were selected by Michael Apted, who has directed every instalment since.

Every seven years, Apted checks in on the original kids, following their path through life. Some personalities truly stand out: Tony, from a working-class background in London's East End, wanted to be a jockey at age seven. At age 14, we see him working in a stable.

At age 21, we find him learning to become a London cabbie. That career actually leads to him leading a comfortable life and, by *63 Up*, retiring.

Others, such as Bruce, stand out for their early strong convictions: as a seven-year-old Bruce already cared a lot about social justice and racial equality. And his life since as a teacher shows how fully formed his personality was from childhood. *The Up Series* has evolved beyond its economic origins to take in a sweeping view of what makes people who they are.

> **"*I hope to do 84 Up when I'll be 99.*"**
>
> Michael Apted (series director)

GREAT OLD AMUSEMENT PARKS

DOCUMENTARY • 1999
RATED: NR • 60 MINS

This nostalgic look at old-fashioned roller-coaster rides and merry-go-rounds pioneered a new style of documentary filmmaking.

How did amusement parks come about? And in this age of theme parks with mega rides and thrills, how do the original parks survive?

These are the questions broadcaster Rick Sebak examines via his homespun narration. He takes us on a tour of old-style rides in Coney Island, New York's Astroland, the Santa Cruz Beach Boardwalk, and Pittsburgh's Kennywood, the "roller coaster capital of the world."

Now over 20 years old, this special has barely aged and remains a perennial favorite in the US. Sebak directed it in his "scrapbook documentary" style, which he developed to celebrate simple pleasures. His films on ice cream and hot dogs are also US TV staples.

LOUIS THEROUX'S WEIRD WEEKENDS

DOCUMENTARY • 1998 • RATED: 18 (UK) • 50 MINS • SEASONS: 3
LOUIS THEROUX, AL SHARPTON, MASTER P

Most TV hosts are defined by their ability to talk. Theroux's greatest virtue is his ability to listen, and this show encouraged an understanding of people who often aren't given a voice.

Spending a little time in somebody else's shoes and learning to empathize with them a bit has been Louis Theroux's modus operandi for well over two decades. From 1998 to 2000, his mission across three seasons and 17 episodes of *Weird Weekends* was to delve into subcultures a little less visited than most, interviewing porn stars, survivalists, wrestlers, self-fulfillment experts, Indian gurus, body builders, and even self-professed alien abduction survivors (one person he speaks to claims to have personally killed 20 aliens).

The show is now over 20 years old and, unsurprisingly, some of it hasn't aged well: it's hard to imagine why Al Sharpton (politician, civil rights activist, and baptist minister) was lumped into Theroux's episode on black nationalists, while another installment presents gangsta rap in the American South as a niche culture rather than one that's part of the mainstream. It also features Theroux, rather embarrassingly, rapping himself.

But some episodes remain revelatory, such as the examination of a group of South African white supremacists who attempted to wall themselves off after the end of apartheid. And even if some of the show could use a refresh, the format Theroux pioneered inspired many others—notably W. Kamau Bell and his series *United Shades of America* (see p299).

MYTHBUSTERS

DOCUMENTARY • 2003
RATED: TV-14 • 44 MINS

This long-running US-Australian series goes to great lengths to test the truth behind urban legends and whether what happens in the movies could happen in real life.

Could someone actually die like the Bond girl painted gold played by Shirley Eaton in the movie *Goldfinger*? Can you swing across a chasm like Luke Skywalker and Princess Leia

in *Star Wars*? These are the kind of questions that *Mythbusters*' hosts Adam Savage and Jamie Hyneman like to explore in the nearly 300 episodes that comprise this 17-season series.

Rather than just debunk such legends outright, the pair test them in a scientific way. In the *Star Wars* case that means rigging a makeshift chasm and setting up a way to swing over it (it turns out it can be done with great difficulty and a lot of pain). So, if you want to find out whether you get less wet walking or running in the rain, or whether talking to plants helps them grow, you have to check this out.

BLOWN AWAY

REALITY TV • 2019
RATED: PG (UK) • 23 MINS

Part soothing exercise in "slow TV," part examination of obsessive perfection, this quirky Canadian series focuses on a subculture worthy of your attention: competitive glass-blowing.

Bless Canada for this show. Watch 10 glass-blowers create works of art before your eyes as they compete for a (modest) $60,000 prize and a residency at New York's Corning

Museum of Glass. Each of the 10 installments see another contestant eliminated, based on the quality of the work they have produced. The competition takes place in a special facility custom-built to accommodate all 10 glass-blowers (and their furnaces) working at once.

Artist and professor Katherine Gray serves as chief judge on this one-season show, which isn't just mesmerizing to watch, but soothing, too. Seeing fiery globs of molten glass shaped into beautiful forms is almost guaranteed to melt away your stress.

UNITED SHADES OF AMERICA

DOCUMENTARY • 2016
RATED: TV-PG • 42 MINS

W. Kamau Bell examines largely unexplored subcultures. His focus is on listening to what people have to say, even when it's completely vile.

The first episode of this four-season series features W. Kamau Bell exploring the white supremacist group Ku Klux Klan. He interviews

several of its members and even attends a cross burning – the last sight many African-Americans beheld in the early 20th century before they were murdered by the group.

That Bell, himself African American, is willing to listen to people who have no interest in listening to him shows his method here: he totally immerses himself in his subjects' experiences, whether he's exploring the lives of Native Americans on a reservation, listening to disability activists discussing their struggles, or talking to Chicago gangs.

ANTHONY BOURDAIN: PARTS UNKNOWN

**DOCUMENTARY • 2013 • RATED: TV-14 • 42 MINS
SEASONS: 12 • ANTHONY BOURDAIN, ERIC RIPERT**

The late chef and presenter showed a different side of travel: not the fancy hotels or daredevil adventures, but the conversations—the value of learning about a place through talking to the locals and simply listening ... often while sharing a delicious meal.

There never has been another travel show quite like *Anthony Bourdain: Parts Unknown*. Most of its type present fantasies of travel, down to suggested itineraries you can follow. But often what you see Bourdain do, you wouldn't want to do yourself—nor would he have recommended it.

In one episode he spends several days drinking with locals in a Borneo longhouse, during which time he gets a tattoo applied somewhat excruciatingly to the center of his chest, then goes out and slaughters a pig for dinner. His are footsteps you're unlikely to walk in.

If that example seems extreme, perhaps that's unfair, because Bourdain is always most interested in something more subtle: learning about a place through the people who live there. Travel for him is total immersion into his surroundings' culture, politics, music, history, and (of course) food—Bourdain made his initial mark with the book *Kitchen Confidential*, about his own career as a chef.

Watching *Parts Unknown*, you can find yourself learning about how different waves of immigration led to the political divisions in Trinidad or what fueled civil war in Sri Lanka.

You could argue *Parts Unknown* is the most globally minded US television has ever been. Each of the 104 episodes offers something of value that you should know, from who kicked off the haute cuisine movement in Lyon to who helped start hip-hop in the Bronx. And that knowledge is imparted with cinematic flair—sometimes the series takes minutes at a time without narration to just let the sights and sounds of a place speak for it.

Pay particular attention to the episodes featuring acclaimed chef Eric Ripert as Bourdain's sidekick and "straight man" on adventures to Peru, Sichuan, the French Alps, and beyond. Be prepared, wanderlust will be inevitable.

CREATOR: Zero Point Zero Production Inc.
PRODUCTION CO: Zero Point Zero Production Inc.

HOW THE
UNIVERSE WORKS

DOCUMENTARY • 2010
RATED: TV-PG • 60 MINS

If you stop to think about the cosmic vastness of space, and its billions of years of history, it can be mind-boggling. This series makes it comprehensible.

Over eight seasons, hosts Mike Rowe and Erik Todd Dellums use animation and experiments to explain basic concepts of astronomy,

physics, and cosmology to help us make sense of the universe. Each episode is devoted to a single concept, such as "The Big Bang," "Black Holes," or "The Birth of the Earth."

From Season 3, *How the Universe Works* starts to explore more esoteric subjects, such as the "Secret History of Pluto," which explains how Pluto might be conducive to alien life. Another installment examines what the universe was like in the first second after the Big Bang. For every borderline sci-fi episode— there's one on time travel—there's another on a more serious idea, such as space-time.

13TH

DOCUMENTARY • 2016
RATED: TV-MA • 100 MINS

The US comprises just 5 percent of the world's population but has 25 percent of the world's prisoners. Director Ava DuVernay powerfully asks, did slavery ever end in America?

The director of the critically acclaimed 2014 Martin Luther King, Jr. drama *Selma* turned her lens from the 1960s to the present in this Netflix documentary. The title comes from the

13th Amendment of the U.S. Constitution, which ended slavery in 1865, near the end of the American Civil War. But *13th* argues that through racist Jim Crow laws, housing discrimination, and police violence, African Americans have continually been denied opportunities in the US—the legacy of which is their disproportionate incarceration.

DuVernay argues her case through powerful testimonials, archive footage that sheds light on neglected histories, and disturbing videos of police brutality. *13th* is hard to watch but important for understanding our world today.

NIGHT ON EARTH

DOCUMENTARY • 2020
RATED: TV-PG • 53 MINS

Using experimental ultrasensitive lenses, this miniseries captures the greatest nighttime footage of animals you've ever seen. It's a revealing look at habitats after dark and their wide-awake inhabitants.

Watching this seven-part Netflix series feels like seeing the world through a whole new set of eyes. And that's at least partly true, because

cameras capable of picking up light levels this low never existed before. The revelations just keep coming: in the first episode, which follows both lionesses on the hunt and a pack of hungry hyenas, the single most successful hunter we see is a Mexican desert mouse that defeats a scorpion in one-on-one combat and feasts on the insect afterward.

Night on Earth takes you to jungles and frozen wastelands and devotes an entire episode to the animal life in human cities after dark. But the most dazzling sight of all? A look under the ocean surface at night, which is truly awesome.

LONG WAY ROUND

DOCUMENTARY • 2004
RATED: TV-PG • 45 MINS

Even movie stars get wanderlust. Actor Ewan McGregor teams up with best friend Charley Boorman to ride motorcycles from London to New York, with a few surprises on the way.

McGregor and British TV presenter Boorman hop aboard BMW motorcycles for the road trip of a lifetime. Airing over seven episodes, most of the series takes place in Russia and the former Soviet republics, as well as Mongolia. Riding across continental Europe to Volgograd in Russia is a snap; after that, things get a bit more complicated as the quality of the roads starts to vary widely and the pair find themselves having to navigate rivers aboard their bikes. They also need to deal with shifty mafia members, injuries, breakdowns, and emotional meltdowns.

The last episode covers their journey across North America before their triumphant entry into the Big Apple. This is travel as roughing it, but it is essentially joyful and upbeat.

RICK STEVES' EUROPE

DOCUMENTARY • 2000 • RATED: TV-G • 30 MINS
SEASONS: 10 • RICK STEVES

The New York Times once called Rick Steves as fine an ambassador to the world as the US could hope for, and it's hard to disagree. Watching him, you'll learn how to be a better global citizen.

Experience a place like the locals do: that's the approach taken by Rick Steves who has been a staple on US public broadcasting for over 20 years. When watching Steves explore a different European city or region in each episode, you'll never see him stay in five-star hotels. He resides at small family-run bed-and-breakfasts, showing you that cost doesn't have to be a barrier to exploring the world.

Come for the travel tips and stay for the art history. Rick Steves' Europe spends much more time on painting, sculpture, and classical music (not to mention cathedral architecture) than many other American travel shows. Steves won't just show the pageantry of the Christmas celebration at the Vatican, he'll explain how the idea of living Nativity tableaux goes back to St. Francis.

> **"Travel is intensified living."**
>
> **Rick Steves** (host)

Special episodes of the show include deep dives into the continent's many festivals; a look at the "Little Europe" of Liechtenstein, San Marino, and other small states; and an examination of the rise of fascism. Steves evangelizes that travel itself can make our lives better, and by watching him you quickly become a convert.

SAMANTHA BROWN'S PLACES TO LOVE

DOCUMENTARY • 2018
RATED: NR • 30 MINUTES

Ready for a travel adventure? Avoiding the art and history that Rick Steves would cover, the jovial Samantha advocates for pure fun.

Samantha Brown understands, first and foremost, that travel is about people. She makes you fall in love with a place, whether she's traveling to Xi'an in China or the Texas Hill Country. Her approach isn't the most intellectual, but it's about what people often most care about: the best places to stay, eat, drink, and have fun. How do you want to make the most of a weekend away? Samantha's the person to tell you.

Samantha was a longtime host on the Travel Channel in the US before making the switch to public broadcasting. It's a good fit as she provides a useful service: throughout three feel-good seasons she shows us just how easy it is to get out and see the world.

THE AMAZING RACE

REALITY TV • 2001 • RATED: TV-PG • 60 MINS • SEASONS: 31
PHIL KEOGHAN

Can a frenetic travel competition show have educational value? *The Amazing Race* answers yes, even if there's always a bit of risking life and limb on top of its cultural immersion.

Since the summer of 2001, *The Amazing Race* has been taking contestants all over the world in two-person teams. The aim of each team is to hop frantically around the world in order to cross the finish line first and collect a $1 million prize. The teams are responsible for booking their own flights and navigating ground transportation as they scramble from country to country.

Along the way, they have to complete various challenges—or "Roadblocks" and "Detours" to use the parlance of the show—which can be physical or more cerebral. These often involve the local culture or sights: teams might find themselves walking a cow across town to a temple or zip-lining over Victoria Falls.

It's such a hectic dash that the result is usually a pretty bad travel experience for the contestants, but the show's exploration of rituals around the world can be illuminating for the viewer.

> **"** We present a world that seems inviting, with people who are warm and helpful. **"**
>
> **Phil Keoghan** (host)

Even if the teams can be rude to people along the way, you always see how kind and helpful the locals guiding them are. *The Amazing Race* has done much to encourage viewers to get out and see the world, without fear of language barriers or culture clashes.

THE BLUE PLANET

DOCUMENTARY • 2001
RATED: TV-G • 60 MINS

How often does a nature documentary break new ground in scientific understanding? This one did, when its production answered some questions that had long stumped oceanographers.

The Blue Planet has become such a phenomenon that it even spawned a live concert tour, in which orchestras accompanied select moments from the show. What more can be said about this brilliant landmark series? Well, the fact that it resulted in the first-ever mapping of blue whale migration routes, for one.

Over its single season, the series also captures new animal behaviors and even new species (such as the Dumbo octopus) on camera for the first time. The effort the BBC Natural History Unit put into The Blue Planet's production is legendary—the years of filming included more than 400 days that producers simply spent waiting around trying to get the shots they wanted and nothing was recorded at all. A sequel, Blue Planet II, aired in 2017.

FROZEN PLANET

DOCUMENTARY • 2011
RATED: TV-PG • 60 MINS

What's it like at the Earth's poles? This David Attenborough–narrated BBC series whisks you off to the frosty climes of the Arctic and Antarctic.

The aim of Frozen Planet was to examine the effects of climate change on some of the most vulnerable animal populations in the world: polar bears and white wolves in the Arctic, and Adélie penguins and albatrosses in Antarctica and nearby islands, such as South Georgia. The series follows these animals and their struggles to survive through the seasons. It also shows the challenges facing humans in these areas, including the residents of the Arctic Norwegian island of Svalbard and the Yupik people of far-eastern Russia.

Like The Blue Planet (see p304) and Planet Earth (see p305) before it, this eye-opening, seven-episode series is yet another amazing nature documentary from BBC Natural History Unit chief Alastair Fothergill and his team.

OUR PLANET

DOCUMENTARY • 2019
RATED: TV-G • 50 MINS

The creators of Planet Earth and Planet Earth II bring you this nature series that looks more closely at the effect humans are having on their animal neighbors around the world.

Producer Alastair Fothergill and narrator David Attenborough's nature documentaries for the BBC are some of the most stunning ever filmed. For this series of eight episodes—as globe-spanning as anything they've ever made—they went to Netflix. The images are as staggering as ever: from hundreds of birds dive-bombing to catch fish off the coast of Peru, to an ant colony working as if with one mind in a rainforest.

But here Attenborough's narration has an even greater sense of urgency. These habitats are being lost, and Our Planet shows what humanity must do to combat climate change across the globe, from the polar ice caps to the woodlands next door. If we don't, the series starkly warns, even fresh water could become scarce.

PLANET EARTH

DOCUMENTARY • 2006 • RATED: TV-PG • 60 MINS • SEASONS: 2
DAVID ATTENBOROUGH

Sometimes seeing is believing, and seeing this you'll believe more than ever in the need to respect and protect our natural world. Has there ever been another series with more images of beauty, awe, and terror per minute?

By any measure *Planet Earth* is a milestone. The 2006 documentary series from the BBC Natural History Unit—revived as *Planet Earth II* in 2016—was the first nature program filmed in high-definition. But the clarity and crispness of the images wouldn't matter as much if what was being photographed wasn't so extraordinary.

> **"** *People must feel that the natural world is important and valuable and beautiful and wonderful....* **"**

David Attenborough (narrator)

You'll never forget the sight of a great white shark launching itself into the air off the coast of South Africa, its jaws clamping down on a slippery seal as the massive eating machine rotates its entire body 360 degrees before hitting the surface of the water again with a great crash. Or a black-and-teal bird of paradise (the greater lophorina) in Papua New Guinea, puffing its feathers until its body appears flat like a lady's fan, in a strange display to catch the eye of a female.

Planet Earth and its sequel are presented by David Attenborough, the legendary British broadcaster and naturalist. Other markets used different narrators: in the US, the actor Sigourney Weaver took over from Attenborough.

Ten years later, *Planet Earth II* continues to break ground with an episode entirely about animals that call human cities their habitats, including peregrine falcons that hunt prey amid the skyscrapers of New York City. But implied in every installment of both seasons is humanity's own responsibility for looking after the natural world. As Attenborough puts it himself in his closing narration for Season 1, "Our planet is still full of wonders. As we explore them, so we gain not only understanding, but power ... We can now destroy or we can cherish. The choice is ours."

CREATORS: Alastair Fothergill, Keith Scholey
PRODUCTION CO: BBC

WHEN THEY SEE US

CRIME DRAMA • 2019 • RATED: TV-MA • 64–88 MINS • SEASONS: 1
JHARREL JEROME, MICHAEL K. WILLIAMS, FELICITY HUFFMAN

Telling the harrowing true story of five African American and Latino teenagers convicted of a brutal crime they did not commit, this dramatic miniseries has much to say about enduring institutional racism in the US. It's time to meet The Exonerated Five.

It was one of the biggest crime stories of the 1980s in the US: five teenagers ranging in age from 14 to 16, all African American or Latino, were charged with beating and raping a 28-year-old woman who was out jogging in New York City's Central Park. The victim's injuries were so severe that she was in a coma for 12 days. But the desire to give her justice was so strong that these five youths were charged with the crime on the scantest of evidence, including false confessions they gave after hours of interrogations without lawyers present.

Filmmaker Ava DuVernay dramatizes their story in this four-part Netflix miniseries that looked at the frenzy to arrest someone—anyone—in the wake of the attack. Future US President Donald Trump spent $85,000 to take out full-page newspaper ads calling for the return of the death penalty in the case.

DuVernay, who previously delivered the definitive cinematic portrayal of Martin Luther King Jr. in *Selma*, balances the larger social ramifications with an intimate, suspenseful portrait of what it would be like to be a teenager and seemingly have the whole world against you.

Jharrel Jerome won an Emmy for his portrayal of Korey Wise, the one member of "The Central Park Five" who was tried as an adult.

The performances of everyone else involved drew critical acclaim as well, including Felicity Huffman as prosecutor Linda Fairstein, who seemingly led the charge for swift justice.

DuVernay follows the case over decades as a chance prison encounter with the real perpetrator leads to a dramatic turn in the story of the Central Park Five—now The Exonerated Five. The result is a chilling indictment of how systemic biases not only undermine justice, but lead to two wrongs that don't make a right.

> **"***I decided to firmly root the story in the men's voices and their stories.***"**
>
> **Ava DuVernay** (Creator)

CREATOR: Ava DuVernay
PRODUCTION CO: Forward Movement, Harpo Films, Participant, Tribeca Productions

HALT AND CATCH FIRE

DRAMA • 2014
RATED: TV-14 • 60 MINS

Imagine *Mad Men*, but for the computer age. This drama set in the 1980s and early '90s charts the personalities who drove the computer revolution and the birth of the internet.

How did we go from computers being the preserve of NASA and huge companies to nearly every home having a PC? This drama shows how, as seen through the eyes of an entrepreneur (Lee Pace), a computer engineer (Scoot McNairy), and a technology prodigy (Mackenzie Davis). Reflecting the actual shift in the development of computers, the first two seasons of *Halt and Catch Fire* are set in Dallas-Fort Worth—the "Silicon Prairie"—while the last two move the action to the Silicon Valley of the San Francisco Bay Area.

The series dramatizes just how rapidly computers changed every aspect of our lives, even as it inspires chuckles with its depictions of early antivirus software, web browsers, and search engines.

THE ROYAL HOUSE OF WINDSOR

DOCUMENTARY • 2017
RATED: NR • 45 MINS

Many actors have played Britain's royals over the years, but none are as interesting as the real people. Rare archive footage puts them in a new light.

Built around never-before-seen footage and talking-head interviews, this century-spanning series examines the British royal family from their rebranding as the House of Windsor from the House of Saxe-Coburg and Gotha amid profound anti-German sentiment during World War I all the way up to Kate and Wills.

A lot of the expected beats are there: the abdication of Edward VIII, Diana, the "*annus horribilis.*" Over six episodes, it also explores how much of a threat to tradition Prince Philip was seen as being, and how much Prince Charles—who comes across as a Berkeley radical with the manners of an 18th-century gentleman—intends to shake up the monarchy as king.

THE TOYS THAT MADE US

DOCUMENTARY • 2017
RATED: TV-14 • 46 MINS

How did LEGO bricks first come about? And why have *Star Wars* toys always been more popular than *Star Trek* ones? You'll learn more than you thought possible about your beloved playthings.

Over three seasons and counting, this Netflix documentary series dives deep into the toys you probably grew up with. It explores how they came about, and why they inspire such enduring affection. Each episode is devoted to just one line of toys, and while some are obvious—Barbie, He-Man, G.I. Joe—it's easy to forget just how much merchandising also reinforced the TV success of the likes of *Teenage Mutant Ninja Turtles* and *Power Rangers*.

Insights abound—who knew that the original colors chosen for LEGO bricks were based on those found in the paintings of Dutch modernist Piet Mondrian? If you packed away your childhood toys, this may make you want to pull them out of the attic again.

THE WATER MARGIN

PERIOD DRAMA • 1973 • RATED: 15 (UK) • 45 MINS • SEASONS: 2
ATSUO NAKAMURA, SANAE TSUCHIDA, KEI SATÔ

There had never been anything like it before: 26 episodes of Japanese television dubbed into English. When *The Water Margin* aired over three months in the 1970s, it was like opening a window to another world.

Talk about a multicultural project. In 1973 Japan's Nippon TV set out to adapt 14th-century masterpiece *The Water Margin*, one of the so-called Four Great Classical Novels of Chinese literature. Attributed to author Shi Nai'an, it tells the epic tale of 108 outlaws who gather their forces and build a huge army.

> **"***Nine dozen heroes and one wicked man.***"**
>
> (S1 E1 title)

In exchange for clemency from the emperor, the outlaws agree to use their army to defend against rebellion and foreign incursion. The novel thus becomes a nationalist statement about the importance of bending the knee to government authority. However, it's no unquestioning authoritarian manifesto: the "nine dozen heroes" run up against a government official who serves as the story's primary antagonist.

The series' broadcast on the BBC three years after it was made introduced the tale to many in the English-speaking world for the first time. Nippon TV's production features an all-Japanese cast playing the legendary Chinese characters. Yet it maintains the sweep and complexity of the source material, with philosophical quotes peppered throughout such as "Do not despise the snake for having no horns, for who is to say it will not become a dragon?"

AROUND THE WORLD IN 80 DAYS

DOCUMENTARY • 1989
RATED: TV-PG • 49 MINS

Monty Python star Michael Palin takes on a timed circumnavigation of the globe more than 100 years after Jules Verne published *Around the World in 80 Days*.

The French author unveiled his adventure classic in 1872. More than a century later, was it still possible to replicate the journey its hero

Phileas Fogg undertakes? Forgoing air travel and other post-1872 conveniences, Palin sets off to find out. The resulting seven-part BBC series is built around some startling connections with the people he encounters along the way. In one beautiful moment aboard the dhow taking him across the Indian Ocean, he lets an older crewman rock out to Bruce Springsteen on his cassette player.

Palin begins his quest from London's Reform Club, just like Fogg, with the goal being to end it there. Does he succeed before the 80 days are up? Why not find out for yourself?

CHASING THE MOON

DOCUMENTARY • 2019
RATED: TV-PG • 108 MINS

How did the US go from losing out to the USSR in the race to launch the first satellite in 1957 to putting a man on the moon 12 years later? Archive footage here shows how.

First broadcast as part of PBS's *American Experience* anthology series, this three-episode film shows the journey that thousands of scientists, mathematicians, engineers, politicians, and, of course, astronauts undertook to put a human being on the moon. What's extraordinary is the amount of archival footage NASA shot that had never been seen before this series.

The images tell the story, from the years of failure at the start of the US's journey into space, to the *Apollo 1* disaster that killed three astronauts in a fire on the launchpad, and finally the moon landing itself on July 20, 1969. *Chasing the Moon* also spends time examining the landing's cultural impact—how it made the world believe anything was possible.

MASTERS OF SEX

DRAMA • 2013
RATED: TV-MA • 60 MINS

William Masters and Virginia Johnson were pioneering researchers of human sexuality. This '50s and '60s-set drama shows just how much thought they gave to what goes on between the sheets.

Want an even sexier *Mad Men?* Michael Sheen and Lizzy Caplan have palpable chemistry as two scientists who greatly advanced our understanding of sex. Sheen's Masters was always a tweedy professor, but Caplan's Johnson was a nightclub singer before switching to the laboratory life. His perspective—clinical, remote—matched with her free-wheeling carnality make for a potent will-they-won't-they combination throughout the series' four seasons.

The show is notable for its attention to accuracy, which is impressive considering its production designers even found drawings of period condoms and sex toys hard to find—that's how taboo they were. A show not to watch with your parents!

TREME

DRAMA • 2010
RATED: TV-MA • 60 MINS

How did New Orleans recover from the devastation wrought by Hurricane Katrina in 2005? *The Wire* **creator David Simon shows how, in this panoramic portrait of a city's recovery.**

What *The Wire* (see p320) did for Baltimore, *Treme* does for New Orleans. The show begins a few months after Hurricane Katrina, as many in the city are wondering how to proceed in the wake of the destruction. Among others, the series follows a bar owner (Khandi Alexander), a jazz musician (Rob Brown), a chef (Kim Dickens), a civil rights lawyer (Melissa Leo), and a professor (John Goodman).

Over four seasons, these characters experience tragedies and triumphs—you'll love the moment Goodman tosses the microphone of a journalist questioning whether New Orleans is even worth rebuilding into the water—and show how everyone in a great city is connected. *Treme* is the kind of series that reminds you we're all in this together.

CIVILISATIONS

DOCUMENTARY • 2018 • RATED: TV-14 • 60 MINS • SEASONS: 1
SIMON SCHAMA, MARY BEARD, DAVID OLUSOGA

Kenneth Clark's 1969 series *Civilisation* was one of the most influential TV documentaries ever broadcast. Its update a half-century later expands the view of art history even further.

What's the earliest known example of human artistic creation? Host Simon Schama, the famed British historian, offers up one possibility in the opening moments of *Civilisations*: a dagger with a jagged pattern on it found in Spain and presumed to be more than 70,000 years old.

That's just the start of a monumental foray into art history and how the things we create fuel the idea of civilization, our beliefs, and our idea of the self, from distant antiquity all the way to the near-present. In subsequent installments, Mary Beard and David Olusoga take over presenting duties for what continue to feel like the most fascinating college lectures you've ever heard—but in TV episode form.

The original *Civilisation* looked primarily at Western art. However, *Civilisations* takes a wider gaze, looking at artistic traditions around the world and devoting an installment to the impact of imperialism and colonialism on our understanding of culture.

The show was heavily re-edited for broadcast on PBS in the US—with actor Liev Schreiber added as a narrator. But even like that, it remains a font of knowledge, if less true to its creators' original intentions.

> **"***Let the exhilaration, the disturbance, the power, and the beauty sink in.***"**
>
> **Simon Schama** (cohost)

NOW HEAR THIS

DOCUMENTARY • 2019
RATED: TV-PG • 56 MINS

You know classical music masterpieces such as Vivaldi's *The Four Seasons* and Handel's *Messiah*? This show tells you exactly why they matter and how it is they've endured.

Scott Yoo, the telegenic conductor of the Mexico City Philharmonic, takes you to the places where classical masterworks were created and shares how they came to be.

Just why is Bach so foundational? A visit to Leipzig helps put his life in context. And on a trip to Venice, Yoo interviews a historian who just rediscovered a piece by Vivaldi lost for centuries.

But each episode of *Now Hear This* is much more than just liner notes in TV form. You'll hear exquisite performances as well. One dazzling moment occurs in the Vivaldi episode when a pianist plays a melody from the Baroque master but transposed into the style of composers who have come since: Mozart, Liszt, and Bill Evans. Exquisite.

THE BLUES

DOCUMENTARY • 2003 • RATED: 15 (UK) • 60 MINS • SEASONS: 1
MARTIN SCORSESE, TAJ MAHAL, ALI FARKA TOURÉ

Intended as a counterpoint to Ken Burns' Jazz, this Martin Scorsese-produced documentary series never pretends to be like a series of classroom lectures. First and foremost, it wants you to listen to and feel the music.

Even the best documentaries usually prioritize the dispensing of information above film-making style. Scorsese wanted to change that with an anthology series in which a different filmmaker would lend their distinct personal aesthetic point of view to each installment. Wim Wenders gets cosmic, contrasting the relatively obscure life of Texas gospel blues artist Blind Willie Johnson with the fact that one of his songs was included on a record placed inside the *Voyager 1* space probe as a greeting to extraterrestrial life.

Eschewing the documentary format of all the other episodes, famed African American filmmaker Charles Burnett directs a narrative film about a young boy torn between gospel music and the blues. And Mike Figgis, Clint Eastwood, and Scorsese himself assume directing responsibilities for installments as well. The result is a prismatic view of blues music, which has shaped so many musical movements that have come since while remaining a distinct form unto itself.

The entire series is performance-led, meaning the act of listening to music gets priority over talking heads rambling on. And the roll call of artists is spectacular: Taj Mahal, B. B. King, Ali Farka Touré, and Ray Charles, among others.

> **"** *I can't imagine my life, or anyone else's, without music.* **"**
>
> **Martin Scorsese** ("Feel LIke Going Home")

MASTERWORKS

DOCUMENTARY • 1988
RATED: NR • 10 MINS

What if you had to pick just one defining masterpiece to represent one of the world's great museums and then study it closely? That's the idea behind this series of mini episodes.

Sometimes you can become more cultured not by looking wider but deeper. *Masterworks* suggests that spending time with one work of art can be more valuable than a survey. You'll explore Millais' *Ophelia*, Caspar Friedrich's *Sea of Ice*, and Rembrandt's *The Return of the Prodigal Son*. Each work comes from a different museum, though none are stereotypical choices: it's not the *Mona Lisa* for the Louvre but Andrea Mantegna's *Crucifixion of Christ*.

As the camera pans and zooms across these triumphs of visual culture, your eye is trained to appreciate the virtuosity of the brushstrokes, the attention to minute detail. *Masterworks* isn't a series about accumulating trivia; it's about adding pleasure to your life.

DOCUMENTARY NOW!

COMEDY • 2015
RATED: TV-14 • 23 MINS

There's nothing funnier than people who take themselves a little too seriously, and that's the case in these parodies of classic documentaries. This is the definition of smart comedy.

These sendups of classic documentaries are so good you don't even need to see the original films to get the jokes. If anything, *Documentary Now!* will inspire you to seek out the films they're making fun of and increase your media literacy. A roster of today's best comedians—Fred Armisen, John Mulaney, and Bill Hader—play spoofs of documentary subjects over three seasons.

If you've never seen *Grey Gardens*, about Jacqueline Kennedy's cousins who lived in squalor, there's a sendup here. Perhaps the best of all is the parody of *Marina Abramović: The Artist Is Present* with Cate Blanchett as a solipsistic performance artist committed to outlandish stunts. You'll laugh, and learn to think critically even about nonfiction.

THE JOY OF PAINTING

DOCUMENTARY • 1983
RATED: TV-G • 30 MINS • SEASONS: 31 • BOB ROSS

Not everyone can become a great painter, but everyone can learn to paint. That was the message of Bob Ross, the late public television host, whose show might be the best program ever to watch if you want to de-stress.

From 1983 to 1994, Bob Ross was a staple of public broadcasting, but it can be argued his fame only reached transcendent heights more than a decade after his death of lymphoma in 1995 with the advent of YouTube. In his show he'd create a painting upon a canvas in real time, imparting techniques viewers could use to conjure their own artworks, often of "little happy trees" or "happy clouds." Each episode—and hundreds of them aired—was a quiet affair, with Ross dispensing pearls of wisdom in a hushed tone, such as, "And there's no secret to this. Anybody can paint. All you need is a dream in your heart and a little practice."

The popularity of Ross has skyrocketed in the years after his death. His presence is inherently welcoming and kind, and his subtle words of encouragement have taken on new life on the internet, where a dense repository of moments from his show, along with full episodes, exists.

> **"** *Let's paint several little happy trees.* **"**
>
> **Bob Ross** (host)

THE CIRCLE

REALITY TV • 2018
RATED: TV-MA • 49 MINS

Think you've got what it takes to be a social-media influencer? This game show puts contestants' thumbs to the test to see if they can win people over through their digital prowess alone.

This British series began with a group of contestants willing to sequester themselves in a block of apartments in London (Salford for Season 2), but only interact digitally—

they never meet in person. Instead they have to learn all they can about each other via the profiles they create online—which could all be just lies—before rating each other from most to least popular. It all sounds somewhat similar to the fictional *Black Mirror* (see p470) episode "Nosedive," which aired two years before.

The two-season series shows how most reality competitions are just popularity contests, and serves as a metaphor for the disconnect between what happens online and IRL*.
*"In real life" for you "olds."

TIDYING UP WITH MARIE KONDO

REALITY TV • 2019
RATED: TV-PG • 40 MINS

Most of us could stand a good declutter, but few have the organization skills, willpower, or cult following of Japanese tidiness expert Marie Kondo.

It's Marie Kondo's world, we're just living in it. She became a pop-culture sensation following this one-season instructional series about how

to make the spaces we live in a little more harmonious. Her advice may seem a tad draconian to some—she's not a fan of keeping lots of books that have sat around for years unread—but if you have a pile of odds and ends taking up so much room in your garage that you can't park your car, she's the one to call.

Kondo assists new parents, empty-nesters, and college students, among others. She is guided by her beliefs and her own "KonMari" aesthetic: the idea you should only save that which gives you joy.

WHO DO YOU THINK YOU ARE?

DOCUMENTARY • 2004
RATED: NR • 60 MINS

Do you know exactly where you come from? This BBC series puts your beliefs to the test and maps family trees down to branches you couldn't imagine.

The 21st-century trend of people investigating their own genealogies owes much of its life to this long-running series. In each episode, the

family history of a different celebrity comes under the microscope: Stephen Fry, Gurinder Chadha, and Nigella Lawson were among the first to put their lineages to the test. But it is *EastEnders* star Danny Dyer whose family tree perhaps most impresses, revealing royal roots.

The show proved so popular that nearly 20 countries created their own versions. In the US, the spin-off even spawned an imitator: a slightly different series on public broadcasting called *Finding Your Roots with Henry Louis Gates Jr.* The UK original remains the longest running, with 17 seasons and several specials.

FEUD

DRAMA • 2017 • RATED: TV-MA • 45 MINS • SEASONS: 1
SUSAN SARANDON, JESSICA LANGE, CATHERINE ZETA-JONES

Don't go into this expecting one long catfight. Ryan Murphy's miniseries is heavy on the barbed bon mots, but ultimately examines the forces that pit powerful women against each other.

The fact that Bette Davis and Joan Crawford disliked each other is well known by fans of Old Hollywood. How they exploited their tabloid-fueled conflict to stage a late career revival is the subject of this Ryan Murphy miniseries. The eight episodes center on the making of *Whatever Happened to Baby Jane?*, the horror film about aging sisters (who are also feuding) who live together in gothic misery until one of them descends into madness and murderousness.

Susan Sarandon is a cool, whip-smart Bette Davis, while Jessica Lange plays a conniving Joan Crawford, the subject of the infamous movie *Mommie Dearest*. But Murphy doesn't perpetuate that film's popular, and disputed, version of events, which included a depiction of Crawford abusing her children; instead, he paints a more well-rounded Crawford, ultimately making her the heart of the series.

The result is a sad, sympathetic view of what Hollywood does to women that offers more than just a cackling good time. That said, Catherine Zeta-Jones's Olivia de Havilland is certainly played for laughs—spawning a libel lawsuit from the centenarian de Havilland that was dismissed in court. *Feud* ultimately reveals a slice of Hollywood history that's far too close to present realities for comfort.

> **"** *You mean all this time we could have been friends?* **"**
>
> **Bette Davis** (S1 E8)

THE STORY OF FILM

DOCUMENTARY • 2011
RATED: 15 (UK) • 60 MINS

There's so much more to cinema than Hollywood. In over 15 hours, film critic Mark Cousins presents a sweeping history, with an emphasis on how moviemaking has always been global.

How did the movies become "the movies?" That's the question the Northern Irish film critic addresses in this groundbreaking documentary looking at the development of the defining art form of the past century. Cousins kicks things off on a poetic note: to demonstrate how one visual idea can evolve over time and in the hands of different directors, he shows how the image of bubbles in a coffee cup was used by Carol Reed, then Jean-Luc Godard, and, finally, Martin Scorsese.

From the very specific he moves toward the expansive, presenting a global view of film history. For Cousins, who narrates the entire series in hushed tones, the canon of classic film has been racist and sexist by omission. This series corrects that.

FIVE CAME BACK

DOCUMENTARY • 2017
RATED: TV-14 • 60 MINS

They were among the most successful Hollywood directors ever. But during World War II they put their careers and their lives on the line to serve a higher cause.

Frank Capra, William Wyler, George Stevens, John Huston, and John Ford directed some of Hollywood's most beloved movies—*Gunga Din* and *The Maltese Falcon*, among so many others.

When the US entered World War II, they volunteered their filmmaking skills to the fight. Each made movies showing the evil of fascism and the struggle of ordinary soldiers. This documentary chronicles their wartime work.

They risked life and limb: Ford filmed the Battle of Midway and also shot color footage of D-Day itself that is now apparently lost. The experience changed the direction of their careers as well. After the war, their newfound ways of seeing the world inspired Wyler to make *The Best Years of Our Lives* and Capra to make *It's a Wonderful Life*.

MOGULS AND MOVIE STARS

DOCUMENTARY • 2010
RATED: NR • 60 MINS

The studio founders who built Hollywood came from nothing. They fled persecution and poverty, but in following the American Dream they created the ultimate fantasy factory.

The lives of the studio heads in Hollywood of the 1920s, '30s, and '40s, were as colorful as the characters in any of the films they made. There's larger than life Louis B. Mayer,

cofounder of MGM, who made some of the most lavish and lush of all Hollywood movies, but whose relentless drive set some of his stars, including Judy Garland, on self-destructive paths. And just who were the Warner brothers, you might ask? Over seven hours you'll find out.

This documentary series was produced by the Turner Classic Movies TV channel, which has done a remarkable job of raising awareness of older films from Hollywood and around the world. *Moguls and Movie Stars* is one of the network's finest achievements.

HISTOIRE(S) DU CINEMA

DOCUMENTARY • 1989
RATED: 18 (UK) • 27 MINS

Jean-Luc Godard is considered one of the greatest filmmakers of all time, but what are the films that inspire him? This documentary-essay series explores his own favorites.

Like an even more poetic version of Mark Cousins' *The Story of Film* (see p314), French New Wave master Godard cobbles together a very personal journey through some of the

films he loves the most, many of which inspired his own work. Blurring the line between documentary, TV series, and video essay, *Histoire(s) du Cinema* first aired on French and Swiss television.

Though the first two episodes were broadcast in 1989, it took until 1997 and 1998 for Godard to finish the other six installments. More than anything, it's a triumph of editing: most of it is comprised of clips from hundreds of films—*Bicycle Thieves*, *Scarface*, and *Rear Window*, among them—letting the sounds and images say all that needs to be said.

QI

COMEDY GAME SHOW • 2003 • RATED: TV-PG • 30 MINS • SEASONS: 17
SANDI TOKSVIG, ALAN DAVIES, STEPHEN FRY

This comedic quiz may not have the most competitive spirit, but you're unlikely to learn more moment-by-moment on any other show. And with its rotating lineup of hilarious panelists, *QI* guarantees laughter.

Not only do its questions often border on the impossible, the BBC's trivia show is happy to skirt the edges of respectability. On *Jeopardy!* (see p317) you probably won't be asked how far germs can travel if a person vomits in an open space, but you may on *QI*, followed by an in-studio regurgitation demonstration from a prop named "Vomiting Larry."

> **"** We all agree that nobody in this universe understands *QI*'s scoring system.**"**
>
> **Stephen Fry** (S1 E2)

It's not winner-takes-all like usual game shows, but a contest of egos and wits in which points are doled out and taken away (to the sound of a klaxon alarm) based on whim more than logic. On occasions, the studio audience can even be declared the "winner" or suffer defeat, as when they sing the wrong lyrics to the German national anthem.

You're always guaranteed to learn something watching *QI*—whether it's about how airlines reduce weight to save money (down to their favoring white paint over heavier dark paint), or how early Portuguese king Peter I exhumed the body of his mistress so she could undergo a coronation to become his queen. And, like that one, you'll learn some things you wish you could forget, too.

Part quiz program, part improv comedy, *QI* devotes each season to the exploration of minutiae related to a single letter of the alphabet. (As of March 2020, the series was on Season Q, with episodes devoted to "Queens" and "Quantity and Quality," among others.) Stephen Fry was the original host, with Sandi Toksvig taking over in 2016; their duty is to pose trivia questions to permanent guest Alan Davies and a rotating group of comic panelists, whose answers often take the conversation to unexpected and hilarious places.

CREATOR: John Lloyd
PRODUCTION CO: Talkback Thames

JEOPARDY!

GAME SHOW • 1964 • RATED: TV-G • 22 MINS
SEASONS: 36 • ALEX TREBEK

Remember to always respond in the form of a question! So if *Jeopardy!* is the "answer," what you surely need to ask is: "What is the most successful quiz show of all time?"

Jeopardy! isn't just the single greatest repository of pub-quiz facts for 30 minutes each and every night in the US, it's often what Americans enjoy watching while they sit with a beer at their local bar. Each episode features three contestants, who choose from 30 questions divided into six categories and then repeat the process in a second round, before making a last wager with their winnings in a single-answer Final Jeopardy showdown. This rapid-fire trivia-based game show is an American institution.

In fact, a prime-time edition airing in early 2020 that reunited some of its most successful former players for a "Greatest of All Time" match drew the kind of massive ratings almost unheard-of for broadcast television in this age of streaming. Old episodes of *Jeopardy!* now appear on Netflix.

Canadian American presenter Alex Trebek has steered each show since 1984—there's "The Moustache Era" and "The Post-Moustache Era" in Trebek's long hosting—until his unfortunate cancer diagnosis in 2019 put his long-term future on the show in doubt. One thing that will remain everlasting is the theme song "Think!," which plays while contestants write down their Final Jeopardy response. It's so well known that its composer, show creator Merv Griffin, claimed he earned $70 million in royalties from it.

TOP WINNING STREAKS

KEN JENNINGS (2004)
74 GAMES

JAMES HOLZHAUER (2019)
32 GAMES

JULIA COLLINS (2014)
20 GAMES

JASON ZUFFRANIERI (2019)
19 GAMES

DAVID MADDEN (2005)
19 GAMES

MATT JACKSON (2015)
13 GAMES

AUSTIN ROGERS (2017)
12 GAMES

SETH WILSON (2016)
12 GAMES

ARTHUR CHU (2014)
11 GAMES

Successful *Jeopardy!* contestants are defined by their speed—many argue that a fast thumb that can "buzz in" with the clicker on answers is as crucial as getting your response right—and their strategizing—how you wager your previous winnings on Daily Doubles and during Final Jeopardy separates the merely smart from champions. There's a little Vegas-style gambling strategy needed in addition to your trivia knowledge. Long may *Jeopardy!* tease our brains and bruise contestants' thumbs.

ESCAPE AT DANNEMORA

PRISON THRILLER • 2018
RATED: TV-MA • 60 MINS

It was one of the most daring prison breaks in recent US history—and it was all enabled by the escapees' alleged romance with a prison worker.

In 2015, convicted murderers Richard Matt and David Sweat escaped from an upstate New York prison and a massive manhunt followed. It was revealed later that an employee of the prison helped them escape.

Ben Stiller directs this dramatization, with Benicio del Toro and Paul Dano playing Matt and Sweat, respectively.

But the true standout is Patricia Arquette as Joyce, the woman who enabled their flight and ended up in prison herself. Arquette won a Golden Globe award for her performance, which reveals her character's swirling emotions and complex motivations over the seven-episode series. Her real-life inspiration has criticized the portrayal in which she is depicted as having intimate relationships with the convicts, an allegation which she firmly denies.

ALIAS GRACE

HISTORICAL DRAMA • 2017
RATED: TV-MA • 60 MINS

This adaptation of author Margaret Atwood's surreally dystopian account of the real-life Grace Marks, who was convicted of two murders in 1843, is both a gripping psychodrama and a compelling history of Canadian life.

After she was sent away for the murders, Marks, a poor immigrant to Canada from Ireland, was hauled out of prison and put on display for various dignitaries in the government house of the city of Kingston (in present-day Ontario). Played by Sarah Gadon, she is a compelling, unknowable figure whom you can't help but empathize with. Much of this six-episode miniseries is dedicated to Marks's interviews with psychologist Dr. Simon Jordan (Edward Holcroft), as he tries to figure her out.

This is a feast of Canadian talent: each episode is written by *Stories We Tell* auteur Sarah Polley and directed by *American Psycho* filmmaker Mary Harron. And master director David Cronenberg even plays a clergyman.

THE KEEPERS

CRIME DOCUMENTARY • 2017
RATED: TV-MA • 60 MINS

It's a 50-year-old cold case only kept open through the efforts of a few friends and a dogged reporter. Who killed Sister Cathy? This documentary miniseries attempts to find out.

In November 1969, Sister Cathy Cesnik, a nun and English teacher at Baltimore's Archbishop Keough High School, suddenly disappeared after she said she was going out to buy an engagement present for her sister. Her body was discovered in the woods several months later, clearly hidden by her killer.

For decades the case went nowhere, and by the mid-2010s, only a couple of her old students, now senior citizens, were keeping the inquiry going. Filmmaker Ryan White interviews family, ex-pupils, friends, journalists, and others to try to uncover what happened. *The Keepers* links Sister Cathy's death to a priest at the school: it's alleged he may have been connected to her death after she discovered his pattern of sexual abuse. But is this the end of the case?

MCMILLION$

CRIME DOCUMENTARY• 2020
RATED: TV-14 • 60 MINS

The most beloved McDonald's promotion every couple of years is its peel-off sticker-based Monopoly game. For over a decade, someone found a way to rig it and win millions.

If this were a fictional crime drama, it'd be laughed out of cinemas for being too far-fetched. But it's all true, down to its extremely colorful cast of personalities. The six-part documentary begins with the Jacksonville financial office of the FBI, which discovered that a number of the winners of the popular McDonald's Monopoly game were related—suggesting a conspiracy to win the game, and its massive prize money, fraudulently.

At one point, an FBI agent meets with representatives of McDonald's wearing a bright yellow suit to pay tribute to the chain's famous Golden Arches—you'd never believe it if it happened in fiction! The focus then shifts to the people who set up the scheme, which was far-ranging and was said to involve the mafia.

PISTORIUS

CRIME DOCUMENTARY • 2018
RATED: 18 (UK) • 60 MINS

He was an inspiration to a nation: a double amputee who competed at the Olympics and took the popularity of the Paralympics to new heights. Now he's a convicted murderer.

This four-part documentary begins on a rousing note with the story of the South African sprinter known as "The Blade Runner," who competed against able-bodied athletes at the 2012 Olympics and became one of the most successful Paralympians of all time. His popularity transcended race and other barriers. But just months after his Games success, Oscar Pistorius killed his girlfriend by shooting her four times.

Was this a horrible accident, as Pistorius claimed? Or cold-blooded murder? This series tracks the case across his trial and appeal—an initial verdict was considered so lenient that the South African state handed down a lengthier sentence—and delves deep into what led to this tragic event.

WHO KILLED LITTLE GREGORY?

CRIME DOCUMENTARY • 2019
RATED: 15 (UK) • 60 MINS

It's the unsolved murder that's puzzled France for decades. In 1984, a young child was found dead—and his father claimed he knew who killed him.

Four-year-old Grégory Villemin was found dead on October 16, 1984—drowned in a river, with his hands and feet bound.

For three years prior to the death, his family had received mysterious threatening letters and phone calls from someone who called him or herself "The Crow." The day after the little boy's murder, the family received a letter from "The Crow" saying, "I have taken vengeance."

Netflix's five-part documentary account of the case brings the case nearly up to the present day, and it is no understatement to say that the twists and turns in this story are about as shocking as they could get. "The Crow" knew so much about the Villemins ... was he or she actually one of them?

319

THE WIRE

CRIME DRAMA • 2002 • RATED: TV-MA • 60 MINS • SEASONS: 5
MICHAEL K. WILLIAMS, IDRIS ELBA, LANCE REDDICK

In the film *It's a Disaster*, the world is coming to an end and one of the characters is lamenting all the great works of art they'll miss. "All of those things are overrated," another responds. "Except for *The Wire.*"

The greatness of *The Wire* is so obvious it has become a punchline. It is to TV what *Sgt. Pepper's Lonely Hearts Club Band* is to pop music or what *Citizen Kane* is to cinema. *The Chicago Tribune* has said that it gives "rewards not unlike those for readers who conquer Joyce, Faulkner, or Henry James." Former President Barack Obama has called it his favorite TV show of all time. Jón Gnarr, the comedian and former mayor of Reykjavík, said that he would not enter a coalition government with anyone who had not watched it.

So yes, *The Wire* is highly acclaimed. But that could make it sound like homework: don't hold its greatness against it. This is the thrilling, bracingly alive story of a city—Baltimore—and the cops, criminals, kingpins, and politicians who run it. The series begins with a first season that is a murder mystery centered on the cops investigating the crime (Dominic West and Lance Reddick), a drug-dealing gang, and a stickup man named Omar Little (Michael K. Williams) who lives his life "one day at a time" robbing drug dealers.

> **"***All in the game yo, all in the game.***"**
>
> Omar Little (S1 E13)

Its panoramic view of the city expands with each new installment. Season 2 shifts much of the action to the docks and its struggling workers, whose lives have been negatively

CREATOR: David Simon
PRODUCTION CO: Blown Deadline Productions, Home Box Office (HBO)

THE WIRE LOCATIONS

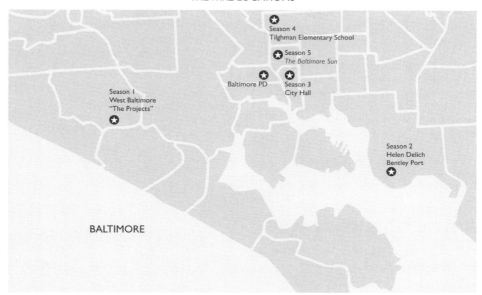

affected by corporate America. Season 3 introduces the politicians who lead Baltimore, including the man who will become the city's mayor (Aidan Gillen). Season 4 focuses on the underfunded public school system, while Season 5 looks at the news media, particularly the reporters of *The Baltimore Sun* newspaper.

That last season comes directly from the experience of *The Wire's* creator, David Simon. Before producing acclaimed TV dramas, he worked as a crime reporter for *The Baltimore Sun* himself, and the knowledge he gained there lends a particular degree of authenticity throughout the show.

"It's about how institutions have an effect on individuals," Simon says of *The Wire* on the commentary track for the episode "The Target." Later, he would elaborate on that idea in a Q&A with fans on HBO's website. He says, "We are not selling hope, or audience gratification, or cheap victories with this show. *The Wire* is making an argument about what institutions—bureaucracies, criminal

enterprises, the cultures of addiction, raw capitalism even—do to individuals. It is not designed purely as an entertainment. It is, I'm afraid, a somewhat angry show."

Omar Little, based on a real-life criminal turned anti-crime crusader named Donnie Andrews, has since become regarded as a kind of urban folk hero. And a star was born in Michael K. Williams, with viewers thrilled by the elaborate stings Little staged to entrap and rob Baltimore's worst, his repetitive singing of *A-Hunting We Will Go*, and his motto: "A man's gotta have a code." Williams went on to repeat that very line and parody Omar Little on cult comedy *Community* (see p212).

The Wire went beyond even *The Sopranos*, (see p341) in its ability to entertain and impress with its writing, its characterizations, and its profoundly visual storytelling. But more than just a work of art, it is a window into an inner-city life far removed from the clichés of TV crime dramas.

MAKING A MURDERER

CRIME DOCUMENTARY • 2015
RATED: TV-14 • 60 MINS

This is a Kafkaesque look at how structural deficiencies and personality-driven biases can lead to injustice in US courts of law. It will leave you hoping you are never at the mercy of an unjust justice system.

A chill will be sent up your spine as you see how Wisconsin man Steven Avery is convicted of a rape charge in 1985 and spends 18 years in prison partly because his first cousin didn't like him and was married to a sheriff's deputy capable of arranging his arrest. When finally released, he was charged with murder in a completely unrelated case.

Regardless of whether you think Avery is innocent or guilty, you'll be riveted by this two-season, 20-episode look into some truly shocking procedural deficiencies in the US law system. This sensation of a documentary is, as series codirector Moira Demos puts it, less a "whodunnit" than a "howdunnit."

HITLER: THE RISE OF EVIL

HISTORICAL DRAMA • 2003
RATED: 12 (UK) • 120 MINS

He personifies evil. But thinking of Hitler as just a monster ignores how it is possible for others to be capable of equal monstrosity. That's the premise driving this historical miniseries.

Robert Carlyle portrays Adolf Hitler from the end of World War I through his rise within the ranks of the Nazi Party to his appointment as German Chancellor in 1933. He doesn't portray him as an implacable force but as a rather unremarkable individual—one scene shows him taking inspiration for his moustache from silent-film star Charlie Chaplin—all the better to show how a mediocrity like Hitler could rise again.

The two-part miniseries also follows journalist Fritz Gerlich (Matthew Modine), who dies in the Dachau concentration camp, and Ernst Hanfstaengl (Liev Schreiber), who becomes a close friend of Hitler and turns the sports team songs he wrote while a student at Harvard into Nazi and Hitler Youth anthems.

MINDHUNTER

CRIME THRILLER • 2017
RATED: TV-MA • 60 MINS

Can you get inside the mind of a killer? This slick procedural thriller shows you the first attempts to do just that, with the development of criminal behavior studies in the 1970s.

Jonathan Groff stars as special agent Holden Ford in the FBI's behavioral science unit in this Netflix drama from British playwright and screenwriter Joe Penhall. In the 1970s, as cases of serial killers dramatically rise, Ford tries to explain the perpetrator's crimes with psychology. The horrors they unleash can't be explained in the same way that those of gangsters, drug lords, and bank robbers can.

David Fincher, who directed one of the most intricate true-crime procedural films of all time in *Zodiac*, brings his precise eye to several episodes in both seasons of *Mindhunter*, along with other first-class directors such as Asif Kapadia and Andrew Dominik. Though a lightly fictionalized account of actual events, its horrors are very real.

MANHUNT: UNABOMBER

THRILLER • 2017
RATED: TV-14 • 60 MINS

The Unabomber killer was responsible for nearly a bombing a year in the US between 1978 and 1995. This is a thrilling account of his capture.

Ted Kaczynski, nicknamed the Unabomber, was a Harvard-educated mathematician who became the youngest tenured professor of math ever at the University of California, Berkeley. He also began a campaign of bombings by sending explosives to victims in packages via the mail. Three people died as a result of his devices, and 23 others were injured.

This historical dramatization, unfolding over eight episodes, stars Paul Bettany as Kaczynski, with Sam Worthington as Jim Fitzgerald, the FBI agent who doggedly pursued him. Season 2 of *Manhunt*, subtitled *Deadly Games*, looks at the 1996 Olympic Park bombing in Atlanta, Georgia, and the media frenzy surrounding the security guard wrongly accused of the attack, Richard Jewell.

CONVERSATIONS WITH A KILLER

CRIME DOCUMENTARY • 2019
RATED: TV-MA • 60 MINS

Ted Bundy is the most notorious serial killer ever and one of the most baffling. Not only handsome and a good son, he also lived an otherwise normal life.

That the US press spent so much of their coverage talking about how handsome Ted Bundy was shows what a strange place he occupied in the American psyche: the underlying subtext always was, how could someone that good-looking be such a deviant?

This compelling four-episode documentary series from Joe Berlinger lets Bundy speak for himself through his prison recordings, and the result is terrifying. The interviews are harrowing to listen to. Bundy describes his crimes in every grisly detail and explains the motivations that drove him to commit them. He calls himself, "the most cold-hearted son of a bitch you'll ever meet," and you won't disagree.

THE JINX: THE LIFE AND DEATHS OF ROBERT DURST

CRIME DOCUMENTARY • 2015
RATED: TV-14 • 46 MINS

The millionaire had it all. But he left a string of bodies in his wake—literally. HBO's landmark documentary helped get him arrested and charged.

It's arguable that no series has caused a surge in popularity for true crime like *The Jinx*. In just six episodes, director Andrew Jarecki tells the story of the heir to a massive New York real-estate fortune, Robert Durst, whose life was marked by three mysterious deaths: the disappearance without a trace of his first wife in 1982, the execution-style murder of a friend, journalist Susan Berman, in 2000, and the murder and dismemberment of a neighbor in 2001.

On the day before the finale of *The Jinx* aired, Durst was arrested and charged with first-degree murder for Berman's death. But the final episode would hold an even more shocking revelation....

BIG LOVE

DRAMA • 2006
RATED: TV-MA • 60 MINS

They exist at the intersection of free love and religious fundamentalism: polygamists in the US had never been portrayed as anything but parodies or predators until this show.

Big Love shows two things can be true at the same time. First, that polygamy, as practiced by fundamentalist Mormons who've broken away from the mainstream Church of Latter Day Saints, is deeply unfair to women. Second, that those women are not necessarily the robotic Stepford Wives they're at times portrayed as.

Over five seasons, this HBO drama shows the complexity of that experience and provides a deep subjectivity to the women married to Bill Henrickson (Bill Paxton): Barb (Jeanne Tripplehorn), Nicky (Chloë Sevigny), and Margie (Ginnifer Goodwin). For what it's worth, women in polygamous marriages belonging to breakaway LDS sects told *The New York Times* in 2006 that they found the show accurate and sensitive.

BIKRAM: YOGI, GURU, PREDATOR

DOCUMENTARY • 2019
RATED: TV-MA • 90 MINS

He popularized an exercise craze that revolutionized wellness: yoga. He has also faced sexual assault and rape allegations which are explored in the documentary.

Bikram Choudhury is as responsible as anybody else for introducing yoga as a workout staple into the West. But though his success—and the millions he made—was very real, almost everything else, as revealed in this show by Eva Orner, was suspect. Even his yoga techniques were allegedly repackaged from Bishnu Charan Ghosh, under whom he claimed he'd studied.

The documentary also suggests Choudhury was an alleged serial predator who made unwanted advances against female students before fleeing the US to escape a civil court judgment, claims which are all denied by Choudhury. *Yogi, Guru, Predator* shows how through charm, bluster, and deception he was able to build his empire.

SURVIVING R. KELLY

DOCUMENTARY • 2019
RATED: TV-MA • 50 MINS

He produced some of the biggest pop hits of all time, but his catchy melodies and danceable grooves masked a dark accusation: the years of alleged sexual abuse he perpetrated, allegations which he has denied.

This six-part documentary series, built largely around the testimonials of women who say Kelly abused them or allege they witnessed his abuse, was a sensation when it aired over three nights in January 2019, pulling in some of the largest ratings that women-focused TV channel Lifetime has ever received.

Kelly is the R&B superstar behind *I Believe I Can Fly* and *Ignition (Remix)*. He's also been repeatedly accused of sexual relationships with underage girls, including with the late R&B star Aaliyah when she was 15, claims he has denied. The series, which yielded a second season centered on the victims, may have helped force prosecutors to bring sex crimes charges against him.

DIRTY MONEY

DOCUMENTARY • 2018
RATED: TV-14 • 60 MINS

Is greed good? This anthology series answers "No" with its scathing look at white-collar misdeeds—including alleged cases from within President Trump's inner circle.

Corporate scandals are more rampant than you might think. Over two seasons, this anthology explores the dark side of capitalism, from HSBC's alleged involvement in money laundering for Hezbollah, to the Volkswagen emissions scandal, the Wells Fargo account fraud scandal, and even the allegedly suspect deals made by Donald Trump himself.

That episode about the US president ends Season 1, and one of its most notable Season 2 installments is about his son-in-law, Jared Kushner, an episode titled "Slumlord Millionaire." That one shows the alleged predatory practices Kushner used to drain low-income families—often people of color—of what little financial resources they had.

THE LOUDEST VOICE

DRAMA • 2019
RATED: TV-MA • 50 MINS

No media figure had more influence on shaping American public discourse than Roger Ailes. This miniseries tells how he built the Fox News Empire and how it came crashing down.

Russell Crowe was unrecognizable when he transformed himself in order to play Roger Ailes, the founder of Fox News in this seven-episode miniseries, based on the book by Gabriel Sherman. Unlike the film *Bombshell*, which covered similar ground but focused more on the women, *The Loudest Voice* traces Ailes's rise to power and pivotal moments in his leadership of Fox News: 9/11, the 2004 election, and the 2016 campaign that propelled Donald Trump to the presidency.

Naomi Watts plays Gretchen Carlson, one of the news anchors whose sexual harassment allegations against Ailes brought him down, while Simon McBurney is Robert Murdoch, and *Family Guy* creator Seth MacFarlane is the network's spinmeister Brian Lewis.

THE STAIRCASE

CRIME DOCUMENTARY • 2004
RATED: TV-MA • 45 MINS

It seemed like an accident, but law enforcement quickly investigated it as a homicide. An acclaimed author's wife apparently fell down the stairs, or was she pushed?

It's rare that someone convicted of murder tells the story of their own case in such a detailed way, but that's what happens in this French docuseries (presented in English) about a notable author's trial and appeal. Did he do it? Through listening to him speak, Michael Peterson sure sounds innocent, as he presents a blow-by-blow account of what happened on the last day of his wife's life. But things are more complicated than they first seem.

His wife's death bears striking similarities to the fate of a friend of Peterson's years before. Did he think that was a convincing enough "accident" to arrange his wife's death himself? Though a jury found him guilty, the twists in this 13-episode series don't end there.

30 FOR 30

DOCUMENTARY • 2009 • RATED: NR • 60 MINS • SEASONS: 3
DONNIE WAHLBERG, ICE CUBE, STEVE JAMES

Think sports is more physical than intellectual? Think again. This long-running documentary anthology series uses athletics as a lens for viewing culture, society, and history—from Muhammad Ali's last fights to the strange saga of Tonya Harding.

Sports channel ESPN has produced dozens of high-quality documentaries over the past decade. These *30 for 30* films are filmmaker-driven, with some of the leading names in the documentary world involved. *Hoop Dreams's* auteur Steve James's installment, *No Crossover: The Trial of Allen Iverson*, typifies the series at its best. It uses an incident of apparently race-based violence from the early life of the NBA star to examine larger societal fault lines in the American South.

So named because it was originally intended to comprise 30 documentaries to celebrate ESPN's 30th anniversary (it has now far eclipsed that initial remit), *30 for 30* is never less than fascinating—and often it's challenging, too. One multi-episode, eight-hour documentary commissioned for the series titled *O. J.: Made in America* looked at the nation-spanning ramifications of the O. J. Simpson murder case and not only won numerous TV awards but also received the Oscar for best documentary feature. One side series especially worth exploring is *30 for 30: Soccer Stories*, which includes a damning film about the 1989 Hillsborough stadium tragedy.

> **"***There is no shortage from the incredible world of sports.***"**
>
> **Connor Schell** (cocreator)

THIS IS FOOTBALL

DOCUMENTARY • 2019
RATED: TV-14 • 60 MINS

For all the fanatical passions it rouses, is there anything that brings people together like soccer? This six-part series looks at the transformative power of what happens on the pitch.

Soccer is called "the beautiful game" (and "football" outside the US—hence, the show name), but this series doesn't focus solely on the preternatural skill of Ronaldo or Messi.

Unfolding over six episodes—each with a one-word theme as its title, such as "Redemption," "Belief," or "Chance"—it spans the globe. One episode takes a look at how soccer helped mend seemingly irreconcilable divides in Rwanda. Others examine England's "blind" soccer club, and explore the success of the Japanese women's soccer team following the devastating 2011 earthquake and tsunami.

And, of course, there's Iceland's fanatical devotion to its national team, Viking clap included. *This Is Football* is essential viewing for both obsessives and casual observers alike.

BASEBALL

DOCUMENTARY • 1994
RATED: TV-PG • 120 MINS

Ken Burns is one of the most beloved and important documentarians of all time. His 18-hour look at America's pastime is also the story of a nation.

Baseball may be America's "national pastime," but no one knows with absolute certainty when it officially began. Ken Burns ventures about as good a guess as anyone, telling the story of what some believe was the first recorded baseball game, in Cooperstown, New York, in 1839. From there, Burns shows how the sport evolved and digs into the lives of legends such as Ty Cobb, Babe Ruth, Jackie Robinson, Hank Aaron, and many more.

Over nine episodes (plus a 10th that aired in 2010), each two hours long (though several are longer), you get to see how the game has both reflected American history and pushed it forward—Robinson "breaking the color barrier" anticipated the American civil rights movement by a decade.

LOSERS

DOCUMENTARY • 2019
RATED: 15 (UK) • 30 MINS

There's the thrill of victory and the agony of defeat. This anthology series looks unflinchingly at the latter, showing how much can be learned from failure.

Football coach Vince Lombardi famously said "Winning isn't everything. It's the only thing." That mentality dominates sports. Over eight episodes, *Losers* shows how much value is to be found in failure. Canadian curling legend Pat Ryan shows how a terrible loss made him devise a new technique that changed the way the sport is played. French figure skater Surya Bonaly dazzled spectators with her backflips, but never found much success in competition, in part because being black in a (at the time) mostly white sport meant she wasn't judged fairly.

Losers's one and only season also features the story of a female dog sledder, an Olympian's struggle in a sandstorm during an endurance race, and the saga of Torquay soccer team.

REAL SPORTS WITH BRYANT GUMBEL

DOCUMENTARY • 1995
RATED: TV-PG • 60 MINS

How much do sports affect people's lives? This long-running series goes beyond the headlines to deliver serious investigative journalism.

Bryant Gumbel was one of the most famous TV journalists in America when he left hosting the popular *Today* show to pursue sports reporting and the creation of this series. It was a decision, Gumbel said, that was "spawned by the fact that sports have changed dramatically, that it's no longer just fun and games, and that what happens off the field, beyond the scores, is worthy of some serious reporting."

Countless awards have followed the series' groundbreaking work over 22 seasons and counting. This includes a report on the abuse suffered by south Asian youths forced into racing camels in the UAE, and research into football's head-injury epidemic. Gumbel shows sports isn't all fun and games.

THE CIVIL WAR

DOCUMENTARY • 1990
RATED: TV-14 • 69 MINS

Not many directors have a cinematic technique named after them: the "Ken Burns Effect" reached its perfect expression in this landmark series about the war that shaped America.

Burns had never before directed a documentary of this scale—11 hours and 30 minutes—but you'd never know it. The nine-episode film covers the four-year conflict that split the US, killed 600,000 Americans, and finally ended slavery, and does so with a profoundly personal dimension.

Burns makes wonderful use of voice-over actors, including Sam Waterston as Abraham Lincoln and Morgan Freeman as Frederick Douglass, to bring quotations from the participants to life. All the while, he employs his namesake pan-and-zoom effect to give greater dynamism to the 1860s photographs. It's never used better than during the reading of a touching letter written by Major Sullivan Ballou to his wife, just before he died.

THE WORLD AT WAR

DOCUMENTARY • 1973
RATED: TV-PG • 52 MINS

Laurence Olivier narrates this 22-hour documentary built around interviews with World War II figures. It was the most expensive factual TV series ever made at the time.

Assembled over four years at a then-unprecedented cost of $115 million, the 26 episodes aired once a week on ITV over six months. There's a massive amount of archival footage throughout, but most of the series is driven by interviews. Some of these are with famous names, including Karl Dönitz, the German admiral who signed the official surrender to the Allies, and Albert Speer, Hitler's chief architect. Even Hollywood actor Jimmy Stewart shows up to talk about the bombing missions he executed over Europe.

But the most revealing interviews are with some of the aides to key players. Himmler's attaché admits on camera that he witnessed a mass execution in his boss's presence. Few series are this historically valuable.

THE LOOMING TOWER

THRILLER • 2018
RATED: TV-MA • 50 MINS

What convergence of events allowed 9/11 to happen? This Hulu drama shows how internal squabbles in the US intelligence community led to tragedy.

A 10-episode miniseries based on Lawrence Wright's Pulitzer Prize-winning book about the lead-up to 9/11, *The Looming Tower* is suffused with a sense of dread. You know how it all ends but the journey there is revelatory.

Much of the drama centers on the head of the New York City-based FBI counterterrorism office, John O'Neill (Jeff Daniels), and one of his top agents, Ali Soufan (Tahar Rahim), who years later also led the charge against the US use of waterboarding.

As dramatized here, Soufan has claimed he might possibly have been able to stop the 9/11 attacks if the CIA had shared some of its critical intelligence with him and the FBI. You will see red at how so much red tape seemingly prevented saving so many lives.

THE GREAT WAR

DOCUMENTARY • 2017
RATED: TV-PG • 120 MINS

It was the war that reshaped Europe forever, toppling emperors and introducing technologies. As this *American Experience* docuseries shows, the First World War also turned the US into a great power.

PBS's long-running anthology series *American Experience* has presented documentaries of exceptionally high quality for years, and its examination of the First World War is no exception. It shows how President Woodrow Wilson tried to keep the country out of the conflict, but also, when US entry became inevitable after the sinking of the *Lusitania*, he hired writer George Creel to create a massive propaganda campaign to whip up enthusiasm with the public.

Much of the three-part series focuses on the war's cultural effects, such as the impact it had on the women's suffrage movement and the development of mass media, showing how rapidly the nation evolved in such a short time.

THE PACIFIC

WAR DRAMA • 2010
RATED: TV-MA • 50 MINS

Compared to the European conflict, the Pacific battles of World War II are slightly neglected. Tom Hanks helps correct that in miniseries form.

It's striking to think that of all the real-life soldiers depicted in this 10-episode miniseries, none are still alive—though many were until quite recently. It's that sense of urgency to record those memories that compelled actor Hanks to produce this series about the island-hopping campaigns of US servicemen against Imperial Japan, from Guadalcanal and Peleliu to Iwo Jima and Okinawa.

The Pacific is essentially a parallel miniseries to HBO's even-more-acclaimed 2001 *Band of Brothers* (see p130), which focused on a company of soldiers fighting across Europe after D-Day. Given the sprawling nature of this war, *The Pacific*'s cast is even larger, and includes James Badge Dale as marine Robert Leckie and future Oscar-winner Rami Malek as Merriell "Snafu" Shelton.

THE VIETNAM WAR

DOCUMENTARY • 2017
RATED: TV-MA • 90 MINS

Twenty-seven years after *The Civil War*, Ken Burns delivered the most expansive documentary he's ever made about another key American conflict— one that affected an entire generation in both the US and Vietnam.

More than 16 hours long, *The Vietnam War* may be Burns' crowning achievement, an astonishingly in-depth examination of the conflict centered on the years 1961 to 1973. As he did with his World War II film *The War*, Burns doesn't let famous figures drive this story: instead the narrative is propelled by former US soldiers and antiwar protesters, as well as Vietnamese combatants and civilians from both the North and the South.

Despite its length, the series never sags. Fascinating interviews abound, such as with US Secretary of Defense Robert McNamara's son Craig, who was a staunch protester against the war his father helped unleash. Burns spent over 10 years making this series, and it shows.

THE ICE CREAM SHOW

DOCUMENTARY • 2018
RATED: TV-MA • 22 MINS

What's even better than eye candy? How about ice cream for the eyes? That's the essence of this show, which takes viewers to some of the best ice-cream parlors in the US.

Ice cream is a global obsession, but possibly nowhere more than in the US. Host Isaac Lappert, a third-generation ice-cream maker himself, travels America to find out just why it's such a part of the nation's cultural fabric—and big business. The first installment looks at the economics of the ice-cream industry, and just how much money is to be made from scoops and cones.

In the remaining nine episodes, Lappert travels across the States, stopping off for cornets and cups galore. In Los Angeles there's a different ice cream for seemingly every ethnic group in the city: Persian saffron ice cream and Mexican *paletas*, among them. And in New York City he samples classic Italian Ice, and tours the ice cream trucks. Yum!

UGLY DELICIOUS

DOCUMENTARY • 2018 • RATED: TV-MA • 50 MINS • SEASONS: 2
DAVID CHANG

While most food shows instruct you in the art of conjuring elaborate culinary creations, this one looks at the everyday. What's the story behind the food items you eat all the time? Pizza, barbecue, tacos—there's more history there than you can imagine.

Who knew that some foodies consider the pizza in New Haven, Connecticut to be the best on Earth? People who watch *Ugly Delicious*, that's who. Host and chef David Chang lasers in on the hidden histories of the food you may very well be eating as you read this.

In the pizza episode Chang goes from Naples, the traditional birthplace of the dish, all the way to Japan where he visits a sushi chef who makes his own pizza using only Japanese ingredients. What becomes clear is that the locals in each place consider their own version to be the best. That competitiveness boils over into a debate in the episode on barbecue: which is better—American or Korean BBQ?

Sometimes Chang is accompanied on his culinary explorations by celebrity friends such as Aziz Ansari, Ali Wong, and Steven Yeun. For all the pleasure food gives us, many of us are shockingly short on knowledge about the history of what's actually on our plate. Watching *Ugly Delicious* will change that.

> **" We really wanted to lean into things we were clueless about. "**
>
> **David Chang** (host)

MAN V. FOOD

DOCUMENTARY • 2008
RATED: TV-G • 30 MINS

Sometimes size does matter. Well, at least it does to host Adam Richman, who spends four seasons of this series travelling the US to highlight the nation's most bounteous food choices.

What is the defining food of a city? Every place has one. If you decide to eat the largest portion of it imaginable, you're already living this show. Each episode ends with a competition in which Richman either tries to eat as much of a city's defining food—or as extreme a variant of it—as possible.

That means racing against the clock to devour a six-pound steak in Amarillo, Texas, or downing six "Atomic" wings covered in a sauce rating 150,000 on the Scoville scale (which measures spiciness) in Pittsburgh. While filming, Richman exercised twice a day to try to stay in shape through all the eating, before passing the baton to new host Casey Webb in 2017 for the next four seasons. Dig in and discover who wins each bout—man or food.

SALT FAT ACID HEAT

DOCUMENTARY • 2018
RATED: PG (UK) • 40 MINS

What if all great cooking—even the most complex recipes—can be boiled down to just four basic elements? Host Samin Nosrat thinks she's on to something.

This is one of the most stunningly beautiful food shows to look at, with each ingredient and dish photographed like it's out of a magazine spread. But it's also thought-provoking, with chef Nosrat's insistence that understanding the variations in salt, fat, acid, and heat accounts for a dish's flavor. Each of the series' four episodes is dedicated to a different one of these elements.

For salt, Nosrat travels to Japan to learn its importance in soy sauce and miso. For fat, she visits Italy, where chefs employ copious amounts of cheese and olive oil. What's especially interesting is that she doesn't just visit Michelin-starred chefs, but also explores meals made at home by ordinary people. Either way, though, you'll end up hungry.

ZUMBO'S JUST DESSERTS

REALITY TV • 2016
RATED: TV-14 • 52 MINS

Stepping into a real-life Willy Wonka–style factory, amateur dessert chefs offer up their sweet creations to be judged by master pâtissier Adriano Zumbo, the self-dubbed "dark lord of the pastry kitchen."

"I'm just waiting for Oompa-Loompas to walk out," one contestant says in the first episode of this Australian reality TV series. With its bright lighting and brilliant colors, the set looks like something you need a golden ticket to visit. It's also the stage for fierce competition: one contestant is eliminated each week based on the judges' decision regarding the most inferior dessert in that round.

Participants have to make cakes, soufflés, and other confections, with Zumbo, who rose to fame on *MasterChef Australia*, casting stern judgment on each. His nicknames include "Lord Voldecake" and "the pâtissier of pain," so you can expect plenty of bon mots served up with the bonbons in this two-season series.

YOU FEEL LIKE WALLOWING

Written by Maggie Serota

Just dumped by your partner? Laid off from your job? It's fine.
Load up on snacks, plant yourself on the sofa for a few days,
and mainline stories about people whose stress, bad luck,
and misery far outweigh your own. In fact, after about three
episodes of *The Handmaid's Tale*, you'll almost certainly feel
better about whatever you've got going on in your own life.

SUCCESSION

DRAMA • 2018 • RATED: TV-MA • 60 MINS • SEASONS: 2
BRIAN COX, JEREMY STRONG, KIERAN CULKIN

They say blood is thicker than water, and that notion is tested to the limits as the Roy children battle for control of the multibillion-dollar family media business their ailing father built from the ground up. With relatives like these, who needs enemies?

When Logan Roy (Brian Cox), CEO of media conglomerate Waystar Royco, suffers a stroke, his children are forced to reckon with both the patriarch's failing health and the realization that he's no longer fit to lead the corporation he founded. The Roy children vying for control of the empire are Kendall Roy (Jeremy Strong), the eldest son from Logan's second marriage and a struggling addict seeking his father's approval; Siobhan "Shiv" Roy, a sharp-elbowed political operative; and Roman Roy (Kieran Culkan), an immature and impulsive layabout competing with Kendall and Shiv for Logan's limited affection. Then there's also eldest son Connor Roy (Alan Ruck), a right-wing conspiracy theorist who's wholly uninterested in corporate power grabs, partly because he's never had to work a day in his life. The Roy children also weather a frosty relationship with Logan's third wife, Marcia Roy (Hiam Abbass), with neither side entirely trusting the other.

> **"** *The dinosaur is having one last roar at the meteor before it wipes him out.* **"**
>
> **Kendall Roy** (SI E4)

The tensions between Logan, Kendall, Shiv, and Roman comprise most of the drama. But much of the levity is provided by the less consequential characters. There's Greg Hirsch (Nicholas Braun), aka Cousin Greg, Logan's awkward stoner grand-nephew who inserts himself into Logan's branch

AWARD-WINNING HIGHS OF SUCCESSION

2018

AMERICAN FILM
INSTITUTE AWARDS:
Top 10 TV Programs
of the Year

DIRECTORS GUILD OF
AMERICA AWARDS:
Outstanding Directorial
Achievement

2019

AMERICAN FILM
INSTITUTE AWARDS:
Top 10 TV Programs
of the Year

BAFTA TV AWARDS:
Best International Series

PRIMETIME EMMY AWARDS:
Outstanding Writing and
Title Theme Music

SATELLITE AWARDS:
Best Television Series
and Best Supporting Actor

ONLINE FILM AND
TV AWARDS:
Best Guest Actor, Best Writing
in a Drama Series, Best New
Theme Song, and Best
Ensemble in a Drama Series

IGN MOVIE AWARDS:
Best Dramatic TV Performance,
Best Drama TV Series, and
Best TV Ensemble

2020

GOLDEN GLOBE AWARDS:
Best Television Series
and Best Actor

CRITICS' CHOICE
TELEVISION AWARDS:
Best Drama Series and
Best Actor in a Drama Series

PRODUCERS GUILD
OF AMERICA AWARDS:
Outstanding Producer
of Episodic Television

WRITERS GUILD OF
AMERICA AWARDS:
Best Dramatic Series and
Best Episodic Drama

of the family tree after screwing up every other possible career path. Cousin Greg's grandfather is Logan's estranged brother, Ewan Roy (James Cromwell), an avowed leftist who hates everything Logan stands for. Cousin Greg finds an unlikely ally in Tom Wambsgans (Matthew Macfadyen), a middle-class lawyer from the heartland. He's also Shiv's profoundly insecure fiancé, who is desperate to ingratiate himself with the rest of the Roys despite being treated as a punching bag. Tom is viewed less like an equal partner in the family enterprise and more like a malleable bumpkin the Roys can control.

When the Roys aren't warring with each other, they're trying to fend off hostile takeovers and other market forces threatening to crush the family empire, or save the company from a self-inflicted scandal. Sometimes that involves family members blackmailing each other or trying to convince one another to publicly fall on their sword when the time comes to answer for corporate malfeasance. You'd think being a member of the 1 percent of the 1 percent would come with a certain level of comfort and security, but it turns out extreme wealth and power is a gilded cage. Sure, the Roy kids can hop on to a private jet whenever they feel like it, but they also might be subjected to a humiliating game of "boar on the floor" (in which they're forced to crawl around like pigs and fight for sausages) should their dad suspect there's a traitor in his midst.

Shows about dysfunctional rich people are nothing new, but *Succession* succeeds where others fail thanks to its crackling dialogue, cutting humor, and damn-near surgical ability to parody current events without feeling forced or obvious. The Roys could easily be stand-ins for present-day dynasties such as the Murdochs or Trumps, where the interpersonal squabbles have a way of bleeding into the headlines and influencing the global economy. However, this fictional family of oligarchs is far more entertaining than anything in the real world.

CREATOR: Jesse Armstrong
PRODUCTION CO: Gary Sanchez Productions, Project Zeus, HBO

UTOPIA

THRILLER • 2013
RATED: TV-MA • 45 MINS

Online fans of a mysterious graphic novel find themselves hunted by a sinister international cabal after getting hold of its original manuscript.

Five comic-book lovers brought together by an internet forum are targeted by a nefarious organization known as "The Network" after one of them obtains the original manuscript of a cult graphic novel titled *The Utopia Experiments*, rumored to predict global disasters past and present. Now the unwitting targets, including orphaned postgrad student Becky (Alexandra Roach), awkward IT guy Ian (Nathan Stewart-Jarrett), and conspiracy theorist Wilson Wilson (Adeel Akhtar), must decode the secrets laid out in the manuscript to save both themselves and civilization.

This UK series doubles as both a wickedly funny satire about life in the surveillance state and a gripping, shockingly violent thriller. Although never a ratings winner, it attracted an obsessive following during its two seasons.

WEEDS

COMEDY • 2005
RATED: TV-MA • 26 MINS

With no marketable skills to speak of, a suburban mom gets in too deep when she starts dealing marijuana to support her family after her husband's death. What could possibly go wrong?

Nancy Botwin (Mary Louise Parker) is a southern California housewife saddled with the burden of supporting her two sons after her husband, Judah (Jeffrey Dean Morgan), unexpectedly dies while out jogging. Nancy begins making what she thinks will be easy cash by dealing weed to the bored housewives and stoner dads populating her upper-middle-class community. But her impulsive and self-destructive nature means she finds herself way over her head as she tackles hardened criminals, drug traffickers, and an ill-fated romance with a drug enforcement agent.

Spanning seven seasons, the show grows a bit far-fetched toward its end but always retains a darkly comic edge that makes it worth sticking with.

THE KNICK

PERIOD DRAMA • 2014
RATED: TV-MA • 44 MINS

Blood, guts, and gore abound in this dark drama about a turn-of-the-century New York City hospital led by corrupt administrators and a brilliant but self-destructive surgeon.

Dr. John Thackery (Clive Owen) is a passionate and talented chief surgeon with an unfortunate appetite for narcotics working at Manhattan's Knickerbocker hospital in the early 1900s. The assistant chief surgeon, Harvard-educated Dr. Algernon Edwards (André Holland), is arguably the best doctor in the building. As the lone black surgeon, however, he is regularly disrespected by his peers in a struggling institution that is desperate to attract rich white patients.

The show depicts 1900 New York as bloody, brutal, and cruel, dominated by racism, gross wealth inequality, and corruption. Cliff Martinez's driving score and Steven Soderbergh's direction enhance the sense of dread hanging over the two seasons.

YES MINISTER

COMEDY • 1980
RATED: TV-PG • 30 MINS

A clueless cabinet minister finds his policy reforms undermined at every turn by scheming civil servants in this classic satire of a government operating behind closed doors.

After the unnamed opposition party assumes power, bumbling MP James Hacker (Paul Eddington) is appointed to head the fictional Ministry of Administrative Affairs. Eager to introduce ambitious changes, Hacker has no idea how woefully unprepared he is to navigate the bureaucracy and backbiting in the upper echelons of British government. He finds his reform attempts frequently undercut by the career civil servants in his employ, namely his manipulative undersecretary Sir Humphrey Appleby (Nigel Hawthorne), who is hell-bent on maintaining the status quo.

Across three seasons, bungler Hacker fails upward, from cabinet minister to PM, paving the way for sequel *Yes, Prime Minister*, in which he faces the same crippling bureaucracy.

A.P. BIO

COMEDY • 2018 • RATED: TV-14 • 22 MINS • SEASONS: 2
GLENN HOWERTON, PATTON OSWALT, PAULA PELL

How does a hotshot Harvard philosophy professor cope after his academic career takes a nosedive? He heads back to his hometown and takes it out on staff and students at the local high school.

After losing a plum teaching gig to a rival scholar and getting blackballed out of academia, professor Jack Griffin (Glenn Howerton) moves back to his late mother's house in Ohio and takes a job teaching advanced placement biology at a local high school. Unfortunately for his overachieving students, Griffin has no intention of teaching them anything, instead preferring to use them to get back at his enemies, including the professor to whom he lost his dream post.

Griffin makes no bones about the fact that he plans to sleepwalk through his new duties, wandering into class late, unshaven, and sometimes still in his bathrobe. His bad behavior is enabled by Principal Durbin (Patton Oswalt), a school administrator torn between his responsibility to hold Griffin accountable and his profound need for the misanthropic teacher's approval.

While it doesn't tell much of a cohesive story, the series is highly watchable as a collection of blackly comic moments showcasing Griffin's downward spiral, witnessed by a captive audience of precocious geeks.

> **❝** *You know, this incessant happy talk is a form of harassment.* **❞**
>
> **Jack Griffin** (S1 E7)

ONE FOOT IN THE GRAVE

COMEDY • 1990
RATED: TV-PG • 30 MINS

A crotchety senior discovers early retirement can be a curse as much as a blessing as he falls victim to a constant series of embarrassing misfortunes.

After getting laid off from his job as a security guard, cranky Victor Meldrew (Richard Wilson) struggles to adjust to his new life and finds himself embroiled in a string of complex messes and misunderstandings, much to the chagrin of his long-suffering but devoted wife, Margaret (Annette Crosbie). Victor's misery is compounded by Margaret's intrusive friend Mrs. Warboys (Doreen Mantle) and the neighbors who constantly catch him in bizarre situations.

Over the course of six seasons and seven Christmas specials, Victor's missteps include accidentally killing his goddaughter's pet tortoise by setting it on fire and buying a pile of radioactive horse manure—with cries of his beloved catchphrase "I don't believe it!" accompanying every fresh ignominy.

UNBELIEVABLE

CRIME DRAMA • 2019
RATED: TV-MA • 46 MINS

A teenager finds herself ostracized from her community after being accused of lying to police about her rape—until two dogged female detectives come along.

Marie (Kaitlyn Dever) is a young woman living in a home for teens transitioning out of foster care. After a masked intruder breaks into her room and sexually assaults her, she reports the incident to police. But when her former foster parents question her credibility, the authorities pressure her to recant the testimony, and her housing and job come under threat. Meanwhile, two dedicated female investigators, Detectives Karen Duvall (Merritt Wever) and Grace Rasmussen (Toni Collette), are investigating attacks that sound shockingly similar to the one Marie describes.

Based on a true story, this single-season miniseries is an exquisitely paced crime drama as well as a damning indictment of the US criminal justice system.

GETTING ON

COMEDY DRAMA • 2013
RATED: TV-MA • 30 MINS

Death, incontinence, and dementia are all part of a day's work for the world-weary nurses and doctors caring for patients in the geriatric wing of an under-resourced hospital.

The ethically dubious, self-absorbed Dr. Jenna James (Laurie Metcalf) and nurses Dawn Forchette (Alex Borstein) and Denise "Didi" Ortley (Niecy Nash) work in a terminally depressing long-term care facility in Southern California. Care of the elderly patients seems to take a backseat to the greed and Medicaid fraud practiced by the doctors and hospital administrators, leaving all the hard work to the put-upon nurses.

This bleak dramedy never really caught on with audiences while it was on, perhaps because a comedy where people are constantly dying is a hard sell. But the humor is both subtle and masterful, even if it was acutely uncomfortable, and remained so during the show's three-season run.

SIX FEET UNDER

**DRAMA • 2001 • RATED: TV-MA • 46 MINS • SEASONS: 5
PETER KRAUSE, MICHAEL C. HALL, FRANCES CONROY**

Death really is part of life for the dysfunctional Fishers—they are the proprietors of a struggling funeral home. But the family is forced to come together and deal with personal loss when the patriarch dies unexpectedly.

Death sets the tone for this moody family drama from the mind of Alan Ball (*True Blood*, see p162). The passing of funeral director Nathaniel Fisher Sr. (Richard Jenkins) forces an uncomfortable family reunion between prodigal son, Nate Jr. (Peter Krause); his in-the-closet younger brother, David (Michael C. Hall); their troubled teenage sister, Claire (Lauren Ambrose), and their aloof, repressed mother, Ruth (Frances Conroy).

The two sons couldn't be more at odds, struggling to put aside their differences in order to run the family business and help clients deal with their losses at the same time as they have to process their own grief.

Indeed, all the surviving Fishers are haunted by the passing of Nate Sr. and sometimes talk to an imagined version of him, and other deceased characters, as if they were still alive.

Each episode begins with a death, caused by anything from murder to natural causes, or a freak accident, such as getting hit on the head by a golf ball or choking on a TV dinner. The aftermath of each passing sets the theme for what follows—always an exquisite blend of moving drama and darkly comic moments.

> **"***That's one of the perks of being dead: you know what happens after you die.***"**
>
> Nathaniel Sr. (S1 E6)

JERICHO

**ACTION DRAMA • 2006
RATED: TV-14 • 43 MINS**

The residents of a small Kansas town are forced to reckon with a lawless postapocalyptic landscape when their community is rocked by an atomic blast.

After a nuclear catastrophe wipes out their infrastructure, the inhabitants of Jericho have to figure out how to survive in a dystopian hellscape. Not only do survivors of the explosion have to solve how to get the lights back on, but they're also racked with further confusion and fear when they discover the blast was premeditated.

As citizens try to keep themselves safe from nuclear fallout and fend off attacks from aggressive neighboring communities, Jake Green (Skeet Ulrich) emerges as an unlikely leader when he returns to town having fled in disgrace five years before.

Although the show ran for only two seasons, it picked up a devoted cult following among fans of postapocalyptic sci-fi.

FLEABAG

COMEDY • 2016 • RATED: TV-MA • 26 MINS • SEASONS: 2
PHOEBE WALLER-BRIDGE, SIAN CLIFFORD, OLIVIA COLMAN

Fleabag is a hilarious and heartbreaking look at how one acerbic woman uses sex and humor to deflect from the grief gnawing at her soul. Its main character engages directly with the audience as she tries to distract herself from dealing with the mostly self-inflicted wreckage of her past.

"Fleabag" was the nickname given to series writer and star Phoebe Waller-Bridge by her family, which subsequently became the title of her one-woman stage show. Although the series never reveals its main character's real name, it grants you an unflinching look at her inner life through her tendency to break the fourth wall and tell viewers what she's thinking.

As it turns out, Fleabag has a lot on her mind. The coffee shop she owns is failing, she's saddled with unprocessed grief over the death of her best friend, Boo, and she's constantly butting heads with her passive-aggressive stepmother (Olivia Colman). She also has a front-row seat to the unhappy marriage of her overachieving, highly strung sister Claire (Sian Clifford) to Martin, an impotent time bomb of rage and self-loathing.

> ## "I get a rush writing women who don't care what you think."
>
> Phoebe Waller-Bridge (writer/actor)

Rather than unpack and deal with her pain and inner turmoil, Fleabag prefers to redirect that energy into sabotaging her own life. She does this by chasing the ultimate unavailable love interest in the form of a hot priest (Andrew Scott), and giving her doormat of an on-again/off-again boyfriend, Harry, the runaround.

The series begins with Fleabag acting as a detached observer to the dysfunction around her, occasionally turning to the camera and offering the audience a pointed glance or dry witticism. But as the show progresses, you start to realize that Fleabag confides in the audience because she's unable to do so with those closest to her. The cutting asides to the viewer are defense mechanisms designed to keep her friends and family from scaling the walls she's built around herself. Given Waller-Bridge's formidable acting and writing skills, the tragic elements are every bit as affecting as the comedy.

CREATOR: Phoebe Waller-Bridge
PRODUCTION CO: Two Brothers Pictures

THE SOPRANOS

**CRIME DRAMA • 1999 • RATED: TV-MA • 50 MINS • SEASONS: 6
JAMES GANDOLFINI, EDIE FALCO, LORRAINE BRACCO**

Even if you've never watched an episode, you've probably heard of *The Sopranos*. The series is equal parts finely tuned, darkly comic mafia saga and Shakespearean tragedy. Prepare to meet Tony Soprano, the suburban dad living a dangerous double life.

Tony Soprano (James Gandolfini) is a middle-aged dad living a suspiciously well-heeled life in the upper-middle-class New Jersey suburbs by earning a living as a "waste management consultant." Or at least, that's his cover story. His wife, Carmela (Edie Falco), and kids, Meadow and Anthony "A. J." Jr., have a comfortable lifestyle in a

sprawling mansion, far removed from Tony's other life as the philandering underboss of a local mafia crime family.

When Tony isn't at home in his dressing gown with a cigar in hand, he can usually be found at his "office," aka a topless joint called the Bada Bing, surrounded by a crew of wiseguys and miscreants. These include pompadoured strip-club owner Silvio Dante, loyal henchman Paulie "Walnuts" Gaultieri, and Christopher Moltisanti, a distant cousin who Tony treats more like a son.

Perhaps the most compelling relationship on the show exists between Tony and his therapist, Dr. Jennifer Melfi (Lorraine Bracco). He starts seeing a psychiatrist amid the pressure of caring for his aging mother, Livia, balancing his affairs with his marriage, and routinely dodging assassination attempts while running North Jersey's largest organized crime racket. Life isn't easy for Tony.

The Sopranos set the gold standard for what would later be termed prestige TV, namely awards-collecting cable series, typically praised as high art. Thanks to the late Gandolfini's brilliant performance, Tony Soprano emerges as a fascinatingly complicated antihero, one who would set the template for a generation of difficult male protagonists such as *Breaking Bad's* Walter White (see p10) and *Mad Men's* Don Draper (see p102).

CREATOR: David Chase
PRODUCTION CO: HBO, Brillstein Entertainment Partners, The Park Entertainment

ABSENTIA

THRILLER • 2017
RATED: TV-MA • 42 MINS

An FBI agent declared dead in absentia after disappearing while on the trail of a serial killer is found barely alive years later. Then her troubles really begin.

Special agent Emily Byrne (Stana Katic) is discovered in a cabin in the woods with no memory of what has happened to her in the intervening six years since she disappeared while pursuing a serial killer in Boston. In the meantime, she has lost everything, including her husband and fellow FBI special agent, Nick Durand (Patrick Heusinger), who has remarried and is now raising Emily's child with his new wife, Alice (Cara Theobold). Above all else, Emily needs to get her memory back, and fast, because someone is trying to frame her for murder.

As well as being a taut thriller, this three-season mystery series also functions as gripping drama, given the tensions and longing between Nick, the wife he thought had died, and the woman he married in her place.

LONDON IRISH

COMEDY • 2014
RATED: 18 (UK) • 23 MINS

Four profane 20-somethings from Belfast move to London and embark on drunken misadventures in a crass sitcom that dances right on the knife's edge of offensive.

In the vein of The Inbetweeners (see p251) or It's Always Sunny in Philadelphia (see p273), London Irish is another sitcom about unpleasant people doing unpleasant things.

This particular crew of miscreants consists of four Northern Irish 20-somethings—two men and two women—who move to London in search of something resembling a future. They mainly end up drinking, doing drugs, and getting themselves into absurd and degrading situations of their own making.

The one-season series from Derry Girls (see p250) creator Lisa McGee came and went amid criticism that it trafficked in stereotypes. For all its failings, London Irish does hit a sweet spot for those who like their humor gross, mildly deranged, and borderline outrageous.

TAKEN

ACTION THRILLER • 2017
RATED: TV-14 • 42 MINS

Based on the blockbuster action movie franchise, this prequel series reveals how former Special Forces soldier Bryan Mills acquired his "very particular set of skills" made famous in the film trilogy.

Long before Bryan Mills (Clive Standen) avenged his kidnapped wife and daughter, he was a young Green Beret hell-bent on avenging the death of his sister, Cali (Celeste Desjardins), after she is targeted by a drug kingpin with a personal vendetta against him. His expertise makes him a prime recruit for an elite wing of CIA superspies headed by Christina Hart (Jennifer Beals), who are tasked with undertaking dangerous missions.

Despite a major cast overhaul in the second and final season, the show never really found its audience. Perhaps that's because it doesn't quite work as a spiritual successor to the film series starring Liam Neeson. Nevertheless, as a fast-paced action thriller, Taken certainly is decent entertainment.

AMERICAN GODS

FANTASY DRAMA • 2017
RATED: TV-MA • 53 MINS

Released from prison early to attend his wife's funeral, an ex-con crosses paths with a mysterious man on his way home and is unwittingly drawn into a battle between warring gods.

This adaptation of Neil Gaiman's fantasy novel is essentially a show about a road trip. Well, a road trip through a hidden magical world where the passenger is the Norse god Odin disguised as a charming con man named Mr. Wednesday (Ian McShane), and the driver is a recently freed prisoner known as Shadow Moon (Ricky Whittle). Things get weirder from there. Far, far weirder.

People expecting traditional narrative storytelling should manage their expectations as, over the course of the show's two seasons, plot often takes a back seat to dreamlike sequences and arresting imagery. As was the case with codeveloper Bryan Fuller's previous series *Hannibal*, the visuals are the real star here.

DIABLO GUARDIÁN

DRAMA • 2018
RATED: TV-MA • 45 MINS

A Mexican teen steals her parents' money and runs off to New York City where she becomes a call girl and the muse of a thrill-seeking writer.

This two-season Spanish-language neo-noir series follows the journey of a bored youngster (Paulina Gaitán) from Mexico to the Big Apple after stealing several hundred thousand dollars from her parents.

Determined to start a more exciting new life, she reinvents herself as a call girl named Violetta. She's also just the kind of fascinating muse a writer named Pig (Adrián Ladrón) has been waiting for. The question is not if the pair are going to meet, but when. And once they do, will they ever be the same again?

Events take an even darker turn when Violetta's cash runs out and she gets caught up in the criminal underworld, transforming her American dream into a waking nightmare. Perhaps she didn't have it so bad back home with Mom and Dad after all.

GOOD GIRLS

COMEDY DRAMA • 2018
RATED: TV-14 • 42 MINS

A trio of cash-strapped housewives resort to desperate measures when they try to score some easy money by knocking off a supermarket.

Beth (Christina Hendricks) is about to lose her house and her sister, Annie (Mae Whitman), is locked in a custody battle with her ex. Their friend Ruby (Retta) is buried under mountains of medical debt from taking care of her daughter. Tired of always losing out, the three suburban housewives decide to turn to crime to get their heads above water. Unfortunately for them, they soon find out there's no such thing as easy money in the wake of their planned supermarket heist.

Prestige dramas and black comedies were getting pretty crowded with male antiheroes, so it's refreshing to see a group of women going astray rather than playing scolds who nag their criminal husbands. Stretched over three seasons, this fun comedy crime drama has a trio of strong performances at its heart.

THE ACT

DRAMA • 2019
RATED: TV-MA • 49 MINS

A toxic relationship between a domineering mother and her supposedly chronically ill daughter reaches breaking point in this drama based on a shocking true story.

Gypsy Blanchard (Joey King) is a sweet but lonely teenager afflicted with several debilitating illnesses, including cancer and diabetes. She also has a disability, requiring the use of a wheelchair, or so she thinks. Overprotective mom, Dee Dee Blanchard (Patricia Arquette) is Gypsy's devoted caretaker. But as Gypsy grows up and gets a taste for life beyond her mother's apron strings, she starts to wonder whether instead of helping her get better, her mom is purposefully making her sicker. Then Gypsy meets her first boyfriend (Calum Worthy), and things come to a head.

A dark one-season drama about a tragic childhood, the desperate measures to escape it, and the lives ruined along the way.

SEE

SCI-FI DRAMA • 2019
RATED: TV-MA • 60 MINS

In a world where humans have lost their sight, the mysterious birth of a set of twins who can see inflames tensions between rival tribes living in darkness.

Welcome to the Earth of the future where a disease has killed off most of humanity and left the survivors blind. A few centuries after the plague, society has reorganized into tribes who mainly survive by hunting and gathering. In this dystopian world, Baba Voss (Jason Mamoa), chief of the Alkenny tribe, accidentally ignites a war between competing tribal units when he welcomes in an outsider (Hera Hilmar), who gives birth to twins who can see.

Made for Apple TV+, this heady one-season sci-fi epic envisions a primitive landscape where survivors believe in witchcraft and wear animal skins like cavepeople. At times, it borders on the ridiculous, with a queen who communes with the spirit world by bringing herself to orgasm, but the concept, action, and visuals make it worth a look.

THIS WAY UP

COMEDY • 2019
RATED: NR • 24 MINS

After a stint in a psychiatric ward following a breakdown, an Irishwoman living in London tries to get her life back on track with the help of her high-powered sister.

A young English-as-a-foreign-language teacher named Aine (series creator Aisling Bea) has her work cut out trying to get her life back together upon her release from a psychiatric hospital. As her recovery from her nervous breakdown progresses in fits and starts, Aine tries to maintain a brave face for her older sister, Shona (Sharon Horgan), a businesswoman who can worry enough for the both of them.

This quietly devastating one-season show handles mental illness with a sensitivity and care not often found in comedies. But that's not to say it holds back on the laughs, either, as it charts its delightfully drawn characters' search for happiness and the meaning of it all. Humorous and heartwarming.

CRASHING

COMEDY • 2017
RATED: TV-MA • 28 MINS

After splitting up with his wife, a Christian wannabe comedian finds himself couch surfing in New York while trying to eke out a career in stand-up.

Comedian Pete Holmes plays a fictionalized—and less successful—version of himself in this often hilarious sitcom about a struggling comic. Finding himself essentially homeless after catching his wife, Jess (Lauren Lapkus),

cheating on him in their suburban New Jersey house, Pete throws himself into stand-up, crashing on the sofas of his more famous friends (T .J. Miller, Artie Lange) as he seeks to make it on the New York comedy scene.

As a practicing Christian who once aspired to become a youth pastor, Pete deviates from the typical dysfunctional dirtbags who drive most dark comedies with his wholesomeness. Rather than cynical wisecracks, it's Pete's naivety that drives much of the humor in a three-season show that charts his steady rise to the brink of stardom.

PRODIGAL SON

CRIME DRAMA • 2019
RATED: TV-14 • 43 MINS

A brilliant but troubled former FBI profiler with a gift for hunting down multiple murderers worries about succumbing to the same tendencies as his serial-killer father.

Malcolm Bright (Tom Payne) is a disgraced FBI profiler who uses his uncanny ability to view crime scenes through the eyes of a killer to help the New York City police catch criminals.

Bright's talent in part stems from his childhood when he helped the authorities catch his own father, Dr. Martin Whitly (Michael Sheen), the notorious serial killer known as "The Surgeon." Over the course of one season, Bright is forced to get back in touch with his dad as he tries to catch a copycat killer, aggravating his fears that he will end up a sociopathic murderer like him.

While his alcoholic mother Jessica (Bellamy Young) is often too sloshed to provide any guidance, Bright finds a surrogate father figure in police lieutenant Gil Arroyo (Lou Diamond Philips), who gives him the stability he needs.

SERVANT

HORROR THRILLER • 2019
RATED: TV-MA • 32 MINS

A grieving mother hires a nanny to move in and look after the doll that she believes is her dead baby son, much to the chagrin of her husband and brother.

Dorothy (Lauren Ambrose) is a local TV news reporter coaxed out of a catatonic state with a therapy tool in the form of a doll fashioned to look like her recently deceased infant.

Her husband, Sean (Toby Kebbell), humors Dorothy's belief that the doll is their living baby to the point that he goes along with the plan to hire a nanny, a mysterious and oddly obedient 18-year-old named Leanne (Nell Tiger Free). But it's not long before Sean starts to wonder whether there's something more sinister going on with the new caregiver.

From executive producer M. Night Shyamalan, this one-season series is a master class in pacing and claustrophobic moods. Rather than hinge on a huge, shocking twist, it unfurls through a series of creepy, drawn-out reveals.

THE HANDMAID'S TALE

SCI-FI DRAMA • 2017 • RATED: TV-MA • 45 MINS • SEASONS: 3
ELISABETH MOSS, JOSEPH FIENNES, ALEXIS BLEDEL

Margaret Atwood's ominously prescient 1985 novel provides the source for this tense dystopian drama where fertile women are enslaved in a repressive theocracy that rose from the ashes of the former United States.

Welcome to the Republic of Gilead, a fundamentalist Christian regime where fertility rates have plummeted amid the spread of STDs and rampant pollution. The few women still able to conceive children are treated as precious commodities known as "Handmaids." Owned by Gilead's elite families, they are forced to undergo ritualized rape in a process called "the ceremony." The Handmaids wear a distinctive uniform of shapeless red robes and oversized white bonnets that obscure their bodies and faces in public. As well as being treated like livestock, women under the new regime aren't allowed to read or have their own money. There's no sugarcoating it—life in Gilead is miserable for anyone who isn't a male member of the ruling class. To add insult to injury, the Handmaids are also stripped of their identities and referred to as "Of," followed by the name of the man who owns them.

The series centers on a Handmaid named "Offred" (Elisabeth Moss), who belongs to Commander Fred Waterford (Joseph Fiennes) and his wife, Serena Joy (Yvonne Strahovski), a powerful couple instrumental in the rise of the brutal new government. While enduring forced servitude to the Waterfords, Offred is haunted by the memory of her former life with husband, Luke (O-T Fagbenle), and their daughter, Hannah, from whom she was separated after getting caught trying to flee to Canada.

Although life in Gilead is oppressively grim, with women being forced to endure public executions after breaking seemingly innocuous rules, there is a glimmer of hope in the form of an underground resistance movement known as Mayday. Unfortunately, the rebels are up against the Eyes, Gilead's Gestapo-style secret police, another oppressive hurdle in an overwhelmingly bleak hellscape. This brilliant futuristic drama packs a powerful emotional punch that's sure to leave you reeling for some time.

CREATOR: Bruce Miller
PRODUCTION CO: MGM Television, MGM/UA Television

HOUSE OF CARDS

THRILLER DRAMA • 1990
RATED: TV-14 • 55 MINS

Hell hath no fury like a chief whip scorned. After being denied a plum cabinet post when his party assumes power, Francis Urquhart plots the new prime minister's downfall.

Francis Urquhart (Ian Richardson) is an MP and the Conservative Party's chief whip in the House of Commons, but he'd much rather be sitting in the new prime minister's cabinet.

Working with his Lady Macbeth-esque wife, Elizabeth (Diane Fletcher), he works to oust his former ally and grab control of the party.

A distinct Shakespearean air, especially of *Richard III*, hangs about this '90s BBC drama, with the ruthless Urquhart intermittently letting the audience in on his scheming by breaking the fourth wall to utter vicious barbs. While the original one-season miniseries spanned just four episodes, it spawned two sequels, as well as providing the basis for the US Netflix series of the same name.

IN TREATMENT

DRAMA • 2008
RATED: TV-MA • 22 MINS

Oh, to be a fly on the wall when patients spill their darkest secrets to their psychotherapists. And when you get to see the therapists undergo their own counseling, it's doubly fascinating.

Dr. Paul Weston (Gabriel Byrne), a middle-aged Ivy League–educated psychotherapist, struggles to balance seeking help for his own issues with treating patients in his Baltimore

home office. Plagued by insecurities about his effectiveness, Weston seeks the help of fellow shrink and former mentor Gina Toll (Dianne Wiest), with whom he hasn't spoken in a decade. Their complicated past comes into focus as Weston's treatment progresses.

While unpacking his issues across the show's three seasons, Weston also conducts sessions with his regular patients, including Laura (Melissa George), a young woman with a fixation on him; Alex (Blair Underwood), a fighter pilot suffering from PTSD; and Sophie (Mia Wasikowska), a suicidal teen.

SIBLINGS

COMEDY • 2014
RATED: 15 (UK) • 30 MINS

The two worst people in the world happen to be related and share an aparment in London. Siblings Hannah and Dan can't seem to stop inflicting misery on everyone they meet.

Hannah French (Charlotte Ritchie) is an unrepentant 20-something slacker who would rather die than put in an honest day's work at her job in an insurance company. She shares a

London apartment with Dan (Tom Stourton), a chronically unemployable idiot with no discernible gifts and a brief prison stay under his belt. The self-absorbed siblings' insistence on cutting every possible corner while indulging their every whim has disastrous results for the unlucky souls they encounter.

Over two seasons, the duo get involved in all manner of outrageous situations, from Hannah ruining her best friend's engagement party with a dumb gift to Dan pretending to be disabled so he can join a wheelchair basketball team. Crass is definitely the word for this pair.

DRIFTERS

COMEDY • 2013
RATED: TV-MA • 23 MINS

Join three young women sharing their first post-college apartment in Leeds. And watch them fall face-first into their quarter-life crisis.

Billed as a gender-flipped *The Inbetweeners* (see p251), this delightfully fun comedy follows the exploits of Meg (series creator Jessica Knappett), her cousin Bunny (Lydia Rose Bewley), and their friend Laura (Lauren O'Rourke) as they navigate the wilderness of early adulthood. After moving into their first post-college apartment in Leeds, they find themselves working humiliating low-level jobs while trying to grow into self-sufficient and upwardly mobile adults. The girls distract themselves by making a series of disastrous but undeniably fun decisions, such as drinking too much and dating aimless guys.

Over the course of four seasons, *Drifters* accurately depicts the overwhelming growing pains that come with trying to make your way in the world after college.

THE TRIP

COMEDY • 2010 • RATED: TV-14 • 30 MINS • SEASONS: 4
STEVE COOGAN, ROB BRYDON, CLAIRE KEELAN

Two top comedians play exaggerated versions of themselves on food tours of England, Italy, Spain, and Greece. As they tuck into their meals, they discuss their ennui, while ridiculing each other and doing impressions of film stars.

Commissioned to go on a food tour around northern England for a newspaper article, actor Steve Coogan's hopes for a romantic trip with his foodie girlfriend, Mischa (Margo Stilley), are dashed when she dumps him. As a last-minute replacement, he seeks out fellow comedian and frenemy Rob Brydon.

Coogan is the more famous and successful of the two characters but also profoundly unhappy given his romantic failures and fears that his career has long since peaked. By contrast, Brydon is almost infuriatingly content, with a happy marriage and fulfilling family life. On the road, the two men bicker and snipe but above all delight in making each other laugh. Things get competitive as they perform their impressions of Hollywood stars, battling it out to see who can do the definitive Michael Caine.

Later seasons have the two men eating and bantering on food tours of Italy, Spain, and Greece, where the gorgeous scenery is as much of a draw as the back-and-forth between the two stars.

> **"***I would never have such a toxic conversation with a friend.***"**
>
> **Rob Brydon in interview** (*The Guardian*)

BETTER CALL SAUL

CRIME DRAMA • 2015 • RATED: TV-MA • 46 MINS • SEASONS: 5
BOB ODENKIRK, MICHAEL MCKEAN, RHEA SEEHORN

The story of a crooked lawyer's path from low-level loser to slick con artist ensconced in the drug trade makes for one of the few spin-off series that's every bit as engaging as the original.

Set six years before *Breaking Bad* (see p10), this wildly successful prequel series follows the transformation of reformed con-man-turned-low-rent-lawyer Jimmy McGill (Bob Odenkirk) into crafty criminal *consigliere* Saul Goodman, who fans loved so much in the parent show. Jimmy is saddled with taking care of his more successful brother, Charles (Michael McKean), a partner in law firm Hamlin, Hamlin & McGill (HHM). Charles is on sick leave with electromagnetic hypersensitivity, which makes him ill in the presence of any electrical object. While trying to establish himself as a legitimate lawyer and win the affections of HHM attorney Kim Wexler (Rhea Seehorn), Jimmy becomes embroiled in the dealings of local drug traffickers, including former cop-turned-cartel-fixer Mike Ehrmantraut (Jonathan Banks) and crystal-meth kingpin Gus Fring (Giancarlo Esposito).

Ehrmantraut and Fring are two of the familiar faces from the original *Breaking Bad* peppered among a cast that is otherwise composed of new characters. Although the writing is exquisite and the performances masterful, it's probably best you enjoy *Breaking Bad* first in order to fully appreciate all the nuances and Easter eggs in *Better Call Saul*.

> **"** *Perfection is the enemy of the perfectly adequate.* **"**
>
> Jimmy McGill (S3 E10)

DEAD TO ME

COMEDY • 2019
RATED: TV-MA • 26 MINS

An angry widow makes an unlikely friend in a pathologically optimistic hippie she meets in a support group for grieving spouses. But their bond is threatened when dark secrets emerge.

Recently widowed real-estate agent Jen Harding (Christina Applegate) is still processing her anger after the recent hit-and-run death of her husband, Ted. She finds solace in a support group for grieving widows where she befriends free-spirited Judy (Linda Cardellini), who lost her fiancé, Steve (James Marsden) to a heart attack. The two are polar opposites: Jen is bitter and cynical, while Judy is relentlessly positive. Despite their differences, the two 40-somethings become close friends until a secret threatens to tear them apart.

This tragicomedy never allows you to get too comfortable with the plot twists coming at breakneck speed. The two seasons both end in big surprises—designed to make your jaw hit the floor.

FLOWERS

COMEDY DRAMA • 2016
RATED: 15 (UK) • 30 MINS

How much dysfunction and misery can you fit under one creaky, crumbling roof? When it comes to the Flowers family, quite a bit.

Things are tense in the crowded Flowers home with children's book author Maurice (Julian Barratt) suffering from severe depression and his eternally chipper music-teacher wife, Deborah (Olivia Colman), wondering why her husband doesn't seem attracted to her anymore. The couple's 25-year-old twins, aspiring inventor Donald (Daniel Rigby) and goth recluse Amy (Sophia Di Martino), are also living in the claustrophobic country home along with Maurice's batty mother, Hattie (Leila Hoffman), and his Japanese illustrator Shun (series creator Will Sharpe).

As much as the show is a wickedly dark comedy about familial dysfunction, it's also a nuanced and imaginative look at mental illness that sacrifices nothing in the way of laughs throughout its two-season run.

SEARCH PARTY

COMEDY • 2016
RATED: TV-MA • 22 MINS

Five self-absorbed hipsters find themselves in peril when one of them goes off in search of her missing college acquaintance and drags the rest along.

Dory Sief (Alia Shawkat) is stuck in a dead-end relationship and working a thankless job as the assistant to a wealthy housewife (Christine Taylor) when she decides to break the monotony by investigating the disappearance of her college acquaintance Chantal (Clare McNulty). Dory is not a private investigator, nor does she have any clue what she's doing, but she does have a crew of misfit friends and a hapless boyfriend to help her comb New York City in search of a woman she never knew that well in the first place.

Over the course of three seasons, Dory's boyfriend, Drew; her friends Portia and Elliott; and her ex, Julian, join her on her ill-fated adventures, finding nothing but trouble along the way, along with a few laughs of the darkly comic kind.

THE BIG C

COMEDY DRAMA • 2010
RATED: TV-MA • 28 MINS

A middle-aged teacher realizes she needs to make the most of her time on Earth after getting diagnosed with late-stage cancer.

Minneapolis high-school teacher Cathy Jamison (Laura Linney) must finally put herself first after receiving a stage-four cancer diagnosis. As she reckons with the fact that her time left is short, she hesitates to tell her family, including estranged husband, Paul (Oliver Platt); unstable, homeless brother, Sean (John Benjamin Hickey); and moody teen son, Adam (Gabriel Basso). Cathy finds an unlikely confidante in elderly crabby neighbor Marlene, who has her own health problems. Meanwhile, personal and professional lines blur between Cathy and her handsome young doctor.

Over four seasons, Cathy struggles to assuage her family's fears while stealing every last moment of happiness possible for herself, until the inevitable occurs.

SILICON VALLEY

COMEDY • 2014 • RATED: TV-MA • 28 MINS • SEASONS: 6
THOMAS MIDDLEDITCH, MARTIN STARR, KUMAIL NANJIANI

Californian tech culture never looked more absurd than in this comedy satire about a lowly software developer trying to market a new app in a cut-throat world beholden to the whims of warring billionaires.

Software engineer Richard Hendricks (Thomas Middleditch) is a faceless drone at behemoth internet company Hooli, run by egotistical billionaire cofounder Gavin Belson (Matt Ross). Believing he's developed a revolutionary new app called Pied Piper, he is eager to strike out on his own. But if he wants to found a viable company and become the next great tech visionary, he has to navigate the unwritten rules and overbearing personalities dominating the bizarre power center that is Silicon Valley.

Hendricks thinks he's well on his way when he sells a stake of Pied Piper to eccentric tech guru Peter Gregory (Christopher Evan Welch), founder of investment group Raviga Capital.

But he soon finds himself caught up in a battle of egos between two old rivals while the future of his company hangs in the balance.

Joining Hendricks is a ragtag crew of tech geeks in the "Hacker Hostel," a house owned by abrasive software designer/burnout Erlich Bachman (T .J. Miller). Full of hilarious characters and biting satire, this is essential viewing for budding tech titans and comedy fans alike.

> **❝ I don't want to live in a world where someone else is making the world a better place better than we are. ❞**
>
> **Gavin Belson** (S2 E1)

THE END OF THE F***KING WORLD

COMEDY • 2017
RATED: TV-MA • 22 MINS

An aspiring teen psychopath goes on a road trip with the girl he intends to murder, and an unlikely romance sparks between them.

James (Alex Lawther) is a 17-year-old self-diagnosed psychopath who decides to murder his angry classmate Alyssa (Jessica Barden) after he grows tired of killing animals. But he's forced to delay his plan when the two embark on an impromptu road trip, resolving to kill her later. Will he off her? Or will unexpected feelings get in the way? And is it possible that James isn't a psychopath at all?

For her part, Alyssa is desperate to escape her dysfunctional home, managing to cajole James into stealing his dad's car and setting off with her for parts unknown. Across two seasons, Alyssa and James learn a lot about each other and not very much about love as they leave a trail of wreckage in their wake.

BORED TO DEATH

COMEDY • 2009
RATED: TV-MA • 26 MINS

After his girlfriend leaves him, a struggling stoner writer fills his free time by trying some amateur private detective work. What could possibly go wrong?

A Brooklyn writer named Jonathan (Jason Schwartzman) distracts himself from heartbreak and a flat-lining career by getting a side hustle as an unlicensed private detective.

He solves cases using methods gleaned from old pulp novels, ably helped and hindered by his comic-book artist best friend Ray (Zach Galifianakis) and editor George (Ted Danson).

The quirky, noirish comedy spends three seasons following its main character—based on series creator and writer Jonathan Ames—through the publishing world and downtown scene. A top-of-the-line supporting cast features the likes of Oliver Platt, Kristen Wiig, and Patton Oswalt, as well as the occasional indie film director (Jim Jarmusch) and actor (Kevin Bacon) playing themselves.

THE FALL AND RISE OF REGINALD PERRIN

COMEDY • 1976
RATED: 12 (UK) • 30 MINS

A middle manager in the throes of a midlife crisis fakes his own death in order to escape the comfortable yet dull hamster wheel that is his life.

Reginald "Reggie" Perrin (Leonard Rossiter), a sales executive at Sunshine Desserts, is driven mad by the crushing predictability

of his life as a married middle manager in his mid-40s. Suffering a nervous breakdown, he starts to act erratically at work before taking drastic measures to escape the daily grind and the boredom of his loving but stale marriage to wife, Elizabeth (Pauline Yates).

Perrin fakes his suicide and assumes a new identity as a humble pig farmer. But over the course of three seasons, he finds himself gradually getting drawn back into the life he had so desperately sought to escape and suffering the unintended consequences of faking his death.

TIN STAR

CRIME DRAMA • 2017
RATED: TV-14 • 43 MINS

In a sleepy Canadian mountain town, a local police chief's violent past catches up with him when his family is threatened by criminal elements and a behemoth energy company.

Jim Worth (Tim Roth) is a recovering alcoholic cop who moves his wife and two children from London (UK, not Ontario) to a mountain town in Canada for a much-needed fresh start.

But Worth finds his dream of a quiet life threatened after he's appointed local police chief, has his authority constantly questioned, and attracts the ire of a giant oil company. And as if all that weren't enough, he is always just one drink away from unleashing his murderous inner psycho.

Like *Ozark* (see p365) and *Breaking Bad* (see p10), this two-season crime drama is driven by a deeply broken man trying to protect his family through dubious means. As the bodies pile up around him, it's clear he's only further endangering them and himself.

EVER DECREASING CIRCLES

COMEDY • 1984
RATED: PG (UK) • 30 MINS

When a dashing ex-army officer moves in next door, middle-aged control freak Martin worries that his self-appointed role as a neighborhood community organizer is under threat.

Martin Bryce (Richard Briers) is a neurotic busybody who's taken it upon himself to organize the activities of his suburban Surrey community through a raft of committees and projects. But when effortlessly charming military-man-turned-hair-salon-owner Paul Ryman (Peter Egan) moves in next door, he feels his position threatened, especially given the chemistry between Paul and Martin's long-suffering wife, Ann (Penelope Wilton).

Over four seasons, Martin finds himself engaging in a hilariously one-sided rivalry with a man who seems to be absurdly good at everything and makes him painfully aware of his own inadequacies. And through it all, Paul's unfaltering friendliness toward Martin only serves to infuriate him further.

GIRLS

COMEDY • 2012 • RATED: TV-MA • 26 MINS • SEASONS: 6
LENA DUNHAM, ALLISON WILLIAMS, ZOSIA MAMET

Moving to New York after graduation, Hannah's grand literary dreams are brought crashing to Earth when her parents shut off the money tap. But at least she has her clueless friends to lean on in the tough times that lie ahead.

Recent college grad Hannah Horvath (show creator Lena Dunham) fancies herself as the next great American writer. But she's given a sharp reality check when her parents visit from Michigan and tell her they'll no longer be subsidizing her life in hipster Brooklyn. Determined to figure things out despite her narcissism, immaturity, and acute sense of entitlement, she has her equally misguided pals to help her. These include pathologically self-centered Marnie Michaels (Allison Williams), free-spirited Brit Jessa Johansson (Jemima Kirke), and deeply neurotic Shoshanna Shapiro (Zosia Mamet).

Together, the four women weather their share of emotionally unavailable men, ill-considered surprise weddings, pregnancies, and Brooklyn loft parties, while trying to figure out exactly what they're doing with their lives.

Their friendships are tested as they swap romantic partners, but they carry on fumbling toward adulthood with each other in tow in this frank, funny, and risk-taking comedy.

> **"**I think that I may be the voice of my generation. Or at least, a voice of a generation.**"**
>
> Hannah Horvath (SI EI)

353

PEEP SHOW

COMEDY • 2003 • RATED: TV-MA • 23 MINS • SEASONS: 9
DAVID MITCHELL, ROBERT WEBB, OLIVIA COLMAN

Meet Mark and Jez, roommates wandering aimlessly through their 30s, grasping desperately for any shred of happiness and shooting themselves (and each other) in the foot along the way. They have nothing in common except for their loathing of each other, themselves, and the world at large.

Mark Corrigan (David Mitchell) and Jeremy "Jez" Usborne (Robert Webb) are the "El Dude Brothers"—two former college roommates who have spent their entire adult lives in a deeply codependent living arrangement. Mark is a sexually repressed, tightly wound loan manager, who owns a modest apartment. Jez is a terminally unemployable slacker man-child with no discernible talents. He fancies himself as a great musician, but he mainly just freeloads off Mark and hangs out with crack-smoking degenerate Super Hans (Matt King). Mark is a

black hole of insecurity and self-consciousness, while Jez is a talentless void lacking anything resembling self-awareness.

The living arrangement is mutually beneficial in that Jez gets a roommate who will subsidize his incessant weed smoking and half-baked artistic endeavors, and Mark gets to feel superior to his aimless friend who has a better batting average with the ladies. They are both the best and worst thing that's ever happened to each other.

> "*God, it's so easy being a freak!*"
>
> **Mark Corrigan** (S2 E1)

JEREMY'S RELATIONSHIP GUIDE

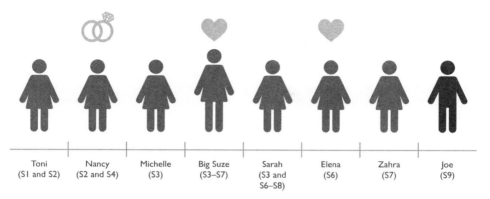

Toni	Nancy	Michelle	Big Suze	Sarah	Elena	Zahra	Joe
(S1 and S2)	(S2 and S4)	(S3)	(S3–S7)	(S3 and S6–S8)	(S6)	(S7)	(S9)

The most innovative aspects of the show are its point-of-view camerawork, which sees most of the action filmed from a perspective matching that of the characters', and its use of voice-over to convey Mark and Jez's innermost thoughts. Seeing the world through the eyes of the protagonists and eavesdropping on their unspoken desires, you get to experience their deepest insecurities firsthand—with all the discomfort and hilarity that entails. Watching the pair struggling to navigate awkward interactions with love interests, bosses, potential bandmates, and each other, as well as satisfying their baser impulses while trying to maintain the appearance of decent people who adhere to social norms is a key part of the show's rich humor.

Every season follows a predictable pattern, with Mark and Jez both fixating on an unavailable love interest. Mark's crushes include his flighty credit-union coworker Sophie (Olivia Colman) and quirky IT geek Dobby. Jez falls for a series of married women, space cadets, ex-girlfriends who no longer want anything to do with him, his downstairs neighbor who lives with her girlfriend, and even Mark's sister. At some point in a season, Mark and Jez will usually end up ruining each others' relationships in one way or another. For anyone else, such transgressions would end a friendship, but for these two misanthropes it's just business as usual. It's almost as if the two are actively sabotaging the other's happiness so one doesn't end up abandoning the other.

The formula for each season never changes with the pair clumsily grasping for love, fulfillment, and professional success that remains just out of reach before culminating in some grand humiliation only to have the cycle begin anew. However, as predictable as it is, the series never gets stale, even after repeated rewatches. It's an impressive feat for such a long-running show.

Like *Curb Your Enthusiasm* (see p360) and *The Office* (see p153), *Peep Show* traffics in cringe comedy stemming from the pair's clumsy attempts at deception, social faux pas, and general inability to get out of their own ways. The more pain Mark and Jez are forced to endure, the better it is for the rest of us.

CREATORS: Jesse Armstrong, Sam Bain, Andrew O'Connor
PRODUCTION CO: Objective Productions

PORRIDGE

PRISON COMEDY • 1974
RATED: TV-14 • 30 MINS

An inmate locked up on a five-year sentence tries to keep his head down and his nose clean as he serves out his time, while taking a clueless young first offender under his wing.

Sent to the fictional Slade prison, repeat offender Nigel Norman Fletcher (Ronnie Barker) is paired with cellmate Lennie Godber (Richard Beckinsale), a naive first-time inmate unaccustomed to life on the inside. The canny Fletcher teases Lennie but also serves as a father figure, teaching him to avoid trouble and find the small pleasures that make life behind bars almost bearable. That includes staying out of the crosshairs of authoritarian warden Mr. Mackay (Fulton Mackay) and ruthless gang leader "Grouty" (Peter Vaughan).

Over three seasons, this classic BBC sitcom also finds the wily Fletcher manipulating bleeding-heart prison guard Mr. Barrowclough (Brian Wilde) and getting involved in schemes such as an ill-fated gambling racket.

HIGH FIDELITY

COMEDY • 2020
RATED: TV-MA • 30 MINS

Rob, a record store owner, navigates heartbreak in this reimagining of *High Fidelity*, the 2000 movie, which was an adaptation of a Nick Hornby novel.

This 10-episode reboot sees a gender flip for the role of Rob, who is played by effortlessly cool Zöe Kravitz. Now set in Brooklyn, the premise is the same: Rob stews over her ex-fiancé by making top-five lists (such as top-five desert island artists and top-five heartbreaks) and revisits those past heartbreaks to figure out what she did wrong.

The show works best when it deviates from the movie and book. A scene in which Rob is ignored by a middle-aged music fan, who talks to her male friend instead, stands out. As does the episode that focuses on Simon (David H. Holmes), Rob's gay ex and employee, as he recounts his own heartbreaks.

Just one season (so far), *High Fidelity* is a cover version with heart.

THE LEFTOVERS

SCI-FI DRAMA • 2014
RATED: TV-MA • 60 MINS

After 2 percent of the world's population mysteriously vanishes one October day, those who are left try to make sense of their loved ones' disappearance amid spiraling chaos.

Small-town police chief Kevin Garvey Jr. (Justin Theroux) has his life torn asunder when his wife, Laurie (Amy Brenneman), and son, Tommy (Chris Zylka), abandon the family to join competing cults that have sprung up since the unexplained disappearance of 140 million people in a cataclysmic event known as the "Sudden Departure." Those who remain, the titular "leftovers," struggle to balance grieving for their missing loved ones and their need to maintain order in a world enveloped by insidious sects.

Across three seasons, the show's intricately interconnected network of tormented survivors broadens, moving from New York to Texas to Melbourne. The result is a surreal meditation on trauma and loss.

ORANGE IS THE NEW BLACK

**PRISON COMEDY • 2013 • RATED: TV-MA • 51 MINS • SEASONS: 7
TAYLOR SCHILLING, LAURA PREPON, NATASHA LYONNE**

A decade-old crime comes back to bite a privileged New Yorker as she's sent to a women's prison and has to learn how to handle the horrors of life behind bars.

Piper Chapman (Taylor Schilling) has her comfortable upper-middle-class existence in New York City with her fiancé, Larry (Jason Biggs), turned upside down when she's sentenced to 15 months for having run drug money over a decade before. On the inside, Chapman is reunited with her drug-trafficker ex-girlfriend Alex Vause (Laura Prepon), causing old feelings to return, despite the fact that it was Vause who ratted her out.

Behind bars, Chapman learns to navigate the unspoken rules and rival gangs of prison life. These include trying not to upset hardened inmates such as erratic former methhead preacher Pennsatucky (Taryn Manning) and intimidating Russian kitchen chief "Red" (Kate Mulgrew).

Chapman also has to deal with unethical and corrupt prison officials, including world-weary, homophobic counselor Sam (Michael Harney), and oafish prison guard "Pornstache" (Pablo Schreiber), who trafficks drugs to prisoners.

From *Weeds* (p336) creator Jenji Kohan, this Netflix comedy drama doesn't shy away from dealing with the dark realities of prison life head on, including riots, guards impregnating inmates, and prisoners struggling to adjust to life on the outside after spending decades in the system. But it always remains outrageous and hilarious entertainment.

VICE PRINCIPALS

**COMEDY • 2016
RATED: TV-MA • 30 MINS**

Nothing brings two rival school administrators together faster than the desire to destroy the highly qualified woman who's just beaten them to the role of principal.

Disgruntled, bad-tempered vice principal Neal Gamby (series cocreator Danny McBride) forges an unlikely alliance with his nemesis, manipulative dandy co–vice principal Lee

Russell (Walton Goggins), when the job they were both competing over is awarded to the infinitely more qualified Dr. Belinda Brown (Kimberly Hebert Gregory). While plotting to unseat her as head, the two men leave a trail of destruction in their wake.

Like McBride's other projects (he is also the creator of *Eastbound and Down*, see p359), this black comedy makes small-town South Carolina feel like a bizarre world of its own. Over its all-too-brief two seasons, it reveals itself to be as much a critique of toxic masculinity as it is a darkly comic masterpiece.

BIG LITTLE LIES

DRAMA • 2017 • RATED: TV-MA • 45 MINS • SEASONS: 2
REESE WITHERSPOON, NICOLE KIDMAN, ZOË KRAVITZ

A murder at a school parents' event exposes the dark underbelly of an otherwise quiet Californian coastal community, laying bare tensions between rival moms and their complicated relationships.

Small-town secrets slowly come to light after five mothers in the well-to-do beachside community of Monterey, California, become involved in a murder investigation. Among those under the magnifying glass are alpha firebrand Madeline (Reese Witherspoon); her wealthy queen-bee rival Renata (Laura Dern); ex-lawyer and mother of twin boys Celeste (Nicole Kidman); Madeline's ex-husband's hippie wife, Bonnie (Zoë Kravitz); and single mom Jane (Shailene Woodley), who's new in town and has a mysterious past.

Through a series of time jumps and flashbacks, an intertwined tale of domestic abuse, sexual assault, unresolved trauma, and marital

infidelity unfolds against a backdrop of elaborate kids' birthday parties and school fundraisers, including the absurdly stylish trivia night where the murder unfolds.

Initially conceived as a one-off miniseries, the show proved so popular that a second season was commissioned. Although it wasn't as well received as the first, the addition of Meryl Streep to the cast makes it worth a watch.

> **"** *It was a unique opportunity to have five really talented, diverse women on screen together.* **"**
>
> **Reese Witherspoon** (Madeline Mackenzie)

RESCUE ME

COMEDY DRAMA • 2004
RATED: TV-MA • 42 MINS

A New York City firefighter with a weakness for booze and women is haunted by the trauma of watching his cousin and colleague die during the 9/11 attacks.

Veteran firefighter Tommy Gavin (Denis Leary) is heroic and dedicated when he's on the job. But off the clock, Gavin is a drunk, self-loathing womanizer separated from his

wife and kids. Fueling his self-destruction is his survivor's guilt over the death of his cousin Jimmy (James Caffrey), a fellow firefighter who died responding to the World Trade Center attacks on September 11, 2001. Rather than unpack his trauma, Gavin is predisposed to fits of rage when he's not screwing up his own life and disappointing his family and coworkers.

There are times where the show can skew a little too dark, but anchored by actor-comedian Leary's performance, it never loses its cracking wit over its seven seasons.

EASTBOUND & DOWN

**COMEDY • 2009 • RATED: TV-MA • 30 MINS • SEASONS: 4
DANNY MCBRIDE, JOHN HAWKES, MICHAEL PEÑA**

After his major league baseball career peters out, a delusional former star pitcher returns to his hometown to teach middle-school gym and plot his comeback.

Former baseball superstar Kenny Powers (series cocreator Danny McBride) refuses to admit his life is in a tailspin as he returns to his hometown in North Carolina, moves in with older brother, Dustin (John Hawkes), and sister-in-law, Cassie (Jennifer Irwin), taking a job as a substitute middle-school gym teacher.

In his new post, the foul-mouthed Powers decides to pursue his coworker and former high-school flame April (Katy Mixon), who is engaged to school principal Terrence (Andy Daly). Although Powers's sports career has tanked, he hasn't dropped the rock-star ego and abrasive personality he cultivated while he was a celebrity. At the same time, his doughy frame, absurd mullet, and gargantuan appetite for booze and drugs make it hard to believe he was ever an elite athlete.

The dark comedy follows Powers from his hometown to Mexico and Myrtle Beach, South Carolina, as the one-time ace pitcher tries to reclaim his past glory aided by desperately devoted sidekick Stevie Janowski (Steve Little). Music teacher Janowski idolizes the obnoxious Powers and doesn't seem to mind that he does nothing but insult and degrade him.

The show features appearances from some genuine star names over its four seasons, including Will Ferrell, Matthew McConaughey, Adam Scott, and Lily Tomlin, a testament to its hilarious humor.

THIS IS ENGLAND '86

**DRAMA • 2010
RATED: TV-MA • 44 MINS**

Check back in with the characters from skinhead movie drama *This Is England* as they leave their pasts behind and embrace the mid-'80s mod revival.

Set during the 1986 World Cup, this four-part miniseries revisits a handful of characters three years after where director Shane Meadows's 2006 movie left off. Shaun (Thomas Turgoose) is finishing school, facing bleak employment prospects, and ingratiating himself back in with his old gang. Meanwhile, ex-skinhead leader Woody (Joseph Gilgun) is a scooter-riding mod having second thoughts about marrying Lol (Vicky McClure), who is coming to terms with the years of extreme emotional and sexual abuse she suffered at the hands of her father, Mick (Johnny Harris).

Like its movie predecessor, this spin-off series vacillates between coming-of-age saga and hyper-violent drama. At times, it can be too difficult to watch but was popular enough to spawn two sequels, set in '88 and '90.

CURB YOUR ENTHUSIASM

COMEDY • 2000 • RATED: TV-MA • 26 MINS • SEASONS: 10
LARRY DAVID, JEFF GARLIN, CHERYL HINES

The cocreator of *Seinfeld* is worth hundreds of millions of dollars, is married to a gorgeous woman light-years out of his league, and will go down in history as a comedy legend. So what does he find to complain about? Literally everything.

Comedy star Larry David plays a fictional, ostensibly more curmudgeonly, version of himself in this meta part-improvised comedy about his semiretired life in Los Angeles. With *Seinfeld* (see p278) behind him, Larry spends his life as a multimillionaire picking fights with friends and service workers alike over such minutiae as the customary cut-off time for an evening telephone call, the unspoken "lose an item, get an item" law of laundrettes, and whether a high-powered HBO executive stole shrimp from Larry's Chinese take-out order.

> **"*I'm going to hate myself more than normally.*"**
>
> Larry (S7 E3)

The bulk of each episode is spent hilariously exploring the consequences of eschewing widely held conventions and customs of social interactions. In every episode, Larry has deliciously spiteful and petty showdowns that have been set up by a series of happenstance run-ins. All the story lines then wrap up in a humiliating if overly convenient bow. In most cases, the bow is David's humiliation or defeat soundtracked to a whimsical tuba and mandolin ditty. As the series continues, the setups become more predictable, but the mostly improvised performances from Larry's friends, including Ted Danson, Mary Steenburgen, and Richard Lewis, are worth the price of admission. The most memorable blowouts come courtesy of Susie Greene, the overly confrontational, loud, foul-mouthed wife of his agent Jeff Greene (Jeff Garlin).

What makes *Curb* arguably more effective than *Seinfeld* is the additional creative freedom afforded to David after he made the jump to pay TV network HBO. He capitalizes on it by creating cruder humor and story lines that dance right on the knife's edge of risky and offensive. The end product is an uproariously hilarious portrayal of a deeply petty man held prisoner by his own neuroses.

CREATOR: Larry David
PRODUCTION CO: HBO, Production Partners

VEEP

**COMEDY • 2012 • RATED: TV-MA • 26 MINS • SEASONS: 7
JULIA LOUIS-DREYFUS, MATT WALSH, ANNA CHLUMSKY**

In the *Veep* universe, Washington, DC, is a viper's nest of petty and vapid dead-eyed careerists who are driven more by their pathologically fragile egos than any desire to serve Joe Public. So is the real DC, but the fictional one is at least funny.

Selina Meyer (Julia Louis-Dreyfus) is the increasingly irrelevant vice president to an unseen POTUS who can't be bothered to return her calls. Meyer's political ambitions far exceed her desire to help anyone but herself. However, her rise is hampered by the team of burnouts, conniving snakes, and assorted incompetents she calls her staff.

Meyer's team includes codependent, hopelessly devoted "body man" Gary Walsh (Tony Hale); chief of staff and simmering cauldron of rage Amy Brookheimer (Anna Chlumsky); ambitious Dan Egan (Reid Scott); middle-aged space cadet

Mike McLintock (Matt Walsh) as director of communications; and her ruthlessly efficient personal secretary Sue Wilson (Sufe Bradshaw). The veep's office is also constantly besieged by visits from absurdly confident low-level cog Jonah Ryan (Timothy Simons), who is all too happy to rub his West Wing lanyard in the faces of the staffers exiled in the dreaded Eisenhower Executive Office Building, far from POTUS.

> **"** *If there is any dirty trick I cannot stand, it is honesty.* **"**
>
> **Amy** (S3 E8)

Veep makes no bones about the fact that it's populated by irredeemable swamp creatures, motivated solely by their own self-interest. Like *Curb...*, the show relies on the impeccable improv skills of its cast when the time comes for the characters to roast each other within an inch of their lives with surgical precision. It's a reliable formula: the more brutal the insults, the funnier the episode. A particularly memorable barb entails VP Meyer knocking the gangly Jonah, dubbed "Jonad" by his colleagues, down a few pegs by calling him "Jolly Green-Jizz Face."

Veep also thrived because it wasn't afraid to shake up its premise from season to season. The vice presidency was just a starting point for Selina Meyer and her staff as each character experiences modest triumphs and devastating failures in their quests to satisfy their endless ambitions.

CREATOR: Armando Iannucci
PRODUCTION CO: Dundee Productions

COLLATERAL

CRIME THRILLER • 2018
RATED: TV-MA • 60 MINS

Assigned to investigate the shooting of a Muslim pizza delivery man, London detective Kip Glaspie uncovers a miry plot implicating multiple sectors of society—from the criminal underworld to the army to the government.

After a pizza delivery man is gunned down on the job in central London, DI Kip Glaspie (Carey Mulligan) is assigned to the case.

Her inquiries lead her through a complicated web of dubious characters, some of whom occupy the upper echelons of government. Unlike more standard police procedurals, this one has loftier ambitions, tackling issues such as racism and the refugee crisis.

With all its twists and turns, this highly addictive single-season, four-part thriller makes an easy binge watch. But you're likely to find it even more rewarding the second time around when you can appreciate how all the pieces of the puzzle fit together into a complex web of conflicting political forces.

ONE MISSISSIPPI

COMEDY DRAMA • 2015
RATED: TV-MA • 25 MINS

Can you ever truly go home again? A dry-witted Los Angeles radio host gets to find out when she returns to the Deep South to be with her dying mom.

While recovering from a double mastectomy and suffering from another mystery illness, LA radio presenter and cancer patient Tig Bovaro (series creator Tig Notaro) is forced to leave her progressive bubble and return to small-town Mississippi to be with her mother as she's taken off life support. Along with having to endure the culture shock of being a lesbian in a conservative town, Tig also has to negotiate complicated relationships with her idiot brother, Remy (Noah Harpster), and uptight stepfather, Bill (John Rothman).

Despite dealing with heavy topics such as grief and childhood sexual abuse, this two-season series also has plenty of levity thanks to Tig's acerbic delivery. The most uplifting moments come from Tig's discovery of unknown details about her late mother's life.

THE LAST MAN ON EARTH

SCI-FI COMEDY • 2015
RATED: TV-14 • 22 MINS

A lonely man desperately seeks other human beings after a virus wipes out most of humanity. But will he regret his search for company once his wish comes true?

What if the apocalypse doesn't entail fire, brimstone, and/or zombies? What if it's just profoundly lonely? That's what bank employee Phil Miller (Will Forte) discovers after most of humanity is killed off by disease, leaving him to roam the country in search of fellow survivors, especially women. He gets his wish when he happens upon fellow survivor Carol Pilbasian (Kristen Schaal) but lives to regret it when the two end up getting on each other's nerves.

As Phil finds other survivors over the show's four-season run, he becomes overwhelmed by the prospect of rebuilding society alongside such a ragtag mix of eccentrics and weirdos. Maybe he was better off just lounging in his kiddie pool full of booze and having spirited conversations with athletic equipment.

BLOODLINE

DRAMA • 2015 • RATED: TV-MA • 48 MINS • SEASONS: 3
KYLE CHANDLER, BEN MENDELSOHN, SISSY SPACEK

When their black-sheep older brother returns to town to claim a piece of the family empire, the children of the owners of a Florida Keys resort are forced to reckon with dark secrets.

Nothing is ever the same again for the well-to-do Rayburn clan after prodigal son and petty criminal Danny (Ben Mendelsohn) arrives back in the Florida Keys to celebrate the 45th anniversary of his parents' opening of their upscale tropical resort, the Rayburn House. Danny's return kicks up forgotten family secrets and turns the lives of his siblings—local sheriff's deputy John (Kyle Chandler), attorney Meg (Linda Cardellini), and impulsive marina owner Kevin (Norbert Leo Butz)—upside down.

Tensions arise after Danny tries to insert himself into the family business, creating concern that he has sinister motives. But the respectable Rayburn children reluctantly welcome him back at the insistence of their mother, Sally (Sissy Spacek). The cause of Danny's initial falling out with his family is revealed through flashbacks and nonlinear storytelling, unearthing a long-buried tragedy.

The first season is a taut, satisfying slow-burn anchored by masterful performances. The second and third seasons are less cohesive but nonetheless gratifyingly suspenseful.

> **"***I always thought the greatest thing that happened to me was being born a Rayburn. Now I'm not so sure.***"**
>
> John Rayburn (SI EI)

THE OA

SCI-FI MYSTERY • 2016
RATED: TV-MA • 50 MINS

A young blind woman missing for seven years mysteriously returns home with her sight restored. Is it a miracle, or is something even more bizarre and insidious going on?

After disappearing seven years before, blind youngster Prairie Johnson (Brit Marling) returns home to her elderly adoptive parents in Michigan with scars on her back and the ability to see. Dubbing herself "The OA" or "original angel," Prairie prefers to stay silent about her lost years, except to a group of four troubled teens she enlists for a secret mission.

Is Prairie the victim of an abduction? Is she tapped into a secret portal allowing her to move between worlds? And what's with all the weird dancing? This sci-fi series delves into surreal territory in its two seasons, sometimes verging on silliness and raising more questions than it answers as a result of its unreliable narrator, but the journey is always thrilling enough to get away with it.

PATRICK MELROSE

DRAMA • 2018
RATED: TV-MA • 60 MINS

A life of privilege can't keep one fortunate son's demons at bay in this saga of a wealthy Englishman's journey from addiction to recovery.

Based on the Edward St. Aubyn novel series, *Patrick Melrose* stars Benedict Cumberbatch as a semibiographical version of the author, a wealthy but boorish Brit dealing with unprocessed trauma imparted by his sadistic father, David (Hugo Weaving), and negligent mother, Eleanor (Jennifer Jason Leigh). The five-episode, single-season miniseries follows Patrick's descent into heroin addiction as he attempts to suppress memories of childhood abuse against a backdrop of fancy parties, five-star hotels, and all the elegant trappings of the upper crust.

The series spans several decades in Melrose's life, including his journey from hopeless but clever junkie to an adult forced to confront his demons and free himself from the cycle of addiction after he spends the family fortune.

THE AFFAIR

DRAMA • 2014
RATED: TV-MA • 50 MINS

How can an extramarital fling cause so much damage in so many seemingly unrelated people's lives? A frustrated novelist and a grieving resort-town waitress are about to find out.

Married dad and struggling novelist Noah Solloway (Dominic West) and Long Island beach-town waitress/grieving mother Alison Bailey (Ruth Wilson) begin an affair after a chance meeting in a restaurant. The consequences of their fling prove both predictable and devastating, as its butterfly effect ripples out to include a murder inquiry, the details of which unravel over time.

Don't bother trying to find a reliable narrator over the course of this mind-bending five-season series. Each episode is broken in half, beginning with Noah and Alison both telling their version of events and often remembering things differently. The multiple-points-of-view premise later extends to the loved ones they devastated during their tryst.

THE POLITICIAN

COMEDY DRAMA • 2019
RATED: TV-14 • 56 MINS

Washington, DC, has nothing on the Machiavellian power plays and cut-throat machinations behind the election for student-body president at posh Saint Sebastian High School.

Creator Ryan Murphy goes full camp in this nighttime soap send-up centered on pathological overachiever Payton (Ben Platt), a privileged southern California high-school student with his sights set on the Oval Office. Unfortunately, he's running against his ex-lover, River (David Corenswet), a hunk blessed with a movie-star's jaw line and charm to spare, so Payton decides on chronically ill wheelchair user Infinity Jackson (Zoey Deutch) as his vice president for the sympathy vote. Things only get uglier from there.

Despite this being a Ryan Murphy show set in a school, don't expect another *Glee* (see p213). There's far more scheming, and even more in Season 2 as Payton sets his sights on the New York State Senate race.

WANDERLUST

DRAMA • 2018
RATED: TV-MA • 56 MINS

A psychotherapist goes to creative lengths to save her marriage after a cycling accident throws a spanner into her sex life.

Marriages are complicated things, as couples therapist Joy (Toni Collette) learns firsthand when a biking accident throws her pelvis out of whack—and along with it her sex life with Alan (Steven Mackintosh), her husband of more than 20 years. The two decide to inject new life into their relationship by opening it up and seeing other people. In Alan's case, it's fellow English teacher Claire (Zawe Ashton), and for Joy, it's Marvin (William Ash), a hot cop she ogles at the swimming pool.

Across one season, Joy and Alan suffer the unforeseen consequences of inviting other people into their marriage, all while trying to raise two teenagers (who have plenty of issues all their own). Both Collette and Mackintosh's performances make this one-season series well worth watching.

OZARK

CRIME DRAMA • 2017 • RATED: TV-MA • 60 MINS • SEASONS: 3
JASON BATEMAN, LAURA LINNEY, JULIA GARNER

A financial adviser flees the Chicago suburbs with his family and lands in a remote Missouri resort town where he must launder money to get back into the good books of his drug kingpin boss.

Financial adviser Marty Byrde (Jason Bateman) finds his life turned upside down when the drug cartel for which he's been laundering money discovers his business partner has been embezzling funds. After the cartel kills the partner, Marty bargains for his own life and those of his wife, Wendy (Laura Linney), and children. He convinces drug lord Del (Esai Morales) to let him launder $500 million. But the Byrdes find that doing this in the Ozark Mountains is more difficult than they imagined when they run up against local crime family, the Langmores, and heroin dealers.

The Byrdes appear to be a clean-cut couple, so they use this to their advantage when investing cartel cash in failing businesses. Unfortunately, those locals unlucky enough to get entangled with them never seem to figure out their firms are being used to wash drug money until it's too late. They might look respectable, but the Byrdes seem to have a talent for ruining the lives of everyone they touch.

It's an uncomfortable watch at times—tense and stressful. Season 2 is the weakest, but stick with it because the third is worth waiting for.

> **"**Money is not peace of mind. Money is not happiness. Money is, at its essence, that measure of a man's choices.**"**

Marty Byrde (S1 E1)

EUPHORIA

DRAMA • 2019
RATED: TV-MA • 54 MINS

A gaggle of troubled high-school kids, including a 17-year-old fresh out of rehab, struggle to stay on the straight and narrow in this cautionary tale against absentee parenting.

High-school student Rue Bennett (Zendaya) has a tough road ahead of her when she returns to her hard-partying classmates after a brief stint in rehab, knowing there's no way she's staying clean. Complicating matters is her unexpected infatuation with the new girl in town, Jules (Hunter Schafer), who comes with secrets of her own. In fact, all of Rue's classmates carry some kind of baggage, especially Nate Jacobs (Jacob Elordi), the popular football captain fighting to suppress the rage boiling just below the surface.

Like a seedy *Degrassi* (see p74), this (so far) one-season drama can be hard to watch, with self-destructive teens finding themselves in harm's way. But at other times, it's also a tender coming-of-age love story. Worth a look.

BROTHERS & SISTERS

DRAMA • 2006
RATED: TV-PG • 42 MINS

A father's death kicks off a series of uncomfortable revelations for a wealthy California family running a lucrative food firm. But nothing quite brings them together like a bottle of wine from their vineyard.

This schmaltzy drama walks the line between heartfelt tearjerker and soap. Like *Six Feet Under* (see p339), it deals with dark secrets that emerge after a family patriarch bites the dust. In this case, Pasadena widow Nora Walker (Sally Field) learns her late husband had a secret, illegitimate daughter (Emily VanCamp) and embezzled pension funds from the family's Ojai Foods empire. Unlike *Six Feet Under*, however, there are far more feel-good moments where the clan set aside their differences over a bottle or 10 of wine.

Over five seasons, the Walkers deal with every possible tragedy, from fertility struggles to marital infidelity, financial ruin, and death. Thank goodness they own a vineyard.

A MILLION LITTLE THINGS

DRAMA • 2018
RATED: TV-14 • 42 MINS

A group of friends in Boston are forced to reevaluate what's important in life after they are rocked by the unexpected suicide of a pal.

Three buddies try to find the meaning of it all after their seemingly successful friend Jon (Ron Livingston) inexplicably throws himself off a balcony after closing a business deal. Jon's suicide forces his pals—music teacher Eddie (David Giuntoli), breast cancer survivor Gary (James Roday), and aspiring filmmaker Rome (Romany Malco)—to confront their own issues, whether it's mental illness, failing marriages, or recovery from a life-threatening illness. Think *This Is Us* (see p179), but instead of a family, it's about four guys who bonded over their love of their favorite hockey team, the Boston Bruins.

Over the course of two seasons, the remaining trio confront their grief while unanswered questions over Jon's death loom. It turns out moving on will be harder than they thought.

TUCA & BERTIE

ANIMATED COMEDY • 2019
RATED: TV-MA • 25 MINS

Two 30-something cartoon birds deal with some very human problems, including career anxiety, relationship troubles, and alcoholism.

Tuca (Tiffany Haddish) is a newly sober codependent toucan dealing with separation anxiety now that she no longer lives with best pal Bertie (Ali Wong), a career-minded songbird climbing the corporate ladder at publishing giant Conde Nest. Together, the pair help each other through life's highs and lows, including Bertie's relationship with her just-moved-in boyfriend, Speckle (Steven Yeun), an architect robin.

For two cartoon birds, Tuca and Bertie are shockingly relatable. Over the course of a single season, the show explores complex themes such as childhood trauma and fear of abandonment, while doubling as a wonderfully weird buddy comedy about two 30-something women masquerading as cartoon animals living in a colorful wonderland known as Bird Town.

PARTY OF FIVE

DRAMA • 1994
RATED: TV-PG • 43 MINS

Five young siblings have to grow up before their time, raise each other, and run the family business after their parents are killed by a drunk driver.

Aimless 20-something Charlie Salinger (Matthew Fox) needs to get his act together fast after becoming the guardian of his newly orphaned siblings following their parents' death in a car crash. He is overwhelmed by his newly acquired responsibility. Charlie has to bring up 16-year-old wild child Bailey (Scott Wolf), bright-but-sensitive 15-year-old Julia (Neve Campbell), 11-year-old master violinist Claudia (Lacey Chabert), and baby Owen. As if that weren't enough, the surviving Salingers also have to run the family restaurant while grieving for their parents. Sometimes good things happen to them, too.

The Salinger kids spend six seasons on the bumpy crash course in adulthood, dealing with the pressures of having to raise a small child together and finding love along the way.

WENTWORTH

PRISON DRAMA • 2013
RATED: TV-MA • 45 MINS

A woman convicted of the attempted murder of her abusive husband must learn to survive the brutal Australian prison system while awaiting sentence.

This gritty seven-season Aussie drama begins with surburban mom Bea Smith (Danielle Cormack) getting separated from her daughter as she is sent to Wentworth prison while awaiting sentencing for the attempted murder of her violent husband. Bea learns hard lessons about whom to trust and whom to avoid as she's turned into a drug mule by Franky Doyle (Nicole da Silva), the first inmate to befriend her.

A reworking of classic 1980s Australian soap opera *Prisoner: Cell Block H*, this series set in a women's jail doesn't have the same levity and humor you encounter in *Orange Is the New Black* (see p357). Instead, it's a dark drama of rival prison gangs and morally compromised guards that feels closer to the grim despair of *Oz* (see p21).

KILLING EVE

THRILLER • 2018 • RATED: TV-14 • 42 MINS • SEASONS: 3
SANDRA OH, JODIE COMER, FIONA SHAW

A game of cat and mouse between a stylish, psychopathic assassin and a bored British intelligence officer takes a sexy turn when the two women become obsessed with each other.

Based on Luke Jennings's *Codename Villanelle* novellas, *Killing Eve* centers on the growing obsession between Eve Polastri (Sandra Oh), a dowdy British intelligence officer assigned to a clandestine mission in MI6, and Villanelle (Jodie Comer), a young cold-blooded assassin who can.wear the hell out of a pink tulle evening gown.

Writer Phoebe Waller-Bridge of *Fleabag* (see p340) fame puts her trademark acerbic touch on this homoerotic spy drama that's equal parts dark comedy and nerve-jangling thriller. The dynamic between the assassin and the spy is buoyed by the electrifying chemistry between the two leads.

Eve and Villanelle's paths collide after Eve, an intelligence analyst fascinated by female killers, is unceremoniously bounced from her desk job to a secret British intelligence unit chasing an impeccably dressed international assassin who seems to kill as much for pleasure as she does for profit.

The series feels like a gender-flipped *Hannibal* (see p430) in the way its subjects explore their taboo desires through their mutual fascination for each other, with both Eve and Villanelle taking turns playing the hunter and the hunted. As the pair get closer to each other, Eve begins to realize some hard truths about how interconnected her employers are with the criminals hiring the object of her obsession.

It is also a true delight for the senses, with the action taking place against gorgeous European landscapes and accompanied by an exquisitely curated soundtrack. This is a show that doesn't fumble a thing. The moments of comic relief elicit thunderous guffaws rather than appreciative chuckles, while the violence is shockingly graphic and visceral.

But above all else, *Killing Eve* delivers wonderfully complex female characters who are often vastly more interesting than the unremarkable men holding them back. Watch out especially for Fiona Shaw's masterfully slippery supporting performance as Carolyn Martens, head of MI6's Russia division. Although Seasons 2 and 3 aren't as cohesive as Season 1—perhaps owing to Waller-Bridges' departure as head writer—this witty, subversive series still makes for satisfying binge material.

CREATOR: Phoebe Waller-Bridge
PRODUCTION CO: Sid Gentle Films, Endeavor Content, BBC America

FARGO

**CRIME DRAMA • 2014 • RATED: TV-MA • 46 MINS • SEASONS: 4
BILLY BOB THORNTON, MARTIN FREEMAN, KIRSTEN DUNST**

A spin-off from the Coen brothers' Oscar-winning movie of the same name, this darkly comic crime series explores a different murderous Midwest tale per season, with a handful of oddball overlapping characters connecting it all together.

Quirky characters abound in Noah Hawley's anthology crime series. From vicious assassins to violent gang members and crooked probation officers, its tales of ordinary folks getting their first taste of ill-gotten gains, only to realize they've gotten in way over their heads in the criminal underworld, are peopled by a motley ragbag of personalities you wouldn't like to meet.

The series begins in the obscure town of Bemidji, Minnesota, in 2006, with unwitting middle-aged insurance salesman Lester Nygaard accidentally putting a hit out on the guy who bullied him in high school after bumping into hardened criminal Lorne Malvo (Billy Bob Thornton) and making an off-handed joke. Instead of distancing himself from Malvo, Nygaard begins an ill-fated association that results in more bloodshed. Meanwhile, salt-of-the-earth Minnesota state patrol deputy Molly Solverson (Allison Tolman) teams up with mild-mannered Duluth police deputy Gus Grimly (Colin Hanks) to solve the wave of murders happening in Nygaard and Malvo's wake.

Season 2 serves as a prequel to the first with young hairdresser Peggy Blumquist (Kirsten Dunst) accidentally killing a member of the powerful Gerhardt crime family in Fargo, North Dakota in 1979.

Season 3 jumps to small-town Minnesota in 2010, where a parole officer and his parolee girlfriend (Ewan McGregor and Mary Elizabeth Winstead) get wrapped up in a double murder.

RECTIFY

**DRAMA • 2013
RATED: TV-14 • 43 MINS**

When a man is freed from death row 19 years after a wrongful murder conviction, he finds readjusting to life in a small Georgia town can be just as difficult as being locked up.

After spending almost 20 years awaiting execution, Daniel Holden (Aden Young) is released from jail when a reexamination of DNA evidence casts doubt on whether he did in fact rape and murder his 16-year-old girlfriend. Returning to a family he barely recognizes, Daniel has trouble adjusting to life as a free man, having spent his entire adult existence enduring the brutality of prison. All must shoulder the burden of helping him reacclimatize to life in his small Georgia hometown where the cops and locals are still wary of him.

A slow-burn Southern Gothic tale sprawling out over four seasons, Daniel's painful journey is a fascinating study of the trauma wrought by stolen time and the search for redemption.

HEARTBREAK HIGH

DRAMA • 1994
RATED: NR • 50 MINS

Addiction, racism, teen pregnancy, and homelessness are just some of the issues addressed in this gritty, long-running drama about high-school teens in Sydney.

The students of Hartley High, a fictional Australian inner-city high school, have some brutally real problems. On any one day, they might have to tackle drug use, class struggles, the debate over free speech, or homophobia—all before lunch. Aside from the hot-button issues, the youngsters—including popular Nick Poulos (Alex Dimitriades), his cousin and classmate Con (Salvatore Coco), and their friends—also deal with the ordinary pressures of school life, such as trying to make the football team and dating.

Over seven seasons, the show eventually drifts away from its high-school setting to focus more on the kids hanging out. But it never stops being a true-to-life nighttime soap unafraid to tackle heavy subject matter.

DARK MATTER

SCI-FI • 2015
RATED: TV-14 • 43 MINS

Imagine waking up on a spaceship in a remote corner of the cosmos with no idea of how you got there, or who stole your memories. That's the situation six space travelers find themselves in before their real troubles begin.

Deep in the future, the crew members of the spaceship *Raza* awake to find their minds have been wiped clean. They have no idea who they are or how they got aboard this ghost ship, but slivers of memories return to them over time. All they know for sure is that they have a cargo of weaponry and are bound for a remote mining colony.

The travelers name themselves One (Marc Bendavid), Two (Melissa O'Neil), Three (Anthony Lemke), Four (Alex Mallari Jr.), Five (Jodelle Ferland), and—you guessed it—Six (Roger Cross). Over the three-season series, they pull together to figure out what happened to them and to fend off threats to the ship and their lives.

THE CROSSING

SCI-FI THRILLER • 2018
RATED: TV-PG • 42 MINS

A small-town sheriff in the Pacific Northwest discovers that a group of refugees who mysteriously washed ashore in his sleepy town might be time travelers from the future.

Sheriff Jude Ellis (Steve Zahn) finds his life upturned when dozens of refugees suddenly rock up in his Oregon town. Before Jude can figure out what's going on, he's frozen out by FBI Agent Emma Ren (Sandrine Holt). She has come to town on behalf of the Department of Homeland Security to investigate who the arrivals are and why they claim to be from 180 years in the future.

In what feels like a nod to *The Terminator* movies, these time travelers say they jumped back to the past to escape a holocaust and possibly prevent a war waged by a genetically altered authoritarian race called Apex. This slow-burn single-season mystery thriller doesn't really break any new ground, but it's a fun, meticulously plotted ride.

LEGION

SCI-FI • 2017
RATED: TV-MA • 44 MINS

A young man with schizophrenia who spent most of his life in institutions learns his mental illness may be super-powers in disguise.

This surreal, mind-bending Super Hero drama centers on David Haller (Dan Stevens), a troubled young man with tremendous powers who has nevertheless spent most of his days wasting away in psychiatric wards

being treated for schizophrenia. It isn't until he meets equally troubled fellow patient Syd (Rachel Keller) that he realizes his hallucinations might be real and he could be the most powerful mutant in existence.

Although this three-season series is connected to the *X-Men* comic books, it's more bizarre and experimental than most Marvel series and avoids linear storytelling. David's confusion over what is real and what isn't extends to the viewer as you're treated to bizarre visuals and unexpected time jumps. The uncertainty, however, is what makes the ride so much fun.

FLESH AND BONE

DRAMA • 2015
RATED: TV-MA • 60 MINS

An aspiring dancer discovers that the seemingly refined world of professional ballet has a dark side after she runs away to New York City from Pittsburgh to become a star.

When Kiira (Irina Dvorovenko), the American Ballet Company's coked-out veteran prima ballerina, suffers an injury, the future of the prestigious troupe rests on the shoulders of

Claire Robbins (Sarah Hay), a promising but self-destructive young dancer with a dark past—that is, if she can survive the rampant exploitation, intense pressure, and other trappings that come with being a professional ballet dancer in the big city.

This single-season miniseries has drawn comparisons with the films *Showgirls* and *Black Swan* with its fixation on the seedy underbelly of the cut-throat professional dance world and draws heavily from familiar tropes. At times, the plot can run a little thin, but the dancing is always a joy to watch.

VICIOUS

COMEDY • 2013
RATED: TV-MA • 23 MINS

Two grumpy old men who've been together for almost 50 years insult each other to within an inch of their lives in this sharp-tongued sitcom.

Having spent nearly five decades under the same roof, elderly gay couple Freddie (Ian McKellan) and Stuart (Derek Jacobi) enjoy a bit of a love/hate dynamic. Their favorite pastime is hilariously insulting and sniping at

each other, as well as their friends, including the ditzy Penelope (Marcia Warren) and the oversexed Violet (Frances de la Tour)—that is, when they're not acting as surrogate father figures to Ash (Iwan Rheon), their handsome, wide-eyed young neighbor.

Although struggling character actor Freddie and househusband Stuart are at their best when being their bitchiest to each other, it's clear there's also a deep and abiding love keeping them together. The occasional tender moment sneaks into the show's two-season run.

LITTLE FIRES EVERYWHERE

DRAMA • 2020
RATED: TV-MA • 53 MINS

An overbearing, upper middle class mother's life is upended when a mysterious artist and her teenage daughter move into her rental property in a quiet Ohio suburb.

Set in the late '90s, this moody adaptation of the Celeste Ng novel of the same name, centers around two mothers from two vastly different backgrounds whose lives become intertwined when Mia Warren (Kerry Washington), a transient artist new to town, rents a flat from uptight married mother of four Elena Richardson (Reese Witherspoon). Before she arrived, Mia was living in her car with her daughter Pearl (Lexi Underwood).

Over the course of eight episodes, the mini-series ambitiously dissects issues such as race, class, and the meaning of motherhood as it delves into the fraught and uncomfortable relationship between Elena and Mia. The show becomes compulsively watchable as their secrets come bubbling up to the surface.

THE MISSING

MYSTERY DRAMA • 2014
RATED: TV-14 • 60 MINS

A family's holiday in France takes a dark turn after their five-year-old son mysteriously vanishes from a crowd watching the World Cup semifinal outside a pub.

Nothing is ever the same for Tony (James Nesbitt) and Emily Hughes (Frances O'Connor) after losing their five-year-old son, Oliver (Oliver Hunt), in 2006 during a family vacation in France for the World Cup. Tony's dedication to finding his son turns into an all-consuming obsession, causing his marriage to fall apart. Years after police close the case, Tony stumbles upon a new clue and pushes to have the investigation reopened, roping the soft-spoken retired lead detective Julien Baptiste (Tchéky Karyo) back into the hunt.

Season 2 of this anthology series has world-weary detective Baptiste move on to a new investigation, this time involving the mysterious return of a girl who went missing from a British military base in Germany.

WAYWARD PINES

SCI-FI THRILLER • 2015
RATED: TV-14 • 42 MINS

An idyllic small town in Idaho seems like a peaceful getaway, if you ignore the fact that its residents are imprisoned by an electric fence and anyone caught trying to escape is publicly executed.

US Secret Service agent Ethan Burke (Matt Dillon) sets out to investigate the disappearance of two fellow agents in Wayward Pines, Idaho, only to end up a prisoner there after he's hospitalized by a car crash. Digging deeper, Burke discovers that one of his colleagues is dead and the other, his ex-mistress Kate Hewson (Carla Gugino), has settled into small-town life. Forbidding him from leaving is Sheriff Pope (Terrence Howard), who executes failed escapees in a ceremony known as a "reckoning."

What is going on in Wayward Pines? After two seasons, the answer is revealed in a shocking twist that feels par for the course when you consider that master-of-surprise filmmaker M. Night Shyamalan is an executive producer.

LONGMIRE

CRIME DRAMA • 2012
RATED: TV-14 • 42 MINS

Struggling to move on after his wife's death, a Wyoming sheriff throws himself back into his work, which involves running for reelection against an ambitious deputy.

Based on Craig Johnson's mystery novels, this neo-western sees grizzled Absaroka County Sheriff Walt Longmire (Robert Taylor) returning to work after grieving the death of his wife. There, he finds his job threatened by young deputy Branch Connally (Bailey Chase), who plans to run against him for sheriff.

Amid the intrigue, Longmire continues to solve major crimes with the help of new deputy Victoria "Vic" Moretti (Katee Sackhoff). There's also his daughter and local attorney Cady (Cassidy Freeman), and his childhood best friend Henry Standing Bear (Lou Diamond Phillips), an expert tracker and local restaurant owner. This is a procedural series that takes its time. You should take your time, too, and enjoy six seasons of western mysteries.

HEMLOCK GROVE

HORROR • 2013
RATED: TV-MA • 45 MINS

Witness the weird goings-on of a remote Pennsylvania town, home to a stark mix of rich families and impoverished ex-steel workers—not to mention a few supernatural creatures.

It doesn't take long for Romani newcomer Peter Rumancek (Landon Liboiron) to realize that strange things are afoot in his new home of Hemlock Grove, a small Pennsylvania steel town presided over by the wealthy and powerful Godfrey family. Shortly after he and his mom, Lynda (Lili Taylor), move into his late uncle's trailer, the 17-year-old becomes prime suspect in the murder of two girls, with rumors circulating he may be a werewolf. Peter teams up with neighbor Roman Godfrey (Bill Skarsgård), heir to the Godfrey biochemical engineering empire, to investigate.

This hotchpotch horror thriller ran for three seasons—barely long enough to get acquainted with all its monsters, or the cult that rises up to drive them out of town.

DIRTY JOHN

CRIME DRAMA • 2018
RATED: TV-14 • 42 MINS

A successful interior designer thinks she's found true love with a handsome doctor after several failed marriages. She's wrong. Dead wrong.

Based on a harrowing true story adapted into a podcast, wealthy interior designer and four-time divorcée Debra Newell (Connie Britton) is convinced her luck has changed when she meets John Meehan (Eric Bana), a handsome anesthesiologist. But Debra's daughters, Terra (Julia Garner) and Veronica (Juno Temple), suspect that John is too good to be true—and they're right. The hard part is convincing their mom, who has already fallen head over heels for the charming stranger.

Debra's descent into terror is slowly laid out over the course of its one season as she comes to realize her knight in shining armor is a terrifying con man. Can she escape his clutches with her bank account intact in this nail-biting thriller? Or will John try to draw some blood on the way down?

BOJACK HORSEMAN

ANIMATED COMEDY • 2014 • RATED: TV-MA • 25 MINS
SEASONS: 6 • WILL ARNETT, AARON PAUL, AMY SEDARIS

Who knew a washed-up sitcom star horse could have such a deeply complex inner life? Ride along as anthropomorphic cartoon equine BoJack stares into the abyss.

Hulking half man, half horse BoJack Horseman (Will Arnett) exists in a quirky and colorful version of Los Angeles where humans happily coexist with anthropomorphic creatures. He enjoys a complicated relationship with his ex-fling/former agent Princess Carolyn (Amy Sedaris), a pink human-housecat hybrid in red heels. BoJack's also a horse of appetites, which he indulges in his palatial bachelor pad amid the Hollywood Hills, one of the few remaining spoils from the glory days of his career.

Now, after a long and agonizing professional dry spell following the cancellation of his '90s family sitcom *Horsin' Around*, the former television star is awash in a sea of drinking, complaining to his lovable slacker human houseguest, Todd Chavez (Aaron Paul), and wallowing in self-pity as he watches reruns of his old show.

BoJack is constantly tormented by his frenemy, the aggressively cheerful Labrador retriever-human hybrid Mr. Peanutbutter, whose success has eclipsed BoJack's since he began starring in a sitcom conspicuously similar to *Horsin' Around*. It also doesn't help that BoJack is competing with a far more successful rival for the affections of his biographer, feminist writer Diane Nguyen (Alison Brie).

" *He's so stupid, he doesn't realize how miserable he should be. I envy that.* **"**

BoJack on Mr. Peanutbutter (SI EI)

BoJack Horseman is as much a meditation on the nature of fame as it is an unflinching examination of what it means to live a fulfilling life. Fortunately, it also entails plenty of cute cartoon animals doing cute things to make sure it remains on the enjoyable side of depressing.

There's no shortage of silly animal puns and goofy sight gags to provide the much-needed shots of levity amid the pathos: BoJack's memoir is titled *One Trick Pony*, while there are also references to a popular television show called *Crazy Ex-Squirrel Friend*.

This offbeat, outrageously inventive show holds up well under repeat viewings, with each frame almost certain to reveal an Easter egg of one kind or another.

CREATOR: Raphael Bob-Waksberg
PRODUCTION CO: Tornante Company, ShadowMachine, Moris Talent Hunt, Netflix

RUSSIAN DOLL

FANTASY COMEDY • 2019
RATED: TV-MA • 24 MINS

A wisecracking New Yorker gets stuck in a torturous time loop in which she's forced to relive her 36th birthday over and over. Not even dying helps her escape her fate.

Death is a daily occurrence for Nadia Vulkokov (series cocreator Natasha Lyonne), a smart-mouthed New York woman forced to relive her 36th birthday on an endless loop.

Vulkokov is desperate to escape her tormenting *Groundhog Day* scenario, but snuffing it just reboots the cycle, depositing her back to her birthday party. No matter how many times Nadia dies, she can't seem to break free. And she dies a lot.

Although Nadia is damned to repeat the same day over and over, the show itself never feels dull or repetitive during the course of its single season. The series is as much a mind-bending puzzle as it is an entertaining adventure wrapped in an ambitious concept that never loses steam.

THE THICK OF IT

COMEDY • 2005 • RATED: TV-MA • 30 MINS • SEASONS: 4
PETER CAPALDI, CHRIS ADDISON, REBECCA FRONT

The workings of the British government are ruthlessly lampooned in this dark satire about a fictional department staffed by weasels and incompetents who are routinely terrorized by a foul-mouthed spin-doctor.

The Department of Social Affairs and Citizenship (DoSAC) is constantly on the verge of a public-relations crisis owing to the bungling misfits and conniving operatives within its ranks. As such, it regularly finds itself in the firing line of brutal Number 10 spin-master Malcolm Tucker (Peter Capaldi).

One of TV's most gleefully demonic creations, Tucker keeps officials in a state of constant fear with his scene-stealing, expletive-ridden tirades. His targets include sad-sack party loyalist Glenn Cullen (James Smith), put-upon director of communications Terri Coverley (Joanna Scanlan), and arrogant Oxbridge-grad adviser Ollie Reeder (Chris Addison).

Created by Armando Iannucci (*I'm Alan Partridge*, see p267; and *Avenue 5*, see p261), *The Thick of It* is that rare series that can introduce new characters and changes in focus without other aspects of the show suffering. It has also proved immensely influential, spawning both acclaimed spin-off movie *In the Loop* and *Veep* (p361), a wildly popular adaptation for those across the pond.

> **"***Don't you ever, EVER, call me a bully. I'm so much worse than that.***"**
>
> **Malcolm Tucker** (first 2007 special episode)

KIDDING

COMEDY DRAMA • 2018
RATED: TV-MA • 26 MINS

A kindhearted children's television personality teeters on the edge of a nervous breakdown as his family falls apart in the wake of tragedy.

Jeff Piccirillo (Jim Carrey) is known to millions of children across the world as "Jeff Pickles," the genial-seeming host of the long-running TV series *Mr. Pickles' Puppet Time*. When he's off the clock, Jeff struggles to reconcile his job as a beacon of joy to kids with the grief he's experiencing over the death of his 13-year-old son, Phil (Cole Allen), and the resulting split from his wife, Jill (Judy Greer).

Also starring Frank Langella as Jeff's father and producer and Catherine Keener as Jeff's sister, this two-season series shows Carrey's character struggling to work through his issues as a man who built a multimillion dollar empire teaching life lessons to children but fails to find any comfort in what he preaches. It's an inner conflict that carries explosive consequences for Jeff's career and his personal life.

PEN15

COMEDY • 2019
RATED: TV-MA • 28 MINS

Follow the journey of two inseparable 13-year-old misfits as they endure the daily humiliations of middle school. They may not have the respect of their peers, but they have each other.

Grown-up actresses Maya Erskine and Anna Konkle play 13-year-old versions of themselves as two best friends determined to make a splash as they enter middle school in the year 2000. Remarkably, they look young enough to blend in with the actual 13-year-olds playing their classmates in this often raunchy coming-of-age comedy about the unbearable awkwardness of the tween years.

Over the single-season series, Maya and Anna discover the joys and indignities of masturbation, making out, getting their first period, and accidentally falling into possession of a popular girl's thong with a hyperrealism that is rarely seen in teen dramas and comedies. Sometimes, it's a little too real, in the best way.

DEAD LIKE ME

FANTASY COMEDY • 2003
RATED: TV-14 • 50 MINS

After getting killed by a falling toilet seat, an aloof college dropout is ordered to collect souls from the living before she can move on to the afterlife.

Georgia "George" Lass (Ellen Muth), an aimless teenage temp worker, finds that more drudgery awaits her in the afterlife as she's assigned to work as a "grim reaper," snatching souls from the living, after she's killed by a toilet that fell from a Mir space station. She's supervised by her boss Rube (Mandy Patinkin), who is also in charge of fellow grim reapers Mason (Callum Blue), Roxy (Jasmine Guy), and Betty (Rebecca Gayheart).

Although the show lasted two seasons, there's a decline in quality after showrunner Bryan Fuller and actor Rebecca Gayheart depart in the middle of the first season. Still, the remainder of the series isn't without its charms amid all the morbid comedy, while Patinkin's performance as a type of afterlife father figure is a standout.

BETTER OFF TED

COMEDY • 2009
RATED: TV-PG • 22 MINS

A handsome single dad tries to reconcile working in an evil corporation with raising his daughter to be a good person in this quirky satire.

This two-season comedy revolves around Ted Crisp (Jay Harrington), the respected and well-liked head of research at the soulless, evil conglomerate Veridian Dynamics, who had a one-off fling with his intimidating boss

Veronica (Portia de Rossi). Ted is also a single dad raising Rose (Isabella Acres), a precocious primary-age schoolkid who often acts as her father's voice of reason.

Ted is undoubtedly in need of moral guidance as Veronica is constantly ordering him to do things such as cryogenically freeze his coworkers, develop an office chair so uncomfortable that it forces employees to be more productive, or just invent more lethal weapons of mass destruction. This is an original sitcom that examines modern morality from a uniquely oblique and witty perspective.

BLUE EYES

MYSTERY DRAMA • 2014
RATED: TV-14 • 58 MINS

A group of far-right extremists wreaks havoc on Sweden in the lead-up to an election in this Nordic mash-up of political intrigue and murder mystery.

After the chief of staff to a justice minister disappears, Elin Hammar (Louise Peterhoff)—previously fired from the ministry after punching a journalist—is called back in to replace her. It's not long before she's digging in to what

happened to her predecessor. Meanwhile, Annika (Anna Bjelkerud), a right-wing party supporter, ends up dead, leaving behind her two adult children: young mother Sofia (Karin Franz Körlof) and sweet-natured Simon (David Lindström). The two stories converge to paint a grim picture of rising anti-immigrant sentiment and right-wing populism in Sweden.

There are few moments of levity in this single-season series that at times feels more like a documentary than a work of fiction. Of course, the fact that the show seems so real makes the terror all the more effective.

NURSE JACKIE

COMEDY • 2009
RATED: TV-MA • 30 MINS

A busy mom working as an ER nurse in a big-city hospital must balance the stresses of her job with the growing drug addiction she hides from her family and coworkers.

Jackie Peyton (Edie Falco) is a devoted mother and wife by day and an equally devoted ER nurse in a busy Manhattan hospital by night. How does she do it? Well, the drugs she

pockets on the job help. How does she get those drugs? By having an affair with Eddie (Paul Schulze), the hospital pharmacist and Jackie's personal Dr. Feelgood. For a woman who appears to have her life together on the surface, Jackie certainly knows how to unleash havoc on herself and everyone who cares about her.

Jackie can keep her double life from her family for only so long. Over the course of seven seasons, she's forced to confront her demons and the devastation she has caused along the way.

YOU JUST WANT TO SWITCH OFF

Written by Matthew Turner

You know how it is—when you're feeling frazzled, sometimes all you want to do is veg out and relax with a guilty pleasure, a soothing story, or some quality lightweight entertainment. Whether it's binge-watching all six seasons of *Gossip Girl* or enjoying the salacious shenanigans of *UnREAL*, this chapter has you covered.

DOWNTON ABBEY

**PERIOD DRAMA • 2010 • RATED: TV-PG • 50 MINS • SEASONS: 6
HUGH BONNEVILLE, MICHELLE DOCKERY, MAGGIE SMITH**

British drama doesn't come much cozier than *Downton Abbey*—well, at least if you ignore the various traumatic deaths. Join the Crawley family and the domestic staff of the Downton Estate as they experience triumph and suffering in the early 20th century.

Created by screenwriter Julian Fellowes, *Downton Abbey* is set on the fictional Downton Estate in Yorkshire and takes place between 1912 and 1926. It centers on the Crawley family, headed by Robert Crawley, Earl of Grantham (Hugh Bonneville), and the downstairs domestic staff of the family home, Downton Abbey. In the opening season, the estate is in severe financial trouble, leaving Robert in need of a male heir. In desperation, he turns to distant cousin Matthew Crawley (Dan Stevens), whom he hopes will fall in love with—and eventually marry—his headstrong eldest daughter, Lady Mary (Michelle Dockery).

Meanwhile, the downstairs staff are overseen by the formidable duo of head butler Mr. Carson (Jim Carter) and housekeeper Mrs. Hughes (Phyllis Logan), whose relationship throughout the series is genuinely touching. Key characters include practical and long-suffering head housemaid Anna (Joanne Froggatt), Lord Grantham's injured-in-the-Boer-War valet Mr. Bates (Brendan Coyle), and ambitious, secretly gay first footman Thomas Barrow (Robert James-Collier). Barrow is jealous of Bates's position and schemes against him, together with Lady Grantham's duplicitous maid, O'Brien (Siobhan Finneran).

Throughout the show's six seasons, plotlines unfold against the backdrop of great historical events, most of which impact the story to a greater or lesser degree. The first episode, for example, begins with the sinking of the *Titanic*. Subsequent seasons involve the outbreak of World War I—"I very much regret to

DOWNTON LOVE LINES (BELOW STAIRS)

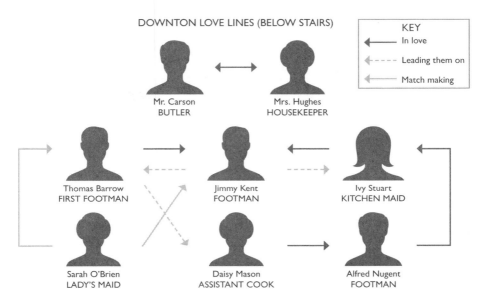

KEY
In love
Leading them on
Match making

Mr. Carson
BUTLER

Mrs. Hughes
HOUSEKEEPER

Thomas Barrow
FIRST FOOTMAN

Jimmy Kent
FOOTMAN

Ivy Stuart
KITCHEN MAID

Sarah O'Brien
LADY'S MAID

Daisy Mason
ASSISTANT COOK

Alfred Nugent
FOOTMAN

announce that we are at war with Germany," intones Robert at a garden party—and the Spanish influenza pandemic. The series moves through the Irish War of Independence (causing problems for Irishman Tom Branson, the Crawley family chauffeur), the British general election of 1923, and the Beer Hall Putsch (the attempted overthrow of the German government by Hitler's Nazi Party).

At its heart, *Downton Abbey* is essentially prime-time melodrama, a chocolate-box soap opera that elicits the full range of emotions. Consequently, as befits a soap, there are a huge number of characters in the show and it's a testament to both the acting and the writing that you come to care deeply about each and every one of them. The standout, of course, is the irrepressible Maggie Smith as the Dowager Countess Violet Crawley, who reliably steals every scene with her imperious manner and caustic one-liners.

The show made stars of several of its cast members, and some characters got killed off in deeply upsetting fashion when the actors who played them left to pursue movie careers.

The series also proved it was capable of delivering genuine shock and horror with its infamous "Red Dinner" moment in Season 6, widely considered the *Downton Abbey* version of *Game of Thrones*' (see p8) infamously bloody "Red Wedding" scene.

> *"You'll find there's never a dull moment in this house."*
>
> **Violet Crawley** (S2 E2)

Sold to multiple countries, *Downton Abbey* became a worldwide phenomenon, attracting an estimated global audience of 120 million, making it one of the most successful British TV shows of all time. The series sadly ended in 2015, but it was followed by a 2019 movie, *Downton Abbey*, that effectively served as a feature-length finale to the show and wrapped up all the remaining story lines.

THE GIRLFRIEND EXPERIENCE

DRAMA • 2016 • RATED: TV-MA • 27 MINS • SEASONS: 2
RILEY KEOUGH, PAUL SPARKS, ANNA FRIEL

Sex. Desire. Companionship. Corruption. A Chicago law student and intern takes a job as a high-class prostitute specializing in something called "The Girlfriend Experience" in this genre-spanning anthology series based on a 2009 movie by Steven Soderbergh.

Law student Christine Reade (Riley Keough) lands an internship at a prestigious law firm but struggles to pay her bills. When her classmate Avery (Kate Lyn Sheil) reveals she's been making money as a high-end call girl, Christine is curious and soon begins working for manager/pimp Jacqueline (Alexandra Castillo) under the pseudonym "Chelsea Rayne." Meanwhile, Christine discovers corruption at her law firm and draws closer to her boss David (Paul Sparks).

Created and written by filmmakers Lodge Kerrigan and Amy Siemetz, *The Girlfriend Experience* has little in common with its film predecessor, other than the fact that the lead character is also named Christine/Chelsea. Anchored by a complex, multilayered performance from Keough, the show is consistently surprising in its storytelling, going to some unexpected places and skillfully spanning several genres, while also taking an honest, unflinching look at female sexuality and identity.

Season 2 switches from a character study to an ensemble drama, telling separate stories with a completely different cast, including Anna Friel as Erica Myles and Carmen Ejogo as Bria Jones.

THE DEUCE

DRAMA • 2017
RATED: TV-MA • 59 MINS

Ever wondered how the porn industry got started? The creator of *The Wire* lays down the ins and outs of the erotic picture business.

Set during the 1970s and 1980s in New York, *The Deuce* tells the story of the rise and legalization of the porn industry. James Franco plays identical twins Vincent and Frankie, who begin working as fronts for

the mafia in Times Square. Meanwhile, street-level prostitute Eileen "Candy" Merrell (Maggie Gyllenhaal) sees opportunity in the emerging porn industry and becomes both an actress and a director.

The Deuce (the nickname for a stretch of 42nd Street) splits its three seasons into three time periods between 1971 and 1985. With its vivid characters, strong cast, and remarkable plotlines, the show combines emotionally engaging storytelling with an exploration of the sexual, cultural, and socioeconomic dynamics of the era.

MAGNIFICA 70

DRAMA • 2015
RATED: TV-MA • 55 MINS

Sex, lies, and celluloid in Brazil. A film censor's life is turned upside down when he falls for the beautiful porn star of a film he's just banned.

In 1970s Brazil, then a military dictatorship, mild-mannered Vicente (Marcos Winter) is a film censor married to the daughter of an army general. Tasked with censoring porn film *The Wild Schoolgirl,* Vicente becomes instantly smitten with lead actress Dora Dumar (Simone Spoladore). Seeking to make amends for banning her film, Vicente approaches producer Manolo and catches the directing bug, secretly helping the Magnifica studio make movies that will get past the censors.

Sumptuously produced with impeccable attention to period detail, *Magnifica 70* has a strong underlying message about freedom of expression. Throughout its three seasons, the show cleverly blurs fantasy and reality and proves consistently entertaining with its compelling characters and racy content.

SNEAKY PETE

CRIME DRAMA • 2015
RATED: TV-MA • 50 MINS

What would you do if a vicious mobster was after you? Chances are, probably not assume your ex-cellmate's identity and hide out with their family—but then not everyone's as sneaky as Pete.

When con man Marius Josipović (Giovanni Ribisi) gets out of jail, he's dismayed to find that Vincent Lonigan (Bryan Cranston), the vicious gangster he stole from, wants revenge. In desperation, Marius pretends to be his former cellmate Pete (Ethan Embry) and hides out with his estranged family, who are none the wiser about his true identity. However, they also have troubles of their own, putting Marius in your classic frying-pan/fire situation.

With a superb cast that includes Margo Martindale as Pete's suspicious grandmother, *Sneaky Pete* delivers three seasons of nail-biting suspense, emotionally engaging drama, and sharply observed character comedy wrapped up in a fun, twisty crime plot. Cranston's on great form, too, but that goes without saying.

TIPPING THE VELVET

PERIOD DRAMA • 2002
RATED: 18 (UK) • 59 MINS

Like a bit of costume drama? In the mood for an erotic coming-of-age tale? Then this Victorian-era lesbian romance has your name written all over it.

Described by scriptwriter Andrew Davies as being like *Pride and Prejudice* "with dirty bits," *Tipping the Velvet* is based on the debut novel of Sarah Waters and set in Victorian England. Rachael Stirling stars as innocent Nancy "Nan" Astley, a young girl whose life is completely upended when she falls in love with the exciting theater star and male impersonator Kitty Butler (Keeley Hawes).

Emotionally intense and powerfully erotic, the three-episode serial attracted both praise and controversy for its explicit depiction of sex and sexuality. The cast, including Jodhi May and Anna Chancellor, are exceptional, with Stirling in particular displaying white-hot charisma and charm. Watch out, too, for a baby-faced Benedict Cumberbatch—in only his second screen appearance—as Nan's boyfriend.

DYNASTY (1981)

DRAMA • 1981 • RATED: TV-PG • 45 MINS • SEASONS: 9
JOAN COLLINS, JOHN FORSYTHE, LINDA EVANS

Sex, shoulder pads, and soapy shenanigans. Those are the key ingredients of *Dynasty*, a glossy, prime-time soap opera that dominated the 1980s, treating viewers to weekly battles between the Carringtons and the Colbys, two oil-rich families in Colorado.

The Carringtons include oil baron Blake (John Forsythe), his new wife, Krystle (Linda Evans), gay son Steven, and headstrong daughter Fallon, who marries Jeff Colby as part of a secret business deal. The arrival of Blake's ex-wife, Alexis (Joan Collins), transforms the show, giving it a truly memorable villain.

Dynasty revels in some fabulously lurid story lines. Highlights include the regular appearance of previously unmentioned relatives—notably vengeful long-lost son Adam and Blake's African American half sister Dominique Devereaux. There is also the so-called poison paint plot (in which Adam poisons Jeff by having his office decorated with toxic paint), Krystle getting kidnapped and replaced by her look-alike double, and Alexis being put on trial

for the murder of Krystle's ex-husband. And, of course, there's the famous Moldavian wedding massacre, one of the all-time great cliffhangers, which saw the entire cast gunned down and left for dead at the end of Season 5.

Alongside its outrageous plots, *Dynasty* has a progressive attitude to representation, not just in its casting of middle-aged women in high-profile, powerful roles, but also in giving mainstream visibility to both LGBTQI+ characters and African American women. However, it's better known for its multiple catfights, notably a knock-down, drag-out slap-fest between Alexis and Krystle in a koi pond.

At the height of its fame, *Dynasty* was the number-one show in America, with an estimated global audience of 120 million. It attracted high-profile guest stars (including Rock Hudson and George Hamilton), spawned a spin-off show *(The Colbys),* and influenced fashion trends, thanks to its glorious costumes. Would we even have had shoulder pads in the '80s without *Dynasty*?

DYNASTY FAMILY TREE

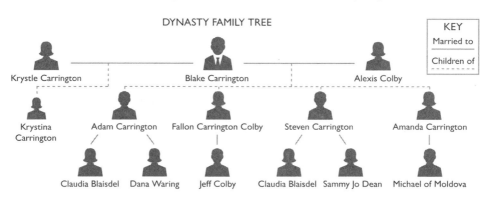

KEY
Married to
Children of

Krystle Carrington — Blake Carrington — Alexis Colby

Krystina Carrington | Adam Carrington | Fallon Carrington Colby | Steven Carrington | Amanda Carrington

Claudia Blaisdel | Dana Waring | Jeff Colby | Claudia Blaisdel | Sammy Jo Dean | Michael of Moldova

CREATORS: Esther Shapiro, Richard Alan Shapiro
PRODUCTION CO: Aaron Spelling Productions

DALLAS

DRAMA • 1978
RATED: TV-PG • 50 MINS

Meet one of TV's greatest villains. Oil baron J. R. Ewing blackmails and manipulates with impunity in this glossy soap. No wonder someone shot him.

An enormous hit in the 1980s, *Dallas* centers on wealthy Texas family the Ewings, who live on a sprawling cattle ranch at Southfork. The series kicks off with oil baron J. R. Ewing (Larry Hagman) becoming enraged when his brother Bobby (Patrick Duffy) marries Pamela (Victoria Principal), the daughter of his sworn enemy, Cliff Barnes.

Throughout *Dallas's* 14 seasons, J. R. enacts scheme after scheme, frequently clashing with Bobby, Cliff, and Sue Ellen, his long-suffering, alcoholic wife. Its most famous story lines include the "who shot J. R.?" mystery (which drew nearly 360 million viewers worldwide) and the so-called "Dream Season," in which the entirety of Season 9 (including Bobby's death) was revealed to be a dream experienced by Pam while Bobby was in the shower.

DYNASTY (2017)

DRAMA • 2017 • RATED: TV-14 • 42 MINS • SEASONS: 3
ELIZABETH GILLIES, GRANT SHOW, ALAN DALE

Strap in for salacious story lines and sassy one-liners. This raunchy reboot of an old favorite successfully updates the classic '80s soap, cranking up the camp factor to the max as it follows fabulously rich feuding families the Carringtons and the Colbys. Let the catfights, catastrophes, and caustic put-downs ensue.

Aside from relocating the series to Atlanta and cleverly gender-swapping and race-swapping several characters (the Colbys are now African American), it's pretty much business as usual for the Carringtons.

Season 1 sees energy magnate Blake Carrington (Grant Show) marrying and promoting employee Cristal Flores, prompting jealous daughter Fallon (Elizabeth Gillies) to go into business with Blake's rival, Jeff Colby (Sam Adegoke). And Blake's son, Steven, begins a relationship with Cristal's nephew, Sammy Jo (one of the aforementioned gender-swaps from the original series).

Subsequent seasons introduce a host of characters familiar from the original series. Long-lost Carrington son Adam arrives, as does Blake's ex-wife, Alexis. The plots frequently revisit famous story lines such as the so-called "poison paint plot" and Alexis causing Cristal to miscarry. And, of course, there are the catfights, because what's *Dynasty* without them?

What really distinguishes the reboot is its knowing sense of humor and its eagerness to embrace the out-there factor. This is evident in its cheerful attitude to recasting— the show is already on its third Cristal in three seasons. And at one point, Gillies plays both Fallon and Alexis due to an outrageous plastic-surgery plot. This is a trashy treat.

REVENGE

DRAMA • 2011 • RATED: TV-14 • 43 MINS • SEASONS: 4
EMILY VANCAMP, MADELEINE STOWE, GABRIEL MANN

Revenge is a dish best served over four glorious seasons of twists, turns, and caustic one-liners. Hang out in the Hamptons as a socialite enacts elaborate vengeance over the wealthy family responsible for her father's death.

Emily Thorne (Emily VanCamp) arrives in the Hamptons carrying a dark secret. She's actually Amanda Clarke, the daughter of David Clarke, who was framed over a connection to a terrorist plot and killed in prison. Enlisting the help of wisecracking tech-genius Nolan Ross (Gabriel Mann), Emily embarks on her carefully plotted mission to bring down the wealthy family who destroyed her father.

Emily's primary target is matriarch Victoria Grayson (Madeleine Stowe), who had an affair with her father and later betrayed him. Seducing Victoria's son, Daniel Grayson (Josh Bowman), is first on the agenda.

Most episodes center on Emily finding someone linked to the conspiracy (she has a book of photos she strikes red lines through) and ruining their lives, usually by exposing their secrets. But her meticulous plans are often disrupted by new information about her father.

With its luxurious settings, its love-to-hate characters, and its deliciously barbed dialogue, *Revenge* is a trashy delight. But the real joy of the show lies in its steady stream of increasingly outrageous twists.

> *"Blackmail—it isn't just for breakfast anymore."*
>
> Nolan Ross (S1 E11)

WHAT/IF

THRILLER • 2019
RATED: TV-14 • 50 MINS

What would you do if a mysterious stranger offered you a ludicrous amount of money to spend a night with your significant other? Renée Zellweger plays a billionaire making an indecent proposal in this soapy morality drama.

Lisa (Jane Levy) is a scientist on the verge of a breakthrough that would save millions of children's lives. Attending what she thinks is a pitch meeting, she's taken aback when billionaire Anne Montgomery (Renée Zellweger) says she'll give her the funding she needs, in return for a single night with Lisa's hunky firefighter husband, Sean (Blake Jenner).

Created by Mike Kelley, this one-season show starts out as a gender-flipped remake of '90s erotic thriller *Indecent Proposal* but swiftly takes the premise to soapy extremes, with suspense and shocking twists galore. It's worth watching for Zellweger alone, who has a whale of a time playing the sort of bad-to-the-bone villain who practices archery in her office.

FOOTBALLERS' WIVES

DRAMA • 2002 • RATED: TV-14 • 49 MINS • SEASONS: 5
ZÖE LUCKER, GILLIAN TAYLFORTH, LAILA ROUASS

Sex, drugs, affairs, kidnap, baby-swapping, murder—*Footballers' Wives* has it all. Pass the bubbly and prepare to be shocked as the wives and players of fictional Premier League football club Earls Park FC get up to all sorts in this gleefully trashy British drama.

The opening season of *Footballers' Wives* centers on team captain's wife, Tanya Turner (Zöe Lucker). She's had enough of alpha male hubby, Jason (Cristian Solimeno), screwing around and schemes to get back at him.

Meanwhile, Donna Walmsley (Katherine Monaghan) searches for the child she and husband, Ian (Nathan Constance), gave up for adoption when they were teenagers, and footballer mom Jackie Pascoe (Gillian Taylforth) agrees to let son, Kyle (Gary Lucy),

and wife, Chardonnay (Susie Amy), pass off her baby as their own. One small problem: Jason is the father.

Fast-moving and frequently hilarious, *Footballers' Wives* packs more drama into a single episode than most shows manage in an entire season. Cast turnover is high and barely half an hour goes past without someone getting cheated on, kidnapped, hospitalized, or murdered.

The series' star player is the irrepressible Tanya Turner, who nabs all the juiciest plotlines and has a catty comment for every occasion. Over five seasons, she gets through three husbands, has multiple affairs, and, most famously, swaps her newborn baby with that of love rival Amber (Laila Rouass). Debauched, deranged, and utterly delightful.

MELROSE PLACE

DRAMA • 1992
RATED: TV-14 • 44 MINS

Bed-hopping, back-stabbing, betrayal, blackmail, and murder—that's just business as usual at this soap's LA apartment complex. Revel in some of the most outrageous plotlines around.

Talk about a course correction. *Melrose Place* begins as a slightly po-faced show about a group of young professionals living in an LA apartment building. But it soon explodes into

a highly addictive soap that redefines the term "jaw dropping." Key characters include ruthless ad exec Amanda (Heather Locklear), psychotic doctor Kimberly (Marcia Cross), and photographer Jo (Daphne Zuniga).

Over the show's seven seasons (as well as its 2009 revival), it undergoes several cast changes and delivers increasingly deranged story lines. Cults are joined, the same baby gets kidnapped twice, and Kimberly blows up the building. The cliffhangers are legendary, too—who can forget the hand emerging from the grave? Gloriously trashy.

BOSTON LEGAL

COMEDY DRAMA • 2004
RATED: TV-14 • 42 MINS

Laughs, lawsuits, and legal wrangling—courtroom drama gets a great comedy double-act in this popular spin-off series about two colleagues at a Boston law firm.

A spin-off from long-running lawyer show *The Practice* (see p389), *Boston Legal* stars James Spader as ethically dubious lawyer Alan Shore, who takes a job alongside eccentric attorney Denny Crane (William Shatner) in the law firm of Crane, Poole & Schmidt. Their colleagues include senior partner (and Denny's ex) Shirley Schmidt (Candice Bergen), paralegal Tara Wilson (Rhona Mitra), and associate Sally Heep (Lake Bell).

Fast-paced and funny, *Boston Legal* has a postmodern style all its own. As a result, the characters are aware they're in a TV show (sample line: "Denny! I've hardly seen you this episode") and often break the fourth wall. The show ran for five seasons, giving its two lead characters a cleverly contrived ending.

ALLY MCBEAL

COMEDY DRAMA • 1997 • RATED: TV-PG • 45 MINS • SEASONS: 5
CALISTA FLOCKHART, GREG GERMANN, JANE KRAKOWSKI

You don't have to be wildly eccentric to work at Boston law firm Cage and Fish, but it helps. Join Ally McBeal and her kooky colleagues as they navigate their topsy-turvy love lives and do a bit of lawyering.

Single lawyer Ally McBeal (Calista Flockhart) takes a job at a law firm co-owned by former classmate Richard Fish (Greg Germann). On her first day, she's horrified to discover that her still-pined-for ex-boyfriend Billy (Gil Bellows) also works there and, worse, that he's married to fellow lawyer Georgia (Courtney Thorne-Smith). Ally's eccentric coworkers also include wisecracking secretary Elaine (Jane Krakowski) and oddball cofounder John Cage (Peter MacNicol).

Created by David E. Kelley, the show is characterized by its surreal fantasy sequences, involving everything from a dancing baby (an early internet sensation) to Ally hearing music in her head, which gives everyone their own theme tune. Though nominally a legal drama, case-related plots take a back seat to the love lives and interpersonal dramas of the characters, though they are occasionally used to explore topical social issues or underscore whatever Ally is going through in that episode.

At the height of its popularity, the show was featured on the cover of *Time* magazine and was famously parodied on *Futurama* as "Single Female Lawyer"! It was canceled after five years, despite gaining a ratings spike in Season 4 after the casting of Robert Downey Jr.

> **"** I like being a mess. It's who I am. **"**
>
> Ally McBeal (S1 E16)

SUITS

DRAMA • 2011
RATED: TV-14 • 42 MINS

What happens if your super-smart lawyer isn't qualified to practice law? A high-flying attorney takes a chance on a talented college dropout in this smartly tailored legal drama.

Maverick lawyer Harvey Specter (Gabriel Macht) is ordered to take on an associate by his boss, Jessica Pearson (Gina Torres). When Harvey meets stoner dropout Mike Ross (Patrick J. Adams), he's impressed by his quick-thinking and photographic memory, so he gives him the job, despite the fact he isn't qualified. Together, the pair take on cases while hiding the fact that Mike is a fraud.

Suits effortlessly weaves gripping courtroom action, light comedy, and interpersonal drama, not least in Mike's relationship with senior paralegal Rachel Zane (future Duchess of Sussex, Meghan Markle). Loyalties shift back and forth over the show's nine seasons, but the compelling central dynamic between Harvey and Mike remains strong throughout.

HOTEL BABYLON

DRAMA • 2006
RATED: TV-MA • 60 MINS

Ambition, romance, partying, affairs— and that's just the staff. Wait till you see what the guests get up to when they check into London's premium establishment for saucy shenanigans.

Based on a novel by Imogen Edwards-Jones, this cheerfully raunchy British drama centers on a five-star London hotel where the high-flying guests expect the utmost discretion from the staff, with good reason. Under the watchful eye of manager Rebecca Mitchell (Tamzin Outhwaite), the team—including troubled deputy manager Charlie (Max Beesley) and all-seeing concierge Tony (Dexter Fletcher)—have their work cut out for them covering up their guests' illicit activities.

With its luxurious backdrop, great characters, and salacious story lines, the show is a delightfully guilty pleasure with a mix of frothy comedy and light drama. Be warned: it was canceled after four seasons, so perhaps not every tantalizing cliffhanger will be resolved.

THE PRACTICE

DRAMA • 1997
RATED: TV-14 • 44 MINS

Ever found yourself in an ethical quandary? At Robert Donnell and Associates, they eat ethical quandaries for breakfast. Join their justice-hungry legal team as they take on their cases.

Bobby Donnell (Dylan McDermott) is the founder of Robert Donnell and Associates, a successful Boston law firm. Said associates include Ellenor Frutt (Camryn Manheim), who has a nose for shady clients; Eugene Young (Steve Harris), a stickler for the letter of the law; and Lindsay Dole (Kelli Williams), who's romantically involved with Bobby.

Created by legal drama supremo David E. Kelley, the show explores the conflict between legal ethics and personal morality as the firm takes on a variety of cases, from misdemeanors to murders. Kelley's sardonic dialogue is the icing on the cake. *The Practice* ran for eight seasons, during which it crossed over with shows such as *Ally McBeal* (p388), and spawned spin-off *Boston Legal* (p388).

GOSSIP GIRL

**DRAMA • 2007 • RATED: TV-14 • 42 MINS • SEASONS: 6
BLAKE LIVELY, LEIGHTON MEESTER, PENN BADGLEY**

How are back-stabbing BFFs Serena and Blair supposed to maintain their fragile friendship when a mysterious blogger keeps revealing all their darkest secrets? Their tumultuous love lives, ruthless rivalries, and scandalous shenanigans spice up this salacious Manhattan-set teen drama.

Adapted from the young adult novels by Cecily von Ziegesar, the first season of *Gossip Girl* opens with privileged Manhattan teen Serena van der Woodsen (Blake Lively) returning to the Upper East Side after an unexplained absence. Serena's reappearance ruffles the feathers of her ostensible BFF, Blair Waldorf (Leighton Meester), a would-be queen bee who's always in Serena's shadow.

Adding further fuel to the fire are the rumors of an illicit assignation between Serena and Blair's boyfriend, Nate Archibald (Chace Crawford). That revelation pushes Blair into the arms of deliciously amoral Chuck Bass (Ed Westwick), sparking a will-they-won't-they love affair that had viewers gripped throughout the series.

Meanwhile, Serena has relationship issues of her own when she falls for less-privileged Brooklynite Dan Humphries (Penn Badgley), which makes things super-awkward when it turns out Serena's mom used to have a thing with Dan's dad. As the scandals mount up, mysterious blogger "Gossip Girl" (voiced perfectly by Kristen Bell) instantly e-blasts the salacious details to all and sundry (the sound of several phones all going off at once is a frequent occurrence).

> **"***Gossip Girl here, your one and only source into the scandalous lives of Manhattan's elite.***"**
>
> **Gossip Girl** (episode intro)

Over the course of six seasons, *Gossip Girl* managed every conceivable romantic combination of its cast members and occasionally made headlines for its "shocking" content, most notably a threesome scene in Season 3. The various plots are a near-constant swirl of secrets and lies (often stirred up by a guest-starring baddie, such as Desmond Harrington's ultra-manipulative Uncle Jack Bass), though the show also tackles darker themes such as drug addiction. However, the real joys of the series lie in Blair's searingly sarcastic dialogue and her screwball comedy-style back-and-forth sparring with Chuck.

CREATORS: Stephanie Savage, Josh Schwartz **PRODUCTION CO:** 17th Street Productions, Alloy Entertainment, CBS Paramount Network Television, CBS Television Studios, College Hill Pictures Inc., Warner Bros. Television

YOU

**THRILLER • 2018 • RATED: TV-MA • 45 MINS • SEASONS: 2
PENN BADGLEY, ELIZABETH LAIL, VICTORIA PEDRETTI**

What if that cute guy you met in the bookstore was a dangerously obsessive killer? That's the premise of *You*, a seriously twisted thriller that's practically a stalker's guide to winning the love of your life.

Based on the novel by Caroline Kepnes, *You* centers on Joe Goldberg (*Gossip Girl's* Penn Badgley, brilliantly cast), a charming New York bookseller who seems like the perfect catch, except for one thing—he's a total psycho. When aspiring writer Guinevere Beck (Elizabeth Lail) walks into his store, Joe takes her mild flirting as a sign that they're meant to be together and immediately begins stalking her, obsessively mining her social media profiles for ways to inveigle himself into her life.

> **" *Well, hello there.
> Who are you?* "**
>
> Joe (S1 E1)

Soon, the pair are in a relationship and with Joe narrating the story—much like in *Dexter* (see p47), a clear inspiration—you're pulled into his worldview as he rationalizes the increasingly extreme actions (up to and including kidnapping and murder) he takes to maintain their romance. There's also the ongoing question of what happened to Joe's previous girlfriend, Candace (Ambyr Childers), who has mysteriously disappeared.

Season 2 (based on Kepnes's second novel, *Hidden Bodies*) sees Joe moving to Los Angeles, where he adopts a new identity and quickly finds another object of obsession in the shape of Love Quinn (Victoria Pedretti). Can he stop his dark history from repeating itself and find true love with Love? Or will a returning figure from his past bring everything crashing down?

Cleverly blending romantic comedy conventions with a deliciously dark and twisted psychological thriller plot, *You* is a horror story for the social media age, with Joe's internet-enabled stalking skills serving as a highly effective cautionary tale—try watching even just the first episode without immediately changing all your passwords afterward. As well as genuinely chilling, it's also cheerfully ridiculous (Joe keeps a glass cage frequently occupied with his victims in the bookstore basement) and chock-full of jaw-dropping twists that make it highly conducive to binge-watching.

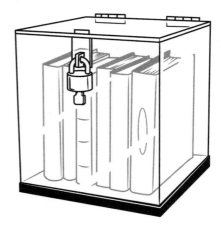

CREATORS: Sera Gamble, Greg Berlanti
PRODUCTION CO: A+E Studios, Alloy Entertainment, Berlanti Productions, Warner Horizon Television

SKINS

DRAMA • 2007
RATED: TV-MA • 46 MINS

Sex, drugs, alcohol, and social issues—it's not easy being a teen. Follow the angst-ridden adolescents in this show that launched a generation of stars.

Each episode of *Skins* focuses on one Bristol teenager, exploring the problems in their personal lives, while other characters' plotlines unfold in the background. Characters in the first season include manipulative Tony

(Nicholas Hoult), selective Muslim Anwar (Dev Patel), and eccentric Cassie (Hannah Murray), with a selection of well-known British comedy actors (Harry Enfield, Bill Bailey, and Josie Lawrence) playing their largely useless, barely seen parents.

As well as featuring authentic depictions of casual sex, drug use, and drinking, the show explores a number of social issues over its seven seasons, including eating disorders, depression, suicide, and sexuality. In a genius move, the cast was replaced every two years, allowing the show to retain its teen focus.

FAME

MUSICAL DRAMA • 1982
RATED: 12 (UK) • 60 MINS

"Fame costs and right here's where you start paying ... in sweat!" Learn how to fly (high!) watching the talented students who attend the New York City High School for the Performing Arts.

Based on the hit 1980 film, the six-season TV version intersperses the struggles of a group of talented performing arts students with regular song-and-dance numbers.

Key characters include dance instructor Lydia Grant (Debbie Allen); gifted, from-the-streets dancer Leroy Johnson (Gene Anthony Ray); introverted musician Bruno Martelli (Lee Curreri); and German music teacher Benjamin Shorofsky (Albert Hague), with all four actors reprising their roles from the movie.

Passionate, charming, and often funny, *Fame* delivers an abundance of feel-good vibes, thanks to its eclectic ensemble cast. The show spawned a smash-hit album, including songs "Hi Fidelity" and "Starmaker." More gleeful than *Glee*, it's a perfect hit of '80s nostalgia.

JACKASS

REALITY TV COMEDY • 2000
RATED: TV-MA • 21 MINS

There's stupid, there's dangerous, and then there's *Jackass*. The thing is, it's also *really* funny. Join Johnny Knoxville and the boys for eye-watering stunts, dangerous dares, and tasteless pranks.

A team of nine friends perform perilous stunts and play practical jokes on each other and the unsuspecting public. Ringleaders include Johnny Knoxville, Steve-O, and Chris Pontius,

as well as Bam Margera, whose parents are frequent victims of their pranks, which include fireworks in their bedroom.

The team's affection for each other somehow makes even the most obnoxious antics weirdly charming. Stunts across its three seasons range from the insane (riding a giant rocket, fighting a bear) and childish (supergluing themselves to each other), to the sublimely ridiculous (crawling across a room full of mousetraps) and utterly disgusting (being locked in a used porta potty as it's turned upside down). It's hilarious—just don't try any of it at home.

SCANDAL

THRILLER DRAMA • 2012
RATED: TV-14 • 43 MINS

A crisis management genius finds her job as fixer for the US president complicated by the fact that they're having an affair.

Kerry Washington stars as Olivia Pope, the head of crisis management firm OPA (that's Olivia Pope & Associates), who takes a job coordinating damage control for President Fitzgerald Grant III (Tony Goldwyn). She has her work cut out because, as well as managing the president's other secrets, Olivia also has to deal with the fact that her own affair with Fitz is one of these secrets.

Created by prolific producer Shonda Rhimes and anchored by a powerhouse performance from Washington, *Scandal* owes its authenticity to the fact that Olivia is based on Judy Smith, former press aide to George H. W. Bush. The compelling plotlines ramp up over the show's seven seasons, moving from crisis of the week to election rigging, White House coups, and assassinations. Enormous fun.

MR. ROBOT

THRILLER • 2015
RATED: TV-MA • 49 MINS

A mentally troubled hacker is recruited into a mysterious activist group trying to take down a corrupt corporation in this twisty cyber-thriller.

Elliot Alderson (*Bohemian Rhapsody*'s Rami Malek) is a skilled hacker and occasional cyber-vigilante who suffers from dissociative personality disorders. Recruited by mysterious insurrectionary anarchist Mr. Robot (Christian Slater), Elliot joins "fsociety," a collective of hacktivists dedicated to destroying the consumer debt records of a corrupt corporation. But is Mr. Robot all he seems?

Acclaimed for its striking visuals, spot-on technical wizardry, and the accurate depiction of Elliot's mental health issues, *Mr. Robot* is a darkly pessimistic thriller that takes a dim view of capitalism's excesses and puts the boot in accordingly. Packed with rug-pulling twists and turns, and anchored by Malek's soulful performance, the show ran for four seasons before wrapping things up in style.

THE SECRET LIFE OF THE AMERICAN TEENAGER

DRAMA • 2008
RATED: TV-14 • 43 MINS

Band camp has a lot to answer for. A high schooler finds her life turned upside down after getting pregnant and deciding she wants to keep the baby.

The Fault in Our Stars' Shailene Woodley plays Amy Juergens, who finds herself pregnant at 15 after losing her virginity to handsome Ricky Underwood (Daren Kagasoff) at band camp. Amy's boyfriend Ben (Kenny Baumann) proves surprisingly supportive, but things get complicated when Ricky decides he wants to be part of the baby's life.

Created by Brenda Hampton, *The Secret Life ...* goes all in on its pregnancy angle, with at least three characters getting pregnant during its five seasons, including Amy's mom (Molly Ringwald). Satisfyingly soapy in the romance department, the show compellingly explores the frustrations of teen motherhood, while also fast-tracking Woodley to stardom.

UNREAL

DRAMA • 2015 • RATED: TV-MA • 42 MINS • SEASONS: 4
SHIRI APPLEBY, CONSTANCE ZIMMER, CRAIG BIERKO

Ever wondered what goes on behind the scenes on a reality dating show? Sex, drugs, manipulation, and betrayal for starters, at least according to *UnREAL,* a (hopefully) fictional portrayal of the making of such a program. Prepare to be shocked.

Cocreated by a former producer on real-life reality dating show *The Bachelor, UnREAL* begins with TV producer Rachel Goldberg (Shiri Appleby) returning to work on the fictional show *Everlasting* after a public meltdown on the previous series. Under pressure from ratings-obsessed executive producer Quinn King (Constance Zimmer), Rachel swallows her principles and manipulates the contestants into creating outrageous, ratings-grabbing television—tearful confessions, angry outbursts, full-on punch-ups, that sort of thing.

Despite her moral qualms, Rachel is exceptionally good at her job, befriending the contestants so they think she's on their side and pulling their strings like a puppet master.

But she's also a monumental screw-up and frequently indulges in self-destructive behavior, such as acting on her own attraction to the suitor. Meanwhile, Quinn is engaged in a constant battle with her boorish boss-slash-lover Chet (Craig Bierko) in order to retain control of the show.

Subsequent seasons continue in the same vein, but with small tweaks to *Everlasting,* such as introducing the first black suitor, or gender-swapping the format with a female "suitress." Meanwhile, the production crew's behind-the-scenes shenanigans are even more outrageous than the show they're producing, with multiple affairs, repeated betrayals, and subplots involving murder, suicide, various cover-ups, and takeover bids.

> **"** *We don't make it up; we make it happen.* **"**
>
> **Quinn** (S2 E5)

Throughout the course of its run, *UnREAL* goes to some extremely dark places, and it's all the more fascinating for its total absence of morality in the way it refuses to judge or punish its characters for the terrible things they do. It also cleverly explores the audience's complicity in the reality TV industry, while providing a revealing look at how such programs are made. It's a measure of the show's impact that it leaves you hoping against hope that it's all exaggerated, because surely it couldn't *really* be as twisted as that. Could it?

CREATORS: Marti Noxon, Sarah Gertrude Shapiro
PRODUCTION CO: Wieden+Kennedy Entertainment

CALIFORNICATION

**COMEDY DRAMA • 2007 • RATED: TV-MA • 28 MINS • SEASONS: 7
DAVID DUCHOVNY, NATASCHA MCELHONE, EVAN HANDLER**

Sex, drugs, more sex, and a bit of rock 'n' roll thrown in for good measure. That's the life of creatively blocked novelist Hank Moody, whose seeming inability to resist temptation forms the basis of this raunchy adult comedy.

David Duchovny (The X-Files) plays Hank Moody, a hedonistic New York novelist suffering from writer's block who moves to California to help raise his teenage daughter, Becca. Still yearning for his ex-wife, Karen (Natascha McElhone), Hank tries to win her back, but his sex addiction, drug problem, and alcoholism keep getting in the way.

Throughout the series, Hank is constantly embroiled in scandalous situations. In the pilot episode, he sleeps with Mia (Madeline Zima), who turns out to be the underage daughter of Karen's fiancé—Mia subsequently blackmails him and steals his novel, passing it off as her own. Meanwhile, Hank's repeated screw-ups are frequently eclipsed by those of his best friend and agent Charlie Runkle (a scene-stealing Evan Handler).

> **❝** *I see myself as an enthusiast. A drug and alcohol enthusiast.* **❞**
>
> **Hank Moody** (S6 E2)

Darkly funny and possessed of a wryly fatalistic worldview, *Californication* drew both criticism and praise for its frank depictions of nudity, sexual practices, masturbation, and drug taking. It also takes several knowing swipes at Hollywood, not least in an inspired running joke whereby Hank's novel *God Hates Us All* gets adapted into a bland but hugely popular movie called *A Crazy Little Thing Called Love*. That's show business.

PRETTY LITTLE LIARS

**MYSTERY DRAMA • 2010
RATED: TV-14 • 44 MINS**

What would you do if a mysterious enemy threatened to reveal your darkest secrets? Four teenage girls discover that their murdered best friend is trying to ruin their lives.

Based on a novel series by Sara Shepard, this glossy mystery drama centers on best friends Spencer (Troian Bellisario), Aria (Lucy Hale), Hanna (Ashley Benson), and Emily (Shay Mitchell), whose clique breaks apart after the disappearance of their manipulative group leader, Alison. A year later, Alison's body is discovered and the four friends are drawn back together as they begin receiving messages from "A," an anonymous enemy who threatens to expose secrets only Alison knew.

Conceived as *Desperate Housewives* (see p243) for teens, *Pretty Little Liars* delivers thrills galore as it surrounds its attractive cast with a deluge of scandals. These range from shoplifting and cover-ups to multiple illicit hook-ups over seven steamy seasons.

PLANET OF THE APES

SCI-FI • 1974
RATED: PG (UK) • 47 MINS

"These humans are dangerous, don't you understand that? They think they're as good as we are!" Two human astronauts and a sympathetic ape become fugitives on a future Earth.

Based on the 1968 *Planet of the Apes* movie and its sequels, the TV adaptation centers on astronauts Alan Virdon (Ron Harper) and Pete Burke (James Naughton) who, much like Charlton Heston in the movie, crash-land on an ape-controlled Earth in the distant future. Befriended by sympathetic ape Galen (movie series veteran Roddy McDowall), the trio are forced to go on the run, pursued by sadistic military gorilla General Urko (Mark Lenard).

Removed from the movies' themes, the single-season series takes time to explore the ape world, stopping by Center City and Oakland's ruins. Plotlines follow the structure of *The Fugitive*, with Virdon, Burke, and Galen helping different people each episode, before being forced to evade capture.

ROSWELL

SCI-FI • 1999
RATED: TV-14 • 42 MINS

What if that cute guy you liked was actually an alien from another planet? Teen romance and extraterrestrial angst collide in this fantasy sci-fi series.

After being caught in a shooting, high schooler Liz (Shiri Appleby) is mysteriously healed by Max (Jason Behr), an apparently normal teenager. Investigating, she discovers that Max, his sister, Isabel (Katherine Heigl), and their friend Michael (Brendan Fehr) are aliens whose ship crash-landed in Roswell in 1947. A love triangle swiftly ensues between Max, Liz, and her boyfriend Kyle (Nick Wechsler), the son of the local sheriff.

Based on the young adult novels by Melinda Metz, *Roswell* focuses on teen-angst drama in Season 1 before ramping up the sci-fi content with time travel, royal alien dynasties, shape-shifters, clones, invasions, and even ghosts (sort of) in two further seasons. Attracting a passionate fan base, the show was rebooted in 2019 with different characters.

THE 100

SCI-FI • 2014
RATED: TV-14 • 43 MINS

Live on a space station? Want to check whether the Earth is habitable again after a nuclear war? Just send down all the young offenders. What could possibly go wrong?

Ninety-seven years after a nuclear war, the last humans are struggling to survive aboard orbiting space station *The Ark*. With resources rapidly dwindling, a group of 100 juvenile detainees are sent down to Earth to determine whether it's habitable. Led by Clarke Griffin (Eliza Taylor) and Bellamy Blake (Bob Morley), the 100 quickly discover they are not alone.

Loosely based on a novel series by Kass Morgan and fronted by an implausibly attractive cast (their hair and makeup are suspiciously perfect considering they live in the woods), *The 100* combines postapocalyptic survival thrills with hard-hitting issue-based drama and provocative sci-fi concepts. Later episodes in the six-season series take it in some unexpectedly bold directions.

12 MONKEYS

SCI-FI • 2015
RATED: TV-14 • 43 MINS

How do you stop a deadly virus from destroying the human race? Time traveler James Cole is on a mission to save the world in this sci-fi mystery drama.

In 2043, the human race is all but destroyed after a deadly virus released in 2017 wipes out 7 billion people. Recruited by scientist Katarina Jones (Barbara Sukowa), scavenger James Cole (Aaron Stanford) is sent back in time to 2015 to stop an organization named the Army of the 12 Monkeys from unleashing a plague. Fortunately, virologist Cassie Reilly (Amanda Schull) is on hand to help.

Loosely adapted from Terry Gilliam's 1995 movie of the same name, *12 Monkeys* delivers sci-fi thrills, great characters, and startling twists over four seasons, while also serving as a thought-provoking meditation on free will versus predestination. Costar of the original film, Madeleine Stowe, makes a cameo in a small but pivotal role in Season 2.

THE EXPANSE

SCI-FI • 2015
RATED: TV-14 • 47 MINS

In space, no one can hear you scream ... or hear you unravel a giant conspiracy. A detective, a spaceship captain, and a UN representative are drawn into a plot that threatens peace in the solar system in this sci-fi thriller.

Set in a future where humanity has colonized the solar system, *The Expanse* begins with the disappearance of rich-girl-turned-activist Julie Mao (Florence Faivre). Asteroid belt detective Joe Miller (Thomas Jane) teams up with UN executive Chrisjen Avasarala (Shohreh Aghdashloo) and starship captain James Holden (Steven Strait) as they uncover a conspiracy that threatens the fragile peace between Earth, the belt, and Mars.

Acclaimed for its production values, world-building, and accurate science, *The Expanse* blends sci-fi concepts, detective thrills, and contemporary political elements to compelling and often provocative effect. Spanning four seasons, this is a space odyssey to remember.

THRESHOLD

SCI-FI • 2005
RATED: NR • 42 MINS

"I have a plan to stop them. That plan is called 'Threshold.'" A secret task force races to save the world in this alien-invasion thriller with a difference.

When a UFO lands in the Atlantic, the crew of a Navy ship is exposed to sonic radiation that rewrites their DNA, giving them superhuman strength and the urge to infect others. Dr. Molly Caffrey (Carla Gugino) leads a "Red Team" of top scientists—including microbiologist Dr. Nigel Fenway (Brent Spiner) and math and linguistic genius Arthur Ramsey (Peter Dinklage)—tasked with stopping the aliens before they take over the world.

Threshold takes its imaginative concept and runs with it, experimenting with different genres, ranging from sci-fi to medical thriller to straight-up horror. The cast are a constant highlight, particularly the interplay between Dinklage and Spiner. Criminally canceled after just 13 episodes, it's one of the great one-season wonders.

ONCE UPON A TIME

FANTASY DRAMA • 2011 • RATED: TV-PG • 43 MINS • SEASONS: 7
JENNIFER MORRISON, LANA PARRILLA, ROBERT CARLYLE

What if an evil queen's powerful curse caused fairy-tale characters to forget their true selves and live in the real world? Welcome to Storybrooke, Maine, where the arrival of a young boy starts to wake up memories.

Bail bonds collector Emma Swan (Jennifer Morrison) is visited by Henry (Jared Gilmore), the 10-year-old son she previously gave up for adoption. He takes her back to Storybrooke, where Emma discovers that, as the long-lost daughter of Snow White and Prince Charming, she's the only one capable of breaking the curse enacted by Evil Queen Regina (Lana Parrilla). But there's one small problem—Regina is Henry's wicked adoptive mother.

Episodes typically follow the same structure, centering on a particular fairy-tale character (such as Cinderella) and advancing the main story in the present day while flashing back to their lives in fairy-tale world.

Trickster Rumplestiltskin (Robert Carlyle) is the main antagonist, responsible for much of the town's misery, including Regina's curse and Emma's separation from her parents.

Later seasons involve more fairy tale–related plots as the characters' memories return in the present day. There are many new additions to the cast—both heroes and villains—including Captain Hook, King Arthur, and the Queen of Hearts. The arrivals also include characters from Disney movies (such as Elsa and Anna from *Frozen*), an advantage of network ABC having Disney as its parent company.

> **"***All magic comes with a price.***"**
>
> **Rumplestiltskin** (S1 E4)

CHARMED

FANTASY DRAMA • 1998
RATED: TV-14 • 42 MINS

Three powerful witch sisters attempt to live normal lives, while using their magic to protect the innocent from warlocks and demons.

When Phoebe Halliwell (Alyssa Milano) moves in with her sisters, Prue (Shannen Doherty) and Piper (Holly Marie Combs), an ancient spell is triggered, revealing the trio to be the most powerful witches ever known.

Supernatural scrapes quickly follow as the Halliwells fend off the forces of evil. Season 4 sees half sister Paige (Rose McGowan) replace Prue, after Doherty left the show.

Characterized by its witty dialogue and strong female ensemble, *Charmed* mixes magical adventures and spellbinding story lines with relatable day-to-day problems and emotional melodrama. Producers intended to end the show after its seventh year and duly wrapped up all the remaining plot threads, but a passionate fan campaign led to a final eighth season. A reboot followed in 2018.

HEX

FANTASY DRAMA • 2004
RATED: TV-14 • 45 MINS

A teenage witch and a lovestruck phantom fend off a malevolent demon with dark desires at a supernatural school.

Boarding-school student Cassie (Christina Cole) discovers she's a witch, attracting the attentions of seductive demon Azazeal (future star Michael Fassbender). Cassie's smitten roommate Thelma (Jemima Rooper) is killed by Azazeal but returns as a ghost that only Cassie can see. Together they attempt to defeat the demon, while unraveling the secrets of Meadenham Hall. The second and final season centers on two new characters: 500-year-old "anointed one" Ella (Laura Pyper) and Azazeal's son, Malachi (Joseph Beattie).

Surprisingly grown-up for a teen fantasy show, *Hex* explores complex sexual relationships and dark desires in among all the demon bashing. The dialogue's a lot of fun, too. "Do you have any idea how frustrating it is being a lesbian ghost?" asks Thelma.

TITANS

ACTION ADVENTURE • 2018
RATED: TV-MA • 45 MINS

Sweary Super Heroes and shocking violence? Batman would not approve. Former sidekick Robin assembles a new team of heroes in this DC Comics action-adventure series.

Tired of being bossed around by Batman, Dick Grayson (Brenton Thwaites), aka Robin, goes it alone, but he's drawn to the case of teen goth Rachel (Teagan Croft), who has powers she doesn't understand. Joined by space princess Kory (Anna Diop) and shape-shifter Gar (Ryan Potter), the new super-friends attempt to save Rachel from falling under the spell of her demon father, Trigon.

Not to be confused with kids' cartoon *Teen Titans Go!* (see p81), which features the same characters, *Titans* is distinguished by its extreme violence and surprisingly sweary dialogue. Layered with dark humor, the two-season show delivers exciting action and engaging character dynamics, with later episodes adding even more heroes and villains.

CHILLING ADVENTURES OF SABRINA

FANTASY HORROR • 2018
RATED: TV-14 • 55 MINS

It's not easy being a teenage witch. Just ask Sabrina Spellman, who's expected to pledge herself to Satan on her birthday. What if she has other plans?

With her 16th year approaching, half witch, half mortal Sabrina Spellman (Kiernan Shipka) must choose between the supernatural side of her family and the human world of her friends. Her aunts Zelda (Miranda Otto) and Hilda (Lucy Davis) assume she'll pledge herself to the dark lord, but Sabrina isn't so sure, not least because it would jeopardize things with boyfriend Harvey Kinkle (Ross Lynch).

Based on the Archie Comics character, *Sabrina* is both a companion show to *Riverdale* (see p414) and a reinvention of '90s sitcom *Sabrina the Teenage Witch* (see p93). Deliciously dark and stylish, its two seasons deliver an enchanting mix of horror and high camp, with a spellbinding turn from Shipka.

EUREKA

SCI-FI • 2006
RATED: TV-14 • 44 MINS

Clones, time travel, doomsday devices, and spontaneous combustion. These are just a few of the everyday problems when you're the sheriff in a town full of geniuses. Welcome to Eureka.

Transporting his delinquent daughter, Zoe (Jordan Hinson), Sheriff Jack Carter (Colin Ferguson) stumbles upon the secret town of Eureka, where the US's greatest scientific minds are building futuristic inventions for the government. When an experiment goes disastrously wrong, Carter's quick thinking saves the day, and he becomes the new sheriff. But his troubles are only just beginning.

Over five seasons, *Eureka* (aka *A Town Called Eureka*) delivers a winning combination of engagingly quirky characters, light comedy, and inventive sci-fi plots, with the odd murder-mystery thrown in—think *Northern Exposure* (see p237) but with mad scientists. Canceled during Season 5, the show was granted an extra closing episode to wrap everything up.

SAPPHIRE & STEEL

SCI-FI • 1979
RATED: TV-PG • 25 MINS

A pair of superpowered beings adopt human bodies and investigate cracks in time made by malevolent forces in this weird British sci-fi-fantasy series.

Interdimensional operatives Sapphire (Joanna Lumley) and Steel (David McCallum) take human form and materialize on Earth. Their mission: to protect the universe from evil forces exploiting cracks in the timeline.

Throughout their cases, the duo occasionally exhibit superhuman powers (such as super-strength or the ability to manipulate time) and encounter other operatives, including Lead (Val Pringle) and Silver (David Collings).

Combining science fiction and ghost stories (one mission involves a couple from the 35th century, another centers on the spirits of WWI soldiers), the show heightens its strangeness by keeping everything tantalizingly unexplained. The show was spread over six serials, each consisting of several episodes, just like classic *Doctor Who* (see p452).

AGENTS OF S.H.I.E.L.D.

ACTION ADVENTURE • 2013
RATED: TV-PG • 43 MINS

Saving the world from superhuman foes is just part of the day job for this team of misfit do-gooders led by back-from-the-dead Agent Coulson.

Operating in the same universe as the Marvel films, *Agents of S.H.I.E.L.D.* (Strategic Homeland Intervention, Enforcement, and Logistics Division) finds resurrected Agent Phil Coulson (Clark Gregg) battling all manner of alien and superhuman menaces. Aiding him are a loyal team who include hacking genius Daisy Johnson (Chloe Bennett) and martial-arts expert Melinda May (Ming-Na Wen).

Gleefully embracing a host of comic-book concepts, this show from *Buffy* (see p428) creator Joss Whedon has impressed with its dedication to putting obscure Marvel villains on the screen over its seven seasons. The plots are thrillingly pulpy, and the action is often first rate, while the cast generate sparky chemistry.

TORCHWOOD

**SCI-FI • 2006 • RATED: TV-MA • 55 MINS • SEASONS: 4
JOHN BARROWMAN, EVE MYLES, BURN GORMAN**

"Torchwood: outside the government, beyond the police. Fighting for the future on behalf of the human race. The 21st century is when everything changes. And Torchwood is ready." Hostile aliens don't stand a chance against Jack Harkness and his team.

When a time rift opens in Cardiff, the city is beset by alien menaces and strange phenomena. Fortunately, help is at hand in the form of Torchwood, a secret organization led by immortal time traveler Captain Jack Harkness (John Barrowman). In the opening episode, policewoman Gwen Cooper (Eve Myles) joins the team, which also includes medical officer Owen (Burn Gorman) and tech expert Toshiko (Naoko Mori).

Conceived by Russell T. Davies as a grown-up spin-off of *Doctor Who* (see p58, and note the titles are anagrams of each other), the show lives up to that remit by including violence, swearing, and sex scenes, with a strong emphasis on bisexuality—a running joke is that Jack will sleep with anyone and anything.

Throughout its four-season run, the show mixes weird story lines (such as Gwen getting pregnant from an alien bite) with emotional moments, while maintaining the humor. It's also capable of surprising depth, notably in Season 3 miniseries "Children of Earth," which explores humanity's reaction to an alien demanding 10 percent of the world's children.

> **"** *That's what Torchwood does ... it ruins your life and saves everyone else's.* **"**
>
> **Gwen Cooper** (S3 E5)

PRIMEVAL

**SCI-FI • 2007
RATED: TV-14 • 45 MINS**

Dinosaurs *and* time travel? A team of scientists track down prehistoric creatures and battle to stave off the apocalypse in this British series.

After mysterious time portals ("anomalies") release dangerous dinosaurs all over Britain, Professor Nick Cutter (Douglas Henshall) and his team—including student Connor Temple (Andrew Lee-Potts) and zookeeper Abby Maitland (Hannah Spearritt)—attempt to return them to their time periods. Cutter's believed-dead wife Helen (Juliet Aubrey) is somehow linked to the anomalies and her reappearance causes chaos.

Created by the team behind the *Walking with Dinosaurs* documentary series, *Primeval* mixes a smart concept and strong characters with impressive creature effects. Throughout its five seasons, the show delivers exciting, fast-paced plots and takes a number of bold character decisions, one of which serves as a stark warning about the dangers of time travel.

ANOTHER LIFE

SCI-FI • 2019
RATED: TV-MA • 45 MINS

What would you do if a giant alien object landed on Earth? Would you try to communicate with it or head into space to discover its origins? Or both?

Astronaut Niko Breckenridge (Katee Sackhoff) leads a crew of impossibly attractive experts on a space mission to discover the origins of "The Artifact," a strange monolith that lands in a field in America. Meanwhile, her left-behind scientist husband, Erik (Justin Chatwin), is tasked with trying to communicate with the structure, while also looking after their seven-year-old daughter.

The first season cleverly combines a space mystery (the nature and purpose of The Artifact) with cliffhanger thrills—Niko and her crew face a different threat in every episode (space viruses, mutinous crew members—you name it). It's anchored by a committed performance from Sackhoff (no stranger to deep space after *Battlestar Galactica*), and heightened by some satisfyingly gloopy effects.

BATTLESTAR GALACTICA

SCI-FI • 1978
RATED: TV-PG • 45 MINS

Spaceships, heroic fighter pilots, and killer robots. Best friends Apollo and Starbuck protect a fleet of civilian ships as they embark on a search for Earth, pursued by murderous Cylons.

Created by TV producer Glen A. Larson, *Battlestar Galactica* is set in a galaxy that's not that far away. When killer robot Cylons attack the Twelve Colonies, Commander Adama (Lorne Greene) leads a ragtag fleet of 220 civilian spaceships in search of the planet Earth, mythical home to the lost 13th colony. With the Cylons in hot pursuit, fighter pilots Apollo (Richard Hatch) and Starbuck (Dirk Benedict) assist Adama in protecting the fleet.

Capitalizing on the big-screen success of *Star Wars*, the show is essentially a survival drama in space, notable for its engaging characters and impressive robots. A second season, *Galactica 1980*, sees the characters landing on Earth, while a remake followed in 2004 (see p29).

BUCK ROGERS IN THE 25TH CENTURY

SCI-FI • 1979
RATED: TV-PG • 52 MINS

Swashbuckling space adventures abound as defrosted astronaut Buck Rogers, Wilma Deering, and robot sidekick Twiki battle hostile aliens.

In 1987, NASA astronaut William "Buck" Rogers (Gil Gerard) is frozen in space after a freak accident. Revived 500 years later, he finds Earth under attack by the Draconian Empire, led by scheming space princess Ardala (Pamela Hensley). In the second and final season, Buck, Wilma (Erin Gray), and Twiki (voiced by Mel Blanc) seek out new worlds.

Produced by Glen A. Larson, *Buck Rogers* was based on a character created in 1928, who'd appeared in novellas, comic strips, and a 1939 movie serial starring Buster Crabbe. With exciting space battles and charismatic leads, the show delivers enjoyably pulpy plots, heightened by a distinctive look—just check out those gleaming white space uniforms.

FARSCAPE

SCI-FI • 1999
RATED: TV-14 • 47 MINS

Wormholes, curious creatures, and a pregnant spaceship? It could only be this inventive series about an astronaut saved by fugitives aboard a living spacecraft.

Fleeing the militaristic Peacekeepers, the crew of biomechanical spaceship *Moya* rescue John Crichton (Ben Browder), a modern-day astronaut from Earth flung into deep space after a wormhole incident. Tensions rise when they're joined by a second passenger, renegade Peacekeeper Aeryn Sun (Claudia Black). Attempting to return to their home planets, the crew experience a series of outlandish occurrences, including *Moya* giving birth to a Peacekeeper warship.

Farscape's imaginative story lines and offbeat characters are enhanced by a colorful array of aliens created by Jim Henson's Creature Shop. The show was canceled after four seasons, but a fan campaign led to *Farscape: The Peacekeeper Wars*, a miniseries that wrapped up the loose ends.

SPACE: 1999

SCI-FI • 1975
RATED: PG (UK) • 49 MINS

When a nuclear blast on its surface sends the moon hurtling through space, the inhabitants of Moonbase Alpha are along for the ride, encountering alien civilizations and unexplained phenomena on their strange journey.

Epic in scope and imagination, *Space: 1999* was the most expensive British series ever produced at the time. Base leader John Koenig (Martin Landau), medical officer Helena Russell (Barbara Bain), and science officer Victor Bergman (Barry Morse) are the core characters, with Bergman replaced by shape-shifting alien—and fan favorite—Maya (Catherine Schell) in Season 2.

With its stunning model work (courtesy of *Thunderbirds* creator Gerry Anderson) and outlandish plots, the show attracted a slew of notable guest stars over its two seasons, including future *Star Wars* actors Christopher Lee, Peter Cushing, and David Prowse, as well as Ian McShane and Brian Blessed.

STARGATE SG-1

SCI-FI • 1997
RATED: TV-14 • 44 MINS

What happens when you go through a portal to another world? Secret military team SG-1 battles aliens, discovers new technologies, and learns the secrets of the universe in this sci-fi series.

Based on 1994 movie *Stargate*, this series centers on a military team tasked with exploring other worlds via interplanetary portals known as Stargates. Led by Colonel Jack O'Neill (*MacGyver*'s Richard Dean Anderson), the crew includes scientists Daniel Jackson (Michael Shanks), and Samantha Carter (Amanda Tapping), as well as scene-stealing alien Teal'c (Christopher Judge). Later in its 10 seasons, *Farscape* alumni Ben Browder and Claudia Black also joined the cast.

The team battle all manner of alien races, from snakelike parasites the Goa'uld, to beings drawn from Egyptian, Greek, and Norse legends. A huge success, the show spawned multiple spin-offs, including *Stargate: Atlantis* and animated series *Stargate Infinity*.

BATMAN

ACTION ADVENTURE • 1966 • RATED: TV-G • 25 MINS • SEASONS: 3
ADAM WEST, BURT WARD, CESAR ROMERO

Holy dynamic duo! Caped crusaders Batman and Robin fight fistfuls of fiendish foes in the tantalizingly tongue-in-cheek 1960s TV series. Gadgets, guest stars, and giggles ensue as Gotham City's garishly garbed good guys get results. Quick, Robin! To the Bat-poles!

Developed by executive producer William Dozier (who also served as the show's bombastic narrator), the first TV adaptation of DC Comics's Batman adopts a campy and colorful comedic approach that proves irresistible. Adam West and Burt Ward play billionaire Bruce Wayne and his young ward Dick Grayson, who live in stately Wayne Manor with their faithful butler Alfred (Alan Napier). Summoned by Commissioner Gordon (Neil

Hamilton), the pair spring into action as costumed crime fighters Batman and Robin whenever various villains threaten Gotham City.

Unlike the 1940s Columbia film serial *Batman and Robin,* the TV show introduces Batman's rogues' gallery of villains from the comics. A key part of the show's appeal is that the villains are frequently played by Hollywood actors, including Cesar Romero (The Joker), Burgess Meredith (The Penguin), and Frank Gorshin (The Riddler). Sometimes a villain is portrayed by more than one actor, most notably in the case of The Catwoman, who's incarnated by both Julie Newmar (Seasons 1 and 2) and Eartha Kitt (Season 3). Mr. Freeze is even played by three actors—George Sanders, Eli Wallach, and famous movie director Otto Preminger. Early episodes of the show also frequently adapt plots from Batman comics, often involving giant deathtraps that provide exciting cliffhangers for two-part episodes.

> **"** *Tune in next week, same Bat-time, same Bat-channel.* **"**

Narrator (end of every episode)

The show's cheerfully upbeat theme music, colorful costumes, cartoonish violence, and pop-art aesthetic all contribute to the high camp factor. The masterstroke is that West and Ward play the whole thing completely seriously, tongues firmly in cheek. This is particularly evident in the show's frequent lessons in good citizenship, which range from

FAMOUS FOES

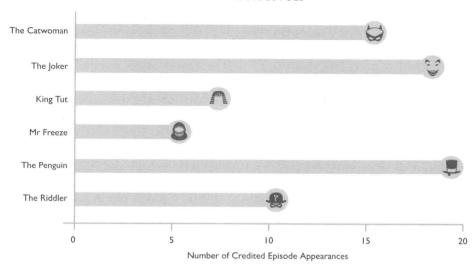

Number of Credited Episode Appearances

Batman reminding Robin to always look both ways before he crosses the road to musings on subjects such as world peace: "Language is the key to world peace. If we all spoke each other's tongues, perhaps the scourge of war would be ended forever."

Throughout its three seasons (and the 1966 movie, filmed after Season 1), the show displays a deep-seated love of language, notably in its frequent use of alliteration; its repeated catchphrases (Robin says a variation of "Holy something-or-other, Batman!" 359 times in the series); and even its rhyming episode titles—Season 1's "Zelda the Great" was followed by "A Death Worse than Fate," for example.

Similarly, Batman's vast array of meticulously labeled gadgets all have fun Bat-names such as "Shark Repellent Bat-Spray" and "Extra-Strong Bat-Knockout Gas." In addition, the onomatopoeic text super-imposed over the fight scenes in comic-book style had multiple variations other than just "BAM!" and "POW!", including made-up words such as "ZLOPP!" and "GLIPP!"

Each episode sticks to a rigid structure (briefly: call from commissioner's office, dash to Batmobile, clues followed, villains discovered, deathtrap, fight), allowing plenty of opportunity for self-parody. One inspired running gag involves "the Batclimb," whereby Batman and Robin scale a wall using Bat-ropes, a sequence filmed on a horizontal surface but with the camera rotated 90 degrees. This became a coveted spot for celebrity cameos, with the likes of Sammy Davis Jr. and Jerry Lewis opening windows for a short conversation during the climb.

The third and final season adds Batgirl (played by Yvonne Craig) to the mix, briefly turning the Dynamic Duo into the Terrific Trio. When the show was canceled, a different network offered to pick it up for a fourth season, but the expensive Batcave set had already been destroyed, so it sadly never happened. Holy terrible timing, Batman!

CREATORS: Lorenzo Semple Jr., William Dozier
PRODUCTION CO: 20th Century Fox Television, Greenway Productions

CHARLIE'S ANGELS

ACTION ADVENTURE • 1976
RATED: TV-PG • 50 MINS

Action, comedy, and outrageous undercover outfits ensue when three beautiful police graduates work for a detective agency run by a mysterious, never-seen millionaire.

Assigned boring, low-risk jobs after graduating from the LA police academy, Sabrina Duncan (Kate Jackson), Jill Munroe (Farrah Fawcett), and Kelly Garrett (Jaclyn Smith) are employed by the Charles Townsend Detective Agency, where they're given weekly assignments by a voice on a speakerphone (John Forsythe). Their cases often involve elaborate undercover work, necessitating a variety of outfits, accents, and hairdos.

With its combination of action and glamour, the show smartly appealed to both sexes, showcasing strong female role models. Only Smith lasted all five seasons, with Fawcett replaced by Cheryl Ladd and Jackson by Shelley Hack and Tanya Roberts. There was a short-lived attempt at a remake in 2011.

TRU CALLING

FANTASY DRAMA • 2003
RATED: 15 (UK) • 43 MINS

***Groundhog Day* meets *The Sixth Sense* is the setup for *Tru Calling*, in which a morgue attendant discovers she can travel back in time after receiving messages from dead people.**

Forced to take a job in a morgue, medical student Tru Davies (Eliza Dushku) gets quite the shock when a dead person asks her for help. Discovering she has the ability to relive each corpse's last day, Tru tries to save them from the mortuary slab. Complications ensue when she meets Jack Harper (Jason Priestley), who shares the same "calling" but wants to prevent Tru from meddling with history.

Anchored by a charismatic performance from Dushku (who could generate on-screen chemistry with a cardboard box), *Tru Calling* smartly blends time travel and the paranormal to entertaining effect. The show was canceled six episodes into Season 2, but writer Doris Egan kindly published a blog post providing fans with closure on all the story lines.

VERONICA MARS

MYSTERY DRAMA • 2004
RATED: TV-14 • 42 MINS

What would you do if your best friend was murdered? If you're high-school student Veronica Mars, you turn detective and investigate.

Sharp-witted teen Veronica Mars (Kristen Bell) has her life turned upside down when her best friend Lily Kane (Amanda Seyfried) is murdered. Having learned the tricks of the trade from her detective father, Sheriff Mars (Enrico Colantoni), Veronica investigates and uncovers the dark underbelly of her super-rich California community, especially in her dealings with Logan Echolls (Jason Dohring), the privileged son of a Hollywood A-lister.

Blending case-of-the-week plots, season-long mysteries, and issue-based teen drama, *Veronica Mars* grafts a neo-noir sensibility on to its high-school setting, heightened by quip-laden dialogue, and Bell's star-making turn. Canceled after three superlative seasons in 2007, the show refused to die, gaining both a 2014 movie and a final season in 2019.

IZOMBIE

COMEDY HORROR • 2015
RATED: TV-14 • 42 MINS

Who knew being a zombie and eating brains could help you solve crimes? A Seattle morgue assistant turns undead detective in this show based on a DC Comics series. Mmmm ... brains.

When medical resident Liv Moore (Rose McIver) is bitten by a zombie, she finds she needs a steady diet of brains in order to maintain her humanity. Taking a job at the morgue, Liv discovers that when she eats the brains of a murder victim, she gets memory flashes from their lives, so she uses her ability to help Detective Clive Babineaux (Malcolm Goodwin) solve cases. Later seasons expand the plot, bringing more zombies into the mix.

Cocreated by Rob Thomas (*Veronica Mars*) and Diane Ruggiero-Wright, this five-season show hits that *Buffy the Vampire Slayer* sweet spot, delivering an appealing mix of snappy dialogue, likable characters, and the supernatural. In other words, this is a horror comedy with brains. Tasty, tasty brains.

SEVEN SECONDS

CRIME DRAMA • 2018
RATED: TV-MA • 60 MINS

What happens when four white cops cover up the death of a black teen? A distraught mother tries to get justice for her son in this gritty drama.

When white police officer Peter Jablonski (Beau Knapp) accidentally runs over and critically injures a black teenager during a snowstorm in Jersey City, he calls his colleagues for help, and a cover-up ensues.

Devastated, the boy's churchgoing mother Latrice Butler (Regina King, superb as always), pushes for an investigation with the aid of alcoholic assistant prosecutor K. J. Harper (Clare-Hope Ashitey) and internal affairs detective Joe "Fish" Rinaldi (Michael Mosley).

Based on the Russian film *The Major*, this hard-hitting, topical, and powerfully emotional single-season crime drama explores racial tensions and the difficulty of getting justice in a broken system. The title refers to the length of time in which Jablonski could have done the right thing right after the accident.

STUMPTOWN

CRIME DRAMA • 2019
RATED: TV-14 • 42 MINS

"Forget it, Dex. It's Stumptown." A PTSD-afflicted ex-Marine turns PI in this Portland-set detective drama. Will solving cases and punching bad guys help her process her past?

Based on the comic-book series of the same title (a nickname for Portland), *Stumptown* stars Cobie Smulders as military veteran Dex Parios, who turns private eye after solving a kidnapping. Aided by Detective Miles Hoffman (Michael Ealy) and best friend Grey McConnell (Jake Johnson), she investigates a series of cases the police can't (or won't) handle.

Smulders smoulders in the lead role, sparking strong chemistry with both Johnson and Ealy. Sharply scripted and featuring a likable support cast, the one-season show delivers a steady stream of pleasingly old-fashioned detective thrills, including some enjoyably messy fight scenes. It also has a great soundtrack, thanks to a smart running gag involving a mixtape and Dex's dodgy car stereo.

COLUMBO

MYSTERY • 1971
RATED: TV-PG • 85 MINS

"Just one more thing...." Don't let that crumpled raincoat fool you. Dogged detective Columbo collars killers with his celebrated catchphrase in this series of satisfying murder mysteries.

Less "whodunnits" and more "howcatchems," *Columbo* episodes upend the usual mystery format by showing the killer upfront. You then get to watch them squirm as twinkly-eyed detective Lieutenant Colombo (Peter Falk) slowly tightens the noose before revealing their guilt. His shabby raincoat, ever-present cigar, unassuming demeanor, and rambling anecdotes are all part of the plan, lulling the culprits into a false sense of security.

Notable guest stars throughout the 10-season series, which aired sporadically for more than 30 years, include Dick Van Dyke, Johnny Cash, and Patrick McGoohan, who played four murderers in total. Bonus fact: "Murder by the Book," the first episode of Season 1, was directed by 25-year-old Steven Spielberg.

DEATH IN PARADISE

MYSTERY • 2011
RATED: 12 • 60 MINS

Sun, sea, sand ... and suspense. A series of detectives solves Agatha Christie–style murders on a fictional Caribbean island in this cozy mystery drama.

Death in Paradise begins with deadpan detective Richard Poole (Ben Miller) arriving on the island of Saint Marie to investigate the murder of a British police officer. When he solves the case, Poole is ordered to stay on as the island's murder rate is surprisingly high. Later seasons repeat the setup with different detectives, including clumsy Humphrey Goodman (Kris Marshall), grieving widower Jack Mooney (Ardal O'Hanlon), and the highly allergic Neville Parker (Ralf Little).

Distinguished by its Caribbean setting and strong cast (including Danny John-Jules's Officer Dwayne Myers), the nine-season series sticks closely to the Agatha Christie formula, whereby a murder is discovered, clues are followed, and the suspects gathered before the astute cop reveals the culprit.

MAGNUM, P.I.

CRIME DRAMA • 1980
RATED: TV-PG • 48 MINS

A Ferrari, a cigar, a Hawaiian shirt, and a luxurious moustache—that's private investigator Thomas Magnum in a nutshell. Join the detective as he solves crimes in Hawaii.

Cocreated by prolific producers Donald P. Bellisario and Glen A. Larson, *Magnum, P.I.* stars Tom Selleck as the titular detective, who lives in Oahu on the grounds of an estate owned by a never-seen novelist (voiced by Orson Welles). Frequently clashing with estate manager Higgins (John Hillerman), he solves crimes, assisted by his sidekicks, helicopter pilot "TC" and bar owner Rick.

Anchored by Selleck's charming performance, the show delivers all the gumshoe action you could ask for, right down to Magnum's film noir-esque voice-over. Over its eight seasons, *Magnum* features a surprising array of guest stars, and even crosses over with fellow sleuthing shows *Murder, She Wrote* (see p82) and *Simon & Simon* (see p409).

IRONSIDE

CRIME • 1967
RATED: TV-PG • 47 MINS

What if Sherlock Holmes had to solve cases from a wheelchair? That's the basic premise of *Ironside*, an ensemble cop drama fronted by a supersmart detective paralyzed by a spinal injury.

Raymond Burr plays San Francisco Chief of Detectives Robert T. Ironside, who's forced to retire after a sniper's bullet paralyzes him from the waist down. But Ironside isn't about to let a spinal injury stop him fighting crime, so he gets himself appointed as a special consultant and works with a team of assistants, including detective Ed Brown (Don Galloway) and ex-con Mark Sanger (Don Mitchell).

The idea of a disabled lead character was groundbreaking for 1967, and Burr's charming, witty performance (punctuated by bouts of grumpiness) propelled the series to eight seasons. The show is also notable for its fully rounded supporting cast (each of them has their own story lines) and its Quincy Jones–composed theme tune.

REMINGTON STEELE

CRIME DRAMA • 1982
RATED: TV-PG • 49 MINS

"It was working like a charm, until *he* walked in, with his blue eyes and mysterious past." Detective thrills and will-they-won't-they romance combine in this devilishly charming crime drama.

Private eye Laura Holt (Stephanie Zimbalist) struggles to attract clients because she's a woman, so she invents a male boss named Remington Steele and is inundated with cases. Then a twinkly-eyed con man (Pierce Brosnan) walks through her door, claiming to be the boss she invented and she can't get rid of him without revealing her deception. Season 2 sees the addition of scene-stealing secretary Mildred Krebs (Doris Roberts).

Brosnan and Zimbalist's chemistry forms the heart of the series, which teases out their romance over five seasons of sparkling dialogue. The show was a huge influence on *Moonlighting* (see p158)—writer Glenn Gordon Caron worked on this before creating the Bruce Willis–starring series.

SIMON & SIMON

MYSTERY • 1981
RATED: 12 (UK) • 47 MINS

Squabbling siblings Rick and A. J. are like chalk and cheese, but they run a detective agency together anyway. Join the disparate duo as they solve crimes in downtown San Diego.

Private eye Rick (Gerald McRaney) is a Vietnam vet who favors cowboy boots, denim, and his beloved pickup truck; his brother and colleague A. J. (Jameson Parker) is a college grad who prefers tailored suits, classical music, and French cuisine. Putting aside their differences to solve cases, the bickering siblings occasionally receive help from assistant district attorney Janet Fowler (Jeannie Wilson).

After a ratings boost from a crossover with *Magnum, P.I.* (see p408), *Simon & Simon* ran for eight seasons. The easygoing show comfortably embraces different tones, ranging from a dramatic episode exploring Rick's Vietnam experience to a lighter outing in which the duo go undercover in a nudist camp.

BILLIONS

**DRAMA • 2016 • RATED: TV-MA • 60 MINS • SEASONS: 5
PAUL GIAMATTI, DAMIAN LEWIS, MAGGIE SIFF**

A thrilling game of fat cat and mouse, this clash of New York titans is loosely based on the legal battles between two real-life figures: former New York Attorney Preet Bharara and billionaire hedge-fund manager Steve Cohen.

In this fictionalized version, US Attorney Chuck Rhoades (Paul Giamatti) becomes convinced that hedge-fund king Bobby "Axe" Axelrod (Damian Lewis) is guilty of insider trading and resorts to dirty tricks to trigger an investigation against him. Caught in the middle is Chuck's wife, Wendy (Maggie Siff), who works for Axe as an in-house psychiatrist and performance coach.

Thankfully, it's not necessary to have a firm grasp of the ins and outs of hedge-fund management to enjoy *Billions*. The show's chief pleasure lies in watching two top-of-their-game actors hurling weapons-grade dialogue at each other. It's particularly fascinating because you never know quite whose side you're meant to be on—both leads play morally questionable characters

with complex shades of gray, and even Wendy, the show's most ostensibly sympathetic figure, isn't above a spot of backstabbing.

Billions already had a diverse supporting cast—Axe's right-hand man Wags (David Costabile) is a constant joy—but it made history in Season 2 with the introduction of Axe-Cap employee Taylor Mitchell (Asia Kate Dillon), the first regular nonbinary character on mainstream American television. An instant fan favorite, Taylor becomes a gripping counterpoint to the central Rhoades vs. Axelrod battle, as they go from being Axe's unflappable, super-competent intern to his direct competition (with John Malkovich as an evil Russian backer, no less).

As well as the trashy thrills of seeing the two leads constantly wriggle out of each other's carefully laid traps, *Billions* is laced with dark humor and positively revels in skewering the macho posturing and male egos associated with the real-life worlds of politics and finance. In other words, it's a show that amply repays your investment.

> *"The only enemy more dangerous than a man with unlimited resources is one with nothing to lose...."*
>
> Chuck (S1 E12)

CREATORS: Brian Koppelman, David Levien, Andrew Ross Sorkin
PRODUCTION CO: Showtime Entertainment, Best Available!

GOLIATH

DRAMA • 2016
RATED: TV-MA • 60 MINS

Can a disgraced lawyer find redemption and stick it to his old firm at the same time? Ambulance-chaser Billy McBride finds out as he takes on a risky case.

Cocreated by David E. Kelley (*Ally McBeal*), *Goliath* centers on Billy McBride (Billy Bob Thornton), a washed-up, alcoholic lawyer who agrees to take on a wrongful death suit against the biggest client of the successful law firm he founded with ruthless recluse Donald Cooperman (William Hurt). Supported by an unconventional team (including Tania Raymonde's prostitute-slash-legal assistant), he uncovers a deadly conspiracy and finds his old partner will stop at nothing to derail the case.

Cleverly structured and laced with sharp dialogue, *Goliath* delivers superlative courtroom drama with a strong focus on its offbeat characters over three seasons. The performances are a real highlight: Thornton is on blistering form, while Hurt makes an intriguingly bizarre villain.

NIP/TUCK

DRAMA • 2003
RATED: TV-MA • 44 MINS

You wouldn't believe the things plastic surgeons get up to. Join cutting-edge scalpel-wielders Sean and Christian as they slice their way through a series of jaw-dropping plotlines.

Created by Ryan Murphy (*Glee, American Horror Story*), this outrageous drama centers on plastic surgeons Sean McNamara (Dylan Walsh) and Christian Troy (Julian McMahon), whose sex lives are every bit as unusual as the operations they perform. Caught between them is Sean's wife, Julia (Joely Richardson), who still has feelings for Christian after a one-night stand when they were in college.

Over the course of six seasons, the show's salacious story lines take in everything from sex addiction to a slasher who targets the pair for fixing his victims. Each episode is named after the patient scheduled to receive surgery (including real-life guest star Joan Rivers), and the series became famous for its extremely graphic depictions of surgical procedures.

SPIN

THRILLER DRAMA • 2012
RATED: TV-MA • 52 MINS

How far would you go to achieve your political goals? Morality goes right out the window when two rival spin doctors battle for supremacy in this French political thriller.

Known as *Les Hommes de l'ombre* (or "The Shadow Men") in its native France, *Spin* begins with a literal bang as the president is killed in what looks like a terror attack. As the race to replace him heats up, spin doctor Simon Kapita (Bruno Wolkowitch) and his protégé-turned-rival Ludovic Desmeuze (*Spiral's* Grégory Fitoussi) resort to increasingly underhand tactics to secure victory for their candidates.

With a cynical outlook that feels more topical then ever, *Spin* is packed with edge-of-the-seat cliffhangers as it explores the murky world of politics and PR. And this being a French drama, there are, *naturellement*, a few affairs of the heart thrown in for good measure across its three seasons. This is *Borgen* with an adrenaline shot.

HART TO HART

MYSTERY • 1979
RATED: TV-PG • 44 MINS

**"When they met, it was murder."
Get comfortable on the couch for
cozy crime-solving fun with glamorous
detective duo Jonathan and Jennifer
Hart. Oh, and their dog, Freeway.**

Created by novelist Sidney Sheldon and set
in Los Angeles, *Hart to Hart* stars movie star
Robert Wagner as self-made millionaire
Jonathan Hart, who enjoys a jet-setting lifestyle

with his wife, Jennifer (Stefanie Powers),
a freelance journalist. Accompanied by their
gravelly voiced butler-chauffeur-cook Max
(Lionel Stander) and their dog, Freeway,
the pair can't go five minutes without
stumbling into a crime to solve, be it
smuggling, espionage, or murder.

The lavish lifestyle and playful chemistry of
Jonathan and Jennifer recalls that of *The Thin
Man's* Nick and Nora Charles, to equally
winning effect. Effortlessly charming, the show
ran for five seasons, which were followed by
eight TV movies between 1993 and 1996.

THE PERSUADERS!

ACTION ADVENTURE • 1971
RATED: PG (UK) • 50 MINS

**Mix two movie stars with crime plots,
beautiful women, and international
locations. That's the recipe for *The
Persuaders!*, starring Tony Curtis and
Roger Moore as playboy detectives.**

Tony Curtis plays rough diamond Danny
Wilde, who grew up on the streets of New
York before making his fortune and becoming
a wealthy playboy. When he gets into a

fistfight with British nobleman Lord Brett
Sinclair (Roger Moore) on the Riviera, Judge
Fulton (Laurence Naismith) blackmails them
into working together as investigators in order
to avoid a jail sentence.

Produced by Lew Grade's ITC Entertainment,
The Persuaders! was briefly the most expensive
show on television, thanks to its steady supply
of fast cars, fashionable clothing, and fancy
locations, as well as a host of glamorous guest
stars. A big success in Britain, the show was
sadly halted after only one season when
Moore was cast as James Bond.

CAGNEY & LACEY

CRIME DRAMA • 1982
RATED: TV-PG • 47 MINS

**Tired of all the male-dominated
detective shows? Then spend some
time with New York City's Christine
Cagney and Mary Beth Lacey, TV's first
female buddy cops.**

Sharon Gless (who took over the role from
Meg Foster in Season 2) and Tyne Daly play
Cagney and Lacey, detectives at Manhattan's
14th Precinct, known as Midtown South.

As well as showing them solving crimes, the
series also explores their contrasting home
lives, with Cagney as a career-minded single
woman, and Lacey as a married, working mom.

Throughout the course of seven seasons, the
show tackles a wide variety of difficult issues,
ranging from domestic abuse, rape, and drug
addiction to Cagney's alcoholism and Lacey's
breast cancer. It also features a diverse,
interesting supporting cast and a surprising
amount of comedy. After Season 2, either
Gless or Daly won best actress Emmys for
the show every year it was on the air.

STARSKY & HUTCH

ACTION DRAMA • 1975
RATED: 15 (UK) • 50 MINS

Seventies cop action doesn't come much cooler than this. Join undercover detectives David Starsky and Kenneth "Hutch" Hutchinson as they bust bad guys in Bay City, California.

Brooklyn-born Starsky (Paul Michael Glaser) and blond Californian Hutch (David Soul) are the ultimate buddy cops as they go undercover for the Bay City police department. Notable supporting characters include Bernie Hamilton as Captain Dobey and Antonio Fargas as friend and informant Huggy Bear, but the real star is Starsky's red-with-a-white-stripe Gran Torino, nicknamed the "Striped Tomato."

In contrast to other cop shows, Starsky and Hutch have quite the touchy-feely relationship, with frequent displays of affection in the form of manly hugs, back-slapping, hair tousling, and so on—a bromance before bromances were a thing. But the four-season show had its gritty side, too, most notably in Season 1's "The Fix," in which Hutch is forcibly addicted to heroin.

STRIKE BACK

ACTION ADVENTURE • 2010
RATED: TV-MA • 45 MINS

"Brutal. Ruthless. Deadly. And they're the good guys." The men and women of secret military intelligence unit Section 20 conduct a series of high-risk missions across the globe.

Based on the novel by former SAS soldier Chris Ryan, Season 1 of *Strike Back* centers on John Porter (Richard Armitage), who returns to military action following the kidnap of journalist Katie Dartmouth (Orla Brady). Across eight seasons, the series intermittently reboots with new protagonists, including Philip Winchester as Sergeant Michael Stonebridge and Sullivan Stapleton as disgraced ex-Delta Force operative Damian Scott.

With plots ripped from the headlines and stylish action, *Strike Back* delivers visceral shoot-'em-up thrills to rival the *Call of Duty* video games. As well as depicting the unit's banter-laden camaraderie and spicing things up with sex scenes, the show also finds room to explore more serious issues, such as PTSD.

THE MAN FROM U.N.C.L.E.

SPY ADVENTURE • 1964
RATED: PG (UK) • 50 MINS

Guns, gadgets, and good-looking superspies. The Cold War heats up as American secret agent Napoleon Solo teams with Russian spy Illya Kuryakin to thwart the forces of T.H.R.U.S.H.

The first of a wave of secret-agent shows produced in the wake of James Bond movie *Dr. No*, this stylish spy thriller stars Robert Vaughn and David McCallum as Solo and Kuryakin, an American and a Russian agent working together for U.N.C.L.E. (United Network Command for Law and Enforcement) to defeat T.H.R.U.S.H., a sinister organization bent on world domination.

Notable for its gadgets, weaponry, and cool little details (like the secret entrance to U.N.C.L.E. HQ in Del Floria's Tailor Shop), the show attracted high-profile guest stars such as Joan Crawford, Vincent Price, and Sonny and Cher. Canceled halfway through Season 4, it also spawned single-season spin-off *The Girl from U.N.C.L.E.*, starring Stefanie Powers.

RIVERDALE

MYSTERY DRAMA • 2017 • RATED: TV-14 • 44 MINS • SEASONS: 4
K. J. APA, LILI REINHART, COLE SPROUSE

A murder mystery. A serial killer. Biker gangs. Underground fight clubs. A deadly game. A brainwashing cult. And another murder mystery. Welcome to Riverdale, a town just like any other town. As long as that other town is Twin Peaks.

Based on the classic characters from Archie Comics, *Riverdale* is a compelling mix of sassy teen drama and small-town mystery thriller. The show centers on four key characters: kind-hearted Archie Andrews (K. J. Apa), wholesome girl-next-door Betty Cooper (Lili Reinhardt), former New York queen bee Veronica Lodge (Camilla Mendes), and philosophical beanie-wearing Jughead Jones (Cole Sprouse), who also serves as the show's narrator.

Season 1 focuses on a mystery surrounding the death of wealthy teenager Jason Blossom, whose mean sister, Cheryl (Madeleine Petsch),

quickly becomes the show's best character, thanks to her whip-smart dialogue and haughty attitude. In subsequent seasons, the plots get increasingly darker and weirder, taking in a serial killer, a creepy cult, and a deadly, highly addictive game called Gryphons & Gargoyles.

> **"** *Sardonic humor is just my way of relating to the world.* **"**
>
> **Jughead** (S1 E2)

Appropriately for a show about a seemingly perfect town hiding dark secrets, *Riverdale* features some nods to *Twin Peaks* (see p456), from its body-in-the-water opening and the typeface used for the title, to the casting of *Twin Peaks'* Mädchen Amick as Betty's mother, Alice Cooper. Fun film references abound, too.

THE TICK

ACTION COMEDY • 2017
RATED: TV-MA • 25 MINS

"Spoon!"—a weird catchphrase for an even weirder hero. Join our costumed do-gooder The Tick as he takes on The Terror with the help of his sidekick, Arthur.

Mild-mannered accountant Arthur Everest (Griffin Newman) believes his city is being controlled by The Terror (Jackie Earle Haley), a long-thought-dead super-villain. When

Arthur is befriended by exuberant, blue-suited Super Hero The Tick (Peter Serafinowicz), he becomes his sidekick, complete with a bulletproof mothlike costume. Together, they attempt to track down The Terror and rid the city of evil.

Created by Ben Edlund, based on his own comic-book character, *The Tick* both parodies and embraces the Super Hero genre. Anchored by Serafinowicz's fully committed performance throughout its two seasons and packed with witty dialogue, it's exciting, emotionally engaging, and laugh-out-loud funny.

DOOM PATROL

FANTASY ADVENTURE • 2019
RATED: TV-MA • 52 MINS

How many Super Hero shows have their heroes facing a magical farting donkey? Meet super-weirdos the Doom Patrol. Can they stop bickering long enough to save the world?

Dr. Niles Caulder (Timothy Dalton) assembles a team of super-powered misfits who include Robotman (Riley Shanahan), Elasti-Woman (April Bowlby), Negative Man (Matthew Zuk), and Crazy Jane (Diane Guerrero). Joined by Cyborg (Joivan Wade), the group face numerous adversaries, including revenge-driven Mr. Nobody (Alan Tudyk) and a magical farting donkey that can open a portal to another dimension.

Having first introduced its characters in an episode of DC Comics sister show *Titans* (see p399), this two-season series distinguishes itself with its ridiculous plots, entertainingly weird characters, and silly humor. As the flatulent donkey indicates, there's a knowing level of tongue-in-cheek to it all.

HEROES

FANTASY ADVENTURE • 2006
RATED: TV-14 • 42 MINS

"Save the cheerleader, save the world." A number of ordinary people discover they have super-powers. All well and good, except there's also the small matter of an oncoming apocalypse.

After a solar eclipse, people all over the world discover they have super-powers. Cheerleader Claire Bennett (Hayden Panettiere) gains the ability to regenerate, Japanese nerd Hiro (Masi Oka) can manipulate time, and nurse Peter Petrelli (Milo Ventimiglia) can absorb the powers of anyone near him. Together with other heroes, they must unite to prevent a prophesied apocalypse and stop serial killer Sylar (Zachary Quinto) from stealing their powers.

Conceived by Tim Kring as a televised comic book with multiple characters and overlapping story arcs, *Heroes* delivers thrills, gripping drama, and shocking twists. Canceled after four seasons, the show returned in 2015 with *Heroes: Reborn,* a stand-alone miniseries.

THE INCREDIBLE HULK

ACTION ADVENTURE • 1977
RATED: TV-PG • 48 MINS

"Don't make me angry. You wouldn't like me when I'm angry." A scientist goes on the run when an experiment transforms him into a raging monster with incredible strength.

Based on the Marvel Comics character, *The Incredible Hulk* stars Bill Bixby as Dr. David Banner, a scientist who transforms into rampaging green monster the Hulk (Lou Ferrigno) whenever he becomes stressed or angry. After the Hulk is falsely accused of murder, Banner is forced to turn fugitive, obsessively pursued by tabloid reporter Jack McGee (Jack Colvin), who believes Banner is connected to the monster.

Each episode follows a similar structure, with Banner helping out a different person before moving on, usually to the sound of a haunting piano theme. The show ran for five seasons and was followed by three made-for-TV movies before Bixby's death in 1993.

I AM NOT OKAY WITH THIS

FANTASY COMEDY • 2020
RATED: TV-MA • 23 MINS

It's not easy being a teenager, especially when you have telekinetic powers you can't control. An awkward high schooler discovers that her rage issues have explosive consequences in this funny fantasy drama.

Still shaken by the mysterious death of her father, teen Sydney Novak (Sophia Lillis) is dealt another blow when her best friend and secret crush Dina (Sofia Bryant) starts dating an obnoxious jock. When her anger manifests in bursts of telekinetic energy, she turns to smitten comics nerd Stan Barber (Wyatt Oleff) to help her figure out what's going on.

Based on a comic book by Charles Forsman—whose *The End of the F***ing World* (see p351) shares the same blackly comic tone—the one-season show mixes teen drama, high-school comedy (there's even a *Breakfast Club*–inspired episode), sci-fi, and horror to richly entertaining effect. It's anchored by a terrific performance from rising star Lillis.

PREACHER

FANTASY DRAMA • 2016
RATED: TV-MA • 54 MINS

A superpowered priest, his vampire buddy, and his ex-girlfriend embark on a violence-strewn search for God in this fantasy drama.

After a crisis of faith, hard-drinking preacher Jesse Custer (Dominic Cooper) is visited by a mysterious entity and awakes to discover that he has gained the power to make anyone do as he asks. Accompanied by vice-loving vampire Proinsias Cassidy (Joseph Gilgun) and trigger-happy ex-girlfriend Tulip (Ruth Negga), Jesse sets out to find God and quickly encounters various denizens of hell.

Based on the comic-book series by Garth Ennis and Steve Dillon, *Preacher* strikes the perfect balance between black comedy and horror, deploying gallons of gore. The mythology expands over its four seasons (an organization called the Grail is introduced, Hitler becomes a recurring character …), while the show remains cheerfully blood-soaked, violent, and profane till the end.

LAND OF THE GIANTS

SCI-FI • 1968
RATED: PG (UK) • 52 MINS

What happens when a spaceship from Earth crash-lands on a planet of giants? The crew of the *Spindrift* are forced to deal with some colossal problems as they try to return home.

Set in the then-distant future of 1983, *Land of the Giants* begins when the crew and passengers of orbital cruise ship the *Spindrift* crash-land on a planet that is almost exactly like Earth, except everything is 12 times bigger. Led by Captain Steve Burton (Gary Conway), the tiny humans face all manner of dangers as they struggle to repair their craft.

Created by legendary producer Irwin Allen, *Land of the Giants* is notable for its impressive effects work, enabled by a sizable budget. Over the course of two seasons, the giants' society is shown to be increasingly complex and fascinating, while the humans deal with a variety of sci-fi menaces (androids, clones, time travelers, you name it), as well as the constant fear of being stepped on.

THE VAMPIRE DIARIES

FANTASY DRAMA • 2009
RATED: TV-14 • 43 MINS

What if that cute guy you liked was a vampire? And what if that other cute guy you liked was also a vampire? Three words: vampire love triangle.

Life in Mystic Falls, Virginia, perks up for teenager Elena Gilbert (Nina Dobrev) when she falls for kindhearted Stefan Salvatore (Paul Wesley), who just happens to be a 162-year-old vampire. Things get complicated when Elena also falls for Stefan's malevolent brother Damon (Ian Somerhalder) and realizes that both siblings were previously in love with Katherine Pierce, her exact double (also played by Dobrev).

Based on the popular book series by L. J. Smith, *The Vampire Diaries* delivers all the romance action you could possibly hope for. Over the course of its eight seasons, the show explores the brothers' tortured history and spices up its mythology by introducing other supernatural threats to Mystic Falls, including werewolves, witches, and ghosts.

HERCULES: THE LEGENDARY JOURNEYS

FANTASY ADVENTURE • 1995
RATED: 15 (UK) • 44 MINS

Join demigod do-gooder Hercules as he clobbers creatures and delivers wisecracks in this action-adventure series based on Greek myth.

Kevin Sorbo stars as muscle-bound hero Hercules, who roams the ancient world with his alternating companions Iolaus (Michael Hurst) and wheeler-dealer Salmoneus (Robert Trebor). Together they save villagers from warlords, monsters, and angry gods. By far, the angriest is Hercules's evil stepmother, Hera, who wants him dead because his mere presence reminds her of husband Zeus's infidelity.

Blending action, mythology, and cheerful humor, *Hercules* is renowned for its fun fantasy plots and nudge-nudge jokes, such as "This is one big web site" (in a spider's lair). The show ran for six seasons and spawned two spin-offs: *Xena: Warrior Princess* and *Young Hercules*, starring, wait for it, Ryan Gosling.

XENA: WARRIOR PRINCESS

FANTASY ADVENTURE • 1995
RATED: TV-PG • 45 MINS

How to atone for misdeeds so terrible that they earned you the name "Destroyer of Nations"? By fighting gods and monsters, that's how! Join Xena as she battles evil.

Seeking to redeem herself, warrior princess Xena (Lucy Lawless) travels the ancient world, fighting for the greater good alongside steadfast companion Gabrielle (Renée O'Connor). Their adversaries range from Norse gods to Roman emperors, with a few mythical creatures thrown in, too.

Having originally appeared in three episodes of *Hercules: The Legendary Journeys*, Xena's popularity quickly surpassed that of her beefy counterpart when she got her own series. Over six action-packed seasons, Xena's adventures spanned everything from cheerful comedy to high tragedy, taking in body-swap plots, musical episodes, and even a bizarre excursion to the present day, where she's forced to watch clips from her own show.

BLACK SAILS

PERIOD ADVENTURE • 2014
RATED: TV-MA • 56 MINS

Yarrrrr. Here be a lusty tale of pirates to shiver ye timbers. Cap'n Flint and new recruit "Long" John Silver pursue a Spanish galleon loaded with pieces of eight in this swashbuckling adventure.

Intended as a prequel to Robert Louis Stevenson's *Treasure Island*, this buccaneering action drama is set in the West Indies during the Golden Age of Piracy. Toby Stephens plays

Flint, a pirate captain whose obsessive pursuit of a Spanish treasure galleon has blinded him to the fact his crew are becoming mutinous. Wily new recruit John Silver (Luke Arnold) secretly holds the key to locating the treasure.

Festooned with lashings of sex and violence, *Black Sails* delivers plenty of cutlass-swishing action over its four seasons but also finds time for meditations on the evils of greed. It's notable for its colorful characters, especially the fictionalized versions of several real-life pirates, including Jack Rackham, Charles Vane, Anne Bonny, and Blackbeard.

DOLLHOUSE

SCI-FI • 2009
RATED: TV-14 • 46 MINS

Ethical quandaries abound in Joss Whedon's sci-fi series, set in a facility that programs mind-wiped "dolls" with made-to-order personalities.

Eliza Dushku plays Echo, a memory-wiped "doll" in an LA "Dollhouse," who is imprinted with different memories, skills, and personalities when she's hired out to rich clients. After assignments ranging from fulfilling

sexual fantasies to committing crimes, Echo develops her own personality, which she conceals from Dollhouse director Adelle DeWitt (Olivia Williams). Meanwhile, obsessed FBI agent Ballard (Tahmoh Penikett) tries to prove the Dollhouse's existence.

Dollhouse starts out as a mission-of-the-week action-adventure show before embracing and exploring complex themes of identity, humanity, and the misuse of technology. Like *Buffy the Vampire Slayer* creator Whedon's *Firefly* (see p91), it was canceled prematurely, after two seasons. It deserved better.

THE TIME TUNNEL

SCI-FI • 1966
RATED: TV-PG • 50 MINS

What happens when a time machine goes wrong? Two scientists find themselves trapped tumbling through history in this 1960s sci-fi adventure.

Created by producer Irwin Allen, the series centers on a top-secret government time-machine project. When testing the titular tunnel, scientists Doug Phillips (Robert Colbert) and Tony Newman (James Darren)

become lost in time, bouncing between different periods in history. They are supported by their colleagues in the present, who can see and communicate with them.

Throughout the single-season show's 30 episodes, Doug and Tony visit key moments in history, such as the sinking of the *Titanic* and the attack on Pearl Harbor, allowing the producers to use sets, stock footage, and props from various 20th Century Fox period dramas. On rare occasions, the time travelers would visit the future and even encounter aliens from other planets.

BAYWATCH

DRAMA • 1989
RATED: TV-PG • 45 MINS

Sun, sea, sand, and slow-motion running. A team of good-looking lifeguards patrol an LA beach, saving lives and catching criminals while also dealing with their relationship problems.

Watching *Baywatch,* it's easy to believe that a California beach must be one of the most dangerous places in the world. Throughout the show's 11 seasons, Mitch Buchannon (David Hasselhoff) and his loyal team of lifeguards—including C. J. Parker (Pamela Anderson) and Stephanie Holden (Alexandra Paul)—face all manner of threats, from earthquakes and bombs to serial killers and shark attacks.

Fondly remembered (and often parodied) for its scenes of impossibly attractive cast members running along the beach in slow motion, *Baywatch* is notable for its remarkably high levels of suspense, especially when it comes to saving people from drowning. The show moved to Hawaii for its last two seasons and also spawned spin-off *Baywatch Nights*.

GILLIGAN'S ISLAND

COMEDY • 1964
RATED: TV-G • 25 MINS

"Join us here each week, my friend, you're sure to get a smile, from seven stranded castaways, here on Gilligan's Isle." A shipwreck begets slapstick in this popular US comedy.

Following the sinking of the *SS Minnow,* seven castaways—including a millionaire (Jim Backus), a movie star (Tina Louise), and a professor (Russell Johnson)—are stranded on a desert island. Their attempts to seek rescue are frequently fouled up by bumbling first mate Gilligan (Bob Denver), much to the annoyance of The Skipper (Alan Hale Jr.).

Suspension of disbelief is part of the fun on *Gilligan's Island,* as the isle often receives guest-star visitors who are somehow unable to help the castaways escape. Over three seasons, the show delivers a steady stream of gentle character humor, with Gilligan and The Skipper's slapstick routines directly lifted from Laurel & Hardy, right down to Hale's fourth-wall-breaking looks to camera.

HAWAII FIVE-0

ACTION DRAMA • 1968
RATED: TV-PG • 45 MINS

Detective Captain Steve McGarrett leads TV's most exotically located police procedural as he busts bad guys in Hawaii. Cue that theme tune!

Immaculately coiffed DC McGarrett (Jack Lord) leads a fictional police force in Hawaii, rooting out secret agents, petty crooks, and organized crime syndicates, as well as clashing with criminal mastermind Wo Fat (Khigh Dhiegh). McGarrett's second-in-command is DS Danny Williams (James MacArthur), who's often on the receiving end of his catchphrase: "Book 'em, Danno."

Blessed with one of the all-time great TV theme tunes, *Hawaii Five-0* stands out for its distinctive scenery and Lord's charismatic performance. The supporting players include a real-life cop in the form of 16-year Honolulu police veteran Kam Fong Chun, who was cast as Detective Chin Ho Kelly after auditioning to play Wo Fat. The original 12-season series ended in 1980, but a remake followed in 2010.

ZOO

THRILLER • 2015 • RATED: TV-14 • 42 MINS • SEASONS: 3
JAMES WOLK, KRISTEN CONNOLLY, NONSO ANOZIE

What if the animals decided to fight back? That's the premise of this gloriously trashy thriller that sees genetically mutated creatures orchestrating coordinated attacks on humans. Our only hope against the four-legged apocalypse is a crack team of experts.

Based on a novel by James Patterson and Michael Ledwidge, *Zoo* centers on animal expert Jackson Oz (James Wolk) and his best friend, safari guide Abraham Kenyatta (Nonso Anozie), as they investigate an outbreak of homicidal animal behavior. They're joined by journalist Jamie Campbell (Kristen Connolly), French intelligence agent Chloe Tousignant (Nora Arnezeder), and animal pathologist Mitch Morgan (Billy Burke).

The team quickly discover that a genetic mutation involving a "defiant pupil" is a common factor in the attacking animals, which also display suspiciously intelligent behavior

patterns. That simple premise allows the show to serve up delightfully absurd scenarios on an episode-by-episode basis, beginning with the pilot, in which a group of shifty-looking cats appear to be holding secret meetings in trees and hatching murder plots.

> *"They were raised in cages. In a way, they're kind of the victims here."*
>
> Mitch (SI EI)

That's just the start of the animal uprising. Soon, dogs are forming covert hit squads, wolves are organizing a prison break (to free an inmate with a defiant pupil, naturally), and technology-hating bats are ingeniously destroying cell phones and taking out a pair of Arctic scientists by blocking their solar panels until they freeze to death.

The subsequent seasons introduce new characters (notably Alyssa Diaz as Dariela Marzan, a ranger who joins the team) and new animal threats in the form of hybrids, such as a telepathic gorilla and an invisible snake. Things get a lot more complicated, with a shocking 10-year time jump, a host of family secrets, and an increasingly apocalyptic plot involving a cure for the mutant gene. However, it's the gruesome action sequences that stay with you, not least the images of an elevator filled with rats or Chloe taking a flamethrower to a basement full of squeaking baby rodents.

CREATORS: Josh Appelbaum, André Nemec, Jeff Pinkner, Scott Rosenberg
PRODUCTION CO: James Patterson Entertainment, Tree Line Film, Midnight Radio, CBS Television Studios

SPARTACUS

HISTORICAL ACTION • 2010 • RATED: TV-MA • 55 MINS • SEASONS: 4
ANDY WHITFIELD, LIAM MCINTYRE, LUCY LAWLESS

Who knew history could be so much fun? This extremely violent tale of the Thracian gladiator who led a slave rebellion against the Romans is drenched in blood, saturated with sex, and laced with licentious language. Try watching without blushing.

Season 1 (*Spartacus: Blood and Sand*) follows Spartacus (Andy Whitfield) up to the rebellion, as he is betrayed by the Romans and cast into slavery. Forced to fight as a gladiator by his new owner Batiatus (John Hannah), he rises through the ranks, making an enemy of arena champion Crixus (Manu Bennett) in the process. Meanwhile, Batiatus and his wife, Lucretia, (Lucy Lawless) scheme to improve their standing in Roman society.

After the success of Season 1, *Spartacus* was hit by tragedy when Whitfield was diagnosed with lymphoma. The six-episode second season, *Gods of the Arena*, was in fact a prequel series, shot while producers waited for Whitfield to complete his treatment. Sadly, Whitfield died before production on the official Season 2 began, but not before giving his blessing to producers to recast the lead role. Subsequently, actor Liam McIntyre played the title character for two further seasons, *Spartacus: Vengeance* and *Spartacus: War of the Damned*.

Every episode of *Spartacus* is characterized by extreme, gory violence, explicit sex, and some hilariously creative swearing, usually involving the body parts of the gods. The show's particular stroke of genius is to have ordinary conversation scenes take place during outrageous sexual encounters, as if such

behavior were commonplace. Consequently, the show's commitment to nudity is unprecedented—even the extras in the crowd scenes are frequently naked.

It's true to say that *Spartacus* takes a fair few liberties with historical detail, but its depiction of the debauchery of Roman society, its cast of compelling characters, and its powerfully dramatic storytelling make for riveting television. You'll never look at the Kirk Douglas film *Spartacus* in quite the same way again, that's for sure.

> *"Prove yourselves more than a common slave— more than a man!"*
>
> **Batiatus** (S1 E2)

CREATOR: Steven S. DeKnight
PRODUCTION CO: Tapert / Donen / Raimi, Starz!

421

BLACK LIGHTNING

FANTASY DRAMA • 2018
RATED: TV-14 • 43 MINS

High-school principal by day, electricity-channeling Super Hero by night. That's the life of family man Jefferson Pierce, aka costumed crime fighter Black Lightning, who sets sparks flying as he defends his city.

Based on the DC Comics character, *Black Lightning* stars Cress Williams as African American high-school principal Jefferson Pierce, who previously retired as Black Lightning because of the strain it put on his family. However, when the rise of a local gang threatens his home city, Jefferson decides it's time to suit up and shoot sparks again.

Alongside improbable, pulpy comic-book plots (the main antagonist is Tobias Whale, a murderous, super-powered albino), *Black Lightning* tackles real-life issues such as racial injustice, police brutality, and gang violence. Over the course of three seasons, Jefferson's daughters discover their own super-powers and become heroes Thunder and Lightning.

THE PUNISHER

ACTION DRAMA • 2017
RATED: TV-MA • 53 MINS

How do you humanize a comic-book character best known for being a gun-toting vigilante? Casting Jon Bernthal is a great start.

Having enacted revenge on the men who killed his family, former soldier Frank Castle, aka The Punisher (Bernthal), is drawn back into violence when expert hacker Micro (Ebon Moss-Bacharach) seeks his help in exposing a military cover-up. In the second and final season, Frank comes to the aid of a teenage runaway when she's targeted by dog collar–wearing killer, John Pilgrim.

Though characterized by its thrillingly violent action sequences, *The Punisher* stops short of painting Frank as just a thuggish vigilante and instead uses the character to explore the effects of violence, PTSD, and the government's duty of care to returning veterans. It's led by a compelling, complex performance from Bernthal, who's both tender and terrifying.

THE UMBRELLA ACADEMY

FANTASY DRAMA • 2019
RATED: TV-14 • 54 MINS

Dysfunctional Super Heroes, time travel, and a talking chimpanzee. Those are just a few elements of *The Umbrella Academy,* in which a disbanded family of super-powered orphans reunite to save the world.

The Umbrella Academy centers on seven children with supernatural abilities, adopted by eccentric billionaire Sir Reginald Hargreeves and turned into a crime-fighting team. Decades later, the Super Heroes have drifted apart but are brought back together when time-traveling Number Five (Aidan Gallagher) returns from the future, warning of an apocalypse.

With great performances (most notably Robert Sheehan as telekinetic drug addict Klaus and Ellen Page as violin-playing Vanya), this stylish, blackly comic one-season show stands out with its offbeat characters, inventive action sequences, and striking set design. The effects are great, too, not least talking chimp Pogo, Sir Reginald's faithful assistant.

STAN LEE'S LUCKY MAN

CRIME FANTASY • 2016
RATED: TV-14 • 45 MINS

What happens when a gambling-addicted cop gains the power to control his luck? Murder Squad detective Harry Clayton finds his mysterious lucky bracelet is both a blessing and a curse.

Conceived by Marvel Comics's Stan Lee, *Lucky Man* stars James Nesbitt as Harry Clayton, a Murder Squad detective who gains the power to control luck after a mysterious woman

(Sienna Guillory) snaps an ancient bracelet on his wrist. However, Harry soon discovers that his new power comes with a price, as the bracelet ensures that every positive event is balanced with a negative.

Cleverly grafting comic-book fantasy elements on to a gritty British cop show, *Stan Lee's Lucky Man* delivers plenty of thrills, thanks to gripping crime plots, exciting action sequences, and Nesbitt's strong performance. Seasons 2 and 3 (the last) expand the mythology of the bracelet, with the discovery that there are other bracelet holders.

SMALLVILLE

FANTASY DRAMA • 2001
RATED: TV-PG • 42 MINS

Ever wondered what Clark Kent's teenage years were like before he became the Man of Steel? Look no further than *Smallville* and its smart blend of small-town teen drama and Super Hero mythology.

Effectively a 10-season origin story for Superman, *Smallville* centers on teenager Clark Kent (a perfectly cast Tom Welling) coming to

terms with his alien origins and super-powers, as well as navigating his relationships with best friend Chloe Sullivan (Allison Mack), love interest Lana Lang (Kristin Kreuk), and a young Lex Luthor (Michael Rosenbaum). Later seasons relocate Clark to Metropolis and introduce Lois Lane (Erica Durance).

Throughout its run, *Smallville* sticks rigorously to its "no flights, no tights" rule, which dictates that Clark never flies or is seen in costume. But the show also packs in loads of Superman mythology, with multiple plots and characters drawn from the comics.

THE SIX MILLION DOLLAR MAN

ACTION ADVENTURE • 1974
RATED: TV-PG • 50 MINS

"We can rebuild him. We have the technology." Badly injured in a plane crash, an astronaut is given bionic implants for a mere six million dollars.

The Six Million Dollar Man stars Lee Majors as Steve Austin, an injured astronaut who has his right arm, left eye, and both legs replaced with

bionic implants, giving him superhuman strength, speed, and vision. Using his enhanced abilities, Steve works for the Office of Scientific Intelligence and fights crime as a secret agent.

Based on the novel *Cyborg* by Martin Caidin, the show had a significant impact on 1970s pop culture thanks to its slow-motion action sequences and innovative sound effects. It ran for five seasons, including three preseries TV movies that were split into two-part episodes. It also spawned *The Bionic Woman*, a popular spin-off starring Lindsay Wagner.

KNIGHT RIDER

ACTION ADVENTURE • 1982
RATED: TV-PG • 46 MINS

**"One man *can* make a difference."
Providing he has a talking car, that is.
Crime fighter Michael Knight takes on
the forces of evil with the help of his
artificially intelligent automobile.**

David Hasselhoff plays Michael Long, a
law-enforcement officer who's taken in by the
billionaire head of a crime-fighting organization
and given plastic surgery after a near-fatal

shooting. Reborn as Michael Knight, he battles
bad guys alongside KITT (the Knight Industries
Two Thousand), an artificially intelligent
supercar capable of incredible speed.

With its winning combination of fast cars and
exciting stunts, *Knight Rider* lasted four seasons
and spawned several spin-offs. The highlight
was KITT (calmly voiced by William Daniels),
whose crowd-pleasing turbo-boost function
was reliably deployed at least once an episode.
And who can forget KITT's revenge-driven evil
nemesis KARR, the Knight Automated Roving
Robot? A thrilling ride!

THE A-TEAM

ACTION ADVENTURE • 1983
RATED: TV-PG • 48 MINS

**"If you have a problem, if no one else
can help, and if you can find them,
maybe you can hire ... The A-Team."
A team of fugitives-turned-heroes
lead this 1980s action comedy.**

Heralded by their famous theme tune, the
titular A-Team consists of "Hannibal" Smith
(George Peppard), B. A. Baracus (Mr. T),
Templeton "Faceman" Peck (Dirk Benedict),

and "Howling Mad" Murdock (Dwight Schultz).
They are an ex-commando unit who escape
military prison after being jailed for a heist
they'd been ordered to do. Pursued by the
government, they exist as heroes for hire.

The A-Team ran for five seasons, using a
successful formula. Packed with running jokes
and catchphrases ("I love it when a plan comes
together"), every episode invariably involves
the team building weaponry from discarded
junk. Producers were always careful to show
that no one got hurt, despite the prevalence
of gunfire and explosions.

AUTOMAN

ACTION ADVENTURE • 1983
RATED: NR • 50 MINS

**What would happen if a cop's artificially
intelligent computer program came to
life as a hologram? Meet Automan, a
computer-generated superhero who
fights crime alongside detective-slash-
programmer Walter Nebicher.**

Automan (short for Automatic Man) stars
Chuck Wagner as the titular hero—who poses
as government agent Otto Mann—and Desi

Arnaz, Jr. as his creator. They're aided by
Walter's associate Roxanne (Heather McNair)
and by Automan's cheeky sidekick Cursor, a
floating polyhedron that can create handy
physical objects like the Autocar, the
Autochopper, and the Autoplane.

Automan is distinguished by its impressive
production values and imaginative design
work, as well as a fabulous theme tune.
The show's highlight is the Autocar, which
is able to perform instant 90-degree turns,
thereby slamming Walter into the window at
least once an episode for comedy purposes.

MANIMAL

ACTION FANTASY • 1983
RATED: TV-PG • 60 MINS

What would you do if you could turn into an animal? Would you use that ability to fight crime? Of course you would! Welcome to the wonderful world of *Manimal*.

Simon MacCorkindale plays Dr. Jonathan Chase, who can transform into any animal he chooses. Together with his best friend Ty (Michael D. Roberts), Chase uses his unique ability to help Police Detective Brooke Mackenzie (Melody Anderson) fight crime, transforming into an animal when necessary.

It may have been canceled after just eight episodes, but *Manimal* is fondly remembered by those who watched it at the time as one of the weirdest TV shows of the 1980s. A limited budget meant that the show had transformation sequences only for a panther and a hawk, so Chase transformed into both in nearly every episode, though he would occasionally change into a third animal (horse, dolphin, bear, etc.) off-screen.

MISSION: IMPOSSIBLE

ACTION ADVENTURE • 1966
RATED: TV-PG • 50 MINS

"Your mission, should you choose to accept it...." Latex masks and gadgets at the ready as the Impossible Missions Force (IMF) embark on a series of dangerous assignments on foreign soil.

Led by Dan Briggs (Steven Hill) in Season 1, then Jim Phelps (Peter Graves) in the next six seasons, the members of the IMF undertake their "impossible" missions knowing they'll be disavowed by the US government if they get caught. Key operatives include master of disguise Rollin (Martin Landau), fashion model Cinnamon (Barbara Bain), tech genius Barney (Greg Morris), and muscle man Willy (Peter Lupus).

Each episode begins with a mission recorded on a self-destructing tape. The team are frequently asked to topple dictators, which they do with elaborate deceptions instead of resorting to gunfire. Lalo Schifrin's famous theme tune provides the perfect soundtrack for their stylish and sophisticated spy capers.

THE FALL GUY

ACTION ADVENTURE • 1981
RATED: 12 (UK) • 48 MINS

He might fall from a tall building, he might roll a brand-new car, 'cause he's the unknown stuntman.... There's action aplenty with stunt performer–turned–bounty hunter, Colt Seavers.

Developed by TV producer Glen A. Larson, *The Fall Guy* stars Lee Majors as Hollywood stuntman Colt Seavers, who moonlights as a bounty hunter between movie gigs. He's frequently assisted by his trainee stunt-performer cousin Howie "Kid" Munson (Douglas Barr) and stuntwoman Jody Banks (Heather Thomas).

Given the setup, it's no surprise that the key feature of *The Fall Guy* is its regular dose of death-defying stunts, many of which feature Colt's trusty pickup truck with an eagle painted on its hood. The Hollywood setting also allows for multiple guest appearances from movie and TV stars during its five-season run, including Richard Burton, Tony Curtis, and Britt Ekland.

YOU WANT TO BE SCARED WITLESS

Written by Mark Morris

We all love being scared, don't we? At least, we do when in reality we know we're safe and cozy and warm. Here's a guide to shows that get your adrenaline surging and the hairs standing up on the back of your neck—and all while hiding behind a cushion on your sofa or snuggled up under your duvet.

BUFFY THE VAMPIRE SLAYER

FANTASY • 1997 • RATED: TV-14 • 44 MINS • SEASONS: 7
SARAH MICHELLE GELLAR, ALYSON HANNIGAN

"In every generation, there is a chosen one ... she alone will stand against the vampires, the demons, and the forces of darkness. She is the Slayer." But when the "chosen one" is a teenage girl who just wants to live a normal life, there's going to be trouble....

Having burned down her previous school's gymnasium, Buffy Summers (Sarah Michelle Gellar) arrives in Sunnydale with her mom, Joyce (Kristine Sutherland), hoping for a fresh start. She soon makes friends with perky academic Willow (Alyson Hannigan) and wisecracking Xander (Nicholas Brendon). She is reminded of her responsibilities by her "Watcher," the oh-so-English Rupert Giles (Anthony Head), who oversees her slaying activities and informs her that her new school is built on a Hellmouth— a gateway to demonic realms, from which all manner of evil entities pour forth.

Over seven seasons, Buffy battles a plethora of hellish monstrosities, while also trying to come to terms with the kinds of issues that beset teenagers worldwide, from identity and acceptance to dependence, sexuality, inclusion, and alienation. She is aided and abetted, and sometimes thwarted and betrayed, by a variety of humans and nonhumans. Among them are friends and acquaintances, foes who become friends, friends who becomes foes, and foes who become friends who later become ... well, let's just say that in *Buffy* relationships— as in real life—are slippery, ever-changing, and full of surprises.

Notable characters who weave in and out of the narrative during the show's 144 episodes include Angel, a vampire cursed with a soul, who becomes Buffy's early love interest, and Spike, the vampire world's answer to punk musician Sid Vicious. Then there's Oz the werewolf, Anya the vengeance demon, and Cordelia the cheerleader—whose story arc is one of the most satisfying in the show—not to mention Buffy's mysterious younger sister, Dawn, who appears in Season 5.

Never afraid to push the narrative format, some of *Buffy*'s most outstanding episodes are among its most unconventional. "Hush"(1999) is an almost silent episode; "Once More, With Feeling" (2001) is a musical comedy; and "The Body" (2001) is an unflinching, at times almost unbearable, examination of grief.

CREATOR: Joss Whedon
PRODUCTION CO: Mutant Enemy, Kuzui Enterprises, Sandollar Television, 20th Century Fox Television

ANGEL

FANTASY • 1999
RATED: TV-14 • 44 MINS

What does a vampire with a soul do when he is forced to face the fact that he can never have a relationship with the woman he loves? He moves to LA and opens a detective agency, of course!

An offshoot of *Buffy the Vampire Slayer*, *Angel* is darker and follows the fortunes of its titular antihero as he continues his quest for redemption. Aided by half-human, half-demon Doyle (Glenn Quinn), who receives visions from the mysterious Powers That Be, Angel (David Boreanaz) sets up Angel Investigations with the intention of "helping the helpless."

Over the course of five seasons, Angel and an expanding roster of associates, including streetwise demon hunter Charles Gunn, pacifist demon Lorne, and *Buffy* regulars Cordelia Chase and Wesley Wyndam-Pryce, battle the forces of evil—most notably in the guise of law firm Wolfram and Hart, a multinational corporation underpinned by demonic forces.

CARNIVÀLE

PERIOD FANTASY • 2003
RATED: TV-MA • 55 MINS

In the US dust bowl during the 1930s Great Depression, a traveling carnival becomes the focus for the ultimate tussle between Good and Evil. But in this era of terrible deprivation, who can tell the difference between the two?

When his mother dies, young farmer Ben Hawkins (Nick Stahl) joins a traveling carnival as a roustabout. Ben, though, is no ordinary man. He can heal the most grievously afflicted simply by touch and suffers vivid nightmares about trench warfare and a tattooed man in a field. His dreams are shared by Methodist preacher Brother Justin Crowe (Clancy Brown), who has the power to influence the minds of others.

Richly detailed, esoteric, and compelling, the two-season series is steeped in mythology and Christian prophecy. *Carnivàle*'s parallel stories twist and turn and reveal ever more shattering secrets, until the two antagonists are drawn toward their apocalyptic confrontation.

IT

HORROR • 1990
RATED: TV-PG • 95 MINS

Derry, Maine, is a cursed town. Every 30 years, children die. But the adults seem unaware of the ravening evil inhabiting the sewer system. The children must face the monster alone.

Based on Stephen King's novel, *IT* is both a love letter to the horror genre and a piercing examination of friendship, loyalty, fear, grief, and love. Sprawling across two time periods—1960 and 1990—in one very scary season, it is also a story about the trials and tribulations of adolescence and the difficult journey to adulthood.

The shape-shifting entity that is blighting the lives of the disparate band of friends, who call themselves "The Losers' Club," is embodied in the shape of Pennywise the Clown, played with psychotic relish by Tim Curry. Perhaps the most terrifying aspect of *IT* is that, having survived terrible childhood traumas, the Losers must return to Derry as adults and face their worst fears all over again.

HUMANS

SCI-FI • 2015
RATED: TV-14 • 42 MINS

At what stage of evolution do robots become like us? In a world where synthetic humans are commonplace, the lines quickly become blurred.

Set in a parallel world where anthropomorphic robots called "synths" have been created to perform menial tasks, *Humans* is a thought-provoking, sometimes touching, sometimes harrowing, examination of what it means to be human. Central to the drama are the Hawkins family and their synth Anita (Gemma Chan), who, the family soon realizes, is capable of emotional responses and independent thought.

When a consciousness program is released that affects all synths, society changes overnight. We see the best and the worst of humanity—understanding and acceptance on one side, intolerance and fear on the other. This three-season series follows a range of characters, both human and synth, as they make their way through this brave new world.

HANNIBAL

HORROR THRILLER • 2013
RATED: TV-14 • 44 MINS

FBI profiler Will Graham is able to empathize with serial killers to help solve the crimes they've committed. But when using his gift takes its toll, he visits psychiatrist Hannibal Lecter.

The *Hannibal* scripts are erudite, thought-provoking, and enigmatic, and the three-season series has psychological heft, too. Season 1's killer-of-the-week format evolves into a more complex narrative, with Dr. Lecter (Mads Mikkelsen) fascinated by the ability of Graham (Hugh Dancy), toying with him like a cat does a mouse. As a prequel to the novels *Red Dragon* and *The Silence of the Lambs*, most viewers will know where *Hannibal* is heading, but that doesn't dilute its considerable effect.

The word that comes to mind when considering *Hannibal* is "elegance." Yes, it's about killers who commit shockingly gory murders, but it's meticulously constructed, painterly in its cinematography, and beautifully weighted in terms of direction and acting.

ALFRED HITCHCOCK PRESENTS

HORROR THRILLER • 1955
RATED: TV-14 • 25 MINS

The true stuff of horror is not the gory payoff but the suspense leading up to it. That was the belief of Alfred Hitchcock, and these 268 episodes prove him right.

Filmmaker Hitchcock introduces every story in this seven-season anthology show, and his blackly humorous monologues and deadpan delivery are worth the price of admission alone. The stories, focusing on the darkest aspects of human nature—cruelty, greed, lust, ruthless ambition—are of a high standard and enhanced by some top acting talent: Vincent Price, Robert Redford, Walter Matthau, Bette Davis, and many more.

Among the best episodes are "Man from the South," starring Steve McQueen and Peter Lorre, in which a man offers his little finger in a bet; and "The Glass Eye," about a ventriloquist (William Shatner) and his number-one fan (Jessica Tandy). Keep the lights on!

SALEM'S LOT

HORROR • 1979
RATED: 15 (UK) • 100 MINS

When he was a boy, Ben Mears saw a ghost in the Marsten House. Now a bestselling author, he returns to Salem's Lot to find something else has taken residence in the old mansion, something much worse than a ghost....

Based on Stephen King's hit novel, the single season of *Salem's Lot* is steeped in atmosphere. It follows Ben (David Soul), who returns to his childhood home to find it has fallen prey to vampires. The master vampire is the mysterious Kurt Barlow (Reggie Nalder), whose hideous appearance is based on Count Orlok in the film *Nosferatu*.

Imbued with an almost palpable sense of insidious menace, *Salem's Lot* contains many memorable set pieces. One, where vampirized character Ralphie Glick (Ronnie Scribner) floats outside his brother's bedroom window, scratching at the glass, appeared in *Empire* magazine's "Top 10 Scariest Movie Scenes" in 2018. And with good reason—it's terrifying.

BLACK SPOT

HORROR • 2017
RATED: 15 (UK) • 52 MINS

The forest surrounding Villefranche is a very strange place. A wolf is found protecting a newborn baby. Mysterious vehicles roam the forest at night. And people die there. Lots of people.

Captain Laurène Weiss (Suliane Brahim) is head of the Gendarmerie in the isolated French mountain town of Villefranche, which has no phone reception and is surrounded by 50,000 acres of dense forest. Prosecutor Franck Siriani (Laurent Capelluto) turns up, concerned by the fact that Villefranche's murder rate is six times the national average. It soon becomes apparent, though, that there is far more going on here than meets the eye.

Well-crafted, captivating, and with stunning cinematography, this two-season French-Belgian series is a real find. It is graced with excellent character development, a dark thread of humor, and an unsettling folk-horror vibe. A gripping show that, like the forest itself, draws you into its embrace and refuses to let go.

FORTITUDE

THRILLER • 2015
RATED: TV-MA • 60 MINS

The town of Fortitude in Svalbard, Norway, is a peaceful place. Crime is almost nonexistent. But then a ghastly murder tears it apart. There are dark secrets churning beneath the ice.

Halfway through Season 1 of this compelling Arctic-set thriller, events take an unexpected turn. What begins as a standard murder mystery suddenly delves into primeval, possibly even mystical territory. *Fortitude* intrigues and tantalizes for several episodes, then hits you like a bus. And those of a sensitive disposition be warned: there's intensely graphic violence here of a level rarely seen on TV.

A stellar script is enhanced by an equally stellar cast, including Stanley Tucci, Dennis Quaid, and Michael Gambon. A diverse range of subplots throughout this three-season series all eventually link back into the complex but never confusing narrative. Moody, gory, and claustrophobic, this is top-drawer stuff.

KOLCHAK: THE NIGHT STALKER

CRIME HORROR • 1974 • RATED: TV-PG • 51 MINS • SEASONS: 1
DARREN MCGAVIN, SIMON OAKLAND, JACK GRINNAGE

For down-at-the-heels reporter Carl Kolchak, Chicago is not just the Windy City but a haunted one. The crimes he investigates are committed by criminals not of this world. But can he ever persuade anyone to believe him?

Kolchak: The Night Stalker originated from a pair of successful TV movies, *The Night Stalker* (1972) and *The Night Strangler* (1973).The TV series follows a "monster-of-the-week" format, with Kolchak (Darren McGavin) usually drawn to the investigation by reports of bizarre or gruesome deaths.

Although featuring many horror and sci-fi staples—vampires, werewolves, zombies, aliens, etc.—the show also ventures into more unusual territory. Several episodes focus on Native American spirits; others deal with spontaneous human combustion, a moss monster, a prehistoric apeman, and a headless motorcyclist. The TV series lasted for only one season (largely due to Darren McGavin's dissatisfaction with the show's inflexible format and punishing filming schedule) but is hugely popular to this day and is cited by writer Chris Carter as the main influence for his *The X-Files* (see p442).

The two TV movies were produced by Dan Curtis and written by renowned novelist Richard Matheson, while the list of celebrated TV and movie creatives who contributed to *Kolchak*'s legacy is also impressive. Hammer Horror films veteran Jimmy Sangster wrote the script for what was arguably the show's best episode, "Horror in the Heights," and David Chase, creator of *The Sopranos* (see p341), cut his teeth as a story editor on the series.

LORE

HORROR DOCUMENTARY • 2017
RATED:TV-14 • 40 MINS

Werewolves, witches, vampires, ghosts, ancient curses ... where does the stuff of horror movies really come from? *Lore* delves into history and folklore in an attempt to find out.

Lore started as a podcast created by Aaron Mahnke, and each episode of the two-season series follows the same format, with a different "lore" explored each week. The subject matter ranges from ventriloquism to icepick lobotomies and often focuses on specific historical cases. For example, the werewolf episode, "The Beast Within," looks at a series of killings in the village of Bedburg, Germany, in 1589, while the episode "Black Stockings" tells the story of Bridget Cleary, who was murdered by her husband in Ireland in 1895 because he believed she was a changeling.

Dramatic reconstructions of the events under discussion are juxtaposed with documentary and/or news footage, plus other media such as animation, to keep the stories vibrant.

AFTERLIFE

HORROR • 2005
RATED: TV-14 • 47 MINS

Robert Bridge and Alison Mundy are the archetypal odd couple. He's an academic and a staunch nonbeliever, and she's a psychic who communicates with the dead. When fate throws them together, their lives change forever.

Although *Afterlife's* 14 episodes are mostly stand-alone stories, a thread that runs throughout the two-season series concerns grieving university lecturer Robert (Andrew Lincoln) trying to come to terms with the death of his young son and the efforts of Alison (Lesley Sharp) to ease his pain using her psychic gifts. But Alison also has family traumas that have left her emotionally scarred, which all leads to one of the most heart-wrenching final episodes you are ever likely to see.

Five years before achieving fame as Rick Grimes in *The Walking Dead* (see p434), Lincoln's on-screen chemistry with Sharp gives *Afterlife* a real emotional punch.

THE HITCHHIKER

HORROR • 1983
RATED: TV-MA • 26 MINS

Insanity, greed, lust, obsession. The Hitchhiker wanders the psychological darklands of human nature, and he has hundreds of stories to tell.

Only a smattering of the 85 episodes in this six-season series has a supernatural element; the majority are embedded in the sleazy grime of humankind's basest instincts and most venal excesses. *The Hitchhiker* is an uneven show, with stories ranging from tedious to compelling, from facile to inspired. Keep digging, though, and you'll unearth plenty of gems.

Highlights include "The Killer," about a wheelchair-using woman (Jenny Seagrove) trying desperately to escape a shotgun-wielding assassin who has murdered her family; "W.G.O.D.," about a radio evangelist (Gary Busey) who receives a call from a boy informing him that Judgment Day is near; and "True Believer," about a detective (Tom Skerritt) investigating some bizarre suicides.

THE STONE TAPE

HORROR • 1972
RATED: PG (UK) • 90 MINS

A research team from Ryan Electrics takes up residence in Taskerlands, a Victorian mansion. But the oldest room in the house remains uncompleted as workmen believe it to be haunted.

The Stone Tape is one of the most intelligent, imaginative, and downright creepy BBC dramas ever made. Combining hard science and ancient superstition, the story explores the idea that hauntings are caused by the emotional energy from traumatic past events becoming absorbed by the fabric of buildings. Computer programmer Jill Greeley (Jane Asher) is particularly sensitive to the phenomenon, hearing footsteps and a gut-wrenching scream, and seeing a young maid run upstairs before falling to her death.

The tension builds in such a way throughout this TV film that *The Stone Tape* seems to transcend its production limitations and affect the viewer on a visceral, primal level. It is, quite simply, a masterpiece.

THE WALKING DEAD

HORROR • 2010 • RATED: TV-MA • 44 MINS • SEASONS: 10
ANDREW LINCOLN, NORMAN REEDUS, MELISSA MCBRIDE

Waking from a coma to find the hospital you're in abandoned and the deserted streets strewn with corpses is not the best way to start the day. Returning home to find your house empty and your family gone is even worse. Surely things can only get better? Can't they?

Not necessarily! The Season 1, Episode 1 pre-credits sequence of *The Walking Dead* starts several weeks after the bullet injury that put police officer Rick Grimes (Andrew Lincoln) into a coma. Now recovered and heading for home in eerie silence, Rick passes a cluster of wrecked vehicles and negotiates a makeshift campsite populated by flyblown corpses. Beyond is an abandoned gas station where he hopes to find fuel but instead finds a handwritten sign proclaiming "No Gas" and the series' first zombie: a small girl in bunny slippers holding a teddy bear. The girl—with the flesh around her mouth ripped away—

regards him for a moment then snarls and lopes toward him. Rick raises his gun and shoots her in the head. And with this shocking action, so our journey begins.

Although *The Walking Dead* chronicles a zombie apocalypse, the word "zombie" is never actually uttered on screen. Instead the dead are called "walkers," or "rotters," or "biters." The idea is that in the world of the show, the deceased returning to senseless, ravenous life is a hitherto unimagined phenomenon for which our characters must find their own solutions.

Season 1 focuses on Rick's quest to find his family and then the family making their way across a hostile landscape to the Center for Disease Control in Atlanta, where it is hoped answers may be found. En route they meet other survivors, and by the end of Season 1, a community of disparate (and desperate) personalities has formed.

TIMELINE OF TERROR

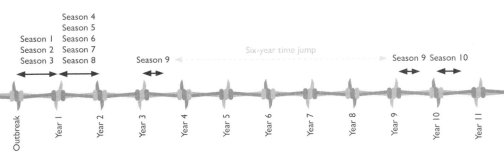

Season 4
Season 5
Season 1 Season 6
Season 2 Season 7
Season 3 Season 8
Season 9   Six-year time jump   Season 9 Season 10

Outbreak | Year 1 | Year 2 | Year 3 | Year 4 | Year 5 | Year 6 | Year 7 | Year 8 | Year 9 | Year 10 | Year 11

Answers are never easily found in *The Walking Dead*, though. In some ways, it is a downbeat show, and at times it has been described as nihilistic. But what continues to drive the narrative forward is the determination and desire of the survivors to keep going against all the odds, and not only to survive but to thrive and prosper, to try to find some peace and equilibrium in a perilous world.

> **"Are we sure they're dead? I have to ask at least one more time."**
>
> Rick Grimes (SI EI)

The fact that equilibrium is fleeting and often temporary is, of course, what creates the drama. Life is by no means a given in this new, lawless society that Rick and his group find themselves in, and no one is safe. Over the 10 years that the show has been on air, it has had a huge and constantly shifting ensemble cast of characters, who have suffered a shockingly high mortality rate, with long-standing, well-loved figures falling by the wayside often in violent, nonheroic ways.

It is not the "walkers" themselves who are the main threat, however. Although, like wild animals, the walkers are a constant

danger, the real, ongoing peril comes from bands of ruthless, murderous humans. Among many survivors, morality has been replaced by a dog-eat-dog mentality, and some of the human antagonists Rick and his group battle against are far more terrifying than the roaming dead.

In Seasons 3 and 4, the insane and sadistic Governor (David Morrissey), ruler of the fortified town of Woodbury, is the constant thorn in Rick's side. From Seasons 6 to 8, smiling sociopath Negan (Jeffrey Dean Morgan), leader of the Saviors, becomes his nemesis. From Season 9, a group known as the Whisperers, who wear the flesh of the dead and are led by the brutal Alpha (Samantha Morton), emerge to threaten what have now become the settled communities of Alexandria, Hilltop, and the Kingdom. Needless to say, for as long as *The Walking Dead* remains on our screens, our heroes will be fighting for their lives. But that's the law of the jungle for you.

CREATORS: Frank Darabont, Angela Kang PRODUCTION CO: AMC, Circle of Confusion, Valhalla Motion Pictures, Darkwoods Productions, AMC Studios, Idiot Box Productions

THE TWILIGHT ZONE (1959–1964)

SCI-FI • 1959 • RATED: TV-PG • 30 MINS • SEASONS: 5
ROBERT REDFORD, BURT REYNOLDS, MICKEY ROONEY

"You're traveling through another dimension, a dimension not only of sight and sound, but of mind; a journey into a wondrous land whose boundaries are that of imagination. That's the signpost up ahead—your next stop, The Twilight Zone."

So says creator Rod Serling in his voice-over, which plays across the show's opening credits. It's the perfect summing up of an anthology show that is widely regarded as the granddaddy of the many genre anthology shows that have appeared on our screens since the series was first broadcast.

Over five seasons, The Twilight Zone presents its viewers with stories that are, by turns, scary, whimsical, fantastical, and surreal. Although the tone and content of the tales varies widely, the general format is that a character, or set of characters, is faced with an uncanny or disturbing situation that concludes with a twist ending carrying a moral message.

Of The Twilight Zone's 156 episodes, Rod Serling himself wrote or cowrote 92, seeing the show as a way of tackling contentious issues such as racism or social injustice that might have been toned down in a straight drama. Of the 64 remaining episodes, 35 were written by either Richard Matheson or Charles Beaumont. Serling's personal favorites were "Time Enough at Last," in which henpecked book lover Henry Bemis (Burgess Meredith) finds himself happily alone after a nuclear war;

and "The Invaders," in which an old woman hears a commotion on her roof and discovers a miniature spaceship with small, robotic creatures emerging from it.

In 1997, TV Guide's 100 Greatest Episodes of All Time ranked the best-ever US TV show installments. It placed The Twilight Zone's "To Serve Man," in which a race of seemingly benevolent aliens offers humankind a solution to its escalating crises, at number 11 and "It's a Good Life," in which a six-year-old boy wields terrifying powers over the small American town in which he lives, at number 31.

CREATOR: Rod Serling
PRODUCTION CO: Cayuga Productions, CBS Television Network

THE TWILIGHT ZONE (1985–1989)

SCI-FI • 1985
RATED: TV-PG • 45 MINS

Ominous music, a midnight landscape, a window slamming. Within a spinning globe, images—a fetus, a tarantula, an owl mask—appear and fade....

You are now entering *The Twilight Zone* 1980s-style. In "Shatterday," a man (Bruce Willis) is hounded by his unscrupulous alter ego; in "A Little Peace and Quiet," an overstressed mom finds a necklace with the power to freeze time; and in "Nightcrawlers," the traumatic memories of a Vietnam vet come to vivid and terrifying life in a roadside diner.

Beset with numerous scheduling, format, and production problems, this three-season set of 65 episodes is uneven in style, quality, and length. But with a roster of unbelievable talent—from directors Wes Craven and William Friedkin, to writers Harlan Ellison and Stephen King, and actors Bruce Willis and Morgan Freeman—there are still many gems.

THE TWILIGHT ZONE (2019–)

SCI-FI • 2019
RATED: TV-MA • 60 MINS

A good idea is timeless and a great idea is worth repeating. Welcome to the modern-day iteration of *The Twilight Zone*.

If the ethos of *The Twilight Zone* is to comment on society through the allegory of fantastical conceits, this new version of the show checks all the boxes, but does it do this effectively? The infrastructure is in place; production values are superb. The stories, though, are a mixed bag, ranging from clever, thought-provoking, and creepy at best to unimaginative and preachy at worst.

Season 1 is topped and tailed by two excellent episodes. "The Comedian" is about jokes that prove lethal to their subjects. "Blurryman" sees a writer for *The Twilight Zone* haunted by a terrifying entity. Best of the bunch, though, is Episode 3, "Replay," about a camcorder that can turn back time.

THE LOST ROOM

SCI-FI • 2006
RATED: TV-PG • 90 MINS

At 1:20:44 p.m. on May 4, 1961, the event happened. At that moment, the room and its contents (or objects) were erased from history.

But now Detective Joe Miller (Peter Krause) has lost his daughter in the room, and the only way he can get her back is to find the prime object. The room in question is Room 10 of the now-derelict Sunshine Motel in New Mexico.

After the event occurs, no one remembers that the room existed. The hundred or so objects, although seemingly ordinary—a pen, a comb, a clock—are now powerful artifacts that are indestructible outside of the room. Various groups, or cabals, such as the Collectors and the Legion, want the objects.

If that all leaves you scratching your head, join the club. Watching this one-season series is like having the rule book of the most complicated board game ever read out to you. The labyrinthine plot will leave you either frustrated by its incoherence or wowed by its ambition.

GOOSEBUMPS

HORROR • 1995
RATED: TV-Y7 • 22 MINS

"Viewer beware: you're in for a scare."
Such was the warning at the beginning
of every episode of Goosebumps, the
anthology show that launched a
thousand preteen nightmares.

Based on the books by R. L. Stine, *Goosebumps*
is not subtle, but it is a lot of fun. It employs
every horror trope you can imagine. Over
its four seasons, the show features ghosts,
haunted houses, werewolves, zombies,
vampires, mummies, ventriloquist dolls, and
living scarecrows, plus all manner of cursed
objects, from a cuckoo clock and a piano
to a remote control and a board game.

Most of the episodes feature themes that tap
into children's fears. Moving is a big one;
visiting a distant—and usually sinister—relative
is another. The child protagonists are usually
trapped or isolated. Adults are disbelieving,
incompetent, or both. And all this is played out
over a background of creaking doors, shadowy
hallways, and howling storms. Wonderful.

SWAMP THING

HORROR • 2019
RATED: TV-MA • 60 MINS

Something sinister is stirring in the
Louisiana swamp. After a young girl
falls ill from a virus known as Green Flu,
disease control doctor Abby Arcane
becomes entwined in a mystery.

Cut from 13 episodes to 10, then canceled
before it had a chance to bloom, this DC
Comics adaptation is a case of what might
have been. Crystal Reed makes medic Abby
an empathic and convincing heroine, and other
characters are well fleshed out—even the main
villains, greedy businessman Avery Sunderland
(Will Patton) and obsessed scientist Jason
Woodrue (Kevin Durand), come across as
people first and bad guys second.

But what really makes this involving and scary
series stand out is its gorgeously murky visuals.
The images of vines bursting and coiling from
dead bodies are unsettling and brilliantly
rendered, while the Thing itself (Derek
Mears)—a man mountain of gooey weeds
and roots—is quite the sight to see.

DEAD SET

HORROR COMEDY • 2008
RATED: TV-MA • 25 MINS

Reality show meets zombie apocalypse
in this blackest of comedies. But should
its Big Brother contestants be grateful
they're safe from the undead or miffed
that no one's watching them on TV?

Dead Set's reconstruction of reality show *Big
Brother*—not only in terms of its sets and
production details but also in the way it nails
the banal concerns and petty self-interests of
some of its contestants—is so convincing that
the resulting zombie mayhem is genuinely
shocking. To see *Big Brother* host Davina
McCall as a ferocious, blood-drenched
member of the undead is both dismayingly
disorientating and an unadulterated joy.

Created and written by Charlie Brooker,
Dead Set can almost be seen as a precursor
to his anthology series *Black Mirror* (see p470).
With a biting satirical edge, doom-laden
atmosphere, and surreal juxtaposition of the
mundane and the fantastical, this one-season
serial is a fascinating watch.

AMERICAN HORROR STORY

HORROR • 2011 • RATED: TV-MA • 60 MINS • SEASONS: 9
SARAH PAULSON, KATHY BATES, JESSICA LANGE

A haunted house, an asylum, a freak show, a school for witches, and a summer camp stalked by a serial killer. This is horror, American-style: big, brash, and unrelenting. You want scares? You want gore? You got it!

Over nine seasons, *American Horror Story* not only gives viewers what they want: it bombards them with it. The show covers demonic possession, alien abduction, witchcraft, voodoo, cannibalism, and nuclear apocalypse. It features killer clowns, sideshow freaks, vampires, vengeful spirits, and the Antichrist.

Created by Ryan Murphy and Brad Falchuk, the concept is irresistible. Each of its seasons is a self-contained miniseries, featuring new characters and settings. What neatly links them all are the recurring cast members, with many actors—Jessica Lange, Evan Peters, Lily Rabe, Sarah Paulson, and others— regularly returning to the show to play different roles.

Of the seasons to date, all but three have featured contemporary stories. The exceptions are Season 2: "Asylum," set in 1964; Season 4: "Freakshow," set in 1952; and Season 9: "1984," set in—guess when? Although each season has its fans, some are considered better than others. Particular praise has been lavished on "Freakshow" and "1984" as well as "Coven" and "Apocalypse."

American Horror Story is not subtle and is not for the fainthearted. But if you like your horror frenetic, demented, and stomach-clenchingly gory, this is the show for you.

GHOUL

HORROR • 2018
RATED: TV-MA • 45 MINS

India, the near future. Society is in turmoil. Interrogation specialist trainee Nida Rahim is recruited by the government to interrogate a dangerous terrorist. But she discovers to her cost that he is far more than he seems....

An Indian production, written and directed by Brit Patrick Graham, this three-episode miniseries takes place in Meghdoot 31, a detention facility for dissidents. The location is almost a character in itself: the narrow, featureless corridors of the dark, grimy, blood-drenched hellhole add to the show's sense of dread as Rahim (Radhika Apte) grills sinister inmate Ali Saeed (Mahesh Balraj).

Although about as subtle as a baseball bat to the head, *Ghoul* is a fascinating watch for the way it differs from westernized horror. The ghoul (or ghul) of the title is a shape-shifting demonic entity from Arabic folklore, though its modus operandi—dispensing murder and mayhem for its own sake—is familiar enough.

GHOSTWATCH

HORROR • 1992
RATED: 12 (UK) • 91 MINS

"Welcome to 41 Foxhill Drive, dubbed 'the most haunted house in Britain.' Tonight BBC1 will be broadcasting live from number 41 to see if the stories are true...."

Transmitted on Halloween night 1992, the short film *Ghostwatch* is landmark TV. Filmed in such a convincing documentary style that many viewers didn't realize it was fiction, it features BBC presenters Sarah Greene, Craig Charles, Michael Parkinson, and Mike Smith as themselves, with Greene and Charles on location at the house and Parkinson and Smith coordinating a studio discussion and phone-in.

Events soon spiral out of control, leading to a shocking conclusion. The BBC received 30,000 calls from distressed viewers and questions were asked in Parliament. The adverse reaction led to the BBC imposing a 10-year ban on *Ghostwatch* being repeated or released on video. Despite this, *Ghostwatch* is regarded as hugely influential.

KINGDOM HOSPITAL

FANTASY • 2004
RATED: TV-14 • 40 MINS

Built on the site of a Civil War–era mill, Kingdom Hospital is haunted by the ghosts of the children who died when the mill burned down, including a girl who carries a warning of disaster.

Kingdom Hospital is an adaptation by horror writer Stephen King of Lars von Trier's *Riget*, a surreal, blackly humorous serial about a neurosurgical ward in Copenhagen's Rigshospitalet. In the one-season series, several earthquakes that shake the hospital coincide with the arrival of two new patients—a man left comatose after an accident (Jack Coleman) and an elderly female psychic (Diane Ladd).

While retaining the spirit of Von Trier's original, King's adaptation is an uneasy marriage of European oddness and glossy commercialism—though King himself called it "the thing I like best out of all the things I've done." Somewhat disjointed and lacking focus, *Kingdom Hospital* is sporadically effective and at least tries to do something different.

SCREAM

HORROR • 2015
RATED: TV-14 • 45 MINS

In the town of Lakewood, teenagers are being stalked by a masked serial killer. The murders are connected to Emma Duval and the town's murky past.

Emma (Willa Fitzgerald) must find out the truth before she, too, becomes a victim. If this sounds familiar, it's because the series is based on the *Scream* film franchise. The TV spin-off follows pretty much the same format, albeit set in a different location and with a new cast. The beauty of a TV series is that it can develop characters and interweave complex plot lines in a way a film cannot. Despite this, Season 1 received lackluster reviews, which spurred its creators to produce a more compelling and better-received Season 2.

Season 3, after a three-year gap, is a complete reboot, with cast and location shifting again. And for the first time, *Scream* has a male lead, Deion Elliot (R .J. Cyler), who lives with the trauma that his twin brother Marcus was a victim of the killer.

CRAZYHEAD

COMEDY HORROR • 2016
RATED: 15 (UK) • 60 MINS

Amy sees a demon. Then the demon attacks her. Then she meets Raquel the demon hunter. Then Amy's best friend gets possessed. This is turning into quite a night—and she only came out for a few drinks.

Crazyhead is a bright, fizzy show about a pair of adorable, socially awkward 20-somethings who become friends during an impending demonic apocalypse. Raquel (Susan Wokoma) already knows about demons, but Amy (Cara Theobold), who works in a bowling alley, picks it up as she goes along. Together, they fumble and stumble their way through a series of perilous and romantic situations.

The humor is bawdy and witty, the action fast moving, the story well paced, and the cast excellent. But it's the friendship between Amy and Raquel, plus the offbeat characters around them, which makes this show click. There's such warmth in this one-season series that you'd have to be a demon not to love it.

THE OUTSIDER

CRIME HORROR • 2020
RATED: TV-MA • 60 MINS

When the corpse of a young boy is found, the evidence points to Terry Maitland. But equally compelling evidence proves that Terry was miles away at the time.

Based on Stephen King's novel, *The Outsider* is an uneasy blend of police procedural and supernatural horror story. It begins when a mutilated body is found and local sports coach Maitland (Jason Bateman) is accused. The performances are excellent, particularly Ben Mendelsohn as Ralph Anderson, the detective leading the investigation, and Cynthia Erivo as autistic private eye Holly Gibney, who injects the downbeat proceedings with some much needed fizz and humor.

As a supernatural horror story, it isn't quite creepy enough, and as a murder mystery, it lacks complexity, but *The Outsider* is a well-made, thoughtful drama worth watching. It may have worked better as a movie than a 10-episode miniseries. See what you think.

FRIDAY THE 13TH: THE SERIES

HORROR • 1987
RATED: NR • 60 MINS

An antiques dealer makes a pact with the devil to sell cursed collectables. After he dies, his store's new owners must recover the demonic goods.

The new proprietors are Micki Foster (Louise Robey), her cousin Ryan Dallion (John D. LeMay), and their friend, occult expert Jack Marshak (Chris Wiggins). Each episode of this anthology show (which has no link to the *Friday the 13th* film series) sees the trio hunting for another antique to lock away in the vault. The objects are generally being used for revenge or personal gain.

Among the best episodes of the three-season series are "The Inheritance," about a creepy antique doll and a possessed child; "Scarecrow," about a killer scarecrow, whose leather mask is particularly unsettling; and "Faith Healer," about a glove that can transfer sickness from one person to another.

THE X-FILES

SCI-FI • 1993 • RATED: TV-MA • 45 MINS • SEASONS: 11
DAVID DUCHOVNY, GILLIAN ANDERSON, MITCH PILEGGI

FBI agent Fox "Spooky" Mulder's life philosophy is double-edged. He believes that "the truth is out there" and that he should "trust no one." But when skeptic Dana Scully is assigned to the X-Files, soon neither of them know what to believe.

The X-Files are unsolved and unwanted FBI cases, often involving the bizarre and the downright inexplicable. Fox Mulder (David Duchovny), a believer in all things paranormal, has made it his mission in life to pursue the cases that the rest of his colleagues consider problematical or just plain kooky. New recruit Dana Scully (Gillian Anderson), a medical doctor, is employed to keep loose cannon Mulder in check. Her brief is to scientifically evaluate each X-Files case, a tactic that Mulder's superiors hope will undermine and maybe even discredit him.

Over the course of the show's 11 seasons, however, Scully's initially rigid worldview is gradually eroded. She and Mulder become not just colleagues but best friends, the kind that will die for one another. Although they have allies—Assistant Director Walter Skinner

(Mitch Pileggi); conspiracy theorists Byers, Frohike, and Langly, known collectively as the Lone Gunmen; and fellow FBI agents John Doggett and Monica Reyes—it is the chemistry between the two leads that drives the central story line and keeps viewers hooked.

Around 70 percent of *The X-Files's* episodes are monster-of-the-week-style stories. Mulder and Scully roam the United States investigating everything from urban legends to mythological creatures; from ghosts and evil spirits to demonic entities; from humanoid mutations to ordinary people with destructive mental powers.

The rest of the episodes involve an extraterrestrial/government conspiracy story line that evolves and develops. Often confusing, though ultimately rewarding, it is a story that takes in the kidnapping by aliens of Mulder's sister as a child, alien super soldiers, a sentient virus known as the black oil, and a shadowy government faction, the Syndicate. The leader of the Syndicate is the series' main antagonist, the ruthless and sinister Cigarette Smoking Man, whose fate is inextricably linked to that of both Mulder and Scully.

CREATOR: Chris Carter
PRODUCTION CO: Ten Thirteen Productions, 20th Century Fox Television, X-F Productions

MILLENNIUM

HORROR CRIME • 1996
RATED: TV-MA • 45 MINS

With the world hurtling toward a new millennium, dark forces are gathering. Former FBI agent Frank Black, who can see through the eyes of killers, is employed by the mysterious Millennium group—but what is its real agenda?

Although *Millennium* is not a spin-off of *The X-Files* (see p442), the creator of both, Chris Carter, saw it as operating within the same milieu. Indeed, when *Millennium* was canceled after its third season, leaving many loose ends, writers Vince Gilligan and Frank Spotnitz wrote an *X-Files* episode titled "Millennium" that effectively provided Frank Black (Lance Henriksen) with a fitting finale.

Perhaps *Millennium* never clicked with viewers because it was so grim and humorless. Its Season 1 preoccupation with serial killers saw its ratings drop so alarmingly that in Season 2 it became more like *The X-Files*. *Millennium* was a classy show and had an excellent lead in Henriksen but never found its true identity.

IN THE FLESH

HORROR DRAMA • 2013
RATED: TV-14 • 56 MINS

What if a drug could convert flesh-eating zombies back into their human selves? How would the undead cope with their traumatic memories? And would the living trust and accept them?

Teenager Kieren Walker (Luke Newberry) suffers from PDS—Partially Deceased Syndrome. Several years before, he had died by suicide after his boyfriend Rick Macy (David Walmsley) was forced to join the army by his homophobic father and ended up dead in Afghanistan. Afterward, Kieren was reanimated during "The Rising," an event that saw the dead return as zombies. Now, rehabilitated, he's heading back to his home village of Roarton.

It's not an easy homecoming, though. Kieren's sister, Jem, is part of a group largely responsible for quelling The Rising. In this thought-provoking two-season series, Kieren must try to cope with his ongoing mental-health issues and integrate himself back into a community rife with intolerance and mistrust.

CHANNEL ZERO

HORROR • 2016
RATED: TV-MA • 44 MINS

A half-remembered kids' show with an insidiously creepy aura; a house that appears from nowhere full of personal fears; a mysterious staircase in the woods; a secret door in the basement....

The four story lines that comprise each of *Channel Zero*'s four stand-alone seasons are based on "creepypastas," flesh-crawling urban legends copied and pasted around the internet. Although distinct from one another, they all share common themes—traumatic childhood memories impacting on the present; suburban and social paranoia; the unsettling nature of abandoned places; and familial angst or trauma.

Together, the overall sense is of being trapped in a bizarre and disorienting dreamscape, in which monsters from the id run rampant. Some of the imagery in *Channel Zero* is truly disturbing. Although gore is kept to a minimum, watching the strangeness unfold is akin to the sensation of insects burrowing deep into your psyche.

THE RETURNED

HORROR MYSTERY • 2012 • RATED: TV-MA • 52 MINS • SEASONS: 2
ANNE CONSIGNY, CLOTILDE HESME, FRÉDÉRIC PIERROT

Why are the dead of a French mountain town returning to their homes, fully clothed and seemingly intact, with no memory of what has happened to them? Why are strange blemishes appearing on both their bodies and those of the living? And what is causing the power outages and the falling water level in the local reservoir?

A supernatural mystery with an escalating sense of dread, The Returned—known as Les Revenants in French—unflinchingly examines how people would feel if their deceased loved ones really started returning to them. Would they be overjoyed? Terrified? Accepting of the miracle or unsettled by it?

The situation is played out in various fascinating ways. Jérôme (Frédéric Pierrot) and Claire Séguret (Anne Consigny), whose grief has led to their separation, are shocked and then overjoyed when their 15-year-old daughter

Camille (Yara Pilartz) returns to them, having been killed in a bus crash four years earlier. Léna (Jenna Thiam), Camille's twin sister, however, is now 19 and finds it hard to reconcile the fact that time has apparently stood still for her sibling. Other "revenants" include fiancé Simon, who wants to rekindle his relationship with Adèle, even though he died by suicide on their wedding day a decade earlier, and serial killer Serge, who was killed by his brother Toni seven years before.

Why have the revenants returned, what does it mean, and what horrors have they brought back with them?

"I died 29 years ago."

Peter (S1 E9)

THREADS

SCI-FI DRAMA • 1984
RATED: 15 (UK) • 112 MINS

A nuclear bomb falls on Sheffield. The lucky ones die quickly. Those who don't try to survive in a poisoned, lawless world where nothing grows.

To say that TV film Threads made an impact when it was shown on British TV would be an understatement. In 1984, the US and the USSR were at loggerheads, and the possibility of nuclear war was seen as a realistic threat.

Instead of reassuring an anxious nation, Threads is one of the most horrifying films you'll ever see.

Filmed in a documentary style, with minimal dialogue, a voice-over spouting cold scientific facts, and with stock footage punctuating the "action," Threads depicts not only the immediate effect of a nuclear attack but its long-term aftermath. There is no hope here for pregnant Ruth (Karen Meagher) or any of the other characters—only misery, death, suffering, and deprivation. The stark message is that in a nuclear war, there can be no winners.

AMERICAN GOTHIC

HORROR • 1995
RATED: TV-PG • 60 MINS

Sheriff Lucas Buck rules Trinity, South Carolina, with a rod of iron. Bribery, corruption, and even murder are the tools of his trade. How can 10-year-old Caleb stay out of his evil clutches?

American Gothic is set in the seedy underbelly of a small US town where odd and mystical events occur. The action centers on the attempts of Buck (Gary Cole) to ensnare Caleb (Lucas Black), presumably in order to shape him in his own image, and the forces of good who work to save the boy, most notably reporter Gail Emory (Paige Turco) and Dr. Matt Crower (Jake Weber).

Cole is excellent as the menacing, manipulative Buck, and Black is outstanding as Caleb, battling with outer and inner demons. Although absorbing, *American Gothic* suffers from erratic pacing, an inconsistent tone, and narrative cul-de-sacs, elements that may have contributed to its cancellation after only one season.

HAUNTED

HORROR • 2018
RATED: TV-MA • 24 MINS

An abused boy is tormented by the spirit of a hanged woman; three dead children in a well try to coax another boy to join them; a US Marine is confronted by a demon in Afghanistan. Can these stories really be true?

Haunted is a very odd two-season show. Presented as factual accounts of paranormal experiences by the people involved, the stories these supposed traumatized survivors recount are so unbelievably clichéd that they come over as bad, low-budget horror movies.

Episode 2, "The Slaughterhouse" has come in for particular criticism. Two sisters tell of their horrific childhoods with their possibly demon-possessed serial killer of a father, whom they say slaughtered perhaps hundreds of strangers, then buried the bodies in the woods. But where is the evidence? Short answer: there doesn't seem to be any. So is *Haunted* meant to be a spoof? Your best bet is to treat it as such, and that way you'll have a hoot.

HARPER'S ISLAND

HORROR • 2009
RATED: TV-14 • 40 MINS

On Harper's Island, a series of gruesome murders take place. The killer is John Wakefield, who is killed by the local sheriff. Seven years later, the sheriff's daughter, Abby, returns to the island. And the murders begin again....

The slasher genre, popularized in the late '70s and early '80s by films such as *Halloween* and *Friday the 13th*, gets an Agatha Christie-style "whodunnit" element in this tense and gory single-season show. The premise is great: Abby Mills (Elaine Cassidy) returns to the titular island to attend the wedding of her friend Henry (Christopher Gorham), along with a bunch of other guests—but there is a murderer on the island.

Over the course of 13 labyrinthine episodes, more and more of the cast fall victim to the killer in various gruesome ways, and the list of suspects grows shorter. Many secrets are unearthed and many revelations come to light before the culprit is finally unmasked.

STRANGER THINGS

SCI-FI HORROR • 2016 • RATED: TV-14 • 51 MINS • SEASONS: 3
WINONA RYDER, DAVID HARBOUR, FINN WOLFHARD

Hawkins, Indiana, is a very strange town. What is really going on at the research center? Why has 12-year-old Will Byers vanished? Who is the mysterious shaven-headed girl known only as Eleven? And what is the Demogorgon?

Stranger Things has become a worldwide phenomenon. In July 2019, Netflix announced that Season 3's launch had broken viewing records for the streaming service, with more than 40 million households watching the show within its first four days. So what is it about Stranger Things that makes it so addictive?

First, the writing is superb. The scripts sparkle with wit and energy and are full of quirky, vulnerable, real characters, which makes the show feel fresh and instantly compelling. Second, the cast is uniformly excellent: old hands such as Winona Ryder and David Harbour deliver career-defining performances, while the young actors—particularly Millie Bobby Brown as Eleven and Gaten Matarazzo as Dustin, arguably the smartest and funniest of the gang—are full of charm and star quality.

Then there's the story. The elements may seem familiar—small American town, a sinister government facility, a terrifying otherworldly entity, a group of ordinary kids facing overwhelming odds—but it's told with such chutzpah, such verve, such joy, that it makes Stranger Things feel like a landmark show, and one that will be watched and rewatched for years to come.

In many ways, Stranger Things shouldn't work. Set in 1983, it is defiantly derivative, chaneling everything from Stephen King (particularly the novels Firestarter, It, and Needful Things—which inspired the show's title—and the movie Stand by Me) to Steven Spielberg films (E.T. and Close Encounters of the Third Kind); and the movies of John Carpenter and Wes Craven. On top of that, its main protagonists are mostly preteen kids in a series that's aimed at a plus-15 audience. But, as with any successful TV show, Stranger Things is a combination of elements all aligning in perfect harmony.

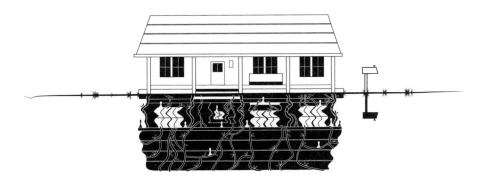

CREATORS: Matt Duffer, Ross Duffer
PRODUCTION CO: 21 Laps Entertainment, Monkey Massacre, Netflix

INSIDE NO. 9

COMEDY • 2014 • RATED: TV-MA • 30 MINS • SEASONS: 5
STEVE PEMBERTON, REECE SHEARSMITH, DENIS LAWSON

The beauty of venturing *Inside No. 9* is that you never know what you'll find. Will it be horror, laughter, heartache, redemption, love, revenge … or something altogether stranger? Only one thing is certain—all human life is here.

Inside No. 9 is a scintillating blend of stories of all kinds, many of which have a dark thread running through them. Most episodes pull the rug out from under your feet with a totally unexpected twist or startling revelation, and not a single one is predictable or boring.

The show's sheer invention is its greatest strength, and a variety of filming styles and approaches are employed to keep things fresh. "A Quiet Night In," in which a pair of burglars are horrified to discover a house they've targeted is not unoccupied, has virtually no dialogue and is one of the funniest and grimmest episodes. "Cold Comfort" is a story about a Samaritans-like call center told through CCTV footage. "Once Removed," about a house move that goes disastrously wrong, is a tale related backward. The genuinely frightening 2018 Halloween special, "Dead Line," is about a live broadcast beset by technical difficulties.

Inside No. 9 is inspired by an episode of Steve Pemberton and Reece Shearsmith's previous series *Psychoville*, which was filmed in a single room, and was itself inspired by the Alfred Hitchcock movie *Rope*. Having previously written series with convoluted plotlines, the duo wanted their new project to be an anthology show in which each story would take place in a single location with a minimal cast.

They further decided they wanted to subvert audience expectations by mixing and matching genres. They have done this superbly. You can enjoy trying to guess the endings, but it is unlikely you ever will.

ARES

HORROR DRAMA • 2020
RATED: 18 (UK) • 32 MINS

How did a small country like the Netherlands become so rich and powerful in the 17th century? The answer is Ares, a secret society for the elite, which not only still exists but is flourishing 400 years later.

Student Rosa Steenwijk (Jade Olieberg) is invited to join Ares—but here is one of the inconsistencies that pepper this sombre, often oblique eight-part, single-series drama—Rosa is not wealthy and privileged like the rest of Ares's members. So why is she invited to join?

This is never explained, and it's not the only element that remains obscure. Despite its short running time (the series is under four hours long, so it's easy to binge-watch), *Ares* is characterized by overlong scenes and opaque dialogue, which won't be everyone's cup of tea. Some viewers may find the obfuscation confusing, though there are plenty of others who will find that this approach makes for an eerie and atmospheric viewing experience.

FEAR THE WALKING DEAD

HORROR • 2015
RATED: TV-MA • 44 MINS

The dead are rising and attacking the living. As society crumbles, the Clark/Manawa family knows that the only way to survive is to flee LA. But where can they go that's safe?

A companion show to *The Walking Dead* (see p434), *Fear the Walking Dead* backtracks to the start of the apocalypse and chronicles events from a different location and a fresh set of perspectives. Even without the mayhem going on around them, though, the extended Clark/Manawa family has problems galore. Madison Clark (Kim Dickens) is the mom of a heroin addict, while the son of her fiancé, Travis Manawa (Cliff Curtis), has anger issues.

Somehow, though, the family members must pull together and overcome their differences if they want to live. Like its parent show, *Fear the Walking Dead* maintains its momentum over five seasons by keeping its ever-evolving cast constantly on the move in their search for a safe haven.

FRINGE

SCI-FI • 2008 • RATED: TV-14 • 46 MINS • SEASONS: 5
ANNA TORV, JOSHUA JACKSON, JOHN NOBLE

Very weird science, a totally mad scientist, an FBI agent, lashings of mystery, nasty body horror, other worldly enemies, and a sinister multinational conglomerate. Put them all together and what do you get? Something very strange indeed....

Often compared to *The X-Files* (see p442), *Fringe* follows the fortunes of FBI Agent Olivia Dunham (Anna Torv), who teams up with father and son scientists Walter (John Noble) and Peter Bishop (Joshua Jackson) to investigate a series of macabre and inexplicable occurrences involving fringe science and weird technology.

A bit of a slow burner, the show spends most of its first season exploring stand-alone stories (a flesh-eating protein is unleashed on a passenger plane; a man has the ability to affect electrical energy; a computer program liquefies its victim's brains), drip-feeding elements of the story arc into the individual episodes.

In later seasons, the development of this connecting narrative—about a parallel universe and a series of events known as "The Pattern"—takes precedence and propels things along. Season 3 episodes jump between the two universes; Season 4 begins in an alternate timeline; and Season 5 leaps 20 years into the future in order to provide answers to the many questions raised along the way.

Boasting a fine cast, excellent production values, and scripts that mystify and enthral in equal measure, *Fringe* is an intelligent, ever-evolving, thrilling show that doesn't talk down to its audience. Although complex, the story line remains consistent and is ultimately very rewarding.

TERRAHAWKS

SCI-FI • 1983
RATED: U (UK) • 23 MINS

In the futuristic year of 2020, Earth is under threat from the evil Zelda, a witchlike android, and her band of monstrous minions. All that stands between them and world domination are high-tech taskforce the Terrahawks!

Employing a knowing, sometimes broad humor—hyperbolic catchphrases are commonplace and Zelda's sister's constantly swiveling blond wig is a running joke—each episode of *Terrahawks*' three seasons documents a new attempt by Zelda to destroy our heroes and their continual thwarting of her dastardly schemes. It's formulaic but enormous fun.

Terrahawks is the final puppet show made by *Thunderbirds* (see p59) creator Gerry Anderson. While his previous efforts used "Supermarionation" (string-operated puppets with electronic components), *Terrahawks* employs "Supermacromation"—stringless latex hand puppets that allow smoother movement.

SLASHER

HORROR • 2016
RATED: 18 (UK) • 60 MINS

Three casts of characters, each of which has a dark secret. Three masked killers, each with an unknown motive. Who is the murderer, and who will be the victims? And will anyone survive?

Inspired by *American Horror Story* (see p439), each of *Slasher*'s three seasons is a stand-alone story. Also like *AHS*, some of its actors are recycled to play different roles in later seasons (Dean McDermott plays Chief Iain Vaughn in Season 1 and Dan Olenski in Season 3, with a brief appearance as Alan Haight in Season 2). Each run combines creator Aaron Martin's three passions: contemporary crime drama, the detailed whodunnit plots of Agatha Christie, and 1980s slasher movies.

The result is pretty outstanding, with strong stories, a fascinating set of characters played by an excellent cast, top-notch production values, plenty of twists, lashings of gore, and far more fingernail-chewing tension than is probably good for you.

THE MIST

HORROR • 2017
RATED: TV-14 • 42 MINS

An impenetrable mist descends upon the town of Bridgeville. Mist can't harm you, though, can it? Trouble is, it's what is in the mist that you have to watch out for. It's not just harmful—it's deadly.

Coming 10 years after Frank Darabont's movie, which was itself based on Stephen King's 1980 novella, this series is an extrapolation of its predecessors. Instead of the mist trapping the protagonists in a single place (a supermarket), this one-season show alternates between three locations—a shopping mall, a church, and a hospital. Those stranded include author Kevin Copeland (Morgan Spector) and junkie Mia Lambert (Danica Curcic).

Siege stories are a staple of the horror genre and rely on the characters' interactions. In this iteration of *The Mist*, the characters are mostly unlikable and make frustratingly bad decisions. The fascination comes in watching their interactions and their various strategies for coping with the terrifying unknown.

JEKYLL

HORROR • 2007
RATED: TV-14 • 60 MINS

When Dr. Tom Jackman leaves his family and moves into a heavily secured flat, his wife thinks he's having a midlife crisis. But Jackman is only trying to protect his loved ones. Inside him is a monster trying to get out.

At first, you're unsure whether Jackman's condition is psychological or physical, a supernatural manifestation or the result of a scientific experiment. James Nesbitt is superb in the lead, portraying Jackman's monstrous alter ego, Hyde, as a terrifying force of nature.

Writer Steven Moffat's *Jekyll* can be seen as a forerunner to *Sherlock* (see p30), the hugely successful Sherlock Holmes adaptation he cocreated with writer Mark Gatiss. Here, Moffat tackles another Victorian literary classic, Robert Louis Stevenson's *The Strange Case of Dr. Jekyll and Mr. Hyde.* The result is a dynamic single-season, six-episode series that expands on the book's original ideas and is full of thrills and surprises.

TALES OF THE UNEXPECTED

DRAMA • 1979
RATED: 12 (UK) • 25 MINS

Betrayal, duplicity, greed, selfishness ... all of these and more are exposed in these dark stories adapted from, or inspired by, the works of Roald Dahl.

Debuting in 1979, *Tales of the Unexpected* became a British TV staple for almost a decade. Seasons 1 and 2 are arguably the strongest, featuring author Dahl's fondly remembered fireside introductions to classic adaptations of his works such as "Lamb to the Slaughter," "The Landlady," "Royal Jelly," and "Poison."

After that, Dahl's intros mostly disappear and, beginning from Season 2, other authors' tales are increasingly adapted as the show marches on to nine seasons. However, the standard generally stays high throughout, aided by an impressive roster of stars, including Peter Cushing, Derek Jacobi, Siân Phillips, Joseph Cotten, and Janet Leigh.

GLITCH

FANTASY DRAMA • 2015
RATED: TV-MA • 45 MINS

When Sergeant James Hayes attends a disturbance in the local graveyard, he gets more than he bargained for. Half a dozen dead people clamber from their graves, one of them his former wife.

In *Glitch,* the "Risen" are not zombies but living, breathing, physically intact versions of the people they once were, bearing none of the wounds or illnesses that killed them. Hayes (Patrick Brammall) sets out to discover what links the resurrected bodies and why they have returned. The drama revolves not only around the mystery of why the Risen have come back to life but also how their loved ones respond to their resurrection—and, in some cases, how the Risen respond to the news that they died decades before.

A riveting Season 1 leads to a decent Season 2, only for the third to be something of a fumbling misstep. Nonetheless, this Australian series is intriguing and unsettling, with a definite sense of the uncanny.

ASH VS EVIL DEAD

HORROR COMEDY • 2015
RATED: TV-MA • 30 MINS

Ash Williams works at Value Stop, lives in a trailer, and spends most of his time getting wasted. But he has a secret. He is guardian of the *Necronomicon*, the most dangerous book in the world.

Twenty-odd years after the final film in writer and director Sam Raimi's *Evil Dead* trilogy, Ash (Bruce Campbell) is back, older and not the remotest bit wiser. After unwittingly

reawakening the old curse and unleashing a new wave of evil Deadites on the world, he has no option but to strap on his trusty chain saw and get back to work, aided by coworkers Pablo (Ray Santiago) and Kelly (Dana DeLorenzo).

Fans of the films will adore this continuation of the franchise. The move to TV has not toned down the salty humor and outrageous gore one iota. Campbell is hilarious in the lead, and the energy never lets up throughout the entire three-season run. *Ash vs Evil Dead* is an absolute blast.

CASTLE ROCK

HORROR MYSTERY • 2018
RATED: TV-MA • 60 MINS

Who is the mysterious "Kid" in the Shawshank State Penitentiary? Could he really be the devil? And why does he whisper the name "Henry Matthew Deaver"?

A death-row lawyer who is drawn back to his hometown, Henry Deaver (André Holland) is the center of this mystery. As a child, he went missing the day his father died, only to reappear

11 days later in the middle of a frozen lake. What happened? Henry can't remember. The more the questions multiply, the more they become like bonds tightening around him.

If you're a fan of Stephen King, you'll love *Castle Rock*. As fans will know, Castle Rock is the name of the fictional Maine town where numerous King stories take place, many of them referenced here. It's a haunted place, or at least a blighted one, and in this addictively mystifying two-season show it also becomes a puzzle box, brimming with tantalizing questions.

ARE YOU AFRAID OF THE DARK?

HORROR • 1990
RATED: TV-Y7 • 30 MINS

Every story in this anthology series starts the same way: a group of children sit around a campfire and take turns telling scary stories.

Each time, one child extracts a handful of powder from a leather bag and tosses it into the flames. As they flare up, the immortal

words are uttered: "Admitted for the approval of the Midnight Society...." A precursor to the better-known *Goosebumps* (see p438), *Are You Afraid of the Dark?* is more atmospheric than its successor.

Most of the episodes are really scary. Among the highlights are "The Tale of the Super Specs," about a pair of glasses that reveal sinister black figures; "The Tale of the Ghastly Grinner," about a grinning harlequin who turns people into giggling zombies; and "The Tale of the Dead Man's Float," whose underwater zombie design is startlingly ghastly.

DOCTOR WHO

SCI-FI • 1963 • RATED: TV-PG • 25/45 MINS • SEASONS: 26
WILLIAM HARTNELL, JON PERTWEE, TOM BAKER

What constitutes the ultimate TV show concept? How about a mysterious, intelligent, witty, and charismatic hero who travels through time and space, meeting historical figures, thwarting mad scientists and alien invaders, and exploring far-flung planets? And to ensure the show's longevity, why not make the main protagonist an alien with the ability, at times of crisis, to transform his entire appearance and character? Why, with such a concept, a show could last forever!

The first episode of *Doctor Who* was broadcast on Saturday, November 23, 1963, the day after President John F. Kennedy's assassination. In the initial four-part serial, the Doctor

(William Hartnell), his granddaughter Susan (Carole Ann Ford), and her schoolteachers, Ian Chesterton (William Russell) and Barbara Wright (Jacqueline Hill), travel back in time and become involved with a cave-dwelling tribe who have lost the secret of fire. This first story is a brooding, rather static affair, but it was the second story, "The Mutants," (aka "The Daleks"), written by Terry Nation, that cemented the show's popularity and earned it its long-standing reputation as one of the scariest children's TV shows ever made.

> *"Have you ever thought what it's like to be wanderers in the fourth dimension?"*
>
> **The Doctor** (SI EI)

Despite the show's creator, Sydney Newman, stipulating that the series should contain no "B.E.M.s" (Bug-Eyed Monsters), the Daleks—ranting, pepper-pot-shaped machines, each of which houses a slimy, tentacled monstrosity—became not just a success but a nationwide phenomenon, almost single-handedly launching the TV merchandizing market in the UK. Children loved them but were also terrified of them, and so *Doctor Who* quickly gained a reputation as the show that youngsters watched "from behind the sofa."

It was during William Hartnell's last story, "The Tenth Planet" in 1966, that an alien foe finally emerged to rival the popularity of the Daleks. The Cybermen were originally humanoid, whose bodies, ravaged by disease, were gradually replaced by metal and plastic, until eventually their emotions were totally eradicated. Like the Daleks, they have returned to plague the Doctor time and again, as have a variety of other foes, most notably the reptilian Ice Warriors, the potato-headed Sontarans, the Great Intelligence and its robotic Yeti, the subterranean-dwelling Silurians and their marine cousins, the Sea-Devils, and the Nestene Consciousness with its army of plastic Autons.

When, after three years, William Hartnell became too ill to continue in the role, the production team came up with the idea of the Doctor regenerating his body, becoming literally a new man, a notion that eventually led to seven actors playing the Doctor during its initial 26-year run. In the final story starring the second Doctor (Patrick Troughton), "The War Games," his mysterious origins are finally revealed. The third Doctor (Jon Pertwee), whose run of stories, beginning in 1970, was the first produced in color, is exiled to Earth

and employed as scientific advisor to a military organization called UNIT. During this period, we are introduced to the Master, a renegade of the Doctor's own race, who, like the Daleks and the Cybermen—and often in tandem with one or the other—has been a continual thorn in the Doctor's side.

Doctor Who was the brainchild of Sydney Newman, a Canadian film and TV producer, widely regarded as one of the most significant figures in the development of British television drama. Newman intended *Doctor Who* to be an educational science-fiction serial with a family appeal to bridge the teatime gap on BBC1 between the afternoon's sports and the evening's entertainment. Of course, it grew to be much more than that.

Doctor Who's story is a breathtakingly rich and complex one, and judging by the success of the revamped 21st-century series (see p58), which brought the Doctor back after a 16-year hiatus, it is one that may never end.

NUMBER OF STORIES IN WHICH THE DOCTOR HAS ENCOUNTERED THE DALEKS ON SCREEN

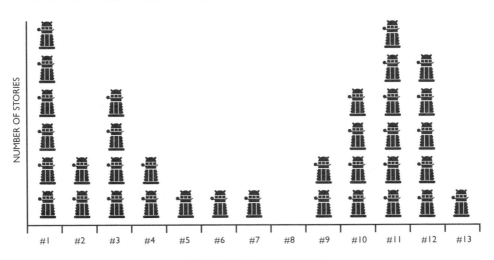

NUMBER OF STORIES

INCARNATION OF THE DOCTOR

#1 #2 #3 #4 #5 #6 #7 #8 #9 #10 #11 #12 #13

CREATOR: Sydney Newman
PRODUCTION CO: BBC

THE RAIN

SCI-FI THRILLER • 2018
RATED: TV-MA • 45 MINS

What do you do when the world turns against you? When the rainfall itself becomes lethal, you're going to need far more than a decent umbrella to survive.

Postapocalyptic teen drama *The Rain* suffers from a teeth-grindingly annoying first episode, in which too many characters make too many decisions that are too stupid. But stick with it, and eventually the sun starts to break through the clouds, though only in a metaphorical sense. The two-season Danish series begins when a brutal virus carried by the rain leads to widespread death and panic. Six years later, teen siblings Simone (Alba August) and Rasmus (Lucas Lynggaard Tønnesen) emerge from the bunker, where their scientist father left them, to find a decimated world.

Polished and fast moving, *The Rain* is a story not only about survival but of hope for a better future. The siblings desperately want to find their father, but when they do, will they discover a hero or a villain?

THE FADES

HORROR • 2011
RATED: TV-14 • 55 MINS

Paul is a troubled teenager. He has apocalyptic dreams and can see the dead all around him. He thinks he's going mad, but then he's told about the Fades and the Angelics and of the oncoming war between them.

Although only one season long, *The Fades* feels like an epic, mythologically rich story, albeit conveyed in a domestic setting. Paul (Iain De Caestecker) is a timid and reluctant hero, his best friend Mac (Daniel Kaluuya, who has since gone on to star in Oscar-nominated movie *Get Out*) is a computer and movie nerd.

As the conflict ramps up between trapped spirits the Fades and the human Angelics who can see them, Paul and Mac muddle along as best they can, discovering answers to the mysteries around them at the same rate as the viewers. Vibrant and innovative, *The Fades* is packed with fascinating characters and terrific ideas. It may have had a short life, but it burned brightly while it was around.

TALES FROM THE CRYPT

HORROR COMEDY • 1989
RATED: TV-MA • 25 MINS

Hello boils and ghouls, are you ready for some campy, pulpy fun, and to see lowlifes and sleazeballs get their comeuppance? If so, let the Cryptkeeper show you the way....

Based on the popular 1950s *EC (Entertaining Comics)* horror comic, *Tales from the Crypt* is a seven-season show that tells simple, satisfying tales with a moralistic message. True to the ethos of the source material, these ultraviolent, lewd, sleazy, and often hilarious tales feature a myriad of prosthetic-based and animatronic monsters—one of which is the aforementioned Cryptkeeper (John Kassir), a rotting corpse with a penchant for puns.

The brand alone is iconic enough to have attracted a staggering array of Hollywood talent. William Friedkin, Tobe Hooper, Arnold Schwarzenegger, and Tom Hanks have all directed episodes, while Demi Moore, Christopher Reeve, Joe Pesci, and Martin Sheen number among the guest stars.

V

SCI-FI • 1983
RATED: TV-14 • 100 MINS

Vast flying saucers hover above Earth's major cities. The Visitors have arrived, offering technology in exchange for resources to aid their dying world. But are they as friendly as they appear?

V was originally conceived as a thriller about the rise of fascism in the US, but NBC wanted a sci-fi hit to cash in on the success of Star Wars. This two-part miniseries became an amalgamation, with the Visitors—reptiles in human guise—presented as a thinly veiled version of the Nazis, who spread propaganda, persecute a minority group (here, scientists), and conduct hideous biological experiments.

A high-budget production, V is epic in scope, boasting a huge cast led by TV cameraman and journalist Mike Donovan (Marc Singer), state-of-the-art special effects, and an enthralling script. Ending on a cliffhanger, the miniseries was followed by V: The Final Battle in 1984, which led directly into a 19-episode series, involving many of the original cast.

THE STAND

HORROR • 1994
RATED: 15 (UK) • 90 MINS

A weaponized strain of influenza is accidentally released from a California research lab, wiping out 99.4 percent of the world's population. The survivors dream of two people: the saintly Mother Abagail and the demonic Randall Flagg.

Based on Stephen King's novel, The Stand stars Gary Sinise and Molly Ringwald as two of those survivors, quiet man Stu Redman and pregnant Frannie Goldsmith. The story tracks them and others through an apocalyptic landscape as they follow their visions either to Nebraska, where Mother Abagail awaits, or to Las Vegas to join up with Flagg.

Abagail and Flagg represent good and evil, which gives The Stand the feel of a modern-day Biblical epic, albeit with a slightly soap-opera vibe. The constraints of squeezing King's huge novel into a six-hour miniseries result in some sketchy characterization and plotting. The horrific excesses of the book are toned down for TV, but this is still a gripping watch.

UNSOLVED MYSTERIES

DOCUMENTARY MYSTERY • 1987
RATED: TV-PG • 60 MINS

This world of ours is a mysterious place. In hundreds of episodes, you'll find out just how mysterious. Questions are asked, theories postulated, and sometimes—just occasionally—answers are provided.

Each episode of Unsolved Mysteries uses a combination of dramatic reenactment and interviews with victims, witnesses, and law enforcement officials to investigate real-life mysteries. What makes the series unique compared with others of its ilk is the sheer range of subjects it covers. Whereas most shows concentrate on either supernatural phenomena or crime cases, Unsolved Mysteries has it all. Murders, kidnappings, and robberies rub shoulders with investigations into UFOs, ghosts, and cryptozoological creatures.

Although Unsolved Mysteries now runs to 16 seasons, it has been canceled and revived on numerous occasions. It's easy to see why it keeps coming back—the premise is irresistible.

TWIN PEAKS

MYSTERY • 1990 • RATED: TV-MA • 47 MINS • SEASONS: 3
KYLE MACLACHLAN, MICHAEL ONTKEAN, MÄDCHEN AMICK

Wrapped in plastic, the body of homecoming queen Laura Palmer is washed ashore in the logging town of Twin Peaks, Washington. FBI agent Dale Cooper arrives to find a town that's steeped in secrets, and also serves excellent cherry pie.

Twin Peaks is not a standard murder-mystery show. As with all of writer and director David Lynch's work, the series has an eerie, off-kilter atmosphere, characterized by portentous dream sequences, uncanny—often surreal—occurrences, black humor, and deeply odd characters who converse using coded messages and non sequiturs.

As an outsider to the seemingly quaint Twin Peaks, FBI agent Dale Cooper (Kyle MacLachlan) is the character with whom you are most encouraged to identify, yet even he is highly unconventional. A major part of his investigation is conducted as a reaction to the messages he receives in his dreams of a room lined with red curtains. The messages come from characters including a one-armed man called Mike, a dwarf in a red business suit, and a giant who informs him that "the owls are not what they seem."

Although the identity of Laura Palmer's killer is revealed midway through Season 2, when *Twin Peaks* was canceled in 1991, it left many questions unanswered. In 2017, after an interval of more than 25 years (and a 1992 prequel movie, *Twin Peaks: Fire Walk with Me*), the series returned to enthral and baffle TV viewers once again. Will it be back a fourth time? Who knows? But whether it will or not, you're left with the impression that the town has many more secrets to reveal.

David Lynch's initial concept for *Twin Peaks* was a show chronicling the many intertwining lives of the inhabitants of a small town. He took inspiration from the complex, sprawling Victorian novels of Charles Dickens and, working with his friend and collaborator Mark Frost, came up with the idea of a series based on popular US soap opera *Peyton Place* (1964–1969). He hoped to hook viewers by opening with a murder investigation, then expand the drama to encompass a range of different overlapping story lines. But as ideas developed further, the murder-mystery concept took over and became the driving force. The result is a strange, surreal series that—like the coffee served in Twin Peaks' Double R Diner—is never less than damn fine.

CREATORS: Mark Frost, David Lynch
PRODUCTION CO: Lynch/Frost Productions, Propaganda Films, Spelling Entertainment, Twin Peaks Productions

GRIMM

CRIME FANTASY • 2011
RATED: TV-14 • 45 MINS

Portland homicide detective Nick Burkhardt starts having hallucinations. For a second, he sees certain people transform into hideous creatures. Is he going mad, or is the world a stranger place than he thought possible?

Burkhardt (David Giuntoli) has a dying aunt who informs him that he is a "grimm," whose job is to maintain the balance between humans and mythological creatures known as Wesen. It's tricky trying to keep his secret from his partner and girlfriend, but at least he has help from Monroe (Silas Weir Mitchell), a werewolf (or Blutbad) with a penchant for one-liners.

Grimm is a blend of police procedural and the dark side of fairy tales—some of the episodes are loosely based on stories by the Brothers Grimm. Replete with scares, gore, and some nasty magical creatures, the mythology and character interactions of this moody, violent, thrilling series are satisfyingly developed over the course of its six seasons.

THE WOMAN IN BLACK

HORROR • 1989
RATED: 15 (UK) • 100 MINS

What is the secret of Eel Marsh House? Why can the sounds of a terrible accident be heard out on the causeway? What is the fearful significance of the woman in black?

Broadcast on Christmas Eve 1989, *The Woman in Black* is a deeply disquieting experience. Set in 1925, it follows the fortunes of London solicitor Arthur Kidd (Adrian Rawlins), who is sent to the small town of Crythin Gifford in northeast England to settle the estate of the reclusive Alice Drablow.

Kidd finds the villagers surly and taciturn, and at Drablow's funeral he sees a woman in black (Pauline Moran) standing among the graves. Back at Eel Marsh House, which is reached via a narrow causeway across the marsh and cut off for long periods by the tide, the tension and scares really begin to ramp up. This TV film is a superb production, the titular character a malign presence whose every appearance is a jolt to the system.

THE KIRLIAN FREQUENCY

ANIMATED HORROR • 2017
RATED: TV-14 • 10 MINS

Kirlian, a lost city somewhere in Argentina, doesn't appear on any map, and the roads that supposedly lead there are a tangled maze that double back on themselves.

The Kirlian Frequency is something of an oddity, a quirky animated anthology show, consisting of just five episodes of less than 10 minutes each, meaning you can watch the entire thing in under an hour. The narrator is a silky-voiced radio DJ, who hosts a midnight news and chat show and calmly chronicles the bizarre and otherworldly events that occur within Kirlian.

With its rich palette of blacks, pinks, purples, and reds, the animation that accompanies these mini episodes is elegantly simple but atmospheric. Figures are seen only in silhouette, their features limited to the glowing glint of their eyes, or white light reflecting off the lenses of their glasses. It's not really a scary show, but it does have a moodily hypnotic effect.

THE CHALET

THRILLER • 2017
RATED: TV-MA • 52 MINS

Dark secrets begin to rise up from the dark soil of the past and impact on the present in this story told across two timelines, set 20 years apart.

In 1997, while renting a chalet in the French Alps, the Rodier family disappears without trace. Twenty years later, a group of friends, including Manu Laverne (Marc Ruchmann) and pregnant Adèle (Emilie de Preissac), stay in the same chalet—and the murders begin. As events unfold, you find out more about the history of the chalet, the isolated town of Valmoline, and its inhabitants.

A murky, gruesome thriller, *The Chalet* starts slowly, but the tension builds as it progresses. When unsettling things begin to happen—a rockslide cuts the group off from the outside world; all phone and internet connections go down; and accidents start to befall the group—it seems clear that the group is being victimized, but why? And by whom? And more important, who will survive?

PENNY DREADFUL

PERIOD HORROR • 2014
RATED: TV-MA • 60 MINS

In Victorian London, a brilliant young doctor named Victor Frankenstein succeeds in bringing life back to the dead, while the charismatic Dorian Gray searches for ways to offset the stultifying boredom of immortality.

Penny Dreadful is a heady, intoxicating brew. Using a plethora of characters from classic horror fiction, albeit given interesting, sometimes startling new twists, it weaves together a multitude of plotlines into a richly complex story, the focus of which is the enigmatic Vanessa Ives (Eva Green).

Although its foundations are lodged in the dark soil of gothic melodrama, *Penny Dreadful* is not a campy production. London is a disease-ridden sewer, and the violence that takes place within its filthy streets is bloody and brutal. Vampires are ravening beasts and witches are scarred, hairless harpies. The cursed Vanessa must face them all, and more besides, as she seeks to avoid a terrible destiny.

TOKYO VAMPIRE HOTEL

HORROR • 2017
RATED: 18 (UK) • 52 MINS

Two opposing vampire clans fight to take possession of 21-year-old Manami who, unbeknownst to her, holds their future, and possibly that of the entire world, in her hands.

Written and directed by cult Japanese director Sion Sono, this 10-episode series (originally nine, but the eighth part was split into two for streaming purposes) blends bright colors and stunning visuals, meticulously choreographed and exceptionally bloody mayhem, outrageous concepts, and larger-than-life characters. The result is a mind-blowing sensory experience.

The story is meandering and confusing at times, to the point where you might find yourself wondering whether you dreamed some of it. But the mostly young, incredibly cool, and gorgeously dressed cast—headed by Ami Tomite as Manami—give it their all. If you're looking for a new slant on vampires and aren't too fussed about plot coherence, you'll love it. If nothing else, it will give your eyes a treat.

UFO

SCI-FI • 1970
RATED: TV-PG • 45 MINS

In 1980, aliens abduct humans to harvest body organs, Earth has a moon base to repel extraterrestrial attacks, and the women of secret defense organization SHADO wear silver jumpsuits and purple wigs. Groovy!

Made in 1970, *UFO's* predictions for a decade hence were a little ambitious. It featured a secret international agency, operating from a hidden base and equipped with a vast array of highly advanced vehicles, weapons, and other gadgets, whose task was to defend Earth against the evil machinations of a sinister enemy.

Created by Gerry Anderson of *Thunderbirds* fame (see p59), this live-action show differs from Anderson's earlier, more family-friendly marionette series in its tone and presentation. *UFO* is a more adult affair, featuring marital breakdowns, family betrayals, drug use, and the senseless, brutal deaths of likable characters over its single season.

THE HAUNTING OF HILL HOUSE

HORROR • 2018 • RATED: TV-MA • 50 MINS • SEASONS: 1
HENRY THOMAS, OLIVER JACKSON-COHEN, KATE SIEGEL

Whatever walks in Hill House walks alone. At least until the Crain family move in. What Olivia and Hugh Crain and their five children encounter within the blighted walls of the accursed house will haunt them forever.

The Haunting of Hill House plays out across two timelines. In 1992, as mom Olivia (Carla Gugino) becomes increasingly unstable as a result of the house's malign influence, dad Hugh (Henry Thomas) keeps himself busy as a way of denying the deep rifts opening up within the family. Meanwhile, their largely unprotected kids are tormented by supernatural phenomena that will lead to mental-health problems and drug addiction in later life. Twenty-six years later, the dysfunctional Crain family are brought back together by tragedy, and the haunting begins anew—though, in reality, it has never gone away. An intricate and compelling story line unravels family mysteries and secrets, while providing enraptured viewers with shocking revelations and lots and lots of behind-the-sofa scares.

If *The Haunting of Hill House* doesn't put the heebie-jeebies up you, nothing will. Some of the ghosts that haunt the beleaguered Crains are downright terrifying—most notably the bent-neck lady and the bowler-hatted man. Then there are the 43 hidden ghosts—peering around corners or standing in the shadows—scattered throughout the series, which are designed to give viewers a constant, subliminal feeling of being watched. Oh, and to cap it all, in one episode, there's the biggest jump-shock since the head popped out of the boat in the film *Jaws*.

MARIANNE

HORROR • 2019
RATED: TV-MA • 50 MINS

Imagine if you were a horror writer and all your darkest imaginings began to come true. When her friend dies by suicide, author Emma Larsimon returns to her childhood home to confront the demons of her past.

In a mere eight episodes, this single-season French series weaves a dark and insidious spell upon you. Constructed like a novel, complete with chapter headings and cutaway shots of riffling pages, it is often difficult to tell where fiction ends and reality begins.

Central to the show is Emma (Victoire Du Bois), whose stories about a witch named Marianne unleash a terrifying supernatural force that begins to poison the lives of Emma's family and friends. There are prolonged scenes of unbearable tension, wince-inducing episodes of body horror, and jump-shocks aplenty as Marianne relentlessly tears Emma's world apart. This is not a show for the fainthearted.

CHILDREN OF THE STONES

HORROR • 1977
RATED: PG (UK) • 30 MINS

Combining hard science, folk horror, and occult mysticism, this seven-part serial was a scary, heady brew for adolescents when it was first on TV. How will you feel watching it now?

Professor Brake (Gareth Thomas) and his teenage son, Matthew (Peter Demin), arrive in rural Milbury to study the ancient stone circle that surrounds the village. They quickly discover that Milbury's inhabitants are curiously placid and happy and that astronomer Rafael Hendrick (Iain Cuthbertson) has a sinister plan involving dark magic and psychic power.

Children of the Stones is a surprisingly adult, complex supernatural drama for children. The eerie opening titles alone,, featuring standing stones looming threateningly amid a discordant soundtrack of groans, whispers, and druid-style chanting, were enough to induce nightmares. It is fondly remembered today for its sense of menace and its shockingly downbeat ending.

LOCKE & KEY

FANTASY HORROR • 2020
RATED: TV-14 • 48 MINS

Welcome to Keyhouse, ancestral home of the Locke family. When Nina Locke and her children, Tyler, Kinsey, and Bode, take up residence, the children find a series of powerful keys, which unlock some very strange doors indeed.

Locke & Key is both a dark fairy tale and a sombre coming-of-age story about childhood trauma and loss. Mom Nina (Darby Stanchfield) moves the Locke family to Keyhouse to make a fresh start after her husband Rendell (Bill Heck) is murdered. The house is somewhere between a haunted mansion and a magical kingdom, full of evil and wonder. The locks to which the keys fit are obvious symbols for the children's feelings, which are in turmoil after their father's death.

Despite the psychology, *Locke & Key* is not all that deep. The dark forces gathering within the house never feel threatening enough. Even so, the one-season show is sumptuous, full of delightful ideas and gorgeous visuals. It may lack emotional depth, but it's still spooky fun.

THE TERROR

HORROR • 2018
RATED: TV-14 • 60 MINS

In 1847, the Franklin expedition becomes stuck in the Arctic ice and is beset by untold horrors. In 1941, Japanese Americans in a US internment camp are terrorized by a spirit from Japanese folklore.

These two 10-episode miniseries, though entirely stand-alone, are thematically linked by the fact they're rooted in real-life historical events. In Season 1, two ships become stuck in the Arctic ice while searching for the fabled Northwest Passage. The crewmen find themselves battling not only starvation and the elements but also a vast and cunning predator. Oozing class, this is a production with a dread-inducing atmosphere that will gnaw into your bones like the Arctic cold.

Season 2, subtitled *The Terror: Infamy*, is both a creepy ghost story and a thoughtful, timely tale about human dignity and fortitude. Although more worthy than its predecessor, it is chilling with spine-tingling tension and grisly horror.

TALES FROM THE DARKSIDE

HORROR • 1983
RATED: TV-14 • 30 MINS

"Man lives in the sunlit world of what he believes to be reality. But there is, unseen by most, an underworld. A place that is just as real, but not as brightly lit. A darkside ..."

So runs the opening narration of *Tales from the Darkside*, uttered menacingly over pastoral scenes that bleed into darkness. Conceived by zombie supremo George A. Romero, this fun and creepy anthology show features adaptations of stories by top writers such as Stephen King, Clive Barker, and *Psycho* author Robert Bloch.

Filmed on video and so a bit cheap-looking, the four-season series has many memorable episodes. In "Inside the Closet," a student (Roberta Weiss) hears something scuttling about in the upstairs closet of her rented rooms. In "A Case of the Stubborns," Grandpa (Eddie Bracken) refuses to accept he's dead, even when he starts to decompose. In "Seasons of Belief," a father (E. G. Marshall) terrifies his children with tales of a demonic anti-Santa.

ULTRAVIOLET

HORROR • 1998
RATED: 15 (UK) • 50 MINS

Investigating the disappearance of his friend Jack just before his wedding, Detective Sergeant Michael Colefield finds himself involved with a para-military organization with a startling directive—to hunt and kill vampires.

Starring Jack Davenport, *Ultraviolet* is a slick and classy one-season serial that brings vampire lore into the late 20th century. The bloodsuckers here are a sophisticated force, who, after years of living in the shadows, are mobilizing due to the threat of global warming and aim to wipe out humanity with a bio-engineered plague.

Both sides use science in their quest for dominance. While vampires indulge in medical experiments to find an alternative food source, the government and other opponents fight back with carbon bullets and gas grenades filled with a garlic-derived compound. Focusing on trauma, grief, and the psychological consequences of warfare, *Ultraviolet* is an adult show with a tough but emotional heart.

DEATH NOTE

ANIMATED HORROR • 2006 • RATED: TV-14 • 24 MINS • SEASONS: 1
MAMORU MIYANO, RYÔ NAITÔ, SHIDÔ NAKAMURA

If you could kill evil people simply by writing their names in a book, what would you do? That's the question Light Yagami faces. But with the power of life and death in his hands, does that make him a force for good or for evil?

Widely regarded as one of the best anime series ever, *Death Note* is more considered, layered, and complex than the usual action-led fare. Disgusted by the moral corruption he sees all around him, top student Light Yagami (Mamoru Miyano) one day finds a "Death Note" lying on the ground, a notebook discarded by a Japanese demon called a shinigami, which grants the user the ability to kill anyone whose name they write in its pages.

At first, Light thinks it's a prank, but he soon discovers that it's anything but. Initially, he is shocked by the power he wields, but soon he's scribbling names like nobody's business, and criminals and ne'er-do-wells drop like flies.

A sprawling, constantly expanding narrative that encompasses several years, *Death Note* is epic in scope. Most of the action plays out as a tactical battle of wills between Light—known as "Kira" to the Japanese people, who regard him not as a murderous vigilante, but as a godlike force for good—and an enigmatic detective known only as L (Kappei Yamaguchi), who is trying to uncover Kira's true identity and end his killing spree. A morally intricate tale about power, corruption, and responsibility, *Death Note* is fascinating and unpredictable.

> **"***This world is rotten, and those who are making it rot deserve to die!***"**
>
> Light Yagami (SI EI)

INVASION

**SCI-FI • 2005
RATED: 15 (UK) • 60 MINS**

Hurricane Eve strikes and lights are seen in the water. Some of the town's inhabitants start behaving oddly. Is an unknown virus to blame or something altogether stranger?

Like Shaun Cassidy's previous series *American Gothic* (see p445), *Invasion* is often considered a lost treasure. Canceled after one 22-episode season, it's an eerie drama full of suspense.

The swampland locations and the ambiguous characters add to an aura of claustrophobic murkiness, with viewers uncertain whether even lead characters such as Sheriff Tom Underlay (William Fichtner) and his wife, Dr. Mariel Underlay (Kari Matchett), have succumbed to the influence of the "lights."

Invasion was partially scuppered by the fact that its first episode aired only three weeks after Hurricane Katrina had devastated the southern states. Promotion for the show was stopped by the ABC network in case viewers connected it with the real-life tragedy.

THRILLER

HORROR • 1973
RATED: 15 (UK) • 65 MINS

Sun-dappled woods, lakes, country houses ... unthreatening, tranquil English settings. But film them through a fish-eye lens, add a blood-red border and ominous music, and they become something else entirely.

Thriller is a gem of an anthology series, perfect for watching when curled up under a blanket on a cold winter night. These 43 stand-alone episodes spread over six seasons are a blend of psycho-thrillers, murder mysteries, and supernatural spook fests.

Highlights of this remarkably consistent and often genuinely chilling series include "A Coffin for the Bride," starring a young Helen Mirren; "Won't Write Home, Mom—I'm Dead," which is set in a deeply creepy hippy commune; "Someone at the Top of the Stairs," in which two female students move into a house full of sinister residents; and "I'm the Girl He Wants to Kill," in which a murder witness is trapped inside an office building at night with the killer.

REQUIEM

HORROR THRILLER • 2018
RATED: TV-MA • 60 MINS

In 1994, a four-year-old girl goes missing from a Welsh village; in 2017, in London, just before going on stage, celebrated cellist Matilda Gray sees her mother slip into a trancelike state and then slash open her own throat....

The shocking opening to this six-part serial also includes an elderly resident of the same Welsh village throwing himself from the roof of the country house where most of the spooky happenings take place. However, these suicides are only the first mysteries in a complex and multilayered plot that heaps twist upon twist.

Part psychological thriller, part supernatural drama, *Requiem* is deliciously creepy and utterly compelling. The cast is uniformly excellent, particularly Lydia Wilson as Matilda, the dogged heroine. A story about identity, secret lives, moral corruption, and how the sins of the past bleed through to impact on the present, this is a class act.

SCOOBY-DOO, WHERE ARE YOU!

ANIMATED COMEDY • 1969
RATED: TV-G • 22 MINS

Where will Scooby and friends go? An empty museum? A deserted castle? An abandoned fairground? Wherever it is, there'll be a mystery to solve!

Scooby-Doo is a TV phenomenon. More than 50 years old, the lovable Great Dane and his human chums Shaggy, Fred, Daphne, and Velma, have appeared in numerous animated series, television specials, and direct-to-video movies. Arriving in their brightly colored van, the Mystery Machine, the groovy gang invariably becomes embroiled in a sinister mystery at a spooky location. And the location is always haunted by a seemingly supernatural creature.

Over its three-season original series, Scooby and his friends find themselves up against a living suit of armor, a caveman, a ghostly clown, and even the triple whammy of Dracula, Frankenstein's Monster, and Wolfman. Zoinks, indeed!

QUATERMASS QUADRILOGY

SCI-FI HORROR • 1953 • RATED: 15 (UK) • 30 MINS • SEASONS: 4
REGINALD TATE, JOHN ROBINSON, ANDRÉ MORELL

A lost British rocket ship reappears on radar, then crash-lands in London. When opened, only one of its crew members is left inside, despite the ship having remained sealed since takeoff. What has happened? Mission chief Professor Quatermass investigates.

Between 1953 and 1979, four *Quatermass* serials were broadcast on British television, each written by Nigel Kneale, and each featuring a different actor in the role of Professor Bernard Quatermass, head of the British Experimental Rocket Group.

Starring Reginald Tate in the lead, *The Quatermass Experiment* (1953) was the first original science-fiction serial made for an adult British TV audience, and it caused a sensation. Its story line, in which surviving rocket-ship crew member Victor Carroon (Duncan Lamont) slowly transmogrifies into a giant, plantlike creature, incorporated elements of body horror considered shocking for its time. Sadly, only the first two of its six half-hour episodes survive—the others have been lost—but it remains a hugely significant TV landmark, influencing many films and TV shows, from Ridley Scott's *Alien* to the BBC's own *Doctor Who* (see p58 and p452).

So successful was the BBC show that a second serial was commissioned, closely followed by a third. In *Quatermass II* (1955), Quatermass (John Robinson) investigates a meteorite shower, which leads him to an industrial plant where possessed humans are protecting

a huge vat in which something monstrous is growing. *Quatermass and the Pit* (1958), with André Morell in the title role, is often considered the crowning glory of the series, combining science fiction, folklore, and occultism to great effect in a deeply creepy story about a strange skull and a mysterious craft found buried in central London.

The final serial, simply titled *Quatermass*, underwent a long gestation before appearing as a miniseries on ITV in 1979. The most downbeat of the *Quatermass* serials, it depicts a retired, reclusive, embittered Quatermass (John Mills) unable to come to terms with a corrupt and dystopian society as he investigates mass disappearances of young people at various stone circles around the country. Its reputation as the least effective of the four serials is unfair. Although unremittingly grim, it is, in its way, just as relevant and compelling as its forebears.

CREATOR: NIGEL KNEALE
PRODUCTION CO: BBC, Euston Films, Thames Television

MASTERS OF HORROR

HORROR • 2005
RATED: TV-MA • 60 MINS

Get together the best horror writers and directors in the business; give them a budget, 60 minutes of airtime, and free rein to indulge themselves; then sit back and watch the results.

Masters of Horror is the brainchild of director Mick Garris, who in 2002 organized a series of dinners that brought together many of the top horror directors of the day, including Guillermo del Toro, Stuart Gordon, and Joe Dante. The outcome was 26 one-hour horror movies, spread over two seasons and displaying a wide range of approaches, styles, and moods.

Masters of Horror is an exhilarating experience—you never know quite what you're in for with each episode. But that also means the series can't help but lack a certain cohesion. Nevertheless, there's some excellent work here, notably John Carpenter's "Cigarette Burns," about an obscure movie that causes everyone who watches it to go insane.

Z NATION

HORROR COMEDY • 2014
RATED: TV-14 • 44 MINS

Having been forced to participate in a government experiment, an ex-con is the only person in the world to have survived a zombie bite—and the only one who can save humanity.

Z Nation opens three years after a zombie plague has laid waste to civilization. The only hope of pulling humankind back from the brink is to get Alvin Murphy (Keith Allan) from New York to the last remaining disease control lab, in California, so that a vaccine can be developed from the antibodies in his blood. Thus begins this five-season journey through a postapocalyptic America, with peril waiting beyond every turn.

Despite drawing inevitable comparisons to *The Walking Dead* (see p434), *Z Nation* is a faster-moving show, with a lighter feel, and plenty of humor. Its characters may be somewhat throwaway, but what the show lacks in angsty psychological depth, it makes up for in sheer pedal-to-the-metal chutzpah.

BLACK SUMMER

HORROR • 2019
RATED: TV-MA • 40 MINS

It may be a long, hot summer, but lazing in the sunshine is the last thing on anyone's mind, because six weeks ago the zombie apocalypse began and the world is now in chaos.

A prequel series to *Z Nation*, albeit one that shares no characters or situations with its parent show, *Black Summer*'s breathless, panicky style perfectly encapsulates the desperation of its various groups of characters as they try to stay alive in their new perilous environment.

Hurling us headfirst into the action, the show is often a disorientating experience, especially when events jump abruptly forward from one episode to the next. Although it's an ensemble piece, Rose (Jaime King) is the touchstone character. Her—and everyone else's—desire to reach "the Stadium," a sanctuary where she believes her missing daughter can be found, is what drives the action in this single season of eight frantic, blood-drenched episodes.

DARK SHADOWS

HORROR DRAMA • 1966 • RATED: TV-PG • 30 MINS • SEASONS: 6
JONATHAN FRID, GRAYSON HALL, ALEXANDRA ISLES

Kidnappings, blackmail, curses, and murder surround the wealthy Collins family in the town of Collinsport, Maine. Then into their melodramatic world arrives cousin Barnabus from England. How odd that he so closely resembles the original Barnabus Collins, whose 200-year-old portrait hangs in the hall....

Dark Shadows is an American TV phenomenon. A daily gothic soap opera, it aired in the afternoons on ABC and came close to cancellation in its first year because of falling ratings. But once the character of Barnabus Collins (Jonathan Frid) was introduced in April 1967, the show became a roaring success, gaining a cult following among teenagers arriving home from school. Barnabus, you see, is a vampire and has spent the last 200 years imprisoned in a chained coffin after being cursed by the witch Angelique (Lara Parker).

The shift into the supernatural proved so successful that *Dark Shadows*' 1,200-plus episodes soon gave rise to stories involving ghosts, werewolves, zombies, and a Frankenstein-like monster named Adam. There's also a time-travel plotline, and one featuring a parallel dimension—all of it borrowed from a rich melting pot of gothic influences, including Edgar Allan Poe, Henry James, the Brontës, Mary Shelley, and even Charles Dickens and Oscar Wilde.

But that's not to say *Dark Shadows* was in anyway sophisticated over its five-year run. Indeed, its trashiness is a huge part of its appeal. Filmed "as live," the show is as famous for its bloopers as it is for its bombastic performances, overblown story lines, and dramatic plot twists. Like watching a never-ending stage play performed by enthusiastic amateurs, *Dark Shadows* is a guilty delight.

EERIE, INDIANA

HORROR SCI-FI • 1991
RATED: TV-Y7 • 30 MINS

The prosperous small town of Eerie, Indiana (population 16,661), is the American Dream come true. But look again. For beneath its squeaky-clean façade, something weird is going on....

Marshall Teller (Omri Katz) has recently moved to Eerie from New Jersey with his family. Together with his friend Simon (Justin Shenkarow), he uncovers weirdness at every

turn. What makes *Eerie, Indiana* so refreshing is that unlike most creepy kids' shows, the usual horror tropes—vampires, werewolves, zombies—are largely absent. Instead the threats are more innovative. Watch out for plastic containers that keep things (and people) fresh for years, tooth braces that enable you to read dogs' minds, and a sentient tornado.

Add witty in-jokes, references to horror films and TV shows, and great performances from the two leads, and here is a smart one-season, 19-episode series that is mostly played for fun but at times also has a darker edge.

BRAINDEAD

HORROR COMEDY • 2016
RATED: TV-14 • 44 MINS

Politics is a hotbed of double-dealing at the best of times. But when brain-eating bugs infiltrate Washington, DC, it's hard not only to tell friend from foe, but also human from alien—at least until someone's head explodes.

Part political satire, part body-horror nightmare, part adorably goofy comedy, *BrainDead* aims for a whole bunch of targets and manages to hit most of them. And in Laurel Healy (Mary Elizabeth Winstead), a documentary filmmaker who takes a job as constituency caseworker for her US Senator brother, Luke (Danny Pino), it has the kind of lead character it's fun to hang out with.

Witty and intriguing—the songs that act as episode recaps are an innovative delight — *BrainDead* was originally planned with a four-series arc but was canceled after just one season. Those who bought into it, *really* bought into it, but for the majority, it perhaps tries to do too much at once.

WYNONNA EARP

HORROR WESTERN • 2016
RATED: TV-14 • 60 MINS

Seventy-seven—that's how many outlaws Wynonna Earp's famous great-great-granddaddy Wyatt killed. Trouble is, the Earps' hometown of Purgatory is cursed, and those outlaws are returning from hell bent on revenge.

To describe *Wynonna Earp* as a Wild West version of *Buffy the Vampire Slayer* (see p428) is not entirely inaccurate. Nor is it doing *Wynonna Earp* a disservice because, like *Buffy*, this is a witty, action-packed, and entertaining show fronted by a sassy kick-ass heroine.

On her 27th birthday, Wynonna (Melanie Scrofano) inherits the power to send returning revenants back to hell using her great-great-grandpa's revolver, "Peacemaker." Over three seasons, she is assisted in her quest by Special Agent Xavier Dolls (Shamier Anderson) from secret government agency the Black Badge Division, a possibly immortal Doc Holliday (Tim Rozon), and Waverley (Dominique Provost-Chalkley), her younger half sister.

HAMMER HOUSE OF HORROR

HORROR • 1980
RATED: 15 (UK) • 54 MINS

A country house at twilight. A haunting tune plays as branches stir in the wind ... a stone gargoyle ... a cowled statue ... a dark figure moving across a window ...

The opening titles of *Hammer House of Horror* are peculiarly English and suggestive of gentle, even genteel, hauntings. Nothing, though, could be further from the truth. The one-season show's 13 episodes are modern, downbeat, and often surprisingly gruesome. After more than two decades of making top-quality movie horror, Hammer seemed to be on its last legs by this point—but what a way to go!

Witchcraft, werewolves, satanism, and voodoo all rear their horned and leering heads in this well-crafted, entertaining, and creepy series. Top of the pile, though, is "The House that Bled to Death," about a family who moves into a suburban house where a grisly murder took place, and things are not what they seem.

THE STRAIN

HORROR • 2014
RATED: TV-MA • 43 MINS

A plane lands at JFK airport with all but four of its passengers dead, victims of an unknown virus. Meanwhile, down in the hold, something is stirring inside a mysterious casket.

Based on the novels by film director Guillermo del Toro and writer Chuck Hogan, *The Strain* chronicles humanity's struggle to quell an epidemic in which people transform into hideous vampires. Dr. Ephraim Goodweather (Corey Stoll), head of a disease-control team, races against time to stem the plague, aided by Dr. Nora Martinez (Mía Maestro) and Professor Abraham Setrakian (David Bradley), a Holocaust survivor and vampire expert.

Intense and apocalyptic, if at times unfocused, *The Strain* is enhanced by arresting visuals and a smart political subtext. Early episodes in its four seasons have a procedural feel, but once the mayhem of the vampire invasion kicks in, it adopts more of a comic-book style, with the screen bathed in fluorescent blues and reds.

REMEMBER ME

HORROR • 2014
RATED: TV-14 • 60 MINS

How can a social worker fall from a seemingly closed fourth-floor window? How can a woman drown in her own home? And why is a young care assistant having nightmares about a veiled figure on a deserted beach?

All these events center on mild-mannered pensioner Tom Parfitt (Michael Palin). From the outset, it is clear that strange things happen around Tom, and those who try to influence his life end up in danger, or worse—including care assistant Hannah (Jodie Comer) and her family.

Reminiscent of writer M .R. James's supernatural tales, *Remember Me* is genuinely creepy–the first episode in particular evokes an escalating sense of dread, before culminating in a tour de force of heart-thumping, sweat-inducing tension. A proper ghost story, this one-off, three-part drama is proof positive that less is more and that what we don't see is often far more frightening than what we do.

HOTEL BEAU SÉJOUR

HORROR MYSTERY • 2016
RATED: NR • 50 MINS

Teenager Kato wakes in a hotel room, beaten and bloody, with no memory of how she got there. She is shocked to find a corpse in the bathtub—and even more shocked to discover it is her own.

Although *Hotel Beau Séjour* has the sombre tone and color palette of a Euro-noir thriller, the supernatural element adds an intriguing twist. Unsatisfied with the police investigation into her murder, Kato (Lynn Van Royen) decides to solve it herself, unearthing mystery upon mystery.

In a way, this Flemish-Belgian crime drama's greatest innovation is also its weakest element. As the main character, Kato should be our emotional touchstone, but the nature of the mystery means she's also something of a blank slate. However, as with all good crime thrillers set in insular communities, the fact that the narrative's murky secrets coil and twist together like a nest of snakes will be enough to keep most viewers hooked.

CREEPSHOW

HORROR COMEDY • 2019
RATED: TV-MA • 44 MINS

A young girl finds a creepy toy head in her new dollhouse. A man with strange powers is found squeezed into a suitcase. A woman goes looking for a monster in Lake Champlain....

Creepshow is an anthology series based on the 1982 movie written by Stephen King and directed by George A. Romero. Like the original film (and its sequel *Creepshow 2*), it's an homage to the EC horror comics of the 1950s, and, like *Tales from the Crypt*, the host is an animatronic zombielike creature with a penchant for bad puns.

Season 1 consists of six episodes, each containing two stories, and the style is campy old-school horror with a comic-book feel—colorful, fast-moving, and crammed with great-looking monsters and gruesome effects. Adaptations of stories by top names—Stephen King, Joe Hill, Josh Malerman, Joe R. Lansdale—ensure that it is strong in terms of ideas, not to mention hugely entertaining.

CONSTANTINE

HORROR • 2014
RATED: TV-14 • 43 MINS

Unable to save the soul of a young girl, occult sleuth John Constantine has himself checked into an asylum. But even there the demons won't leave him be.

Based on the character from DC Comics' *Hellblazer* series, Constantine (Matt Ryan) is an archetypal antihero, a former con man-turned-occult detective and demon hunter, driven by the need to atone for past sins. Each of the 13 episodes in this single-season series see Constantine and his loose band of companions battling demons and other supernatural entities as the "Rising Darkness" threatens to extinguish more and more innocent lives and overwhelm the world with evil.

Stuffed with occultist and mythological mumbo jumbo, *Constantine* is an uneven but fun show, graced by excellent effects and impressive production values. Holding it all together is Ryan, who makes an engaging lead—by turns dishevelled, wisecracking, irreverent, and cynical.

TIDELANDS

CRIME FANTASY • 2018
RATED: TV-MA • 60 MINS

There's something fishy going on in Orphelin Bay. Just arrived home from prison, an ex-con gets thrown in at the deep end when the body of a local fisherman washes ashore.

Fresh out of jail, Cal McTeer (Charlotte Best) heads back to her hometown, an Australian coastal village where tensions simmer between the human population and the Tidelanders—half human, half siren hybrids. Cal finds herself with secrets, lies, betrayals, and sins to uncover, as she struggles to contain visions of her own traumatic past.

The acting is variable: Tidelanders' leader Adrielle (Elsa Pataky) has what is meant to be a fey and mystical air about her but at times comes across as dopey. And while *Tidelands* may feel a bit soapy, it's no family show. There are gruesome killings and, as strong as the female characters are purported to be, most shed their clothes at frequent intervals. It may not be the most masterful of shows but it's atmospheric.

BLACK MIRROR

SCI-FI HORROR • 2011 • RATED: TV-MA • 60 MINS
SEASONS: 5 • DANIEL KALUUYA, BRYCE DALLAS HOWARD

A woman awakes to find the whole world filming her on their cell phones. Robotic bees pollinate flowers and act as government surveillance drones. In a log cabin, a minute lasts 1,000 years. When you stare into the black mirror, your darkest technological fears are reflected back.

Inspired by Rod Serling's *The Twilight Zone* (see pp436–437), which tackled sensitive and controversial subjects through a filter of fantasy and speculation, writer and satirist Charlie Brooker first decided to develop the idea of an anthology series examining technology and its implications back in 2010.

Since the first three *Black Mirror* episodes aired in December 2011, 20 more have been produced to date, spanning five seasons and two feature-length specials, each shining a harsh light on many of the technological innovations that either already underpin society or are just around the corner. From artificial intelligence and robots to social media, CCTV, virtual reality, video games, online dating apps, downloads, reality shows, and eugenics, Brooker and his writing team have scrutinized, dissected, and hypothesized them all with acerbic and witty clarity.

Most episodes are set in a near-future but still highly recognizable society and take the form of cautionary tales, the main protagonists of which are trapped in a situation that is gradually escalating out of their control. The standard of each episode is high—most are sharply observed and surprisingly poignant. "White Bear" (S2 E2) is a highlight, in which a woman wakes up in a strange house and

finds herself the target of armed hunters. Also seek out "San Junipero" (S3 E4), a love story set in an ideal holiday destination that is not what it seems. "USS Callister" (S4 E1) is a black comedy that mostly takes place in a *Star Trek*–like simulation. "Hang the DJ" (S4 E4) is a bittersweet examination of what would happen if we allowed technology to choose our life partners for us. "Metalhead" (S4 E5), starkly filmed in black and white, sees a fugitive pursued by a ferocious robotic dog.

And then there's special feature-length episode "Bandersnatch." This interactive drama—about a programmer adapting a branching narrative-type book into a video game—lets you make key plot decisions at certain points, with more than a trillion potential paths. No question, *Black Mirror* is TV at its most innovative.

CREATOR: Charlie Brooker
PRODUCTION CO: Zeppotron, Channel 4 Television Corporation, Gran Babieka

BATES MOTEL

HORROR DRAMA • 2013
RATED: TV-MA • 45 MINS

We all know the story of *Psycho*, about Norman Bates and his mother. But what happened to turn Norman into the man he became? *Bates Motel* challenges what you thought you knew.

Norma Bates (Vera Farmiga) and her 17-year-old son, Norman (Freddie Highmore), move to Oregon after the death of Norma's husband and buy the Seafarer motel. It's a new start for mother and son, but it's not easy to escape the past. They're soon at the center of a missing persons investigation, and their new hometown seems full of dark undercurrents.

Bates Motel is a sensitive, intricate, compelling drama that, over five seasons, shows real psychological progression. At its heart is the relationship between Norma and Norman, roles played to perfection by the two leads. Both characters are damaged and do terrible things yet remain sympathetic—so much so that even though we know what's coming, we wish we could somehow stop it.

THE INVADERS

SCI-FI • 1967
RATED: TV-PG • 51 MINS

Driving home one night, an architect pulls over on an isolated country road to take a nap. It is a decision that will change his life forever.

US Senator Joseph McCarthy's communist witchhunt of the 1940s and '50s, during which he accused left-leaning Americans of subversive activity, inspired much science fiction, including *The Invaders*. Tapping into Cold War fears of infiltration, this taut, edgy show starts with David Vincent (Roy Thinnes) witnessing the arrival of an alien spacecraft.

He spends the series' two seasons trying to convince the authorities not only that aliens are among us but that they mean us harm. He is invariably met with hostility and disbelief and finds himself in frequent peril, targeted by the aliens' human allies or the aliens themselves in human guise. Although formulaic, the variety of locations, characters, and story lines keeps things fresh. Sweaty-palmed paranoia has never been so much fun.

KINGDOM

PERIOD HORROR • 2019
RATED: TV-MA • 45 MINS

What is wrong with the king of Joseon? Why is no one allowed to visit him? And what is the mysterious plague that threatens to wipe out not only the dynasty but society itself?

Set in late 16th-century Korea, *Kingdom* blends court intrigue with a plague from which the dead come back to ferocious life. When the king falls ill, Crown Prince Lee Chang (Ju Ji-hoon) is accused of treachery by the Cho clan, the family of the king's pregnant second wife, and is forced to set out to investigate the mysterious epidemic sweeping through the southern provinces.

Yes, this is another zombie series, but the setting and circumstances, plus the cultural and political ramifications underpinning the story, keep things fresh and invigorating over two seasons. It's also helped immensely by an enthralling narrative, gripping set pieces, and cinematography so stunning that every shot could be framed and hung on the wall.

DRACULA

HORROR • 2020
RATED: TV-14 • 90 MINS

We all know about vampires. And we all know how to kill them—don't we? But what if all we knew was wrong? How then do you go about stopping the most dangerous man in the world?

Having already presented BBC viewers with dynamic 21st-century reimaginings of Dr. Jekyll and Mr. Hyde and Sherlock Holmes, Steven Moffat—again accompanied by his *Sherlock* (see p30) cocreator Mark Gatiss—turns his attention to another icon of Victorian literature, Count Dracula.

The result is a production that outraged the purists but had everyone else punching the air in glee. Playing fast and loose with the source material—to be honest, most of the material from the novel is there, just in a different order, twisted into new shapes, and peppered with additions—this is an electrifying retelling of the familiar story. At its center, Danish actor Claes Bang gives us a Dracula who oozes both charisma and bestial menace.

THE OUTER LIMITS

SCI-FI HORROR • 1963 • RATED: TV-PG • 51 MINS
SEASONS: 2 • ROBERT CULP, ROBERT DUVALL, MARTIN LANDAU

"There is nothing wrong with your television set. Do not attempt to adjust the picture...." Heed the message kicking off each episode and prepare to shudder on the sofa as an hour of terrifying stories and creatures takes over your TV.

Although influenced by *The Twilight Zone* (pp436–437), *The Outer Limits* is a different beast entirely. While the former landmark series covers all aspects of speculative fiction, moving from horror to sci-fi to fantasy, ABC's *The Outer Limits* sticks firmly to science-fiction concepts, albeit often underpinned by horror elements.

It also tends to be grimmer and moodier than *The Twilight Zone*, both in the way it looks (regular cinematographer Conrad Hall, who would go on to win three Academy Awards, favors a film noir approach) and its reliance on suspense. A common story theme is to pitch human protagonists against malevolent—and often visually disturbing—alien threats.

The series' many memorable creatures were dubbed "bears" by producer and writer Joseph Stefano. Considered key to hooking viewers and creating fear and suspense, many of them can still induce nightmares, from the bug-eyed, antlike Zanti in "The Zanti Misfits," to the shuffling, zombielike creatures in "A Feasibility Study," and the Thetan in "The Architects of Fear." The latter was considered so terrifying that when the episode was first broadcast, some ABC stations showed only a black screen when the creature appeared.

The show was revived in 1995 for a seven-season run. It had over 100 more episodes than the original series, including adaptations of tales by Stephen King and *Game of Thrones* (see p8) creator George R. R. Martin.

THE PURGE

HORROR • 2018
RATED: TV-MA • 42 MINS

In the not-too-distant future, the US is ruled by a totalitarian government. To allow its citizens to let off steam, once a year, for 12 hours, all crimes are legalized—including murder.

Based on the popular movie series, *The Purge* uses the longer TV-show format to expand its premise by focusing on "Purge Night" from several angles. In Season 1, the action moves between three wildly disparate stories on Purge Night, whereas Season 2 shifts its focus to its immediate aftermath and repercussions.

The better stories are those with characters involved in the action, like Miguel Guerrero (Gabriel Chavarria), a US Marine searching for his sister, who he fears may have joined a death cult. Other narrative strands are less engaging, such as that involving a pair of entrepreneurs attempting to secure capital from a wealthy businessman. Admittedly, this approach highlights societal divides, but it also results in inconsistent pacing.

ROUND THE TWIST

FANTASY COMEDY • 1989
RATED: U (UK) • 25 MINS

"Have you ever ... ever felt like this?" Fun magical adventures abound in the Australian coastal town of Port Niranda after three siblings and their widowed dad move into its haunted lighthouse.

Widower Tony Twist and his children, twins Pete and Linda and younger son Bronson, become caught up in a series of bizarre, fantastical adventures in this frothy Australian kids' show. The first two seasons, based on stories by author Paul Jennings, are widely considered the best, featuring such fun concepts as magic underpants, circus clothes that come to life, a green baby found under a cabbage patch, and ghosts galore.

Seasons 3 and 4, by which time Jennings had withdrawn the rights to his stories, are more patchy but have their moments. The gaps between seasons meant that *Round the Twist* was regularly recast, with sometimes as many as three different actors playing the same role over the show's 12-year run.

THE ORDER

HORROR FANTASY • 2019
RATED: TV-MA • 60 MINS

The Hermetic Order of the Blue Rose is an urban legend—or is it? College freshman Jack Morton doesn't think so. But when a series of strange murders sweeps the campus, he finds himself out of his depth.

Coming across like a rich but slightly cheesy stew of *Twilight*, *Harry Potter*, and *Buffy the Vampire Slayer*, with a side helping of superhero salad, *The Order* follows Jack Morton (Jake Manley), who joins a secret magical society to avenge his mother's death. As his affiliations deepen, he discovers an ongoing conflict between members of the Order and the Knights of Saint Christopher, a secret society of werewolves whose mission is to eliminate all black magic practitioners.

Slick and fast moving, the two seasons of *The Order* can take themselves too seriously at times, but there are moments of goofy humor to leaven the pomposity.

INDEX

PRODUCTION COMPANY KEY

AMC	American Movie Classics
ATV	Associated Television
ABC	Australian Broadcasting Corporation
BBC	British Broadcasting Corporation
BSkyB	British Sky Broadcasting
CBC	Canadian Broadcasting Corporation
HA	Henson Associates
HBO	Home Box Office
ITC	Incorporated Television Company
MRC	Media Rights Capital
NBC	National Broadcasting Company
NTV	Nippon Television Network
PGP	Procter & Gamble Productions
UMS	Universal Media Studios
VAP	Video Audio Project

Senior Editor Ruth Amos
Project Art Editor Sam Bartlett
Cover design Studio Noel and Lisa Lanzarini
Production Editor Siu Yin Chan
Senior Production Controller Lloyd Robertson
US Editors Jennette ElNaggar, Karyn Gerhard
Managing Editor Paula Regan
Managing Art Editor Jo Connor
Publisher Julie Ferris
Art Director Lisa Lanzarini
Publishing Director Mark Searle

DYNAMO LIMITED
Managing Editor Claire Lister
Design Project Manager Judy Caley

Acknowledgments
DK would like to thank Tori Kosara, James McKeag,
Helen Murray, Nicole Reynolds and Nishani Reed.

The number of TV seasons given in each
data file is correct as of May 2020.

First American Edition, 2020
Published in the United States by DK Publishing
1450 Broadway, Suite 801, New York, New York 10018

Page design copyright ©2020 Dorling Kindersley Limited
DK, a Division of Penguin Random House LLC
20 21 22 23 24 10 9 8 7 6 5 4 3 2 1
001–321184–Oct/2020

A catalog record for this book is available from the Library of Congress.
ISBN 978-0-7440-2513-2

DK books are available at special discounts when purchased in bulk for sales
promotions, premiums, fund-raising, or educational use. For details, contact:
DK Publishing Special Markets, 1450 Broadway, Suite 801, New York, New York 10018
SpecialSales@dk.com

Printed and bound in China

For the curious
www.dk.com